Dublin

timeout.com/dublin

Penguin Books

PENGUIN BOOKS

Published by the Penguin Group
Penguin Books Ltd, 80 Strand, London WC2R ORL, England
Penguin Books USA Inc., 375 Hudson Street, New York, New York 10014, USA
Penguin Books Australia Ltd, Ringwood, Victoria, Australia
Penguin Books Canada Ltd, 10 Alcorn Avenue, Toronto, Ontario, Canada M4V 3B2
Penguin Books (NZ) Ltd, cnr Rosedale and Airborne Roads, Albany, Auckland, New Zealand

Penguin Books Ltd, Registered Offices: Harmondsworth, Middlesex, England

First published 1998
Second edition 1999
Third edition 2002
10 9 8 7 6 5 4 3 2 1

Copyright © Time Out Group Ltd, 1998, 1999, 2002
All rights reserved

Colour reprographics by Icon, Crown House, 56-58 Southwark Street, London SE1
and Precise Litho, 34-35 Great Sutton Street, London EC1
Printed and bound by Cayfosa-Quebecor, Ctra. de Caldes, Km 3 08 130 Sta, Perpètua de Mogoda, Barcelona, Spain

Edited and designed by
Time Out Guides Limited
Universal House
251 Tottenham Court Road
London W1T 7AB
Tel + 44 (0) 20 7813 3000
Fax + 44 (0) 20 7813 6001
Email guides@timeout.com
www.timeout.com

Editorial

Editor Sophie Blacksell
Deputy Editor Ros Sales
Consultant Editor Nicholas Kelly
Researchers Rachel Askham, Siobhan Ayres, Janice Fuscoe, Andrew Harkness, Chris Kanal
Proofreader Marion Moisy
Indexer Selena Cox

Editorial Director Peter Fiennes
Series Editor Ruth Jarvis
Deputy Series Editor Jonathan Cox
Guides Co-ordinator Jenny Noden

Design

Group Art Director John Oakey
Art Director Mandy Martin
Art Editor Scott Moore
Designers Benjamin de Lotz, Lucy Grant
Picture Editor Kerri Littlefield
Deputy Picture Editor Kit Burnet
Picture Librarian Sarah Roberts
Scanning & Imaging Dan Conway
Ad make-up Glen Impey

Advertising

Group Commercial Director Lesley Gill
Sales Director Mark Phillips
International Sales Co-ordinator Ross Canadé
Advertisement Sales (Dublin) Noted Marketing & Design
Advertising Assistant Sabrina Ancilleri

Administration

Publisher Tony Elliott
Managing Director Mike Hardwick
Group Financial Director Kevin Ellis
Marketing Director Christine Cort
Marketing Manager Mandy Martinez
US Publicity & Marketing Associate Rosella Albanese
Group General Manager Nichola Coulthard
Production Manager Mark Lamond
Production Controller Samantha Furniss
Accountant Sarah Bostock

Features in this guide were written and researched by:
Introduction Sophie Blacksell. **History** Orlaith O'Sullivan, Nicholas Kelly (*First ladies of Ireland* Sophie Blacksell).
Dublin Today Nicholas Kelly (*One hundred thousand welcomes?* Neil Hegarty). **Architecture** Nicholas Kelly, Luke Dodd.
Literary Dublin John Boyne, Nicholas Kelly (*Word of mouth* John McManus; *Write on* John McManus). **Accommodation**
Kerry Sinanan. **Sightseeing Introduction** Nicholas Kelly, Sophie Blacksell (*Trips and tours* Rachel Askham). **Southside**
Fran Cassidy (*Bridging the gap* Neil Hegarty; *Education, Education, Education* Orlaith O'Sullivan; *Really wired city?* Neil
Hegarty; *Statue spotting* Sophie Blacksell). **Northside** Nicholas Kelly (*Joking apart* Fran Cassidy; *Walking the Ulysses trail*
Sophie Blacksell, David Wheatley). **Beyond the City Centre** Fran Cassidy. **Dublin Bay & the Coast** Sophie Blacksell.
Restaurants & Cafés John McKenna, Samantha Fanning. **Pubs & Bars** Nicholas Kelly, Fran Cassidy. **Shops & Services**
John Boyne (*Dedicated followers of fashion* Emily Hourican). **By Season** Samantha Fanning. **Children** Ann-Marie Hardiman.
Film Sean McGowan. **Galleries** Sean McGowan. **Gay & Lesbian** Tim Ilsley. **Music: Classical & Opera** John Boyne;
Rock, Pop, Trad & Jazz Ann Marie Hardiman (*Trad ain't bad* Fran Cassidy). **Nightlife** Rory O'Keefe (*Bored of the black stuff?*
Samantha Fanning; *Endless weekend* Rory O'Keefe, Sophie Blacksell). **Performing Arts** Emily Hourican. **Sport & Fitness**
Fran Cassidy. **Getting Started** Nicholas Kelly, Sophie Blacksell. **Leinster** Fran Cassidy. **Munster** Barry Iremonger, Marie
Gethins. **Connaught** Katie Moylan, Patrick Fleming (*Gael talk* Katie Moylan; *Surfing IRE* Sam Le Quesne). **Ulster** Michael
O'Hanlon, Sinead Morrissey (*Dialling Northern Ireland* Sophie Blacksell; *Out on the town* Sinead Morrissey). **Directory:**
Getting Around, Resources A-Z Neil Hegarty, Janice Fuscoe, Ruth Jarvis. **Further Reference** Nicholas Kelly.

The Editor would like to thank:
Emily, Penny and Simon Blacksell, Portia Clarke, staff at *The Dubliner*, Aine Friel at Chief O'Neill's, Will Fulford-Jones, Sarah
Guy, Simon Jones, Paul Keene at Graphics IT, Sam Le Quesne, Ruth Livingston at the Morrison, the staff at the Leeson Inn,
Lesley McCave, Cath Phillips, Andrew White, and all contributors to previous editions of the guide whose work formed the
basis for this edition.

Quadrophonic has complained that our article 'It's all in the mix' in the previous edition of the Guide on rivalries in the clubbing
world was materially inaccurate in certain respects. We apologise to Quadrophonic for any embarrassment caused to them as a
result of any inaccuracies. WITHOUT PREJUDICE 12 July 2000.

Maps by JS Graphics, 17 Beadles Lane, Old Oxted, Surrey RH8 9JG.

Photography by Paul Avis except: page 6, 8, 12, 18, 204, 209 AKG London; page 17, 254, 265 Corbis; page 163 The Irish
Times; page 223, 226, 231, 238 Bord Fáilte/Irish Tourist Board; page 229, 233, 261 BSK Photo Library; page 235, 244
Cork Kerry Tourism; page 240 Courtesy of Crawford Municipal Art Gallery; page 248 Tina Frohlich & Volker Schutsch Ventry;
page 251 Getty Images; page 252 Image Bank; page 259 Duchas Heritage Service; page 269, 273, 276 Northern Ireland
Tourist Board.

The following images were provided by the featured establishments/artists: 117, 164, 173, 207, 211, 219.

Contents

Introduction

Traditionally Dublin has been the preserve of literary aficionados and long-lost American cousins tracing their Irish roots – a small, provincial city with an interesting history and some admittedly excellent pubs. More recently, its legendary (if often unjustified) reputation for drunken debauchery has attracted an altogether different breed of visitor: young, usually British and intent on having a good time. During the 1990s the city became notorious as the number one destination for stag parties, which would make the most of cheap flights from the UK in order to spend the weekend in a blur of booze and vomit.

Since the millennium, however, Ireland's capital has outgrown this dubious reputation, to achieve a more mature self-confidence. Now visitors to Dublin are as likely to come from Spain, Japan or Australia as from the USA and Britain. And they don't come here to research their ancestors in the National Library or to throw up in the gutters of Temple Bar but rather to enjoy all the benefits of the city's youthful, English-speaking urban population, its compact layout, its vibrant cultural life and its increasingly international perspective.

The exuberance of the Irish economy means that Dublin's hotels, restaurants, cafés and clubs exude a sense of style and class that was unthinkable just a few years ago, and while locals might rue the wholesale changes being wrought in their city, visitors will be happy not to have to endure some of the dowdy guesthouses and eateries of old.

That said, Dublin must tread carefully in these heady times to preserve those aspects of the city that made it so appealing in the first place. Stroll the streets and you'll find buildings, statues and museums that are a testament to Ireland's complex colonial heritage and to the extraordinary number of writers who sought to document or interpret it. There are the advantages of Dublin's location, too: it's on the coast, surrounded by hills and mountains, and has the largest park in Europe right on its doorstep. Although the centre of the city is perennially, irritatingly congested – with both people and traffic – escape is always easy. And there are the pubs, of course, still the hub of the city's social life and a quintessential element of the Dublin experience. Despite the inexorable rise of the identikit chain bar, the best Dub pubs (both old and new) will live up to your expectations in all the right ways.

Now is the time to shake off any lingering preconceptions and enjoy the Dublin of the moment. Ireland's capital has shed its bookish, introspective past to become a lively, young city, where history provides a context for the enjoyment of the present; nostalgia hunters may be disappointed.

ABOUT THE TIME OUT CITY GUIDES

The *Time Out Dublin Guide* is one of an expanding series of Time Out City Guides, now numbering over 35, produced by the people behind London and New York's successful listings magazines. Out guides are all written and updated by resident experts who have striven to provide you with all the most up-to-date information you'll need to explore the city or read up on its background, whether you're a local or a first-time visitor.

THE LOWDOWN ON THE LISTINGS

Above all, we've tried to make this book as useful as possible. Addresses, telephone numbers, websites, transport information, opening times, admission prices and credit card details have all been included in the listings. And, as far, as possible, we've given details of facilities, services and events, all checked and correct as we went to press.

However, owners and managers can change their arrangements at any time, and they often do. Before you go out of your way, we'd advise you to telephone and check opening times, ticket prices and other particulars. While every effort has been made to ensure the accuracy of the information contained in this guide, the publishers cannot accept responsibility for any errors it may contain.

PRICES AND PAYMENT

Prices throughout this guide are given in euros (with the exception of the Belfast and Derry sections of the Ulster chapter, where pounds sterling are used). Wherever possible, the prices quoted are the official euro prices as determined by the venue or institution concerned. However, at the time of going to press, many Irish businesses had not yet confirmed their euro rates for 2002 and beyond. Where this is the case we have converted the price from Irish

pounds (punts) into euros using the official conversion rate (1 euro – 1.27 punts) and then rounded the figure up or down to the nearest five cents. It is important to remember that prices are likely to fluctuate during the first few weeks of the euro changeover until the currency has settled down, and for this reason, the prices we've supplied should be treated as guidelines, not gospel. If prices vary wildly from those we've quoted, please write and let us know. We aim to give the best and most up-to-date advice, so we always want to know if you've been badly treated or overcharged. For more on the euro, see p290.

We have noted where venues such as shops, hotels, restaurants, museums and so on accept the following credit cards: American Express (AmEx), Diners Club (DC), MasterCard (MC) and Visa (V). Many will also accept travellers' cheques, along with other credit cards (Carte Blanche, for example).

THE LIE OF THE LAND

To make the book (and the city) easier to navigate, we have divided Dublin into areas and assigned each one its own chapter in our **Sightseeing** section starting on page 57: Southside, Northside, Beyond the City Centre, and Dublin Bay & the Coast. Although these area designations are a simplification of Dublin's geography and are not official names

There is an online version of this guide, as well as weekly events listings for over 35 international cities, at www.timeout.com.

seen on signposts, we hope they will help you to understand the city's layout and find its most interesting sights. For consistency, the same areas are used in addresses throughout the guide. We've also included postal districts for those venues you might want to write to and website addresses wherever possible. Finally, there's a series of fully indexed colour maps at the back of the guide, starting on page 305. For further orientation information, see p58; for details of addresses and Dublin postal districts, see p283.

TELEPHONE NUMBERS

The area code for Dublin is 01. All telephone numbers listed in this guide take this code unless otherwise stated. For more information on telephones and codes, see p293.

ESSENTIAL INFORMATION

For all the practical information you might need for visiting Dublin, including visa and customs information, advice on facilities and access for the disabled, emergency telephone numbers, useful websites and the lowdown on the local transport network, turn to the **Directory** chapter at the back of the guide. It starts on page 277.

MAPS

Wherever possible, a map reference is provided for every venue listed in the guide, indicating the page and grid reference at which it can be found on our street maps. These fully indexed colour maps are located at the back of the book (see pp306–314) and include Ireland, Dublin & Environs, Dublin City, the DART & Suburban Rail network, Phoenix Park & Kilmainham, Central Dublin, Grand Canal & the Docks.

LET US KNOW WHAT YOU THINK

We hope you enjoy the *Time Out Dublin Guide*, and we'd like to know what you think of it. We welcome tips for places that you consider we should include in future editions and take note of your criticism of our choices. There's a reader's reply card at the back of this book for your feedback, or you can email us at dublinguide@timeout.com.

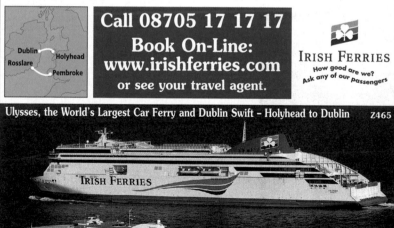

In Context

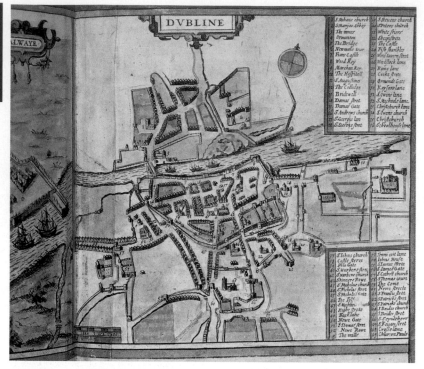

History

Viking fort, Georgian showpiece, dirty old town, hotbed of revolution and Celtic Tiger: Dublin's been all that and more.

Though Dublin celebrated its thousandth birthday in 1988, the area around the city has been inhabited since 8,000 BC. Ireland survived wave after wave of invaders, but with the arrival of the Gaels shortly before the birth of Christ, the language and the culture of the native people were irrevocably changed. The modern names of the capital city – 'Baile Átha Cliath' and 'Dublin'– derive from two distinct settlements in early Gaelic Ireland.

Ath Cliath – 'the ford of the hurdles' – is believed to be the older of the two settlements, a fortified secular enclosure dating from the sixth century. It was most likely a trading post, marking the junction of the long-distance routeways from the four provinces – Leinster, Connaught, Ulster and Munster. Its importance as a meeting of the ways is debatable, but it was certainly of some value, for its ale was renowned throughout the early Christian period; it seems the Guinness family is only continuing a long tradition of brewing in Dublin.

Dubhlinn – 'the black pool' – takes its name from a tidal pool in the estuary of the River Poddle. The settlement was originally a monastic community, located in the area now known as the Liberties, comprising several churches, religious houses and holy wells. Ireland received Christianity early: St Patrick arrived in AD 432 and soon extinguished the rites of the pagans. A golden age of Gaelic Christianity followed, producing magnificent works of religious art such as the Book of Durrow, the Ardagh Chalice and the **Book of Kells**. The city also bears the imprint of the great missionary: legend holds that **St Patrick's Cathedral** (founded in 1191) marks the site where the saint himself baptised the heathen Irish.

ENTER THE VIKINGS

It was only with the arrival of the Norse that the Dublin area became urbanised. Two years after an attack in 839, Norwegian Vikings established themselves in Dubhlinn with the construction of a harbour, or *longphort*. In the following decades, they used Dublin as a base from which to raid and plunder the surrounding regions. The invaders were unimpeded by any unified resistance, and the area became the focal point of Scandinavian settlement in Ireland, developing into an important port and market place for the trade of slaves (native men and women captured during the raids).

Dublin merited mention in the Viking sagas, and a wealth of artefacts has been preserved in its soil, including the largest Viking burial site outside of Scandinavia (at **Islandbridge** and **Kilmainham**). Although politically united during the early years of their reign, after the death of Ivar the Boneless in 873, there was considerable internal dissent among the Scandinavians. In 902, they were driven out by the joint forces of Brega and Leinster.

A second Viking invasion began in 914, and three years later Dublin was reoccupied. This time, though, the settlement was not described as a *longphort*, but as a *dun*, or stronghold. It was a period of great construction, during which **Wood Quay** was developed and several permanent dwellings constructed in the area now flanked by **Christchurch** and **Dublin Castle**. However, the leadership remained radically unstable, as consecutive Scandinavian kings attempted to rule both Dublin and their English centre, the city of York, concurrently.

The Dublin Vikings only concentrated their efforts on Ireland after the collapse of the Scandinavian kingdom of York in 954. From this point, their status changed: they established the first Irish towns, intermarried with the Irish and chose Gaelic names for their children. Yet though the Norsemen became absorbed into the Gaelic world during this period, all was not peaceful. The Vikings continued to plunder the countryside, and monasteries took to building 'round towers' (some of which still stand: at Monasterboice, for example) in order to keep watch for marauders.

Viking Dublin came under regular attack from the Irish after 936, particularly under the leadership of Brian Ború and Mael Sechnaill, the last great High Kings of Ireland. Sechnaill clashed with the Norse leader Olaf at Tara in 979, and in the following years laid siege to Dublin a further four times. His periods in power (980-1002 and 1014-22) mark the transition between Viking and Hiberno-Norse Dublin. The Scandinavians were finally defeated by King Brian Ború at Clontarf on Good Friday 1014, and Dublin became a Christian vassal state, ruled by King Sitric 'Silkbeard' under the protection of the Irish High King. Silkbeard made a pilgrimage to Rome in 1028, precipitating a period of considerable religious activity in Dublin that resulted in the foundation of **Christchurch Cathedral** and the westward expansion of the town. He was eventually deposed in 1036, and Dublin was ruled by Irish over-kings until 1170, when the town – indeed, the whole country – underwent another massive upheaval as the English arrived.

THE MEDIEVAL CITY

In 1169, a small band of English Norman troops landed in County Wexford in the south-east of the country, sent over by the Earl of Pembroke (better known as Strongbow). They helped the king of Leinster, Diarmait MacMurchada, in his war, then returned to England to gather more men. By 1170, Strongbow had taken Dublin from the Hiberno-Norsemen (or Ostmen), rebuilt the wooden Christchurch with a stone foundation, married MacMurchada's daughter, and inherited the kingship of Leinster on the death of Diarmait. The English king, Henry II, then sent in his own army to keep an eye on Strongbow. These Anglo-Normans, like the Vikings before them, became 'more Irish than the Irish themselves', and so began the pattern of invasion and assimilation that would come to characterise the history of Ireland.

In 1171, Henry II proclaimed that the city of Dublin was now under his rule. The Vikings were expelled, and the town had soon become the capital of the English 'colony' in Ireland: it even had its own parliament and exchequer. However, the only area actually brought under English control was 'the Pale', an area of just a few dozen square miles around Dublin (from this comes the expression 'beyond the Pale', meaning something that is uncontrollable).

As the decades progressed, even this small area began to shrink, and the English focused their attention on Dublin itself. However, under Henry II and his son, John, the city was finally established in legal terms, and during the 13th century, it expanded rapidly both as a port and

The **Book of Kells** dates from the golden age of Gaelic Christianity. *See p7.*

merchant centre. Trade within the town became standardised with the gradual development of the craft guilds, which were strictly monitored to exclude any Gaelic elements whatsoever: only men and women 'of English name and blood' were allowed to join.

In many respects, Dublin was a medieval city like any other, but particularly with regard to overcrowding. Its population of 5,000 or so were crammed into a small, walled area full of thatched roofs through which fire raged on a regular basis. And though the burgesses were diligent in establishing water supplies, these were usually limited, in true medieval fashion, to the wealthy. Partly as a result, the large poor population suffered terribly in times of famine and sickness. Fortunately, Dubliners were generous and their wills are filled with bequests to the needy. The citizens also founded a massive leper hospital, which was granted the rents from present-day **St Stephen's Green**. But despite these philanthropic efforts, there was great strife in the city: in 1295, it was reported that there was such a desperate shortage of food that the poor actually ate the criminals hanged on the gallows, while 1317 saw the worst famine of the Middle Ages, when mothers are purported to have devoured their own children.

Infectious diseases were at their most lethal in medieval cities. By modern Western standards, even the wealthy lived in disgusting conditions, coping with open sewers, flea-infested beds, rats, floors covered with soiled straw and filthy streets. In 1348, the plague hit Dublin with appalling effect; it returned regularly, restricting the growth of the city for the next century. In times of disease, all beggars were banished from the city, and regulations concerning health and hygiene were stepped up. In 1489, royal letters even ordered the swine of Dublin to be contained, complaining that they 'infect the air and produce mortality, fevers and pestilence throughout the city'.

Dublin's reputation as the pub capital of the world has a long history, too: in the Middle Ages, the town was full of taverns serving inexpensive ale and beer. Alcoholism was prevalent, but was perhaps the least of the many booze-related problems: in an age where most people went armed, a drunken disagreement could mean serious trouble.

But such mortal dangers did not dissuade the hordes of pilgrims journeying to the shrines of Dublin each year. The plethora of churches and religious houses within the city included two main crowd-pullers, the cathedrals: **St Patrick's**, and the **Church of the Holy Trinity (Christchurch)**, among whose relics was the *bacall Iosa* ('staff of Jesus').

TUDORS AND STUARTS

By the Tudor period, Dublin had expanded beyond its medieval walls and won some considerable privileges from the English government. The rest of Ireland, however, lived under tribal kingdoms, largely beyond English control. In 1534, Henry VIII attempted to quell their anarchy by ordering the surrender of all lands to the English Crown. When Elizabeth inherited the throne in 1558, she set about 'civilising' the primitive people of Ireland. The Anglo-Normans resident in Ireland were hardly one hundred per cent loyal to the crown, so the queen sent over 'true' Englishmen to conquer Ireland. The Irish savages were 'only by force and fear to be vanquished' and by breaking their will, Elizabeth hoped to reform the country completely. She went about the task fervently: unarmed citizens and children were among those slaughtered and one of her deputies in Ireland lined the path leading to his tent with the heads of those killed. Quite apart from the Gaelic, the Anglo-Irish rebelled six times against their queen, yet despite such resistance, Elizabeth's resolve to bring Ireland to its knees prevailed. The final Gaelic battle was fought on Christmas Eve, 1601, when a Spanish fleet landed in Kinsale to aid Hugh O'Neill's rebellion. O'Neill lost and was forced to make a formal submission to the Crown. England had won.

During this century of strife, England kept the capital on a tight rein and Dublin became a place of relative stability, though the Gaelic Irish were always suspect. One way that power was demonstrated was through control of religion: acts of parliament in 1536 and 1539 had dissolved the monasteries of the city, changing the urban landscape in the process. The *bacall Iosa* was ritually burned in Skinner's Row outside Christchurch in 1538, and the following year the removal of all 'superstitious' relics and images was ordered. When the English proclaimed Ireland an Anglican country in 1560, the country split on religious grounds. Protestants took over the Catholic churches, leaving adherents of the old religion to worship in cellars and back rooms, and former religious institutions were appropriated for civic purposes: St Andrew's church became a stable, St George's was turned into a bakery and, in 1591, the defunct monastery of All Saints became **Trinity College**.

The English newcomers settled in Dublin in a climate of acquisition and opportunity, and the royal expansion of the city began. For the latter half of the century, it was run by a war administration, whose heavy military expenditure encouraged economic growth. During this period, the city of Dublin changed dramatically: where once it had been a medieval provincial centre, now it was an Elizabethan stronghold, with its role as a centre of trade and administration increasing dramatically over the course of the century.

But while merchants amassed wealth, the public utilities degenerated. The Liffey bridge and **Dublin Castle** were both teetering, and, in 1562, the south wall and roof of Christchurch Cathedral collapsed. An initiative to clean up the city led to the widening of the streets and the reconstruction of dilapidated buildings, but the poverty problem had worsened with the closure of the monasteries, and the plague of 1575 claimed up to 34 per cent of the population.

'By 1640, Dublin was overwhelmingly Protestant and remained so for over a century.'

Further hardship came in the final decades of the century. The citizens were ordered to fund new troops for the royal army and from 1594 almost every Dublin family also had to 'diet' a soldier to fight in the Nine Years War. On 11 March, 1597, 140 barrels of gunpowder exploded on the quays – the clerk, who should have been keeping an eye on things, had popped off for a pint – wiping out much of the medieval city at a single stroke and killing 126 people. By the end of the century the citizens of Dublin had suffered terrible personal and financial losses, and were being threatened every day with invasion. In London, where rumours abounded that Dublin was run by papists, Elizabeth ignored the pleas of her deputies across the sea.

Under James I, the English government paid more attention to Ireland than it had done previously. In 1607, Hugh O'Neill and the Earl of Tyrconnell fled to Europe, and their lands (the counties of Donegal, Tyrone, Derry and Armagh) were declared forfeit to the Crown. The acquisition of this territory formed the basis for the 'Plantation of Ulster' – essentially, shipping loyal Protestants in from England and Scotland to colonise the land. (The plantations have current ramifications: the plantation of Derry, for instance, was followed by an alliance between the new city and the Corporation of London, which involved both county and city in a name change. Londonderry city and county were born and their titles still remain contentious: people use the names of Derry or Londonderry to indicate where their allegiances lie, though some, with a tired irony, refer to the place as Stroke City.)

Dublin boomed as a garrison town. By 1640, it was overwhelmingly Protestant and remained so for over a century, further widening the gulf between the Anglicised capital and the rest of the country. Outside Dublin, discontent grew as the oppressed Catholic majority congregated in ruined churches or in open fields to practise their religion: rebellion broke out in 1641 and rumbled on until 1649, when Oliver Cromwell landed in Dublin to personally reassert English power over Ireland. Ruthless victories at Drogheda and Wexford ensured his success. Cromwell's bloody campaign and its aftermath did not infringe greatly upon the city of Dublin, however: the most significant effect was the collapse of suburbia, which had been flourishing for 50 years. Now the citizens moved back to the centre of the city, closer to the heart of the colony, and Dublin entered its architectural heyday.

RESTORATION AND GEORGIAN DUBLIN

During the reign of Charles II, the Duke of Ormond was appointed Lord Deputy of Ireland and the city began to expand rapidly, both in terms of population and construction. Most of present-day Dublin dates from this period of magnificent growth and expansion, during which time a neo-classical city was built by the upper classes. The Anglo-Dutch phase dates from the Restoration in 1660 to about 1720, after which time the Georgian style dominated. The two centuries saw a phenomenal amount of work undertaken: urban initiatives salvaged **Dublin Castle**, and started construction on the **Royal Hospital** at Kilmainham, **Phoenix Park** and **Temple Bar**. **Marsh's Library** was built in 1702, and the library at **Trinity College** was begun in 1712. Earlier, in 1664, **St Stephen's Green** had been set out as an urban square, becoming a central focus for the construction of new streets. Inspired by the examples of Paris and Amsterdam, plans were set out to develop the land along the river, and work on the quays began. The Earl of Drogheda, Henry Moore, purchased a large area of land north of the river, developing the newly fashionable Henry Street and its environs.

In 1705, Joshua Dawson got in on the act, buying a plot between Trinity College and St Stephen's Green. Dawson set out the aristocratic boulevards of Dawson Street and Grafton Street, and built a grand house for himself, which, in 1715, became the **Mansion House**, home of the Lord Mayor of Dublin. Five years later, Luke Gardiner built Henrietta Street (named after Henrietta, Duchess of Grafton), a prime aristocratic quarter north of the river, before going on to construct Gardiner Street,

a stunning line of terraced houses overseen by James Gandon. Soon, the Wide Street Commissioners – the body established to regulate the thoroughfares – had created Sackville Street, one of the widest streets in Europe, now known as **O'Connell Street**. The new **Parliament House** was opened in 1731, and, 20 years later, building began on the impressive façade of **Trinity College**, the largest piece of collegiate architecture in Europe.

The penetrating aesthetic influence of the Age of Enlightenment merged with the increased wealth and the growing awareness of Dublin as a capital city, and upper-class life reached the height of extravagance during the 1770s. The intense construction showed no signs of abating: the Fitzwilliam Estate constructed the Georgian lines of Merrion Street, Merrion Square, Baggot Street and Pembroke Street as residential areas for the Protestant ascendancy. Gandon designed Beresford Place, **Custom House**, the **Four Courts** and the Kings Inns.

By now, the city was thriving: the first American ship arrived in 1785, and Dublin was second only to London in terms of music, theatre, publishing and the service industries. The names of those born, educated, or living in the city at this time emphasises the city's pre-eminent cultural status. Handel lived in Abbey Street in 1741-42, and his *Messiah* had its debut in Fishamble Street. Swift was born in Dublin in 1667 and attended Trinity, as did the Dublin-born political philosopher Edmund Burke (born in 1729) and playwrights William Congreve and Oliver Goldsmith. Other Dubliners include the founder of *The Tatler*, Richard Steele (born 1672), and dramatist Richard Sheridan (born 1751).

However, underneath the glorious Protestant façade of the city, dissatisfaction grew. The decisive defeat of Catholic James II at the Battle of the Boyne in 1690 had led to the imposition of strict penal laws by William of Orange. Although the laws did not outlaw the practice of Roman Catholicism, it was actively discouraged. Moreover, no Catholic was permitted to hold any office of state, stand for Parliament, join the armed forces or practise law. And, most crucially, Catholics could neither vote nor buy any land. By the third quarter of the 18th century, barely five per cent of the land of Ireland remained in Catholic hands. The migration of disenfranchised Catholics from the countryside into Dublin meant that by the mid 18th century, the capital had a Catholic majority. As the economic and artistic centre of the country, Dublin also began to spearhead new political movements of a dissenting nature.

Famine sculpture on the quays. *See p89.*

The sectarian animosity was translated, perhaps inevitably, into violence, and Protestant-Catholic riots became common. In the early 1700s, they fought under Whig/Tory factions, but soon gang wars were being fought between (mostly Protestant) tailors' and weavers' apprentices known as the Liberty boys and (mostly Catholic) butchers' assistants known as the Ormond boys.

Quite apart from the multitude of popular disturbances, there was a growing awareness of an 'Irish' identity that transcended religious differences. Henry Grattan's Declaration of Rights in 1782 won legislative independence for Ireland and some of the penal laws were repealed: Catholics were finally allowed to practise law, though they were still excluded from any municipal role. Deeply affected by the French revolution, the oppressed Irish were inspired to take matters into their own hands.

In 1796, a fleet of French republican troops arrived to help in a revolution, which failed. Two years later, Dubliner Protestant Wolfe Tone harnessed urban discontent and orchestrated his own rebellion of 'United Irishmen'; however, the group was unsuccessful in all but convincing the British government that they had given Ireland too much slack. The reins had to be tightened.

THE 19TH CENTURY

The Act of Union of 1800 dissolved Ireland's Parliament, transferring power back to the English Crown. Dublin's importance and prosperity diminished as a result, and the capital became a hotbed of political agitation.

In 1803, the Protestant Robert Emmet led a nationalist uprising, with an ultimate aim to take over Dublin Castle. He failed – dismally, as it happens – but lawyer Daniel O'Connell continued the fight. O'Connell, known as the 'Liberator', initiated a campaign for Catholic Emancipation. He ran for a seat in the British Parliament in 1828, winning by a landslide, but, as a Catholic, he could not take his seat. Faced with this organised display of resistance, the British government passed the Emancipation Act in 1829, dissolving the remaining penal laws discriminating against Catholics, and O'Connell became the first Catholic Lord Mayor of Dublin in 1841. By the 1840s, when O'Connell began to call for a repeal of the Act of Union, Ireland had become wholly concerned with another threatening problem: famine.

In 1845, a fungus ravaged potato crops in Ireland, destroying the staple food of the poor, and the Great Famine began. On hearing the pleas for help, Prime Minister Robert Peel first remarked that the Irish had a tendency to exaggerate, but the government was soon forced to act. It began importing Indian corn, but the food was not to be given out as emergency aid: the people would have to work for it. Concerned that providing food subsidies would undermine the Irish economy and encourage laziness, the government established workhouses. A multitude of projects were thought up to consume the time and energy of the starving Irish.

The evidence of the pointless labour that was enforced on the Irish during the famine years (1845-49) can still be seen: roads begin in a field and go nowhere, perhaps ending on a beach. Again, for fear of damaging the economy, the wages paid to the 'moving skeletons' employed on the public works were lower than average. The reality was that they were often not paid at all, and many died from starvation and exhaustion.

Daniel O'Connell (1775-1847): the champion of Catholic Emancipation.

The terrible irony was that there was plenty of food in Ireland: it was simply not available to the poor. Cargoloads of imported corn sat in depots for months, until the government felt that releasing the corn for sale would not adversely affect food prices. Charles Trevelyan, the head of the Treasury, actually refused food that was en route to Ireland, claiming that the cargo was not wanted. Huge quantities of cattle, pork, sheep, oats, eggs and flour were all being exported from Ireland. One of the only options available to the poor was emigration. During the famine, over one million people left Ireland for good, around three-quarters taking the long voyage to the United States. In 1841, Ireland's population was estimated to be eight million. Cut by death and migration, it had fallen to 6.5 million just a decade later.

Dublin's own famine experience was different. The wealth of the country was focused in the city, and in many respects, life continued as normal for the upper classes. Balls were held at the **Mansion House**, and plans were made to establish a library, museums and a gallery for the people of Ireland. (The buildings were constructed between 1852 and 1871 on the west side of Merrion Square.) But the population of Dublin had surged from some 10,000 in 1600 to approximately 247,000 in 1851, and the city limits were strained: the quality of water, air and housing was degenerating and the mortality rate was high, due to the epidemics spreading from 'fever nests' throughout town. Gerard Manley Hopkins was one famous victim, contracting a fatal case of typhoid while living at St Stephen's Green.

Civic funding was practical and sought to establish a modern infrastructure for the deteriorating city. A commercial rail network was set up, the tramways were completed (*see p13* **Transports of delight**), the Grand and Royal Canals were built, and hospitals were opened. In addition, new bridges across the Liffey were erected, the **GPO** was completed in 1818, and the system of policing was completely overhauled: the Dublin Metropolitan Police made it their priority to clean up the city, and public baths and wash-houses were opened to help contain the grime of the poor, which was thought to spread disease. There was also an initiative to supply permanent social housing for Dublin's needy.

The middle and upper classes, though, simply moved away from the filth and began building sumptuous new homes for themselves in suburbia. The houses of once-fashionable Henrietta Street, along with other aristocratic areas of the city, became derelict and ended up in multiple occupancy as overcrowded slum tenements. The only good thing to come out of this period was the fact that the city's classical architecture was left almost untouched, albeit stagnating in squalor.

THE FIGHT FOR INDEPENDENCE

The horrors of the famine left many in Ireland convinced of the need for total independence. The next nationalist movement to gain popular support was the Fenian Brotherhood, formed by James Stephens and James O'Mahony. Named after the Fianna, the ancient Gaelic warrior elite, the society soon had the backing of thousands of Irish at home and in the USA. However, an 1867 rebellion was thwarted and the Fenians had only minor success, though many remained active within the Irish Republican Brotherhood.

In the late 1870s, with famine threatening once more, Michael Davitt, a Fenian, persuaded

Transports of delight

Anyone who has ever been stuck in Dublin's rush-hour city centre traffic will appreciate just how ineffective the city's transport system is. A modest journey across town can take as long as an hour, and while both the bus and DART train (serving coastal destinations) services are adequate, the city's chronic congestion is bringing it to a virtual standstill.

Things are looking up, however. On the drawing board since 1994, the first phase of the Luas light-rail system is presently under construction, with a projected completion date of 2003. Luas (which is Irish for 'speed') will provide three lines initially, serving the city centre from outlying suburban destinations. The Luas trains will run overground and will be able to accommodate over 200 passengers. Further lines and a supplementary metro system for the immediate city centre are all in the pipeline, with the completion of the entire system planned for 2016. What may come as a surprise, however, is that the capital actually had a very efficient tram system as early as 1900, which was remarkably successful in meeting the demands of commuters in early 20th-century Dublin.

Horse-drawn cars, providing a regular service to commuters, were first introduced to the city in 1872. A skeletal tramway system, drawn by steam engines, followed soon after, and by the early 20th century, the system had been electrified. The green and cream trams, most of which were double-deckers, were owned and operated by the Dublin United Tramways Company, the company which was at the centre of the infamous workers' 'lock out' of 1913 (*see p14*). The service boasted a fleet of over

300 vehicles, bringing passengers to and from the terminus at Nelson's Pillar on O'Connell Street and during its heyday in the 1920s and '30s, it operated some 31 routes, extending as far as Dalkey to the south, the village of Howth to the north and the town of Lucan to the west.

During the early 1940s the tramway system fell into decline, owing to a rise in car ownership and the development of public bus routes. Dublin's trams weren't exactly scrapped, but rather discontinued piecemeal: outlying stations were shut down and the steady closure of lines that followed meant that by the 1950s only a handful of routes were still in operation. There seems to have been little public outcry at the time; the trams were considered outdated and cumbersome, and there was a misplaced but widely held belief that buses were a more effective means of public transport.

Dublin is still paying the price for abandoning its trams: public enthusiasm for exhaust-belching buses has worn thin over the years, with many citizens choosing to crawl through the city in their own vehicles instead. Although Luas has the potential to greatly reduce traffic in the city, only time will tell whether Dubliners are willing to abandon their beloved cars.

Transport enthusiasts will be glad to hear that five refurbished trams including the finely ornate Director's Tram (which unfortunately was set on fire by vandals prior to its acquistion in 1988) stand in the National Transport Museum in Howth (*see p101*). It's a fitting resting place: the city's last tramline, serving the Hill of Howth, ran a minimal service to the village until 1959.

Charles Stewart Parnell, a Protestant landowner from Wicklow, to join him in supporting the Land League of Ireland. The Land League aimed to assist Irish farmers who were struggling with increasing rents and forced evictions, and was entirely run by Fenian men. Parnell took on the cause, and, in the 1880s, came to dominate British parliamentary life, battling against William Gladstone for the cause of the Land League. The Land Acts introduced by Gladstone enabled tenants to buy their land, and, by 1920, some 11 million acres had changed hands.

The achievements of the Land League were a key element in Parnell's drive for Home Rule (self-government for Ireland), an ideal with which Gladstone agreed. The cause suffered a setback when two English officials were murdered in **Phoenix Park** in 1882, and in 1886 the Home Rule Bill was defeated. Progress was further impeded when news broke of Parnell's long-term affair with Mrs Katherine (Kitty) O'Shea. He was deposed from his party soon after, and died in 1891.

Before his liaison became public, Parnell had succeeded in tapping into the burgeoning appeal of the nationalist cause and popular feelings of pride in 'Irishness'. The movement to distinguish and preserve all things distinctly 'Irish' gained momentum with the foundation of the Gaelic Athletic Association (GAA) in 1884 to promote Irish games (*see p215*) and the creation of the Gaelic League in 1889. The League was founded to champion the (dying) Irish language and encourage Irish arts; it was instrumental in the Celtic literary revival spearheaded by writers such as WB Yeats, whose poetry is steeped in Irish myth.

Even so, the standard of living in Dublin continued to be appallingly low, with the slums of the capital city assuming the dubious title of the worst in Europe. In 1913, there were, on average, five families per house, with almost 90,000 people living in tenements.

In such an atmosphere, the fight for political freedom seemed to promise better times. Jim Larkin and James Connolly rebelled against low wages and corporate corruption, forming the Irish Citizen Army to protect workers. During the Great Lockout of 1913, a public meeting that had been prohibited by the authorities went ahead regardless. Over 200 people were batoned by British forces, an event that went down in history as the first Bloody Sunday.

In the first decade of the 20th century, the Irish Republican Brotherhood was revived. Arthur Griffith, who worked on nationalist newspapers *The United Irishman* and *Sinn Féin* ('Ourselves Alone'), called for the Irish MPs to form their own government in Dublin,

and Home Rule was a live issue again. By 1910, it seemed a foregone conclusion, despite vigorous protests from northern Irish Orangemen (so called because their forefathers had been supporters of William of Orange). In January 1913, the Home Rule Bill was read for its third time.

In Belfast Town Hall, half a million men and women signed a covenant to affirm that they would resist Home Rule, with many signing in their own blood. Senior MP Sir Edward Carson threatened to establish a Protestant province of Ulster: he demanded the exclusion of six counties – Derry, Antrim, Tyrone, Down, Armagh and Fermanagh – and had an Ulster Provincial Government standing by. The Ulster Volunteer Force (UVF) was established, consisting of 100,000 men from Orange lodges. The nationalist Irish Volunteers were soon formed as a reaction to the UVF and both societies set about gun-running to arm themselves. The outbreak of World War I put the Home Rule issue on hold, and around 180,000 Irish signed up with the British forces, hoping that their loyalty would win them concessions after the war.

RISING UP

However, the onset of war did nothing to discourage the more determined independence fighters. Old members of the IRB met with younger revolutionaries including the trade unionist James Connolly, Belfast barman Sean MacDermott, schoolteacher Patrick Pearse and the older Thomas Clarke and planned a revolt for Easter 1916. Strategic centres in Dublin were chosen for the uprising – the Four Courts, Jacob's Biscuit Factory, St Stephen's Green, Boland's Flour Mill, and Liberty Hall – and headquarters were set up at the GPO.

> **'Eamon De Valera and Michael Collins filled the power vacuum left in the wake of the Easter Rising.'**

However, the uprising, planned for Easter Sunday, ended in confusion, as the official leader of the Irish Volunteers, Eoin MacNeill, had been kept in the dark about the rebellion. When he finally found out about it, he placed an advertisement in the *Sunday Independent* announcing that the 'manoeuvres' planned for the day were cancelled. The leaders rescheduled the action for Monday, and around 1,000 men turned up to fight. Pearse, Connolly and Clarke marched to the GPO, where Pearse declared Ireland to be a republic. The general public saw an opportunity for disorder and looted Clery's department store. British troops were sent from London, and after almost a week of fighting had enclosed the Irish. By Friday evening, the GPO was ablaze and had to be evacuated. The centre of Dublin was ravaged.

The number of casualties was estimated at 300 civilians, 130 British troops and 60 rebels. Pearse, horrified by the bloodshed, eventually surrendered on Sunday evening: he was imprisoned in Kilmainham and shot, along with Clarke. In all, 77 death sentences were issued, though many were commuted. Last to be killed were Sean MacDermott and James Connolly, who, because of a broken ankle, was unable to stand to face the firing squad and had to be shot sitting in a chair.

Two nationalists filled the power vacuum left in the wake of the Easter Rising. Eamon De Valera was an Irish-American mathematics teacher who had led the garrison at Boland's Mill, while Michael Collins was a West Cork man who had emigrated to England but returned home for the Easter Rising to train and organise the Irish Republican Brotherhood. Anti-British feeling in Dublin was fanned by the list of martyrs from 1916 and by increasing rumours that conscription for the war would extend to Ireland. On his release from prison in 1917, De Valera was elected leader of the rebel party, and in the 1918 General Election, the new party, campaigning under the name of Sinn

Féin, won nearly 75 per cent of all Irish seats. However, voting was rigged, with some supporters casting as many as 20 votes.

Instead of attending the London Parliament, the new MPs met in Dublin at Dáil Éireann (the Irish Parliament) and declared a sovereign independent Irish Republic. De Valera went to the US to rally support among the emigrants and call for political recognition of the Irish Republic. Collins, though, took a different route. Officially Minister of Finance, his main energies were actually spent as director and overseer of the military wing of the Irish Volunteers, later to be called the Irish Republican Army (IRA). The killing of policemen and informers began in earnest, but the Royal Irish Constabulary fought back. Disguising themselves in civilian clothes, they murdered the nationalist Lord Mayor of Cork and targeted other Sinn Féin supporters. There were not enough uniforms to accommodate the new recruits imported from England, who instead wore military khakis and became known as the Black and Tans. The poet Austin Clarke wrote: 'No man can drink at any public house/In Dublin but these roarers look for trouble/And break an open door in…'. The ruthlessness of the Tans and the Auxiliaries did much to encourage nationalist resentment: posters declared that for every Crown servant killed, two Sinn Féiners would be shot, and house-burning became a standard way of

The **General Post Office**, focal point of the 1916 Easter Rising. *See p14.*

First ladies of Ireland

'Instead of rocking the cradle they have rocked the system.' Mary Robinson

Maud Gonne (1865-1953)

Maud Gonne is perhaps most famous as the stunningly beautiful object of WB Yeats's unrequited love and the subject of many of his poems, but she was also an ardent revolutionary, whose contribution to the nationalist cause earned her the soubriquet Ireland's Joan of Arc – and this despite the fact that she was an Englishwoman. During her long-standing affair with the French journalist and politician Lucien Millevoye she joined the secret Irish Republican Brotherhood and, in 1900, founded Inghinidhe na hÉireann (Daughters of Ireland), a women's republican movement. It was, however, her stage performance in 1902 as Yeats's Cathleen ni Houlihan that ensured her notoriety: in the play, the legendary Countess Cathleen symbolises Ireland's national struggle by transforming from an old crone into 'a young girl with the walk of a queen'.

Maud Gonne repeatedly refused Yeats's marriage proposals, instead marrying Major John MacBride, an Irish officer who was later executed for his part in the Easter Rising. Gonne's continued support for the republican cause landed her in prison in 1918 and again in 1923, when she went on hunger strike with Countess Markievicz (see below) and 91 other female prisoners. She spent the last decades of her life at Roebuck House in Dublin, where she died on 27 April 1953. Her son, Sean MacBride, became Irish Foreign Minister, chairman of Amnesty International and joint winner of the Nobel Peace Prize in 1974.

Countess Markievicz (1868-1927)

Another Brit who adopted the nationalist cause was the famously feisty Countess Markievicz (pictured), a pre-eminent figure in Irish politics. Constance Gore-Booth spent most of her childhood on the family estate in County Sligo, before moving to Paris where she married Polish Count Casimir Markievicz. On her return to Ireland she joined Sinn Féin and in 1909 formed the Sinn Féin youth movement – basically a boy scout group for revolutionaries. She was a committed socialist despite her upper-middle-class upbringing, and assisted Connolly and Larkin in the 1913 lockout (see p14). Her finest hour came during the Easter Rising of 1916 when she and Michael Mallin led the rebel forces at St Stephen's Green, holding it for six days until the British brought them a copy of Pearse's surrender order. The Countess was jailed at Kilmainham, but was spared execution on grounds of her sex. When she heard of her reprieve she famously remarked

targeting suspects. Dublin was badly hit: entire sections were cordoned off as suspects were rounded up; ambushes and street shootings made life dangerous for civilians.

The second Bloody Sunday took place on 21 November 1920. At dawn, Michael Collins had 14 undercover British intelligence officers executed in their beds, and that afternoon, British troops opened fire on a crowd of football spectators at Croke Park, killing 12 people. Later the same day, two senior IRA men and an innocent Sinn Féin supporter were put to death in Dublin Castle. Michael Collins came out of hiding to lay a wreath at their funeral.

The tit-for-tat violence of the War of Independence continued on both sides. In December, the Auxiliaries torched the centre of Cork city, and in May 1921, during working hours, 120 IRA men took over the Custom House in Dublin, the centre of the British administration. They set it alight, but were surrounded and eventually surrendered, with their artillery supplies drained. Presumably unaware that the IRA had few men or arms left, British representatives met with De Valera on 9 July 1921, signing a truce two days later. The ensuing negotiations concluded on 6 December 1921, when Michael Collins, Arthur Griffith and representatives of the British government signed the Anglo-Irish Treaty. Collins remarked: 'I have signed my death warrant.'

FROM FREE STATE TO REPUBLIC

The terms of the treaty gave limited independence to 26 counties of Ireland, known as the Irish Free State. The remaining six (largely Protestant) Ulster counties refused to join, thereby effectively partitioning Ireland along geographical, political and religious lines. Moreover, Britain's authority was still evident in the Free State, as under the terms of the treaty, members of the Dáil would have to

to the British officer: 'I do wish your lot had the decency to shoot me.' On release she became president of the Women's Volunteers and a minister in the first Dáil Éireann. During the Civil War the Countess supported the anti-treaty republicans, she was jailed by the Free State government and went on hunger strike with Maud Gonne and others. In 1926 she joined Eamon de Valera's Fianna Fáil Party

and was elected as one of its candidates shortly before her death in 1927. Countess Markievicz is buried in Glasnevin Cemetery and commemorated for her part in the Easter Rising by a bust on St Stephen's Green.

The two Marys

In 1990, the Irish political world was rocked when **Mary Robinson**, a pre-eminent lawyer and member of the Senate, beat the Fianna Fáil candidate to became the first woman president of Ireland and one of only three female heads of state in the world. During her time in office she showed an unprecedented interest in domestic and international affairs and was noted for her religious tolerance and liberal attitude to abortion, divorce and homosexuality. She resigned the presidency in 1997 to accept the position of United Nations High Commissioner for Human Rights, but remains one of Ireland's most popular politicians.

Robinson was succeeded by **Mary McAleese**, the second and current female president of the Republic of Ireland. Between them, the two Marys have transformed the presidency from a retirement home for superannuated politicians into a vital, active post, and successfully promoted Ireland's international status as a dynamic and forward-looking country.

swear allegiance to George V and his heirs. Eamon De Valera disassociated himself from the treaty and Sinn Féin split, leaving the treaty ratified by a small majority. Nationalist Ireland was torn asunder: in Northern Ireland, the death toll for the first half of 1922 was 264 people, some 65 per cent of whom were Catholic.

Civil war broke out in June between the pro- and anti-treaty factions, with O'Connell Street and the Four Courts the main battlegrounds. After eight days of fighting, De Valera's supporters were forced to surrender and emergency anti-terrorist legislation was enacted: any republican carrying arms would be shot by the Free State troops. The Irish Civil War lasted for a year and was characterised by bloody acts and vicious reprisals. In just seven months, 77 people were executed and 13,000 imprisoned, with many on hunger strike. Michael Collins himself was killed in an ambush near Bandon in west Cork on 22 August, 1922.

Unsurprisingly, the Civil War dominated Irish politics throughout the 1920s. De Valera split from the republicans to form Fianna Fáil ('Warriors of Ireland'), speaking against the Free State's betrayal of the country, and won as many seats as the government party in 1927. Fianna Fáil refused the oath of allegiance and, for a period, were locked out of the Dáil before eventually joining the government. In 1932, rigged voting and some voter 'encouragement' by the IRA helped Fianna Fáil take the parliamentary majority. The party remained in power for 17 years, widening the gap between England and Ireland. The enforced oath of allegiance was scrapped, and IRA prisoners were released (some were even offered commissions in the state army). However, when the IRA refused to disarm, De Valera declared it illegal. The 1937 constitution declared the state's name as Eire, and Roman Catholicism was prioritised as the majority religion.

During this time, the Four Courts and O'Connell Street were slowly rebuilt yet again. IRA terrorist activities remained sporadic in Ireland, but were extended to the English mainland, with London targeted for a bombing campaign in 1939. At the outbreak of World War II, Ireland assumed neutral status, though the IRA aided the German war effort by bombing Belfast docks. The government focused on abstract republican ideals, paying little attention to social welfare, and in 1948, Fianna Fáil were ousted by a coalition of Fine Gael ('Tribe of the Gaels') and Seán MacBride's Clann na Poblachta ('Republican Party'). A year later, Ireland was finally declared a republic.

THERE MAY BE TROUBLES AHEAD

The coalition government tackled the enormous problem of tuberculosis, attempting to introduce 'radical' health legislation that would provide pre- and post-natal care for mothers. The Catholic Church took umbrage, and the government was defeated over the issue. In 1955, Ireland joined the United Nations: a significant step that was in stark contrast to the insular, isolationist beliefs of De Valera's party.

More generally, the 1950s were a time of tremendous emigration and migration, with rural communities dying out as young people moved to urban centres, especially the capital.

Eamon De Valera (1882-1975).

Dublin began growing again and never stopped, its radius increasing with each year as villages on the outskirts of the city became engulfed in the sprawling suburbia. Many of the city's 18th-century houses were replaced by uninspiring concrete buildings. By 1957, Fianna Fáil were back in power, with De Valera leading the party until 1959, when he swapped the role of Taoiseach (prime minister; pronounced 't-shook') for that of president of Ireland. Sean Lemass took over Fianna Fáil, and became Ireland's first true economic manager; his expansionist policies led to moves away from an agrarian economy crippled by emigration. International trade grew and Ireland began to compete tentatively on the world market. In 1966, Lemass was succeeded by Jack Lynch.

As the fiftieth anniversary of the Easter Rising, 1966 was the last gasp of the romantic republican spirit. Rallies and celebrations were held all over the country and Nelson's Pillar on O'Connell Street, a surviving emblem of British power, was blown up.

But the high-flown ideals were soon to be overshadowed by reality. To the north, where Catholics were, in effect, second-class citizens, the Northern Ireland Civil Rights Association was founded in 1967, drawing inspiration and methods from the American civil rights movement. The British government banned civil rights marches and in 1968, the Royal Ulster Constabulary baton-charged peaceful demonstrators. Horrific riots ensued over the following months: in Londonderry, the RUC fired machine guns and tear gas at Catholic protesters. In the winter of 1969, the IRA split, leading to the formation of the Provisional IRA.

The third Bloody Sunday occurred in Londonderry in January 1972, when 13 civilians were shot by British paratroopers during a protest march. The Belfast parliament at Stormont was suspended and direct rule from Westminster was imposed. In 1973, the Sunningdale agreement offered concessions: every adult was allowed a vote in local elections, and the RUC was disarmed. The measures were rejected by extreme unionists, and the fighting continued. Meanwhile, several members of Fianna Fáil were accused of gun-running for the IRA: Charles Haughey (who was later acquitted) was one of the Cabinet sacked by Jack Lynch in 1970.

Ireland became increasingly involved in international politics, too, and on 1 January 1973, joined the EEC. (The decision was approved only by a narrow margin, but has since proved a key moment in the country's development.) By the mid '70s Ireland was feeling the effects of the worldwide oil crisis, and industrial unrest resulted in large-scale unemployment. Interest rates were high and inflation soared, at one stage reaching 25 per cent. The late 1970s and early '80s were characterised by political instability, with frequently changing governments struggling to retain political and economic control. In 1985 the first Anglo-Irish agreement was signed, formalising cooperation between the British and Irish governments in the handling of Northern Irish affairs. Unionists were outraged by this development, however, and re-enacted the covenant of 1913 (*see p14*). Emigration increased dramatically during the late 1980s, though this time the emigrants were highly educated graduates.

END OF A CENTURY

However, other issues were soon splitting the country, with abortion proving to be a particularly divisive topic. In 1983, a fanatical campaign had been initiated by a 'pro-life' movement to get the prohibition of abortion enshrined in the constitution. Strenuously encouraged by the Church, the referendum was passed. Then, in 1992, came the 'X Case', when a young Dublin girl who had been made pregnant as a result of rape was restrained from travelling to England to have an abortion. The Supreme Court ruled that not only was it legal for her to travel, but that under those circumstances it was not unconstitutional for her to have an abortion in Ireland. The right-wing element were incensed, organising a further referendum to declare abortion illegal, to prohibit pregnant women leaving the country with the intention of procuring an abortion, and to ban the dissemination of information about abortion. The first issue was passed, but the others were defeated, leaving Ireland in a slightly hypocritical no-man's land. Divorce, too, was – and still is – a controversial issue, and was only finally approved after a referendum in 1995.

By the mid 1990s, the day of the all-powerful Church had passed, its voice chronically weakened by various well-publicised scandals concerning acute mismanagement of clerical funds, numerous priests' children, sexual abuse and paedophilia. In 1994, Labour pulled out of its coalition with Fianna Fáil as a result of allegations of possible collusion between the government, the Church and the Attorney General's office concerning the case of Father Brendan Smith. Smith, a priest living at liberty in the Republic, was wanted in Northern Ireland on charges of paedophilia. Extradition requests by the Northern Irish authorities were allegedly ignored in Dublin, and in retaliation, Labour collapsed the government, reforming with Fine Gael and the Democratic Left.

The 1990s were a time of great economic prosperity for Ireland, and Dublin reaped most of the rewards. The so-called 'Celtic Tiger' economy, in tandem with global dot.com euphoria, gave rise to an unprecedented level of investment. Unemployment, which had always been an issue of grave concern for the Irish administration, fell to its lowest rate on record and the new-found economic confidence bolstered both the spending power and arrogance of the city's newly returned expatriates. Temple Bar was revitalised as the city's 'Left Bank', and tax breaks attracted home-buyers back to central Dublin, causing house prices to spiral. The city was once more a place in which to work and live.

However, Dublin's crime rate and drug problems also grew, curtailing the city's relaxed, informal atmosphere. On 26 June 1996, journalist Veronica Guerin was murdered while investigating the crime lords of Dublin. Her death shocked the nation, and catalysed a movement to root out the drug barons and racketeers of the city. Ireland also became an attractive destination for refugees – particularly Romanians and Nigerians – and despite being famed for its hospitality, Dublin found itself facing the very real and ugly issue of racism (*see p23* **One hundred thousand welcomes?**).

> **'The 1990s were a time of great economic prosperity for Ireland, and Dublin reaped most of the rewards.'**

The chronically embarrassing political fiascos of the past two decades have also been cited as another example of the new hypocrisy at the heart of the Irish psyche. In 1997, it emerged that former Taoiseach Charles Haughey had received £1.3 million from magnate Ben Dunne and allegedly laundered it through the Cayman Islands. The money was pooled in a Cayman bank account for Ireland's obscenely rich, holding more than £40 million. It seemed to many observers that the rich were getting richer and the poor were being ignored.

Around 2000, there were signs that the boom may not last much longer. However, while Ireland in the new millennium faces many real and formidable challenges – not least the repercussions of the Euro currency changeover in 2002 – it's doubtful that the country and its capital will revert to the depressed economic climate of the 1970s and '80s. Culturally, geographically, economically and socially, Ireland remains in a state of transition. Only time will tell how it fares.

Key events

839-902 AD Vikings establish Dublin as a harbour or *longphort* and the focus for Scandinavian settlement in Ireland.
1014-1170 Dublin becomes a Hiberno-Norse settlement following the defeat of the Vikings by Brian Ború at the Battle of Clontarf.

MEDIEVAL CITY
1170-71 The Normans led by Strongbow take Dublin from the Hiberno-Norse and Henry II declares Dublin an English colony.
1171-1300 Expansion of Dublin as a port and city. Christian pilgrims flock to Christchurch Cathedral and St Patrick's Cathedral.
1204 Construction of Dublin Castle begins.

TUDORS AND STUARTS
1534 Henry VIII orders the surrender of all Irish-owned lands to the English crown.
1536-1540 Dissolution of the monasteries. Religious houses and relics are destroyed.
1560 Ireland proclaimed an Anglican country.
1591 Foundation of Trinity College.
1601 Defeat of Irish and Spanish forces led by Hugh O'Neill at Kinsale leads to the Act of Supremacy, establishing English control.
1608 Plantation of Ulster begins.
1649 Oliver Cromwell subdues Ireland.
1660 Duke of Ormond is made Lord Deputy of Ireland; Dublin's influence grows.
1685 Catholic James II ascends the English throne, threatening to undermine Protestant control in Ireland.
1690 James is defeated by William of Orange at the Battle of the Boyne. The powers of the Protestant ascendancy are strengthened. Catholic penal laws introduced.

GEORGIAN DUBLIN
1700-1800 Dublin's prosperity is expressed in a rich cultural life and an unprecedented building boom.The city's medieval layout is replaced by wide streets and neo-classical architecture.
1782 The Irish parliamentarian, Henry Grattan, wins nominal legislative independence for the Irish Parliament.
1798 Unsuccessful rebellion of the United Irishmen led by Wolfe Tone.

THE 19TH CENTURY
1800 Act of Union abolishes Irish Parliament, establishing direct rule from London.
1828 Catholic activist and lawyer Daniel O'Connell wins a parliamentary seat to become the first Catholic MP.
1829 Emancipation Act dissolves remaining penal laws discriminating against Catholics.
1841 O'Connell becomes first Catholic mayor of Dublin.
1845-9 The Great Famine.

THE FIGHT FOR INDEPENDENCE
1879-80 Irish MP Charles Stewart Parnell becomes president of the Irish Land League and leader of the Irish Home Rule Party.
1882 Phoenix Park murders.
1886 Gladstone's first Home Rule Bill defeated in the British parliament.
1913 Jim Larkin and James Connolly lead a public meeting during the Great Lockout; over 200 workers batoned by British forces. Becomes known as the first Bloody Sunday.
Easter 1916 Easter Rising.
1918 Sinn Féin, led by Eamon de Valera, wins 75% of Irish seats in the general election.
1919-1921 War of Independence.
21 Nov 1920 Second Bloody Sunday. Twelve people are killed by British forces at Croke Park, Dublin.
6 Dec 1921 Anglo-Irish Treaty creates the Irish Free State and the partition of Ireland.
June 1922 Civil War breaks out between pro- and anti-treaty factions.
August 1922 Michael Collins killed.
1932-1949 Fianna Fáil led by De Valera is the governing party in the Free State Parliament.
1937 Irish constitution names the country Eire and formalises Roman Catholicism as the state religion.
1949 Ireland leaves the Commonwealth and is declared a Republic.

END OF A CENTURY
1966 Fiftieth anniversary of the Easter Rising.
1969 Formation of the Provisional IRA.
Jan 1972 Third Bloody Sunday. British troops shoot 13 civilian protestors in Londonderry.
Jan 1973 Ireland joins the EEC.
1973-1982 Irish home affairs dominated by political and economic instability.
1985 Anglo-Irish agreement.
1990 EU funding and the creation of jobs in the technology sector introduce a new period of prosperity for Ireland.
1990 Mary Robinson is elected President of Ireland.
1991 Dublin is European City of Culture.
26 June 1996 Journalist Veronica Guerin murdered while investigating Dublin crime.
1998 Good Friday Peace agreement.

Dublin Today

Can Dublin handle the growing pains and potential identity crisis of its cosmopolitan ambitions?

On 7 November 2001 the director of Ireland's Central Bank, Maurice O'Connell, officially announced that the era of the country's Celtic Tiger economy was over. The statement was not unexpected, of course; unsustainable levels of growth at home, the global economic downturn, and the terrorist attacks on New York's World Trade Center all played their role in undermining the buoyancy of an economy that during the 1990s was the fastest growing in Europe. For Dublin, the consequences will be both dramatic and far-reaching.

It's been an exhilarating, slightly surreal, ten years for those who call the city home. The 1990s saw Dublin transformed – culturally, socially and architecturally – from a stagnating provincial city to a thriving cosmopolitan destination, and despite the recent gloomy announcements, that process is continuing. In a 20th-century replay of the city's Georgian heyday, Dublin witnessed a rampant spending marathon reminiscent of London in the 1980s. The city quays were one of the beneficiaries.

Once almost completely derelict, they now boast a Millennium Bridge, a Parisian-style boardwalk, glitzy hotels, super pubs and blocks of new apartment complexes. A native to the city, returning after a long absence may find certain areas of the city virtually unrecognisable; the extensive developments around the Temple Bar area, Smithfield Village and the International Financial Services Centre are all testament to the fact that in the last few years the fabric of Dublin city has been changed utterly.

The economic growth of the 1990s was a blessing in other ways, too. Emigration, which had been a feature of Irish life since the Famine, slowed down to a trickle, while unemployment reached its lowest-ever level in 2000. Dublin benefited hugely from investment by the European Union, with the city receiving what some other member states regarded as more than its fair share of cash. In fact, the Irish economy has responded so well to the injection of EU money that the amount of funding has recently been scaled back.

With plenty of money to go around, it is not only business that has profited. The arts in Dublin are booming, a fact witnessed by the continued success of Irish writers around the world, the healthy state of Irish theatre, the development of an indigenous film industry, and the establishment of arts centres in the city suburbs. Museums and galleries have also continued to flourish, with the recent refurbishment of important national institutions such as the National Museum at Collins Barracks, the Project Arts Centre, City Hall and the Chester Beatty Library. Despite the current economic scaremongering, Dublin is an undeniably lively and cultured place in which to live and work.

'Dublin has become a multicultural city very quickly, and the response in certain quarters has been hostile'.

However, it hasn't all been a bed of roses. Attempts to meet the demands of a modern, cosmopolitan city have pushed resources to breaking point; the last few years have seen staff shortages in the services industry, and during 2000 and 2001 the country was threatened time and time again by industrial disputes. Train drivers, airport staff, health service workers, teachers – all of them took to the picket line in an attempt to secure higher pay and better conditions. In December 1999, the city's taxi-drivers brought the city to a virtual standstill – blocking off access to Dublin Airport and public routes in a show of aggression that could have been viewed as ludicrously comic if it had not been so damn inconvenient.

And then, of course, there's the traffic. Central Dublin remains gridlocked for large parts of the day, with more and more people owning cars and choosing to drive to work. In theory, 2003 will herald the arrival of the first phase of the city's own light-rail system, known as Luas (*see p13* **Transports of delight**), funded by a combination of government money and EU largesse. However, it remains to be seen whether the prospect of an efficient transport network will encourage commuters out of their cars and finally ease congestion in the city.

A cynic might suggest that the Celtic Tiger economy only benefited the rich. As rampant inflation sent house prices through the roof, less affluent Dubliners have found themselves struggling to meet exorbitant rents, while first-time buyers have been squeezed out of the

market almost entirely. The self-congratulatory tone often adopted by the government (and some sections of the media) has been met by sharp disapproval from the general public, as the gap between those benefiting from the boom and those going under has widened. Nor has the situation been helped by the constant media analysis of three separate tribunals investigating the offshore investments and generally dodgy financial transactions of former politicians (including the disgraced former Taoiseach Charles J Haughey), Fianna Fáil deputy Liam Lawlor was jailed in January 2001 (albeit, for a week) for refusing to give evidence.

For many, the cultural and economic sea-change over the past ten years has sharply exposed what many see as a fundamental hypocrisy at the heart of the Irish psyche. While the country has continued to reap the rewards of a vibrant tourist industry – priding itself on the friendliness and good-humour of the Irish people – many visitors to Dublin have found the city an increasingly hostile place to visit. In the late 1990s there were numerous (and particularly vicious) assaults on tourists, a phenomenon indicative of the insidious racism that had crept into Ireland hand in

Reflections of old and new Dublin.

One hundred thousand welcomes?

In the last ten years immigration to Ireland has swiftly transformed the country in general and Dublin in particular into an ethnically diverse society. The changes wrought are visible everywhere: ethnic food shops jostle with traditional market stalls on Parnell and Moore Streets; and goods that would previously have been simply and unquestionably absent are now readily available. The result is a much more vibrant blend of cultures on the streets of the city.

There have, of course, been other consequences. Although for many years Ireland has projected an image of itself as the land of *céad míle fáilte* (one hundred thousand welcomes), the new economic prosperity and its consequences have strained this cosy self-image to breaking point. The presence of asylum seekers and other immigrants, and the establishment of cohesive ethnic communities in Dublin have forced the Irish residents seriously to examine their attitudes to people of other cultures. Or perhaps the problem is that Dubliners are failing to do exactly that – for racism is vigorously alive and well on the streets of the city.

Eleven thousand asylum seekers entered Ireland in 2000 – a substantial number given the size of the country's population, but nevertheless tiny in comparison with the number hosted by other European countries.

Government policy has meant that these refugees are either dispersed around the country or accommodated in Dublin hostels with a small weekly living allowance. Thousands of other immigrants enter Ireland each year as students or workers in the technology sector, and although their experience of Irish society has doubtless been more appealing, they too must make a home in a society still struggling to adjust to the concept of multiculturalism.

It is a moot point whether Ireland's brand of racism is more virulent than the bigotry which exists in other European countries; it seems highly unlikely that the Irish are especially or essentially racist. Rather, it appears that the racist folk of Dublin – egged on by such vile national bodies as the Anti-Immigration Platform – are not particularly concerned about hiding or dissembling their opinions. The result is a particularly lurid, visible and audible racism, deeply depressing for those citizens convinced that the city should be a natural destination for present-day immigrants.

Despite government initiatives to tackle the problem, and some signs of slow improvement, there is a disturbing irony to the fact that a nation with such a long history of emigration and diaspora, should respond with intolerance to those who choose to make Ireland their home.

hand with economic prosperity (*see above* **One hundred thousand welcomes?**). A sharp rise in both the number of refugees in the city (particularly from Bosnia and Nigeria) and the number of temporary workers made up largely of students from Spain, Italy and China has transformed Dublin into a multicultural city very quickly, and the response in certain quarters has been hostile. It would seem that the city is rather selective about which aspects of cosmopolitan life it wants to adopt: Dublin has embraced continental coffeeshops, modern restaurants and designer bars with alacrity, but seems less than willing to take on the responsibilities that accompany its aspirations to become an international destination.

As construction of the Monument of Life gets underway in the middle of O'Connell Street, it is interesting to speculate what this 200-metre (656-foot) spire will come to represent in ten years' time. Some detractors have suggested that the monument, colloquially known as the

'Spike', is an unfortunate symbol of Dublin's still-chronic heroin problem, while for others the spire's height seems a fitting representative of the excess of the 1990s.

Dublin's decade of decadence now appears to be finally reaching an end: inflation is falling, redundancies in certain sectors are on the rise, and while much speculation has been made about a recovery in mid-2002, in these days of uncertainty, the prevailing atmosphere has certainly taken a darker turn. Being such a small, peripheral country, Ireland will always be affected by international events without being able directly to influence them, and the country's dependence on both the tourist industry and foreign investment, make it vulnerable to shifts in the global economy.

Furthermore, since January 2002, the Irish have had to contend with the euro. In late 2001, the complex practicalities of the changeover from punt to the new single European currency were still being implemented,

Temple Bar.

with a fervid advertising campaign to help the Irish adjust to their new money. While statistics suggest that most of the population support the new currency (they did vote for it, after all), there's a healthy sceptism about it, too, with many people fearing price-hikes, bank errors and other fiscal mishaps. Most importantly, the euro's future stability (or lack thereof) against the dollar will play a vital role in Ireland's economic development.

'After a surge in popularity in the 1990s, Dublin's success as a tourist destination shows no sign of diminishing.'

However, once the novelty factor of the new notes and coins wears off and the currency has achieved some kind of equilibrium on the world markets, these factors are unlikely to be pressing issues for most visitors to the city. After its extraordinary surge in popularity during the 1990s, Dublin's success as a tourist destination shows no signs of diminishing. In the last decade, the city's prosperity, its hospitable reputation and the boom in budget

flights from the UK earned Dublin a reputation as a cheap and cheerful party city. The Temple Bar area proved particularly popular with hordes of British stag and hen parties who piled into Dublin at the weekends intent on 48 hours of booze-fuelled mayhem. By the late 1990s most Dubliners were so fed up with the weekly invasion of marauding bachelor Brits, that many pubs and restaurants in Temple Bar banned such spirited shenanigans from their premises altogether. Now it would seem that the British stags and hens have been replaced, or perhaps subsumed, by a more varied international menagerie of visitors from all corners of the globe.

The city remains a perfect destination in so many ways: its proximity to the sea and the mountains; its walkable, human scale; its rich and varied cultural life; its elegant Georgian architecture and fine city parks; its peerless pubs and bars – not to mention its growing sense of cosmopolitanism are all factors in Dublin's continuing appeal.

More than anything else, though, the energy and humour of its citizens remain among the city's greatest assets – as in previous decades, these are the essential factors that will help Dublin muddle through the challenging days that lie ahead.

Georgian doors.
See p28.

Architecture

Revolutionary fires and careless construction have taken their toll, but Dublin's buildings remain a proud testament to the city's complex history.

Over the past decade, the city of Dublin has undergone a startling transition. In the 1990s, an economic boom and a swelling urban population gave rise to an unprecedented level of development, and while things may be slowing down now, the ongoing process of planning for an uncertain future continues to be the source of furious debate. Controversies over preservation issues, the feasibility of high-rise construction, and the city's shamefully inadequate transport system dominate the headlines.

Thankfully, however, the bleak urban landscape of the 1970s and '80s – referred to by the then-Lord Mayor, Jim Mitchell, as having 'as much character as a second-rate knacker's yard' – has been given a long-overdue facelift. One cannot help being overwhelmed by it all: the glittering Financial Services Centre, the public squares in Temple Bar, the Millennium Bridge and even a Parisian-style boardwalk along the quays all stand as a testament to the new prosperity of the city.

Throughout the 18th century, Dublin was regarded as the second capital of the British Empire, and until the 1960s it remained the most intact Georgian city in either England or Ireland. Like the people of any formerly colonised country, however, the Irish have always had a volatile relationship with their architectural heritage. Bad planning and unscrupulous commercial development meant that grave mistakes were made: listed buildings were bulldozed to make way for apartments and hotels, while prominent historical areas (particularly on the city's north side) suffered shamefully through neglect. Recent developments have sought to redress the damage, and the new millennial Dublin is certainly more visually pleasing. However, the challenge for Dublin for the coming years is a monumental one: can the city satisfactorily develop to meet the needs of its citizens without compromising what remains of its character?

VIKING AND MEDIEVAL DUBLIN

The Vikings arrived in Dublin in around AD 841 and established a settlement in the area between the city quays and the site of Christchurch Cathedral. Rich archaeological remains, particularly those discovered in the 1970s around Wood Quay (now occupied by the Civic Offices), have provided valuable information about Viking Dublin, but nothing has survived from the period completely intact. The Normans, who took the city in 1171, accepted the basic design inherited from the Vikings, adding new walls, streets and suburban monasteries. Portions of the original city wall can still be seen in the Cornmarket area next to Christchurch Cathedral, while **St Audoen's** (*see p77*) on Cook Street, is the site of the only surviving gateway to the old city.

Dublin's two great Norman cathedrals, **Christchurch** (founded 1038; *see p76*), and **St Patrick's** (consecrated in 1192; *see p77*) are also to be found in this area. Both were substantially renovated in the 19th century, although sections of the original medieval structures survive. The crypt of Christchurch is the city's oldest intact building and features a 12th-century Romanesque doorway.

The 13th and the first half of the 14th century were times of prosperity and expansion in Dublin. The city was the capital of the English 'colony' in Ireland, and from this period until the Reformation, much effort was expended on keeping the native Irish out. Little is known about the architecture of the time, except that it marked a move from timber to brick construction. The dissolution of the monasteries and the seizure of large amounts of church property by the Tudor monarchy allowed the urban structure of Dublin to be consolidated, signalling the transition from a medieval settlement to a modern city.

THE NEO-CLASSICAL TRADITION

After the Restoration of Charles II in the 1660s, Dublin experienced an economic boom and became a permanent seat of parliament, viceroy and university. The city's new-found stability and prosperity was given physical expression in an unprecedented phase of construction, which saw the development of neo-classical architecture in Ireland.

Dublin Castle, which had been the centre of British colonial power in Ireland since 1204, expanded considerably. Built around two quadrangular yards, the castle is a hotchpotch of styles: the castle crypt still contains carefully excavated Viking and Norman remains, but the public buildings bear witness to Dublin's 18th-century heyday. The lavish state apartments (1685) are open to the public, and the guided tour (*see p74*) is recommended.

Neo-classical **Trinity College**. *See p27.*

The first great classical building in Ireland, however, was the **Royal Hospital** in Kilmainham, completed in 1680. It was built by Sir William Robinson as a home for retired soldiers and was modelled on Les Invalides in Paris. The building consists of a central courtyard surrounded on four sides by an unbroken range of buildings with arcaded walkways at ground level. After lying empty for many years, the quadrangular building was splendidly restored in the 1980s by the Irish government and converted into the **Irish Museum of Modern Art** (*see p82*). Robinson was also responsible for the design of **Marsh's Library** (*see p77*), built in 1701 as Ireland's first public library. Located next to St Patrick's Cathedral, this beautiful scholar's library, purpose-built for Archbishop Narcissus Marsh, remains almost totally unchanged to this day.

Neo-classical Palladianism became the dominant architectural style of the first half of the 18th century. The style was introduced to the city of Dublin by Sir Edward Lovett Pearce (1699-1733) in the late 1720s and although the architect only spent seven years in Ireland, his dozen or so commissions transformed Irish architecture. Not least among them is **Parliament House**, begun in 1729 and now the Bank of Ireland (*see p63*). Consisting of a central section with huge colonnades, Parliament House was the first public building built in the Palladian style in either Ireland or England. Above the portico stand the statues of Wisdom, Justice and Liberty, designed by Edward Smyth. The building was reworked by several architects throughout the 18th and 19th centuries, including James Gandon, who added the east and west porticoes. Pearce's building, the octagonal House of Commons, with its domed ceiling, was the most important chamber in the original building. It was destroyed by fire in 1792 and converted into the Banking Hall by Francis Johnston in 1803. Pearce's oak-panelled House of Lords, however, remains intact.

Although it was founded in 1592, **Trinity College**'s most significant period of expansion took place during the 18th century. Trinity's main quadrangle, known as Parliament Square, is enclosed on three sides by monumental neo-classical buildings: the **West Front** (Theodore Jacobsen; 1752-1759); the **Chapel** (1798) and the **Examination Hall** (1779-1785), both designed by Sir William Chambers. The oldest extant building on the campus, however, is the red-brick **Rubrics** (1700) facing the Square to the east. An attractive red-brick building with numerous tall chimneys and distinctive Dutch gables (added in the 1890s), the Rubrics offer a complete contrast to the neo-classicism of the Square's other structures.

Despite the grandiose architecture of Parliament Square, the pride of Trinity is the old **Library Building** (1712), designed by Thomas Burgh. The library was housed in the **Long Room** on the first floor of the building, while the ground floor was originally an open-sided arcade, designed for ventilation. (The arcade was filled in during the 19th century to create more shelf space, and now houses the library shop and an exhibition gallery; see p62.) Another major 19th-century adaptation was the creation of the Long Room's magnificent, barrel-vaulted ceiling by the architectural partnership of Deane and Woodward, to replace the high, flat ceiling designed by Burgh. Despite the college's decision to rip a hole in the library floor to provide access to the shop, the Long Room remains one of Dublin's most impressive sights.

Also within the confines of Trinity College is the **Printing House** (1734), a small building in the style of a Doric temple, designed by the German-born architect Richard Castle (or Cassels; 1690-1751). Castle dominated Irish Palladian country-house architecture until his death; his most significant work in Dublin is **Leinster House** (1745), home to the Dáil and the Seanad (see p66). It has two formal fronts: the Kildare Street frontage, designed to look like a townhouse, and a Merrion Square frontage. Like a country house, they are connected by a long central corridor.

While Dublin's northside suburbs are not exactly spoilt for architectural highlights, they do boast the **Casino at Marino** (see p97), commissioned by Lord Charlemont from British architect Sir William Chambers in 1758. Chambers never again equalled the elegance and sophistication of the Casino, which is considered the greatest example of neo-classical architecture in Ireland: from the outside, the building appears to be a one-roomed structure, but it hides an inventive interior, featuring 16 finely decorated rooms.

'The Georgian houses and squares distinguish Dublin from other 18th-century cities.'

In the late 18th century, James Gandon (1743-1823) came to dominate the architectural landscape. Gandon had studied under William Chambers, and his two great public buildings, the **Four Courts** (1786) and the **Custom House** (1791; for both see p89), are beautifully balanced exercises in neo-classicism. They were almost completely destroyed by fire during the Irish Civil War, but have since been elegantly restored. More recently, **City Hall** (see p74) on Dame Street has been extensively renovated according to the original design by Thomas Cooley. This fine public space was designed as the Royal Exchange in 1779 and has a giant portico and impressive domed atrium.

Despite the public buildings constructed during the period, it is the prevalence of Georgian houses and squares that distinguishes Dublin from other 18th-century cities. Much of the development in the late 1700s came under the jurisdiction of the Wide Streets Commissioners, overseen by John Beresford. They shifted the main north–south axis of the city eastwards, establishing O'Connell Street and the route south to Trinity College as the city's main thoroughfare. As a result, northside areas like **North Great Georges Street**, **Mountjoy Square** and **Henrietta Street**, with their fine Georgian houses, became some of the most sought-after addresses in Dublin. Laid out by Luke Gardiner in the 1720s, Henrietta Street is the most intact Dublin streetscape from the period. Many of its fine houses are now in a state of disrepair, although significant efforts by the Irish Georgian Society have helped restore some to their former glory.

The **Casino at Marino**: architectural illusion.

Meeting House Square in Temple Bar: a tangible expression of the 1990s boom. *See p29.*

It is the south side of the city, however, in which Dublin's Georgian heritage is most in evidence today, with **Merrion Square** (1760s; *see p70*) and **Fitzwilliam Square** (1790s; *see p71*) representing a high-point in the city's architectural development. The terraced houses on the squares are plain but also elegantly proportioned, with external decoration usually confined to doorways and surrounds (fanlights, door-knockers and elaborate footscrapers). Once inside, the subdued exterior design gives way to exuberant internal plasterwork.

REGENCY AND VICTORIAN

In 1800, the Act of Union dissolved the independent Irish Parliament, and the wealth, power and sophistication of Dublin diminished. However, the classical tradition survived well into the 19th century, particularly in the design of the Catholic churches erected after emancipation in 1829. The Gothic style also enjoyed a brief revival during this period; a fine example is the **Church of Augustine & John** on Thomas Street.

The **General Post Office** (*see p85*), begun in 1814, is the work of Francis Johnston, who was to the 19th century what James Gandon had been to the 18th century. The building was gutted during the 1916 Easter Rising, but the exterior retains all of its original elegance, featuring a hexastyle Doric portico, above which stand the three symbolic statues of Fidelity, Hibernia and Mercury. Inside, a bronze statue depicting the death of the mythical Irish warrior Cúchulainn is dedicated to those who died in the Easter uprising.

All Dublin's national cultural institutions were constructed during the late 19th century, but the **Natural History Museum** (built in the 1850s; *see p70*) is the most distinctive. The architecture, consisting of little more than a single block of granite, is rather pedestrian, but the interplay between the building and the collection (which remains all but untouched) conspires to make it an embodiment of 19th-century museology.

Another national treasure, the **National Botanical Gardens** (1840s; *see p97*) at Glasnevin, features wonderful curvilinear glasshouses by Dubliner Richard Turner. One of the 19th century's great innovators in the use of iron and glass, Turner constructed both the Palm House in London's Kew Gardens and the Botanic Gardens in Belfast. Within easy walking distance of the Botanic Gardens is one of Dublin's hidden architectural jewels, the central building of **St Patrick's College**, Drumcondra. Constructed in the 1890s around an arcaded, Italianate quadrangle, it's good enough to survive the impact of the indifferent 1960s buildings that surround it.

MODERN ARCHITECTURE

A strain of classicism continued to play a part in Dublin architecture during the 20th century, but improved technology and increasing foreign influence also began to change the city's face as new styles were introduced. The Edwardian baroque of the **Government Buildings** (1920s) on Merrion Street is in stark contrast to both the sombre classicism of Edwin Lutyens's **Irish National War Memorial Gardens** (1930-40; *see p82*) at Islandbridge, and the art nouveau exuberance of the **Iveagh Trust Buildings & Baths** (1894-1915) near St Patrick's Cathedral. Although dilapidated, the design of this ambitious rehousing programme, funded by a Guinness family trust, clearly shows the influence of the Arts and Crafts movement. In recent decades, some of the more contemporary Corporation housing around the Iveagh Buildings has also been internationally recognised for the quality of its design.

Busáras (1940s), the city's central bus station, is a modernist landmark. Designed by Irish architect Michael Scott, it takes its influences from Le Corbusier and the early International Style. One of the first modern buildings in the city, it features a glazed façade and a dramatic pavilioned top storey.

In 1967, Trinity College's pioneering **Berkeley Library** by Paul Koralek heralded a new dynamism in the city's architecture. Koralek was obliged to keep the 'footprint' of the building to a minimum, and in doing so, constructed a modernist masterpiece. (Trinity's new state-of-the-art **James Ussher Library** is being constructed next door to the Berkeley and is scheduled to open in 2002.)

The Berkeley was followed by a number of innovative projects, such as the former **Bord na Mona Headquarters** (1977) at Baggot Street Bridge, and the **Civic Offices** (1986) at Wood Quay, both by Sam Stephenson. The 'Bunkers', as these gaunt, bleak twin towers came to be known, aroused controversy less for their appearance than for their location, on a Viking archaeological site. In the 1990s, the banality of Stephenson's design was modified and incorporated into a new building by Scott, Tallon and Walker. The new structure, with its good use of space, natural light and undulating curves, is one of the city's more successful modern buildings. The **Belfield Campus** of University College Dublin, however, is far less distinguished. Constructed post-1968 with the express intention of limiting students' ability to gather and protest, it's a dispiriting and soulless jumble of buildings.

BUILDING FOR THE FUTURE

In the early 1990s, the Irish Government designated Temple Bar (see p75) as the city's cultural quarter. Since then, this area's development has been the most tangible expression of the boom of the late 1980s and 1990s. Although the 18th-century street layout was largely preserved, two squares (Temple Bar and Meeting House Squares) and new thoroughfares (Curved Street and Cow's Lane) were added. Notable buildings in the area include **Arthouse** (Shay Cleary, 1996) and the **Music Centre** (McCullough Mulvin, 1996; see p195), which form the concave and convex sides of Curved Street, the **Gallery of Photography** and **National Photographic Archive** (O'Donnell & Tuomey, 1996; for both see p175) on Meeting House Square, and the

Ark (Shane O'Toole and Michael Kelly, 1996; see p171). The **Irish Film Centre** (1992; see p174), designed by O'Donnell and Tuomey, is housed in an 18th-century Friends' (Quaker) Meeting House and is a good example of how an innovative use can be found for an old building without hiding modern interventions. While few regard the 'cultural quarter' as a complete success, the overall method of integrating new developments with existing structures has marked a refreshing change in urban planning.

'The key to Dublin's future success may be the creation of urban districts that act as alternatives to the immediate city centre.'

The new millennium was given physical expression in Dublin in the form of a pedestrian bridge stretching from Ormond Quay on the north side to Wellington Quay in Temple Bar. Designed by Howley Harrington Architects, the bridge forms an elegant link between the two sides of the river. By the end of 2000, pedestrian access to the bridge had been improved by the addition of a 560-metre (1,837-foot) boardwalk along the north bank of the river. Designed by McGarry Ni Éanaigh, it stretches from O'Connell Bridge to Grattan Bridge, creating a pleasant pedestrian environment alongside the quays.

Much of the recent architectural development in the city is now taking place on the north side of the Liffey. **Smithfield Village** (see p91 **Urban space in the making**), complete with its public square and observation tower, has been one of the more successful developments and suggests that the key to Dublin's future success may be the creation of urban districts that act as alternatives to the immediate city centre. The ambitious **Historic Area Rejuvenation Project** (HARP), which aims to regenerate the O'Connell Street area, is in full swing, and construction for the 120-metre (394-foot) **Monument of Light** (aka the 'Millennium Spike') has already begun. The coming years will see the construction of two further bridges across the Liffey designed by Santiago Calatrava (see p83 **Bridging the gap**), significant (if still-undecided) dockland developments, and even a light-rail system, the first phase of which is scheduled for completion in 2003 (see p13 **Transports of delight**).

Whether such ambitious plans will succeed remains to be seen: as in the 18th century, the ability to foster innovative architectural practice in the city seems to rely heavily on Dublin's economic fortunes.

Literary Dublin

The city has nothing to declare but its genius.

Since the 17th century, Dublin's unique Anglo-Irish culture has produced a peerless collection of writers for which the city is known throughout the world. Foremost among them, perhaps, is James Joyce, whose novel *Ulysses* is regarded by many as the finest in the English language and is compulsory reading if you want to get a flavour of the city. Although the settings have changed in the 80 years since its publication, the Dublin-ness remains and the characters and situations are as convincing now as ever. Other key texts, include the work of Samuel Beckett, which, while not set in a traditionally Irish milieu, contains a pioneering streak that affected a generation. *Malone Dies*, one part of a trilogy of novels, showcases Beckett's distinctive and distinctively Irish mixture of laconic prose and black humour. Probably the best depiction of tenement life at the start of the century can be found in the plays of Sean O'Casey. *The Plough and the Stars, Juno and the Paycock* and *The Shadow of a Gunman* are still performed regularly on the Dublin stage and are worth seeing for O'Casey's once riot-inducing honesty.

For a city that has spawned so many hugely influential novelists and playwrights, however, the topographical landscape of Dublin is surprisingly absent from much of Irish literature. While Joyce's labyrinthine *Ulysses* and the stories in *Dubliners* offer fascinating portraits of a colonial city in transition, until recently a great deal of Irish writing has seemed unconcerned with the reality of the urban experience, taking instead a solipsistic and often surreal approach. Swift's *Gulliver's Travels* delivers its barbed political satire through the creation of imaginary landscapes; Beckett's characters wander aimlessly through barren wastelands; while works by Oscar Wilde, George Bernard Shaw and Bram Stoker are characterised by vividly imagined settings that, for the most part, have got nothing to do with Dublin whatsoever.

The retreat from the city into the world of the imagination is still a theme common in contemporary Irish literature, but Dublin's new-found confidence has played a part in creating a new breed of urban literature that seeks to catalogue and explore life in the capital (*see p32* **Writing the city**).

IN THE BEGINNING

Modern Irish writing begins with **Jonathan Swift** (1667-1745), whose birthplace is marked by a plaque on Little Ship Street by Dublin Castle. Following an undistinguished career at Trinity College, he was ordained a clergyman and served in Antrim, Meath and London. He failed to secure advancement in England, so returned to Dublin, where he became Dean of St Patrick's Cathedral in 1714. His *Drapier's Letters* (1724), a series of pamphlets denouncing British attitudes to Ireland, gained him a reputation as an Irish patriot, and he became famous for satirical masterpieces such as *A Tale of a Tub* (1704) and *Gulliver's Travels* (1726). A bequest in Swift's will helped found St Patrick's Hospital for the treatment of mental illness, or as Swift put it: 'He gave the little wealth he had,/To build a house for fools and mad,/And showed by one satiric touch,/No nation wanted it so much.' Swift now lies in St Patrick's Cathedral (*see p77*).

The statues on either side of Trinity College's front gate commemorate political philosopher **Edmund Burke** (1729-97) and the playwright **Oliver Goldsmith** (1730-74). Arguably – though unintentionally, for he was a Whig – the forefather of British Conservative thinking, Burke was born on Arran Quay on the north side of the Liffey, and was baptised in nearby St Michan's church (*see p90*). However, upon completion of his degree, he left Dublin for England and became MP for Bristol in 1774, going on to write *Reflections on the Recent Revolution in France* 16 years later. Like Burke, Goldsmith didn't stay very long in Dublin: he left for London after finishing his studies at Trinity College, and latterly found success with the plays *The Good Natur'd Man* (1768) and *She Stoops to Conquer* (1773). Much of his childhood was spent in County Roscommon, the inspiration for his great poem *The Deserted Village* (1770).

BOOZE AND BLOOD

Ireland's foremost poet of the 19th century, **James Clarence Mangan** (1803-49), was born in historic Fishamble Street. His colourful appearance and prodigious drinking at taverns such as the Bleeding Horse on Camden Street (*see p131*) made him an easily recognisable Dublin character. When he wasn't knocking back the booze, he worked as a legal scrivener and, later, in the library of Trinity College. However, Mangan merits mention here for his poems and translations, which number almost a thousand and include 'Dark Rosaleen', 'Siberia' and 'The Nameless One'. He died of malnutrition and is buried in Glasnevin cemetery (*see p97*).

Novelist **Joseph Sheridan Le Fanu** (1814-73) was less of a wino. Born into a Huguenot background, after completing his legal studies he became the editor of a series of Dublin magazines and began to publish ghost stories: notable examples include *Ghost Stories* and *Tales of Mystery*, which both appeared in 1853. Echoes of Dublin of yore can be found in his novel *The House by the Churchyard* (1863), set in the Dublin suburb of Chapelizod and a central influence on Joyce's *Finnegans Wake*. In later years, Le Fanu rarely left his home in Merrion Square (*see p70*), where he devoted much of his time to the study of magic and demonology. One of his most famous stories, 'Carmilla', anticipates Bram Stoker with its exotic theme of lesbian vampirism.

And it is **Bram Stoker** (1847-1912) who remains one of Dublin's best-known literary figures, though he can hardly be pinned as its most notable. Born at 15 Marino Crescent in Clontarf, Stoker worked as a civil servant in Dublin Castle (*see p74*) before acting as manager for the celebrated Victorian actor Henry Irving: among other passions, Stoker was a great theatre enthusiast and drama critic. Stoker, of course, is best known for authoring *Dracula*, which appeared in 1897, though he also knocked out a number of other macabre volumes, including *The Jewel of the Seven Stars* (1903) and *The Lair of the White Worm* (1911).

THOSE WHO LEFT…

No trawl around Dublin's literary past would be complete without mention of one **Oscar Fingal O'Flahertie Wills Wilde** (1854-1900; *pictured p30*), even though this great wit and dramatist spent most of his creative life in London. Born at 21 Westland Row to surgeon/architect Sir William Wilde and nationalist poet 'Speranza', Wilde was educated at Trinity College, where he won a gold medal for Greek and became a protégé of the classicist and wit Sir John Pentland Mahaffy. After studying at Magdalen College, Oxford, where he had won a scholarship in 1874, Wilde rarely returned to Dublin. His brilliant conversation and plays, including *Lady Windermere's Fan* (1892), *An Ideal Husband* (1895) and *The Importance of Being Earnest* (1895), helped him conquer London, but an ill-considered libel action led to his downfall and prosecution for homosexuality: *The Ballad of Reading Gaol* (1898) and *De Profundis* (1905) are painful records of his time in prison. Bankrupt, he died in Paris in 1900.

Another playwright who left Dublin for London – you may notice a theme developing here – is **George Bernard Shaw** (1856-1950), born at 33 Synge Street in the south inner city (*see p72*). Between 1866 and 1873, he lived at

Torca Cottage in Dalkey (*see p106*), where the views of the bay impressed the young Shaw greatly. After variously working as a clerk, cashier and estate manager, he headed for London in 1876, and thereafter returned to his native land infrequently. Most of his plays deal with political themes, the class struggle, gender politics and nationalism; among the most successful are *John Bull's Other Island* (1904), exploring Anglo-Irish relations, *Man and Superman* (1903), *Saint Joan* (1924), and *Pygmalion* (1913), which was eventually morphed into *My Fair Lady*. (Woody Allen once jibed that he was trying to raise money to buy the rights to *My Fair Lady* in order that he could turn it back into *Pygmalion*.) Shaw was awarded the Nobel Prize for Literature in 1925. Despite his self-imposed exile, he never lost his fondness for his homeland and left a third of his royalties to the National Gallery (*see p70*), where a statue of him stands.

James Joyce (1882-1941; *pictured p30*) is still supreme among literary chroniclers of Dublin life. Born at 41 Brighton Square in Rathgar, Joyce spend much of his childhood moving around. He was educated at the Jesuit

Writing the city

With playwrights plastered on mugs and poems printed on tea-towels, Dublin's literary heritage is paraded for all to see. Lauded by the academic cognoscenti and exploited by the tourist trade, the extraordinary body of work produced by Dublin writers has become a cultural commodity that defines the city. Yet against this background of almost overwhelming literary precedent, a new generation of Dublin writers has begun to make its collective voice heard. They have been able to observe and articulate the massive physical and social changes that have taken place in this city over the last 15 years.

A central figure among this group is the Dublin poet, novelist and playwright **Dermot Bolger**. As his early novels such as *Nightshift* and *The Journey Home* demonstrate, he was at the vanguard of those attempting to portray Dublin's urban underclass, struggling to eke out a meager living on the margins of society. Also active as a publisher and editor, he has worked tirelessly to promote new writing.

Similarly, fellow Dubliner **Roddy Doyle** (best known for *The Commitments* and *Paddy Clarke Ha Ha Ha*) has achieved huge success by expressing, in hilarious and graphic detail, life as lived in Dublin's dirt-poor suburbs. In *A Star Called Henry* (1999) he brings the same frank observation and life-affirming humour to the difficult subject of Irish history, tracing the life of a boy growing up in Dublin in the turbulent years of the early 20th century. The wit of Doyle's novels is also a feature of the work of **Joseph O'Connor**, whose early novels, such as *Cowboys & Indians,* deal with the emigration of an entire generation of the city's young people.

Other authors have also been prepared to write openly about previously taboo subjects. Writer **Keith Ridgway** in his book *The Long* *Falling* was one of the first to describe aspects of gay life in the city, while **Jamie O'Neill** in *At Swim Two Boys* audaciously takes on two icons of 20th-century Dublin, fusing Joycean language with the events of the 1916 uprising to tell a story of (homo) sexual awakening.

Women writers are increasingly making their voices heard in response to a predominantly male literary heritage. **Emma Donohue**, one of Ireland's first openly lesbian novelists, is among those charting the sexual mores of the Celtic Tiger generation. In her short stories and particularly in her debut novel *Stir-Fry,* we get a sense of a new generation, less in thrall to the moral restrictions and nationalist myths of old. In a similar vein, novelists like **Mary Morrissey** and **Catherine Dunne** and poets such as **Yvonne Cullen, Enda Wyley** and **Paula Meehan** are busy mapping out the emotional terrain of modern Ireland's capital. Meehan in particular, from the north inner city, vividly evokes women's experience of growing up in a locale where despite a strong sense of community, the threat of domestic violence was never far away. In more quirky style, **Anne Enright** casts an original eye on Dublin life in her collection of short stories *A Portable Virgin*, and two novels, *The Wig My Father Wore* and *What are you like?*.

Dublin's strong theatrical tradition has also been given a boost in recent years, as local playwrights **Mark O'Rowe** (*Howie The Rookie* and *Made in China)* and **Conor McPherson** (*The Weir* and *The Port Authority*) make a splash on the international scene. For details, *see p210* **Staging a coup.**

All these writers are intent on telling their own Dublin stories exactly as they see fit. Enjoy them all before they become tomorrow's souvenir.

colleges of Clongowes and Belvedere, and later at University College, Dublin; an early pamphlet, 'The Day of the Rabblement', bore witness to his distrust of Catholic nationalism. After a curtailed stay in Sandycove (*see p105*), Joyce followed in what was becoming something of a literary tradition by leaving Dublin, with his lifelong companion Nora Barnacle in tow. His travels took him to Paris, Pola and Trieste, where he taught English. During this period he wrote poetry, collected as *Chamber Music* in 1907, and short prose sketches or 'epiphanies', some of which appear in his early novel *Stephen Hero*.

The first of his prose books to be published was *Dubliners* (1914), a collection of short stories set in the city and exploring themes of death, disease and paralysis through the lives of its inhabitants. It was followed two years later by *A Portrait of the Artist as a Young Man*, an autobiographical novel charting the growth of Joyce's mind and his decision to abandon Ireland and Catholicism for the 'silence, exile and cunning' of his artistic vocation. By this time Joyce had left Dublin for good. he visited the city in 1909 to help establish the country's first cinema on Mary Street, but did not return again after 1912.

'James Joyce is still supreme among literary chroniclers of Dublin life.'

Joyce began his masterpiece *Ulysses* in Trieste in 1914 and published it under the imprint of Shakespeare & Co in Paris in 1922. Set on 16 June, 1904 – Joyce's first date with Nora Barnacle – it charts a day in the life of Stephen Dedalus, a student, and Leopold Bloom, an advertising canvasser. The novel follows the structure of Homer's *Odyssey*, with Bloom representing Ulysses and Stephen his son, Telemachus. Many of the novel's locations can be visited today, such as Glasnevin Cemetery, Davy Byrne's pub on Duke Street, Holles Street Hospital, Olhausen's butcher shop on Talbot Street, the Thomas Moore statue on College Green, and Sandymount Strand (*see also p95* **Walking the *Ulysses* trail**).

Having finished off the daylight world in *Ulysses*, Joyce plunged into the world of dreams in his last novel, *Finnegans Wake* (1939), which took him 17 years to write. The novel is 'set' in the Mullingar Inn, Chapelizod, in the dreams and dream-language of publican Humphrey Chimpden Earwicker and his wife and children Anna Livia Plurabelle, Shaun the Post, Shem the Penman and Issy. Its last sentence is unfinished ('along the'), connecting with its first ('riverrun'), suggesting the novel's theme of resurrection and

eternal recurrence. It remains a uniquely daunting book, but also a uniquely rewarding one. Driven out of Paris by the German occupation, Joyce died in Zürich in 1941.

Dublin's third Nobel laureate, **Samuel Beckett** (1906-89), was born in Foxrock and educated at Trinity College. Beckett spent much of his life living in Paris and writing in French specifically to disassociate himself from the English literary tradition. While in Paris in the late '20s, he became a friend of Joyce, who dictated some of *Finnegans Wake* to him. Unlike Joyce, however, Beckett returned from his self imposed exile and promptly wrote a collection of stories, *More Pricks Than Kicks* (1934), in a garret in Clare Street. Perhaps in revenge for the Free State government banning the book, a character in *Murphy* (1938) assaults the buttocks of the statue of national hero Cuchulainn in the General Post Office (*see p87*). Careful observers will notice that the statue does not, in fact, possess any buttocks.

Beckett eventually returned to Paris in 1937, but spent much of the war on the run from the Gestapo in the south of France. After the war, he produced the clutch of masterpieces that would bring him international fame, including his most famous play *Waiting for Godot* (1955), characterised by its spare dialogue, stark setting and its powerful and symbolic portrayal of the human condition. Later works, such as *Endgame* (1958) and *Happy Days* (1961), concentrate even further on language with minimal action. Dublin and its environs never completely disappeared from Beckett's work, however, with Dún Laoghaire pier, Dalkey Island, and Foxrock railway station all recognisable in the prose work *Malone Dies* (1958) and the monologue *Krapp's Last Tape* (1959). Beckett was awarded the Nobel Prize for Literature in 1969.

... AND THOSE WHO STAYED

However, not every late 19th-century writer left the country for good. Ireland's greatest poet, **William Butler Yeats** (1865-1939), was born at 5 Sandymount Avenue (in the south-east of the city), but spent much of his childhood in Sligo and London. His father JB Yeats and brother Jack were both painters of note. With Lady Gregory he founded the Irish Literary Theatre, which took as its home the Abbey Theatre in 1904 (*see p86*; the building burned down in 1951, and was replaced by the current model in 1966). Among his early plays are *The Countess Cathleen* (1892) and *Cathleen ni Houlihan* (1902), in which his great love Maud Gonne played the lead. The poem 'Easter 1916' is his response to the Easter Rising and contains the famous line, 'A terrible beauty is born'.

After being made a senator of the Irish Free State and being awarded the 1923 Nobel Prize for Literature, Yeats's work improved still further: 'Sailing To Byzantium', 'Among School Children' and 'The Circus Animals' Desertion' are all undoubted masterpieces. He died in France in 1939 and was reinterred in Sligo in 1948, his headstone reading: 'Cast a cold eye/On life, on death./Horseman, pass by!'

Playwright **John Millington Synge** (1871-1909), his first names commonly abbreviated to JM, was born to an old clerical family in the suburb of Rathfarnham, though it was the family holidays in County Wicklow that gave him a first taste of the country life depicted so vividly in his plays. After studies at Trinity College, he spent several years on the continent before visiting the Aran Islands in 1898; the Islands were to have a long-lasting effect on Synge. Returning to Dublin, he became associated with Yeats and Lady Gregory's Irish Literary Theatre. His early plays include *Riders to the Sea,* set on the Aran Islands, and *The Well of the Saints,* but his masterpiece is *The Playboy of the Western World,* which caused riots when first produced at the Abbey in 1907. However, just two years later, Synge died of Hodgkin's disease in a Lower Mount Street nursing home and now lies in Mount Jerome cemetery in the southern suburb of Harold's Cross.

Another playwright, **Sean O'Casey** (1880-1964), was born at 85 Upper Dorset Street in the north inner city. His working-class childhood and experiences in the Irish labour movement are described in his multi-volume autobiography. O'Casey did not become a full-time writer until he was in his 40s, but quickly got the hang of it: *The Shadow of a Gunman* (1923), *Juno and the Paycock* (1924) and *The Plough and the Stars* (1926) – which, like Synge's *Playboy,* caused a riot at the Abbey – are three wonderful Dublin plays that deal realistically with the dangers of Irish patriotism and the hardship of tenement life. In later years he lived in Devon, where he eventually died.

THE BEST OF THE REST
Elizabeth Bowen (1899-1973) – about time a woman writer got in on the act – spent her early years in Dublin before moving to London, but her life in the city and at the family home in Cork influenced much of her later work. Among her novels is *The Last September* (1929), which tells the story of the decline of a great house in Ireland during the Civil War. Visitors might also be interested in *The Hotel* (1927), a short book about the Shelbourne Hotel (*see p42*) and the lives of the people who stayed there in the early 20th century.

A canal bank statue off Baggot Street (*pictured p30*) commemorates **Patrick Kavanagh** (1905-67). Born in Inniskeen, County Monaghan, he described his country childhood in *A Green Fool* and *Tarry Flynn* (1948). He moved to Dublin in the 1930s, where he wrote his long poem *The Great Hunger* (1942). However, he was never financially secure: he even started his own newspaper, *Kavanagh's Weekly,* which soon collapsed. Many of his best poems celebrate the canal where his statue now sits.

'Living writers continue to make Dublin a vibrant literary capital.'

Brian O'Nolan (1911-66), aka **Flann O'Brien** or Myles na Gopaleen, was born in County Tyrone but brought up in Dublin, where he worked as a civil servant. *At Swim-Two-Birds* (1939) is a burlesque and multi-layered novel about a Dublin student writing a book. It won the praise of James Joyce and contains the poem 'A pint of plain is your only man', to be recited over a round of drinks in the Palace (*see p138*) or any of the (numerous) other bars associated with O'Brien. Of his other works, the darkly surreal *The Third Policeman* (1940, published 1967) and *An Béal Bocht* (*The Poor Mouth*, 1941), a satire of Gaelic autobiography, are both worth a look. He is best remembered by Dubliners, though, for his satirical column in the *Irish Times,* a feature of Irish life for almost three decades before his death on April Fools' Day, 1966.

Playwright, drunkard and general hellraiser, **Brendan Behan** (1923-64) was born in Holles Street Hospital and brought up in Russell Street, off the North Circular Road. He was twice arrested for Republican activities and spent five years in prison, an experience that was to shape his plays *The Hostage* (1958, written circa 1941), set in a Dublin brothel, and *The Quare Fellow* (1954). However, too much time spent in McDaid's pub on Harry Street (*see p135*) and other boozers undermined his talent and hastened his demise.

THE LIVING LITERATI
While some prestigious Dublin-born writers, such as **Jennifer Johnston** (b.1930; *Shadows on Our Skin, The Ginger Woman*), **Colum McCann** (*This Side of Brightness*) and the much-acclaimed **John McGahern** (b.1934; *Amongst Women*) have chosen to make their home elsewhere, there are numerous other writers who continue to make Dublin a vibrant literary capital.

Word of mouth

Although some of the more spontaneous literary events in the city have died out recently, there are still a number of places that host readings and writers' workshops. Most are free, but you should expect to pay for some of the more high-profile events. Phone for further details.

There are a cluster of venues close to each other on the northside. The **Irish Writers' Centre** (19 Parnell Square North; 872 1302/ www.writerscentre.ie) is the literary nerve centre of Dublin and is the place to hear poetry and prose in beautiful surroundings. Its remit to promote the work of Irish writers and create links with artists from other countries is reflected in an interesting programme of readings by local and international authors. Consult the website for details. Nearby is the **James Joyce Centre** (see p88), which hosts a *Finnegans Wake* Reading Group on Tuesday evenings and a Joyce workshop on Thursday evenings. It also hosts a regular series of talks on you know who, and facilitates local literary magazines such as *Incognito* and *The Stinging Fly* with readings and launches. Opposite, the **Cobalt Café** (see p128) specialises in cabaret nights, but also occasionally throws some music and poetry into the mix. On the north quays is the **Winding Stair Café** (see p128; pictured), a favourite haunt of local authors and a good place to catch readings from

up-and-coming writers. This popular café-cum-bookshop is a mainstay of the Dublin scene and hosts regular spoken word events. It's also a reliable spot to catch up on some of the local literary backbiting.

Across the river, writers read from works in progress at the **Dublin Writers' Workshop**, held upstairs at Bowes, a distinctly old-style Dublin pub (31 Fleet Street, Southside; 671 4038) every Monday evening (except the first Monday of the month). The writers are a friendly bunch and usually glad to have an audience. Close by, the **Bank of Ireland Arts Centre** (Foster Place; 671 1488) specialises in low-key music recitals (see p187) but often also features lunchtime poetry sessions. Finally, free author readings and other literary events are held in a lovely raftered room on the top floor of **Waterstone's** (see p146) on Dawson Street. These events tend to be very popular and some are ticketed, so book your seat in advance.

These include **Neil Jordan** (b.1950), best known as a film scriptwriter and director, but also a successful novelist (*Dream of A Beast, Sunrise with Sea Monster*), and **John Banville** (b.1945), one of Ireland's most important literary figures thanks to highly acclaimed novels *Dr Copernicus* (1976), *The Book of Evidence* (1987) and *The Untouchable* (1997). Also resident in the city are **Colm Tóibín** (b.1955), who has achieved success as a travel writer and novelist, with works such as *The Story of the Night* and *The Blackwater Lightship*, and the poet **Eavan Boland** (b.1944), who explores issues of nationality and gender in collected works including the *New Territory* (1969), *The Journey* (1987) and *In a Time of Violence* (1994).

Probably the most successful Dublin literary writer of recent years, however, is **Roddy Doyle** (1958), who has managed to pull off the rare feat of impressing the critics while building a huge audience of loyal readers. Moreover he

has made a virtue of recording life in the city in which he lives, beginning with the Barrytown trilogy – *The Commitments*, *The Van*, and *The Snapper* – set in the working-class suburbs of north Dublin. Doyle's colourful language, combined with an easy sense of humour and realistic characters, brought his initial audience to him, but it was with the publication of *Paddy Clarke Ha Ha Ha*, a semi-autobiographical account of growing up in Dublin, that the wider literary world began to take notice. Rewarded with the Booker Prize in 1993, Doyle has continued to produce well-crafted, intelligent novels dealing with social issues: *The Woman Who Walked Into Doors* and most recently the critically acclaimed *A Star Called Henry* (see also p32 **Writing the city**).

▶ For other suggestions on what to read, see chapter **Further Reference**.

Accommodation

Accommodation

After a hard day's sightseeing and a hard night's partying, sleep well in Dublin's increasingly sophisticated hotels and good quality guesthouses.

Looking at the Dublin skyline the first thing that will strike you won't be the graceful spires (although there are many) but the dozens of cranes – everywhere. The city continues to burgeon, and much of the new development is geared towards providing Dublin with the quantity and quality of accommodation needed for a top international destination.

Several new hotels, such as the **Stephen's Green**, the **Westin** and the **Trinity Capital**, have opened in prime southside city locations, and more established names, encouraged by the competition, have had facelifts. Dublin can now boast an array of tempting places to lay your hat, ranging from luxury 'boutique' hotels to reliable mid-range establishments, with all the amenities you would expect, to a solid stock of convenient guesthouses and hostels.

As a visitor to Dublin, one thing you will notice is the grime: the image of 'dirty old Dublin' is unfortunately not mere nostalgia. Beyond the city-worn exteriors, however, most city-centre hotels, guesthouses and B&Bs today are spruce, fresh and comfortable. The standard of food in hotel restaurants has improved enormously, too. While a few hotels have signature eateries offering some of the finest dining in the city – Halo at the **Morrison** and Peacock Alley at the **Fitzwilliam** are two examples – even less flash dining rooms are usually up to scratch. It is now safe to assume that you won't have to stomach the over-boiled vegetables and leather-like meat that characterised Irish hotel dining in the past. Don't panic, though, the full Irish breakfast is still widely available, and is often better in the less expensive places.

CHOOSING WHERE TO STAY

There are many different Dublin experiences to be had and your choice of accommodation can be key to the success of your visit.

Spearheading the gentrification of the north city quays is the **Morrison**, one of Dublin's most impressive state-of-the-art hotels with a fantastic view of the Liffey. Right across the river is U2's supercool **Clarence Hotel**, and the new **Eliza Lodge** guesthouse, which can give you the same central location without running up a huge bill. For a taste of colonial Dublin, stay in one of the city's Georgian

buildings that house every level of hotel from the top-class **Merrion** on the southside to the humbler guesthouses north of the river on **Lower Gardiner Street**. This area of town has really improved over the last couple of years, making it a safer as well as an amazingly convenient location, within walking distance of the central bus station, Connolly train station and DART line and most city bus routes.

The compact size of central Dublin means you can opt out of the city altogether, yet still be within easy reach of its amenities. Dublin's coastline, from Howth Head in the north to Bray Head in the south, is studded with hotels and guesthouses, while inland a handful of country house hotels offer secluded luxury in beautiful surroundings. The **Portmarnock Hotel**

The best Hotels

For a home away from home
Don't miss the attractive surroundings, great breakfasts and top-notch service at the **Anglesea Town House** (*see p52*) and the incomparable **Number 31** (*see p51*).

For a celeb-spotting, ab-fab stay
Try the glamorous **Westbury**, the elegant **Merrion** (for both, *see p42*) or the super-star **Clarence** (*see p39*), darling.

For 21st-century style
Check into the ultra-hip **Fitzwilliam** (*see p41*), the effortlessly cool **Morrison** (*see p45*) or the modishly upmarket **Westin** (*see p45*).

For party animals
Drink and dance your way around Dublin from the **Trinity Capital** (*see p47*), the **Temple Bar Hotel** (*see p51*) or the ever-open **Abraham House Hostel** (*see p54*).

For a unique experience
Sink into the comforting opulence of the legendary **Shelbourne Meridien** (*see p42*), or relax at the cleverly renovated **School House Hotel** (*see p50*).

You too can enjoy the supercool **Clarence**.

boasts a setting worthy of the wilds of the west coast, and history buffs will love the ancient surroundings of **Clontarf Castle**.

RATES

The rates given here are intended as general guidelines and should always be checked before you make a reservation. Rates will vary depending on the day of the week, the time of year and on special events happening in the city. Most places listed here will give special rates for children and a reduction for children's meals. Check hotel websites for up-to-date information and special offers before you book.

All prices are quoted as room rates and include breakfast, unless otherwise stated. VAT is also included, but at the upper end of the market, you may also have to add a 12½-15 per cent service charge. Hotel rooms are en suite and have a telephone as standard, unless we have indicated otherwise.

Luxurious

Southside

The Clarence

6-8 Wellington Quay, Temple Bar, Dublin 2 (407 0800/fax 407 0820/www.theclarence.ie). All cross-city buses. **Rates** €267-€286 single/double; €572-€1,905 suite. Breakfast €16-€19. **Credit** AmEx, DC, MC, V. **Map** p75.

A triumph of both style and substance, the Clarence is the finest hotel in Temple Bar. The clever conversion of the 1852 building into a mid-1990s style

hotel means the interior is as fashionable as the location. Arts and Crafts detailing, Shaker furniture and natural materials combine to create a calmly chic ambience. The rooms themselves are individually designed around a carefully chosen colour scheme to create a soothing as well as luxurious environment. Well established at the heart of Dublin's dining and nightlife scene, The Clarence offers fine food in the Tea Room (*see p119*) and classy cocktails in the Octagon Bar (*see p136*). It is well known to be owned by members of U2 and you will be able to soak up some of that superstar nightlife in the hotel's nightclub, the Kitchen (*see p199*).

Hotel services *Babysitting. Bar. Beauty salon. Bureau de change. Business services. Concierge. Laundry. Limousine service. Nightclub. Parking. Restaurant.* **Room services** *Air-conditioning. Dataport (Internet & ISDN). Mini bar. Room service (24hr). Safe. TV (satellite/VCR).*

Conrad International

Earlsfort Terrace, Dublin 2 (676 5555/fax 676 5424/www.conrad-international.ie). Bus 10, 11, 13, 14, 15, 44, 46A, 47, 48, 86. **Rates** €248 single; €280 double; €610-€1,067 suite. Breakfast €22. **Credit** AmEx, DC, MC, V. **Map** p313 H7.

The classy Conrad International is popular with business travellers because of its vast range of services. Some rooms have beautiful views of the National Concert Hall opposite, and all of them, from standard boudoirs to deluxe suites, are modern, with colour co-ordinated furnishings, individual temperature controls, a desk you can actually work on and a spacious bathroom, complete with fluffy robes. The gym is excellent and reduced rates are available for the use of the K Club golf course (*see p216*). Alfie

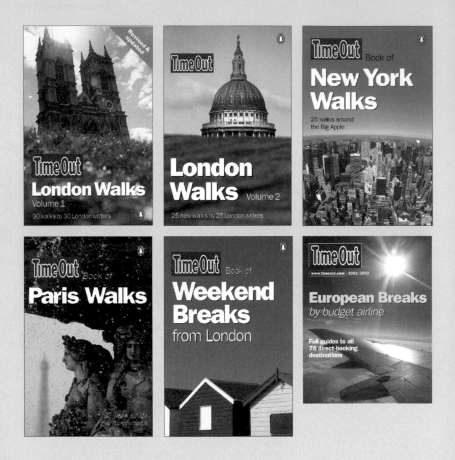

Take a hike...   ...take a break

Available from all good booksellers

Welcome to the **Fitzwilliam**.

Byrnes pub in the hotel is popular with local office workers and the Alexandra restaurant and Plurabelle Brasserie offer the same high standard in food. Within walking distance of Grafton Street yet a social hub in its own right, this is one of Dublin's most impressive hotels.
Hotel services *Babysitting. Bar. Beauty salon. Bureau de change. Business services. Concierge. Conference facilities. Gym. Laundry. Limousine service. No-smoking rooms. Parking. Restaurant.* **Room services** *Air conditioning. Dataport. Mini bar. Room service (24hr). Safe. Trouser press. Turndown. TV (pay movies).*

Davenport Hotel

Merrion Square, Dublin 2 (607 3500/fax 661 5663/www.ocallaghanhotels.ie). Pearse DART/ all cross-city buses. **Rates** *€215-€298 single/double. Breakfast €16.50-€20.* **Credit** *AmEx, DC, MC, V.* **Map** p313 J6.
The impressive façade of this hotel was originally built in 1763 as the front of Merrion Hall and is now a landmark in this elegant part of the city. The warm tones of the façade are carried through to the bedrooms, which are individually styled in bright colours and rich fabrics. Located just behind Trinity College, yet hidden in a relatively quiet corner, the Davenport is a great base for exploring the Georgian southside. The hotel is especially well fitted out for big parties and functions and has every business facility.
Hotel services *Babysitting. Bar. Bureau de change. Business services. Concierge. Conference facilities. Gym. Laundry. No-smoking rooms. Parking. Restaurant.* **Room services** *Air-conditioning. Dataport (Internet & ISDN). Room service (24hr). Safe. Trouser press. Turndown. TV (cable/pay movies).*

Fitzwilliam Hotel

St Stephen's Green, Dublin 2 (478 7000/fax 478 7878/www.fitzwilliam-hotel.com). All cross-city buses. **Rates** *€275 single; €305 double; €440-€640 suite.* **Credit** AmEx, DC, MC, V. **Map** p313 H6.
Proclaiming itself one of the 'hottest' hotels in the world, this Terence Conran-designed hotel is unashamedly aimed at the young executive market. Decorated in chrome and glass in late '90s style, it exudes an ambience of understated contemporary elegance. The jewel in its crown is the award-winning restaurant Peacock Alley (*see p119*) where many visitors to Dublin make a point of dining. It also boasts Ireland's largest roof garden and, from here, looking over St Stephen's Green, you'd be right in thinking you had found something of a city oasis.
Hotel services *Babysitting. Bar. Bureau de change. Business services. Conference facilities. Concierge. Laundry. Limousine service. No-smoking rooms. Parking. Restaurant.* **Room services** *Air-conditioning. CD-players. Dataport (Internet & ISDN). Fax machine. Mini bar. Room service (24hr). Safe. Trouser press. TV (cable/satellite).*

Hilton Dublin

Charlemont Place, Grand Canal, Dublin 2 (402 9988/fax 402 9966/www.dublin.hilton.com). Bus 14, 15, 48A, 44. **Rates** *€??? single; €248 double.* **Credit** AmEx, DC, MC, V. **Map** p309.
This modern hotel overlooks the leafy banks of the Grand Canal, offering a tranquil setting that belies its proximity to the south end of the city centre. The

Georgian style: the **Merrion Hotel**. *See p42.*

Pure luxury at the **Shelbourne Meridien**.

bedrooms are of a good size and decorated in gentle tones to enhance the feeling of space and light; the best ones also have a canal view. The Hilton frequently caters for big parties and conferences and can seem rather impersonal, but it does have a great array of services, including a full complement of business facilities. For relaxation, there's the Champions Bar, a contemporary sports bar with a large and popular beer garden.

Hotel services *Babysitting. Bar. Bureau de change. Business services. Concierge. Conference facilities. Laundry. Parking. Restaurant. Safe.* **Room services** *Dataport (Internet & ISDN). Room service. Trouser press. TV (satellite).*

Merrion Hotel

Upper Merrion Street, Dublin 2 (603 0600/ fax 603 0700/www.merrionhotel.com). Pearse DART/all cross-city buses. **Rates** €280-€356 single; €305-€394 double; €597-€953 suites. Breakfast €19-€23. **Credit** AmEx, DC, MC, V. **Map** p313 J6.

Housed in four restored listed Georgian houses, the Merrion offers a chance to experience uniquely Dublin surroundings at their most lavish and elegant. The service is discreet yet of the highest quality, and many of the rooms and suites overlook 18th-century gardens. Pamper your body in the spa and pool or delight your tastebuds in the top-end Patrick Guilbaud Restaurant (*see p113*). Close to the Irish Parliament buildings and Merrion Square, a stay in such polished finery is a treat to savour.

Hotel services *Babysitting. Bar. Beauty salon. Bureau de change. Business services. Concierge. Conference facilities. Garden. Gym. Laundry. Limousine service. No-smoking rooms. Parking. Restaurant. Spa. Swimming pool.* **Room services** *Dataport. Mini bar. Room service. Safe. Trouser press. TV.*

Shelbourne Meridien

27 St Stephen's Green, Dublin 2 (663 4500/fax 661 6006/www.shelbourne.ie). Bus, 11, 14, 15. **Rates** €197-€445. Breakfast €23. **Credit** AmEx, DC, MC, V. **Map** p313 H6.

A major landmark in Dublin since 1824, the Shelbourne has been extensively refurbished in the last decade and is now part of the Meridien chain. While only the most expensive rooms actually overlook the Green, they are all individually furnished to the highest degree of style and luxury and retain some period features. The Side Door restaurant and bars are popular with fashionable Dubliners, and you definitely shouldn't miss afternoon tea in the Lord Mayor's Lounge. The Shelbourne Club offers a world class fitness suite, including a steam room, sauna and an 18-metre pool. If you want to relax, you can enjoy a massage in the beauty parlour or a traditional hot shave in the barber's. Only steps away from Grafton Street and the National Museum, the Shelbourne fits in perfectly with the grand colonial style of this part of the city.

Hotel services *Babysitting. Bar. Beauty salon. Bureau de change. Business services. Concierge. Conference facilities. Gym. Laundry. No-smoking rooms. Parking. Spa. Swimming pool.* **Room services** *Mini bar. Room service (24hr). Trouser press. TV (cable).*

Stephen's Green Hotel

St Stephen's Green, Dublin 2 (607 3500/fax 661 5663/www.ocallaghanhotels.ie). Bus 10, 11. **Rates** €220-€315 single/double; €315-€380 suite. Breakfast €16.50-€20. **Credit** AmEx, DC, MC, V. **Map** p313 H6.

One of Dublin's newest hotels and already a striking addition to the Green, this hotel typifies the Dublin mix of traditional and cutting-edge design. Its sparkling glass-and-chrome atrium catches the eye and the modern flair continues into the spacious lobby and the comfortable bedrooms. The hotel has a full gym and every possible business amenity, and although you may find a homely atmosphere somewhat lacking, if you want style and efficiency you will be satisfied. The Magic Glasses Bar is already popular in the area.

Hotel services *Babysitting. Bureau de change. Business services. Concierge. Gym. Laundry. No-smoking rooms. Parking.* **Room services** *Air-conditioning. Dataport. Mini bar. Room service. Trouser press. TV (cable/pay movies).*

Westbury Hotel

Grafton Street, Dublin 2 (679 1122/fax 670 7078/ www.jurysdoyle.com). All cross-city buses. **Rates** €248-€292 single; €248-€330 double; €276-€921 suite. Breakfast €23. **Credit** AmEx, DC, MC, V. **Map** p313 H5.

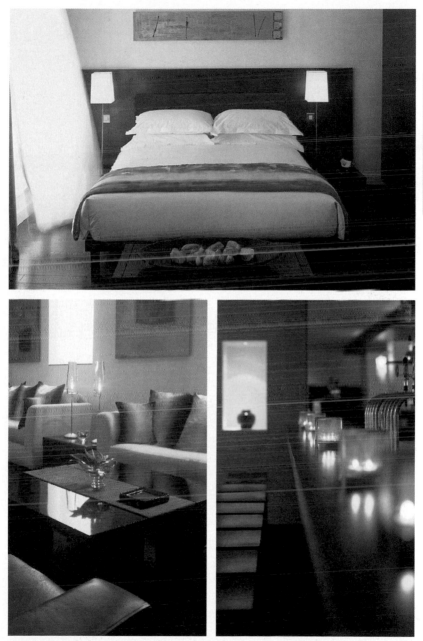

Heaven for lovers of creature comforts and good design: the **Morrison**. *See p45*.

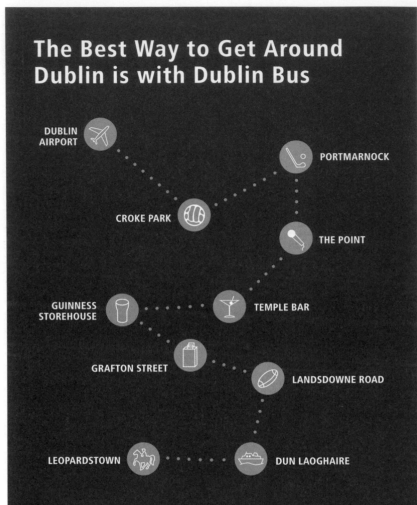

The Best Way to Get Around Dublin is with Dublin Bus

DUBLIN AIRPORT

PORTMARNOCK

CROKE PARK

THE POINT

GUINNESS STOREHOUSE

TEMPLE BAR

GRAFTON STREET

LANDSDOWNE ROAD

LEOPARDSTOWN

DUN LAOGHAIRE

With our network of over 5,000 bus stops and special services such as Airlink and Nitelink, we've got the city covered. The smartest way to use Dublin Bus is with prepaid tickets. Purchase yours at any one of over 250 ticket agents or through Dublin Bus. Better yet, buy your tickets on-line at www.dublinbus.ie or www.ticketmaster.ie

Dublin Bus, 59 Upper O'Connell St., Dublin 1
Travel Information +353 (0)1 873 4222

Dublin Bus
Changing With the City

Clontarf Castle Hotel

Situated right in the heart of Grafton Street, the Westbury has been the setting of many urban legends concerning the doings of the rich and famous, and remains one of the city centre's most glamorous hotels. While the lounge area maintains an aura of exclusivity, the Terrace Bar contrasts with its more cosy library feel. Other hotels exhibit a contemporary style, but the Westbury relies on a more complacent sense of luxury and this is carried through in its rooms and suites, which feature luxury amenities such as TV screens in the bathroom.
Hotel services *Babysitting. Bar. Beauty salon. Bureau de change. Business services. Concierge. Conference facilities. Gym. Laundry. Limousine service. No-smoking rooms. Parking. Restaurant.* **Room services** *Air conditioning. Dataport. Mini bar. Room service (24hr). Safe. Trouser press. TV (cable/pay movies).*

The Westin

College Green, Dublin 2 (546 1000/fax 645 1234/ www.westin.com). All cross-city buses. **Rates** €319 single/double; €1,896 Presidential suite. **Credit** AmEx, DC, MC, V. **Map** p313 H5.
The Westin is one of Dublin's newest luxury hotels and is a reincarnation of two old bank buildings that date back to 1863. As such, it combines new design with traditional grandeur. Three of the façades are original and located right on College Green. Many of the rooms look out on to a stunning atrium courtyard and there are excellent views of the centre of Dublin from the upper storeys. The variously sized bedrooms are decorated in mahogany and relaxing neutral shades, with ultra-comfortable beds and

modern dataports. The hotel's bar, the Mint, is in the old bank's vaults and retains the original counters. In contrast, the Exchange restaurant is bright, new and modernly styled. Don't be put off by the somewhat stark reception area; the rest of the hotel fulfils the potential provided by its historic setting.
Hotel services *Babysitting. Bar. Bureau de change. Business services. Concierge. Conference facilities. Laundry. Gym. No-smoking rooms. Parking. Restaurant.* **Room services** *Air-conditioning. Dataport (Internet & ISDN). Mini bar. Room service (24hr). Safe. TV (cable/pay movies/ satellite).*

Northside

The Morrison

Ormond Quay, Dublin 1 (887 2400/fax 878 3185/ www.morrisonhotel.ie). Bus 30, 90. **Rates** €265 single/double; €570 suites; €1,460 penthouse. **Credit** AmEx, DC, MC, V. **Map** p313 G4.
Designed by fashion guru John Rocha, the Morrison is the epitome of Dublin's new-found sense of style. Its gleaming brick and glass frontage exudes an air of easygoing cool. The colour palette is dark choco late and cream, the furnishings are leather and suede, and in the evening the lighting is just low enough to make everyone look sexy. The generous-sized bedrooms may be stylishly minimalist but there are no compromises when it comes to comfort: spacious bathrooms, king-size beds, mini hi-fi systems and high-speed dataports create the ideal environment for business or pleasure. The surprisingly relaxed bar (*see p140*) is the perfect place for an early evening drink, before moving on to the striking Halo Restaurant (*see p121*) or downstairs to the über-fashionable Lobo club (*see p199*). A treat.
Hotel services *Air conditioning. Babysitting. Bar. Business services. Concierge. Disabled: adapted rooms. Laundry. Limousine service. No-smoking rooms. Parking. Restaurant.* **Room services** *Dataport. Mini bar. Room service. Safe. Turndown. TV (satellite/VCR).*

Dublin Bay & the coast

Clontarf Castle Hotel

Castle Avenue, Clontarf, Dublin 3 (833 2321/fax 833 0418/www.clontarfcastle.ie). Clontarf Road DART/ 130 bus. **Rates** €197-€248 single; €229-€273 double; €286-€445 suites. **Credit** AmEx, DC, MC, V.
Dublin's only genuine castle hotel, Clontarf Castle is a truly historic site and one of the city's most beautiful hotels. The castle was built in 1172 by Hugh de Lacy and today magically combines the authentic features of the castle building with a contemporary luxury to cater for all your needs. The impressive hotel lobby makes a feature of one of the castle walls, with bright tapestries, wood panelling and stone floors. Decorated in rich reds and golds, the rooms have a medieval feel, while at the same time offering 21st-century amenities. Great for business or for short breaks, its proximity to the city centre, several golf courses and the seafront makes this a real gem.

Old-fashioned class is combined with personal service at **Buswells Hotel**.

Hotel services *Babysitting. Bar. Bureau de change. Business services. Concierge. Conference facilities. Disabled: adapted rooms. Garden. Gym. Laundry. No-smoking rooms. Parking. Restaurant. Safety deposit.* **Room services** *Dataport. Room service (24hr). Trouser press. TV (cable/pay movies).*

Portmarnock Hotel & Golf Links

Portmarnock, Co. Dublin (846 0611/fax 846 2442/ www.portmarnock.com). Bus 32. **Rates** €184-€248 single; €267-€330 double; €377-€445 suite. **Credit** AmEx, DC, MC, V.

For a luxurious getaway, complete with spectacular views and a top-class 18-hole golf course, the Portmarnock offers the full package. All the sumptuously decorated bedrooms have either a bay view or a view of the links, enhancing the feeling of space and light pervading the hotel, and the Osborne restaurant promises high-class food in gorgeous surroundings. The hotel caters equally for business and pleasure, with understated but efficient service – if you're here for the golf, you can be sure your outings will be well organised, but non-golfers are equally well looked after with long beachwalks along the sweeping coastline, and opportunities for clay-pigeon shooting or archery.

Hotel services *Babysitting. Bar. Business services. Concierge. Conference facilities. Golf course. Laundry. Parking. Restaurant. No-smoking rooms.* **Room services** *Dataport (Internet & ISDN). Room service (24hr). Safe. Trouser press. Turndown. TV (cable).*

Expensive

Southside

Brooks Hotel

Drury Street, Dublin 2 (670 4000/fax 670 4455/ www.sinnotthotels.com). All cross-city buses. **Rates** €153-€203 single; €222-€280 double. **Credit** AmEx, DC, MC, V. **Map** p313 G5.

This traditionally styled designer hotel has gained an enviable reputation for considerate service and attention to detail. It combines an intimate atmosphere with fin de siècle styling. Francesca's Restaurant and

the Butter Lane Bar offer a sophisticated ambience aiming to give city visitors a welcome refuge from the buzz of Grafton Street only minutes away.

Hotel services *Bar. Bureau de change. Business services. Concierge. Conference facilities. Laundry. Parking. Restaurant.* **Room services** *Air-conditioning. Dataport (Internet & ISDN). Mini bar. Room service. Safe. Trouser press. TV.*

Buswells Hotel

23-27 Molesworth Street, Dublin 2 (614 6500/ 676 2090/www.quinnhotels.com). Pearse DART/ 10, 11, 13, 46A bus. **Rates** €140 single; €215 double; €240 triple; €254 suite. **Credit** AmEx, DC, MC, V. **Map** p313 H5.

A superb hotel with a traditional sense of class, Buswells combines the piquancy of a rarified atmosphere with a really personal and friendly code of service. The promise of charm suggested by the exterior of this Georgian building is fulfilled as soon as you step into the lobby, while the hotel bar is a hub of activity attracting politicians and journalists from the Dáil just across the road. Understated in its tone, it nevertheless provides every service you would expect. The hotel is currently developing an on-site business centre and gym.

Hotel services *Babysitting. Bar. Bureau de change. Concierge. Laundry. No-smoking rooms. Parking. Restaurant. Safe.* **Room services** *Dataport (Internet & ISDN). Room service. Safe. Trouser press. TV.*

Clarion Stephens Hall Hotel & Suites

The Earlsfort Centre, Lower Leeson Street, Dublin 2 (638 1111/fax 638 1122/www.premgroup.ie). Bus 11, 11A, 46A. **Rates** €165 1-bedroom suite (1-2 people); €240 2-bedroom suite (2-4 people). Breakfast €10.16-€12.70. **Credit** AmEx, DC, MC, V. **Map** p313 H/J7.

If you're in Dublin for a while and prefer to stay in a self-catering environment, the all-suite Stephen's Hall is perfect. Housed in a fine Georgian building, all the suites, with the exception of the studios, have separate lounges, fully equipped kitchens and dining areas. The penthouse suites on the top floor provide splendid city views, while the townhouse suites on the ground floor have their own private entrances. The hotel also provides free underground parking. **Hotel services** *Babysitting. Bar. Bureau de change. Business services. Conference facilities. Laundry. No-smoking rooms. Parking. Restaurant. Safe.* **Room services** *CD-player. Dataport (Internet & ISDN). Fax machine. Kitchen. Room service. Safe. Trouser press.*

Morgan Hotel

10 Fleet Street, Dublin 2 (679 3939/fax 679 3946/ www.themorgan.com). All cross-city buses. **Rates** €134-€476. **Credit** AmEx, DC, MC, V. **Map** p75.
Perfectly situated close to College Green, the Morgan is a stylish contemporary hotel. The light, airy rooms combine beech furniture with Egyptian white cotton bedlinen to create an atmosphere of serene comfort. Excellent in-room amenities, including ISDN connections and mini hi-fi systems, ensure that this hotel is popular with business travellers as well as style conscious tourists. A completely different tone is set by the House of Rock diner next door, where breakfast is served.
Hotel services *Aromatherapist. Babysitting. Bar. Bureau de change. Business services. Concierge. Conference facilities. Gym. Laundry. Limousine. No-smoking rooms. Restaurant. Safe.* **Room services** *Dataport (Internet & ISDN). Hi-fi. Mini bar. Room service (7am-10.30pm). Safe. Trouser press. TV (satellite/VCR).*

La Stampa

35 Dawson Street, Dublin 2 (677 8611/www.la stampa.ie). All cross-city buses. **Rates** from €123 single; €152-€210 double. **Credit** AmEx, DC, MC, V. **Map** p313 H5/6.

Opened in 2001 and still very much in the early stages of development, this stylish boutique hotel builds on the reputation of the highly regarded La Stampa restaurant (*see p113*). With a luxury bar (SamSara), two top-notch restaurants and designer accommodation all on one premises, La Stampa promises to become one of the city's most sought-after places to stay. There are currently 21 rooms, with 16 suites to be added during 2002. Definitely one to watch.
Hotel services *Air-conditioning. Bar. Business services. Concierge. Laundry. No-smoking rooms. Restaurants* **Room services** *Mini bar. Room service. Safe. TV (satellite).*

Trinity Capital Hotel

Pearse Street, Dublin 2 (648 1000/fax 648 1010/ www.capital-hotels.com). All cross-city buses. **Rates** €125 single; €151 double; €222 mini-suite. **Credit** AmEx, DC, MC, V. **Map** p313 J5.
This brand new hotel has been superbly designed to offer a high level of comfort that will appeal to both business travellers and pleasure seekers. The brightly coloured rooms are stylishly decorated with art deco influences, and though they're a bit on the small side, they have the advantage of generous black and white tiled bathrooms. Service is very friendly and all your dining requirements will be satisfied by the restaurant and the comfortable lobby lounge, where snacks are served from noon until 6pm. Fireworks, the hotel nightclub and bar, is one of Dublin's newer nightspots and attracts a young, vibrant clientele.
Hotel services *Babysitting. Bar. Bureau de change. Business services. Nightclub. No-smoking rooms. Safe.* **Room services** *Dataport (Internet & ISDN). Iron. Room service. Safe. TV.*

Contemporary comfort at **Chief O'Neill's.** *See p49.*

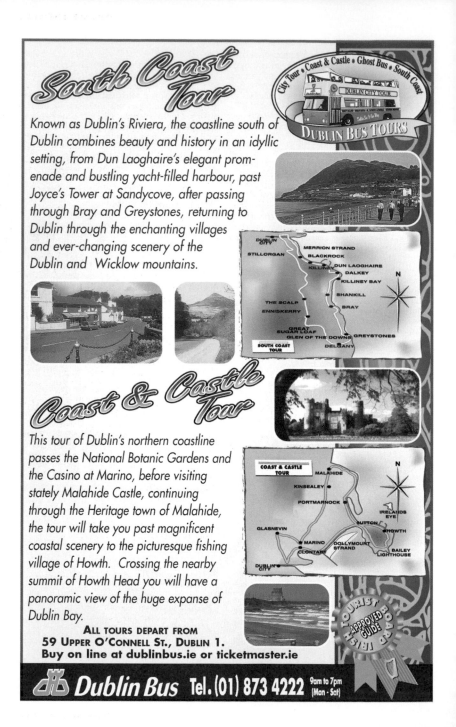

South Coast Tour

City Tour • Coast & Castle • Ghost Bus • South Coast

DUBLIN CITY TOUR

DUBLIN BUS TOURS

Known as Dublin's Riviera, the coastline south of Dublin combines beauty and history in an idyllic setting, from Dun Laoghaire's elegant promenade and bustling yacht-filled harbour, past Joyce's Tower at Sandycove, after passing through Bray and Greystones, returning to Dublin through the enchanting villages and ever-changing scenery of the Dublin and Wicklow mountains.

DUBLIN CITY
STILLORGAN
MERRION STRAND
BLACKROCK
KILLINEY
DUN LAOGHAIRE
DALKEY
KILLINEY BAY
SHANKILL
THE SCALP
ENNISKERRY
BRAY
GREAT SUGAR LOAF
GLEN OF THE DOWNS
GREYSTONES
SOUTH COAST TOUR
DELGANY
N

Coast & Castle Tour

This tour of Dublin's northern coastline passes the National Botanic Gardens and the Casino at Marino, before visiting stately Malahide Castle, continuing through the Heritage town of Malahide, the tour will take you past magnificent coastal scenery to the picturesque fishing village of Howth. Crossing the nearby summit of Howth Head you will have a panoramic view of the huge expanse of Dublin Bay.

COAST & CASTLE TOUR
MALAHIDE
KINSEALEY
PORTMARNOCK
IRELANDS EYE
GLASNEVIN
SUTTON
HOWTH
MARINO
DOLLYMOUNT STRAND
CLONTARF
BAILEY LIGHTHOUSE
DUBLIN CITY
N

**ALL TOURS DEPART FROM
59 UPPER O'CONNELL ST., DUBLIN 1.
Buy on line at dublinbus.ie or ticketmaster.ie**

TOURIST TRAIL
IRISH APPROVED GUIDE

Dublin Bus Tel. **(01) 873 4222** 9am to 7pm (Mon - Sat)

The much-loved **Gresham Hotel**.

Northside

Chief O'Neill's

Smithfield Village, Dublin 7 (817 3838/fax 817 3839/www.chiefoneills.com). Bus 25, 26, 39, 37, 67, 68, 69, 70. **Rates** €165 double; €375 suite. **Credit** AmEx, DC, MC, V. **Map** p312 E4.

A music-themed hotel may sound like an excuse for Disney-esque excess, but Chief O'Neill's (named after a musical historian and collector) carries it off in style. Located in the Smithfield development, this is an efficient modern hotel. Comfortable contemporary bedrooms are designed to make the best use of space, with stylish stand-alone basins and separate shower rooms, while the penthouse suites boast in-room jacuzzis and roof top balconies. Decor is brightened with primary colours and modern glasswork that picks out the musical theme. Redevelopment work in 2002 aims to expand the hotel's conference facilities and remodel the open-plan ground floor area to create a fine dining restaurant and bar.

Hotel services *Air-conditioning. Bar. Business services. Conference facilities. Laundry. No-smoking rooms. Restaurant.* **Room services** *CD player. Dataport (Internet & ISDN). Room service. TV (pay movies/satellite).*

Gresham Hotel

23 Upper O'Connell Street, Dublin 1 (874 6881/fax 878 7175/www.ryan-hotels.com). Bus 11, 13. **Rates** (subject to variation) €143 single; €210 double; €258-€343 suite. **Credit** AmEx, DC, MC, V. **Map** p313 H3.

The Gresham is one of Dublin's oldest and best-loved hotels and remains the place to stay if you are after a quintessentially 'Dublin' experience. Its location near the top of O'Connell Street means that you are right in the hub of the north inner city. The lobby is resplendent with chandeliers and potted palms, while the Gresham lounge has the atmosphere of a relaxed gentleman's club. Rooms have been done up to offer modern facilities along with old-style luxury, and service combines efficiency with personal attention, contributing to the establishment's considerable charm. Special offers are available all year round, making it perfect for a weekend getaway.
Hotel services *Babysitting. Bar. Bureau de change. Business services. Concierge. Disabled: adapted rooms. Gym. Laundry. Limousine service. No-smoking rooms. Parking (€7.50 per day).*
Room services *Dataport. Mini bar. Room service (24hr). Safe. Trouser press. TV.*

Dublin suburbs

Herbert Park Hotel

Herbert Park, Ballsbridge, Dublin 4 (667 2200/fax 667 2595/www.herbertparkhotel.ie). Lansdowne Road DART/ 7, 7A, 8 bus. **Rates** €130-€230 single; €160-€275 double; €210-€340 executive double; €430 suite. **Credit** AmEx, DC, MC, V. **Map** p309.

Light, spacious and contemporary in design, the Herbert Park is now firmly established as one of the city's top venues. Located in the leafy recesses of Ballsbridge, next door to the charming Herbert Park,

it offers all the advantages of a luxury hotel while being a pleasant refuge from the hustle of the city centre. Efficient service from the staff matches the hotel's slick appearance, and the menu at the Pavilion Restaurant holds its own with the high-class restaurants in the Ballsbridge area.
Hotel services *Babysitting. Bureau de change. Business facilities. Gym. Laundry. No-smoking rooms. Parking. Safe. Tennis courts.* **Room services** *Air-conditioning. Mini bar. Playstation. Safe. Trouser press. TV (pay movies/web TV).*

Jury's Ballsbridge Hotel

Pembroke Road, Ballsbridge, Dublin 4 (660 5000/ fax 660 5540/www.jurysdoyle.com). Lansdowne Road DART/7, 8 bus. **Rates** per person €110-€187. **Credit** AmEx, DC, MC, V. **Map** p309.
This five-star hotel offers every conceivable service to guests, including the rare luxury of both indoor and outdoor swimming pools and a full gym. This is very much a social hotel, as you will see from the crowds enjoying the Dubliner bar, Library lounge or the Coffee Dock, which remains open round the clock. If you don't like rugby, avoid this place on Six Nations weekends, when red-faced rugby revellers congregate here before and after matches for hot whiskey. The rooms themselves are pretty unremarkable, but their generous size makes up for their unimaginative styling, and there's plenty more accommodation on offer at The Towers, Jury's sister hotel, next door.
Hotel services *Babysitting. Bar. Beauty salon. Bureau de change. Business services. Concierge. Conference facilities. Gym. Laundry. No-smoking rooms. Parking. Swimming pools (indoor & outdoor). Safety deposit.* **Room services** *Dataport. Mini bar. Room service. Trouser press. TV.*

School House Hotel

2-8 Northumberland Road, Ballsbridge, Dublin 4 (667 5014/fax 667 5015). Lansdowne Road DART/7, 8 bus. **Rates** €151 single; €189 double. **Credit** AmEx, DC, MC, V. **Map** p314 L7.
It is a tribute to those who undertook the refurbishment of this listed 1860 building that they managed to make a Victorian former schoolhouse not only cheerful, but also charming and stylish. The eye-catching redbrick exterior is instantly inviting and inside the award-winning Satchel's restaurant, with its stunning high-beamed ceiling, provides another lure. The well-appointed bedrooms have been furnished in traditional style, in keeping with the building's Victorian heritage, but the chalk and slates that would have been here have been replaced by modern dataports and ISDN lines. Close enough to the city centre to be convenient, the School House also enjoys close proximity to the banks of the Grand Canal, just across the road. Booking ahead is essential, but well worth it for this unique hotel.
Hotel services *Babysitting. Bar. Business services. Garden. Parking. Restaurant.* **Room services** *Dataport (Internet and ISDN). Trouser press. TV.*

Dublin Bay & the coast

Fitzpatrick Castle Dublin

Killiney, Co. Dublin (230 5400/fax 230 5430/www. fitzpatrickhotels.com). Dalkey DART. **Rates** per person €107-€117. **Credit** AmEx, DC, MC, V.
Set in beautiful grounds close to the station, this 18th-century castellated manor house has been refurbished to create a large, well-equipped hotel. Designed to cater for large parties and functions, Fitzpatrick Castle is family-friendly and offers a high standard of service, plus regular night-time entertainment. The rooms are comfortable, if not spectacularly designed.
Hotel services *Babysitting. Bar. Business services. Conference facilities. Gym. Parking. Restaurant. Swimming pool. Safe.* **Room services** *Room service. Trouser press. TV.*

Marine Hotel

Sutton Cross, Dublin 13 (839 0000/fax 839 0442/ info@themarine.ie). Sutton DART/31B, 32B bus. **Rates** €140-€143 single; €210-€229 double. **Credit** AmEx, DC, MC, V.
The Marine Hotel affords instant access to the north Dublin Bay coastline: walk through the lobby, lounge and garden and you'll find yourself right on the beach. The hotel itself is bright, spacious and supremely comfortable. Many bedrooms benefit from an uninterrupted bay view and, on a good day, you could imagine you're in more Mediterranean climes. There's a swimming pool, steam room and sauna on hand for some rest and recuperation, and yet Dublin airport and city centre are only a short drive away. The Meridian Restaurant has a carvery, as well as table service, and the Schooner Bar is a pleasant enough place to while away an evening.
Hotel services *Babysitting. Bar. Bureau de change. Business facilities. Conference facilities. Laundry. No-smoking rooms. Parking. Restaurant. Spa. Swimming pool.* **Room services** *Dataport (Internet & ISDN). Room service. Safe. Trouser press.*

Mid-range

Southside

Central Hotel

1-5 Exchequer Street, Dublin 2 (679 7302/ fax 779 7303/www.centralhotel.ie). Bus 16, 16A. **Rates** per person €70-€95. **Credit** AmEx, DC, MC, V. **Map** p313 G5.
The Central combines an atmosphere of comfortable seclusion with the buzz of being in the city centre. Foot-weary Dubliners and sightseeing-sore visitors are drawn to the Library Bar, a haven of civility offering leather armchairs, blazing fires, rich wood panelling and books to leaf through. Friendly service, spacious rooms and close proximity to cafés, restaurants and shops make this an ideal place to stay that won't break the bank – as long as you avoid rooms overlooking the noisy main road.
Hotel services *Babysitting. Bar. Parking. Restaurant.* **Room services** *TV.*

Eliza Lodge

23-24 Wellington Quay, Temple Bar, Dublin 2 (671 8044/fax 671 8362/www.dublinlodge.com). Bus 90. **Rates** per person €57-€83. **Credit** AmEx, MC, V. **Map** p75.

This guesthouse enjoys a fantastic location overlooking the Liffey and the Millennium Bridge. The rooms are spacious and bright, and all double or luxury rooms guarantee a river view. Amenities are excellent for this price range and the Eliza Blue's restaurant below stairs is proving hugely popular. **Hotel services** *Bar. Restaurant.* **Room services** *Iron. Safe. TV.*

Jury's Inn Christchurch

Christchurch Place, Dublin 8 (454 0000/fax 454 0012/www.jurysdoyle.com). All cross-city buses. **Rates** €84-€89 for 3 adults or 2 adults & 2 children. **Credit** AmEx, DC, MC, V. **Map** p312 F5.

With a magnificent view of Christchurch, Jury's Inn is something of an institution, providing cheap, comfortable and central accommodation for thousands of visitors to the city. The focus may be on function, but the atmosphere is friendly and relaxed. The hotel specialises in family rooms able to accommodate three adults or two adults and two children. The Inn Pub is open until 1.30am for residents on weekend nights and offers live traditional music. There's also an adjoining 24-hour car park costing €9.50 per day. A second branch is located close to the IFSC development at Custom House Quay – the perfect location for business visitors. **Hotel services** *Babysitting. Bar. Business services. No-smoking rooms. Restaurant.* **Room services** *TV.* **Branch: Jury's Inn Custom House** *Custom House Quay, Dublin 1 (607 5000/fax 829 0400).*

Leeson Inn

24 Leeson Street Lower, Dublin 2 (662 2002/fax 662 9963/www.iol.ie/leesoninn). Bus 11. **Rates** €64-€102 single; €102-€140 double. **Credit** AmEx, DC, MC, V. **Map** p313 J7.

Just a few minutes' walk from Stephen's Green, the Leeson Inn is an unassuming hotel housed in an attractive Georgian terrace. The rooms are well equipped and comfortable, and are decorated in inoffensive natural colours. Breakfast is served in a basement dining area, and some excellent eateries are only a short walk away. The hotel's best asset, however, are the relaxed, friendly staff, who are at pains to cater to every guest's needs. **Hotel services** *Business services. No-smoking rooms. Parking.* **Room services** *Dataport. Mini bar. Room service. TV (satellite).*

Molesworth Court Suites

35 Schoolhouse Lane, Dublin 2 (676 4799/fax 676 4982/www.molesworthcourt.ie). **Rates** €160 1-bedroom suite (sleeps 2-4); €200-€280 2-bedroom suite (sleeps 2-4); €350 3-bed suite (sleeps 3-6). **Credit** AmEx, MC, V. **Map** p313 H6.

These three- and four-star self-catering apartments located right in the heart of the city are an excellent option for families. Children are welcome, bed linen is provided and there are shops and places to eat within a stone's throw of the apartments. Rent on a nightly, weekend or three-night mid-week basis. **Hotel services** *Babysitting. Parking.* **Room services** *Dishwasher. Kitchen. TV. Washing machine.*

Number 31

31 Leeson Close, Dublin 2 (675 5011/fax 676 2929/www.number31.ie). Bus 10, 46A. **Rates** per person €54-€115. **Credit** AmEx, MC, V. **Map** p309.

Set in one of the city's most fashionable locales, this unique guesthouse is a real find, combining modern design with an almost rural tranquillity. The soothingly styled bedrooms are housed in a Georgian townhouse, while delicious home-made breakfasts are served in the beautifully designed modern mews building. Chill out in the sunken lounge and wander through the gardens and conservatory for some green therapy. Child-friendly, convenient and elegant – Number 31 seems to have it all covered. **Hotel services** *Babysitting. Garden. Parking.* **Room services** *TV.*

Staunton's on the Green

83 St Stephen's Green, Dublin 2 (478 2300/fax 478 2263). Bus 10, 11, 46A. **Rates** per person €70-€89. **Credit** AmEx, DC, MC, V. **Map** p313 H6.

A wonderful location, just across the road from St Stephen's Green, makes Staunton's one of the most upmarket guesthouses in the city. The Georgian building has modern amenities that offer comfort and convenience, and the gardens fulfil the role of providing a welcome retreat from the grime and bustle of the city. **Hotel services** *Babysitting. Garden.* **Room services** *Trouser press. TV.*

Temple Bar Hotel

15-17 Fleet Street, Temple Bar, Dublin 2 (677 3333/fax 677 3088/www.towerhotelgroup.ie). All cross-city buses. **Rates** per person €64-€102. **Credit** AmEx, DC, MC, V. **Map** p75.

Situated on the edge of Temple Bar, this bright, airy hotel is designed for those visitors looking for close-quarters entertainment. The hugely popular pub, Buskers (under the same management), is right next door, usually crammed to the rafters with tourists swaying to dodgy music. There's a multi-storey car park opposite, offering special rates for overnight parking. With every possible amenity right on its doorstep, this is the place to stay if you are in Dublin to shop all day and party all night. **Hotel services** *Bar. Beauty salon. Bureau de change. Business services. Conference facilities. Laundry. No-smoking rooms. Restaurant. Safe.* **Room services** *Dataport (Internet & ISDN). Trouser press. TV.*

Trinity Lodge

12 South Frederick Street, Dublin 2 (679 5044/fax 679 5223/trinitylodge@eircom.net). All cross-city buses. **Rates** €63.50 per person. **Credit** AmEx, DC, MC, V. **Map** p313 H5.

This three-star guesthouse combines the spaciousness and grace of a well-kept Georgian building with an excellent city-centre location. The rooms cater for modern needs but retain an old-fashioned ambience, and a full-scale suite allows guests the chance to sample the delight of a Georgian apartment. **Hotel services** *Internet access.* **Room services** *Safe. Trouser press. TV.*

Northside

Cassidy's Hotel

Cavendish Row, Upper O'Connell Street, Dublin 1 (878 0555/fax 878 0687/www.cassidyshotel.com). Bus 11, 11A, 13, 16, 16A, 19, 19A, 41. **Rates** €108 single; €146 double. **Credit** AmEx, DC, MC, V. **Map** p313 H3.

Cassidy's provides a warm welcome and a cosy stay in an excellent location on the north side of the city centre. Right beside Parnell Square and opposite the Gate Theatre, yet slightly away from the throng of central O'Connell Street, you can have the best of both the shopping and cultural worlds. Groomes Bar and Restaurant 6 contribute to the hotel's homely atmosphere. **Hotel services** *Babysitting. Bar. Conference facilities. Parking. Restaurant. Safe.* **Room services** *Trouser press. TV.*

Clarion Hotel

International Financial Services Centre, Dublin 1 (433 8800/fax 433 8811/www.clarion hotelifsc.com). Connolly DART/all cross-city buses. **Rates** per person €80-€115. **Credit** AmEx, DC, MC, V. **Map** p313 J4.

The IFSC continues to develop as the heart of Dublin's business world, and the Clarion is one of its newest additions. This light, airy hotel is designed for the business market and built and fitted in a contemporary style that complements its riverside location. It boasts an international selection in its restaurant, bar and café and – just what the weary business person needs – a full gym and 18m pool in which to unwind. **Hotel services** *Babysitting. Bar. Bureau de change. Business services. Conference facilities. Gym. No-smoking rooms. Restaurant. Safe. Swimming pool.* **Room services** *Dataport (Internet & ISDN). Room service. Trouser press. TV.*

Comfort Inn

95-98 Talbot Street, Dublin 1 (874 9202/fax 874 9672/www.premgroup.ie). Bus 33, 41. **Rates** €76 single; €191 double. **Credit** AmEx, DC, MC, V. **Map** p313 H/J3.

You could almost miss this guesthouse, situated as it is, on one of Dublin's busiest thoroughfares. This is the place to stay if you want to shop till you drop then step into your resting place with the minimum fuss. Furnished in contemporary style, the rooms are brightly coloured and stylish. A pleasant surprise, just off O'Connell Street. **Hotel services** *Babysitting. Parking.* **Room services** *TV.*

Hotel Isaac's

Store Street, Dublin 1 (855 0067/fax 836 5390/www.isaacs.ie). All cross-city buses. **Rates** per person €51-€89. **Credit** AmEx, MC, V. **Map** p313 J3.

A smart hotel housed in what was once a wine warehouse, Hotel Isaac's offers elegance for visitors on a budget. Much of the original brickwork remains exposed, though it much of it has been embellished with new features. The bedrooms are bright and comfortable, and the Il Vignardo restaurant serves good Italian food. **Hotel services** *Babysitting. Bar. Concierge. Garden. Laundry. Parking. Restaurant.* **Room services** *Iron. TV.*

Hotel St George

7 Parnell Square, Dublin 1 (874 5611/fax 874 5582/www.indigo.ie/~hotels). Bus 10, 11, 11A, 16, 16A, 19, 19A. **Rates** per person €51-€63.50. **Credit** MC, V. **Map** p313 G3.

Situated on Parnell Square, the St George blends in well with its Georgian surroundings. Its size means that you can benefit from an intimate atmosphere and personal service, yet enjoy the convenience of a central northside location. **Hotel services** *Babysitting. Bar. Parking. Restaurant.* **Room services** *TV.*

Maple Hotel

75 Lower Gardiner Street, Dublin 1 (874 5239/fax 874 5239). Connolly Street DART/41 bus. **Rates** €51-€76 single; €76-€114 double. **Credit** MC, V. **Map** p313 H/J3.

Established for 40 years in a spacious Georgian house, the Maple is Gardiner Street's only two-star hotel. If you're after the charm and comfort of the chintz and doily school of hospitality, then you've hit the jackpot here. The rooms are cosy, the service is warm and welcoming and the small restaurant serves evening meals. **Hotel services** *Bar. Parking. Restaurant.* **Room services** *TV.*

Dublin suburbs

Anglesea Town House

63 Anglesea Road, Ballsbridge, Dublin 4 (668 3877/fax 668 3461). Bus 5, 7. **Rates** per person €57-€61. **Credit** AmEx, MC, V.

This gorgeous four-star guesthouse has one of Dublin's most prestigious addresses. Enjoy the intimacy and elegance of a family-run Edwardian house at a surprisingly affordable rate. You can be sure of a warm welcome as well as a fantastic breakfast, but book well in advance, as there are many others eager to make the most of its charm. **House services** *Babysitting. Garden. Parking.* **Room services** *TV.*

Bewley's Hotel Ballsbridge

Merrion Road, Ballsbridge, Dublin 4 (668 1111/fax 668 1999/www.bewleyshotels.com). Bus 5, 7. **Rates** €88 single/double/family. Breakfast €6.20-€8.80. **Credit** AmEx, DC, MC, V. **Map** p309.

Budget hotels on **Lower Gardiner Street**.

Newly built in the grand style, Bewley's offers the feel of a classy hotel and the ambience of a classy address, although it also represents excellent value for families, since many of the hotel's rooms can accommodate up to two adults and three children at no extra cost. Clearly designed to create a sense of space and comfort, Bewley's is very much in keeping with its Ballsbridge neighbourhood, close to the RDS showgrounds. Enjoy lounging in the downstairs bar area before a meal in the popular O'Connell's Restaurant.
Hotel services *Babysitting. Bar. Parking. Restaurant.* **Room services** *Dataport (Internet & ISDN). Safe. TV (cable). Trouser press.*

Jury's Skylon Hotel

Upper Drumcondra Road, Drumcondra, Dublin 9 (837 9121/fax 837 2778/www.jurysdoyle.com). Bus 3, 13, 16, 16A, 33, 41, 41B, 41C. **Rates** per person €54-€83. **Credit** AmEx, DC, MC, V.
The old Skylon has been given a makeover and now offers good three-star accommodation right between the airport and the city centre. If location is not important to you, there are many better places to stay, but for business visitors with a plane to catch, Jury's fulfils its function well.
Hotel services *Babysitting. Bar. Business services. Parking. Restaurant.* **Room services** *TV.*

Roxford Lodge Hotel

46 Northumberland Road, Ballsbridge, Dublin 4 (668 8572/fax 668 8158/www.roxfordlodge.ie). Lansdowne Road DART/7, 7A, 8 bus. **Rates** per person €70 single; €64 double; €57 triple; €64 suite. **Credit** MC, V. **Map** p314 M7.

A red-brick house on one of Dublin's most charming streets, this hotel offers real value for money without cutting any corners. The rooms are spacious and traditionally decorated and the service makes you feel as if you are staying in a home rather than a hotel. All the rooms are wheelchair accessible and tea or coffee are served at any time for no extra cost.
Hotel services *Bar. Parking. Restaurant.* **Room services** *TV.*

Dublin Bay & the coast

Court Hotel

Killiney Bay, Co. Dublin (285 1622/fax 285 2085/ www.killineycourt.ie). Killiney DART. **Rates** per person €63-€97. **Credit** AmEx, DC, MC, V.
The Court Hotel enjoys pleasant grounds and one of the most enviable views of Dublin Bay. Gables and turrets give the large converted Victorian building the look of a domesticated fairytale castle, while inside you'll find plenty of places to relax. The service here is excellent and children-friendly, and there's quick access to Killiney beach for a run along the sands. Ask for a room with a sea view.
Hotel services *Babysitting. Bar. Bureau de change. Business services. Conference facilities. Laundry. Parking. Restaurant. Safe.* **Room services** *Dataport (Internet & ISDN). Room service. Trouser press. TV.*

Deer Park Hotel & Golf Courses

Howth, Co. Dublin (832 2624/fax 839 2405/ www.deerpark-hotel.ie). Howth DART/31A, 31B bus. **Rates** per person €67-€76; phone for details of golfing rates. **Credit** AmEx, DC, MC, V.
The Deer Park is very good value for money and is a great spot for a family break, with very affordable green fees, a new swimming pool, a child-friendly policy and a relaxed atmosphere, not to mention the stunning scenery of Howth Head on its doorstep. The 1970s exterior is rather off-putting, but the rooms themselves are bright and modern, and the restaurant is decent and the bar is a hive of activity.
Hotel services *Babysitting. Bar. Bureau de change. Golf course. Room service. Safety deposit. Swimming pool.* **Room services** *TV.*

Gresham Royal Marine Hotel

Royal Marine Road, Dún Laoghaire, Co. Dublin (280 1911/fax 280 1089/www.ryan-hotels.com). Dún Laoghaire DART/46A bus. **Rates** per person €83-€165. **Credit** AmEx, DC, MC, V.
This charming three-star hotel has hung on to its 19th-century design and still blends in perfectly with the Victorian resort atmosphere of Dún Laoghaire. A feel of colonial elegance is evident throughout the hotel, and suites come complete with four-poster beds. Surrounded by its own attractive grounds, yet within spitting distance of the ferry terminal, DART station and the east pier, this is a good place from which to explore south Dublin Bay.
Hotel services *Babysitting. Bar. Gardens. Parking. Restaurant. Safe.* **Room services** *Trouser press. TV.*

Island View Hotel

Coast Road, Malahide, Co. Dublin (845 0099/fax 845 1498/www.islandviewhotel.ie). Malahide DART. **Rates** per person €65. **Credit** AmEx, DC, MC, V.

Right above Oscar Taylor's Restaurant, the Island View is intimate and cosy, offering standard accommodation in the most scenic part of Malahide. One to consider for a weekend getaway as the restaurant has possibly the best steaks in Dublin, the village has many good cafés and restaurants, and the surrounding area is good for beach walks.

Hotel services *Bar. Parking. Restaurant.*
Room services *TV.*

Tudor House

Dalkey, Co. Dublin (285 1528/fax 284 8133/ www.iol.ie/tudor). Dalkey DART. **Rates** per person €50-€57. **Credit** MC, V.

There's nothing very Tudor about this gracious listed house, but it's a very pleasant, nonetheless. Located in Dalkey village and surrounded by beautiful grounds, the guesthouse is tastefully and comfortably decorated. All rooms enjoy a sea view.

Hotel services *Garden. Parking.*
Room services *TV.*

Budget

Southside

Other options for backpackers on a budget include the spacious and clean **Ashfield House** (19-20 d'Olier Street, Dublin 2; 679 7734/fax 679 0852), which charges €15-€23 for dormitory beds and €35.50-€38 per person for a private room, and the **Brewery Hostel** (22-23 Thomas Street, Dublin 8; 453 8600/fax 679 0852), which charges €16 for a dormitory bed or €58.50 per person for a double room.

Avalon House

55 Aungier Street, Dublin 2 (475 0001/fax 475 0303/www.avalonhouse.ie). Bus 16, 16A, 19, 22, 155. **Rates** per person €13-€16.50. **Credit** AmEx, MC, V. **Map** p313 G6.

Only minutes from St Stephen's Green and Temple Bar, Avalon House is a friendly hostel with a popular café and good facilities. It may not be the Ritz but it does what it says on the tin.

Services *Bureau de change. Café. Cooking facilities. Internet access. Left luggage. Payphone. Safe.*

Kinlay House

2-12 Lord Edward Street, Dublin 2 (679 6644/ fax 679 7439/www.iol.ie/usitaccm). All cross-city buses. **Rates** per person €16.50. **Credit** MC, V. **Map** p313 G5.

One of the most popular hostels in Dublin and understandably so. It's open 24 hours all year round and there is a friendly if rather raucous atmosphere. Rates include breakfast.

Services *Bureau de change. Cooking facilities. Internet access. Laundry. TV room.*

Trinity College

College Green, Dublin 2 (608 1177/fax 671 1267/ www.tcd.ie). All cross-city buses. **Rates** per person €38-€63.50. **Credit** MC, V. **Map** p313 H5.

From June until the beginning of October, visitors can stay on Trinity College campus. The university enjoys possibly the most central location in the city, and there's the added bonus of fantastic surroundings. Of the 589 rooms, 195 are en suite, and there's a choice of single, double or triple rooms. Rates include a continental breakfast. Campus facilities include a bar, cafés, laundry, parking and a restaurant.

Northside

The small **Goin' My Way Hostel** (15 Talbot Street, Dublin 1; 874 1720/fax 878 8091) has dormitory beds for €12.50 and double rooms for €20.50 per person. There's a midnight curfew, so don't get caught out late. Nearby at 81-82 Marlborough Street, Dublin 1 is the **Marlborough Hostel** (874 7629/fax 874 5172), which charges €16.50 for a dormitory bed or €51 per person.

Abraham House

82 Lower Gardiner Street, Dublin 1 (855 0600/fax 855 0598/abraham@indigo.ie). Connolly Station DART/41 bus. **Rates** €14-€23 dormitory; €32 triple. **Credit** AmEx, MC, V. **Map** p313 H/J3.

One of the city's best hostels, Abraham House is in a prime location for backpackers, close to Busárus and Connolly Station. The wonderfully helpful staff are happy to help you to organise your stay in Dublin, and are particularly good at catering for students' interests. The bedrooms are spacious and clean and the hostel places a strong emphasis on security. Unlike many other hostels, there is no curfew. Good value.

Services *Bureau de change. Cooking facilities. Laundry. Parking (cars & bikes). Safe.*

Gardiner Lodge

87 Lower Gardiner Street, Dublin 1 (836 5229/fax 836 3279/www.dublinhotels.com). Connolly Station DART/all cross-city buses. **Rates** per person €38-€44.50. **Credit** MC, V. **Map** p313 H/J3.

The Gardiner Lodge has a bright, cheery air and is decorated in warm tones. The rooms are spacious and bright, with full-length Georgian windows. Able to cater for families and small groups, the Lodge is a comfortable, well-appointed choice on the popular Gardiner Street strip.

Hotel services *Bar. Restaurant.*
Room services *TV.*

Glen Guesthouse

84 Lower Gardiner Street, Dublin 1 (855 1374/ fax 456 6901/theglen@eircom.net). Connolly Station DART/all cross-city buses. **Rates** (subject to seasonal variation) €32-€38 single; €38-€44.50 double. **Credit** MC, V. **Map** p313 H/J3.

A refurbished Georgian guesthouse, the Glen offers a reliable standard of accommodation along with friendly service, but its location on Gardiner Street is its main draw.
Hotel services *Bar. Parking. Restaurant.* **Room services** *TV.*

Isaac's Hostel
2-5 Frenchman's Lane, Dublin 1 (855 6215/ fax 855 6524/hostel@isaacs.ie). Connolly DART/ all cross-city buses. **Rates** per person €13.50 dormitory; €30.50 single; €25.50 twin. **Credit** MC, V. **Map** p313 J3
Across the road from the central bus station and Connolly train station, Isaac's is a well-run hostel with a decent restaurant, as well as self-catering facilities. One drawback is that the hostel does not allow access to dormitories between 11am and 2.30pm, though you can leave your bags in a safe room during this time.
Services *Bureau de change. Café. Cooking facilities. Internet access. Restaurant. TV room.*

Othello House
74 Lower Gardiner Street, Dublin 1 (855 4271/ fax 855 7460). Connolly Station DART/41 bus. **Rates** €44.50 single; €89 double; €114.50 triple. **Credit** MC, V. **Map** p313 H/J3.
One of Gardiner Street's longest established guesthouses, Othello offers generously sized rooms, especially for families, and a good standard of service. There's also small room in which to relax.
Hotel services *Parking.* **Room services** *TV.*

Phoenix Park House
38-39 Parkgate Street, Dublin 8 (677 2870/fax 679 9769/www.dublinguesthouse.com). Bus 10. **Rates** per person €25-€44.50. **Credit** AmEx, DC, MC, V. **Map** p311 C4
Right beside Phoenix Park, Heuston Station and only ten minutes from the city centre, this family-run guesthouse is the ideal spot if you need to stay at this end of town. Considering the price, the standard of accommodation is high.
Hotel services *Bureau de change. No-smoking rooms. Restaurant.* **Room services** *TV.*

Dublin suburbs

Aran House
5 Homefarm Road, Drumcondra, Dublin 9 (836 7395). Bus 11, 16, 41. **Rates** per person €35.50. **Credit** MC, V.
This family-run B&B is close to the airport and convenient for town. Bright, spacious and full of home comforts, Aran House offers en suite accommodation including breakfast. The leafy environs of Homefarm Road belies its proximity to the centre.
Hotel services *Garden. TV room.*

Dublin City University
Glasnevin, Dublin 9 (700 5736/fax 700 5777/ www.dcu.ie). Bus 3, 13, 16, 19. **Rates** €42 single; €70 double. **Credit** MC, V.

Dublin City University has 609 rooms available for rent from June to September, 253 of which are en suite and three of which have been adapted for disabled use. The campus is 25 minutes from the city centre by bus, and services are frequent.

Egan's Guesthouse
7-9 Iona Park, Glasnevin, Dublin 9 (830 3611/fax 830 3312). Bus 11, 16, 16A, 41. **Rates** per person €37-€41.50. **Credit** MC, V.
This large three-star guesthouse is housed in a beautiful turn-of-the-19th-century building fitted with all modern conveniences. It's superbly run and has spacious communal areas to relax in. The centre of town is only ten minutes' bus ride away.
Hotel services *Babysitting. Parking.* **Room services** *TV.*

Errigal B&B
36 Upper Drumcondra Road, Dublin 9 (837 6615). Bus 16, 13, 33, 41. **Rates** from €32 per person. **Credit** MC, V.
Errigal is an extremely smart, welcoming and well-run B&B, located right on the main airport road and bus routes into the city centre. It's a family-run establishment, and you can always be sure of a warm welcome and a great breakfast. And if you don't fancy the short bus ride into town, the area of Drumcondra itself is full of amenities – shops, bars and restaurants.
Hotel services *Garden.* **Room services** *TV.*

Iona House
5 Iona Park, Glasnevin, Dublin 9 (830 6217/fax 830 6732). Bus 11, 16, 16A, 41. **Rates** per person €44.50. **Credit** AmEx, MC, V.
Make the most of the leafy Victorian charm and relative seclusion of an attractive city suburb at this well established three star guesthouse. Red brick Iona House is close to major bus routes and the National Botanical Gardens (*see p98*).
Hotel services *Bar. Garden.* **Room services** *TV.*

UCD Village
Belfield, Dublin 4 (269 7111/fax 269 7704/ www.iol.ie/usitaccm). Bus 3, 10, 46A. **Rates** per person €33. **Credit** MC, V.
From mid-June to mid-September, 1,200 bedrooms and 350 apartments are available on the UCD campus, which is 20 minutes south of the cith centre by bus. All accommodation is self-catering, but guests can also make use of the campus bar, restaurant, coffee shops and bank.

Camping

Shankill Camping & Caravan Park
Shankill, Co. Dublin (282 0011/fax 282 0108/ www.camping-ireland.ie). Shankill DART. **Rates** €9 tent only; €13 caravan/tent plus car; plus €2 per person. **No credit cards.**
The Shankill has a scenic location, with views of the mountains, and is only a short drive away from the coast. Pitches cannot be booked in advance.

NATIONAL LIBRARY OF IRELAND

Since its foundation in 1877, the National Library of Ireland has maintained an active policy of acquiring heritage items and other materials. Today the Library's collections of books, manuscripts, maps, photographs, newspapers and genealogical material comprise probably the most outstanding collection of Irish documentary material in the world, amounting to some six million items. Among the most notable of the Library's many treasures are the illustrated thirteenth century manuscript Topographia Hiberniae, the Gaelic manuscript collection, the manuscripts and letters of WB Yeats and James Joyce, and the Joly rare book collection.

The Library's Genealogy Service is the starting point for many of the visitors to Ireland who wish to research their Irish ancestry.

Housing the Library's collection of some 300,000 photographs, the National Photographic Archive in the Temple Bar area of Dublin opened in 1998. The programme of exhibitions at the Archive features selected images from the photographic collections.

Facilities:
Exhibitions, Genealogy Advisory Service and Shop
Guided Tours (by appointment)

Open: Mon-Wed 10.00-21.00
Thurs-Fri 10.00-17.00
Sat 10.00-13.00
Closed: Sundays, Bank Holidays, 23 Dec-2 Jan and Good Friday
Admission Free

Kildare Street, Dublin 2
Telephone: +353 1 6030200 Fax: +353 1 6766690
E-mail: info@nli.ie   Website: www.nli.ie

NATIONAL
LIBRARY
of IRELAND

Sightseeing

Introduction

Where to go and what to see.

Dublin crams most of its key sights and attractions into a compact, easily walkable area. Historical sites such as **Christchurch Cathedral** (*see p76*) and **Dublin Castle** (*see p74*) jostle for attention with boisterous **Temple Bar** (*see p75*), while the Georgian elegance of 18th-century streetscapes such as **Merrion Square** (*see p70*) stands in sharp contrast to newly developed and still emerging areas like **Smithfield** (*see p90*). Walk for a short while and you can exchange the bustle of **Grafton Street** (*see p65*) or **O'Connell Street** (*see p84*) for the wide open spaces of

Phoenix Park (*see p93*) or the relative tranquility of the **Grand Canal** (*see p72*).

When you've had enough of wandering the streets, Dublin's museums demand your attention. Chief among them are the **Chester Beatty Library** (*see p74*), the Book of Kells Exhibition at **Trinity College** (*see p61*) and the **National Museum** (*see p66 and p93*), all of which hold fascinating and often unique artefacts and exhibits. Other essential tourist destinations include the Royal Hospital at Kilmainham, home of the **Irish Museum of Modern Art** (*see p82*), the **Municipal**

Gallery of Modern Art (*see p87*), the impressive new **Guinness Storehouse** (*see p81*) and the **James Joyce Centre** (*see p88*) – a tribute to the city's most important writer and most significant cultural export. Finally, don't forget to take full advantage of the city's location. The seaside suburbs around **Dublin Bay** (*see pp99-106*) are easily accessible by DART, and offer a totally different experience from the urban buzz of the centre. Inland there are further attractions, including a couple of interesting museums and grand country houses, that make a journey beyond the city centre worthwhile.

ORIENTATION
Boundaries are difficult in Dublin, with one area merging into another. The most significant demarcation is the River Liffey, which divides Dublin in two along an east–west axis. The city centre spreads across the river, roughly marked by four corners: St Stephen's Green, the top of O'Connell Street, Trinity College and Christchurch. As a visitor, it is likely that most of your time will be spent within this diamond-shaped area. The Royal and Grand Canals also provide a useful boundary, ringing the city centre to the north and south respectively.

TOURIST PASSES AND INFORMATION
For information during your stay, visit the **Dublin Tourism Centre** on Suffolk Street (*see p294*) which has plentiful information about the city and the rest of the country. Dublin Tourism offers a **Combined Ticket** (€9; €5-€8 concessions; €25 family), which admits visitors to any two of the following attractions: Shaw's Birthplace (*see p73*); Dublin's Viking Adventure (*see p76*); Dublin Writers' Museum (*see p88*); Malahide Castle and Fry Model Railway (*see p102*) and the Joyce Museum (*see p105*). Dublin Tourism will also take bookings for tours (*see p60*) and publishes a set of guides, which detail trails around the city and excursions into the surrounding countryside.

Visitors who are planning to visit other parts of the Republic may want to invest in the **Dúchas Heritage Card**, which provides unlimited admission to more than 65 sites administered by Dúchas (the Heritage Service of Ireland), including several in Dublin city and county. The Heritage Card costs €19.05 (€7.62-€12.70 concessions; €45.72 family) and can be bought in advance from Dúchas, over the Internet, or from any member site.

Dúchas (The Heritage Service)
Postal address: 6 Upper Ely Place, Dublin 2 (freephone Ireland only 1-850 600 601/647 2461/ fax 661 6764/www.heritageireland.ie). **Open** 10am-5pm Mon-Fri.

Don't miss Sights

Book of Kells
The stand-out exhibit at Trinity College continues to impress for its exquisite craftsmanship; the Old Library upstairs is pretty special, too. *See p62.*

Chester Beatty Library
This beautiful collection of rare Oriental, Middle Eastern and European art and artefacts is the highlight of Dublin Castle. *See p74.*

Glasnevin Cemetery
A fittingly atmospheric resting place for many of Ireland's heroes. *See p97.*

Guinness Storehouse
Explore the stunningly converted storehouse and then enjoy a perfect pint of Guinness in the Gravity bar. *See p81.*

Irish Museum of Modern Art
One of the city's most important 17th-century buildings provides a lovely setting for the best of Irish modern art. *See p82.*

Kilmainham Gaol
Find out what happened to the Easter 1916 rebels at this famous and evocative prison. *See p82.*

National Gallery
The National Gallery houses some excellent European and Irish art and hosts an annual Turner exhibition. *See p70.*

National Museum
Two sites stuffed with Irish treasures. Marvel at Bronze Age gold at Kildare Street (*see p66*) and decorative art at Collins Barracks (*see p93*).

Natural History Museum
This fusty, musty, old-fashioned place provides a unique insight into Victorian museology. *See p70.*

Phoenix Park
For fresh air, wildlife and acres of space, not many city park's can compete with the green expanses of Phoenix Park. *See p93.*

Temple Bar
Whatever the detractors say, this is still the liveliest part of the city. Avoid the tourist hang-outs and make the most of the area's artistic and cultural venues. *See p75.*

Sightseeing

Trips and tours

Walking tours

Dublin Footsteps Walking Tours

Information (496 0641/269 7021). Start from: James Joyce Room, Bewleys Café, Grafton Street, Southside. **Tours** *June-Sept* 10.30am daily. By appointment only at other times. **Tickets** €6.35. **Duration** 2hrs.
A literary walk through the old city in the footsteps of Joyce, Wilde, Shaw, Yeats et al. Bookings are not required for routine walks; specialist group walks can also be arranged.

Dublin Literary Pub Crawl

Information (670 5602/www.dublin pubcrawl.com). Start from: The Duke (upstairs), 9 Duke Street, Southside. **Tours** *Apr-Oct* 7.30pm Mon-Sat; noon, 7.30pm Sun. *Nov-Mar* phone for details. **Tickets** €8.90; €7.60 concessions. **Duration** 2hrs 15min.
Two actors perform humourous extracts from the works of Dublin's best-known writers. The tour takes in four pubs, and includes a literary quiz (with prizes for the winners).

Musical Pub Tour

Information (478 0193/www.musical pubcrawl.com). Start from: Oliver St John Gogarty's, Fleet Street, Southside. **Tours** *May-Oct* 7.30pm daily. *Nov, Feb-Apr* 7.30pm Fri, Sat. No tours Dec, Jan. **Tickets** €9; €8 concessions. **Duration** 2hrs.
Prepare yourself for a drinking session and a singalong on this jaunt around a dozen of the city's public houses.

1916 Rebellion Walking Tours

Information (676 2493). Start from: International Bar, 23 Wicklow Street, Southside. **Tours** *May-Aug* 11.30am Tue-Sat. *Sept-Apr* phone for details. **Tickets** €7.60; €6.40 concessions. **Duration** 2hrs.
The tour takes you to key sites associated with the Easter Rising and tells the story of the events that led to Ireland's independence.

Walk Macabre

Information (087 677 1512/087 271 1346). Start from: main gates, St Stephen's Green, Southside. **Tours** 7.30pm by appointment only. **Tickets** €7.60; €6.40 concessions. **Duration** 1hr 15min.
Dublin's spooky nooks and crannies are exposed on this scary walk, guided by actors from the Trapeze Theatre Company.

The Zozimus Ghostly Experience

Information (661 8646/www.zozimus.com). Start from: pedestrian gate, Dublin Castle, Dame Street, Southside. **Tours** *Winter* 7pm daily. *Summer* 9pm daily. **Tickets** (bookings essential) €7.60. **Duration** 1hr 30min.
Visit scenes of great escapes, murders and mythical happenings accompanied by Zozimus, the blind storyteller.

Cycle tours

Dublin Bike Tours

Information (679 0899/dublinbiketours@ connect.ie). Start from: Harding Hotel, Christchurch Place, Southside. **Tours** (arrive 15min before start) *Apr-Oct* 2pm Mon-Fri; 10am, 4pm Sat, Sun. *Nov-Mar* phone for details. **Tickets** €15.25 incl bike, guide & insurance. **Duration** 3hrs.
Guided bicycle tours around the capital's quieter streets. The pace is relaxed, with plenty of stops for historical insights. Bike picnics and full day trips are also available.

Bus tours

Dublin Bus

Information: 59 Upper O'Connell Street, Northside (703 3028/www.dublinbus.ie). **Open** 9am-5.30pm Mon-Fri.
The hop-on, hop-off **Dublin City Bus Tour** (€10.20; €5.10 concessions) can be joined at any point on its circuit of the city until 6.30pm, or you can take the **Ghost Bus** (€19) for an evening tour of Dublin's haunted houses. Tours venturing outside the centre (€15.25; €7.60 concessions) include the **Coast and Castle Tour**, which takes in the National Botanic Gardens and Malahide Castle, and the **South Coast Tour** to Killiney Bay and the Wicklow Mountains.

Viking Splash Tours

Information (855 3000/www.vikingsplash tours.com). Start from: Bulley Alley Street, Southside. **Tours** *June-Sept* (every 30min) 10am-5pm Mon-Sat; 10.30am-5pm Sun. *Oct, Nov, Mar-June* phone for details. **Tickets** €13.50; €7.50 concessions; €45 family.
Trawl the streets in a WWII amphibious vehicle (known as a duck; *pictured p38*), with a Viking guide, before taking to the water at the Grand Canal Dock. Great fun for kids.

Southside

Sights, shops, pubs and parks – Dublin's southside has got the lot.

The majority of visitors to Dublin spend most of their time on the southside of the city – and it's not hard to understand why. Not only was this area of central Dublin the site of the original Viking *longhport*, but since the building boom of the mid 18th century, it has been considered by far the more salubrious side of town, with a wealth of cultural and historical sights to interest the visitor. Within a relatively small (and eminently walkable) area, you'll find many of Dublin's key attractions: **Trinity College**, **St Stephen's Green** and the well-heeled squares of **Georgian Dublin**; **Dublin Castle** and the cultural hedonism of **Temple Bar**; the old Viking settlement and the city's two **cathedrals**. What's more, the southside has plenty of restaurants, bars and shops to provide diversions from the serious business of sightseeing. And, while the immediate city centre is heavily touristed, it is possible to head slightly off the beaten track to the working-class neighbourhood of the **Liberties**, the monolithic presence of the **Guinness brewery** and further west to the suburb of **Kilmainham**.

national pride. Literary giants such as Jonathan Swift, Bram Stoker, Oscar Wilde and Samuel Beckett studied at the college, while the statues on either side of the main gate depict Trinity graduates Edmund Burke and Oliver Goldsmith. Today, Trinity is Ireland's most prestigious university and one of Dublin's biggest tourist attractions. The 40-acre (16 hectare) campus boasts the city's finest buildings and one of the country's greatest treasures, the medieval **Book of Kells** held in the Colonnade gallery of the original college library (*see p62*).

Trinity's grounds unfold into a series of elegant quadrangles, gardens, walks and leafy sports fields. The **Old Museum Building**, a large Venetian-style Victorian edifice, was commended by Ruskin, but arguably the finest buildings are those in Front Square, dominated by the twin Palladian façades of Chambers' **Chapel** and **Examination Hall** (*see also p27*). Just beyond, in Library Square and surrounded by some beautiful old maple trees, is Lanyon's remarkable 30-metre (100-foot) **Campanile**. Trinity's architecture is complemented by

The Georgian City

Trinity College & around

Since the late 1700s, all the great streets of Dublin have led off from College Green, a triangular plot with a fine conjunction of buildings, dominated by the neo-classical West Front of **Trinity College**. Unfortunately, College Green is also a busy intersection where it is difficult to cross the road, let alone stand and take in the architecture. Once inside the gates, however, Trinity is so artfully constructed that it cuts out the noise of the city altogether.

The 'College of the Most Holy and Undivided Trinity' was founded in 1592 by Elizabeth I as a place of learning for the Anglo-Irish ascendancy. Although Catholics were first admitted in 1793, it was not until 1970 that they could attend without a special dispensation from the Archbishop of Dublin (*see p62* **Education, education, education**). However, if the college has been perceived as being slightly removed from the affairs of the predominantly Catholic Irish, the achievements of former students are a legitimate source of

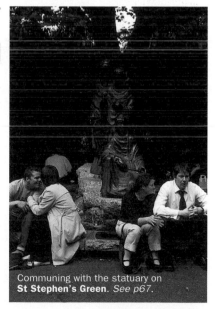

Communing with the statuary on **St Stephen's Green**. *See p67.*

Education, education, education

Women's entrance into Trinity College, Dublin was relatively painless. The university opened its doors to the female sex in 1904 after a few years of campaigning – well before either Oxford or Cambridge dared so radical a step. At first, women were subject to stringent rules and banned from college after 6pm. However, as the women proved themselves academically, the 'Cinderella' hour was moved further back. Eventually, women shared the privileges of the male scholars (although it was not until 1964 that the first female fellow of the college was elected).

These progressive attitudes only helped a minority of women, however: Protestants. For practising Catholics of either sex, things were much tougher. Elizabeth I's original foundation of TCD declared its intention to provide 'our people' (good practising Anglicans) with 'knowledge and civility', motivated by the fact that scholars were returning from continental universities 'infected with popery and other ill qualities'. The establishment was fundamentally anti-Catholic, and remained so for a long time. Even when the college lightened up on such matters in the late 18th century, the Catholic Church focused on the Protestant (and therefore inherently bad) nature of the university: if it couldn't control the institution, then it could at least boycott it. The great

synod of 1927 decreed that, since there were three colleges in Ireland 'sufficiently safe as regards faith and morals', no reason existed to warrant a Catholic attending TCD.

When John Charles MacQuaid became archbishop of Dublin in 1941, he took the moral danger of attending Trinity College very seriously, and set about enforcing the legislation of 1927. This was followed by an outright ban, from which only MacQuaid could grant a dispensation. Trinity responded by relaxing the college statutes so that attendance of the Anglican chapel was no longer compulsory, but this was not enough for MacQuaid, who in 1961 asserted that Catholics were forbidden 'under pain of mortal sin' to study at Trinity.

The resolution of the century-long debate was simple: the archbishop died. In 1970 the Catholic Church lifted the ban – ostensibly to allow Catholics to study veterinary medicine and dentistry, subjects which were only offered by Trinity – and the Protestant Church of Ireland gave up its rights to the college chapel. Given this troubled history of attendance, it is perhaps fitting that two of the college's most prestigious alumni of recent years are Mary Robinson and Mary McAleese – both Catholic, both female and both to become President of Ireland (*see p16* **First ladies of Dublin**).

pieces of artwork dotted around the campus: there's a Henry Moore sculpture on the lawns to the back of the Campanile, and Pomodoro's *Sphere within a Sphere* sits in front of the Berkeley Library.

To find out more about the college join one of 30-minute **guided tours** offered every hour by personable student types operating from a shack inside the main gate. The tours, which only take place during the summer, offer a wealth of well-presented architectural and historical information, and tickets (€7.60) include entry to the Book of Kells exhibition.

Less edifying is the audio-visual **Dublin Experience** (*see below*), which is shown in the Arts Block from late May to October. The **Douglas Hyde Gallery** (*see p177*) in the same block is worth checking out, though, while on the other side of the campus is the high-tech **Samuel Beckett Theatre** (*see p209*), where plays are performed during the college term. The **Pavilion Bar** (or Pav) on the cricket pitch is a popular place to drink outdoors in summer.

Dublin Experience
Arts Block, Trinity College (608 1688). All cross-city buses. **Open** *mid May-Sept* 10am-5pm daily. Closed Oct-Apr. **Admission** €4.10; €3.50 concessions. *Combined ticket with Book of Kells Exhibition* €7.90. **No credit cards. Map** p313 H5.
Clearly designed for tourists, this one. The breathlessly hyperbolic introduction promises 'to portray the history and development of Dublin and its people over the last 1,000 years'. This is rather a tall order for a show that lasts around 45 minutes, and despite the much-vaunted production values and elegiac tone, the Dublin Experience feels like an enthusiastic student project.

Old Library & Book of Kells Exhibition
Trinity College (608 2308). All cross-city buses. **Open** *late May-Sept* 9.30am-5pm Mon-Sat; 9.30am-4.30pm Sun. *Oct-late May* 9.30am-5pm Mon-Sat; noon-4.30pm Sun. **Admission** €5.70; €5.10 concessions; €11.40 family; free under-12s. *Combined ticket with Dublin Experience* €7.90. **Credit** MC, V. **Map** p313 H5.

The **Old Library** at Trinity College. *See p62.*

busts from the 18th century, and the oldest surviving Irish harp, thought to date from the 15th century. Trinity has been a copyright library since 1801, and is thus entitled to a copy of every book published in Great Britain and Ireland: it now stocks about three million volumes, held on campus and in the suburb of Santry.

Bank of Ireland

The grand Palladian building opposite Trinity is now the **Bank of Ireland**, but it began life in 1729 as the seat of the Irish Parliament. The Parliament existed for 71 years, until 1800, when the Act of Union made Ireland a part of Great Britain, governed directly from London. As an exclusive bastion of the Protestant minority, its demise has never been imbued with the tragedy of other Irish defeats.

The former **House of Commons** has been subsumed into the bank, but the **House of Lords** (*see below*) is still intact and is open to visitors. However, as the bank is unwilling to push itself as a tourist attraction, you may have to ask permission first. Also in the complex is the **Bank of Ireland Arts Centre** (*see p187*), which hosts regular classical music concerts and poetry readings (*see p35* **Word of mouth**). Next door is the **Museum of Banking** (*see p65*), which, perhaps surprisingly, is actually worth a look.

House of Lords

Bank of Ireland, 2 College Green (671 1488). All cross-city buses. **Open** 10am-4pm Mon-Wed, Fri; 10am-5pm Thur. *Guided tours* 10.30am, 11.30am, 1.45pm Tue. **Admission** free. **Map** p313 H5.

This vaulted chamber is beautifully panelled in Irish oak. It may lack the stucco extravagance of other Dublin buildings, but it does hold items of note, including an 18th-century crystal chandelier made from 1,223 pieces. Tapestries depict the 1689 Siege of Derry and the 1690 Battle of the Boyne: Protestant victories still celebrated annually (and often controversially) by Orangemen in the north. For more on the architecture of Parliament House, *see p26.*

It's worth trying to get to Trinity College's Old Library early in the day as it attracts huge crowds, especially in summer. One ticket covers the exhibition of illuminated manuscripts, including the Book of Kells, and a visit to the Georgian Long Room.

The **Book of Kells** is an illuminated copy of the Gospels in Latin written around 800 AD by early Christian monks, and is Trinity's most famed treasure. The tonsured scribes used valuable dyes on vellum, creating intricate texts and drawings that are stunning in their delicacy and refinement. Pages of the manuscript are displayed alongside selections from the only marginally less impressive Books of Durrow, Armagh, Dimma and Mulling, as well as an exhibition detailing the history and techniques used to produce early Christian manuscripts.

The library buildings were designed by Thomas Burgh and constructed between 1712 and 1732. At their heart is the **Long Room**, an imposing Georgian library, nearly 65m (213ft) in length, with a lofty barrel-vaulted ceiling, which was added in 1860. The Long Room contains about 200,000 of the library's early books, plus a collection of marble

Old money: **Museum of Banking**.

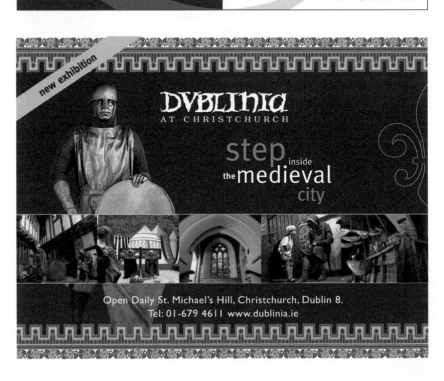

Museum of Banking

*Bank of Ireland Arts Centre, Foster Place
(671 1488). All cross-city buses.* **Open** 9.30am-
4pm Tue-Fri. **Admission** €1.50; €1 concessions.
Credit MC, V. **Map** p313 H5.
This is an interactive museum covering 200 years
of banking history in Ireland and is most interesting when dealing with the interface of banking and
politics. Exhibits include the mace from the House
of Commons and correspondence from the Abbey
Theatre bearing the signatures of JM Synge, WB
Yeats and Lady Gregory.

Grafton Street & around

North of College Green, at the top end of
Westmoreland Street, is a statue of Molly
Malone. Probably the best-known female
associated with the city, Molly was one of a
number of Dublin barrow girls who sold
shellfish 'through streets broad and narrow'
in the 18th century. It is thought she died in
1734 in the parish of St Werburgh's (near
Christchurch). The statue, complete with
a barrow and an impressive cleavage, has
been nicknamed the 'tart with the cart' and
marks the entrance to Grafton Street. This
pedestrianised thoroughfare leading to St
Stephen's Green is the heart of the south inner
city. During the 1950s it was a haunt of the
alcohol-fuelled literati, including the likes of
Brendan Behan, Patrick Kavanagh and Myles
na Gopaleen (Flann O' Brien), and it remained
the hub of 'alternative' Dublin in subsequent
decades. In the early years of the 21st century,
however, it is most notable as the main
shopping street on the southside, although
an array of buskers, flower-sellers and stall
traders help it retain a smidgen of its
bohemian atmosphere.

In fact, Grafton Street on a Saturday
afternoon is a positive cacophony of street
music: teenage string quartets mix it up with
talented guitar players and barbershop
ensembles, while surprisingly tuneful street
urchins make unfounded claims that today is
gonna be the day that they're gonna throw it
back to you (realistically you shouldn't expect
change from a pound). These distractions aside,
Grafton Street is a fairly typical pedestrian
shopping street lined with department stores
and high-street fashion outlets, though there are
also a couple of long-standing institutions here
that are worthy of a closer look.

The first of these is the plush **Brown
Thomas** department store (*see p144*), whose
legendary Christmas window displays light up
Grafton Street throughout December. The
second is **Bewley's Oriental Café** (*see p127*),
a 19th-century eating house with a stunning

mosaic façade. It was founded by the Quaker
Bewley family in 1840 and has been a city
meeting place and landmark ever since, serving
up morning coffee, afternoon teas and simple
hot food in Victorian surroundings. The
Grafton Street branch is most notable for its
distinctive 19th-century stained-glass windows
by Harry Clark; in recent years Bewley's seems
to have adopted a more businesslike approach
that has affected its renowned old-world
ambience a little.

The streets off Grafton Street abound with a
combination of fashionable bars and good
Dublin pubs. Joyceans may like to linger at
Davy Byrne's (*see p132*) – the 'moral pub' in
Ulysses, where Bloom tucked into a gorgonzola-
and-mustard sandwich and a glass of Burgundy
– while **McDaids** (*see p135*) should appeal to
those who wish to follow in the rather shaky
footsteps of Behan and co.

To the west of Grafton Street, but barely
noticeable in the narrow lane beside Bewley's,
is **St Teresa's Carmelite Church &
Friary**. Built towards the end of the 18th
century, before Catholic Emancipation, the
church's once hidden location, catering for
furtive worshippers, now provides an island
of tranquillity in the bustle of the inner city.
Daniel O'Connell was a regular at the church
and held political meetings there between 1813
and 1829. Nearby is **Powerscourt
Townhouse** (*see p145*), a Georgian building
that has been tastefully renovated in soothing
wood and brick to create the most stylish of
shopping malls. The grand front entrance is on
South William Street, an increasingly hip
part of town that has renounced its hitherto
fringe status. Here you'll find a clutch of
decently priced eateries, plus über-fashionable
café-bars and some designer boutiques that
provide a refreshing change from the chain
stores of Grafton Street. If you wish to ponder
such changes to the fabric of the city, the
Dublin Civic Museum (*see below*) makes
an interesting counterpoint.

Dublin Civic Museum

*58 South William Street (679 4260) All cross-city
buses.* **Open** 10am-6pm Tue-Sat; 11am-2pm Sun.
Admission free. **Map** p313 H5.
This admirably unpretentious little museum run by
Dublin Public Libraries aims to collect and present
material contributing to an understanding of the
city. The premises are too small to do justice to
Dublin's rich history, but there are some interesting
exhibits ranging from Viking artefacts to manhole
covers. The highlights are two documents that
depict Dublin at the beginning and the end of the
18th century: Charles Brooking's map of 1728, and
a set of James Malton aquatints from 1793. Regular
exhibitions are also held here.

Street entertainers on **Grafton Street**. *See p65.*

Kildare Street & around

A number of attractive side streets lead east from Grafton Street to Dawson Street and the **Mansion House**. This Queen Anne-style building has been home to the Lord Mayor of Dublin since 1715 and is where the Irish Parliament first assembled in 1919 to ratify the Irish Declaration of Independence. Next door is **St Anne's Church** (tel. 676 7727) where Bram Stoker was married in 1878. The interior dates from 1720, although the incomplete neo-Romanesque exterior by Sir Thomas Dean was added in 1868. The loaves of bread displayed in the chancel are the result of a bequest made in 1723 to provide for the poor of the parish.

From Dawson Street, Molesworth Street runs towards Kildare Street and **Leinster House**, seat of the Dáil (Irish Parliament) since 1922. This area was developed by the Earl of Kildare in the mid 18th century, precipitating a shift by the upper classes from the formerly fashionable northside to the newly developed Georgian southside. **Buswells Hotel** (*see p45*) on the corner has a reputation as a hotbed of political machinations, but for an atmosphere of machiavellian intrigue the **Freemasons' Hall** (*see below*) opposite seems hard to beat. While the Masons have managed to retain their secrets, Irish politicians have not been so fortunate and ongoing corruption tribunals have loomed large on the recent political scene. Harried politicos being pursued by the media and motley groups of protesters are a common

sight in the grounds of Leinster House. Public reaction ranges from outrage at the politicians' rank dishonesty to a sneaking regard for their breathtaking audacity.

Leinster House is flanked by the mirrored façades of the **National Library** to the north and the **National Museum** to the south (for both, *see p67*). Both institutions are the result of enthusiastic activity by the Royal Dublin Society, which owned Leinster House from 1815 until it was acquired by the Irish Free State government in 1922. At the north end of Kildare Street is the small **Heraldic Museum** (*see p67*) located in a Gothic red-brick building that once housed the Kildare Street Club, a conservative bastion of the Anglo-Irish ascendancy.

Freemasons' Hall

17 Molesworth Street (679 5465). Bus 10, 25X, 32, 51X, 66X, 67X, 84X. **Open** *June-Aug* 11.30am-2pm Mon-Fri. Closed Sept-May. **Admission** €1.30. **No credit cards. Map** p313 H5.

This building has been the headquarters of Freemasonry in Ireland since the 1860s and was refurbished in 2000. As well as the meeting rooms, dining rooms, offices and a library, which are all decorated in an assortment of wildly exuberant Victorian styles, there is a museum exhibition and video detailing the Masons' history in Ireland since the foundation of the Irish Lodge in 1725. The Masons assert that theirs is 'a system of morality', but some may find the Hall and exhibitions vaguely anachronistic, not to say sinister – and signs for 'ritual classes' do little to alleviate such unease.

Nevertheless if you can resist knicker-wetting giggles, this place is undeniably fascinating, and a secret handshake is not required for entry.

Heraldic Museum

2 Kildare Street (677 7444). All cross-city buses. **Open** 10am-8.30pm Mon-Wed; 10.30am-4.30pm Thur, Fri; 10.30am-12.30pm Sat. **Admission** free. **Map** p313 J5.

Seals, coins, insignia, papal decorations and a small display of objects sporting armorial bearings enliven the Heraldic Museum, although that's not enough perhaps to make it worth a special trip, especially since the genealogy and family history section has been moved to the National Library. There is a reading room with manuscripts from Yeats' and Joyce's estates but permission to see these is confined to those undertaking legitimate research.

Leinster House

Kildare Street (618 3000). All cross-city buses. **Open** only when parliament is not in session. **Admission** free. **Map** p313 J6.

Leinster House is the home of Irish Parliament, made up of the Dáil (lower house) and the Seanad (senate or upper house). The first of Dublin's great 18th-century houses to be constructed south of the Liffey, it was built by Richard Castle between 1745 to 1748 for the Earl of Kildare, who subsequently became Duke of Leinster in 1766. The Seanad meets in the sumptuous North Wing Saloon; the Dáil in a rather grubby room added as a lecture theatre in 1897.

The house has two formal fronts: the Kildare Street frontage, designed to look like a town-house, and a Merrion Square frontage; they are connected by a long central corridor. Leinster House has been claimed as the prototype for the White House in the United States, whose architect, James Hoban, was born in 1762 in County Kilkenny. The entrance hall and principal rooms were redecorated towards the end of the 18th century with the help of James Wyatt. Note that no cameras or recording equipment are allowed inside the building.

National Library of Ireland

Kildare Street (603 0200/www.nli.ie). All cross-city buses. **Open** 10am-9pm Mon-Wed; 10am-5pm Thur, Fri; 10am-1pm Sat. **Admission** free. **Map** p313 J5.

Although predominantly a research institution, parts of the National Library building are open to the public. These include the grand domed Reading Room – where Stephen Dedalus expounds his views on Shakespeare in *Ulysses* – and the Exhibition Room, with changing displays from the Library's extensive collections. There is also a walk-in Genealogical Service for visitors tracing their family tree. Visitors who wish to obtain a reader's ticket must provide valid identification.

National Museum of Ireland: Archaeology & History

Kildare Street (677 7444). All cross-city buses. **Open** 10am-5pm Tue-Sat; 2-5pm Sun. **Admission** free. **Map** p313 H5.

Established in 1877 by the Science and Art Museums Act, the National Museum is deservedly one of Dublin's most popular attractions. The 19th-century building, designed by Thomas Newenham Deane, is squeezed into a site to the side of the impassive façade of Leinster House. Its domed entrance hall, or Rotunda, looks like a Victorian reworking of the Pantheon, with windows on the upper gallery that jut inwards so that the space appears to cave in towards the spectator.

Kildare Street houses the museum's holdings of archaeological material and artefacts, chiefly relating to Ireland. The most striking exhibition is the permanent display of Bronze Age Irish gold. You'll also find extraordinarily intricate sacred and secular metalwork from the Iron Age to the Middle Ages in the Treasury, displays relating to prehistoric and Viking Ireland, plus Ancient Egyptian artefacts on the first floor. Unfortunately, the exhibition relating to the extraordinary political events in Ireland from 1900 to 1921 does not live up to the museum's other displays. For details of the National Museum at Collins Barracks, *see p93*.

see p93

St Stephen's Green & around

At the bottom of Grafton Street, Dawson Street and Kildare Street is St Stephen's Green, a welcome patch of greenery in the city centre. It has a pretty duck pond, a good playground, a bewildering array of statues and some fine floral displays – and this Victorian park is also a favourite spot for young office workers to take their lunches. Courting couples and 'park-bench aristocrats' also make regular use of the facilities.

Until the 18th century the Green was a common ground used for hangings and whippings, and it remained an inhospitable area until 1800. It was then fenced off, as efforts were made to smarten it up, the lawns were landscaped, gravel paths were laid, and for a period after 1814, entrance to the park was subject to a one guinea annual fee. Finally, in 1877, Lord Arthur Guinness pushed through an Act of Parliament opening the gates to the public and financed the park's new design. His second greatest legacy to Dubliners remains a graceful, slightly formal space to this day.

To the left of the central park and the large flower beds is a curious collection of stone circles and arguably the park's finest statue – George Moore's impression of WB Yeats. In a city where statuary realism rules with an iron fist, Moore's work stands out for its expressionistic curves – not that this appears to mean much to some of the Green's less desirable habitués, who regularly cover the statue with graffiti.

Sightseeing

Other public art in the park includes busts of poet James Clarence Mangan and the revolutionary Countess Marcievicz, and a depiction of the Three Fates at the Leeson Street gate. This statue was presented to Ireland by West Germany as a thank-you for aid given in the aftermath of World War II. On the south-western corner of the Green is a statue of Protestant rebel Wolfe Tone (1763-1798). Tone is a chameleonic figure in Irish history, his legacy being claimed by all shades of Irish Nationalism and Republicanism. Much influenced by English political writer Tom Paine, Tone argued for an Ireland in which Catholic, Protestant and dissenter could live in harmony, an ideal that is still unrealised centuries later. Finally, a statue of the ubiquitous James Joyce stands near Queen Victoria's Jubilee Bandstand, where daily concerts are held during the summer. (Details are usually available near the gates or in the local press.) Also look out for the art exhibitions along the railings on Saturday afternoons.

The Green is lined for the most part with elegant terraces of Georgian houses, though sections of the square's southern and western sides have been spoiled by undistinguished modern buildings, and determinedly chic shops are gaining a stranglehold on the Grafton Street end. Also on this northern side is the illustrious **Shelbourne Hotel** (*see p42*), a byword for luxury in Dublin. If you can't afford to stay here, at least stop in for a drink as the bartenders mix a mean cocktail. Of its two drinking areas, the tiny Horseshoe Bar is more elegant than the Shelbourne Bar, although it can fill up with barristers and media folk after 6pm.

On the southern side of the green is **Newman House** and **Newman University Church** (for both, *see below*). Both buildings are named after Cardinal Newman, who founded the Catholic University in Dublin and left his austere stamp on a generation of Irish thinkers. Gerard Manley Hopkins was professor of Classics here from 1884 until his death in 1889, and Joyce attended the university as a student between 1899 and 1902. There are quotations from Newman and Hopkins in the church, but nothing from the anti-clerical Joyce. Ironically, given Joyce's contempt for the Church and, to some measure, the University, a glance at the comments book reveals that it is his association with the premises that inspires the most interest from visitors.

Newman House backs on to the 19th-century **Iveagh Gardens**, designed by Ninian Neven and created in 1863. The gardens are visible from Hopkins' room, but can only be entered from Earlsfort Terrace or Clonmel Street (off Harcourt Street). Long lawns, a delicate stone

Leinster House. *See p66.*

fountain, a grotto, a maze and a rosarium combine to create one of the most tranquil and under-utilised parks in the city. The secluded entrances give the impression of a private premises, but rest assured, the gardens are open to the public and there is no better place to relax before a concert at the **National Concert Hall** (*see p188*) on Earlsfort Terrace. The concert hall was formerly the main premises of University College Dublin (UCD); although the main UCD campus is now in the suburbs of Belfield, part of the college's engineering faculty remains here. Go to the back of this building to reach the gardens.

Finally, on the western side of the green is the elegant **Royal College of Surgeons**, and, beside it, the glass-domed **St Stephen's Green Centre** (*see p147*), the interior of which cleverly utilises space and natural light. As a shopping centre it is nothing special, but if the weather's good, consider visiting the salad bar in Dunne's Stores and making a picnic to take to the Green.

Newman House

85-86 St Stephen's Green South (706 7422/706 7419). All cross-city buses. **Open** (by guided tour only) *June-Aug* noon, 2pm, 3pm, 4pm Tue-Fri; 2pm, 3pm, 4pm Sat. *Closed Sept-May.* **Admission** €4; €3 concessions. **No credit cards. Map** p313 H6.

These conjoined townhouses, bought as the premises of the Catholic University of Ireland and now owned by University College Dublin, are probably the finest example of 18th-century Georgian architecture open to the public. Two celebrated Victorian converts to Catholicism, Cardinal Newman and Gerard Manley Hopkins, are associated with the Catholic University, though James Joyce is possibly its most illustrious alumnus. One of the classrooms where Joyce attended lectures is preserved. Ongoing restoration since 1989 is being held up through lack of funding, but there is still much to see.

Built in 1738 for Hugh Montgomery, an Irish MP, the sombre façade of No.85 gives way to a spacious, elegant interior with lavish reception rooms and superb plasterwork by the Swiss stuccodores Paolo and Fillipo Lafranchi dating from 1740. When the

Sightseeing

Newman House: Gerard Manley Hopkins slept here. *See p69.*

building was purchased by the Catholic University of Ireland in 1865, the classical plasterwork was considered in bad taste and the female nudes were chastely covered: Juno's curves are still hidden by a rough costume but other figures have been returned to their natural state. The house contains the famous Apollo Room, with panels depicting Apollo and the Muses; and a magnificent saloon where allegories promoting prudent economy and good government are framed by rococo motifs of shells and foliage.

No.86 was begun in 1765 by Richard Whaley, father of a notorious gambler, Buck, and was later acquired by the University. The interior is by Irish stuccodore Robert West. Head up to the top of the house via the flights of back stairs, and you'll find Gerard Manley Hopkins' rather spartan bedroom/ study, perfectly preserved.

Newman University Church

87A St Stephen's Green South (478 0616). All cross-city buses. **Open** 8.45am-6pm Mon-Sat. **Admission** free. **Map** p313 H6.

This church was University College Dublin's answer to the privileged tradition of Trinity College. A favourite place for society weddings, its opulent, neo-Byzantine interior found little favour when it was built between 1854 and 1856, but time has mellowed objections and its extravagant decor now makes it one of Dublin's most fashionable churches.

Merrion Square & around

Between St Stephen's Green and Ballsbridge is the well-preserved heart of Georgian Dublin, the wealthiest quarter of the inner city. It is generally a rather sedate area of town, full of upmarket residences and successful (often hi-tech firms), although Baggot Street is studded with lively shops and restaurants. If yuppies are old hat elsewhere in the world, they are thriving around here.

WB Yeats referred to the Georgian buildings in these parts as 'grey eighteenth-century houses'. Generally four storeys high with large basements, they line squares and streets and have no front gardens. The only exterior ornamentation are the colourful doors and occasionally embellished door-knockers. Like well-bred aristocracy they keep their extravagances well concealed: beautifully proportioned spacious rooms with ornate stucco plasterwork on the walls and ceilings define their interiors (*see also p27*).

Elegant **Merrion Square**, a list of whose former residents reads like a *Who's Who* of 19th-century Ireland, is the most significant square in the district. On its western side is the 'back' entrance to **Leinster House** (*see p67*), flanked by the **National Gallery of Ireland** and the fascinating **Natural History Museum** (for both, *see p71*). Leinster Lawn, in front of the Parliament building, has an obelisk dedicated to some of the founders of the Irish Free State: Michael Collins, Arthur Griffith and Kevin O'Higgins. A statue of Prince Albert by John Henry Foley has been retained, though Queen Victoria's was removed in 1948.

The rest of Merrion Square is now almost exclusively occupied by offices, clubs and organisations, though small oval plaques beside the houses recount the names of famous former occupants. A survey of the plaques along Merrion Square South will reveal the homes of WB Yeats at No.82 (from 1922 to 1928); the poet and mystic George (Æ) Russell two doors down at No.84; the great horror writer Joseph Sheridan Le Fanu at No.70; and the Austrian Erwin Schrödinger, co-winner of the 1933 Nobel Prize for physics, at No.65. The hero of Catholic Emancipation Daniel O'Connell inhabited No.58 – look out for the plaque reading 'The Liberator'. Elsewhere around the square is the Duke of Wellington's birthplace at No.24 and the former site of the British Embassy at No.39 Merrion Square East. The embassy was burnt down in 1972, as a protest against the actions of the British army on Bloody Sunday.

In the centre of the square there are some extremely pretty gardens, which seem labyrinthine until you get to the open space at

Sightseeing

the centre. At the southern end is a bust of Michael Collins, while at the north-western corner the figure of **Oscar Wilde** overlooks his old home at No.1 Merrion Square North (*see p72*). Wilde is sprawled in multi-coloured loucheness atop a rough rock and is surrounded by his bon mots, scrawled as graffiti on two translucent columns. Perhaps inevitably, this unusual memorial has been christened the 'fag on the crag'.

The stretch from Merrion Square East to Fitzwilliam Square was once the longest unbroken line of Georgian houses in the world. Sadly, in 1961, the Electricity Supply Board knocked down 26 of them to build some hideous offices that continue to mar the square's symmetry to this day. This architectural travesty was typical of planning decisions in the 20th century: most of Dublin's finest houses had been built by the British and the developing Irish state showed a marked lack of respect for the city's colonial architecture. Only in recent years have proper efforts been made to protect the city's heritage. In partial recompense for the destruction it had caused, the ESB tarted up **Number Twenty-Nine** (*see p72*), restoring it as a Georgian townhouse with the latest in household fashion circa 1800.

Fitzwilliam Square, completed in 1825, is the smallest, most discreet and most residential of the Georgian squares. It is also immensely charming, although it's a pity that only residents have access to the lovely central garden. Fitzwilliam Square leads on to Leeson Street, a wide, long thoroughfare that slopes up to the canal. Until recently, the basements from Leeson Bridge up to St Stephen's Green – an area known as the Strip – housed nightclubs, where older men would pay through the nose for a bottle of plonk for thirsty young ladies. Since the clubs only had wine licences, entrance was free, provided you could get past the gorillas on the door. The atmosphere was sleazy, the music dire, and the street was deluged in debris every Sunday morning. Some of the better of these old-school drinking dens still remain, despite the revolution in nightlife of recent years.

National Gallery of Ireland
Merrion Square West (661 5133/www.national gallery.ie). Pearse Station DART/5, 6, 7, 7A, 8, 10, 44, 47, 48, 62 bus. **Open** 10am-5.15pm Mon-Wed, Fri, Sat; 10am-8.30pm Thur; 2-5pm Sun. **Admission** donations welcome. **Map** p313 J5.
This gallery houses a fine collection of European work from the 14th to the 20th centuries, including paintings by Caravaggio, Titian, Tintoretto, Monet, Degas, Goya, Vermeer and Picasso. A room is also devoted to the paintings of Jack B Yeats, who evolved an impressionistic style particularly suited

to the Irish landscape. Look out, too, for works by Paul Henry, Roderic O'Conor, William Orpen, Nathaniel Hone and Walter Osbornem. The smaller British collection is also impressive, with works by Hogarth, Landseer and Gainsborough, and every January, an exhibition of Turner's watercolours draws art lovers from all over the world. A multi-media gallery with a user-friendly computer system details one hundred of the gallery's finest works.

Natural History Museum
Merrion Street Upper (677 7444). Pearse Station DART/44, 48 bus. **Open** 10am-5pm Tue-Sat; 2-5pm Sun. **Admission** free. **Map** p313 J6.
This museum is a paean to intrepid 19th-century explorers and to the Victorian mania for collection and collation. Little changed since its foundation in 1857, it's packed with skeletons, fossils and stuffed animals from all over the world. Ireland's native wildlife is also well represented, including animals that were extinct millennia before humans walked the land. The entrance is watched over by a statue of Surgeon Major Thomas Heazle Park, the first Irishman to travel the breadth of Africa.

Statue spotting

As soon as a monument goes up in this city it is given a usually tasteless but always catchy nickname. Here are some of the best.

● **Agitator with the rotavator**: Statue of James Connolly, Butt Bridge. Also known as the **Scut on the Butt**.
● **Bench with the stench**: Statue of Patrick Kavanagh, Grand Canal, Southside (*see p72*).
● **Fag on the crag**: Statue of Oscar Wilde, Merrion Square, Southside (*see p71*).
● **Floozie in the jacuzzi**: Anna Livia Fountain, O'Connell Street, Northside. Also known as the **Whoo-er in the sewer**. (*see p86*)
● **Golden goolie**: *Crann an Ór*, outside Central Bank, Dame Street, Southside (*see p73*).
● **Hags with the bags**: Meeting Place statue, Ormond Quay, Liffey Street, Northside.
● **Half-eaten malteser**: *Sphere Within a Sphere*, outside Berkeley Library, Trinity College, Southside (*see p62*).
● **Stiletto in the ghetto**: Monument of Light, O'Connell Street, Northside (*see p85*).
● **Tart with the cart**: Statue of Molly Malone, top of Grafton Street, Southside (*see p65*).

Number Twenty-Nine

29 Fitzwilliam Street Lower (702 6165). Bus 6, 7, 8, 10, 45. **Open** *10am-5pm Tue-Sat; 2-5pm Sun.* **Admission** *Guided tours* €3.20; €1.30 concessions; free under-16s. **No credit cards. Map** p313 J6.

This 18th-century merchant house, restored by the Electricity Board, is presented as a bourgeois dwelling circa 1790-1820, with furnishings that are comfortable rather than opulent. Particularly interesting from a heritage viewpoint, it also has some good examples of Irish Georgian cabinet-making scattered throughout. The house is on the corner of one of the most elegant vistas in Dublin, a long neo-classical perspective stretching from Merrion Square West down Mount Street.

The Oscar Wilde House

American College Dublin, 1 Merrion Square (662 0281). All cross-city buses. **Open** *Guided tours* 10.15am, 11.15am Mon, Wed, Thur. **Admission** €2.50. **No credit cards. Map** p313 J6.

Sir William Wilde, a controversial eye-surgeon and his wife, the poetess 'Speranza', moved into this elegant Georgian house in 1855, when their son Oscar was one year old; he lived here until 1876. In 1994 the building was taken over by the American College Dublin, which has restored the ground and first floors of the house, including the surgery and Lady Speranza's drawing room. These are now open to the public by guided tour. The nominal admission fee goes towards the continued restoration and upkeep of the house.

Grand Canal & the south docks

Both Baggot Street and Leeson Street cut across the **Grand Canal**, which meanders around the city to the south, flowing into the Canal Basin in the old industrial zone of Ringsend before joining the Liffey at the south docks. Built between 1756 and 1796, it was the longest canal in the British Isles, stretching from Shannon Harbour in Offaly to Dublin Bay. It has not been used commercially since 1960 and nowadays its grassy banks are a focal point for walkers, cyclists, and, in summer, swimmers, who take to the water when the locks are full.

The most pleasant stretch of the canal is probably found between Leeson Street and Mount Street. This was the stamping ground of the poet Patrick Kavanagh, a contemporary of Behan (and equally fond of the booze). In 'Lines Written on a Seat on the Grand Canal' he asks to be commemorated 'with no hero courageous tomb, just a canal-bank seat for the passer by'. Fittingly there is now a statue of him perched on a bench overlooking the canal.

Venture west from here along the canal for a mile to reach the Portobello district, where you'll find **Shaw's Birthplace** at 33 Synge

Street (*see p73*), a clutch of excellent restaurants, and the **Jewish Museum** (*see below*), a poignant space devoted to the often-neglected history of the Jewish community in Ireland. Alternatively, make your way north-east to **St Stephen's Church** on Mount Street Upper, usually known as the Peppercannister Church because of its distinctive shape. The church is more attractive on the outside than within and is best seen from the far end of Merrion Square at night, when it is enigmatically lit up. Its position in the middle of a traffic island has made it a popular beat for local prostitutes, but it is still a functioning Anglican church, specialising in Christmas carol singing, weddings and concerts. It's also a popular film location that featured three times in *Michael Collins* alone. From here, cross Huband Bridge to reach Haddington Road and the **National Print Museum** (*see below*).

At the dock end of the Grand Canal, ten minutes' walk from Baggot Street Bridge, is the floating **Waterways Visitor Centre** (*see p73*), which has informative displays on Ireland's inland waterways. There is a lot of redevelopment work going on in the Canal Basin here, including a brand new DART station at Grand Canal Dock. Look out, too, for the **Ocean Bar** (*see p135*), a great spot for a pricey drink.

Jewish Museum

13-14 Walworth Road, Portobello (453 1797/467 0773/475 8388 appointments). Bus 16, 16A, 19, 19A, 22, 22A. **Open** *May-Sept* 11am-3.30pm Tue, Thur, Sun. *Oct-Apr* 10.30am-3.30pm Sun or by appointment. **Admission** free. **Map** p308.

This collection of documents and artefacts relating to the Jewish community of Ireland includes a reconstruction of a turn-of-the-19th-century kitchen typical of a Jewish home in the neighbourhood, and a synagogue preserved with ritual fittings. The exhibition draws attention to events such as the pogroms against the Jews of Limerick in the 1920s, which have largely been airbrushed out of Irish history. The home of Ireland's first chief rabbi, Rabbi Herzog, at 55 Bloomfield Avenue is commemorated by a plaque, and another plaque at 52 Upper Clanbrassil Street pays homage to Ireland's most famous fictional Jew, Joyce's Leopold Bloom.

National Print Museum

Garrison Chapel, Beggars Bush, Haddington Road (660 3770). Grand Canal Dock DART/5, 7, 7A, 8, 45 bus. **Open** *May-Sept* 10am-12.30pm, 2.30-5pm Mon-Fri; noon-5pm Sat, Sun. **Admission** €3.20; €1.30 concessions; €6.35 family. **No credit cards. Map** p314 L7.

This display of printing apparatus leaves even those who aren't fans of industrial archaeology stimulated and enlightened. The Beggars Bush building was originally a barracks, and the central garrison building houses the Irish Labour History Museum. More of an archive and library than a museum, it is enhanced by documents relating to labour and industrial history in Ireland since the 18th century. The guided tours are good.

Shaw's Birthplace

33 Synge Street, Portobello (475 0854). Bus 16, 16A, 19, 19A, 22, 22A. **Open** *May-Oct* 10am-1pm, 2-5pm Mon-Sat; 11am-1pm, 2-5pm Sun. Closed Nov-Apr. **Admission** €5.10; €2.55-€3.80 concessions; €14 family. **Credit** MC, V. **Map** p309.

This neat Victorian house was the early home of George Bernard Shaw, Ireland's most overlooked Nobel prizewinner. He's commemorated simply – some might say tersely – as 'author of many plays' on the plaque outside. The house is a good example of a Victorian middle-class home, although those who aren't Shaw enthusiasts might find it a bit dull. One of Shaw's greatest contributions to Dublin is the National Gallery on Merrion Square (*see p71*), which he endowed generously and which commemorates his achievements as a playwright with a statue in its front garden.

Waterways Visitor Centre

Grand Canal Quay (677 7510). Grand Canal Dock DART/3 bus. **Open** *June-Sept* 9.30am-6.30pm daily. *Oct-May* 12.30-5pm Wed-Sun. **Admission** €2.50; €1.25-€1.90 concessions; €6.30 family. **No credit cards.** **Map** p314 L5.

The Waterways Centre offers visitors historical and environmental information on Ireland's inland waterways and canals, many of which are in the process of being restored. The building itself deserves some commendation: it's not the floating Portakabin it resembles at first from the outside, but an airy space of wood and glass, whose suggestion of mobility and fluidity reflects the water that flows around and under the building. It's worth a visit if you're in the area.

Temple Bar & the Old City

Dame Street & around

Dame Street has long been dominated by banks and clogged traffic, but now hotels and coffee-shops are popping up like acne in pubescence. The most obvious of the banks is the architecturally bizarre **Central Bank**. The building is not constructed from ground to sky, but is suspended around a central axis, and so looks very top-heavy. It looms over the area like a huge concrete bunker, but admirable efforts have been made to decorate the square outside with trees and the Crann an Ór (tree of gold) sculpture by Eamonn O'Doherty (*see p71* **Statue spotting**). The space is a popular

It's all happening in **Temple Bar**. *See p75.*

Saturday afternoon hangout for skateboarders, punks and other cheerful teenage layabouts, and is also one of the main access points for **Temple Bar** (*see p75*).

Further up Dame Street is the **Olympia Theatre** (*see p209*), an excellent venue with an aura of genteel decay, while opposite is traffic-choked **South Great George's Street**. This thoroughfare has not been blessed with the marketing and planning that other areas have enjoyed, but has nevertheless transformed itself over the past decade into one of Dublin's trendiest streets. Highlights along this stretch include the marvellous **Long Hall** pub (*see p134*) and the red-brick **George's Street arcade** (*see p154* **Market forces**), a Victorian covered market that sells clothes, food and other bargains.

If you continue up George's Street towards Portobello you reach Aungier Street, Wexford Street and Camden Street – an area that is controversially being refashioned as the 'Village Quarter'. Residents of this traditionally unpretentious working-class area at first mocked the developers' upmarket pretensions, but as rents increase in tandem with the area's popularity, angry objections are replacing the derision. This whole area is still in the early

Dublin Castle, once the seat of British power, is now a popular tourist attraction.

stages of redevelopment, but it's worth seeking out the **Whitefriar Street Carmelite Church** (*see p75*), just off Aungier Street. The church stands on the site of a 13th-century Carmelite priory, which was zealously suppressed by Henry VIII in 1537. Its lands and wealth were seized and the priory itself fell into complete ruin. Three centuries later, the Carmelites returned to the site and opened a new church, which was designed mainly by George Papworth, also the architect of St Mary's Pro-Cathedral (*see p86*).

Back on Dame Street, just beyond George's Street, is the complex of **Dublin Castle** (*see below*), the former seat of British power in Ireland and now a benign tourist attraction and a venue for diplomatic functions. The Castle was constructed on the foundations of a Viking fortress, parts of which can be seen in the subterranean undercroft. The oldest surviving visible building is the 13th-century Record Tower, from which the flamboyant Red Hugh O'Donnell escaped in 1591 and again in 1592. Other buildings were gradually added to the castle area over the centuries, resulting in a grand, if rather haphazard, mixture of building styles. You can walk into the peaceful open courtyard, but to get inside, you have to pay for a guided tour.

At the back of the castle lie the Dubh Linn gardens – an attractive place to chill out on a sunny day – and the unmissable **Chester Beatty Library** (*see below*), now located in a beautifully converted 18th-century barracks. Next door to the castle entrance, facing Grattan Bridge, is **Dublin's City Hall** (*see p75*), built as the Royal Exchange in 1779. For many years the building was home to the Dublin Corporation, before being restored and reopened to the public in September 2000. The vaults (entered from a side entrance) now house the Story of the Capital exhibition.

Chester Beatty Library

Clock Tower Building, Dublin Castle, Dame Street (407 0750/www.cbl.ie). All cross-city buses. **Open** *May-Sept* 10am-5pm Mon-Fri; 11am-6pm Sat; 1-5pm Sun. *Oct-Apr* 10am-5pm Tue-Fri; 11am-6pm Sat; 1-5pm Sun. *Guided tours* 1pm Wed; 3pm, 4pm Sun. **Admission** donations welcome. **Map** p313 G5.
This remarkable collection of rare books, manuscripts and artefacts was bequeathed to the people of Ireland in 1969 by Sir Alfred Chester Beatty, an Irish-American mining magnate who had settled in Dublin in 1950. In 2001 the collection moved to this purpose-built conversion behind Dublin Castle, a cool tranquil space that does justice to the beauty of the exhibits. Among them are Japanese prints, Chinese furniture, oriental painted scrolls, ceramics and snuff bottles, Buddhist scrolls and statuary, Arabic scientific instruments, Biblical and Egyptian papyri, Coptic and Armenian icons and German Renaissance woodcuts. The second floor is dedicated to the world's religions and the quality and the rarity of the objects displayed is often breathtaking. Check out the pretty roof garden and the eastern-flavoured Silk Road Café on the ground floor. There are regular events and lectures, and audio-visual programmes on woodblock printing, calligraphy, papermaking and book production.

Dublin Castle

Dame Street (677 7129) All cross-city buses. **Open** (by guided tour only) 10am-5pm Mon-Fri; 2-5pm Sat, Sun. **Admission** €4; €1.50-€3 concessions. **No credit cards. Map** p313 G5.

The worthwhile castle tour encompasses the state apartments and the excavations of one of the Norman towers, which predate the present 18th-century complex. The state chambers contain a fine assortment of antiques, but lack the elegance and delicacy of some of the other buildings erected by the Anglo-Irish ruling class of the time. Look out for the sprightly rococo ceilings, which were removed from Mespil House to the south side of the city when it was demolished. The archaeological part of the tour reveals the lower reaches of the Norman castle, where the river that once fed the moat emerges above ground.

Dublin's City Hall
Dame Street (672 2204/www.dublincorp.ie/cityhall).
All cross-city buses. **Open** 10am-5.15pm Mon-Sat;
2-5pm Sun. **Admission** €3.80; €1.30 concessions;
€8.90 family. **Credit** MC, V. **Map** p313 G5.
Enter through the main portico on Dame Street to view the stunning domed atrium by Thomas Cooley. The walls are decorated with 12 Arts and Crafts-style panels by James Ward, depicting scenes from the early history of Dublin. Also in the atrium are statues of key figures from Irish history, including a vast marble portrayal of Daniel O'Connell created in 1843. Downstairs, the Story of the Capital exhibition traces the history of government in the city through the ages. Well-presented and informative, it includes stand out exhibits such as the Great City Sword presented to the city by Henry IV.

Whitefriar Street Carmelite Church
Whitefriar Street, off Aungier Street (475 8821).
Bus 16,16A, 19, 19A, 22, 22A. **Open** 8.30am-
6.30pm Mon, Wed-Fri; 8am-9pm Tue; 8.30am-7pm
Sat, Sun. **Admission** free. **Map** p313 G6.
This 19th-century church is the scene of many romantic pledges as its altar supposedly contains the remains of St Valentine, donated by Pope Gregory XVI in 1835. There's also a life-sized oak figure of Our Lady of Dublin, believed to be the only wooden statue in town to have escaped the ravages of the Reformation.

Temple Bar

Slotted neatly between Dame Street and the Liffey, Temple Bar is proof that the phrase 'urban renewal project' need not be a death knell for an area. Since its creation and (ongoing) renovation as 'Dublin's Left Bank', Temple Bar has managed to carve itself an international reputation as one of Europe's most happening culture and entertainment districts. The area's 18th-century cobbled streets and public squares are pedestrianised and the good new shops, restaurants and bars are perpetually bustling; it's difficult to imagine that until the late 1980s the whole district was earmarked for a central bus depot.

Super-bars and tourist-oriented restaurants tend to dominate Temple Bar, meaning that while the nightlife is undeniably lively, it can also seem to be lacking in character. Many Dubliners give the area a wide berth at weekends, deterred by a supercharged atmosphere underpinned by energy drinks and copious amounts of alcohol. The banning of stag and hen parties from the bars has improved the overall atmosphere, but it still retains a local reputation as a place for hedonistic tourists to indulge in a spot of debauchery. That said, there are some decent restaurants here (if you can get a table), and a number of excellent cultural enterprises make Temple Bar more than just a glutton's paradise.

One of the first of these was the **Temple Bar Gallery** (*see p179*), founded in 1983 on Temple Bar Square, but redesigned and expanded in 1994. It is now the biggest studio and exhibition space of its kind in the country. Next door is the **Original Print Gallery** (*see p179*) a showcase for national and international printmakers. Elegant Curved Street is framed

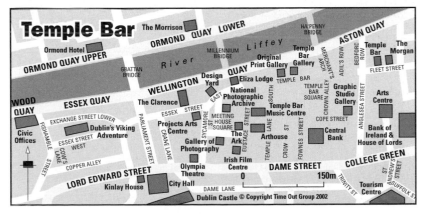

by the architecturally magnificent **Art House** (605 6800), a multimedia resource centre with a database of thousands of contemporary Irish art images, and the **Temple Bar Music Centre** (*see p195*), one of the city's premier live music and club venues. Cross Eustace Street to reach the **Irish Film Centre** (*see p174*), which shows an impressive range of arthouse films in a pleasant setting and has a popular and attractive café.

Behind the Irish Film Centre lies **Meeting House Square** (information 677 2255), a well-designed urban space that is used for public entertainment, notably free film screenings on summer evenings. A small but excellent **food fair** is held in the square on Saturday mornings, and board games are played there on Sunday afternoons. It is also the site of the **Ark** (*see p171*), a children's art centre, and the **Gallery of Photography** (*see p177*), which features some good exhibitions. Nearby is the **National Photographic Archive** (*see p177*) in which the photographic collections of the National Library of Ireland are stored.

Turn left into Essex Street East to reach the **Design Yard** (*see p148, p152*), which showcases beautifully crafted modern Irish jewellery, furniture and accessories, and the **Clarence** (*see p39*), owned by U2 and one of the most stylish hotels in the city. (Its nightclub, the **Kitchen** – *see p199* – is still a contender for the title of ultimate Dublin nightspot.) **Connolly Bookstore** (43 Essex Street East; 676 2554) is a long-standing supplier of left-leaning literature and the tiny attached **New Theatre** (670 3361) is a good-quality fringe venue featuring plays with political undertones. The newly renovated **Project Arts Centre** (*see p209*) next door has re-invented itself as a centre for alternative drama and a range of innovative arts projects.

Bisecting Essex Street is Parliament Street, which leads gently uphill to the **City Hall**. Here you will find the **Porterhouse** micro-brewery and pub (*see p138*) and the **Front Lounge**, one of the city's most successful modern bars (*see p133*). Also look out for the rather grubby but beautiful frieze on the **Sunlight Chambers** building facing Grattan Bridge.

Until recently Parliament Street marked the western edge of the Temple Bar development, but as the eastern end has become more commercialised, gentrification has extended across the road into Essex Street West and the area now styled as the 'Old City'. Here too is the well advertised but rather insipid **Dublin's Viking Adventure** exhibition (*see below*). Off Essex Street West is **Cow's Lane**, where you'll find a concentration of boutiques showcasing

fashion and interior design, and a good organic food market on Saturdays that complements the market in Meeting House Square.

Fishamble Street, where Handel's *Messiah* was famously first performed in 1742, is the oldest street in Dublin and leads from the top of Dame Street down towards **Wood Quay**, through the heart of Viking Dublin. Wood Quay, which dates from 1200, is now dominated by the **Dublin Corporation Buildings** (known as 'the Bunkers'), whose construction in the late 1970s aroused a huge amount of controversy. Excavations on the site revealed artefacts and building remains dating from the tenth century, yet despite a huge protest march in 1978, the Corporation carried on with the project.

Dublin's Viking Adventure

Essex Street West, Temple Bar (679 6040). Bus 25, 51, 51B, 79, 90. **Open** 10am-4.30pm Tue-Sat. Closed until Apr 2002. **Admission** €5.50; €3 concessions; €15 family. **Credit** AmEx, DC, MC, V. **Map** p75. An interactive exhibition that re-creates the sights, sounds and even smells of Dublin as it was 1,000 years ago. The exhibition is partly a response to the Dublin Corporation/Wood Quay controversy, but it's difficult to get too excited about it. Entertainment and education sit uneasily side by side, and the actors give the distinct impression that they would rather be elsewhere. Still, kids seem to enjoy it, and recent refurbishment work may improve matters. Watch out for crowds of school parties.

The cathedrals & around

At the top of Dame Street look out for **Burdocks**, Dublin's most famous 'chipper', where queues for fish and chips often stretch out the door and down the street. Look back at the lovely red-brick curving block of shops, and take a moment to enjoy the new **Peace Garden**. Constructed as a salutary reminder of the country's troubled history, it can only be hoped that the spirit of optimism with which the garden was designed does not prove to be premature. This area of the city is dominated by the grey hulk of **Christchurch Cathedral** (*see p77*), which enjoys a commanding position above Wood Quay.

Ireland may have the most committed church-going population in Europe, but its churches are hardly the finest on the continent. Centuries of poverty and religious repression mean they lack both exquisite historical details and costly fittings, and while the few remnants left over suggest that the medieval period must have been glorious, there has been little of note since then. Extensive and over-enthusiastic Victorian renovations have, in most instances, marred the buildings' original structures. Today all the most important churches in Dublin, including both Christchurch and St Patrick's cathedrals, are Anglican (Church of Ireland), a strange situation given that the denomination currently accounts for only about three per cent of the population.

Built in the 12th century but extensively renovated in the 19th century, Christchurch has had a long and chequered history: Edward VI was crowned king of England here in 1487; Henry VIII burned it down in the 16th century, after which it was turned into law courts. At the time of James II, it even became Catholic for a while. The cathedral's famous arched bridge fans out over Winetavern Street into what was the Synod Hall. Today it leads to the **Dublinia** exhibition (*see below*).

West of Christchurch on the corner of High Street and Bridge Street are two churches dedicated to St Ouen. One is Catholic, and was constructed after Emancipation in 1846; the other is the 800-year-old Protestant **St Audeon's** (*see p78*), now reduced to a nave but open to the public. Behind it is an attractive park with 'forty steps' leading down to an impressive stretch of the old turreted city wall, dating from the 13th century, and **St Audeon's Gate**, the only remaining Norman gateway in the city. The park is a popular haunt for local heroin users whose presence, while not necessarily dangerous, can be off-putting. The area reeks of history and, too often, unfortunately, of urine.

South of Christchurch, meanwhile, is **St Patrick's Cathedral** (*see p78*) the oldest Christian site in Dublin. Although the cathedral itself was founded in the 12th century, St Patrick is supposed to have baptised Irish pagans in a well beside the building back in the fifth century. A statue of the saint was erected inside the cathedral in 2001. The **Viking Splash Tours** (*see p60* **Trips and tours**) leave from St Patrick Gardens, the cathedral green, on Bull Alley Street. Opposite is the Arts and Crafts façade of the **Iveagh Buildings** (*see p28*), a housing project set up by the Guinness family in the 1890s.

If you follow the small lane past the entrance to St Patrick's, you'll come across **Marsh's Library** (*see p78*), which nestles among mature and fragrant gardens. This was the first public library built in Ireland (1701) and its beautiful reading room is well worth exploring.

Christchurch Cathedral

Christchurch Place (677 8099). Bus 50, 78A. **Open** 10am-5pm Mon-Sat; 10-10.45am, 12.30-3pm Sun. **Admission** €3 suggested donation; €3 Treasury Exhibition. **Credit** *Shop* MC, V. **Map** p312 F5.

A wooden cathedral was built on this site in 1038 by Donat, the first Bishop of Dublin, but it was not until 1170 that the conquering Normans under Richard de Clare (Strongbow) decided to rebuild it in a more fitting style. The south transept, the north wall, the western part of the choir and the huge crypt, which extends under the entire church, remain from Strongbow's time; the rest of the cathedral was restored between 1871 and 1878 by the architect George Edward Street. Christchurch is best viewed from the quays, from where it looms upwards, impressive against the hills. The interior features a stone sculpture of Strongbow as well as other sculptures dating from the 16th to the 19th centuries. The crypt houses a permanent display of the cathedral's treasures. For details of services, *see chapter* **Resources A-Z: Religion**; choral evensong is a particular treat.

Dublinia

Christchurch, St Michael's Hill (679 4611/ www.dublinia.ie). Bus 50, 78A. **Open** *Apr-Sept* 10am-5pm daily. *Oct-Mar* 11am-4pm Mon-Sat; 10am-4.30pm Sun. **Admission** €5.80; €4.25-€4.50 concessions; €15.20 family. **Credit** MC, V. **Map** p312 F5.

A lot of work and money went into improving this multimedia presentation on medieval Dublin prior to its relaunch in 2001. The new version is innovative and generally diverting and includes interactive

Great City Sword from **City Hall**. *See p74.*

areas, a reconstructed archaeological dig and a museum. Historical rigour sometimes loses out to entertainment imperatives, but on the whole the exhibition is the best of its kind in the city. The centrality of the gift shop to the whole enterprise seems telling, though.

Marsh's Library

St Patrick's Close (454 3511). Bus 49X, 50, 50X, 54A, 56A, 77X, 150. **Open** 10am-12.45pm, 2-5pm Mon, Wed-Fri; 10.30am-12.45pm Sat. **Admission** €1.30; free children. **No credit cards.** **Map** p312 F6.

Marsh's Library was commissioned by Archbishop Narcissus Marsh and designed by Sir William Robinson, the architect of the Royal Hospital in Kilmainham. Up a flight of ancient stairs is a beautifully preserved scholars' library – the first public library to be built in Ireland – complete with carved and gabled bookcases and three wire 'cages', that were used to lock in readers who were consulting particularly precious works. Apart from its fine architectural qualities, the library possesses a valuable collection of classical, liturgical and humanist texts. There are also early Russian, Hebrew, Arabic and Turkish printed works, and a collection of manuscripts, including a volume of *Lives of the Irish Saints*, written in about 1400. Look out, too, for the collection of memorabilia relating to Jonathan Swift, who was a former governor of the library, including a number of books bearing his extensive annotations.

In contrast to Trinity College's Long Room, where learning is presented in terms of a classicising canon of eminent luminaries, in Bishop Marsh's Library it is the private world of the baroque scholar that is most in evidence.

St Audeon's Church

High Street (677 0088). Bus 123. **Open** *June-Sept* 9.30am-5.30pm daily. Closed Oct-May. **Admission** €1.90; €0.80-€1.30 concessions. **No credit cards.** **Map** p312 F5.

Dedicated to Ouen, the seventh-century bishop of Rouen and patron saint of Normandy, St Audeon's is the only medieval parish church in Dublin that is still in use. It reopened to visitors in 2001, and the admission charge includes entry to a small exhibition on guilds and church history, followed by a guided tour of the church. Look out for the ninth-century graveslabs and the 'lucky stone'. Duchás, the governmental heritage service that looks after the church, offers a well-produced visitors' guide. The staff are knowledgeable and helpful, and while the building, with its cool stone walls, may not be as dramatic as the cathedrals, it nevertheless possesses considerable historical harm.

St Patrick's Cathedral

St Patrick's Close (453 9472/www.stpatricks cathedral.ie). Bus 49X, 50, 50X, 54A, 56A, 77X, 150. **Open** 9am-6pm daily. **Admission** €2.80; €2.60 concessions; €8.25 family. **No credit cards.** **Map** p312 F6.

Travel back 1,000 years at **Dublin's Viking Adventure**. *See p76.*

Really wired city?

Just as 1990s Dublin benefited from a telecommunications boom and the global dot.com euphoria, so the 21st-century city has a lot to lose if the economic turndown in the sector continues. The latest talking point concerns the future of the **Digital Hub** (www.thedigitalhub.com), an ambitious plan to turn the deprived Liberties area of Dublin into a 'digital media district', supporting a host of film, music, animation and Internet studios and regenerating the area's urban fabric in the process. Already set up in the former Guinness Hopstore is **Media Lab Europe** (www.medialabeurope.org), a prestigious offshoot of the Massachusetts Institute of Technology that specialises in cutting-edge multimedia technology and development. The high hopes invested in Media Lab Europe can be gauged from its description in the normally sober *Irish Times* as the 'Holy Grail of multimedia'. However,

this was before the technology and telecom sector really began to take a battering on the world markets.

The transformation of the oldest, most rundown, part of the city into a centre for Europe's wired technocrats would be a dramatic manifestation of the changes that had been brought about by Ireland's Celtic Tiger economy, but by 2001 the project was beginning to look shaky. Originally backed by £100 million of state money, plans for the digital hub were scaled back (amid much hand-wringing about Irish narrow-mindedness, short-term-ism and xenophobia in the pages of the *Wall Street Journal*). If it fulfils anything like its original vision, however, and if the government keeps its nerve, then the Digital Hub has the potential to wholly transform a deprived area of Dublin's inner city, with knock-on benefits for the city and country as a whole.

Built outside the original city walls, St Patrick's Cathedral doesn't have the same commanding position as Christchurch, but it has perhaps the more interesting historical associations of the two. Jonathan Swift was dean of the St Patrick's between 1713 and 1745 and his tomb (along with that of Esther Johnson – 'Stella') lies near the cathedral entrance. Its Latin inscription translates as: 'Here he lies, where savage indignation can no longer lacerate his heart.' Written by Swift himself, it seems an oddly gloomy epitaph for a Christian dean, but most appropriate for the greatest satirist in the English language.

Look out too, for the hole cut in the old door of the chapter house – it has an interesting history. In 1492, a feud between two great Norman earls, Kildare and Ormond, resulted in a battle being fought inside the cathedral. During the fighting, Ormond's representative, Black James, took refuge inside the chapter house, only agreeing to emerge when the Earl of Kildare cut a hole in the door and thrust his arm through it in a gesture of reconciliation. Kildare's act succeeded in restoring peace between the two earls, and gave birth to the expression 'chancing your arm'.

Interpretative panels greatly enhance the Living Stones exhibition, which celebrates the history of the cathedral and its place in the life of the city; in addition, the voluntary curators are extremely helpful and are happy to provide more historical information. The cathedral choir school dates back to 1432 and still sings two services every day during the school terms. For more information on cathedral services, *see chapter* **Resources A-Z: Religion**.

The Liberties & Further West

The Liberties & the Guinness Brewery

West of St Audeon's, Thomas Street is the gateway to the **Liberties**, one of the most disadvantaged, albeit lively, areas of Dublin. In medieval times the Liberties was a furiously independent self-governing district outside the city walls. In the 17th century it was settled by Huguenots, who developed the area as a centre for silk-weaving. However, the introduction of British trading restrictions in the 1770s and increased competition from imported cloth signalled the area's demise. By the 19th century, the Liberties had become a slum district; mass unemployment threatened and outbreaks of violence were common, often between the Liberty Boys (tailors' and weavers' apprentices) and the Ormond Boys (butchers' apprentices from the northside).

In recent decades the tight-knit community has been badly scarred by heroin, and the gentrification process, so obvious in other parts of the city, has only recently shown signs of life here. However, the rebuilding of the **Guinness Storehouse** (*see p81*) as a mecca for fans of

The **Guinness Storehouse** experience is good for you – or so they say. *See p81.*

the black stuff, and (perhaps more importantly in the long run) the establishment in 2000 of **MediaLab Europe** (*see p79* **Really wired city?**) in part of the brewery complex suggest that the pace of change may be set to accelerate. That said, the number of refugees that have settled in the Liberties in recent months enhances the impression that this area is a microcosm of Dublin in flux.

If the Guinness Storehouse has ensured that Thomas Street has a steady stream of daytime tourists – readily identifiable with their distinctive Storehouse bags – then the **Vicar Street** venue (*see p195*) and the revamped **Thomas House** (*see p139*) are leading the charge in making the area a popular nightspot, particularly favoured by students from the nearby National College of Art & Design. This is problematic, since Thomas Street has long been the locus of the city's hard-drugs trade, and retains an edgy undercurrent despite a significant Garda presence.

Off Thomas Street, you'll find **Francis Street**, the centre of the Dublin antiques trade (*see p145*), and also the site of the 18th-century church of St Nicholas of Myra, which features a stained-glass window in the nuptial chapel by Harry Clarke. **Meath Street**, further west, hosts an old-style street market of the type that has largely disappeared from the city. If you like getting off the beaten track, want to experience a vanishing side of Dublin, or just need some very cheap comestibles, copy penny-wise Dubliners and check it out. At the bottom of Meath Street is the **Coombe**, one of the area's main thoroughfares. The warren-like maze of sometimes cobbled streets between the Coombe and South Circular Road were the heart of the Liberties and boast wonderful monikers like Brabazon Street, Fumbally Lane and Blackpitts. Many of the tiny red-brick houses in the Liberties are in the process of being renovated. As the gentrification process gets under way, long-term residents must be hoping that the rising economic tide will finally get around to lifting their boats too.

At the end of Thomas Street is James's Street, synonymous in Dublin's collective imagination with the black brew. The **St James's Gate Brewery** fills all available land north and south of James's Street, right down to the river, and has been producing Ireland's world-famous Guinness over 250 years. There had been a brewery at St James's Gate since 1670, but it was largely derelict by the time Arthur Guinness purchased a 9,000-year lease for the site in 1759 at £45 per annum. Guinness started by brewing ale, but soon switched to a black beer made with roasted barley and known as 'porter' due to its popularity among porters at

Covent Garden and Billingsgate markets in London. The new beer proved extremely successful: by 1838, Guinness at St James's Gate was the largest brewery in Ireland and in 1914 it became the world's largest brewery. It now produces 4.5 million hectolitres of Guinness Stout each year; ten million glasses are consumed around the world every day.

Although most of the complex is closed to visitors, the brewery area remains impressively atmospheric: vast Victorian and 20th-century factory buildings are surrounded by a maze of high brick walls and narrow cobblestoned streets, and the air is suffused with the distinctive, warming odour of hops and malt. At the heart of the complex is the **Guinness Storehouse** (*see below*).

The Guinness Storehouse

St James's Gate (453 6700/www.guinnessstorehouse. com). Bus 51B, 78A, 123, 206. **Open** 9.30am-5pm daily. **Admission** €11.40; €2.50-€5 concessions; free under-6s. **Credit** AmEx, DC, MC, V. **Map** p312 D5. No longer part of the active brewery, this 'visitor experience' is the public face of Ireland's most famous export and a celebration of the Guinness company's corporate soul. The six-storey listed building is designed around a stunning pint glass-shaped atrium and incorporates a retail store, extensive exhibition space, function rooms, a restaurant and two bars. Much of the four acres of floor space

Irish Museum of Modern Art. *See p82.*

A prison with a history: **Kilmainham Gaol**.

is taken up with presentations on the history and making of the humble pint, which, although self-congratulatory in tone, are magnificently realised. Most entertaining, perhaps, is the advertising section – a testament to the company's imaginative marketing. The steep entry fee includes a complimentary pint of the best Guinness you are likely to get, and where better to drink it than in the Gravity bar, at the very top of the building? The circular bar has a 360 degree window and offers a spectacular view over Dublin on a clear day. (Look out for the distinctive shape of St Patrick's windmill on the other side of Watling Street). Despite the crowds, lingering here with a pint or two makes the experience wholly worthwhile.

Kilmainham

Beyond the brewery on the south bank of the Liffey lies **Kilmainham Gaol** (*see p82*) and the **Royal Hospital**. The gaol housed every famous Irish felon from 1798 until 1924, when the Free State government closed it down. Indeed, the list of those who spent time here reads like a roll call of nationalist idols: Robert Emmet, John O'Leary, Joseph Plunkett, Patrick Pearse and Eamon De Valera, who had the dubious honour of being the last ever prisoner released from here before he became Taoiseach. Even Parnell spent some time in Kilmainham, albeit in a cell that is strikingly more spacious than those around it. The boat in dry dock outside the prison is the *Asgard*, Erskin Childers' vessel, which successfully negotiated the British blockade and landed guns for the Irish Volunteers at Howth in 1912.

The Royal Hospital, brilliantly restored in 1986, now houses the **Irish Museum of Modern Art** (*see below*). The building dates from 1684, and was constructed as a hospital for military veterans. Built around a large inner courtyard, it is classically proportioned and the oldest secular non-military building in Ireland.

West of Kilmainham, across the river from Phoenix Park, is **Islandbridge**, site of the **War Memorial Gardens** (entrances on Con Colbert Road and South Circular Road). Designed by Edwin Lutyens as a suitably fine tribute to the 49,000 Irish soldiers who died in World War I, the gardens retain an austere beauty, with granite columns, yew hedges, sunken circular gardens, pergolas, fountains and lily ponds. Being slightly out of the way, they are under-used – a pleasant space for contemplation.

Irish Museum of Modern Art

Royal Hospital, Military Road, Kilmainham (612 9900/www.modernart.ie). Bus 51B, 68, 69, 78A, 79, 206. **Open** 10am-5.30pm Tue-Sat; noon-5.30pm Sun. **Admission** free. **Map** p311 C5.

One of the most important 17th-century buildings in Ireland, the Royal Hospital was designed by Sir William Robinson in 1684 as a nursing home for retired soldiers. In 1991, the hospital was opened as the Irish Museum of Modern Art, with superb exhibition spaces around a peaceful square. The work generally takes the form of a temporary show and a selection from the permanent collection of 20th-century works. The museum favours a kind of scrupulous minimalism, and is occasionally accused of being relentlessly conceptual in a country that suffers from an impoverished visual arts tradition. Still, these are minor quibbles. Even if you are only vaguely interested in art, the museum is worth visiting for its setting alone. The chapel and banqueting hall are open for guided tours, and the imposing grounds include a beautifully restored baroque formal garden.

Kilmainham Gaol

Inchicore Road, Kilmainham (453 5984). Bus 51B, 78A, 79, 206. **Open** (by guided tour only) *Apr-Sept* 9.30am-6pm daily. *Oct-Mar* 9.30am-5pm Mon-Fri; 10am-6pm Sun. **Admission** €4.45; €1.90-€3.20 concessions. **Credit** MC, V. **Map** p311 A5.

Although it ceased to be used in 1924 – offenders are now sent to Mountjoy – this remains the best known Irish prison. It was here that the leaders of the 1916 Easter Rising were executed, and it has since featured in various movies, including *In the Name of the Father*. If you are interested in the 1916 Rising or previous rebellions in Ireland from the 18th century onwards, visit Kilmainham rather than the National Museum. Other displays relate to a variety of 19th-century prisons, with documents that testify to the atrocious conditions of the day. All are grimly informative, though the multimedia display on hanging seems gruesome beyond the call of duty.

Bridging the gap

The waters of the Liffey divide Dublin in half, creating two quite distinct centres on either side of the river and fuelling a rivalry between the northside and the southside that has long been one of Dublin's most salient characteristics (*see p90* **Joking apart**). The differences between the two areas are generally painted in the broadest of brush strokes – the northside is poor and the southside wealthy; the northside is the true heart of the city while the southside is full of uptight middle-class Anglophiles – and so on. A stroll through Dublin will soon convince you that both rich and poor neighbourhoods are scattered throughout the city regardless of their relative position to the river, but enough of a sense of genuine division remains to endue the unusual scale of bridge-building on the Liffey with an intriguing symbolic resonance. The Corporation's efforts

The river and its surroundings, then, are belatedly being seen as a real asset to Dublin. Broad and busy **O'Connell Bridge** is far from being the most distinguished of the city's bridges, but in the evening, when the tide is high and the sun sets over the Guinness buildings upriver, this bustling thoroughfare is one of the most atmospheric spots in Dublin and offers unbeatable views of the city centre.

The city's plans for **Grattan Bridge** (named after the 18th-century politician Henry Grattan) are a good illustration of Dublin's changing attitude to the Liffey. Current redevelopment work includes the construction of a walkway along the bridge that will join up with the existing Boardwalk and provide the site for a book market on the bridge. The intention is to create a pedestrian zone that embraces the alleys of Temple Bar on

to create a genuine pedestrian zone centred around the river may at last give the city a real and unified heart.

Until the last few years, the Liffey and its bridges had seldom commanded the attention they deserve. Instead, the river was mocked for its famous pungency and the traffic-clogged quays meant that even getting a look at the water involved an element of risk.

Now though, the river and its 'furniture' are finally attracting some interest. In 2000, the delicate new **Millennium Footbridge** (*see p89*) was opened to widespread praise, followed a year later by the **Boardwalk**, a handsome, silvery walkway suspended over the northern bank of the river. Little coffee kiosks and benches dot its length and on a sunny day, this is a pleasant spot indeed. The **Ha'penny Bridge** (*see p89*) itself was swept off to the shipyards of Belfast for much-needed repairs and is due to be reopened at the beginning of 2002.

the southside and the shopping zone of Henry Street on the northside, utilising the Ha'penny, Millennium and Grattan Bridges as vital connections between the two areas. It's a cheerful, optimistic vision of the future that looks as if it will transform the river in this part of the city.

Dublin Corporation also has plans for two brand-new bridges: **Blackhall Bridge** will connect the National Museum, the Four Courts and the rejuvenated Smithfield district to the south bank of the river, while further downriver, the €25million **Macken Street Bridge** by Santiago Calatrava Valls will form the centrepiece of Dublin's docklands regeneration scheme. Innovative and daring in design, the bridge will swivel to facilitate the passage of shipping in the river, and looks set to become a brilliant and dramatic addition to the cityscape. Such innovations should help to consolidate the new vision of the Liffey as the focus of the city.

Northside

Explore Dublin's turbulent political history and her challenging urban future on the streets north of the Liffey.

Traditionally seen as less-advantaged, the area of Dublin immediately north of the Liffey has taken its fair share of knocks over the years, but still remains the heart of the city for many Dubliners. In the first half of the 18th century the northside was the residential area of choice for the city's upper classes, but by 1800 new developments south of the Liffey had drawn people away from the district, initiating a long period of decline. In the 20th century, inner-city deprivation and drug-related problems earned the northside a poor reputation as the city's trouble spot, so that by the 1980s and '90s many of the well-heeled citizens of Dublin 4 would have considered crossing O'Connell Bridge a dangerous pursuit. Although not particularly accurate (*see p83* **Bridging the gap**), this view of the northside is a persistent one, with much of the prejudice articulated along class lines. The distinctions are blurring somewhat these days – Ireland's economic boom brought both investment and a new population to the district – but the northside of the city still has an edgier feel to it than the glitzy shopping areas of Grafton Street and Temple Bar.

For the visitor, the northside has particular historical resonance as the site of many key events in the Irish struggle for independence, including the 1916 Easter Rising at the **General Post Office**. The northside also boasts some of the city's most prestigious cultural institutions, such as the **Hugh Lane Gallery** on Parnell Street, and the world-renowned **Abbey Theatre**. Newly developed urban districts, such as **Smithfield** offer an insight into modern Dublin and, further west, the vast, green expanse of **Phoenix Park** provides a welcome retreat from the traffic-clogged centre.

O'Connell Street & around

Still the most historically important and politically contentious of Dublin thoroughfares, O'Connell Street is impossible to miss. Imperially wide, it boasts some grand buildings and a fine collection of statues. It is also presently undergoing a dramatic facelift. While grave mistakes were made in the past, with an unnecessarily generous berth given to motorists, tacky fast-food and budget shopping outlets, history – under the guise of the Historic

Daniel O'Connell keeps watch over O'Connell Street. *See p85.*

The view of Gandon's **Custom House** from George's Quay. *See p89.*

Area Rejuvenation Project (HARP) – is in the process of being rewritten. In addition to a new shopping complex and increased pedestrian access, the centrepiece of the project is the **Monument of Light**, an enormous (and enormously phallic) stainless steel spire that will rise to a height of 120 metres (396 feet) from the centre of the street. Colloquially known as 'the Spike', construction is expected to be completed by January 2002.

O'Connell Street has been through many name changes. It began life in 1700 as Drogheda Street, named after the Earl of Drogheda, but became Gardiner's Mall in 1740 after being widened by Luke Gardiner. In 1794, the completion of Carlisle Bridge (later O'Connell Bridge) raised the street's profile and it became the main thoroughfare in Dublin, known as Sackville Street. Finally, in 1924, it was renamed after Daniel O'Connell.

A street of statues, it is bound bottom and top by the imposing figures of **Daniel O'Connell** and **Charles Stewart Parnell**. O'Connell's statue is the gateway to the street. Built in 1854, it's a fine bronze representation of the stout man, flanked by four winged Victories. Slap bang in the nipple of one of them is a bullet hole, sustained in the fighting of 1916. Indeed, the street gains much of its historical importance from the Easter Rising of that year (*see p14*). It can only have enraged the ghost of O'Connell, who famously said (O'Connell, that is, not the ghost), 'The price

of Irish freedom is not worth the shedding of one drop of blood.' Much of O'Connell Street was destroyed during the fighting and had to be rebuilt in the 1920s.

The **General Post Office** (GPO; *see p87*) is the heart of the street. A landmark as much physical as it is historical, the GPO was designed by Francis Johnston and opened in 1818. In Easter 1916, Patrick Pearse read a proclamation declaring an Irish republic from its steps, then barricaded himself and his army of supporters inside. During the ensuing siege, the building was completely burnt out, and six years later, the outbreak of the Civil War did further damage; it was not reopened until 1929. You can still put your fingers in the bullet holes that riddle the columns and façade. To this day the steps of the GPO are used as a rallying point for demonstrations and protests of every kind, and the building's iconic status remains undiminished.

Nelson's Pillar used to stand near the GPO. The pillar was erected in 1815, predating its better-known sibling in Trafalgar Square, London, by 32 years. In 1966, on the 50th anniversary of the Easter Rising, it was blown up by the IRA; Nelson's head now sits in the **Dublin Civic Museum** (*see p65*). Opposite the GPO is **Clery's department store** (*see p144*), formerly the Dublin Drapery Store and Imperial Hotel. It was from the hotel balcony that trade unionist **Jim Larkin** made a stirring speech to his supporters during the general

Sightseeing

Fruit, veg, flowers and fortunes at markets on **Henry Street** and **Moore Street**.

strike in 1913. He cared more for the welfare of the people than the status of the country, and was universally loved. A fabulous statue of him now stands in the centre of O'Connell Street, throwing his arms in the air in a characteristically vigorous pose.

The 1988 **Anna Livia Millennium Fountain** is a homage to Anna Livia, spirit of the Liffey in Joyce's *Finnegans Wake*. This grotesque fountain, which some have viewed as almost pornographic, has become colloquially known as the 'Floozie in the Jacuzzi' (*see p71* **Statue spotting**) and has taken on the role of city landfill site for discarded burger boxes. The fountain is likely to move to Talbot Street, once the Monument of Light has been completed. Joyce himself appears in bronze on the corner of North Earl Street, gazing sardonically at the hordes of shoppers walking along O'Connell Street.

Cathedral Street to the north leads to **St Mary's Pro Cathedral**, Dublin's principal Catholic Church. Built in the Greek classical style in 1815, the church was the setting for the funeral of Daniel O'Connell in 1847, attended by crowds of mourning Dubliners. The best time to visit the cathedral is on a Sunday at 11am, when you'll will hear Latin mass exquisitely sung by the Palestrina Choir.

Besides its statues and fast-food joints, the O'Connell Street area also boasts some notable cultural institutions. On Abbey Street and Marlborough Street is the **Abbey Theatre** (*see p205*), founded in 1904 by WB Yeats and Lady Gregory. The Abbey has enjoyed a distinguished history, having hosted the premières of radical plays by JM Synge and Seán O'Casey that refused to pander to the myth of Gaelic Catholic Ireland. The performances caused riots in the theatre, forcing Yeats to venture on stage to reprimand the audience. The Abbey is now less of a radical dramatic hotbed and more of a safe establishment playhouse, though the occasional great production redeems it somewhat. **The Peacock** (*see p209*), a smaller theatre on the same premises, has taken up the Abbey's daring mantle, and now presents newer and generally less commercial work. If you're in the area drop into the **Flowing Tide** pub (*see p140*) across the street, which has a long association with the Abbey, and boasts an impressive collection of theatre posters. Staying on Abbey Street, cross over O'Connell Street to reach the **Hot Press Irish Music Hall of Fame** a populist temple to the success of Irish music (*see p87*).

The area north of here is renowned for its lively pedestrian markets along **Moore Street** and **Henry Street**. Aside from the expected fruit and vegetable stalls, numerous other bargains are offered by street traders along these stretches. Moore Street, of late, has adopted a multi-cultural flavour, with several shops specialising in Asian and African cuisine sitting a little uneasily among the street's longer-established businesses.

General Post Office

O'Connell Street (705 7000). Connolly Station DART/all buses to O'Connell Street. **Open** 8am-8pm Mon-Sat; 10.30am-6.30pm for stamps only Sun. **Admission** free. **Map** p313 H4.

Best known as the site of the Easter Rising in 1916, and almost completely destroyed by fire as a result, the GPO remains a potent symbol of Irish indepen-dence. The restored interior is wonderfully spacious and filled with light from the street, and most of the features and fittings have been respectfully pre-served. Near a window and visible from the outside is the beautiful **Death of Cúchulainn**, a statue by Oliver Sheppard commemorating the building's reopening in 1929. Cúchulainn, legendary knight of the Red Branch and admired heroic ideal, is said to have died aged just 27. Such was the awe and terror he inspired in his enemies, however, that even after killing him no one dared approach his body until some ravens landed on his shoulders, proving that he was dead. The way in which Pearse used Cúchulainn, the legendary hero of ancient Ireland, to romanticise the Irish struggle was made explicit by Yeats in his poem 'The Statues': 'When Pearse summoned Cuchulainn to his side/What stalked through the Post Office?'.

Hot Press Irish Music Hall of Fame

57 Abbey Street Middle (878 3345). All buses to O'Connell Street. **Open** 10am-7pm (last entry 6pm) daily. **Admission** €7.60; €5.10 concessions. **Credit** MC, V. **Map** p313 H4.

Although the Hall of Fame is geared to the corpo-rate market – there's even a private bar for VIP guests – it also features a state-of-the-art concert space, a restaurant and an interactive exhibition of the history of Irish music. The emphasis is on the modern rock scene, with lots of material on U2 and all the usual suspects, but trad stuff also gets a look in. If glorified karaoke is your thing, step onto the brightly lit stage, choose the music and grab the opportunity to be a megastar for a moment.

Parnell Square

O'Connell Street Upper gives way to **Parnell Square**, a large Georgian Square made up mainly of museums and public buildings. The south side of the square is taken up by the imposing **Rotunda Hospital**, founded in 1745 by Dr Bartholomew Mosse and occupying its present site since 1757. The building's name and shape coincides nicely with its role as the

first maternity hospital in Europe. It was built by Richard Castle, the architect of Leinster House and share's that building's design scheme. Housed in part of the hospital complex is the other great Dublin theatre, **The Gate** (*see p208*). The theatre was founded in 1929 by two remarkable characters, Hilton Edwards and Micheál MacLiammóir, who were both English and openly homosexual. MacLiammóir changed his name, learned fluent Gaelic and would walk around in full drag, in what was unarguably the most Catholic country in Europe at that time. He gave his last Dublin performance in his one-man show, *The Importance of Being Oscar*, in 1975.

On the north side of the Square is the **Garden of Remembrance**, established on the 50th anniversary of the 1916 Easter Rising to commemorate those who died for Irish freedom. The garden is dominated by a huge sculpture of the Children of Lir, a visual representation of one of Ireland's oldest legends, in which four children are changed into swans by their evil stepmother. Opposite the garden is the **Municipal Gallery of Modern Art** (*see p88*), also known as the **Hugh Lane Gallery**, another cultural spot with an interesting (and Yeats-related) history. Founded in 1908 by art enthusiast Sir Hugh Lane, this elegant gallery houses his collection of works by Dégas, Monet

James Joyce Centre. *See p88.*

Sightseeing

and Courbet, in addition to other fine 19th- and 20th-century paintings and sculptures. Lane first offered his outstanding collection to Dublin on condition that a suitable gallery was built to house them. When plans for such a gallery faded, Lane approached the National Gallery in London, much to the chagrin of WB Yeats, who wrote a number of poems vilifying his compatriots for their philistinism. Lane later decided to leave the collection to the city of Dublin and changed his will accordingly. Although the codicil was not witnessed before his 1915 death on the *Lusitania* and ownership of the collection remains unresolved, an agreement has now been reached whereby the most important works rotate between the two galleries. The gallery's most noteworthy acquisition of late is Francis Bacon's London studio, 7 Reese Mews, which is reproduced in the gallery untouched.

Next door to the Hugh Lane is the **Dublin Writers' Museum** (*see below*), established in 1991 in a house once belonging to the Jameson whiskey distilling family. The museum adjoins the **Irish Writers' Centre**, which is active in hosting a wide range of public lectures, readings and receptions (*see p35* **Word of mouth**), and serves as an excellent resource for those seeking information on contemporary Irish literature. Nearby, on the north-west corner of the square, is the camp'n'kitschy **National Wax Museum** (*see below*).

Head east from Parnell Square to North Great Georges Street to reach the **James Joyce Centre** (*see below*), housed in a beautifully restored 1784 Georgian townhouse. The centre is dedicated to the study of the man and his formidable body of work and contains a scholarly first-floor library. Across the street you'll find the stylish **Cobalt Café & Gallery** (*see p128*), which frequently hosts exhibitions by newer Irish artists, while at the top of the road is **Belvedere College**, the prestigious Jesuit school that Joyce himself attended.

Dublin Writers' Museum

18-19 Parnell Square (872 2077). Bus 3, 10, 11, 13, 16, 19, 22. **Open** *Winter* 10am-5pm Mon-Sat; 11am-5pm Sun. *Summer* 10am-6pm Mon-Fri; 10am-5pm Sat; 11am-5pm Sun. **Admission** €3.80; €1.80-€3.20 concessions. **No credit cards. Map** p313 G2/3.

Comprised of several rooms with displays relating to Irish writers, plus a 'gallery' upstairs that contains images of a selection of literary notables, the museum provides a useful introduction to Irish literature. First editions, correspondence and other memorabilia enliven the displays, although it is disappointing that little information is proffered about the international standing of Irish literature over the last 30 years.

James Joyce Centre

35 North Great George's Street (878 8547). Bus 3, 10, 11, 11A, 13, 16, 16A, 19, 19A, 22. **Open** 9.30am-5pm Mon-Sat; noon-5pm Sun. **Admission** €3.50; €0.90-€2.20 concessions. **Credit** MC, V. **Map** p313 H2.

One of the most interesting cultural venues in the city, the centre is a mixture of Joyce memorabilia and Dublin history. The first floor library has early editions and translations of Joyce's work, portraits of the Joyce family, and critical and biographical texts. Short films, readings (*see p35*) and workshops are presented here on a regular basis. Joyce himself knew the house as Denis Maginni's dance academy. *See also p95* **Walking the *Ulysses* trail**.

Municipal Gallery of Modern Art (Hugh Lane Gallery)

Parnell Square North (874 1903). Bus 3, 10, 11, 13, 16, 19, 22. **Open** *Sept-Mar* 9.30am-6pm Tue-Thur; 9.30am-5pm Fri, Sat. *Apr-Aug* 9.30am-6pm Tue, Wed; 9.30am-8pm Thur; 9.30am-5pm Fri, Sat. **Admission** *Gallery* free. *Francis Bacon Studio* €7.60; €3.80 concessions; free under-18s. Free to all 9.30am-12.30pm Tue. **Credit** MC, V. **Map** p313 G3.

The gallery is probably best known for its collection of Impressionist works including Manet's *La Musique aux Tuileries*, Degas' *Sur la Plage* and Vuillard's *La Cheminée*, but houses Rodin sculptures and a fine selection of modern Irish paintings, too. It is also home to an exhibition of exuberant art nouveau stained glass panels by Harry Clarke, a Beardsley-style illustrator whose most accomplished work was executed in glass (some rather restrained panels can be seen in Bewley's Oriental Café in Grafton Street). Most recently, the gallery acquired the entire contents of the London studio at 7 Reese Mews, rented by artist Francis Bacon from 1961 until his death in 1992. Enclosed within glass, Bacon's notoriously untidy studio sits undisturbed, and visitors can stare in at the half-completed canvases, dirty paintbrushes, bottles of booze, books and shopping bags scattered around the four- by eight-metre room. Such was the desire for authenticity that even the fine layer of dust that covered the room was collected and re-scattered over this strangely voyeuristic exhibit. Free classical music concerts and lectures are also frequently held here.

National Wax Museum

Granby Row, Parnell Square (872 6340). Bus 3, 10, 11, 13, 16, 19, 22. **Open** 10am-5.30pm Mon-Sat; noon-5.30pm Sun. **Admission** €4.50; €2.50-€3.20 concessions. **Credit** AmEx, DC, MC, V. **Map** p313 G3.

Madame Tussaud's it's not, but an eclectic range of figures, including Eamon De Valera, Snow White, Bart Simpson, Elvis and rock superstars U2 are all immortalised here. While it's probably most enjoyable for small children or those with an exaggerated appreciation of kitsch, the museum does feature some genuine oddities, not least its life-size replica of Leonardo Da Vinci's *Last Supper*.

North city quays

The quays are the oldest part of the city and have a distinct character of their own. They follow the Liffey from Phoenix Park in the west to Dublin Harbour in the east, encompassing the city centre at O'Connell Bridge, the most important river crossing in the city. Although the quays fell into disrepair in the 1970s and '80s, with many fine buildings left derelict, much has been done to revitalise the strip, and its environs are now home to countless apartment complexes, shops, pubs and even a Parisian-style **boardwalk** which runs from the corner of Capel Street to O'Connell Bridge.

The area west of O'Connell Bridge is predominantly a residential and business district, but the Docklands Development Authority has done much to revitalise the 'campshires' – the strip of land between the quay walls and the roads. This pedestrianised stretch is home to a number of cafés and hotels,

and also boasts a fine sculpture by Ronan Gillespie commemorating the victims of the Great Famine. Dominating the whole area, however, is the city's most blatant symbol of commerce, the glittering **International Financial Services Centre** (www.ifsc.ie), which employs over 6,500 people and is the Irish home of many of the world's largest banks and financial institutions.

From the Custom House to the Four Courts

The central part of the quays is bounded by the Custom House in the east and the Four Courts in the west, both 18th-century masterpieces by James Gandon (*see p27*). The copper-domed **Custom House** (for visitor centre, *see p90*), topped with a sculpture of Commerce, is a landmark in the city, and is best viewed from across the river at George's Quay. Its classical façade stretches for 114 metres (375 feet), with busts representing the gods of Ireland's 14 major rivers decorating the portico. (Only the Liffey is a goddess: even before Joyce, Dublin's river was represented as female). Gandon's extraordinary building techniques included constructing the foundations of the Custom House on wooden supports over a bog. To this day, the foundations haven't shifted an inch, even surviving a fire during the independence war of 1921 that blazed for five days (courtesy of the IRA) and reduced the building to a shell (*see p16*).

West of O'Connell Bridge, Bachelor's Walk leads to the newly-renovated **Ha'penny Bridge**, a charming pedestrianised arched structure, built in 1816. Its official name is the Liffey Bridge but, as there used to be a halfpenny toll crossing charge, its popular name endures. The **Winding Stair** (*see p147*), the best loved of all Dublin's second-hand bookshops is nearby, while the stylish **Morrison Hotel** (*see p75*) is further west on Ormond Quay. Built on the site of the Ormond Multimedia Centre, the hotel's sleek interiors were designed by Irish fashion guru, John Rocha, and epitomise the cosmopolitan glamour of new-Dublin money. Adjacent to the hotel, is the **Millennium Bridge**. Strikingly well-lit at night, this pedestrian bridge was actually constructed in Carlow, some 50 miles (80 kilometres) from Dublin, and was the single largest object to have ever been transported over land in Ireland.

Further west, Gandon's **Four Courts** (*see p27*) were the site of a key event in the Irish struggle for independence. In 1922, IRA forces, led by Eamon De Valera, occupied the Courts for two months in protest against the Anglo-

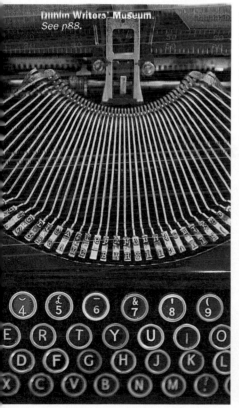

Dublin Writers' Museum. *See p88.*

Joking apart

- What do you call a northside Dubliner in a three-bedroom semi? A burglar.
- What do you call a northsider in a suit? The accused.
- Why do southside women go out with northside men? To get their handbags back.
- What do you call two vehicles colliding on the southside? A crèche.
- Why don't southside secretaries take coffee breaks? It would take too long to retrain them afterwards.

Irish Treaty. They were besieged by the forces of the new Free State government led by Michael Collins, in an action that marked the start of the Civil War. Government shelling destroyed the building, which was eventually rebuilt in 1932.

The task of the reconstruction of both the Four Courts and the Custom House after the ravages of the struggle for independence fell into the hands of the Office of Public Works. It is a great testimony to the original design of the buildings that they survived the restoration process so well. The Four Courts houses the Supreme and High Courts, so only the entrance hall beneath the great cupola is open to visitors.

Custom House Visitor Centre

Custom House Quay (878 7660). Tara Street DART/ 53A, 90A bus. **Open** 10am-5pm Mon-Fri; 2-5pm Sat, Sun. **Admission** €1. **Map** p313 J4.

The Custom House Visitor Centre only offers access to a small area of the building. Displays and a video relate to the history and uses of the Custom House, and to Gandon himself, but unless you have a passionate interest in the administration of customs and excise duties in 18th-century Ireland, the main reason for visiting is architectural. Parts of the interior open to the public include a beautiful octagonal space on the first floor, the only place where the building's original elegant ornamentation remains.

Smithfield & around

Just north of the river and the Four Courts lies **St Michan's Church** (*see p93*), which occupies the site of the first suburban church of Norse Dublin (built in 1096), although sadly, little remains from this era. In fact, St Michan's chief 'attractions' lie below ground in the 17th-century vaults, which are composed of magnesium limestone. The atmosphere in the vaults is so dry that the bodies buried in them have been preserved. It makes a gruesome but hugely popular tourist attraction.

Close by is **Smithfield**, where a network of tiny Victorian streets of redbrick houses converge on a newly-renovated civic square. Still very much a work in progress, Smithfield

The cupola of the **Four Courts**, overlooking the Liffey. *See p89.*

Urban space in the making

If you're new to Dublin it's unlikely that you'll just stumble upon Smithfield. Located near the Four Courts, this dramatic urban space nestles among a warren-like maze of streets that make up one of the oldest parts of the city. The centrepiece, an impressive public square that has been compared rather inappropriately to the Piazza Navona in Rome, is flanked by sharply contrasting aspects of new and old Dublin. If nothing else, a visit to Smithfield offers a rare opportunity to witness the ongoing process of aggressive urban development in action.

Smithfield started out in the mid-17th century as a cobbled marketplace, a function that the square still partly retains. During the '70s and '80s it was most notable for its horsefair, a bustling, spit-and-sawdust farmers' market that took place on the square on the first Sunday of each month (*pictured*). The whole district later fell under the jurisdiction of the HARP plan to revitalise the north inner city and was sold by the state to private enterprise in 1991.

Now hailing itself rather dubiously as the largest purpose-built civic plaza in Europe – the square was already there, after all – Smithfield is austerely decked out with twelve gas braziers, each 26 metres (86 feet) high, that burn brightly on Saturday evenings. It's eerily beautiful, but also representative of the climate of self-aggrandisement so common in Dublin these days. Haggling and horse-shit are seen as no longer compatible with Smithfield's new 21st-century image, so in 2001 the fair relocated, just up the road to Morningstar Avenue, where it remains a living, breathing reminder of the city's more rough-and-ready past.

Smithfield, meanwhile, is looking to the future. In addition to some 220 new apartments in the immediate area, on the east side of the square a complex of buildings from the old distillery have been rebranded to form Smithfield Village. As a purpose-built tourist attraction, complete with hotel and restaurants, the complex feels vaguely dissatisfying and rather divorced from its surroundings: the ingeniously converted **Smithfield Chimney** (*see p92*) is certainly worth a look, but only the most committed whiskey fans will enjoy the **Old Jameson's Distillery Tour** (*see p92*). What's more, Smithfield's most worthy attraction, **Ceol** – an excellent interactive history of Irish music – moved out of the complex in November 2001.

Nightlife in Smithfield is deceptive. Unlike the bustling public squares in Temple Bar that throng with hordes of chatty tourists, Smithfield often feels deserted after dark. There are, however, a number of spots worth seeking out, particularly if you want to avoid the stress-inducing atmosphere of an evening in the immediate city centre. The lively **Cobblestone** pub (*see p139*) at the north end of the square has a fine reputation for traditional music sessions, while the **Dublin Brewing Company**, located nearby, brews up tasty alternatives to the well-known brands, which are served in pubs throughout the area (*see p140*).

Where Smithfield really excels, however, is in the sheer size of the public space itself. The square can accommodate up to 15,000 people, and has been the site of a number of high-profile concerts. March 2000 saw it packed to capacity, as the freedom of the city was conferred on both Dublin rock superstars U2 and Burmese opposition leader Aung San Suu Kyi. As long as it avoids the excesses that have threatened to ruin Temple Bar, and manages to survive the city's economic downturn, Smithfield has the potential to become one of the city's most vibrant areas. For the moment though, it offers a little breathing-space; something for which Dubliners should certainly be thankful.

Sightseeing

Smithfield Chimney.

and the **Smithfield Chimney** (*see p93*), from which an observation tower at the top offers a panorama of the city. Dublin is hardly famed for its skyline, but the 360-degree view is a good way to understand the urban layout, and riding the external glass elevator is ever-so-slightly thrilling.

Smithfield is best visited on a Saturday night, when the square's massive gas-braziers are lit, adding a real air of drama to the proceedings. Sceptics might suggest, however, that the area is little more than an under-developed theme park, and a visit to the area's other principal attraction, the tacky and lucklustre **Old Jameson Distillery** (*see below*), will do nothing to dispel such an argument. That said, enterprising visitors will discover some excellent bars in Smithfield and adjoining Stoneybatter, that make a pleasant change from the overcrowded pubs in the city centre.

Old Jameson Distillery

Bow Street, Smithfield Village (872 5566). Bus 25, 26, 37, 39, 67, 67A, 68, 69, 79. **Open** 9.30am-6pm daily. **Admission** (by guided tour only) €5; €3.80. concessions. **Credit** AmEx, MC, V. **Map** p312 E4. This vapid guided tour, which includes an AV presentation, is not much more than an advert for Irish whiskey, designed to tempt wealthy tourists to buy some seriously expensive bottles. Several claustrophobic rooms concentrate on the manufacturing process: a beautifully crafted model of the distillery vessels and machines made for the 1924 World Exhibition is the most interesting object on show. Although the museum gives plenty of information

is a microcosm of the startling interface of old and new that characterises so much recent development in the city (*see p91* **Urban space in the making**). The west side of the square is home to a series of trade-only vegetable markets and derelict sites, while opposite stands a monolithic complex of newer redbrick buildings, including **Chief O Neill's Hotel** (*see p49*), the **Kelly & Ping** Asian restaurant

Enjoying the great outdoors in **Phoenix Park**. *See p93.*

Collins Barracks, now the second site of the **National Museum**. *See p94.*

about the five brand names of Irish Distillers (Bushmills, Jameson, Paddy, Powers and Tullamore Dew), details are scarce about other, slightly more specialised labels. Be thankful, then, that admission includes a glass of Jameson's.

St Michan's Church

Church Street Lower (872 4154). Bus 25, 26, 37, 39, 67, 67A, 68, 69, 79. **Open** 10am-12.45pm, 2-4.45pm Mon-Fri; 10am-12.45pm Sat. **Admission** €2.50; €1.30-€1.90 concessions. **No credit cards. Map** p312 F4.
There has been a place of worship on this site since 1096 and it remained the only parish church on the north side of the River Liffey until the 16th century. The current building dates from 1686, but was drastically restored in 1828 and again following the civil war, giving the whole place a somewhat inconclusive air. Those with an interest in the macabre will love the church's world-renowned vaults, where mummified bodies, including one of an eight-foot tall crusader, have stood for centuries showing no signs of decomposition. Rumour also has it that Handel gave the first ever performance of his *Messiah* on the church's 18th century organ, predating the work's first public performance on Fishamble Street.

Smithfield Chimney

Smithfield Village (817 3800). Bus 25, 26, 39, 37, 67, 68, 69, 70. **Open** 9.30am-5.30pm daily. **Admission** €6.35; €4.40-€5.10 concessions; €19.05 family. **Credit** AmEx, MC, V. **Map** p312 E4.
Once part of the old Jameson Distillery, this 175ft chimney now functions as a novel skyline observatory. A purpose-built glass elevator ascends the chimney to a two-tiered glass platform from which visitors can view the whole of Dublin city, the surrounding countryside and Dublin Bay.

Towards Phoenix Park

West of Smithfield, opposite the enormous bulk of the Guinness Brewery, is Collins Barracks, the second site of the excellent **National Museum** (*see p94*). This finely renovated 17th-century building is the oldest military barracks in Europe and overlooks a spacious open courtyard. The building principally houses the National Museum's decorative art collections, with silver, ceramics and period furniture dominating the permanent displays.

Beyond the museum, a short walk will take you to the vast expanse of **Phoenix Park**. At 1,752 acres (710 hectares) it is the largest city park in Europe, and a wonderful place to explore, with an invigorating mixture of formal gardens, casual meadows, sports fields, wild undergrowth, mature trees and plenty of easygoing deer. The land making up the park was seized from Kilmainham Priory during the Reformation and converted into a viceregal residence and royal deer park during the 17th century by the Duke of Ormond. In 1747 Lord Chesterfield opened the park to the public. Chesterfield Avenue, the wide main road through the park, is named after him.

The park contains the residence of the Irish president, **Áras an Uachtaráin**, a Palladian lodge that was the home of the lord lieutenant of Ireland. On 6 May 1882, Lord Cavendish, recently arrived chief secretary of Ireland, and TH Burke, the under-secretary, were both stabbed to death within sight of the residence. The episode became know as the Phoenix Park

The **Papal Cross**: the pope woz 'ere.

murders, and it poisoned and embittered Anglo-Irish relations for years to come.

The formal **People's Garden** welcomes visitors at the south-eastern entrance of the park. Across the road is the huge **Wellington Monument** by Sir Robert Smirke, while to the north-west is **Dublin Zoo** (*see below*). The zoo was rather down-at-heel for years, but after a successful expansion and substantial efforts to brighten itself up, it has once more begun to attract visitors other than first-communion children. If you're lucky enough to be blessed with a sunny afternoon, a visit here can be very pleasant indeed.

At the Phoenix Monument in the centre of the park, side roads and pathways lead off in various directions towards the **Phoenix Park Visitors' Centre** (*see below*), the gracious 18th-century home of the American ambassador and the towering **Papal Cross**. Erected in 1979, the cross marks the gathering of some million people who came here to hear Pope John Paul II say: 'Young people of Ireland, I love you.'

It is also well worth taking the time to explore the acres of unspoilt wilderness that make up the bulk of the Phoenix Park; its expansive greenery is an ideal antidote to the overcrowding of the city centre.

Dublin Zoo & Zoological Gardens

Phoenix Park (677 1425). Bus 10, 25, 25A, 26, 51, 66, 67, 68, 69. **Open** *Summer* 9.30am-6pm Mon-Sat; 10.30am-6pm Sun. *Winter* 9.30am-4pm Mon-Fri; 9.30am-5pm Sat; 10.30am-5pm Sun. **Admission** €7.60; €4.50-€5.70 concessions; free under-3s. **Credit** AmEx, DC, MC, V. **Map** p311 B2.
Dublin's very own animal house was first founded in 1830, making it the third oldest zoo in the world. It now houses over 700 animals, including endangered species such as snow leopards, rhinoceroses and golden lion tamarinds. The place is run with children very much in mind, with a Pets' Corner, a Zoo Train, ample picnic facilities and play areas, but recent improvements mean there's plenty to interest adults too. Most significantly, summer 2000 saw the opening of **African Plains**, a Savannah-style environment incorporating a large lake, pastureland and mature woodland, which is now home for many of the zoo's larger residents. Kick-started by a government donation of 32 acres (13 hectares) land from the Áras an Uachtaráin grounds, the expansion has effectively doubled the size of the zoo.

National Museum of Ireland: Decorative Arts & History

Collins Barracks, Benburb Street (677 7444). MuseumLink shuttle/25, 25A, 66, 67, 90 bus. **Open** 10am-5pm Tue-Sat; 2-5pm Sun. **Admission** free. **Map** p312 D4.
This section of the National Museum of Ireland houses the institution's collections of decorative art. Of particular note are the collections of Irish silverware and furniture, in addition to an interesting exhibition on Irish fashion and style since the 1950s, and a regularly updated Curator's Choice room. All of the exhibitions are well-complemented by interactive multimedia displays and frequently supplemented by workshops and talks. An Earth Science Museum is due to open at the Collins Barracks premises in 2003; there are plans for it to house geological collections, fossils and even the odd bit of dinosaur.

Phoenix Park Visitors' Centre

Ashtown Castle, Phoenix Park (677 0095). Bus 37, 39. **Open** *Mid-end Mar* 9.30am-5pm daily. *Apr-May* 9.30am-5.30pm daily. *June-Sept* 10am-6pm daily. *Oct-mid-Mar* 9.30am-4.30pm Sat, Sun. **Admission** €2.50; €1.25-€1.90 concessions. **No credit cards.**
The Phoenix Park Visitor Centre deals with the history of the Park and its wildlife, and is housed in the coach house of the former papal nunciature. Admission to the centre includes a tour of Ashtown Castle, a delicate 17th-century tower house that was enclosed within the later residence.

Walking the *Ulysses* trail

Leopold Bloom's house at **7 Eccles Street** on the northside was demolished to make way for the Mater Hospital, but its front door survives at the **James Joyce Centre** (*see p88*) on North Great George's Street – a good place to start a Joycean walk around central Dublin in the footsteps of Leopold Bloom.

In Joyce's day this building was the dancing academy of Dennis J Maginni, one of the real-life characters who makes an appearance in the novel. Now the house is filled with fascinating memorabilia, with a delightful library room on the first floor. As you leave the centre, look up the street to the red brick façade of **Belvedere College**, which Joyce attended between 1893 and 1898.

At the bottom of North Great George's Street you can join Bloom as he makes his way into the city along Lower Gardiner Street. Pass under the railway bridge, round the side of the **Custom House** (*see p89*) and cross the river via Butt Bridge. On the southside, follow Bloom's route along St George's Quay to Lombard Street, where you, like he, will notice **Nichol Undertakers** – still in existence and barely changed a century later. Then it's on to the post office on Westland Row, now part of **Pearse Station**, and **St Andrew's Church** – called All Hallows in the novel – where Bloom looks in on the sleepy congregation. At the end of Westland Row on Lincoln Place, and still sporting the same shopfront as in 1904, is **Sweny's Chemist**, where Bloom goes to buy some lemon soap for his trip to the baths in Leinster Street (no longer in existence). His route takes him past the back entrance to **Trinity College** (*see p61*) and past **Finn's Hotel**, where Nora Barnacle worked.

After his ablutions Bloom makes his way to **Glasnevin Cemetery** (*see p97*) to attend Paddy Dignam's funeral, but he returns to the southside of the city in chapter eight. Pick up his trail again by heading along Nassau Street to **College Green** (*see p61*) and the statue of the poet, Thomas Moore. Bloom enjoys the irony of the fact that the author of 'The Meeting of the Waters' stands over a urinal. From the 'surly front' of Trinity College follow Bloom to Grafton Street, and turn left on to Duke Street for some lunch – a gorgonzola sandwich and a glass of burgundy, perhaps? – in **Davy Byrne's** (*see p132*). From Duke Street, turn right on to Dawson Street and left on to Molesworth Street towards the **National**

Museum and the **National Library** (for both, *see p66*). Bloom checks out the female statues in the museum foyer, before making his way to the library. When he enters the reading room in chapter nine, Stephen Dedalus is engaged in a heated debate about *Hamlet* with the poet George Russell (Æ).

Bloom leaves the library for **Temple Bar** (*see p75*) to buy a second-hand book for his wife Molly. Make your own way there, then walk through Merchant's Arch and on to Wellington Quay. Continue along the river, past the front of the **Clarence** (*see p39*) and over Grattan Bridge to the **Ormond Hotel** (7-11 Ormond Quay), where Bloom hears Stephen Dedalus sing in chapter 11. From the hotel walk along the north quays and then pause on O'Connell Bridge where Bloom stops to throw bread to the seagulls on his return to the southside in chapter eight. Turn up O'Connell Street and into Abbey Street to visit two pubs that Bloom pops into on his way back from the funeral in chapter seven: the **Oval** (78 Middle Abbey Street) and **Mooney's** (now the Abbey Mooney, Lower Abbey Street). At the end of Lower Abbey Street, on Beresford Place, turn left on to Lower Gardiner Street and left again on to Talbot Street to find the former site of **Olhausen's**, a butcher's shop at No.72, at which Bloom buys a pig's trotter and a sheep's hoof in chapter 15. This is the climactic chapter of the book and is set in nighttown or the 'kips', Dublin's former red-light district, which was cleared of its prostitutes by the Catholic Legion of Mary after Independence. Head up Gardiner Street to reach present-day **Railway Street**, site of the Bella Cohen brothel in the novel, where Stephen Dedalus confronts the ghost of his mother and has to be rescued by Bloom from a skirmish with a soldier. Bloom and Stephen make their way back to Eccles Street, by way of Gardiner Street, Mountjoy Square, Temple Street and Hardwicke Place; follow them as far as Parnell Street, from where you can return to North Great George's Street; the **Cobalt Café** (*see p128*) is the perfect place to recover from your exertions.

Note: this walk does not follow the exact chronology of the novel, nor should it take 24 hours! For a fuller Joyce experience, join the guided walks and other events on **Bloomsday**, held annually on 16 June (*see p165*).

Beyond the City Centre

Discover some hidden gems within the suburban sprawl.

Sightseeing

Away from the coast, the core of the city is ringed by a handful of self-contained suburban areas, including **Phibsboro**, **Drumcondra** and **Glasnevin** on the northside, and **Rathmines**, **Donnybrook** and well-heeled **Ballsbridge** to the south. These are popular residential neighbourhoods, where a young population ensures that the restaurants and pubs are lively, although less varied than in town.

Beyond these flatland villages, the once-rural hinterland of the city has been replaced by a low-density urban sprawl, a process that accelerated dramatically in the last three decades of the 20th century. Socio-economic factors have ensured that some areas are prettier than others, but most were built to be functional and hold little of interest to the visitor. The main routes in and out of Dublin are perhaps most notable for vast office developments and retail parks. Having said that, there are some interesting museums, castles and gardens sprinkled throughout the inland suburbs. Here are the best of them.

Southern suburbs

Directly south-east of central Dublin is the upmarket suburb of **Ballsbridge**, a 19th-century neighbourhood that now houses many of the city's embassies, as well as the **Royal Dublin Showgrounds** and **Lansdowne Road Rugby Ground** (*see p217*). The area's high-quality hotels and restaurants, and its proximity to the centre, make Ballsbridge popular with monied visitors.

South-west of here is **Rathfarnham Castle** (*see below*), which dates from 1583 and is in a state of ongoing restoration. Also in Rathfarnham is a museum dedicated to one of Irish nationalism's most important and charismatic figures, Padraig Pearse. Pearse was a schoolteacher and a leader of the 1916 Easter Rising, and the **Pearse Museum** (*see below*) is housed in the 18th-century premises of his innovative school, St Enda's. Nearby **Marlay Park** is one of the most attractive public spaces in Dublin and an increasingly popular venue for outdoor concerts. Hill-walkers should note that the **Wicklow Way** (*see p225*) starts from here.

Further west, **Tallaght**, in the foothills of the Dublin mountains, is a densely populated area that until recently was shamefully devoid

of facilities. Many inner-city residents moved here – not necessarily by choice – as Dublin was gentrified, and the rapid expansion earned the area the nickname Tallaghtfornia. For a while it was a byword for crime, drugs, and deprivation, but while further investment is still needed, the area has improved dramatically: it now boasts a new theatre, improved sporting facilities (including the arrival of Shamrock Rovers soccer club; *see p217*) and a thriving shopping centre.

There are almost 1,400 hectares of public parks and open spaces in South Dublin: in Tallaght, check out the **Sean Walsh Memorial Park**, which has landscaped parkland, ornamental formal gardens and recreation facilities, and **Tymon Park**, whose lakes attract countless wildfowl. Equally fine is **Corkagh Park** in Clondalkin, further to the south-west, notable for its extensive mature woodlands and water features.

Pearse Museum

St Enda's Park, Grange Road, Rathfarnham (493 4208). Bus 16. **Open** *Nov-Jan* 10am-4pm daily. *Feb-Apr, Sept, Oct* 10am-5pm daily. *May-Aug* 10am-5.30pm daily. **Admission** free.

This museum, dedicated to nationalist leader and educationalist Padraig Pearse, is housed in the premises of his experimental school, the first to adopt the now-ubiquitous system of bilingual Irish-English instruction. Displays document Pearse's life and work, although a little more information on what was taught (and how) would be interesting: many of Pearse's ideas on education were inspired.

In political terms, Pearse is the man most associated with the philosophy of 'blood sacrifice' for Ireland. Imprisoned and later shot for his part in the Easter Rising, any criticism of him or his ideals was, for a long time, effectively beyond the pale in Irish nationalist historiography. If the man holds no fascination, it's still worth going to the museum for its beautiful gardens and park. The tearoom in the stable block is particularly pleasant.

Rathfarnham Castle

Rathfarnham (493 9462). Bus 16A, 16C. **Open** *May-Oct* 9.30am-5.30pm daily. **Admission** (by guided tour only) €1.90; €70-€1.20; €5 family. **No credit cards.** The castle dates from 1583 and was built by Sir Adam Loftus, archbishop of Dublin. It was substantially renovated in the 18th century and has beautiful interiors by Sir William Chambers and

Glasnevin Cemetery: full of famous bodies. *See p98.*

James 'Athenian' Stuart. The castle is undergoing substantial conservation work, but the adjoining park has recently been restored to its former rather formal beauty.

Northern suburbs

Heading north-east from the city centre, the Finglas Road will bring you to **Glasnevin Cemetery**, founded by Daniel O'Connell in 1832. Until O'Connell's intervention, the repressive anti Catholic penal laws had meant that there was no official place for Catholics to bury their dead. The cemetery (also known as Prospect Cemetery) is now the largest in Ireland and sprawls over 120 acres (49 hectares). Some one million bodies have been interred here, including famous names from Irish political history. The older sections exude a suitably melancholic atmosphere – all crumbling walls, worn stone monuments and ivy. The cemetery is accessible through the old gates off Curran's Square, where you'll also find the famous Gravediggers' pub, properly known as **Kavanagh's** *(see p141)*. Adjoining the cemetery are the magnificent **National Botanic Gardens** *(see p98)*. Packed with a variety of plants but often virtually empty of human visitors, the gardens are truly magical – and at eight acres (3.2 hectares), they are also big enough to get lost in.

The vast stadium at **Croke Park** looms over the suburb of Drumcondra to the east of Glasnevin. As the home of Gaelic sports (Gaelic football, hurling and camogie; *see p220* **Going Gaelic**), the stadium also houses the **GAA Museum** *(see p98)*, which explores the development of the Gaelic Athletic Association, from its foundation in 1884, and its role in promoting Gaelic culture. North-east at Marino on the Malahide Road is the **Casino**, a little-visited attraction that is actually one of the most unusual architectural conceits in Dublin. It's not a gambling den of course, but a small house designed in the 18th century by Sir William Chambers for the Earl of Charlemont. Inside, are a host of diminutive rooms housing all the accessories of a home of the period, reproduced in miniature. The Earl of Charlemont's eccentricities clearly irritated some people; in 1792 the painter Charles Folliot contrived to insult him by building a terrace of beautiful houses along Marino Crescent, just where they would obscure the Earl's view of the sea. *Dracula* author Bram Stoker was born at No.15 Marino Crescent.

Further north, the Dublin suburbs come under the auspices of Fingal County Council. There is still a farming hinterland around here, and villages such as Ballyboughal, Naul and Oldtown are more rural than urban in character.

Casino at Marino

Malahide Road (entrance opposite Clontarf Golf Club) (833 1618). Clontarf Road DART/20B, 27, 27B, 27C, 32A, 42, 42A, 42B, 43 bus. **Open** *Feb-Apr, Nov, Dec* noon-4pm Sat, Sun. *May* 10am-5pm daily. *June-Sept* 10am-6pm daily. Closed Jan. **Admission** €2.53; €1.26 concessions; €6.34 family. **No credit cards.**
From the outside the Casino looks like a folly, and you imagine it has one room within. In fact, it's a fascinating complex of tiny rooms spread over three floors and it has in miniature everything that you would expect to find in an 18th-century house, including a butler's pantry and a servants' hall. The windows are deliberately blackened to conceal the presence of these convoluted and cunning rooms. The huge and imposing front door is another trick as entry is actually via a small panel. Inside are a range of cunning techniques of concealment, disguise and deception, including columns that act as drains; huge urns disguising heaters, and wall drapes that turn out to be carvings. There's a zodiac room, a Chinese room, and even a secret underground tunnel leading to Charlemont House. Unfortunately the original furnishings are long since dispersed and have been replaced by less suitable Victorian additions, but this is a minor quibble in an otherwise fascinating building.

Sightseeing

The marvellous glasshouses at the
National Botanic Gardens.

GAA Museum

New Cusack Stand, Croke Park (855 8176).
Drumcondra rail/11, 13, 51A bus. **Open** *May-Sept*
9am-5pm daily. *Sept-May* 10am-5pm Tue-Sat; noon-
5pm Sun. **Admission** €5; €3-€3.50 concessions;
€13 family. **Credit** MC, V. **Map** p309.

The self-guided tour takes the visitor through the
background of this unique organisation and incorporates displays on Gaelic sports and their role in
today's Ireland. The emphasis is on education and
displays are often interactive. If possible, combine a
visit to the museum with watching a match and note
that on match days only those with stand tickets are
permitted access to the museum.

Glasnevin Cemetery

Finglas Road, Glasnevin (830 1133). Bus 40, 40A.
40B, 40C. **Open** 8.30am-5pm daily. **Admission** free.

It is fitting that Glasnevin Cemetery holds the body
of its founder, Daniel O'Connell, whose grave is
imposingly marked by a 19th-century version of an
early Irish round tower. In fact, not all of his body
is interred here; his heart was buried in Rome. The
cemetery is also the final resting place of the other
major name in Irish 19th-century political life,
Charles Stewart Parnell. He requested to be buried
in a mass grave among the people of Ireland, and a
large boulder beside this grave carries his name.
Other famous cadavers include Eamonn De Valera,
Michael Collins, Gerard Manley Hopkins and Phil
Lynott of Thin Lizzy. Different architectural and
cultural movements are well represented by the
sculptures, monuments and gravestones: the Young
Ireland movement (which launched a doomed
rebellion attempt in 1848) is commemorated by a
multitude of shamrocks, harps and wolfhounds.

National Botanic Gardens

Finglas Road, Glasnevin (837 7596/837 4388).
Bus 13A, 19, 134. **Open** *Summer* 9am-6pm Mon-
Sat; 11am-6pm Sun. *Winter* 10am-4.30pm Mon-Sat;
11am-4pm Sun. **Admission** free.

These atmospheric gardens are a judicious blend of
exoticism and genteel dilapidation. Don't miss the
glasshouses, built between 1843 and 1869 by the
architect Richard Turner, who was also responsible
for the glasshouse at Belfast Botanic Gardens and
the Palm House at the Royal Botanic Gardens in
Kew. The yew-walk beside the River Tolka has trees
dating back to the early 18th century.

West of the city

Immediately south-west of Phoenix Park is
the historic riverside village of **Chapelizod**. Its
unusual name is a corruption of 'Seipeal Iosaild'
indicating where the legendary Irish princess
Isolde built a church. The village features in
the Joseph Sheridan Le Fanu ghost story *The*
House by the Churchyard and is the location of
Mullingar Inn in *Finnegans Wake*. Chapelizod
forms the eastern boundary of **Strawberry**
Beds, a shaded valley that is one of the most
attractive spots on the River Liffey. As the
name suggests, the sheltered slopes of the
riverbank were once used to grow strawberries
for the local market. The area was immortalised
in the maudlin folk song 'The Ferryman', in the
line 'where the Strawberry Beds sweep down to
the Liffey' and in the 19th century it was a
popular excursion spot.

Many still make the short trip out to
Strawberry Beds to enjoy the scenery and eat
and drink in the valley's pubs: **Angler's Rest**
(Knockmaroon; 820 4351), the **Wren's Nest**
(821 0949) and **Strawberry Hall** (821 0634)
The latter two both claim to be Ireland's second
oldest pub, with foundations dating back to
the 16th century. To reach Strawberry Beds
take bus nos.25, 26, 66 or 67 to Chapelizod and
then make the short walk over the wonderfully
named Knockmaroon Hill.

Dublin Bay & the Coast

'From swerve of shore to bend of bay.'

If you take the ferry from Holyhead to Dublin, you'll see from afar the lovely horseshoe curve of Dublin Bay, with **Killiney Head** at the south end and **Howth Head** at the north. It's the last view the 19th-century emigrants had of their native land, and still makes for a poignant sight, despite the enormous red and white chimneys of the petroleum factory on Poolbeg Causeway.

The quays stretch for miles through the city centre until they reach Dublin harbour, where ferry services to Holyhead and Liverpool depart and arrive. It's a seedy, old-fashioned harbour with oily smells and dockside pubs, but it's perfect if the trappings of shipping are your particular thing. On the south bank is an empty, haunting view across to the **Pigeonhouse Fort** (now used as a power station) and out to **Poolbeg Lighthouse** set at the easternmost point of the South Wall, a low breakwater stretching far into Dublin Bay. The walk along the South Wall to the lighthouse is one of Dublin's best, particularly on windy days when the sea breaks over the path and the exhilarating atmosphere is just dangerous enough to be fun. There is no public transport to the South Wall; take a taxi to the far end of Pigeonhouse Road in Ringsend to reach it.

Another good spot to blow away any Guinness-induced cobwebs is **North Bull Island**, just off the coast at Clontarf. This low-lying sandy island was constructed in the 19th century, on the suggestion of Captain Bligh (yes, that one) to prevent Dublin Bay silting up, and attracts numerous species of migrating birdlife to its mudflats and dunes, which have been designated a UNESCO Biosphere Reserve. Birdies of a different kind can be found on the island's two golf-courses and if you're desperate for a dip, there are swimming spots along Bull Wall at the south end. Access to the island is via Clontarf Road.

Beyond the city, many of Dublin's most attractive destinations are along the curve of the bay and the way to get to them is by the DART, a suburban rail system that hugs the coast from Bray in Co. Wicklow to Howth and Malahide north of the city. For further information, *see chapter* **Getting Around**. Make sure to sit on the side looking out to sea.

Poolbeg Lighthouse.

Heading north

The north bay and coast have fewer pretty seaside towns than the south, possibly because the coastline does not lend itself so well to swimming and there are fewer convenient coves. However, views at Howth Head are spectacular.

Howth

At the far north-eastern end of Dublin Bay, Howth (it rhymes with 'both') was once the city's main harbour. It was here that Erskine Childers' boat, the *Asgard*, – now grounded outside the Irish Museum of Modern Art (*see p82*) – landed German guns for the Irish Volunteers in 1914. The town is now a centre for fishing and yachting, and can be reached by DART or buses 31 and 31B from the city centre. The latter, which follows the route of an old tram line, goes over the top of Howth Head peninsula; there are great views of Dublin Bay from the top deck.

LOOK INTO THE BEST OF MODERN
AND CONTEMPORARY ART AT THE
IRISH MUSEUM OF MODERN ART.

Admission free
Café and Bookshop

Open Tuesday - Saturday: 10.00am - 5.30pm
Sunday and Bank Holidays: 12 noon - 5.30pm

Irish Museum of Modern Art / Áras Nua-Ealaíne na hÉireann
Royal Hospital Military Road Kilmainham Dublin 8 Ireland

**Irish
Museum
of
Modern
Art**

Tel +353 1 612 9900
Website www.modernart.ie

Woman of the North Sea, detail 1994, by John Bellany

Turn left out of the DART station, past a rather offputting concrete factory and the commercial port to reach the yacht harbour and the attractive waterfront village. Howth is overlooked to the north by the unflinching gaze of **Ireland's Eye**, a rocky island and seabird sanctuary that incorporates the ruins of a sixth-century monastery and a Martello tower. Round, granite, with thick walls and slits for windows, the Martello towers were built as lookouts during the Napoleonic wars, and are a distinctive sight along the coast from Howth to Dalkey. In the distance you'll also see the outline of **Lambey Island**. Motorboat trips (831 4200) to both islands leave regularly from the far end of the East Pier from April to October. It's also a great place for a windy stroll, whatever the time of year.

From the seafront, steep, winding streets lead to the centre of the village. Take Church Street to reach the remains of **St Mary's Abbey**, parts of which dates from the 14th century, or turn out of the DART station to the right for Howth Castle, a fortified mishmash of styles dating from the 16th to the 20th centuries. The castle has been owned by the St Lawrence family for eight centuries; it's not open to the public, but in its grounds you'll find the **National Transport Museum** (*see below*), the Deer Park golf course, an ancient dolmen and a fantastic cluster of rhodendrons that explodes into flower each spring.

Beachlife near **Clontarf**. *See p99.*

Most visitors, however, make straight for the cliff path snaking around **Howth Head**, a dramatic and picturesque 8.5 kilometre (five-mile) route from the village to the Baily Lighthouse and beyond, punctuated by a number of secluded coves. From the harbour, walk along Balscadden Road to the start of the cliff path, or take a shortcut by hopping on the 31B bus, alighting at the **Summit** pub and walking down to the lighthouse from there. Alternatively, you can climb up Howth Head to the transmitter aerial on the **Ben of Howth** for dramatic views of the peninsula, Dublin Bay and the Wicklow Mountains in the distance.

National Transport Museum

Howth Castle Demesne, Howth (848 0831), Howth DART/31, 31B bus. **Open** *June-Aug* 10am-5pm Mon-Fri; 2-5pm Sat, Sun. *Sept-May* 2-5pm Sat, Sun. **Admission** €2.50; €1.25 concessions; €6.30 family. **No credit cards.**

Enjoy the coastal scenery on a walk from **Howth harbour** to **Howth Head**.

Fry Model Railway Museum.

The National Transport Museum offers a chance to see vehicles dating from the 1880s to the 1970s, with shedfuls of trams, buses, commercial and military vehicles, and fire engines on display. Given the state of the city transport service today, it comes as a shock to discover that Dublin transport was among the most advanced in the world a century ago, being one of the first cities to introduce electric trams (*see p13* **Transports of delight**).

Malahide

North from Howth is Malahide: first intended as a summer seaside resort, it's now residential and has kept its villagey air. A new branch of the DART line now stops in Malahide, but you can also take a suburban train or a bus from the city centre.

Malahide town has small charming streets and comfortable houses in a variety of styles. The seashore is never far away (some buses go along the coast road and deliver you straight to the beach) and although it's not strikingly pretty when you get there, you can swim in the eye of Ireland's Eye (watch out for the sea's strong pull). If you fancy a longer walk, start at Malahide and strike out south along the strand for **Portmarnock**. Crow-spotters, incidentally, will enjoy Malahide: the sheer number of them here, especially at twilight, is remarkable, even slightly sinister.

The main reason to visit the village, however, is for **Malahide Castle** (*see below*), a turreted stately home that combines an interesting, if haphazard, arrangement of architectural styles. For 800 years it was the property of the Talbot family, bar a small interlude during Cromwellian times when it was owned by the regicide Miles Corbet. It was opened to the public in 1975.

The castle is situated on the outskirts of town in 300 acres (120 hectares) of delightful wooded parkland. Directly behind the castle is the 20-acre (eight-hectare) **Talbot Botanic Garden** (*see p103*), laid down by Lord Milo Talbot in the 20th century, and the ruins of a 15th-century abbey, dedicated to St Sylvester. Carvings in the ruins included two *sheelagh-na-gigs* (women figures with very pronounced and

exaggerated genitalia), while in the nave is the wonderful effigy tomb of Maud Plunkett who was 'Maid, wife and widow' all in one day: her husband, Lord Galtrim, was called away to battle on their wedding day, Whit Monday 1429, where he was killed, prompting Gerald Griffin to write his maudlin ballad 'The Bridal of Malahide'. In fact, he needn't have bothered: Maud later married Sir Richard Talbot, and outlived him to marry a third time.

Nearby are some craft workshops and the **Fry Model Railway Museum** (*see below*), a delight for kids. The largest of its kind in Ireland, it gives a minutely accurate tour of most of the country's rail system and surrounding terrain. Finally, the grounds also encompass a superb children's **playground** made entirely of wood.

Fry Model Railway Museum

Malahide Castle Demesne, Malahide, Co Dublin (846 3779). Malahide DART/rail/32A, 32X, 42 bus. **Open** *Apr-Oct* 10am-1pm, 2-5pm Mon-Sat; 2-6pm Sun. Closed Nov-Mar. **Admission** €5.50; €3-€5 concessions; €15 family. *Dublin Tourism combined ticket* €9; €5-€8 concessions; €25 family. **Credit** AmEx, MC, V.
The Fry Model Railway Museum houses a collection of handmade models of Irish trains and miniature constructions of Dublin's stations and other landmarks; trees, houses, stations, bridges, barges, rivers and buses are all lovingly recreated to form a very charming overview of Ireland's transport system. It even includes the DART and Irish Sea ferry services. The models are all painstakingly handmade and many date back to the 1920s.

Malahide Castle

Malahide Castle Demesne, Malahide, Co Dublin (846 2184). Malahide DART/rail/32A, 32X, 42 bus. **Open** *Apr-Oct* 10am-5pm Mon-Sat; 11am-6pm Sun. *Nov-Mar* 10am-5pm Mon-Sat; 11am-5pm Sun. **Admission** €5.50; €3-€5 concessions; €15 family. *Dublin Tourism combined ticket* €9; €5-€8 concessions; €25 family. **Credit** AmEx, MC, V.
The most ancient part of the castle is a 12th-century square tower, while the main body is post-medieval. Inside, there's the requisite Robert West swooping rococo plasterwork and remnants of what used to be the finest collection of 18th- and early 19th-century furniture in the country. Part of the National Portrait collection is on loan to Malahide Castle, and the family's own collection is large. In the Great Hall is Van Wyck's magnificent commemoration of the 1690 Battle of the Boyne, a reminder of one of the sadder Talbot family tales: 14 members of the family gathered at breakfast in the hall on the morning of the battle, then rode off together to fight for the Catholic King James. Not one came back.

Also in the Great Hall is a small pointed door leading to Puck's Tower. The story goes that Puck was so misshapen and crooked, he was given the job of watchman in the castle. Unfortunately, he wasn't very good at it. Enemies attacked the castle while he slept and, in shame, he hanged himself. However, he comes back to express his displeasure every once in a while: the last sighting was in 1975, when the castle was being auctioned.

Talbot Botanic Garden

Malahide Castle Demesne, Malahide, Co Dublin (816 9914). Malahide DART/rail/32A, 32X, 42 bus. **Open** *May-Sept* 2-5pm daily. Guided tour 2pm Wed. Closed Oct-Apr. **Admission** €3; free concessions. *Guided tour* €3. **No credit cards.**
Run under the auspices of Fingal District Council, the Talbot Botanic Garden was laid out by Lord Talbot between 1948 and 1973. Five thousand species are represented, with particular emphasis on plants from the southern hemisphere. The guided tour on Wednesday afternoon visits the walled garden, which is normally closed to visitors.

Further north

Beyond Malahide, the northern suburban rail route provides access to a clutch of attractions in Fingal (north Dublin County). At Donabate lies **Newbridge House** (*see p104*) whose coherent 18th-century façade stands in stark contrast to the assortment of styles and turrets that characterises Malahide. Built in 1737 for the Archbishop of Dublin to the designs of Richard Castle, this manor house has one of the most complete and exquisite Georgian interiors in Ireland. Its courtyard

and various estate buildings house artisans' workshops, while the grounds are home to a traditional farm with a variety of domestic and unusual breeds.

Two stops further on is the picturesque coastal town of **Skerries**, said to be the spot where St Patrick first set foot on Irish soil. The area is rich in wildlife, including a colony of seals. If you're in the area, visit **Skerries Mill Complex** (*see p104*), an interesting heritage centre close to the station, with beautifully restored wind- and watermills. Nearby, **Ardgillan Castle & Demesne** (*see below*) enjoys a magnificent location overlooking the coast. The park consists of 194 acres (78.5 hectares) of sweeping grassland, woods and gardens, including a beautiful Victorian conservatory and rose garden, and the 18th-century castle is open to the public.

Ardgillan Castle & Demesne

Balbriggan, Co Dublin (849 2212). Bus 33. **Open** *Apr-June, Sept* 11am-6pm Tue-Sun. *July, Aug* 11am-6pm daily. *Oct-Mar* 11am-4.30pm Tue-Sun. **Admission** €4; €3 concessions; €8 family. **No credit cards.**
The magnificent two-storey castle was built in 1738 and boasts tasteful Georgian and Victorian furnishings. You can visit the kitchen for an insight into how the staff might have coped, and there are regular exhibitions on the first floor. Take time to stroll the extensive grounds; the garden is an excellent spot for a picnic, if weather permits; otherwise there are adequate tearooms on the premises.

Twelfth-century **Malahide Castle**. *See p102.*

Newbridge House & Traditional Farm

Newbridge Demesne, Donabate, Co Dublin (843 6534). Donabate rail. **Open** *Summer* 10am-5pm Tue-Fri; 11am-6pm Sat; 2-6pm Sun. *Winter* 2-5pm Sat, Sun. **Admission** *House* €5; €2.10 concessions; €10.50 family. *Farm supplement* €1.25; 76¢ concessions. **Credit** MC, V.

Newbridge House is decorated in the great house manner, with stunning stucco by Robert West, red damask and gilt frames aplenty. Each room has its own distinct style, virtually unaltered in 150 years. Of particular note are the Red Drawing Room – its ceiling by William Stuccoman – and the Museum of Curiosities, which contains everything from stuffed birds and snakeskins to bricks from Babylon, an African chief's umbrella, a mummified head and an Indian dancing-girl's hair-plait. Like Malahide Castle, Newbridge was acquired by Fingal County Council; however, in this instance the original furnishings were kept intact and a set of private apartments was set aside for the resident Cobbe family (whose coat of arms bears the evocative motto, 'Dying I Sing'). The Cobbes still live in the building.

Artisans' workshops in the courtyard are filled with 19th-century tools. Pay particular attention to the Lord Chancellor's amazing coach in the stables, one of the finest examples of carriagework ever executed. In the 350 acres (142 hectares) of undulating pastureland, watercourses and pleasure grounds is a traditional farm with old-fashioned, storybook breeds of goats, sheep, giant hens and an incredibly ugly Vietnamese pot-bellied pig. Miniature horses and donkeys can be petted and there is an outdoor aviary full of peacocks and partridges.

Skerries Mills Complex

Skerries, Co Dublin (849 5208/http://indigo.ie/ ~skerries/). Skerries rail/33 bus. **Open** *Apr-Sept* 10.30am-6pm daily. *Oct-Mar* 10.30am-4.30pm daily. **Admission** €4; €3 concessions; €10 family. **No credit cards.**

Skerries Mill Complex offers an insight into what 21st-century environmentalists argue should be an important power supply of the future. Comprising three working mills – including a watermill with a five-sail windmill – as well as a millpond and wetlands, this attraction has been particularly well preserved and restored, and with a bakery on site you can even do some grinding of your own. There is also a decent coffeeshop in a lovely stone building.

Heading south

Dún Laoghaire & Sandycove

South Dublin Bay is punctuated with bathing spots and other points of interest. There's a good view from the DART at **Booterstown**, where extensive sands and coastal marshland attract assorted ducks, grebes, snipe, dunlin, tern and gulls. The marshland habitat hides the birds, but if you look towards the coast you'll see great flocks of them. The sands here go on for many miles, so that even when the tide is in, the water is never deep and the birds always have somewhere to cluster. Two stops from Booterstown is **Seapoint**, a Victorian bathing place that is still used for swimming. A group of hardy faithfuls – either fine old ladies or middle-aged gents – swim all year round, and it only gets at all crowded on extremely hot days.

Dún Laoghaire (pronounced 'Dun Leary') is the main port of call on the southside. Although it's an important harbour and the main departure point for ferries to England and Wales, it has the slightly seedy and depressed air of a once-bustling 19th-century shipping town. Settled for over one thousand years, Dún Laoghaire is named after a fifth-century king who was converted to Christianity by St Patrick. In 1821, it was renamed Kingstown to mark George IV's visit (commemorated by a statue on the waterfront), though in 1922 the Free State reverted to the town's old name. Apart from the **Maritime Museum of Ireland** (*see p106*), beautifully housed in a former mariners' church (closed until further notice), there's

The peerless piers at **Dún Laoghaire**.

Forty toes frolic at the Forty Foot in **Sandycove**.

not much to entice you into the town centre, and the main street is grim enough to make you stick to the shore.

The seafront is dominated by a new state-of-the-art ferry depot, and by Dún Laoghaire's famous mile-long granite piers: two arms of the harbour wall, which stretch around the port in a loose embrace. Construction of the vast harbour began in 1815 and rapidly grew into one of the biggest building endeavours ever undertaken in the British Isles. By the time the piers were completed, the project had cost over £1 million, an enormous sum for its time.

The east pier is good for a bracing walk: the stout sea breeze 'encourages' you along to the lighthouse and gun-saluting station, and on Sundays, families with children eating ice-creams are out in force. As you stroll along, look out for the lifeboat memorial and the Victorian anemometer (for measuring wind speed). Sailing is a hugely popular pastime in Dún Laoghaire; the east pier is home to a number of prestigious members-only yacht clubs founded in the 19th century, while on the west pier is the far more accommodating **National Sailing School** (*see p222*); you are likely to see learner sailors capsizing in the harbour here. If you just fancy a one-off trip out to sea, try the

Dublin Bay Sea Thrill (260 0949/ www.seathrill.ie), where you get whizzed around the bay on a high-speed boat. Trips last about 40 minutes and cost between €320 and €380 per boat, with each boat taking a maximum of ten people.

Walk along the seafront to **Sandycove**, a tiny sandy beach that's popular with families and perfect for a gentle swim. Just beyond it is the most famous bathing spot in Dublin, the Forty Foot (the name comes from the Fortieth Foot regiment, who were stationed at the Martello tower here during the 19th century), where you can always get a swim, whatever the tide. The Forty Foot used to be a (nude) gents-only venue. Now it's open to everyone and a sign warns 'Togs must be Worn'. Nude men still lurk resentfully behind rocks a little way from the main changing area. Overlooking the Forty Foot is the Martello tower where James Joyce spent less than a week in 1904, time enough for him to set the great opening sequence of *Ulysses* here and to describe, so charmingly, 'the snotgreen scrotumtightening sea'. The Martello tower now houses the **Joyce Museum** (*see p106*) – a must-visit for Joyce fans. Also in Sandycove, on the main road, is **Caviston's**, the best delicatessen in Dublin, and famous for its seafood restaurant (*see p124*).

Sightseeing

Joyce Museum

*Joyce Tower, Sandycove, Co Dublin (280 9265).
Sandycove DART/8 bus.* **Open** *Apr-Oct* 10am-1pm,
2-5pm Mon-Sat; 2-6pm Sun. **Admission** €5.50;
€3-€5; €15. **Credit** MC, V.

The Joyce Museum contains a collection of memorabilia relating to the great man, but the chief attraction is the reconstructed room where Joyce briefly
resided in 1904, until an argument with his host, the
surgeon and man of letters, Oliver St John Gogarty,
forced him to leave. Joyce found Gogarty fairly insuf-
ferable, and revenged himself by portraying him as
'plump stately Buck Mulligan' in the first chapter of
Ulysses. The tower itself is notable for its cramped
and basic conditions, and for the excellent view of
Dublin Bay and Killiney Hill from the roof.

Maritime Museum of Ireland

*Mariners' Church, Haigh Terrace, Dún Laoghaire
(280 0969). Dún Laoghaire DART/46B bus.*

The museum has a collection of maritime models,
documents and other miscellaneous items connected to the country's seafaring heritage. The stand-out
exhibits are the clockwork lamp used in Baily lighthouse in Howth until 1972 and a French longboat
captured during Wolfe Tone's failed invasion in
1796 (*see p11*). In late 2001 the museum was closed
indefinitely for essential maintenance work.

Dalkey

A short walk south around the coast brings
you to **Bullock Harbour**, overlooked by the
restored **Bullock Castle**, which was built
by St Mary's Abbey in the 12th century. Five
minutes' walk further on is **Dalkey**, a village
of great charm, perfectly poised between Dublin
Bay to the north and Killiney Bay to the south.
In the middle ages, Dalkey was the most
significant port on the east coast, with seven
castles guarding its wealth. As Dublin's
importance increased, Dalkey declined,
becoming a popular seaside retreat for monied
Dubliners, who built grand villas on the slopes
of Dalkey and Killeney Hills. Today Dalkey
retains the feel of a small fishing village and
has access to some lovely beaches, advantages
which have made it a highly desirable place
to live. It is now known, rather unoriginally, as
'Dalkeywood', thanks to the influx of notables
to the area: celebrity inhabitants include film
director Neil Jordan, soul singer Lisa Stansfield,
racing driver Damon Hill, and members of
all-conquering and practically unavoidable
pop combo U2.

In the village, Castle Street is the site of **Goat
Castle** and **Archbold's Castle**, both dating
from the 15th century. The former has been
completely restored and now houses **Dalkey
Heritage Centre** (*see below*), with exhibitions
on the history of the town. From Dalkey village,

The 'gloomy domed living room' at the **Joyce Muse**

walk down Coliemore Road and along the coast
to Coliemore Harbour, from where you can
catch boats (283 4298) in the summer months
out to **Dalkey Island**, which lies just offshore.
This southside version of Ireland's Eye hosts
a bird sanctuary and even some wild goats.
It also has a Martello tower and the ruins of
the medieval **St Begnet's Oratory**.

Above Coliemore Road, you'll reach the most
exclusive address in Dublin: Sorrento Terrace,
where the great houses seem carved out of the
hill with a view across the sweeping grey sands
of **Killeney Bay**. Carry on to Vico Road for
more spectacular views. A detour onto Torca
Road will take you to the childhood home
of George Bernard Shaw – now in private
ownership but marked with a plaque – or you
can continue as far as the lane at the end of
Vico Road, which will bring you to the top of
Killiney Hill. There is a wishing stone here
and an obelisk that was built for the arrival of
Queen Victoria to Kingstown. It's a hard climb
to the summit but worth it for the myriad views
– north to Dublin, south to Wicklow. Take time
to catch your breath here, before returning
along the ridge and down the other side of
Dalkey Hill, past the quarry to Dalkey village.

Dalkey Heritage Centre

*Goat Castle, Castle Street, Dalkey (285 8366). Dalkey
DART.* **Open** 9.30am-5pm Mon-Fri; 11am-5pm Sat,
Sun. **Admission** €6.40; €2.50-€3.20 concessions.
Credit MC, V.

The exhibition, narrated by playwright Hugh
Leonard, traces the development of Dalkey from a
medieval port until the Victorian era, when granite
from Dalkey quarry was used to construct the harbour wall at Dún Laoghaire. Most interesting, however, are the original features of the castle itself and
the great views from the battlements. Admission
includes a tour of St Begnet's churchyard on Castle
Street, which dates from the ninth century.

Eat, Drink, Shop

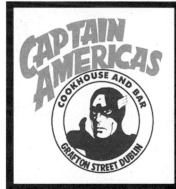

Restaurants & Cafés

Dubliners demand quality, variety and affordablilty. You taste the benefits.

Dublin cuisine gets better and better: **Caviston's** flexes its mussels. *See p124.*

Food-loving visitors to Dublin have reason to celebrate. While prices have risen throughout the city, the standard and variety of restaurant cooking, from the simplest to the grandest, has never been better. A decade ago, people in Dublin either ate simply to take in fuel, or they dined out in order to applaud their financial or social status. Respect for the culinary arts by both cooks and customers was as rare as a stuffed ortolan. But Dubliners have learned a pivotal lesson in recent years. If they don't get what they want, then they don't go back. Dubliners complain by simply withdrawing their custom, and then continuing the search for places that give them what they want, at a price they are happy to pay.

And what the city's dining-out public is now demanding is that quality applies across the board. They want a good zesty juice and a cool shake and a good cup of coffee, just as much as they want a cutting-edge brandade or some baked rock oysters. Brunch needs good Bloody Marys as well as eggs Benedict and waffles

with maple syrup. Basically, when it comes to eating and drinking, Dubliners want the lot.

As usual, Temple Bar provides an accurate yardstick. The best restaurants in TB serve good, creative cooking every day, offer ace brunch at the weekends, respect local trade and aren't content just to lighten tourist wallets. Choose poorly and you will find yourself eating below-par food at above-average prices, served by inexperienced students and surrounded by undiscerning tourists. But choose well and you can enjoy pleasing food, a funky atmosphere and informal but on-the-ball service all day long. Accessibility in terms of price, cooking and ambience are what counts.

This lesson has begun to filter out to the suburbs, too, and there are now affordable and fun places both southside and northside. Smart restaurateurs cater first and foremost for a local audience; something of vital importance to the visitor who wants to experience the inimitable, laid-back, spontaneous and, let's face it, rather deliciously wild, nature of the city.

WHERE TO EAT

Temple Bar has the highest density of eateries, ranging from rip-off tourist traps to cutting-edge restaurants to relaxed coffeeshops and brasseries. Elsewhere on the southside, Georgian houses and hotel dining rooms house some high-end restaurants with prices to match. Other good southside dining districts include upper-crust **Ballsbridge** and increasingly trendy **Portobello** by the Grand Canal, or if you want to mix with the celebrities you can head down the coast to **Dalkey**.

There's less choice north of the river, although some stand-out eateries in the city centre and a clutch of good seafood restaurants further afield are definitely worth checking out.

Southside

American

Bad Ass Café

9-11 Crown Alley, Temple Bar (671 2596). All cross-city buses. **Open** 11.30am-midnight daily. **Main courses** €11.50-t15.50. **Set menu** (evenings only) £11.50 for 3 courses. **Credit** AmEx, MC, V. **Map** p75.
A Temple Bar institution, the Bad Ass does what it has always done – pizzas, burgers, salads – the way it has always done it. Which is pretty well, in fact. The pulley system that transports your order to the kitchen is a great quirky touch.

Elephant & Castle

18 Temple Bar, Temple Bar (679 3121). All cross-city buses. **Open** 8am-11.30pm Mon-Fri; 10.30am-11.30pm Sat; noon-11.30pm Sun. **Main courses** €8.50-€20.50. **Credit** AmEx, DC, MC, V. **Map** p75.

It remains to be seen how the E&C will cope without the guiding hands of Liz Mee and John Hayes, but the staples such as fine burgers, chicken wings and omelettes are just as popular as ever.

Chinese

Fan's Cantonese Restaurant

60 Dame Street, Temple Bar (679 4263) All cross-city buses. **Open** 5.30pm-12.30am Mon-Fri; 12.30pm-12.30am Sat, Sun. **Main courses** €13-€15.50. **Credit** AmEx, DC, MC, V. **Map** p75.
All the usual Chinese suspects that you find on every takeaway menu are on offer here, and are served in a seriously characterless room. But if you ask for something authentic, and show you are serious, then Fan's can produce some great real Chinese food.

Good World Restaurant

18 South Great George's Street (677 5373). All cross-city buses. **Open** 12.30pm-3am daily. **Main courses** €10-€19. **Credit** AmEx, DC, MC, V. **Map** p313 G5.
Dim sum is the speciality here. Try to get a table upstairs at the weekend to really enjoy some very challenging and fun cooking at excellent value. Away from the dim sum, the food is the usual menu of Chinese standards.

Imperial Chinese Restaurant

12A Wicklow Street (677 2580). All cross-city buses. **Open** 12.30pm-midnight Mon-Thur, Sun; 12.30pm-12.30am Fri, Sat. **Main courses** €13-€19. **Credit** AmEx, MC, V. **Map** p313 H5.
There's nothing special about the standard restaurant menu at the Imperial; much better is the excellent dim sum, which, as well as being some of the best value food in town, will show you what the kitchen is really capable of producing.

Bad Ass kicks ass with its pizza/burger menu.

European/International

Bistro

Castle Market (677 6016). All cross-city buses. **Open** noon-11.15pm daily. **Main courses** €9.50-€23.50 **Credit** AmEx, MC, V. **Map** p313 G5.

The likes of Caesar salad, steak sandwiches, pizzas, pastas, omelettes and salads draw a regular clientele to Bistro, all of whom want to nab a table outside when the sun shines.

Cooke's Café/Rhino Room

14 & 14A South William Street (679 053G/G70 5260/www.cookescafe.com). All cross-city buses. **Open** 12.30-3pm, 6-11pm Mon-Sat. **Main courses** *Cooke's Café* €20.50-€25.50. *Rhino Room* €15.20-€24. **Credit** AmEx, DC, MC, V. **Map** p313 H5.

Cooke's Café is still many people's favourite Dublin dining room. John Cooke and his team produce sophisticated and brilliantly turned out modern food using fresh, usually organic, ingredients, and the restaurant is always home to a gaggle of the great and the good. Upstairs, the **Rhino Room** offers American Italian fusion food and fish cocktails in relaxed New York-style surroundings. In 2001, Cooke's opened a branch at the National Museum, offering lunches and light meals.

Branch: National Museum at Collins Barracks, Benburb Street, Northside (677 7599).

Fitzers Café

50 Dawson Street (677 1155/www.fitzers.ie). All cross-city buses. **Open** noon-4.30pm, 5.30-10.30pm Mon-Wed, Sun; noon-4.30pm, 5.30-11pm Thur-Sat. **Main courses** €12-€19. **Credit** AmEx, DC, MC, V. **Map** p313 H5.

A pair of stylish rooms in the Fitzers chain. Although the cooking can be a little self-consciously eclectic (as demonstrated by dishes such as shiitake stuffed chicken poached in stock with a potato risotto) there are fine moments to be enjoyed, especially in the Dawson Street branch.

Branch: Temple Bar Square, Temple Bar, Southside (679 0440).

The Gotham Café

8 South Anne Street (679 5266). All cross-city buses. **Open** noon-midnight Mon-Sat; noon-10.30pm Sun. **Main courses** €6-€16. **Credit** AmEx, MC, V. **Map** p313 H5.

Teenagers' heaven, thanks to some fine pizza cookery and an over-the-top Manhattan theme. Mind you, plenty of grown-ups like the relaxed vibe in the Gotham, too.

Moe's

112 Lower Baggot Street (676 7610). All cross-city buses. **Open** noon-midnight Mon-Sat; noon-10.30pm Sun. **Main courses** €9-€16. **Credit** AmEx, DC, MC, V. **Map** p313 J6.

John Connelly has been doing some smart, relaxed modern cooking here for the last year, and gaining an appreciative audience for food with personality and flair. Service is good, too.

Velure

47 South William Street (670 5585/www.velure.com). All cross-city buses. **Open** 6-11pm Tue-Thur; 6-11.30pm Fri, Sat; noon-6pm Sun. **Main courses** €18-€28. **Credit** AmEx, DC, MC, V. **Map** p313 H5.

One of the grooviest addresses in the city offers sexy decor, scrummy cocktails, a jazzy, funky soundtrack and modern fusion food such as veal with Taggia monk potatoes and pink peppercorn vinaigrette. There's a flashy brunch menu on Sundays, too.

Fish & seafood

Leo Burdock's

2 Werburgh Street (454 0306/www.leoburdocks. com). All cross-city buses. **Open** noon-midnight daily. **Main courses** €4.50-€7. **No credit cards.** **Map** p312-3 F/G5.

The classic Dublin chipper beside Christchurch sells fried and battered fish and chips. What more could you ask for – other than the obligatory pints of porter before you join the queue? There are other branches around town, but this is the best one. Branches: 375 North Circular Road, Phibsboro, Northern suburbs (830 4114); Unit 20 Swan Centre, Lower Rathmines Road, Rathmines, Southern suburbs (497 3117).

Lord Edward Seafood Restaurant

23 Christchurch Place (454 2420) All cross-city buses. **Open** 12.30-2.15pm, 6-10.30pm Mon-Fri; 6-10.30pm Sat. **Main courses** €13-€40.50. **Credit** AmEx, DC, MC, V. **Map** p312 F5.

You don't have to be a barrister to eat in this thirty-something-year-old restaurant, but the bewigged ones make up a substantial part of the crowd. Old-style fish cookery is the speciality and is enjoyably unpretentious, though not cheap. Just about as far from the cutting edge as you can get.

French

La Cave

28 South Anne Street (679 4409). All cross-city buses. **Open** 12.30pm-2am daily. **Main courses** €15.50-€21.50. **Credit** AmEx, DC, MC, V. **Map** p313 H5.

Best known as a wine bar, La Cave is nostalgically decorated with bistro-cliché posters and prints. Cleverly agreeable French cooking is served to an eager and lively late-night audience. A little touch of bohemia, well done.

Dobbins Wine Bar

15 Stephen's Lane (676 4679/www.dobbins winebar.ie). Bus 7, 45. **Open** 12.30-3pm Mon; 12.30-3pm, 8-11.45pm Tue-Fri; 8-11.45pm Sat. **Main courses** €13.50-€25. **Credit** AmEx, DC, MC, V. **Map** p314 K6.

Dobbins is one of the great old troopers of the Dublin restaurant scene, a cultural institution masterminded by John O'Byrne and supported by a faithful team who have given over 20 years' service to the Wine

Eat, Drink, Shop

timeout.com

The online guide to the world's greatest cities

Italian by name, French by nature: the lovely belle époque **La Stampa**.

Bar. It's a fiercely sociable place, which is able some-how to be all things to all people, thanks to approachable, if complacent, cooking and utterly first class service.

Les Frères Jacques

74 Dame Street, Temple Bar (679 4555/www. lesfreresjacques.com). All cross-city buses. **Open** 12.30-2.30pm, 7.30-10.30pm Mon-Thur; 12.30-2.30pm, 7.30-11pm Fri; 7.30-11pm Sat. **Main courses** €23.50-€43. **Set menus** €18.50 lunch; €30.50 dinner. **Credit** AmEx, MC, V. **Map** p75.
Nothing ever changes in Les Frères Jacques, pleas-ingly, given Dublin's hectic restaurant scene. The food is mellow French classical cuisine, and it's very professionally executed, though one tends to wind up with a fairly hefty bill for the experience.

Locks

1 Windsor Terrace, Portobello (454 3391). Bus 49, 49X, 54A. **Open** 12.30-2pm, 7-11pm Mon-Fri; 7-11pm Sat. **Main courses** €26.50-€33.50. **Credit** AmEx, DC, MC, V. **Map** p309.
One of the most professional restaurants in the city, Locks is run with precision and care by Claire Douglas. The room is commodious and character-ful, and the subtle, traditional French-style cooking is very enjoyable.

Restaurant Patrick Guilbaud

The Merrion Hotel, Merrion Square (676 4192/ www.merrionhotel.com). All cross-city buses. **Open** 12.30-2pm, 7.30-10.15pm Tue-Sat. **Main courses** €40.50-€48. **Set lunch** €28 (€48.50 in Dec). **Credit** AmEx, DC, MC, V. **Map** p313 J6.

Patrick Guilbaud and Guillaume Lebrun, along with front of house Stephane Robin, run a slick, meticu-lous operation that has become very much part of the culinary furniture of the city. The cooking and the service are formal, quintessentially French, and – with the exception of the good value set lunch – this place is only for very special occasions.

The Old Mill

Merchant's Arch, Temple Bar (671 9262). All cross-city buses. **Open** 4.30-11pm daily. **Main courses** €12-€21.50. **Credit** AmEx, DC, MC, V. **Map** p75.
This simple upstairs place, at the side of Merchant's Arch, offers enjoyable cooking in French bistro style, set off by a romantic, bohemian ambience.

Pearl Brasserie

20 Merrion Street Upper (661 3627). All cross-city buses. **Open** noon-2.30pm Wed-Sun; noon-2.30pm, 6-10.30pm Thur, Sun; noon-2.30pm, 6-11pm Fri, Sat. **Main courses** €18-€24. **Credit** AmEx, DC, MC, V. **Map** p313 J6.
Sebastian Masi is enjoying quite a success with the Pearl, a cosy basement that suits his simple, rustic style of French food: duck magret; steak with sauté potatoes, or croque monsieur at lunchtime.

La Stampa

35 Dawson Street (677 8611/www.lastampa.ie). All cross-city buses. **Open** 12.30-2.30pm, 6.30-11.30pm Mon-Thur; 12.30-2.30pm, 6pm-12.30am Fri; 6pm-12.30am Sat; 6.30-11.30pm Sun. **Main courses** €18-€28. **Credit** AmEx, DC, MC, V. **Map** p313 H5/6.

The Dublin GHOST BUS TOUR

City Tour • Coast & Castle • Ghost Bus • South Coast

DUBLIN BUS TOURS

Let us put you at your unease on the world's only Ghostbus, and introduce you to the dark romance of a city of gaslight ghosts and chilling legends.

Your professional guide will weave his spell and spirit you away to meet the felons, fiends and phantoms who reach out across a thousand years of Dublin's troubled history.

You'll visit haunted houses, learn of Dracula's Dublin origins and we'll even throw in a crash course in body-snatching.

Near journey's end the lights go out and darkness invites the macabre traditions of the Irish wake. Your host - one blessed with the "gift of the gab" - will conclude the tour by explaining the meaning of life - and death!

ALL TOURS DEPART FROM 59 UPPER O'CONNELL ST., DUBLIN 1.
Buy on line at dublinbus.ie or ticketmaster.ie

Dublin Bus Tel. (01) 873 4222 9am to 7pm (Mon - Sat)

Dar Italia's lunch menu is the real deal. And the coffee's not bad, either. See p116.

It may have an Italian name, but the most gorgeous belle époque brasserie in town has always had a French bias, and is now looking more glamorous than ever before. A boutique hotel and a top-notch Thai restaurant, **Tiger Becs**, opened on the same premises in 2001.

Trocadero
3 St Andrew's Street (679 9772). All cross-city buses. **Open** 6pm-12.15am Mon-Sat. **Main courses** €10-€18. **Credit** AmEx, DC, MC, V. **Map** p313 H5.
The Troc is a smashing room: timeless, calmly lit, a womb of good times. The food may be straight out of a 1970s cordon bleu cookery class, but night owls, thespians and hacks never seem to tire of the place.

Indian

Jaipur
41 South Great George's Street (677 0999/www. jaipur.ie). All cross-city buses. **Open** 12.30-3.30pm, 6pm-midnight daily. **Main courses** €7.50-€18. **Credit** DC, MC, V. **Map** p313 G5.
It's difficult to like this awkwardly shaped and ill-lit room, but the Indian cooking in Jaipur is modern and experimental, and deserves full marks for avoiding Balti-blandness, which makes it essential for curry lovers. There's an interesting wine list, too.

Monty's of Kathmandu
28 Eustace Street, Temple Bar (670 4911). All cross-city buses. **Open** noon-2.30pm, 6-11.30pm Mon-Sat; 6-11.30pm Sun. **Main courses** €11.50-€15.50. **Credit** AmEx, MC, V. **Map** p75.
Monty's is assembling quite a reputation among food lovers for its well conceived ethnic cooking. One of the more interesting and creative addresses in Temple Bar.

Rajdoot Tandoori
26-28 Clarendon Street (679 4274). All cross-city buses. **Open** 12.15-2.30pm, 6-11pm daily. **Main courses** €6.50-€15.50. **Credit** MC, V. **Map** p313 H5.
One of the first Indian restaurants in Dublin remains one of the best for formal service and clever, authentic cooking. Always enjoyable, albeit far from cheap.

Shalimar
17 South Great George's Street (671 0738/ www.shalimar.ie). All cross-city buses. **Open** noon-2.30pm, 5pm-midnight Mon-Thur, Sun; noon-2.30pm, 5pm-1am Fri, Sat. **Main courses** €19-€32. **Credit** AmEx, DC, MC, V. **Map** p313 G5.
The Pakistani-Punjab cooking of the Shalimar comes two ways: formal service with tandoori specialities upstairs; simpler, more rustic balti cooking in the basement at lower prices.

Tulsi
17A Lower Baggot Street (676 4578). Bus 10. **Open** noon-2.30pm, 6-11.30pm daily. **Main courses** €11-€18. **Credit** AmEx, DC, MC, V. **Map** p313 J6.
Tulsi is expanding, with branches throughout Ireland. It's an ambitious and efficient operation, offering pleasing, straightforward Indian food.

Italian

For reliable, if predictable, pizzas and pasta, try branches of **Milano** (an offshoot of the UK's Pizza Express chain), found all over town, including at 38 Dawson Street (670 7744).

Ar Vicoletto
Crow Street, Temple Bar (670 8662). All cross-city buses. **Open** 1-4pm, 6-11pm Mon-Sat; 2-11pm Sun. **Main courses** €10-€25.50. **Credit** AmEx, DC, MC, V. **Map** p75.

Sister of the popular Botticelli and the cult Steps of Rome (*see p117*), the Vic is a cosy trattoria with utterly predictable food that, luckily, is often very neatly done. Spaghetti alla cozze (with mussels) is particularly good.

Il Baccaro
Meeting House Square, Temple Bar (671 4597). All cross-city buses. **Open** 6-11pm daily. **Main courses** €9-€19. **Credit** AmEx, DC, MC, V. **Map** p75.
One of the ultimate cult addresses, Il Baccaro is a popular spot on weekend nights. Never mind the standard food or the extra-rough wine; the atmosphere is everything here.

Bar Italia
Unit 4, The Bookend, Essex Quay, Temple Bar (679 5128). All cross-city buses. **Open** 8am-6pm Mon-Fri; 9am-6pm Sun. **Main courses** €6-€8.50. **Credit** AmEx, DC, MC, V. **Map** p75.
Bar Italia may well serve the best espresso in town, and Stefano Crescenzi's simple but utterly authentic Italian food at lunchtime is also the real deal: be sure not to miss it.

Botticelli
3 Temple Bar (672 7289). All cross-city buses. **Open** 10am-midnight daily. **Main courses** €8.50-€20.50. **Credit** MC, V. **Map** p75.
One of three Italian-style restaurants run by the family who started the cult Steps of Rome (*see p117*), Botticelli is fairly reliable, very popular and an extremely enjoyable place to eat. On offer are decent pastas and pizzas, good desserts and terrific coffee.

Little Caesar's Palace
Balfe Street (671 8714). All cross-city buses. **Open** 12.30pm-12.30am daily. **Main courses** €11-€14. **Credit** AmEx, DC, MC, V. **Map** p313 H5.
A boisterous place that fizzles with gung-ho energy, Little Caesar's specialises in pizzas, and especially in the theatrics of spinning the discs of dough. Great fun, especially if you are ten years old.

Nico's
53 Dame Street, Temple Bar (677 3062). All cross-city buses. **Open** 12.30-2.30pm, 6pm-midnight Mon-Fri; 6pm-midnight Sat. **Main courses** €11-€18.50. **Credit** AmEx, DC, MC, V. **Map** p75.
Nico's is ageless and unpretentiously targetted. The food is enjoyable trattoria stuff – chicken cacciatora, pasta carbonara, zabaglione and so on – but the drama of the evening, especially the hilariously macho waiters trying to chat up any female diners, is what really counts.

Pasta Fresca
3-4 Chatham Street (679 2402). All cross-city buses. **Open** 11.30am-midnight Mon-Sat; 1-10pm Sun. **Main courses** €11.50-€21.50. **Credit** AmEx, DC, MC, V. **Map** p313 H5.
Style-conscious women and their style-conscious daughters still love Fresca's mix of light pasta dishes and decent coffee and baked products. The shop out front sells fresh pasta, oils and sauces.

Da Pino
38-40 Parliament Street, Temple Bar (671 9308). All cross-city buses. **Open** noon-11.30pm daily. **Main courses** €6.50-€16. **Credit** AmEx, DC, MC, V. **Map** p75.
A menu of classic Italian food – spaghetti carbonara, pizza caruso, entrecote pizzaiola, zuppa di cipolla – served in a room that can be guaranteed to buzz with good character and good cheer.

Il Primo
16 Montague Street (478 3373). All cross-city buses. **Open** noon-3pm, 6-11.30pm Mon-Thur; 6-11.30pm Fri, Sat; 5-10pm Sun. **Main courses** €10-€14 lunch; €11.50-€29 dinner. **Credit** AmEx, DC, MC, V. **Map** p313 G6.
A fine wine list with lots of interesting Italian bottles is one of the main attractions of the little Il Primo. The food is familiar modern Italian, and it is very popular with the local office folk and a more sedate evening-time crowd.

QV2
14-15 St Andrew's Street (677 3363/www.qv2 restaurant.com). All cross-city buses. **Open** noon-3pm, 6pm-12.30am Mon-Sat. **Main courses** €11 lunch; €17 dinner. **Credit** AmEx, DC, MC, V. **Map** p313 H5.
QV2 is the most stylish and modern of the cluster of restaurants on St Andrew's Street. Complementing the Italian-influenced specials the regular menu promises ambitiously modern and eclectic food, featuring as many home-grown ingredients as possible, with an Irish twist.

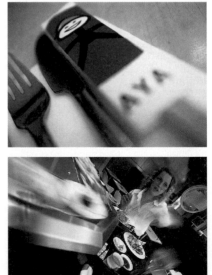

AYA. *See p117.*

Star quality at **The Commons**. *See p118.*

Ristorante Bucci

7 Lower Camden Street (475 1020). All cross-city buses. **Open** 6-10pm Mon, Sun; 12.30-11.30pm Tue-Sat. **Main courses** €9.50-€16. **Credit** AmEx, MC, V. **Map** p313 G7.

Bucci's roll-call of pasta and pizzas may well be another fashionable variation on that modern, grab-bag style of food that has little time for authenticity, but it is well executed and flavoursome

Steps of Rome

Chatham Street (670 5630). All cross-city buses. **Open** 10am-midnight Mon-Thur; 10am-1am Fri, Sat; 1-10pm Sun. **Main courses** €7.50-€9. **No credit cards**. Map p313 H5.

Slacker's paradise. The Steps of Rome is just a single room with a counter, close to Neary's pub (*see p135*), and the young crowd just love it to bits. The pizzas, especially the rather fabulous potato and rosemary, are cool and the red wine is usually warm. Grab a takeaway pizza slice (€3) and a caffe latte for good food on the go.

Unicorn Restaurant

12B Merrion Court, Merrion Row (676 2182/ www.unicornrestaurant.ie). Bus 7, 10, 44, 45, 48A. **Open** 12.30-3pm, 6 11.30pm Mon-Thur; 12.30-3pm, 6pm-midnight Fri, Sat. **Main courses** €10-€21 lunch; €10-€33.50 dinner. **Credit** AmEx, DC, MC, V. **Map** p313 J6.

Truth be told, the Unicorn's main draw is not the familiar Italian-style food it dispenses; it's the crowd who hang out here. There are few better entertainments to be had in the city than ogling this mix of suits, shakers and wannabes.

Japanese

AYA

Brown Thomas, Clarendon Street (677 1544/ www.aya.ie). All cross-city buses. **Open** *Restaurant* noon-4pm, 5.30-11pm Mon-Sat; noon-4pm, 5.30-9.30pm Sun. *Sushi bar* 5-10.30pm Mon-Sat; 5-9.30pm Sun. **Main courses** €13-€17. **Credit** AmEx, DC, MC, V. **Map** p313 H5.

This conveyor belt sushi bar is a massive success, with two new branches opening at the IFSC and in Donnybrook. It's not what you might call authentic, but it is mighty good fun and the staff are ace. Takeaway service is also available.

Branches: Unit 1B, Valentia House, Custom House Square, Northside (672 1852); **AYA 2 Go** 51A Donnybrook Road, Donnybrook, Southern suburbs (219 5780).

Wagamama

South King Street (478 2152/www.wagamama.com). All cross-city buses. **Open** noon-11pm Mon-Sat; noon-10pm Sun. **Main courses** €7-€13. **Credit** AmEx, DC, MC, V. **Map** p313 H6.

It's not a place to linger for the evening, but for a fast bowl of nifty noodles on the way to the movies Wagamama's hard to beat.

Yamamori Noodles

71 South Great George's Street (475 5001). All cross-city buses. **Open** noon-11pm Mon-Wed; 12.30-11.30pm Thur-Sat. **Main courses** €11.50-€16.50. **Credit** AmEx, DC, MC, V. **Map** p313 G5.

The Yamamori has an ever-increasing stream of devotees who love it for its noodles, its hipness and its cheapness. The music is fabulous, the Japanese waitresses are splendid, and Yoshi Iwasaki's cooking is buzzy with flavour. You can't go wrong with well-controlled dishes such as soba noodles and chicken and spring onion, or udon noodles with seaweed and vegetables.

Middle Eastern

The Cedar Tree

11 St Andrew's Street (677 2121). All cross-city buses. **Open** 5.30pm-midnight daily. **Main courses** €11-€18.50. **Credit** AmEx, MC, V. **Map** p313 H5.

A range of popular Lebanese meze and meat dishes (mainly kebabs) are the order of the day at this low-key, left-field place. A popular late-night hangout.

Modern Irish

Browne's Brasserie

22 St Stephens Green (638 3939/www.brownes dublin.com). All cross-city buses. **Open** 12.30-2.45pm, 6.30-10.55pm Mon-Sat; 12.30-2.45pm, 6.30-9.55pm Sun. **Main courses** €21.50-€23. **Credit** AmEx, DC, MC, V. **Map** p313 H6.

This rather grand townhouse on St Stephen's Green houses a handsome first-floor restaurant among its assortment of rooms. The cooking is good, but for brasserie food it can become a little too pricey by the time you've had a few drinks.

Bruno's

21 Kildare Street (662 4724/www.brunos.ie). All cross-city buses. **Open** noon-2.30pm, 6-10.30pm Mon-Sat. **Main courses** €16.50-€25.50. **Credit** AmEx, DC, MC, V. **Map** p313 H/J5/6.

Eat, Drink, Shop

Garrett Byrne is one of the most promising new talents cooking in Dublin today, and when you try that guinea fowl with cep risotto or the boudin of crab with velouté of basil you will see why. Good service and good value make Bruno's a don't miss. There's a branch in Temple Bar, but this is the hot one.
Branch: 30 East Essex Street, Temple Bar, Southside (670 6767).

The Commons
Newman House, 85 St Stephen's Green (478 0530/ www.thecommons.ie). All cross-city buses. **Open** 9am-10.15pm daily. **Main courses** €25.50-€40. **Credit** AmEx, DC, MC, V. **Map** p313 H6.
Aiden Byrne is the new star chef of the city, producing dishes that are a meticulously assembled riot of flavours and demonstrate his awesome technique. It's pricey but worth every penny; just ignore the dull business clientele.

L'Ecrivain
112 Lower Baggot Street (661 1919/www.lecrivain. com). All cross-city buses. **Open** noon-2pm, 7-11pm Mon-Fri; 7-11pm Sat. **Main courses** €30.50-€35.50. **Credit** AmEx, DC, MC, V. **Map** p313 J6.
Derry Clarke and his crew rebuilt and refurbished this sparkling room in the 1990s and since then have been on an unstoppable roll, producing perhaps the best mix of exciting contemporary food and friendly, efficient service in town. You'll need to book about a week in advance to enjoy it, though.

Eden
Meeting House Square, Temple Bar (670 5372). All cross-city buses. **Open** 12.30-3pm, 6-10.30pm Mon-Fri; noon-3pm, 6-10.30pm Sat, Sun. **Main courses** €13.50-€21.50. **Credit** AmEx, DC, MC, V. **Map** p75.
Long past its fashionable days, Eden is now just home to Eleanor Walshe's excellent modern cooking, whose mix of funky pairings and maternal comfort is always a treat.

Ely
22 Ely Place (676 8986). All cross-city buses. **Open** noon-midnight (later if the bar is busy) Mon-Sat. **Main courses** €19-€32. **Credit** AmEx, DC, MC, V. **Map** p313 J6.
The city's only real wine bar is home to a fantastic wine list, chosen with great skill by Erik Robson, along with excellent modern rustic cooking, simply done and packed with great flavours thanks to ingredients from the family farm.

Jacob's Ladder
4-5 Nassau Street (670 3865/www.jacobsladder.ie). All cross-city buses. **Open** 12.30-2.30pm, 6-10pm Tue-Sat. **Main courses** €23-€32 **Credit** AmEx, DC, MC, V. **Map** p313 H5.
This is one of the best, if not the best-known, places to eat in the city. Adrian Roche's imaginative modern Irish cooking has a style unlike any other, and the room, which offers views across Trinity, is quite, quite lovely. It's just a shame that the staff can, on occasion, be less than obliging.

Ely: quality on the plate and in the bottle.

No.10
Longfields Hotel, Fitzwilliam Street Lower (676 1367/www.longfields.ie). All cross-city buses. **Open** 12.30-2pm, 6.30-10pm Mon-Thur; 12.30-2pm, 7.30-11pm Fri; 7.30-11pm Sat; 7-9pm Sun. **Table d'hôte menu** €40. **Credit** AmEx, DC, MC, V. **Map** p313 J7.
Having moved from the kitchen at L'Ecrivain just across the road, Kevin Arundel has been wowing folk with great, grown-up savoury cooking and fantastically keen prices.

The Mermaid Café
69-70 Dame Street, Temple Bar (670 8236/ www.mermaid.ie). All cross-city buses. **Open** 12.30-2.30pm, 6-10.30pm Mon-Thur; 12.30-2.30pm, 6-11pm Fri-Sun. **Main courses** €18-€29. **Credit** MC, V. **Map** p75.
This Temple Bar icon has spawned a soup kitchen next door, wittily called Gruel, but the lean, spare room of the Mermaid remains one of the hottest spots in town. The food is smart, original and forever enjoyable. Don't miss the crab cakes, the seafood platter and the spicy pecans, or the weekend brunch. *See also p181.*

Eat, Drink, Shop

Odessa

13-14 Dame Court (670 7634). All cross-city buses.
Open 6-11pm Mon-Fri; noon-4.30pm, 6-11pm Sat,
Sun. **Main courses** €11.50-€19. **Credit** AmEx, DC,
MC, V. **Map** p313 G5.
Odessa's menu is a typical example of the modern
Irish style; don't expect haute cuisine, but do expect
decent nosh in hip surroundings. Check it out for
brunch at the weekend when a big pitcher of Bloody
Mary should help shift that hangover.

One Pico

*5&6 Molesworth Place, Schoolhouse Lane (478
0307/www.onepico.com). All cross-city buses.*
Open 12.30-2pm, 6-10.15pm Mon-Sat. **Main
courses** €13-€25.50. **Credit** AmEx, DC, MC,
V. **Map** p313 H6.
Eamonn O'Reilly has moved into a handsome building on Schoolhouse Lane, and finally has a room as
swish as his wildly exciting contemporary cooking.
Expect the unexpected.

Peacock Alley

*Fitzwilliam Hotel, St Stephen's Green (677 0708/
671 0854/www.restaurantpeacockalley.com).
All cross-city buses.* **Open** 6-11pm daily. **Main
courses** €30.50-€37. **Credit** AmEx, DC, MC, V.
Map p313 H6.
Having now opened a branch in London, Conrad
Gallagher has relaunched his handsome third-floor
restaurant here in Dublin. Under new head chef
David Cavalier, the cooking retains Gallagher's
trademark Mediterranean flavour and bravado:
guinea fowl with parsley risotto and fava beans;
seared scallops with foie gras butter and sauce
albufera; pastrami cured sea trout with pickled pear.
Intense and artful cooking.

Shanahan's on the Green

*119 St Stephen's Green (407 0939). All cross-
city buses.* **Open** 6-10pm Mon-Sat. **Main
courses** €24-€32. **Credit** AmEx, DC, MC, V.
Map p313 H6.
John Shanahan's big, classy brasserie is styled on
an American steakhouse, but the food is a fusion of
Irish and European flavours; West Coast mussels
and Irish beef are highlights. High prices and fantastic service make for quite an experience.

The Tea Room

*The Clarence, 6-8 Wellington Quay, Temple
Bar (670 7766/670 9000/www.theclarence.ie).
All cross-city buses.* **Open** 12.30-2.30pm, 6.30-
10.30pm daily. **Main courses** €29. **Tasting
menu** €65 per person (last orders 9.30pm).
Credit AmEx, DC, MC, V. **Map** p75.
Antony Ely is cooking some of the best food in
Dublin right now. A regular clientele of other chefs
at the tables testifies to the excitement this fine cook
is pulling out of the pan. Beautiful savoury dishes
include the likes of pot roast pheasant and grati-
nated Rossmore oysters. Great food, then, and a
beautiful room, but in our experience the service
needs to try a little harder.

Thornton's

*1 Portobello Road, Portobello (454 9067/www.
thorntonsrestaurant.ie). Bus 14, 15, 15A, 15B,
54A, 155.* **Open** 12.30-2pm, 6.30-11pm Tue-Sat.
Main courses €19-€40.50. **Credit** AmEx, DC,
MC, V. **Map** p309.
Kevin Thornton's reputation is so sky-high at the
moment that getting a table is difficult in this canal-
side restaurant. Persevere, for the cooking is a
brilliant synthesis of flavours and textures – and is
well worth the very high prices.

Pacific Rim

Café Mao

*Chatham Row (670 4899/www.cafemao.com). All
cross-city buses.* **Open** noon-11pm Mon-Thur; noon-
11.30pm Fri, Sat; noon-10pm Sun. **Main courses**
€10-€15.50. **Credit** MC, V. **Map** p313 H5.
A swish room decorated with oversized Warhol
posters, an open-plan kitchen and laid-back service
are the winning formula at groovy and popular Mao.
The menu is basically Asia's greatest hits, but it's a
fun place and not somewhere to quibble about culinary authenticity. The Dún Laoghaire branch has
slightly different opening hours; phone for details.
Branch: The Pavilion, Dún Laoghaire (214 8090).

Chameleon

*1 Fownes Street Lower, Temple Bar (671 0362).
All cross-city buses.* **Open** 5.30-11pm Tue-Sun.
Main courses €13-€18.50. **Credit** MC, V.
Map p75.
Carol Walshe's Chameleon is one of the simplest and
most loveable eateries in Temple Bar – a shrine created by the caring work of a great hostess. Walk in
the door and you get character and charm, sit down
and you get sassy Indonesian cooking.

Thai

For some stylish Thai cookery, don't miss new,
hip **Tiger Becs** at La Stampa (*see p113*).

Chili Club

*1 Anne's Lane, South Anne Street (677 3721).
All cross-city buses.* **Open** 11.30am-2.30pm,
6-10.30pm Mon-Wed; 11.30am-2.30pm, 6-11pm
Thur-Sat. **Main courses** €15.50-€21.
Credit AmEx, MC, V. **Map** p313 H5.
The Chili Club preceded the boom in all things Thai,
but continues to be successful. It's easy to enjoy the
mildly spicy food on offer in this intimate little room.

Pad Thai

*Richmond Street, Portobello (475 5551). Bus 15,
16, 16A.* **Open** 12.30-3pm, 6-10pm Mon-Thur;
12.30-3pm, 6-11pm Fri; 6-11pm Sat; 6-10pm Sun.
Main courses €11-€16. **Credit** MC, V. **Map** p309.
When diminutive Fon is in the kitchen, you're in for
some snappy, fun Thai cooking at this Portobello
hotspot – the funky room with its loud music is a
favourite hangout for local hipsters.

Total restaurants

A sign of just how savvy a bunch of restaurant users the residents of Dublin have become over the past decade is the fact that today, if a restaurant gets its act together, it is likely to be packed to the rafters within a couple of weeks. In the old days, restaurants had to budget for a long haul before they made a name for themselves. Today, dining-out Dubliners are hunting down every new opening, sure of what they want and eager to distribute their dosh to the deserving. In their quest for good food and a good time, Dubliners have become hooked on what we might call Total Restaurants.

These are restaurants that aim to offer excitement, innovation, creative thinking and good value. They have a singular style, which comes from the input of both the front-of-house staff and the kitchen, and there is no overt 'boss' who tells everyone what to do. The Total Restaurant has signature dishes – the sort of things that the chefs like to cook and that the customers like to eat, often time and again – and it innovates, both with food and service: no standard formality, no obsequious deference.

The most successful restaurants in Dublin over the past five years have all been Total Restaurants – places such as **L'Ecrivain** (*see p118*), **Tribeca** (*see p123*), **101 Talbot** (*see p118*), **Thornton's** (*see p121*), **Caviston's** (*see p124*), the **Mermaid Café** (*see p118*), **Jacob's Ladder** (*see p118*), **Roly's Bistro** (*see p123*) and **O'Connells** (*see p123*). Each is characterised by good food, good fun, good service and good value. They are accessible and affordable; they don't stand on ceremony, and they know that it is important to attract customers through the doors every week, rather than trying to get as much money as possible on a single visit.

The consequence of this increased social and culinary know-how has been simple and startling. In essence, Dubliners have brought about the death of the chef. You are a high profile knife-wielder who reckons folk will flock to your door because you serve cutting-edge food? Forget it; it'll take more than cutting-edge to keep the Dubs coming back. You are a restaurateur who wants to serve very formal food to rich folk in an ultra-posh dining room? Fair enough if you are happy to have a restaurant with all the atmosphere of a mausoleum. Status and swank are out; the Dublin restaurant scene today is dynamic, fun and focused on food. Don't miss it.

Eat, Drink, Shop

Vegetarian

Cornucopia

19 Wicklow Street (677 7583). All cross-city buses. **Open** 5.30-8pm Mon-Wed, Fri, Sat; 5.30-9pm Thur. **Main courses** €7-€9.50. **Credit** DC, MC, V. **Map** p313 H5.
Everyone's favourite vegetarian restaurant has been serving good pulse and staple-based veg cooking for ever and a day, and its popularity shows no sign of diminishing, particularly among parents who want to get their children away from the McDonald's round.

Juice

73 South Great George's Street (475 7856). All cross-city buses. **Main courses** €6.50-€15.50. **Credit** AmEx, MC, V. **Map** p313 G5.
Juice is very cool, almost self-consciously so, and in the evening it fills up with equally cool night owls after a healthy fix – or an antidote to too much Guinness. There are juices and smoothies, of course, but you can also choose from a list of organically produced wines and a menu of reasonable cooking that seems happy to follow largely familiar vegetarian themes. *See p200* **Bored of the black stuff?**

Nectar

7-9 Exchequer Street (672 7501). All cross-city buses. **Open** 9.30am-12.30am daily. **Main courses** €8.50-€14. **Credit** MC, V. **Map** p313 G5.
The city outpost of the Ranelagh juice bar pioneer, Nectar isn't a dedicated vegetarian restaurant but it does take pains to offer a more than decent choice for veggies. Admirably, there are also some coeliac-friendly dishes listed. As well as the inevitable smoothies and salads, the menu lists some more substantial hot dishes, for example piri-piri chicken served with tomato pasta.
Branches: 53 Ranelagh Village, Ranelagh (491 0934); Epicurean Food Hall, 46 Middle Abbey Street & 13-14 Liffey Street (no phone).

Nude

21 Suffolk Street (677 4804). All cross-city buses. **Open** 8am-10pm Mon-Sat; 11am-7pm Sun. **Main courses** €4-€5. **Credit** MC, V. **Map** p313 H5.
Nude has been a runaway success, almost literally, as it has already spawned Nude to Go, a takeaway joint on Leeson Street. Wraps, shakes, smoothies, and lots of vegetarian energy food are the order of the day, and it's extremely well done.
Branch: Nude to Go 103 Lower Leeson Street, Southside (661 5650).

Northside

International

Epicurean Food Hall

Entrances at 46 Middle Abbey Street & 13-14 Liffey Street (no phone). All cross-city buses. **Open** 9am-7.30pm Mon-Sat. **Credit** varies. **Map** p313 H4.

The Epicurean Food Hall is a walkway of international food and beverage treats: Italian coffee stalls, juices and smoothies to go, sushi, Turkish eateries, paninis, hard-to-get foodie items, American ice-cream, French confectionery, bread and wines – it's a calorie-laden heaven. Highlights include **Caviston's Seafood Bar** (*see p124*) and **Nectar** juice bar (*see p120*). There's some seating at the stands and in the central areas but the walkway gets very crammed at lunchtimes.

Mero Moro Café

56A Manor Street, Stoneybatter (670 7799). Bus 37, 38, 39. **Open** 8.30am-7pm Mon Fri; 9am-6pm Sat. **Main courses** €4-€7.50. **Credit** MC, V. **Map** p312 E/D3.

Teresa Hernández's cute café delivers authentic flavours in its tortillas and burritos – a rare chance to experience real Mexican cooking.

Ta Se Mahagoni Gaspipes

17 Manor Street, Stoneybatter (679 8138). Bus 37, 38, 39. **Open** noon-3pm, 6-9.30pm Tue-Fri; 6-9.30pm Sat. **Main courses** €15.50-€33. **Credit** DC, MC, V. **Map** p312 E/D3.

Enjoyable American-style cooking from Drina Kinsley and late night jazz at the weekends is the winning formula at this northside restaurant, on the main strip of newly posh Stoneybatter.

Modern Irish

Bond

Beresford Place (855 9244). All cross-city buses. **Open** 9.30am-9pm Mon-Wed; 9.30am 10pm Thur-Sat. **Main courses** €14-€24. **Credit** MC, V. **Map** p313 J4.

Karl Purdy's wine bar with waiters is a cult locale. Relaxed modern food is accompanied by great wines at terrific prices; what's more, you get to choose your own bottle from the basement.

Chapter One

18-19 Parnell Square (873 2266/www.chapterone. com). All cross-city buses. **Open** 12.30-2.30pm, 6-11pm Tue-Fri; 6-11pm Sat. **Main courses** €22-€25.50. **Theatre menu** €25.50 for 3 courses. **Credit** AmEx, DC, MC, V. **Map** p313 G3.

There's Barbra Streisand on the sound system, but Ross Lewis's cooking is amongst the best contemporary Irish cooking in the entire city. Choose from dishes such as morels stuffed with chicken mousse and roast sea bass with avocado and pistachio purée. Very good value, and fantastic for dinner before and after a performance at the Gate (*see p208*).

Halo

Morrison Hotel, Ormond Quay (887 2421/ www.morrisonhotel.ie). All cross-city buses. **Open** 7-10.30am, 12.30-2.15pm, 7-10pm daily. **Main courses** €18.50-€31.50. **Credit** AmEx, DC, MC, V. **Map** p75.

Fantastic modern food from Jean-Michel Poulot is the big draw in the funky Morrison hotel. No one executes lavish, surprising fusion better than this cook, and it's worth the money. Dishes such as Gressingham duck breast with black truffle mash or tartlet of monkfish are perfectly in tune with the high-ceilinged, stylish room and the cool, mon-eyed crowd who dine here.

101 Talbot

100-102 Talbot Street (874 5011). All cross-city buses. **Open** 5-11pm Tue-Sat. **Main courses** €8.50-€17. **Credit** AmEx, DC, MC, V. **Map** p313 H/J3.

For years the pivotal address on the northside of the river, 101 remains one of the city's best-loved restaurants, thanks to excellent modern cooking and witty, vivacious service. The menu demonstrates Mediterranean and Middle Eastern influences and includes good options for vegetarians. It's particularly popular with the theatre crowd.

Traditional Irish

Paddy's Place

Corporation Markets, Smithfield (873 5130). All cross-city buses. **Open** 6am 2.30pm Mon-Fri, Sun; 7-11am Sun. **Main courses** €6-€7. **No credit cards.** **Map** p312 E4.

This brilliant little caff for market traders and smart shoppers is a good place to track down Dublin's elusive signature dish, coddle: a stew of rashers, sausages and onions.

Southern suburbs

Chinese

China-Sichuan Restaurant

4 Lower Kilmacud Road, Stillorgan (288 4817). Bus 46A. **Open** 12.30-2.30pm, 6-11pm Mon-Fri; 12.30-2.30pm Sat, Sun. **Main courses** €13-€25.50. **Credit** AmEx, DC, MC, V.

You have to book well in advance to get in here for Sunday lunch, which is proof of just how beloved the venerable old Sichuan is. The cooking is excellent and authentic, and service is charming.

Furama Chinese Restaurant

88 Donnybrook Road, Donnybrook (283 0522/ www.furama.ie). Bus 10, 46A. **Open** 12.30-2.30pm, 6-11.30pm Mon-Thur; 12.30-2.30pm, 6pm-midnight Fri, Sat; 1.30-11pm Sun. **Main courses** €11.50-€25.50. **Credit** AmEx, DC, MC, V.

Along with Kilmacud's China-Sichuan (*see p121*), the Furama offers the best Chinese food in town. The cooking is authentic, the service is gracious and it's a great restaurant to take a date, thanks to a pretty and comfortable room.

Eat, Drink, Shop

Instant classic **Tribeca** is generating a southside buzz. *See p123.*

Kites

15-17 Ballsbridge Terrace, Ballsbridge (660 7415/www.kitesrestaurant.com). Lansdowne Road DART/7, 45, 84 bus. **Open** 12.30-2pm, 6.30-11.30pm Mon-Fri; 6.30-11.30pm Sat. **Main courses** €16.50-€19. **Credit** AmEx, DC, MC, V.

A lot of Kites' clientele is drawn from nearby hotels, but don't let that put you off. It's a cosy, Westernised room and serves well-executed food.

Zen

89 Upper Rathmines Road, Rathmines (497 9428). Bus 14, 15, 16, 16A. **Open** 6-11pm daily. **Main courses** €13.50-€23. **Credit** AmEx, DC, MC, V.

Housed in a de-consecrated church, Zen is enjoyably surreal thanks to its surroundings. The cooking is reliable and has lots of verve to set it apart from the average Chinese.

Fish & seafood

Lobster Pot Restaurant

9 Ballsbridge Terrace, Ballsbridge (668 0025/660 9170). Lansdowne Road DART/7, 18, 45, 84 bus. **Open** 12.30-2.30pm, 6.45-9.45pm Mon-Fri; 6.45-9.45pm Sat. **Main courses** €19.50-€50. **Credit** AmEx, DC, MC, V.

Comfy and ageless as any gentleman's club, the Lobster Pot formula survives light years beyond the food fashions of the day. Classic bisques and the catch of the day cooked whichever way you like – but preferably with dollops of wine and cream – are what's on offer, and the team look after you in such a way that every visit is a treat.

French & European

Ernie's

Mulberry Gardens, Donnybrook (269 3260). Bus 10, 46, 46A, 46B, 46C, 46D, 46E, 58, 58C. **Open** 12.30-2pm, 7.30-10.30pm Tue-Sat. **Main courses** €20.50-€36. **Credit** AmEx, DC, MC, V.

Set in a courtyard just off the main strip in Donnybrook (and hard to find), Ernie's is a pampering little place, characterised by old-fashioned dedication to service. The food has nothing to do

with fashion – rack of Wicklow lamb with madeira; lamb's liver with sage; guinea fowl with Puy lentils; prune and Armagnac tart – but that is just how the loyal older clientele like it.

Seasons@The Four Seasons

Simmonscourt Road, Ballsbridge (655 4000). Lansdowne Road DART/7, 45 bus. **Open** noon-3pm, 6.30-10pm daily. **Main courses** €20.50-€34.50. **Set menu** €44.50 for 3 courses. **Credit** AmEx, DC, MC, V.

Terry White's serene food owes as much to French cuisine as to modern American food, and meticulous sourcing of ingredients means that flavours in dishes such as grilled fillet of sea bass and pan-seared beef tenderloin are very pure. Prices are high, of course, but the set menus are decent value. Service could do with some fine tuning, however.

Indian/Pakistani

The Bombay Pantry

Glenageary Shopping Centre, Glenageary (285 6683). Bus 7, 45A, 111. **Open** 5-10pm daily. **Main courses** €6.50-€10. **Credit** DC, MC, V.

A second branch of this authentic Indian takeaway has opened in Rathmines, which is good food news for city folk as the Pantry's Indian cooking is right on the money and hugely enjoyable.

Poppadum

91A Rathgar Road, Rathgar (490 2383/www. poppadum.ie). Bus 15, 65. **Open** 6pm-midnight daily. **Main courses** €14-€19. **Credit** AmEx, MC, V.

This elegant restaurant continues to offer the most highly regarded Indian cooking in the city. Poppadum's dishes excite because of a genuine sense of creativity and exploration.

International

Expresso Bar

St Mary's Road, Ballsbridge (660 8632). Bus 7, 18, 45, 84. **Open** 9am-5pm Mon-Fri; 10am-7pm Sat; 10am-3pm Sun. **Main courses** €7.50-€10. **Credit** MC, V. **Map** p309.

(margin, left side) Eat, Drink, Shop

Ann Marie Nohl's Expresso Bar has become one of the institutions of southside Dublin, regularly packed out at lunchtime with twentysomething women from the business offices tucking into relaxed but stylish international dishes. Standards are consistently high, and it's a great space for weekend brunch. In fact, we like it so much that we'll forgive the rather misleading name.
Branch: Unit 6, Custom House Square, IFSC, Northside (672 1812).

Modern Irish

Dali's
63 Main Street, Blackrock (278 0660). Blackrock DART. **Open** noon-3pm, 6-11pm Tue-Sat; noon-3pm Sun. **Main courses** €15.50/€19 set lunch; €16-€25 dinner. **Credit** AmEx, DC, MC, V.
A swish room and a happy bunch of regular locals explain how the somewhat modern-by-numbers Dali's continues to prosper.

Dish
64 Upper Leeson Street, Ballsbridge (671 1248) All cross-city buses. **Open** noon-11pm daily. **Main courses** €13-€19. **Credit** AmEx, DC, MC, V. **Map** p309.
Recently moved from Temple Bar, Dish continues to serve up sharp yet comforting cooking that hits all the right buttons. It's also a great weekend brunch location for lingering over the papers.

O'Connells
Bewley's Hotel, Merrion Road, Ballsbridge (647 3304/www.oconnellsballsbridge.com). Bus 5, 7, 7A, 45. **Open** 12.30-2.30pm, 6-10.30pm Mon-Sat; 12.30-3pm, 6-9.30pm Sun. **Main courses** €15-€20.50. **Credit** AmEx, DC, MC, V. **Map** p309.
This stylish room in the Bewley's Aparthotel serves great modern food – grills from their wood-fired oven are particularly good. Tom O'Connell runs the room with meticulous efficiency.

Roly's Bistro
7 Ballsbridge Terrace, Ballsbridge (668 2611). Lansdowne Road DART/18, 45 bus. **Open** noon-2.45pm, 6-9.45pm daily. **Main courses** €18-€24. **Credit** AmEx, DC, MC, V.
This Ballsbridge powerhouse has been one of the city's most significant restaurants in recent years, and with Paul Cartwright at the stove the food remains as consistently interesting and engagingly enjoyable as ever. There's a fantastic atmosphere to boot. Book well in advance to get a table.

Tribeca
65 Ranelagh, Ranelagh (497 4174). Bus 11, 18, 44, 48A. **Open** noon-11pm daily. **Main courses** £8.50-£27.50. **Credit** MC, V. **Map** p309.
Tribeca is one of the hottest new addresses on the southside, with folk queuing up in the rain to get in here for brunch at the weekends. The zippy modern food on offer benefits from culinary care and mature service. So hot, it's cool.

Thai & Pacific Rim

Baan Thai
16 Merrion Road, Ballsbridge (660 8833/www.baanthairestaurant.ie). Lansdowne Road DART/7, 45, 84 bus. **Open** 6-11pm Mon, Tue; 12.30-2.30pm, 6-11pm Wed-Fri; 6-11.30pm Sat. **Main courses** €13-€18. **Credit** AmEx, MC, V. **Map** p309.
For many people, Baan Thai is responsible for the best Thai food in town. Certainly, the savoury main courses are a strong point, but desserts are a no-go area (though they're admittedly less important in Asian cuisine). Service is provided by polite staff wearing traditional dress.

Langkawi
46 Upper Baggot Street, Ballsbridge (668 2760). Lansdowne Road DART. **Open** 12.30-2pm, 6-11.30pm Mon-Fri; 6-11.30pm Sat. **Main courses** €18-€24. **Credit** AmEx, DC, MC, V. **Map** p309.
The Langkawi is popular with local office workers thanks to its melange of Far Eastern dishes, including fish stuffed with chilli paste served on a banana leaf and beef rendang.

Northern suburbs

Italian

Il Corvo
100 Upper Drumcondra Road, Drumcondra (837 5727). Bus 16. **Open** noon-11.30pm Mon-Sat; 12.30-11pm Sun. **Main courses** €9-€19. **Credit** AmEx, MC, V.
Nothing ever changes in this popular place in Drumcondra. Il Corvo's clientele like the familiar Italian-style food, including very good pizzas.

Independent Pizza Co
46 Lower Drumcondra Road, Drumcondra (830 2957). Bus 16, 41. **Open** noon-midnight Mon-Sat; noon-10.30pm Sun. **Main courses** €4.50-€12. **Credit** AmEx, MC, V.
The Independent is the classic purveyor of excellent pizzas, from a key address on the northside. A local treasure worth visiting.

Modern Irish

The Old Schoolhouse
Coolbanagher, Swords (840 2846). Bus 33, 41, 41C. **Open** 12.30-2.30pm, 6.30-10.30pm Mon-Fri; 6.30-10.30pm Sat; 12.30-2.30pm Sun. **Main courses** €21-€28. **Credit** AmEx, DC, MC, V.
The Old Schoolhouse is a capable, enthusiastic restaurant, founded on a well-understood notion of service, tuned to the demands of its suburban clientele and very expert at catering to the needs of the ever-growing population of Swords. There's plenty of fish, plus local meaty options such as venison or Irish ostrich (served panfried, with crème fraiche).

Eat, Drink, Shop

American

PD's Woodhouse

1 Coliemore Road, Dalkey (284 9399). Dalkey DART.
Open 6-11pm Mon-Sat; 4-9.30pm Sun. **Main courses** €13-€24. **Credit** AmEx, DC, MC, V.
PD's Woodhouse has carved out a niche as a place to feast on good char-grilled steaks – the speciality – baked potatoes and crisp salads.

Fish & seafood

Caviston's

59 Glasthule Road, Sandycove (280 9120/ www.cavistons.com). Sandycove/Glasthule DART.
Open noon-1.30pm, 1.30-3pm, 3-5pm Tue-Sat. **Main courses** €6.50-€19. **Credit** AmEx, DC, MC, V.
A southside phenomenon, offering three packed-out sittings for lunch. The fish cookery is immaculate and the clientele bourgeois. Also check out the funky, fresh seafood bar in the Epicurean Food Hall. **Branch: Caviston's Seafood Bar** Epicurean Food Hall, Liffey Street, Northside (878 2289).

French

Kish

Coliemore Road, Dalkey (285 0377). Bus 7D, 59.
Open 7-10.30pm Wed, Thur; 12.30-2.30pm, 7-10.30pm Fri-Sun. **Main courses** €24-€30.50.
Credit AmEx, MC, V.

A gorgeous room with views over the bay is enticement enough to tempt you to Kish, but recently the modern French-oriented cooking has also found its feet. Stylish and pricey, Kish is now fulfilling its promise as a big, expensive, special-night-out place, serving patrons the likes of whole roast quail with savoy cabbage and pan-fried foie gras.

Modern Irish

Bistro One

3 Brighton Road, Foxrock Village, Foxrock (289 7711). Bus 46A. **Open** 6.45-10.45pm Tue-Sat.
Main courses €13-€24. **Credit** MC, V.
Bistro One is a local secret. Climb the stairs at the side of a dry-cleaner's to a cosy, comfortable space, where you can enjoy such dishes as Thai fish red curry with basil and coriander, or honey-blackened haddock with a sweet and sour chilli glaze, served with stir-fried egg noodles and pak choi.

Blackrock Café

15 Main Street, Blackrock (278 8900). Blackrock DART/7, 45 bus. **Open** noon-2pm, 5.30-10pm Mon-Fri; 5.30-10pm Sat; noon-3pm Sun. **Main courses** €14.50-€21.50. **Credit** MC, V.
The renamed Blackrock is the foremost dining room in this polite 'burb. Slick modern food and service are offered in an elegant room above Jack O'Rourke's pub. The brioche pain perdu alone is worth the trip.

Duzy's

18 Glasthule Road, Dún Laoghaire (230 0210). Dún Laoghaire DART. **Open** 12.45-2.45pm, 5.30-10pm Mon-Thur; 12.30-2.45pm, 5.30-10.30pm Fri;

007 would feel utterly at home at stylish **Bond**. *See p121.*

Restaurants

For belt-busting on a budget
Dim sum at the **Imperial** (*see p110*), the set menu at the **Bad Ass Café** (*see p110*), fish and chips at **Leo Burdock's** (*see p111*), Italian at the **Steps of Rome** (*see p117*), vegetarian at **Nude** (*see p120*) and **Cornucopia** (*see p120*), and trad Irish at **Paddy's Place** (*see p121*).

For a complete blow out
The Commons (*see p118*), **Thornton's** (*see p119*), and, unless you go for the relatively reasonable set lunch, **Restaurant Patrick Guilbaud** (*see p113*).

For dining in style
Cooke's Café (*see p111*), **La Stampa** (*see p115*), **L'Ecrivain** (*see p110*), **The Tea Room** (*see p119*), **Shanahan's on the Green** (*see p119*), **Halo** (*p121*) and **Roly's Bistro** (*see p123*).

For the perfect brunch
Elephant & Castle (*see p110*), **The Mermaid Café** (*see p118*), **Tribeca** (*see p123*), the **Expresso Bar** (*see p122*) and **Nosh** (*see p125*).

For a taste of distinctively delicious Dublin
Ely (*see p118*), **Jacob's Laddor** (*see p118*), **Caviston's** (*see p124*), **L'Ecrivain** (*see p118*), **Chapter One** (*see p121*) and **Bond** (*see p121*).

6-10.30pm Sat; 12.30-3pm, 6-9pm Sun. **Main courses** €18-€21.50. **Credit** AmEx, DC, MC, V.
John Dunne's cooking is as pitch perfect as ever in the rechristened Duzy's. Feast on duck confit, fillet of beef with green beans and pecan pie, and enjoy the keen service and good-value pricing. Well worth the DART journey south.

Munkberry's
Castle Street, Dalkey (284 7185/www.munkberrys.ie). Dalkey DART. **Open** 5.30-10pm Tue-Sat; noon-10pm Sun. **Main courses** €12-€22.50. **Credit** AmEx, DC, MC, V.
This is a beautiful room, and not surprisingly one of the places that Dalkey-ites use for special occasions. The cooking is reliable modern Irish, and quite pricey. Food can feature modern takes on traditional dishes (such as herb crusted fillet of cod with mushy peas and 'pont-neuf' potato chips), and local ingredients are used wherever possible (roast loin of Wicklow lamb with caramelised onion and a white bean aioli, for example).

Nosh
111 Coliemore Road, Dalkey (284 0666/www.nosh.ie). Dalkey DART. **Open** noon-4pm, 6pm-late Tue-Sun. **Main courses** €14-€20.50 **Credit** MC, V.
The Farrell sisters' pretty room pulls in the crowds in Dalkey for a taste of archetypal modern cooking: Caesar salad, bangers and mash, fish and chips with mushy peas, chargrilled salmon are menu classics. It's a popular place for weekend brunch and very much the Dalkey hotspot.

The Purty Kitchen
Old Dún Laoghaire Road, Dún Laoghaire (284 3576/www.purtykitchen.com). Salthill & Monkstown DART. **Open** 11am-11.30pm Mon-Wed; 11am-12.30am Thur-Sat; noon-11.30pm Sun. **Main courses** €10-€19.50. **Credit** AmEx, MC, V.
This low-lying pub on the edge of Dún Laoghaire has been around for eons. It has a good reputation for bar food, and dishes such as pan-fried Barbary duck with cracked pepper and soy sauce reveal more than a hint of ambition.

The Queen's/Vico
Castle Street, Dalkey (285 4569). Dalkey DART. **Open** *The Queen's* noon-midnight Mon-Thur; noon-12.30am Fri, Sat. *Vico* 5.30-11pm Tue-Sat. **Main courses** *The Queen's* €3-€9. *Vico* €21-€29. **Credit** AmEx, DC, MC, V.
Enjoy good bar food on the ground floor or head upstairs to Vico, a posh room with linen, formal service and decent char-grills.

Roly@The Pavilion
Unit 8, The Pavilion, Dún Laoghaire, Co Dublin (236 0286). Dún Laoghaire DART. **Open** 12.30-2pm, 6-9.45pm Tue-Fri, 6-9.45pm Sat. **Main courses** €13-€21.50. **Credit** AmEx, MC, V.
Roly Saul has always had the gift of creating great rooms, and then serving accessible, affordable smart food in them. Following the success of Roly's Bistro (*see p123*) he seems set fair to do the same again at the Pavilion. Leather banquettes and cubicles in dark mauves and clubby browns is the setting for modern rustic food: braised shoulder of lamb with green beans and mash; roast chicken with fondant potato, and a cheese and dessert selection for afters – if you've left enough room.

Spanish

Valparaiso
99 Monkstown Road, Monkstown (280 1992). Monkstown DART/7, 8 bus. **Open** 6-11pm Mon-Sat; 6-10pm Sun. **Main courses** €15.50-€21.50. **Credit** MC, V.
Eclectic ingredients are combined into interesting dishes such as roast quail with a chestnut and apricot stuffing, served with sweet potato purée; and chicken La Brasa – which comes with a coriander, lime, chilli and cream sauce. The restaurant is a comfy space above a pub.

Thai

Thai House

21 Railway Road, Dalkey (284 7304/www.thaihouse ireland.com.ie). Dalkey DART. **Open** 6pm-midnight Tue-Sun. **Main courses** €13-€20.50. **Credit** AmEx, DC, MC, V.

Tony Ecock's Thai restaurant is now a stalwart of the Dalkey scene. The cooking is authentic – the likes of tod man kappoot (deep-fried corn cakes containing herbs) and larb gai (spicy minced chicken) – albeit somewhat expensive.

Dublin Bay (north)

Fish & seafood

King Sitric

East Pier, Howth (832 5235). Howth DART/31, 31B bus. **Open** noon-2.30pm, 6.30-11pm Mon-Fri; 6.30-11pm Sat. **Main courses** €28-€43. **Credit** AmEx, MC, V.

Aidan MacManus's long-established restaurant has been smartly revamped recently, and now offers comfortable accommodation alongside some very fine seafood cookery.

Red Bank Restaurant

7 Church Street, Skerries (849 1005/redbank @iol.ie). Skerries rail/33 bus. **Open** 7-9.30pm Mon-Sat; 12.30-3.30pm Sun. **Main courses** €13-€44.50. **Credit** AmEx, DC, MC, V.

As well as offering excellent, ageless seafood cookery, TerryMcCoy has now added some rooms in an adjoining guesthouse to the Red Bank package. Staying overnight will make a visit out to this northside eatery even more fun.

Fusion

Citrus

1 Island View House, Howth (832 0200). Howth DART/31, 31B bus. **Open** 12.30-11pm daily. **Main courses** €13.50-€23. **Credit** AmEx, MC, V.

Under the same ownership as Casa Pasta (*see p126*) and just as bustling and boisterous, this is a modern space with eclectic modern cooking that pulls in ideas and influences from all over the globe.

Italian & Mediterranean

Casa Pasta

12 Harbour Road, Howth (839 3823). Howth DART/31, 31B bus. **Open** 6pm-11pm Mon-Thur; 5pm-midnight Fri, Sat; 12.30-10pm Sun. **Main courses** €10-€19. **Credit** AmEx, DC, MC, V.

Casa Pasta has been the success story of Howth ever since it opened up in late 1993, spawning a second outpost in Clontarf. Simple furnishings, keen prices, good views over the bays and straightforward zappy food are key to its continuing popularity. **Branch**: 55 Clontarf Road, Clontarf (833 1402).

Bewley's: gorgeous for gorging. *See p127.*

Modern Irish

Aqua

1 West Pier, Howth (832 0690/www.dineataqua.ie). Howth DART/31, 31B bus. **Open** 1-3.30pm, 5.30-11pm Tue-Sat; 12.30-6pm Sun. **Main courses** €16.50-€50. **Credit** AmEx, MC, V.

Charlie Smith's restaurant is on a roll. The modern Irish cooking served here is savvy and smart, and perfectly suited to this handsome room with its great views over the bay.

Bon Appetit

9 St James Terrace, Malahide (845 0314/845 2206/www.bonappetit.ie). Malahide DART/ rail/42 bus. **Open** 12.30-2pm, 7-10.30pm Mon-Fri; 7-10.30pm Sat. **Main courses** €17-€30.50. **Credit** AmEx, DC, MC, V.

The classical-meets-contemporary cooking at Bon Appetit doesn't date, and the chef remains as youthfully addicted to the stove as ever.

Cafés & Coffeeshops

After years of packaging up 'Oirishness' and flogging it to tourists at home and abroad, the early to mid '90s saw Dublin do an about-turn and embrace the continental café cool associated with Paris and Rome. Out went the dish-water tea and instant coffee, in came espresso beans and white-aproned waiters. Well-travelled entrepreneurs took proven formulas they saw abroad – juice bars, serious coffee retailers and health-conscious food outlets – and brought them home.

But just as Dubliners have got used to the lazy sunny Sunday atmosphere of hanging out in locally owned cafés, the big boys have started to get in on the act. Chains of coffeeshops along the US model are springing up everywhere, squeezing into every vacant lot and buying up independent shops to rebrand them. **Café Sol** is the Irish answer to Starbucks, though it doesn't have quite the aggressive reputation of the US chain.

These days, you can't walk more than five feet before you hit a coffee counter and if you take your caffeine seriously it's a positive godsend. Many Dubs now spend their time racing to and from their offices with caffe lattes scalding their fingers. Luckily, however, there are still plenty of characterful cafés for the visitor with time to spare, where you can linger for hours over a cup of excellent coffee and contemplate Dubliners' wholehearted espousal of the 'other' black stuff.

Southside

Other top spots for coffee include **Bar Italia** (*see p116*) and the **Steps of Rome** (*see p117*).

Bewley's Oriental Café
Grafton Street (677 6761/www.bewleys.ie). All cross-city buses. **Open** 7.30am-11pm daily. **Credit** AmEx, DC, MC, V. **Map** p313 H5.
The first Bewley's café was opened in 1894 on South Great George's Street, since which time they have become a Dublin institution. The main room in the Grafton Street branch, with its exquisite Harry Clarke windows, is beautiful; the perfect place for coffee, buns and all-day breakfast hangover cures. **Branches**: throughout the city.

Blue Room
1 Coppinger Row, off Clarendon Street (670 6982). All cross-city buses. **Open** 11am-6pm Mon-Sat. **Credit** AmEx, DC, MC, V. **Map** p313 H5.
Opposite the side entrance to the Powerscourt Centre and rather elegant, serving upmarket sandwiches and salads and fresh soups with decent, but not dramatically exciting, coffee. It looks dead posh, but isn't overly expensive. Turns into a mellow jazz-flavoured venue on selected evenings.

Brown's Bar
Brown Thomas, Grafton Street (679 5666). All cross-city buses. **Open** 9am-6pm Mon, Wed, Fri, Sat; 10am-6pm Tue; 9am-8pm Thur; noon-6pm Sun. **Credit** AmEx, DC, MC, V. **Map** p313 H5.
Designed as somewhere to see and be seen, Brown's Bar has rather lost its cool factor of late. Still, it must be doing something right as there's hardly room for the customers, never mind the oodles of bulging shopping bags from the store upstairs. Great coffee, and excellent but pricey salads and sandwiches.

Butler's Chocolate Café
24 Wicklow Street (671 0591/www.butlers chocolates.com). All cross-city buses. **Open** 8am-7pm Mon, Wed, Fri, Sat; 8am-10pm Tue, Thur; 11am-6pm Sun. **Credit** AmEx, DC, MC, V. **Map** p313 H5.

For a truly hedonistic experience, pop into one of the Butler's Chocolate Cafés, where you can indulge in good coffee or wicked hot chocolate accompanied by luxurious handmade choccies.
Branches: 9 Chatham Street, Southside (672 6333); 51A Grafton Street, Southside (671 0599); 18 Nassau Street, Southside (671 0772).

Chompy's
Powerscourt Townhouse Centre, Clarendon Street (679 4552). All cross-city buses. **Open** 8am-5.30pm Mon-Sat. **Credit** MC, V. **Map** p313 H5.
The great American breakfast is one of the big attractions in Frank Zimmer's popular place, with folk queuing up for pancakes, smoked salmon bagels, eggs Benedict and French toast.

Gloria Jean's Coffee Co
Powerscourt Townhouse Centre, Clarendon Street (679 7772). All cross-city buses. **Open** 8am-7pm Mon-Sat; 10am-6pm Sun. **Credit** AmEx, DC, MC, V. **Map** p313 H5.
Few venues in Dublin take their coffee as seriously as Gloria Jean's. There's an enormous array of Arabian bean coffees of all varieties and prices, and a broad range of flavoured coffees. The cakes, pastries and muffins are a disappointment, though.

Guy Stuart
George's Street Arcade, South Great George's Street (no phone). All cross-city buses. **Open** 9am-6pm Mon-Sat. **No credit cards. Map** p313 G5.
Jenny Guy and Laura Stuart make terrific sandwiches, picnic foods and fun, funky soups for days when the sun shines and you want to eat al fresco on St Stephen's Green.

Joy of Coffee
25 East Essex Street, Temple Bar (679 3393). All cross-city buses. **Open** 8am-10pm Mon-Fri; 9am-11pm Sat; 10am-10pm Sun. **Credit** AmEx, DC, MC, V. **Map** p75.
An aesthetically pleasing café in the heart of Temple Bar, complete with elegant prints and functional, if vaguely uncomfortable, benches. The punters can be tiresomely trendy but just ignore them – the coffee is good.

Kaffe-Moka
39 South William Street (679 8475). All cross-city buses. **Open** 10.30am-6pm Mon-Sat. **Credit** MC, V. **Map** p313 H/G5.
One of the first of the continental-style cafés, Kaffe-Moka's mini-chain got it right from the beginning, with a winning mix of big windows, myriad varieties of tea and coffee and a chilled atmosphere (chess games and newspapers are readily available). The Rathmines branch has switched management and has been renamed Moda, but it maintains the same high standards.
Branch: Unit 5 The Pavilion, Dún Laoghaire Shopping Centre, Dún Laoghaire, Dublin Bay (284 6544); **Moda** 192 Lower Rathmines Road, Rathmines, Southern suburbs (497 9329); Epicurean Food Hall, Middle Abbey Street, Northside (872 9078).

Eat, Drink, Shop

Queen of Tarts

4 Cork Hill (670 7499). All cross-city buses.
Open 7.30am-7pm Mon-Fri; 9am-7pm Sat, Sun.
No credit cards. Map p313 G5.
Excellent cakes, coffees and savoury baking have
made the Queen something of a cult success.
Branch: Dublin City Hall, Dame Street, Southside
(672 2925).

Simon's Place

*George's Street Arcade, South Great George's Street
(679 7821). All cross-city buses.* **Open** 9am-6pm
Mon-Sat. **No credit cards. Map** p313 G5.
Great soups, chunky sarnies, good coffee and funky
clientele. Try to arrive late morning to sample the
sublime fresh-baked cinnamon buns. *See also p180.*

The Stonewall Café

18 Exchequer Street (672 7323). Bus 19, 83.
Open 11am-5pm, 6-11pm daily. **Credit** AmEx, DC,
MC, V. **Map** p313 G5.
Exposed bricks and a friendly atmosphere set the
tone at this laid-back café. Read the papers and gaze
contentedly at the Dublin streetlife outside, as you
dig into great coffee and light meals. Caesar salad is
delish, and breakfast is top-notch. *See also p180.*

Coffee to go

Café Sol

*Block 4, Harcourt Road (478 1016). All cross-city
buses.* **Open** 8am-6pm daily. **No credit cards.**
Map p313 G6/7.
Café Sol follows the Starbucks philosophy with a
branch, shop or vendor on every corner (though for
the moment they're all on the southside). The sandwiches and muffins are good value, but most people
come for the excellent coffee: cappuccinos, mochas
and lattes, in various sizes and optionally accompanied by every syrup known to man.
Branches: Harcourt Street, Southside (475 1167); 46
Baggot Street Lower, Southside (662 8037); 21 Clare
Street, Southside (678 8690); Unit 1A Earlsfort
Terrace, Southside (678 5895); Upstairs at Habitat, St
Stephen's Green, Southside (672 7457).

Northside

Cobalt Café

*16 North Great George's Street (873 0313). All
cross-city buses.* **Open** 10am-5pm Mon-Fri; 11am-
4pm Sat. **Credit** MC, V. **Map** p313 H3.
Located in the ground floor of a finely restored
Georgian home, this stylish establishment is particularly popular with arty types and office workers in
the area. The Cobalt also doubles as an art gallery,
with a range of distinctive, original work lining the
walls. There are occasional cabaret nights.

Panem

*21 Lower Ormond Quay (872 8510). All cross-city
buses.* **Open** 9am-5pm Mon-Fri; 10am-5pm Sat. **No
credit cards. Map** p313 G4.

Good soups, filled focaccias, fine coffees and a couple of daily pasta dishes are the staples of this fun,
stylish room on Ormond Quay.

West Coast Coffee Company

*63-64 O'Connell Street (878 6790). All cross-city
buses.* **Open** 7am-6pm daily. **No credit cards.**
Map p313 H4.
Squashy couches and an excellent, well-pitched
menu of paninis, pastries and light meals. The coffee has the freshest taste and all the usual frothy,
with-syrup variations are available. Another bonus
is the super-fast service from an outlet that brands
itself as a purveyor of 'gourmet coffee to go'.
Branches: 20 Lower Ormond Quay, Northside (874
9029); 21 Lower Camden Street, Southside (475 6144);
2 Lincoln Place, Southside (661 4253); 144 Lower
Baggot Street, Southside (678 8738).

Winding Stair Café

*40 Ormond Quay Lower (873 3292). All cross-city
buses.* **Open** 10.30am-6pm Mon-Sat. **Credit** MC, V.
Map p313 G4.
The loveliest, most lingerable bookshop in Dublin
has offered cracking lunchtime food for years.
Arrive around 11-ish, browse the shelves, sip some
coffee, have lunch, buy some books, and bliss out.

Coffee to go

Coffee Society

*2 Lower Liffey Street (878 7984). All cross-city
buses.* **Open** 8.30am-6pm Mon-Fri; 10am-5pm Sat,
Sun. **No credit cards. Map** p313 G4.
Yes, there is a sit-down area, but it's bustling, noisy
and cramped: hardly the place to linger. Order coffee to go, cross the road to the Liffey Boardwalk and
enjoy the best mocha in town, by the river.

Southern suburbs

Café Java

*145 Upper Leeson Street, Ranelagh (660 0675). Bus
11, 11A, 46A.* **Open** 7.15am-5pm Mon-Fri; 8am-5pm
Sat; 11am-5pm Sun. **Credit** MC, V. **Map** p309.
The Javas are hugely popular as breakfast,
lunchtime and coffee places, and their clever mix of
light food – bagels, poached eggs with bacon – and
the best hot chocolate in Dublin is confidently handled in comfortable, slightly baroque surroundings.
Branches: 5 South Anne Street, Southside (660
8899); Main Street, Blackrock, Dublin Bay (278 1571).

The Coffee Club

*4 Haddington Road, Ballsbridge (667 5522). Bus 7,
7A, 8, 10.* **Open** 7am-7pm Mon-Fri; 9am-4pm Sat;
10am-4pm Sun. **Credit** MC, V. **Map** p314 L7.
Fine upmarket sandwiches and excellent coffee are
served in this pleasant café. It's best on a weekday:
Sunday brunch gets horribly crowded and the service can deteriorate as a result.
Branch: 81 Morehampton Road, Donnybrook,
Southern suburbs (677 7638).

Pubs & Bars

Stop pretending you're here for anything else.

While members of the city's so-called café society might protest, there's no denying that the social life of most Dubliners still revolves around the pub. It's also a fair assumption that more people come to the city for the drinking than anything else: Irish pubs are legendary and have spawned countless imitations the world over. This reputation has much to do with the associations that the demon drink has with Irish music, politics and literature, but also with something far more intangible. Irish pubs are often perceived as sanctuaries, places where total strangers sing and carouse with you, where the Guinness is perfect, and everyone is welcomed with open arms. It's a great concept – the very epitome of pub culture, perhaps – but these days, particularly in Dublin, it's an experience that is fast disappearing.

Drinking in Dublin can be an exhilarating or a profoundly disappointing experience, depending on your expectations. If your night on the beer is a prelude to clubbing or a party, you should have no problem getting in the mood: the pubs in the city centre are plentiful (there are over 700) and usually buzzing with life. The city's swelling population is young, stylish and energetic, but while the atmosphere in most pubs usually remains good-humoured, the pace may seem too frenetic. Although most pubs in Temple Bar have banned travelling hen and stag parties, and a Friday night no longer quite resembles the Visgoths invading Rome, Dublin can still be an extraordinarily rowdy place after dark. When faced with a surging crowd ten-deep at the bar and a seemingly unending queue for the toilet, a cynic might suggest that having a pint these days is often more trouble than it's worth.

Most Dubliners distinguish between the newer, bigger, brighter 'superpubs' and the traditional public houses of old. The city's newer bars ooze an occasionally smug sense of style and sophistication that at worst makes them virtually indistinguishable from one another, and from the glitzy café-bars of any other modern European city. There are exceptions, of course – places like the **Front Lounge**, **Voodoo** or the **Modern Green Bar** manage to pull off an effortless cool that is great fun. In general, however, Dublin's newer bars are often a triumph of style over substance: exposed brickwork, polished beechwood and some well-selected art are certainly very pleasant distractions, but the atmosphere can be disappointingly anonymous.

While the indiscriminate are usually happy anywhere, and most of them are to be found in the tourist traps around Temple Bar, those seeking a more authentic experience should beat a hasty retreat to the nearest no-nonsense, dark-panelled public house, where the interior hasn't changed in a century and you don't have to shout at the person beside you to make yourself heard. Sadly these older, reputable venues are also falling victim to the modernising trend. If there's one issue that can move a jaded barfly to fervour, it's the argument that Ireland's buoyant economy has destroyed the most distinctive aspect of Dublin city life. Many of the city's finer pubs have been butchered beyond recognition – either stripped of their fading grandeur entirely or expanded so much that any sense of character falls by the wayside. Others, sadly, appear to be in terminal decline.

A pint of plain: Ireland's icon in a glass.

new order

We pride ourselves on the quality and unique taste of the stouts and beers we brew, so much so that Porterhouse stouts and beers are only available in a Porterhouse Pub, this ensures quality from grain to glass.

3 great stouts, 3 ales, 3 lagers & specials all on the premises. Including one of the largest selection of bottled beers. Only available in Temple Bar Dublin, Bray and Covent Garden London.

The Porterhouse
Parliament Street, Dublin 2
Strand Road, Bray &
22 Maiden Lane, Covent Garden London
LIVE MUSIC - for more info visit
www.porterhousebrewco.com

the porterhouse
BREWING COMPANY
STOUT & OYSTER BAR

PRIDE
in everything we brew

A real Dublin pub – if you can find a seat in one – is truly something special, however. It's not just the eccentric decor or unusual architecture that make them winners; legendary establishments like the **Long Hall**, the **International Bar**, **Grogan's Castle Lounge**, the **Stag's Head** or **Kehoe's** are famed for their genuine atmosphere, where time can stand still, and the emphasis remains on conversation, conviviality and a sly, often self-deprecating, good humour. Generally speaking, the better pubs in the city are the ones that have defied the pressure to move with the times, so you'll find all the charming pub ephemera here: the fine, mahogany bars, the charming snugs and antique clocks. Most importantly, the better Dublin pubs still have 'regulars'. It's the punters – the spoofers, layabouts, crooks, artists, writers and alcoholics – that really dictate the atmosphere. On a good night, you can really see what all the fuss is about.

A WORD OF WARNING

Finally, while not wishing to spoil the party, it's worth mentioning that a healthy proportion of Dublin's drinking population has no social outlet that doesn't involve alcohol. While the image of the 'drunken Paddy' is the kind of racial slur that the nation appears to have outgrown, alcohol-related social problems are making the headlines once again: under-age drinking is a major problem, and a disturbingly high level of road deaths, suicides and street violence suggest the city is struggling with the effects of upholding its boozy reputation. Enjoy a drink by all means; enjoy several – but keep your wits about you.

OPENING TIMES

Early 2000 finally saw the long-awaited extension of pub opening times. Last orders are at 11.30pm from Monday to Wednesday, at 12.30am from Thursday to Saturday and at 11pm on Sunday. A handful of 'late' bars serve until 2.30am on one or more nights of the week. Although some pubs open their doors as early as 7am, most of the pubs in the city start serving some time between 10.30am and 11am (slightly later on Sundays).

Southside

AKA

6 Wicklow Street (670 4220). All cross-city buses. **Open** 4-11.30pm Mon-Wed; 4pm-2.30am Thur-Sat; 4-11pm Sun. **Credit** MC, V. **Map** p313 H5.
Attracting a young businesslike crowd, AKA does a good line in reasonably priced Asian food. The long submarine bar downstairs has a pleasantly aquatic feel, easy listening, ambient sounds, and is better stocked than most Dublin pubs.

Music biz meets media at the **Bailey**.

Auld Dubliner

17 Anglesea Street, Temple Bar (677 0527). All cross city buses. **Open** 10.30am-11.30pm Mon-Thur; 10.30am-12.30am Fri, Sat; 12.30-11pm Sun. **Credit** (minimum €10 spend) AmEx, MC, V. **Map** p75.
Even after redecoration, the Auld Dub looks much as it has ever done. As a place to wait when there are no free tables in the Elephant & Castle (*see p109*) just across the street, it serves its purpose nicely. The atmosphere is busy and lively, though tourists tend to predominate.

The Bailey

2 Duke Street (670 4939). All cross-city buses. **Open** 11.30am-11.30pm Mon-Sat; 4-11.30pm Sun. **Credit** AmEx, DC, MC, V. **Map** p313 H5.
A part of Dublin's social and cultural history, the super-trendy Bailey attracts everyone from record company hipsters to minor-league musicians, self-conscious thespians and aspiring journalists. You used to enter the pub through the door of Leopold Bloom's house, but this has now been relocated to the James Joyce Centre (*see p87*). *See also p200* **Bored of the black stuff?**

Bleeding Horse

24 Camden Street Upper, Portobello (475 2705/ restaurant 478 2101). Bus 16, 16A, 55, 83. **Open** noon-midnight Mon-Wed; noon-1am Thur; noon-2am Fri, Sat; noon-11.30pm Sun. **Credit** MC, V. **Map** p309.
The Bleeding Horse has traded on this prominent Camden Street site for over 200 years. These days, the bar attracts local boozers and an energetic student crowd in equal proportions. The bar rambles over several storeys: the interconnected rooms downstairs are replete with heavy beams and a dark, medieval atmosphere. There's a restaurant upstairs.

Eat, Drink, Shop

Come to **Dakota** for cocktails and a wide range of beers.

Brazen Head

20 Bridge Street Lower (679 5186). Bus 21, 21A.
Open 10.30am-12.30am daily. **Credit** AmEx, DC,
MC, V. **Map** p312 F5.
The haunt of foreign students who come to Dublin
to learn English, as well as almost everyone else who
visits the city and must – just must – have a pint in
what is reputedly the oldest bar in town.

Bruxelles

*7-8 Harry Street, off Grafton Street (677 5362).
All cross-city buses.* **Open** 10.30am-1.30am Mon-Wed,
Sun; 10.30am-2.30am Thur-Sat. **No credit cards.**
Map p313 H5.
Situated just off Grafton Street, the Bruxelles
delights in extremely loud rock music. It's a raucous
place, cheerful and full of character. If your
eardrums can't stand it, then head for the basement
bar, which is a little quieter. *See also p191.*

Chocolate Bar

*Hatch Street Upper, off Harcourt Street (478 0166).
Bus 15A, 15B, 15C, 20, 86.* **Open** 5-11.30pm Mon-
Thur; 5pm-1am Fri; 6pm-1am Sat; 6-11.30pm Sun.
Credit DC, MC, V. **Map** p309.
The Choc is impossibly trendy: a vivid Gothic fantasy in twisted metal, it boasts the weirdest loos in
the city. The high balcony seating overlooks the
main action of the bar, which opens at 5pm (6pm at
weekends). The cocktails, incidentally, are great. *See
also p200* **Bored of the black stuff?**

Dakota

*9 South William Street (672 7696). All cross-city
buses.* **Open** 3pm-midnight Mon-Thur, Sun; 3pm-3am
Fri, Sat. **Credit** AmEx, DC, MC, V. **Map** p313 H5.
A tastefully converted fabric warehouse that tends
to get very packed, particularly at weekends, Dakota
aims to attract a professionals in the 25-30 age
group. A combination of good floor service, a wide
range of cocktails and one of the best selections of

bottled beers in Dublin means that if you are lucky
enough to get one of the huge leatherette armchairs,
you'll probably still be sitting in it at closing time.
See also p200 **Bored of the black stuff?**

Davy Byrne's

21 Duke Street (677 5217). All cross-city buses.
Open 10am-11.30pm Mon-Wed; 10am-12.30am
Thur-Sat; noon-11pm Sun. **Credit** AmEx, MC, V.
Map p313 H5.
This is the pub where Leopold Bloom partook of a
gorgonzola sandwich and a glass of burgundy in
James Joyce's *Ulysses*. Nowadays, however, Davy
Byrne's has a fairly nondescript interior that is not
in keeping with its past literary connections.
Nevertheless – and partly thanks to its location off
Grafton Street – the bar attracts a pretty swish
crowd, a mix of locals who haven't read Joyce's
unique slice of Dublin life and tourists who've
devoured the book several times over and are only
too keen to discuss it.

Dawson Lounge

25 Dawson Street (677 5909). All cross-city buses.
Open noon-11.30pm Mon-Thur, Sat; noon-12.30am
Fri. **Credit** AmEx, DC, MC, V. **Map** p313 H6.
A tiny downstairs bar at the bottom of a corkscrew
staircase, the Dawson Lounge markets itself as the
'smallest bar in Dublin'. Unsurprisingly, it's cosy in
winter and, well, cosy in summer, though it's also
always, somehow, curiously surreal.

The Dockers'

*5 Sir John Rogerson's Quay (677 1692). Tara Street
DART.* **Open** 10am-11.30pm Mon-Wed; 10am-
12.30am Thur-Sat; noon-11pm Sun. **Credit** MC, V.
Map p314 K4.
U2 have made this riverside pub famous by hang-
ing out here when they're recording in the nearby
Windmill Lane recording studios. Even without the
musical legends, it's still a neat wee pub.

Doheny & Nesbitt
5 Baggot Street Lower (676 2945). Bus 10, 11, 11A.
Open 10.30am-11pm Mon-Wed; 10.30am-12.30am
Thur-Sat; 12.30-11pm Sun. **Credit** AmEx, DC, MC,
V. **Map** p313 J6.
At weekends, this glorious old pub is packed to the
gills with lawyers, all of them getting squiffy and
quoting Archbold, Blackstone and the hottest law
library gossip at each other. However, Nesbitt's may
actually be best during the week for a contemplative
sup in the company of the sage barmen.

Doyle's of College Street
9 College Street (671 0616). All cross-city buses.
Open noon-1am Mon-Thur; noon-2.30am Fri, Sat;
4pm-1am Sun. **Credit** MC, V. **Map** p313 H4.
There is usually plenty of room in Doyle's. Situated
opposite Trinity College, it's popular with students
and (for no obvious reason) Dublin's stagecrew
community. The latter will regale you with tall tales
of stars that they have known. A heavy-drinking
atmosphere prevails.

The Duke
9 Duke Street (679 9553). All cross-city buses. **Open**
11.30am-11.30pm Mon-Wed; 11.30pm-12.30am Thur-
Sat; noon-11pm Sun. **Credit** MC, V. **Map** p313 H5.
Stalled academics, minor novelists and archetypal
Dublin characters, all wearing tweed jackets and
holding an appropriate disdain for Life, pile in here
from noon on a daily basis. Indifferently refurbished
a few years ago, it's a less than characterful establishment, but the crowd is both cheerful and mellow.

Farringdon's
*27-29 East Essex Street, Temple Bar (671 5135/679
8372). All cross-city buses.* **Open** 11am-11.30pm
Mon-Wed; 11am-12.30am Thur-Sat; 11am-11pm Sun.
Credit MC, V. **Map** p75.
While locals still remember the former Norseman
with fondness, the pub's location in Temple Bar
means it's now almost permanently stuffed with
wide-eyed tourists seeking the authentic pub experience. Having said that, it remains one of the better
pubs in Dublin's much-maligned 'cultural quarter'.

Foggy Dew
*1 Upper Fownes Street, Temple Bar (677 9328).
All cross-city buses.* **Open** noon-11.30pm Mon, Tue;
noon-12.30am Wed; noon-1am Thur; noon-2am Fri,
Sat; 1-11pm Sun. **No credit cards. Map** p75.
Once a firm favourite of teenagers trying to pass
themselves off as 18, the Foggy was one of the first
central pubs to undergo the ubiquitous pine and
brass revamp. It now attracts a mixture of old punk
types and workers from nearby offices. Good for a
late drink, accompanied by loud rock music and age-
ing rockers (*see p192*).

The Front Lounge
*33-34 Parliament Street, Temple Bar (670 4112).
All cross-city buses.* **Open** noon-11.30pm Mon, Wed,
Sun; noon-midnight Tue; noon-1.30am Thur, Fri;
noon-12.30am Sat. **Credit** MC, V. **Map** p75.

The best Pubs & bars

For a good pint of Guinness
Mulligan's (*see p135*) still unofficially
serves the best pint in the city, although
there's stiff competition from the **Gravity
Bar** in the Guinness Storehouse (*see
p81*). The snugs at **Ryan's** (*see p138*)
and the **Stag's Head** (*see p138*) are
both great places to savour the black
stuff in peace.

For getting into furious debates
The emphasis remains on argumentative
but good-humoured conversation at the no-
nonsense **Palace** (*see p138*), boisterous
Grogan's Castle Lounge (*see p134*), and
the theatrical **Flowing Tide** (*see p140*).

For hanging out
with the cool crowd
Hogan's is home to a fair share of Dublin
students, hipsters and beautiful people
(*see p134*). You'll also find plenty of
eligible candidates at the **Life Café-Bar**
(*see p140*). Oh, and there's a mirrored
ceiling, too. The **Odeon Bar's** (*see p140*)
understated cool attracts the more
discriminate of Dublin's trendoids.

For listening to trad music
The **Cobblestone** (*see p139*) is a lively,
good-humoured pub with free sessions
every night. **O'Donoghue's** (*see p137*) is
a bit of a tourist trap but still a safe bet,
or there's **O'Shea's Merchant** (*see p137*),
one of the few places in Dublin where you
can still see traditional Irish dancing.

For seeing & being seen
Models, magazine editors and It-girls
congregate in the **Morrison Hotel Bar** (*see
p140*). Mobile phones, designer eyewear
and gourmet coffees are the lowest
common denominator at the **Bailey** (*see
p131*), while impressive glass frontage
provides ample exposure for the lively
shenanigans at **Viva** (*see p139*).

For a little piece of history
The **Long Hall** (*see p134*), with its
cluttered ephemera, remains charmingly
unaffected by the vagaries of changing
bar fashions. Also don't miss Brendan
Behan's favourite, **McDaid's** (*see p135*)
and the magnificent carved bar at the
International Bar (*see p134*).

Also known as the Back Lounge, depending on which entrance you use, this is the quintessential new Dub pub. Couches and chaises longues, plaster casts, fountains and spot-lighting make the Front Lounge about as slick as they get, which may explain why the Chardonnay crowd, who pack the place out, scrutinise each new arrival so carefully.

Ginger Man

40 Fenian Street (676 6388). All cross-city buses. **Open** 11am-12.30am Mon-Thur, Sun; 11am-1.30am Fri, Sat. **Credit** MC, V. **Map** p314 K5.
This small, old-fashioned pub is only just around the corner from Merrion Square, and so is great for a tasty lunch and a pint or nine after a jaunt around the museums. Regular pub quizzes are a nice touch, and the relaxed atmosphere is even better.

The Globe

11 South Great George's Street (671 1220). Bus 12, 16, 16A, 55. **Open** noon-11.30pm Mon-Thur, Sun; noon-midnight Fri, Sat. **Credit** AmEx, DC, MC, V. **Map** p313 G5.
A fashionable, dimly lit pub in the middle of South Great George's Street, the Globe was one of the first of the new breed of Dublin pubs. The lunches are excellent, and there's also a good line in Sunday afternoon jazz (ring for details). By night, the Globe becomes the chill-out room for Ri Ra (*see p201*).

Grogan's Castle Lounge

15 South William Street (677 9320). All cross-city buses. **Open** 10.30am-11.30pm Mon-Wed; 10am-12.30am Thur, Fri, Sat; 10.30am-10.30pm Sun. **No credit cards**. **Map** p313 H5.
A former haunt of Flann O'Brien, Grogan's is a traditional pub, unashamed in its eccentricity – and all the more attractive for it. Drawing a diverse range of punters, including artists, writers and a selection of general chancers, the atmosphere is as chaotic as the artwork that lines the walls. *See also p136* **Solitary pint**.

Hogan's

35 South Great George's Street (677 5904). Bus 12, 16, 16A, 55. **Open** 1-11.30pm Mon-Wed; 1pm-12.30am Thur; 1pm-2.30am Fri, Sat; 3-11.30pm Sun. **No credit cards**. **Map** p313 G5.
Hogan's was one of the first superpubs in the city, and its open-plan design, with wooden floors and huge windows, attracts a generally young crowd, who spend their evenings eyeing each other up with casual suspicion. It's popular as a serious clubbers' pre-club venue, where art students mix with hair-dressers and compete to see who has the baggiest pants. The soundtrack is progressive house, soul and jazz fusion, and while the atmosphere is often predictable, it's rarely dull.

Horseshoe Bar

Shelbourne Hotel, St Stephen's Green (676 6471). All cross-city buses. **Open** *Winter* 11am-11pm Mon-Sat. *Summer* 11am-11.30pm Mon-Sat. **Credit** AmEx, DC, MC, V. **Map** p313 H6.

If you want to see how the Irish government really operates, then forget Leinster House: this is really where it all happens. Affairs of state can get pretty wild late on a weekend evening, when the executive, legislative and judicial arms get a little woozy. An essential and amusing slice of Dublin life.

International Bar

23 Wicklow Street (677 9250). All cross-city buses. **Open** 11am-11.30pm Mon-Wed; 11am-12.30am Thur-Sat; 11am-11pm Sun. **No credit cards**. **Map** p313 H5.
International by name but very much local by nature, this long-established pub can be a little intimidating at first: the long bar and narrow seating area offer few places to hide from prying eyes. Don't be put off, though, this exuberant, wood-suffused temple with superb natural lighting, is friendly and unpretentious, and the atmosphere's as good as you'll get. Head upstairs for live music (*see p193*) or down to the basement for comedy (*see p213*).

JJ Smyths

12 Aungier Street (475 2565). Bus 16, 16A, 19, 19A, 83. **Open** 10.30am-11.30pm Mon-Wed; 10.30am-12.30am Thur-Sat; 10.30am-11pm Sun. **No credit cards**. **Map** p313 G6.
Downstairs it's an old-fashioned locals' bar; upstairs there are regular quality jazz sessions (*see p193*).

Kehoe's

9 South Anne Street (677 8312). All cross-city buses. **Open** 10.30am-11.30pm Mon-Wed, Thur; 10.30am-12.30am Fri, Sat; noon-11pm Sun. **Credit** MC, V. **Map** p313 H5.
Many drinkers' fave Dub pub, Kehoe's offers grand old snugs but difficult-to-get-to loos. John Kehoe himself used to live upstairs, but since he died you can drink in his living room from 4.30pm daily. It hasn't been changed in any way since his death. Try not to think about it. *See also p136* **Solitary pint** and *p200* **Bored of the black stuff?**

Long Hall

51 South Great George's Street (475 1590). All cross-city buses. **Open** 11am-11.30pm Mon-Wed; 11am-12.30am Thur; noon-12.30am Fri; 10.30am-12.30am Sat; 2-11pm Sun. **No credit cards**. **Map** p313 G5.
If there is a bar in heaven, it will look something like the Long Hall. One of the most exuberant pieces of design in town, the Long Hall is a cathedral of booze. Sacrifice your brain cells at this shrine without guilt, and the evening will just waste away.

Long Stone

10 Townsend Street (671 8102). All cross-city buses. **Open** noon-11.30pm Mon-Wed; noon-12.30am Thur, Fri; 4pm-12.30am Sat; 4-11pm Sun. **Credit** Amex, MC, V. **Map** p313 H/J4.
The Long Stone is a fairly run-of-the-mill establishment next door to Mulligan's that's very handy for a drink after a visit to the Screen on d'Olier Street (*see p174*). It gets madly crowded, but the craic's good.

Long Hall: a shrine to booze. *See p134.*

Lord Edward

23 Christchurch Place (454 2420). All cross-city buses. **Open** 11am-11.30pm Mon-Wed; 11am-12.30am Thur-Sat, 11am-11pm Sun. **Credit** AmEx, MC, V. **Map** p312 F5.
The circular bar downstairs is a typical old-fashioned boozer serving good Guinness, but the cosy little room upstairs is a well-kept secret. If local office-workers aren't having a night out, it can be virtually empty at peak times. There is a decent seafood restaurant on the top floor, too (*see p111*). A solid choice.

McDaid's

3 Harry Street, off Grafton Street (679 4395). All cross-city buses. **Open** 10.30am-11.30pm Mon-Wed; 10.30am-12.30am Thur-Sat; 12.30pm-11pm Sun. **No credit cards. Map** p313 H5.
Popularly known as the Brendan Behan, McDaid's is a major place of pilgrimage for tourists who want to discover the real literary Dublin and to ask everyone intelligently daft questions about it. The decor is strictly unreconstructed Gothic. *See also p200* **Bored of the black stuff?**

Messrs Maguire

1-2 Burgh Quay (670 5777). All cross-city buses. **Open** 10.30am-1.30am daily. **Credit** AmEx, MC, V. **Map** p313 H4.
One of the city's few pubs to boast a micro-brewery, Maguire's is a slightly disorientating mix of old and new Dublin. The bookshelves, wooden staircases and nooks and crannies suggest an intimate atmosphere, but the crowd is generally young and boisterous.

Modern Green Bar

31 Wexford Street (478 0583). Bus 19, 19A, 83. **Open** noon-11.30pm Mon-Wed, Sun; noon-12.30am Thur-Sat. **Credit** MC, V. **Map** p313 G6.
A New York-inspired watering hole, the Modern Green Bar pulls the imitation off effortlessly, with intentionally scruffy, funky urban decor. The colour scheme is green, of course, with intimate booths, a long bar, subtle lighting and some fine photographs of Dublin. MGB draws a slightly older crowd than the student favourite Club Mono next door (*see p197*). Food is served from noon to 8pm, and DJs spin classy sounds most nights of the week.

Molloys

13 High Street (677 3207). Bus 123. **Open** 11am-11.30pm Mon-Wed; 11am-2.30am Thur-Sun. **Credit** AmEx, MC, V. **Map** p312 F5.
Unremarkable decor and occasionally haphazard service notwithstanding, Molloys is an admirably innovative and friendly pub. Running over three small floors, the place hosts lesbian nights, singer-songwriter competitions and a range of DJ sets of unpredictable quality. Probably not worth travelling too far out of your way for, but Molloys' heart is in the right place.

Mother Redcap's Tavern

40-48 Back Lane (453 8306). Bus 50, 78A. **Open** 5-11.30pm Mon-Thur; 5pm-12.30am Fri, Sat; 5-11pm Sun. **No credit cards. Map** p312 F5.
Since the demise of the adjoining market, Mother Redcap's has been quieter than of yore, and there's some talk of it closing altogether. Despite its obvious attraction for depressed-looking locals, the large wooden interior is rarely filled to capacity. There are popular sing-along sessions and free live music that ranges from good to atrocious (*see p193*).

Mulligan's

8 Poolbeg Street (677 5582). Tara Street DART. **Open** 10.30am-11.30pm Mon-Wed; 10.30am-12.30am Thur-Sat; 12.30-11pm Sun. **Credit** V. **Map** p313 J4.
A legendary pint of Guinness – perhaps the most celebrated and discussed in the entire town – is served at Mulligan's by blokes who have seen it all and heard it all before. The bar attracts a curious crowd who boast their authentic Dubliner status by talking loudly and pretending to ignore you. Don't miss either the pints or the regulars.

Neary's

1 Chatham Street (677 8596). All cross-city buses. **Open** 10.30am-11.30pm Mon-Thur; 10.30am-12.30am Fri, Sat; 12.30pm-11pm Sun. **No credit cards. Map** p313 H5.
With a location right at the back door of the Gaiety Theatre, Neary's is inevitably a slightly theatrical boozer. However, late at night – and, especially, on rugby weekends – the drama affects everyone. Though Neary's gets crowded late in the evening, the little lounge to the left is charming and quieter. Just a step away from Grafton Street, it's perfect for a Saturday afternoon pint.

Eat, Drink, Shop

Ocean Bar

The Millennium Tower, Charlotte's Quay Dock, off Ringsend Road (668 8862). Grand Canal Dock DART. **Open** noon-12.30am Mon-Thur; noon-1.30am Fri, Sat; 12.30pm-12.30am Sun. **Credit** AmEx, DC, MC, V. **Map** p314 L5.

This new upmarket dockside establishment claims to have Dublin's only waterfront public licence. The patios overlooking the canal basin are ideal for drinking if there is even the smallest hint of sunshine, and the bistro serves decent food until 10pm. It seems to be a favoured hangout for Dublin's IT entrepreneurs, for whom the sound of gently lapping waves is probably a welcome distraction from the bursting dotcom bubble. The Ocean Bar must be as pleasant a place as any other to sit out a recession.

Octagon Bar

Clarence Hotel, 6-8 Wellington Quay, Temple Bar (670 9000). All cross-city buses. **Open** 11am-11pm Mon-Sat; 12.30-10.30pm Sun. **Credit** AmEx, MC, V. **Map** p75.

The Octagon in the Clarence Hotel (*see p39*) is delightful, with a central bar surrounded by seating. The cocktails, especially the dry Martinis, are good, the decor is stylishly understated, the staff are exemplary and the clientele is made up of megastars, mates of U2 and supermodels. Don't let this last fact put you off.

Odeon

57 Harcourt Street (478 2088). Bus 14, 15, 16. **Open** noon-1am Mon-Fri; 8pm-3am Sat; 1pm-midnight Sun. **Credit** AmEx, MC, V. **Map** p313 G7.

Solitary pint

There's something indescribably charming about having a drink on your own. It's not a pursuit that suits everybody; it requires a curious synergy of bravado, indifference and, sometimes, even a modicum of despair for the human race. The experience can be a rare pleasure, however; offering a stolen opportunity to ruminate on one's status in the greater scheme of things, scowl at the *Irish Times* crossword for hours on end, or maybe, just maybe, make some new friends. There's nothing wrong with going out for a drink with yourself sometimes. There's nothing wrong with it at all. Only it pays to be prepared.

There are few cities that are good to explore alone and Dublin is no exception. If you're visiting solo, you may find it difficult to locate places where you can hang out without feeling shamefully self-conscious. Dubliners – and particularly the predominant group of twentysomethings – prefer to socialise in large numbers, so a lone customer at a bar stool is often assumed to be a lech, a lush, an alcoholic or a day-care patient. In fact, unless you're either very good-looking or have some prominent physical deformity, it's unlikely that anyone is going to pay the slightest heed to you whatsoever. It's not that Dubliners are an unfriendly bunch – quite the opposite in fact – it's just that they're rather preoccupied with themselves at the moment, and who can blame them?

So, here is a foolproof way to risk an enjoyable evening with a solitary pint. As in any urban village, walking into a Dub pub without knowing anything about its character is a risky proposition, so do your research first. Having pored over our listings, find a

nice, dark, traditional pub with no inflated opinion of itself; and find one that suits your temperament. **Grogan's Castle Lounge** (*pictured; see p134*) for example, has a certain, almost riotous, eccentricity to it, or for those blessed with a glummer, more introspective disposition, there's **Kehoe's** (*see p134*) or the **Palace** (*see p138*). Alternatively, if you fancy yourself as a bit of an international jetsetter, you'll enjoy the New York cool of the **Dice Bar** (*see p140*) or the cavernous, pseudo-Russian ambience of **Pravda** (*see p140*). Wherever you choose, you should be showered, dressed (semi-casual, no trainers; unless you're female, in which case, it doesn't matter), and at the bar by 7pm. Seven is the ambiguous hour, when a casual pint before, perhaps, 'meeting friends' or 'returning home' appears entirely reasonable. If you're lucky, there may even be others like you – 'just out for a quiet one'.

Have your pint in blissful anonymity. Do the crossword. Engage in a healthy debate with the self. You've got a decent hour here, before the 'real pub people' arrive and if you're bored by 8pm you can leave without shame. If you want to go the whole hog and actually speak to somebody, though, proceed with caution. There are many ways of meeting Dubliners, but introducing yourself is not generally considered to be one of them. It is not advisable to join a table unless you're first invited to do so, nor should you buy drinks for strangers. Instead exchange salutations at the bar in the short interval between ordering and receiving a drink (anything between three and 15 minutes). Throw yourself in there. Say something

A large and very stylish art deco bar housed in the old Harcourt Street Station. There aren't too many seats here, but no one really cares: people come in to see and be seen. Odeon is an especially pleasant place to visit on a Sunday, when you can deliciously fritter the whole afternoon away with free newspapers and tasty food.

O'Donoghue's

15 Merrion Row (660 7194/lounge 676 2807). All cross-city buses. **Open** 10.30am-11.30pm Mon-Wed; 10.30am-12.30am Thur-Sat; 12.30pm-11pm Sun. **Credit** AmEx, MC, V. **Map** p313 J6.

Good impromptu music sessions can be enjoyed in this smoky old pub, famous as the haunt of musical legends the Dubliners. In fact, O'Donoghue's draws in actual Dubliners, visitors and denizens, young

The International. *See p134.*

and old. Its fame as a guidebook staple has not made the staff even a bit self-conscious: they just get on with the business of pulling pints.

Oliver St John Gogarty

58-59 Fleet Street, Temple Bar (671 1822). All cross-city buses. **Open** *Bar* 10.30am-2am daily. *Lounge* 3pm-3am daily. **Credit** AmEx, MC, V. **Map** p75.

Popular with tourists and offering good free trad music throughout the day, Oliver SinGin's tends to get very full during the evening but is nonetheless a good place for a night on the town. The traditional Irish menu contains dishes rarely dreamed of in your average Irish kitchen, and the prices are distinctly modern Irish.

O'Neill's

37 Pearse Street (677 5213). Pearse DART **Open** noon-11.30pm Mon-Wed; noon-12.30am Thur-Sat. **Credit** AmEx, MC, V. **Map** p313 J5.

Lots of besuited folk drink here, but don't be put off: O'Neill's is, in fact, a relaxed and comfortable pub with a gratifying number of seats. The great big fires are wonderful in winter.

O'Neill's

2 Suffolk Street (679 3671). All cross-city buses. **Open** 10.30am-11.30pm Mon-Wed; 10.30am-12.30am Thur-Sat; 10.30am-11pm Sun. **Credit** AmEx, MC, V. **Map** p313 H5.

A veritable warren of a pub: O'Neill's has recently expanded and now rambles over many different levels. The main bars are complemented by lots of little snugs and lounges tucked away in the corners. Very comfortable and very central.

O'Shea's Merchant

12 Bridge Street Lower (679 3797). Bus 21, 21A. **Open** 10.30am-midnight Mon-Wed, Sun; 10.30am-2.30am Thur-Sat. **Credit** AmEx, MC, V. **Map** p312 F5.

O'Shea's is very much a country pub set in the city and it tends to get very busy when there is a major GAA game on. A centre for set dancing and occasionally austere traditional music (*see p194*), it also serves reasonably priced traditional food until 10pm daily.

devastating. If you can't think of anything clever, something stupid should serve equally well. The key is to attract either attention or curiosity, and after that, it's up to you. Your chances of getting involved in any remotely interesting conversations beyond the immediately cursory are, well, slim, and we can't guarantee you'll end up with dozens of firm friends, but you should get a few Dublin pleasantries, a bit of banter and maybe a tantalising taste of that famous craic that people keep grinding on about.

The **Stag's Head**

The Palace

21 Fleet Street, Temple Bar (bar 677 9290/lounge 679 3037). All cross-city buses. **Open** *Bar* 10.30am-11.30pm Mon-Wed; 10.30am-12.30am Thur-Sat; 12.30-11pm Sun. *Lounge* 5-11.30pm Wed; 5pm-12.30am Thur, Fri; 6.30pm-12.30am Sat. **Credit** MC, V. **Map** p75.

This elegant Victorian bar hit the headlines in January 2001 when a member of English teen pop sensation Five was arrested on the premises for disorderly behaviour. (Apparently he got into an argument about whether or not Five were a better band than Westlife.) The event was particularly newsworthy as the Palace is not usually renowned for such shenanigans; it's a lovely old bar that vaults and swirls with wood and glass and is one of the few premises that has managed to avoid the crassness of the Temple Bar area. Boy-bands, keep out, please. *See also p136* **Solitary pint.**

Peter's Pub

1 Johnston's Place (677 8588). All cross-city buses. **Open** 10.30am-11pm Mon-Wed; 10.30am-midnight Thur-Sat; 10.30am-11pm Sun. **Credit** MC, V. **Map** p313 G5.

At the top of South William Street, Peter's is small, modern and quite charming. If you're shopping in the area, it is perfect for a pint, soup or a basic cheap sandwich, and the tables in the market outside are a welcome addition.

Porterhouse Brewing Company

16-18 Parliament Street, Temple Bar (679 8847). All cross-city buses. **Open** noon-11.30pm Mon-Wed; 10.30am-1am Thur-Sat; 10.30am-11pm Sun. **Credit** MC, V. **Map** p75.

This excellent microbrewery-pub has some of the best brews in the city, among them Wrassler, An Brainblásta, Oyster Stout and Porterhouse Porter.

Created by Belfast man Brendan Dobbin, the beers show a clean pair of heels to conventional, bland brews. It's a nice room, too. *See also p200* **Bored of the black stuff?**

Ryan's

28 Parkgate Street (bar 677 6097/restaurant 671 9352). Bus 23, 25, 26. **Open** *Restaurant* 5-10pm daily. *Bar* 12.30-11.30pm Mon-Wed; 12.30pm-12.30am Thur-Sat; 12.30-11pm Sun. **Credit** AmEx, MC, V. **Map** p311 C3.

Ryan's is a beautiful old bar, with a famous counter that you'll immediately recognise, having seen it a thousand times in photographs and picture postcards. There are some truly wonderful snugs at the back of the pub, and some pretty decent meals upstairs in the restaurant. A well-maintained slice of authentic Dublin Victoriana.

Sheehan's

17 Chatham Street (677 1914). All cross-city buses. **Open** 11am-11.30pm Mon-Wed; 11am-12.30am Thur-Sat; noon-11pm Sun. **Credit** AmEx, MC, V. **Map** p313 H5.

Formerly a pleasingly comfortable, elbow-patchy and much-loved pub, Sheehan's is now a slightly over-designed and quietly self-conscious watering hole. Irrespective of the changes, the bar continues to attract lawyers, writers and a smattering of the creatively funky classes.

Smyth's

10 Haddington Road, Grand Canal (660 6305). Bus 10. **Open** 10.30am-11.30pm Mon-Wed; 10.30am-12.30am Thur-Sat; noon-11pm Sun. **Credit** MC, V. **Map** p314 L7.

Just a stroll from the National Print Museum (*see p72*) on the banks of the Grand Canal, Smyth's is a real neighbourhood pub, with a disarmingly laid-back atmosphere.

Sosumi

64 South Great George's Street (478 1590). All cross-city buses. **Open** 5-11.30pm Mon, Tue; 5pm-2.30am Wed-Fri; 2pm-2.30am Sat; 4pm-1am Sun. **Credit** MC, V. **Map** p313 G5.

Look in through the large plate glass window and you may well witness ugly scenes of boisterous civil servants loosening their collars and trying to cop off with travelling hen parties. The place can seem labyrinthine after you've had a few, but it's a commendably lively spot.

Stag's Head

1 Dame Court, off Dame Street (679 3701). All cross-city buses. **Open** 10.30am-11.30pm Mon-Wed; 10.30am-12.30am Thur-Sat. **No credit cards.** **Map** p75.

A lovely, oaky, smoky pub that is splendid for idling away the afternoon hours or for motoring through the evening hours, and you can eat here too: the Stag's serves some of the best pub food in town. Were it not closed on Sundays, it'd be perfect. *See also p200* **Bored of the black stuff?**

Temple Bar
48 Temple Bar (672 5286). All cross-city buses.
Open 11am-midnight Mon-Wed; 11am-12.30am
Thur-Sat; noon-12.30am Sun. **Credit** MC, V.
Map p75.
Refurbished a few years back to make it resemble
an age-old, authentic Dublin boozer, the Temple Bar
is permanently stuffed to bursting point with
raucous trendies and age-old authentic citizens.
Everything and everyone spills out on to the streets
in the summertime, though there's also a large beer
garden   a rare phenomenon in Dublin – at the
rear of the pub.

Thing Mote
15 Suffolk Street (677 8030). All cross-city buses.
Open 10.30am-11.30pm Mon-Wed, Sun; 10.30am-
12.30am Thur Sat; 3-11pm Sun. **Credit** V.
Map p313 H5.
A little bar at the top of Grafton Street that attracts
tired shoppers, students from Trinity College and
almost every other sort of passer-by. It can get loud
and packed during the evening, but it's a pleasant
spot in which to linger awhile during the afternoon.
The name, in case you were wondering, is an Anglo-
Saxon term for 'meeting place'.

Thomas House
*86 Thomas Street, Liberties (671 6987). Bus 51B,
78A.* **Open** 11am-11.30pm Mon-Wed; 11am-12.30am
Thur-Sat; 11am-11pm Sun. **No credit cards.**.
Map p312 E5.
At the vanguard of Thomas Street's surge for credibility as a night-spot, this small dark pub is gaining
a reputation as a place to see quality leftfield DJs –
the Wednesday dub night in particular has an
unassailable reputation. It is very small but in some
ways that only adds to the cachet. During term time
it does a roaring trade with students from the nearby
art college. Some consider it a dump, of course.

Thomas Read
*1 Parliament Street, Temple Bar (671 7283). All
cross-city buses.* **Open** 11am-11.30pm Mon-Wed;
11am-12.30am Thur; 11am-2.30am Fri, Sat; 11am-
11pm Sun. **Credit** AmEx, MC, V. **Map** p75.
For a Dublin pub, Thomas Read's does one hell of a
good imitation of a Viennese coffee house during the
day. In the evening, though, the focus switches to
the bar and the building is transformed into a lively spot with a wide selection of international brews
(*see p200* **Bored of the black stuff?**). Connected
to the main room is the Oak bar: simple, wooden,
and a relief, perhaps, from all that coffee.

Toner's
*139 Baggot Street Lower (676 3090). Bus 10,
11, 11A.* **Open** 10.30am-12.30am Mon-Sat; 12.30-
11.30pm Sun. **Credit** AmEx, MC, V. **Map** p313 J6.
Toner's is an authentic Dublin pub that has survived
being tarted up over the years: the character that
made it popular to begin with still remains, and the
bar itself is still particularly pleasing. Agreed, by all
and sundry, to be 'a good place for a pint'.

Turk's Head
*27-30 Parliament Street, Temple Bar (679 9701).
All cross-city buses.* **Open** 4.30pm-2am daily.
Credit AmEx, MC, V. **Map** p75.
A stylistically varied bar, to say the least: the whole
effect has been succinctly summarised as 'gaudy
Gaudí'. It's all rather fun, but you may find yourself
feeling rather isolated in the midst of the indiscriminate late-night crowd.

Viva
*52 South William Street (677 0212). All cross-city
buses.* **Open** 11.30am-midnight Mon-Wed; 11.30am-
1.30am Thur; 11.30am-2am Fri, Sat; 4pm-midnight
Sun. **Credit** MC, V. **Map** p313 H5.
This spacious DJ bar and café is spread over three
floors. Downstairs is fiery red and, unfortunately,
gets as hot as hell at times. The middle floor is
brighter thanks to the large front window, while
the top floor is a relaxing airy blue. Comfortable
when not too crowded, Viva does decent food until
7pm and the DJs know their stuff. The crowd is late
20s and older.

Whelan's
25 Wexford Street (478 0766). Bus 55, 61, 62, 83.
Open 10.30am-11.30pm Mon, Tue; 10.30am-1.30am
Wed-Sun. **Credit** AmEx, MC, V. **Map** p313 G6.
While the front bar is pleasantly boisterous and
good-humoured, the main attraction at Whelan's is
its gig venue (*see p195*), admission to which is
gained from an alleyway around the corner. It's
arguably the best place in the city to see live rock,
roots and country. Look out for the rather eerie
sculpture of a bloke nursing his pint at the bar.

Northside

Cobblestone
*77 North King Street, Smithfield (872 1799). **Open***
Bus 25, 26, 37, 39, 67, 67A, 68, 69, 79. **Open**
4-11.30pm Mon-Wed; 4pm-12.30am Thur-Sat;
12.30-11.30pm Sun. **No credit cards. Map** p312 E4.
With posters of yesteryears' folk festivals, a musicians' corner and genuine old school wooden décor,
the Cobblestone is one of the best places to hear living trad music in the city (*see p192*). Don't expect
too many frills but if you want to avoid excessive
Paddywhackery in favour of a more genuine taste
of Dublin, then don't miss it. *See also p200* **Bored
of the black stuff?**

Conways
70 Parnell Street (873 2687). All cross-city buses.
Open 10am-11.30pm Mon-Wed, Sun; 10am-12.30am
Thur-Sat. **No credit cards. Map** p313 G3.
Situated opposite the Rotunda Hospital, this is
where new fathers – including Jimmy Rabbitte Snr
in the film version of *The Snapper* – celebrate their
new responsibilities. Otherwise, there's a curious
mixture of bicycle couriers and teacher-types. A
good place to start a session or for a quiet drink,
but if you are seeking excitement, go elsewhere.

Eat, Drink, Shop

Dice Bar

Queen Street, off Arran Quay, Smithfield (872 8622). All cross-city buses. **Open** 10.30am-11.30pm Mon-Wed; 10.30am-12.30am Thur-Sat; 10.30am-11pm Sun. **Credit** AmEx, MC, V. **Map** p312 E4.

You can't help being suspicious of any establishment that displays the words 'Phat Joint' in red neon outside, but as New York-style bars go, the Dice Bar is a winner. Its no-nonsense decor – almost entirely black – is lit by dozens of church candles, and if you get a seat at the long bar you'll certainly feel like an international superstar. There's an eclectic, quality music policy, too. *See also p200* **Bored of the black stuff?** and *p136* **Solitary pint**.

Dublin Brewing Company

141-146 North King Street, Smithfield (872 8622/ www.dublinbrewing.com). Bus 25, 26, 37, 39, 67, 67A, 68, 69, 79. **Open** 9am-5pm daily. **No credit cards. Map** p312 E3/4.

The best and most energetic of the new generation of microbreweries is situated in newly sexy Smithfield. It's not a bar as such – hence the rather office-esque opening hours – but it is open to visitors, though staff prefer it if you call ahead. The finest natural ingredients go into D'Arcy's Dublin Stout, Beckett's Dublin Beer, Maeve's Crystal Beer and Revolution Red. *See also p200* **Bored of the black stuff?**

Flowing Tide

9 Abbey Street Lower (874 4106). All cross-city buses. **Open** 11.30am-11.30pm Mon-Wed; 11.30am-12.30am Thur-Sat; noon-11pm Sun. **No credit cards. Map** p313 H4.

Forever a haunt of thespians and die-hard locals who refuse to be swayed by the winds of change, the Tide, as it's colloquially known, is a solid, reliable Dublin pub, which can get pretty busy after 11pm as the crowds flock in from the Abbey Theatre across the street. With an impressive collection of theatre posters adorning the walls, it's a great place to soak up the kind of authentic atmosphere that is fast disappearing from the city.

Hughes' Bar

19 Chancery Street, off Church Street (872 6540). All cross-city buses. **Open** 7am-11.30pm Mon-Wed; 7am-12.30am Thur-Sat; 11am-11pm Sun. **No credit cards. Map** p312 F4.

During the day, young men contemplating an imminent spell inside may quaff their last drink in freedom here in the company of pitiful relatives and pitiless lawyers. In the evenings, excellent sessions and fine set-dancing fill the place.

Isaac Butt

Opposite Busárus, Store Street (855 5021). All cross-city buses. **Open** 11am-1am Mon-Thur, Sun; 11am-3am Fri, Sat. **Credit** MC, V. **Map** p313 J3.

A range of techno club nights made this place popular among student northsiders and backpackers from the nearby hostels, but the emphasis now

seems to be shifting to live indie music (*see p193*). The bar is as good a place as any to get hammered and has a big screen for football matches. Many of the punters seem to be looking for a quick snog.

Jack Nealons

165 Capel Street (872 3247). All cross-city buses. **Open** noon-11.30pm Mon-Wed; noon-12.30am Thur-Sat; 12.30-11pm Sun. **Credit** AmEx, MC, V. **Map** p313 G4.

Popular with Northsiders preparing to go clubbing, Nealons is stylish but relaxed. Look out for the juggling barmen and enjoy freshly squeezed juices with your tipple. Nealons is on the pricey side, but the happily braying punters don't seem to object.

JB Smith's

10 Jervis Street (872 4031). All cross-city buses. **Open** 11.30am-11.30pm Mon-Wed; 11.30am-midnight Thur-Sun. **Credit** MC, V. **Map** p313 G4.

An attractive bar close to the Jervis Centre, with lots of fine wood fittings, crackling fires and mosaics on the walls. A spiral staircase links the three floors, and there's live music on Sunday.

Life Café-Bar

Irish Life Centre, Abbey Street Lower (878 1032). All cross-city buses. **Open** noon-11.30pm Mon-Wed; noon-12.30am Thur; noon-1.30am Fri; noon-2am Sat; 5-11pm Sun. **Credit** AmEx, MC, V. **Map** p313 H4.

A very lovely bar: trendy and expensive, with a fine range of beers and some excellent coffees. The design is cool and very stylish, with plenty of sofas and polished wood. Life is close to Busáras and Connolly Station, so it's a good place for tired travellers to stop and refuel.

Morrison Hotel Bar

Lower Ormond Quay (887 2400). All cross-city buses. **Open** 10.30am-11.30pm Mon-Wed, Sun; 10.30am-12.30am Thur-Sat. **Credit** AmEx, MC, V. **Map** p75.

With an interior designed by fashion guru John Rocha, the Morrison's bar is stylish and expensive, with plenty of comfy black couches and windows looking out on to the Liffey. Dress to impress here, and arrive early.

Pravda

35 Liffey Street Lower (874 0076). All cross-city buses. **Open** noon-11.30pm Mon-Wed; noon-12.30am Thur; noon-2.30am Fri, Sat; 4-11pm Sun. **Credit** AmEx, MC, V. **Map** p313 G4.

Cyrillic script stencilled on the walls doth not an authentic Russian bar make, but Pravda has pulled off the pseudo-Russian thing pretty well. The building is large and rambling, the punters are relaxed and the atmosphere is chilled during the day and vibrant at night. *See also p200* **Bored of the black stuff?** and *p136* **Solitary pint**.

Slattery's

29 Capel Street (872 7971). All cross-city buses. **Open** 11am-11.30pm Mon-Wed; 11am-12.30am Thur; 11am-2am Fri, Sat; 11am-11pm Sun. **No credit cards. Map** p313 G4.

Times don't change at the **Flowing Tide**. *See p140*

Slattery's used to be a dingy kind of place where punters would grudgingly shell out a few quid to see new rock or trad music. Now completely refurbished, it resembles most other Dublin pubs: it's spacious, spotless, a little bland perhaps, and there's not a band in sight. Its rather unsalubrious location still virtually guarantees a seat on a Friday night, however.

Voodoo Lounge
39 Arran Quay, Smithfield (873 6013). All cross-city buses. **Open** 11am-12.30am Mon-Wed; 11am 2am Thur-Sat; noon 1am Sun. **Credit** MC, V. **Map** p312 E4.
Part-owned by Huey from the Fun Lovin' Criminals, Voodoo is a huge, flashy bar-club, with a long bar and candlelit tables nicely complemented by eerie murals on supernatural themes. The music policy seems to differ from night to night, but there's an emphasis on hip hop, and the crowd are an attractively mixed bunch. *See also p200* **Bored of the black stuff?**

Zanzibar
36 Ormond Quay Lower (878 7212). All cross-city buses. **Open** 5pm-3am Mon-Wed; 4pm-3am Thur-Sat; 4pm-2am Sun. **Credit** AmEx, MC, V. **Map** p313 G4.
A vast bar on the north quays, Zanzibar is a mite over the top. An African theme has been grimly pursued, with palm trees in every direction and a general ornate lavishness dominating proceedings. It might get on your nerves after a while, as might the slightly snotty staff. As an essay in weirdness, however, it's worth checking out.

Southern suburbs

Johnny Fox's
Glencullen, Co Dublin (295 5647/www.johnniefoxs com). Bus 44B. **Open** 10.30am-11.30pm Mon Sat; 11am-11.30pm Sun. **Credit** AmEx, DC, MC, V.
Something of an Irish institution and claiming to be the 'highest pub in the country', Johnny Fox's is perched in the hills above the city. Maybe it's delightful for your American cousins, maybe it's the epitome of tack. Either way, it's a very busy pub with 'traditional' music, dancing and all that hoopla every evening. One of the main draws is the excellent seafood menu (main courses €12-€43). On Sundays, the pub – and the car parks – are packed; instead, come during the week and relish the good view and the fresh air.

Northern suburbs

Kavanagh's
1 Prospect Square, Glasnevin (no phone). Bus 13. **Open** 11am-11.30pm Mon-Wed; 11am-12.30am Thur-Sat; 11am-11pm Sun. **No credit cards.**
Out at Glasnevin cemetery, this famous boozer – which is also known as the Gravediggers' – hasn't changed a jot in the century and a half that it's been trading. After spending some time poking around the gravestones in the cemetery, you might welcome the mellow atmosphere.

Eat, Drink, Shop

*For the best in style, Marks & Spencer is streets ahead.
With our 3 Dublin stores in Mary Street, Grafton Street &
Liffey Valley and our Cork store in Patrick Street, we've even
more than ever to offer you. The word is on the street –
Marks & Spencer has it all.*

MARKS & SPENCER

Shops & Services

Shop for everything from designer fashion and Irish crafts to organic foodstuffs and second-hand vinyl – without ever hopping on a bus.

Dublin may not yet have made an impression on the world as the shopping capital of Europe – after all, you don't generally see Naomi, Kate or Claudia buying off the rack in Temple Bar like you might in Paris or Milan – but the city does have a wide range of department stores, boutiques, chain stores and craft shops. For British tourists, many of the shops will be familiar from their English high-street equivalents, but if you're prepared to push your way through the inevitable Saturday crowds, you'll also find some more unusual stores.

As a rough idea of layout, the **Grafton Street** area is home to department stores, boutiques and chain stores, while **Temple Bar** has some of the city's hippest shops, among them record shops and vintage clothes outlets. On the northside, **O'Connell Street** is the site of two Dublin institutions: Eason's and Clery's. You'll find more department stores on **Henry Street**.

BARGAIN HUNTING

If you're a hardened bargain hunter and want to get away from the familiarity of the high street, you'll have to do a bit of exploring. On the southside, Camden, Francis and Thomas Streets offer a wide range of reasonable clobber without the designer labels or designer prices, while on the northside, Liffey Street is good for cheap clothes and household goods. Also north of the river, Capel Street is probably the best spot for hardware, survival gear and naff furniture and North Earl Street is excellent for cheap luggage. Along the river, on Crampton Quay and Aston Quay, you'll find cheap books, music, videos and electrical goods in abundance, alongside comic book stores and sporting goods.

OTHER INFORMATION

Shops are generally open from 9am to 6pm Monday to Saturday, and in the afternoon on Sunday. Almost all stores also stay open for late-night shopping on Thursday until 8 or 9pm. Sales take place in different shops throughout the year, although most shops can be relied on to offer post-Christmas and early summer reductions. Mastercard and Visa credit cards are widely accepted, although AmEx and Diners Club cards may only be accepted in major stores. Sales tax (VAT) is 20 per cent; visitors from outside the EU can get a refund at the airport.

One-stop shopping

Department stores

Reliable, familiar British stores include **Debenham's** (Jervis Centre, Jervis Street, Northside; 878 1222/www.debenhams.com), and **Marks & Spencer** (15-20 Grafton Street, Southside; 679 7855 and Mary Street, Northside; 872 8833/www.marksandspencer.com).

Arnotts

12 Henry Street, Northside (872 1111/www. arnotts.ie). All cross-city buses. **Open** 9am-6.30pm Mon-Wed, Fri, Sat; 9.30am-9pm Thur; noon-6pm Sun. **Credit** AmEx, DC, MC, V. **Map** p313 G/H4.
Although traditionally known as the store where your mother took you to buy your new school uniform, recent years have seen a smarter image being imposed on one of Dublin's oldest stores. Arnott's holds a vast range of goods, but specialises in ladies' and gents' clothing.

Stylish **Brown Thomas**. *See p144.*

Clery's: a northside landmark.

Brown Thomas
88-95 Grafton Street, Southside (605 6666). All cross-city buses. **Open** 9am-6pm Mon-Wed, Fri, Sat; 9am-8pm Thur; noon-6pm Sun. **Credit** AmEx, DC, MC, V. **Map** p313 H5.

Got your credit card with you? Good; you'll need it. Plush surroundings and expert staff all lend the shop a well-heeled atmosphere, suited to the high-class goods on sale. Following a major redesign a few years ago, the store now oozes a truly cosmopolitan and sophisticated air, and stocks all the big-name designers. Watch out for the sales assistants determined to spray you from head to foot with CK1. Brown Thomas's December window displays are an integral part of the Dublin Christmas shopping experience.

Clery & Co
18-27 Lower O'Connell Street, Northside (878 6000/ www.clerys.com). All cross-city buses. **Open** 9am-6.30pm Mon-Wed; 9am-9pm Thur; 9am-8pm Fri; 9am-6pm Sat. **Credit** AmEx, DC, MC, V. **Map** p313 H4.

The oldest, most famous and generally most reliable of Dublin's department stores, Clery's takes pride of place in the centre of O'Connell Street and its clock has, for decades, been a popular meeting place for dates, so watch out for the groups of nervous looking young men standing outside with their hands in their pockets. It stocks everything from clothes to computers, operates over many floors and is generally reasonably priced with lots of decent bargains. There's a good selection of Irish gifts for our American cousins who take particular pleasure in fridge magnets and tea towels with pictures of leprechauns on them.

Dunnes Stores
Henry Street, Southside (671 4629/www.dunnes stores.ie). All cross-city buses. **Open** 9am-6pm Mon-Wed, Fri, Sat; 9am-9pm Thur; 2-6pm Sun. **Credit** MC, V. **Map** p313 G/H4.

Another long-established family-run store, Dunnes is as well known for the scandals of its past as it is for its stock. It's mostly gents' and ladies' casual-wear here, though it also caters for children and babies. The shops may not have a designer reputation, but they're actually pretty good for cheap and cheerful summer fare – clothes that will see you quite comfortably through a season without cluttering up your wardrobe for years to come. Some of the larger stores also sell groceries.
Branches: throughout the city.

Guiney & Co
79 Talbot Street, Northside (878 8835). All cross-city buses. **Open** 9am-6.30pm Mon-Wed, Fri, Sat; 9am-7pm Thur. **Credit** MC, V. **Map** p313 H3.

The fashionable male or trendsetting female will not necessarily want to be caught dead in Michael Guiney's; it's the kind of shop that stocks 'em high and sells 'em cheap. To your left – a three piece suit. To your right – hundreds of pairs of boxer shorts. In front of you – new kettles. Behind you – sweeping brushes. Bring a five pound note and go crazy.

Roches Stores
54 Henry Street, Northside (873 0044). All cross-city buses. **Open** 9am-6pm Mon-Wed, Fri, Sat; 9am-9pm Thur. **Credit** MC, V. **Map** p313 G/H4.

A popular department store with an emphasis on home accessories and furnishings, along with the standard clothing departments. It's generally well air-conditioned, and prices are decent.

Shopping centres

The completion of the **Liffey Valley Centre** in Lucan to the west of Dublin (Clondalkin, Southern suburbs; 623 3300) is likely to provide stiff competition for the city centre malls. Already boasting some big-name stores and smaller fashion shops, it will soon become a much larger cinema and retail complex, with parking for over 3,000 visitors.

Also outside the city centre, try **Blackrock Shopping Centre** (Frascati Road, Blackrock, Dublin Bay; 283 1660), a nicely designed shopping mall with some decent restaurants and coffeeshops, and **The Square Towncentre** (Tallaght, Southern suburbs; 414 1404). This large centre may be out of the way, but it has loads of reasonably priced shops, and the added bonus of a UCI multiplex cinema (*see p175*). The **Dún Laoghaire Shopping Centre** (Marine Road, Dún Laoghaire, Dublin Bay; 280 2981) and the **Dundrum Shopping Centre** (Dundrum, Southern suburbs; 298 4123) are far less appealing. There's talk that the latter will be demolished soon and rebuilt in brand spanking new fashion, but it's more likely that it will just receive a lick of paint.

ILAC Shopping Centre

Henry Street, Northside (704 1460). All cross-city buses. **Open** 9am-6pm Mon-Wed, Fri, Sat; 9am-9pm Thur; noon-6pm Sun. **Credit** varies. **Map** p313 G/H4.
The ILAC was one of the first multi-purpose centres to arrive in the city and caused a mini sensation when it opened in the early 1980s, but it's starting to show its age now. ILAC is spread out like an octopus and although there are often bargains to be found, it is difficult to negotiate.

Irish Life Shopping Mall

Talbot Street, Northside (704 1452). Connolly Station DART/all cross-city buses. **Open** 7.30am-6.20pm Mon-Wed, Fri, Sat; 7.30am-7pm Thur. **Credit** varies. **Map** p313 H3.
The Irish Life Shopping Mall has been around for a long time but people seem to pass through it rather than shop at the cluster of stores. Like the ILAC, it needs an overhaul.

Jervis Centre

Jervis Street, Northside (878 1323/www.jervis.ie). All cross-city buses. **Open** 9am-6pm Mon-Wed, Fri, Sat, 9am-9pm Thur; noon-6pm Sun. **Credit** varies. **Map** p313 G4.
The Jervis Centre is the baby brother of Dublin's shopping centres, having been in existence for only about four years. Containing a wide range of shops over several floors, the Jervis is worth visiting for its customer-friendly layout and wide range. Flagship shops include Debenham's, Waterstone's and Dixons: indeed, you'll find that most of the major British chain stores are here.

Powerscourt Townhouse Centre

Powerscourt Townhouse Centre, 59 South William Street, Southside (679 4144). All cross-city buses. **Open** 10am-6pm Mon-Wed, Fri Sat; 11am-8pm Thur; noon-6pm Sun. **Credit** varies. **Map** p313 H5.
Converted from an elegant Georgian townhouse, the salubrious Powerscourt Centre is more than just a shopping mall. In addition to fashion shops, ranging from Kookaï to Karen Millen and the Design Centre (*see p152*), there are also antique shops, galleries (including the Solomon Gallery, *see p179*) and a number of restaurants. At weekends you'll often find a pianist playing Chopin to accompany your shopping experience.

St Stephen's Green Centre

St Stephen's Green, Southside (478 0888/www. stephensgreen.com). All cross-city buses. **Open** 9am-7pm Mon-Wed, Fri, Sat; 9am-9pm Thur; noon-6pm Sun. **Credit** varies. **Map** p313 H6.
A huge complex with excellent parking facilities, the St Stephen's Green Centre combines a selection of pricey, specialist shops with bargain emporia. It's light, bright and attractive inside.

Antiques

Although Dublin, unlike other more rational cities, does not usually devote whole streets or areas to the retail of a specific product or service, the world of antiques is an exception. **Francis Street** is the heart of the city's antiques trade and is lined from top to bottom and on both sides with small, welcoming shops crammed with antiques of varying historical, aesthetic and monetary value. Dealing mainly in later-period furnishings and ornamentation, the shops here exude a dusty, dreamy atmosphere, but don't be fooled: the easygoing façade hides a world of experienced dealers running a big business with a brisk turnover.

On **Clanbrassil Street** there is a scattering of smaller, junkier antique shops, where, armed with copious amounts of time and alertness, you might just manage to unearth that oil lamp you've always wanted. Lovers of finer jewellery and silverware will be better off in the Grafton Street area. **South Anne Street** is home to several silver merchants, as well as an antique prints dealer and an antique bookshop, while **Johnson Court** is home to a fine antique jeweller. In the **Powerscourt Townhouse Centre** (*see above*) you'll find plentiful riches, while opposite the tourist office on Andrew

Powerscourt Townhouse Centre.

Greene's: a bookshop made for browsing.

Street is **Rhinestones** (679 0759), which offers an eclectic selection of curious, colourful collectibles and paraphernalia from across the spectra of time and taste.

Books

General

Book Stop
Dún Laoghaire Shopping Centre, Dún Laoghaire, Dublin Bay (280 9917/www.bookstop.ie). Dún Laoghaire DART/7, 8, 46A bus. **Open** 9am-6pm Mon-Wed, Sat; 9am-9pm Thur, Fri. **Credit** MC, V.
Book Stop is good for general titles and children's literature: it has a particularly wide range of school-books, both new and secondhand.
Branch: Blackrock Shopping Centre, Blackrock, Dublin Bay (283 2193).

Books Upstairs
36 College Green, Southside (679 6687/ www.booksirish.ie). All cross-city buses. **Open** 10am-7pm Mon-Fri; 10am-6pm Sat; 1-6pm Sun. **Credit** AmEx, DC, MC, V. **Map** p313 H5.
A very popular and well-stocked small bookshop opposite Trinity College, Books Upstairs has a particularly good Irish literature section, alongside a good selection of drama, women's studies and gay and lesbian material, plus American imports. There are always bargains to be found in their centre aisles and advertised in the windows.

Eason's
40 O'Connell Street, Northside (873 3811/ www.easons.ie). All cross-city buses. **Open** 8.30am-6.45pm Mon-Wed, Fri; 8.30am-8.45pm Thur; 8.30am-7.45pm Sat. **Credit** MC, V. **Map** p313 H4.
This large, busy shop sells books on the ground floor, along with stationery, art supplies and a good selection of magazines. The main contenders are popular fiction, new titles and Irish books; you won't find much beyond the mainstream, but bargains are often available.
Branches: throughout the city.

Hodges Figgis
56-58 Dawson Street, Southside (677 4754/ www.hodgesfiggis.com). All cross-city buses. **Open** 9am-7pm Mon-Fri; 9am-6pm Sat; noon-6pm Sun. **Credit** AmEx, MC, V. **Map** p313 H5.
Having made a cameo appearance in *Ulysses*, Hodges Figgis remains one of the best known – and best – bookshops in Dublin. The upside is the huge range of books and good ordering facilities; the downside is the dull lighting and the fact that it's so easy to get lost in here. There's a great coffeeshop on the first floor and a terrific bargain basement. Watch out for the Christmas and summer sales.

Hughes & Hughes
St Stephen's Green Shopping Centre, Southside (478 3060). All cross-city buses. **Open** 9.30am-6pm Mon-Wed, Fri, Sat; 9.30am-8pm Thur; noon-6pm Sun. **Credit** AmEx, DC, MC, V. **Map** p313 H6.
A literary chain store with a good mix of popular titles, Irish works and fiction, plus a decent collection of children's books.
Branches: Blackrock Shopping Centre, Blackrock, Dublin Bay (283 4316); Dublin Airport, Northern suburbs (704 4034); Nutgrove Shopping Centre, Rathfarnham, Southern suburbs (493 6633).

Waterstone's
7 Dawson Street, Southside (679 1415/www. waterstones.co.uk). All cross-city buses. **Open** 9am-8pm Mon-Wed, Fri; 9am-8.30pm Thur; 9am-7pm Sat; 9am-6pm Sun. **Credit** AmEx, DC, MC, V. **Map** p313 H5.
Stocking 10,000 John Grishams at €3 each now seems more important to Waterstone's than sticking to its original, successful and proven formula of selling good-quality books at the publisher's price. That said, the Dawson Street branch remains a good, solid book-buying emporium, with friendly staff, appealing surroundings, literary events (*see p.35*) and talk of a coffeeshop on the horizon.
Branch: Jervis Centre, Jervis Street, Northside (878 1311).

Second-hand & rare

Cathach Books
10 Duke Street, Southside (671 8676/www.rare books.ie). All cross-city buses. **Open** 9.30am-6pm Mon-Sat. **Credit** AmEx, MC, V. **Map** p313 H5.
Although it can be quite pricey, Cathach specialises in rare Irish titles and is worth a visit if only to inspect the signed editions of everyone from Yeats to Heaney. It also buys used books and stocks a good range of rare maps and prints.

Greene's
16 Clare Street, Southside (676 2554/www.greenes bookshop.com). All cross-city buses. **Open** 9am-5.45pm Mon-Fri; 9am-5pm Sat. **Credit** AmEx, DC, MC, V. **Map** p313 J5.
A large, sprawling bookshop selling mostly second-hand and Irish titles, plus a range of rare books. It's a great place to browse.

Secret Book & Record Shop

15A Wicklow Street, Southside (679 7272). All cross-city buses. **Open** 10.30am-6pm Mon-Sat; noon-6pm Sun. **No credit cards. Map** p313 H5.

This is a great second-hand bookshop with records towards the back, also worth checking out for its few out-of-print paperbacks and recently remaindered titles. Hardly a secret any more, but still a fab place in which to lose yourself for an hour.

The Winding Stair

40 Ormond Quay Lower, Northside (873 3292/ www.windingstair.ie). All cross-city buses. **Open** 10am-6pm Mon-Sat; 1-6pm Sun. **Credit** AmEx, DC, MC, V. **Map** p313 G4.

A great old-fashioned bookshop. You'll find cheap paperbacks and bargains both downstairs and up, but upstairs has the added bonus of a popular café overlooking the Liffey (*see p128*). The tables are surrounded by books, making it a fine place to while away an afternoon. Readings are sometimes held here (*see p35*).

Specialist

Forbidden Planet

Aston Quay, Southside (671 0688/www.forbidden planet.glo.cc). All cross-city buses. **Open** 10am-6pm Mon-Wed, Fri, Sat; 10am-7pm Thur. **Credit** AmEx, DC, MC, V. **Map** p313 H4.

A science fiction and fantasy bookshop, with a huge range of comics, books, mags, videos, toys, action figures and posters from all over the world, plus a good range of movie stills and posters.

Crafts & gifts

There are two types of indigenous crafts available in Ireland: the 'traditional' stuff (woolly jumpers, shillelaghs, anything with a shamrock, harp or the word 'Guinness' on it); and the more creative, 'modern' crafts, which, being less stereotyped, are in reality more genuinely Irish. While it's a common mistake to think that all Irish crafts are of the traditional variety, it is an equally dangerous error to think all the traditional crafts are necessarily tacky. Honest.

If you find yourself in Dublin in early December, make your way to the RDS for the **Craft Fair** (670 2186), where a small admission fee will grant you access to the broadest range of Irish crafts (traditional, modern, iron, linen, wood, wax) under one roof.

Traditional craft shops

Nassau Street is home to a number of large, well-stocked, traditional craft shops. **Lord Edward Street** is also a good source of Irish crafts, both traditional and modern.

Blarney Woollen Mills

21-23 Nassau Street, Southside (671 0068/ www.blarneywoollenmills.ie). All cross-city buses. **Open** 9am-6pm Mon-Wed, Fri, Sat; 9am-8pm Thur; 11am-6pm Sun. **Credit** AmEx, MC, V. **Map** p313 H5.

The mills themselves, situated in Cork, have a well-deserved and long-standing reputation for producing the finest hand-woven garments. The Dublin branch of the operation stocks a full range of the mills' products at relatively reasonable prices.

China Showrooms

33 Abbey Street Lower, Northside (878 6211/ www.chinashowrooms.ie). Connolly Station DART/rail/all cross-city buses. **Open** 9.30am-6pm Mon-Wed, Fri, Sat; 9.30am-9pm Thur. **Credit** AmEx, DC, MC, V. **Map** p313 H4.

If you have either a penchant for porcelain and crystal or a pet bull in tow, the China Showrooms may make a fun pitstop.

Dublin Woollen Mills

41 Lower Ormond Quay, Northside (677 5014/ www.woollenmills.com). All cross-city buses. **Open** 9.30am-6pm Mon-Wed, Fri, Sat; 9.30am-8pm Thur; 1-6pm Sun. **Credit** MC, V. **Map** p313 G4.

Set up by the Roche family more than a century ago, Dublin Woollen Mills offers high-quality knitwear: kilts, shawls and Aran jumpers – the kind of stuff of which your granny would approve. There are usually a few stalls selling handmade jewellery out front, too. The Wellington Quay branch stocks fabrics and haberdashery.

Branch: 46 Wellington Quay, Temple Bar, Southside (677 0301).

House of Ireland

38 Nassau Street, Southside (671 6133/www. houseofireland.com). All cross-city buses. **Open** 9am-6pm Mon-Wed, Fri, Sat; 9am-8pm Thur; 10.30am-6pm Sun. **Credit** AmEx, MC, V. **Map** p313 H5.

The House of Ireland carries expensive cut glass, porcelain, leather, wool and linen products from around the country.

Irish Celtic Craftshop

12 Lord Edward Street, Southside (679 9912). All cross-city buses. **Open** 9am-6pm daily. **Credit** AmEx, DC, MC, V. **Map** p313 G5.

This shop stocks a comprehensive selection of Irish knitwear, T-shirts, bodhrans, Celtic jewellery, dolls and ceramic miniatures.

Kilkenny Shop

6 Nassau Street, Southside (677 7066/www.kilkenny group.com). All cross-city buses. **Open** 9am-6pm Mon-Wed, Fri, Sat; 9am-8pm Thur; 11am-6pm Sun. **Credit** AmEx, MC, V. **Map** p313 H5.

The Kilkenny Shop stocks the usual range of traditional knitwear, as well as some expensive Irish designerwear and an excellent selection of Irish-made pottery, from delicate Belleek porcelain to more robust Shanagarry.

Treasure Ireland

37 Wicklow Street, Southside (679 4560). All cross-city buses. **Open** 10am-6pm Mon-Wed, Fri, Sat; 10am-8pm Thur. **Credit** AmEx, MC, V. **Map** p313 H5.

Good for brass-and-tack fetishists.

Modern craftshops

Design Yard

12 East Essex Street, Temple Bar, Southside (677 8453). All cross-city buses. **Open** 10am-5.30pm Mon, Wed-Sat; 11am-5.30pm Tue. **Credit** AmEx, MC, V. **Map** p75.

Located in a converted china warehouse, Design Yard comprises two spaces: downstairs there's a retail outlet for Irish and international jewellery, specialising in unusual wedding or engagement rings (*see p152*), while upstairs you'll find Irish applied art and sculpture.

Natural Interiors

The Mill, Mill Street, Southside (473 7444). Bus 50, 56A, 77, 150, 210. **Open** 9am-5.30pm daily. **Credit** MC, V. **Map** p312 E/F6.

This shop does not restrict itself to Ireland in its quest for beautiful natural fabrics, wood and rope mirrors, cane furniture and so on.

Whichcraft

5 Castlegate, Lord Edward Street, Southside (670 9371/www.whichcraft.com). All cross-city buses. **Open** 9am-6pm Mon-Sat; 10am-6pm Sun. **Credit** AmEx, MC, V. **Map** p313 G5.

Through hard work, Whichcraft has become one of Dublin's most exciting and comprehensive stockists of contemporary work of all kinds from all counties. From wooden bowls and rocking chairs to jewellery, ceramics and terrific ironwork, it's essential for visitors interested in the crafts of modern Ireland. **Branch**: Cow's Lane, Southside (474 1011).

Electronics

General

Beyond 2000

2 Chatham Row, Southside (677 7633). All cross-city buses. **Open** 9am-6pm Mon-Wed, Fri; 9.30am-7.30pm Thur; 9am-5.30pm Sat. **Credit** AmEx, DC, MC, V. **Map** p313 G/H5.

Primarily a computer specialist shop, Beyond 2000 also sells hi-fi equipment and computer accessories.

Compustore

25 St Stephen's Green, Southside (676 2050/ www.compustore.ie). All cross-city buses. **Open** 9am-5pm Mon-Fri; 11am-5pm Sat. **Credit** AmEx, DC, MC, V. **Map** p313 H6.

An excellent computer specialist shop that stocks a range of new systems and every accessory you can think of: games, printers, scanners and rewritable CDs for the music terrorist.

Dixons

15 Jervis Centre, Jervis Street, Northside (878 1515/www.dixons.co.uk). All cross-city buses. **Open** 9am-6pm Mon-Wed, Sat; 9am-9pm Thur; 9am-7pm Fri; noon-6pm Sun. **Credit** AmEx, MC, V. **Map** p313 G4.

A standard but broad range of electrical equipment, televisions, stereos, computers and Walkmans. **Branches**: Blanchardstown Shopping Centre, Blanchardstown, Northern suburbs (820 2333); The Square, Tallaght, Southern suburbs (452 2855).

Hi-fi Corner

14 Aston Quay, Southside (671 4343/www.hifi corner.ie). Bus 78A. **Open** 9.30am-6pm Mon-Wed, Fri, Sat; 9.30am-8pm Thur. **Credit** MC, V. **Map** p313 H4.

Attached to the Virgin Megastore, Hi-fi Corner covers the top end of the market in terms of both cost and quality. It stocks a good range of hi-fi equipment and separates, and also sells laser discs. **Branch**: 18 Merrion Road, Ballsbridge, Southern suburbs (667 0990).

Peats World of Electronics

197-200 Parnell Street, Northside (872 7799/ www.peats.com). Bus 19, 19A, 40, 40A, 134. **Open** 9.30am-6pm Mon-Sat. **Credit** AmEx, MC, V. **Map** p313 G3.

A huge range of electrical goods is sold at this well-known, good-value Dublin store. Peats can also be relied upon for after-sales service. **Branches**: throughout the city.

House of Ireland. *See p147.*

Sony Centre
17 O'Connell Street, Northside (872 1900). Bus 19, 19A, 40, 40A, 134. **Open** *9.30am-6pm Mon-Sat.* **Credit** *AmEx, MC, V.* **Map** *p313 H3.*
This specialist branch of the Peats chain stocks all the Sony goodies you could want, and is particularly adept at putting together systems out of separates at reasonable enough prices.

Photography

Camera Centre
56 Grafton Street, Southside (677 5594/www. cameracentre.com). All cross-city buses. **Open** *9am-6pm Mon-Wed, Fri, Sat; 9am-7pm Thur.* **Credit** *AmEx, MC, V.* **Map** *p313 H5.*
A reliable choice for anything in the photographic field: cameras, camcorders, binoculars and telescopes, and a one-hour film processing service, too. **Branches:** throughout the city.

Camera Exchange
9B Trinity Street, Southside (679 3410/www.camera exchange.com). All cross-city buses. **Open** *9am-6pm Mon-Wed, Fri, Sat; 9am-7pm Thur.* **Credit** *AmEx, MC, V.* **Map** *p75.*
Stockists of both new and used cameras, Camera Exchange is a good place to go if you're shopping on a budget but still want a camera that will take good pictures and isn't going to break down after one roll of film.

Fashion

In a city where half of the population is under 25 years of age, it's not surprising that the most dominant elements of Dublin's fashion culture are the mid-priced, mass-produced clothing retailers. The city has literally dozens of these shops, from small single-outlet stores in the suburbs and backstreets to larger Irish department stores and fashion chains, and instantly recognisable branches of British and international fashion franchises, such as **Next** (67 Grafton Street, Southside; 679 3300); **Principles** (72 Grafton Street, Southside; 679 5078) and **Benetton** (1 St Stephen's Green, Southside; 478 1799).

A-Wear
26 Grafton Street, Southside (671 7200). All cross-city buses. **Open** *9.30am-6.30pm Mon-Wed, Fri, Sat; 9.30am-8.30pm Thur; noon-6pm Sun.* **Credit** *AmEx, DC, MC, V.* **Map** *p313 H5.*
Range of modern, reasonably priced clothes, mainly by younger Irish designers.

Airwave
36 Grafton Street, Southside (671 5550). All cross-city buses. **Open** *9.30am-6pm Mon-Wed, Fri, Sat; 9.30am-8pm Thur.* **Credit** *AmEx, MC, V.* **Map** *p313 H5.*
Decently made, reasonably stylish but no-nonsense clobber for men and women.

French Connection
Unit 10, Powerscourt Townhouse Centre, Clarendon Street, Southside (670 8199). All cross-city buses. **Open** *10am-6pm Mon-Wed; 10am-8pm Thur; 10am-7pm Fri, Sat; 2-6pm Sun.* **Credit** *MC, V.* **Map** *p313 H5.*
Stylish clothes for men and women, plus covetable undies and toiletries.

Hobo
6-9 Trinity Street, Southside (670 4869). All cross-city buses. **Open** *9.30am-6pm Mon-Wed; 9.30am-8pm Thur; 9.30am-7pm Fri; noon-6pm Sun.* **Credit** *MC, V.* **Map** *p75.*
Hobo stocks a decent range of youth clothing, and is usually the first stop for any country student arriving in the city who aspires to rise from the bog to the ghetto.

Jigsaw
42 Grafton Street, Southside (671 3456). All cross-city buses. **Open** *9.30am-6pm Mon-Wed, Fri, Sat; 9.30am-8pm Thur; 1-6pm Sun.* **Credit** *AmEx, DC, MC, V.* **Map** *p313 H5.*
Jigsaw may not offer the most outrageous designs on the high street, but it can be relied on for good-quality fabrics and slick modern tailoring for both men and women. This Dublin branch is well designed and airy.

Kookaï
21 Wicklow Street, Southside (677 6321). All cross-city buses. **Open** *9.30am-6pm Mon-Wed, Fri, Sat; 9.30am-8pm Thur.* **Credit** *AmEx, MC, V.* **Map** *p313 H5.*
If you're a young, slim fashionista you can't go far wrong with the catwalk-conscious clothing that's served up here. Small sizes, small prices.
Branch: Arnott Centre, Henry Street, Northside (805 0564).

Levi's Store
5 Grafton Street, Southside (679 9917). All cross-city buses. **Open** *9.30am-6pm Mon-Wed, Fri, Sat; 9.30am-8pm Thur; 2-5pm Sun.* **Credit** *AmEx, MC, V.* **Map** *p313 H5.*
Engineered jeans and all manner of branded clothes from the denim specialists.

Miss Selfridge
41 Grafton Street, Southside (679 3473). All cross-city buses. **Open** *10am-6pm Mon-Wed, Fri; 10am-9pm Thur; 9.30am-6pm Sat; 2-6pm Sun.* **Credit** *AmEx, MC, V.* **Map** *p313 H5.*
Skimpy, sparkly stuff for the younger generation of clubbers and wannabes.

Monsoon
38 Grafton Street, Southside (671 7322). All cross-city buses. **Open** *9.30am-6pm Mon-Wed, Fri, Sat; 9.30am-8pm Thur; noon-6pm Sun.* **Credit** *AmEx, DC, MC, V.* **Map** *p313 H5.*
Monsoon's clothes combine a strong, ethnic look with good quality fabrics and bright colours. There are brill accessories, too.

Eat, Drink, Shop

Oasis

*3 St Stephen's Green, Southside (671 4477). All
cross-city buses.* **Open** 10am-6pm Mon-Wed, Thur
Sat; 10am-8pm Thur; noon-6pm Sun. **Credit** AmEx,
MC, V. **Map** p313 H6.
Probably the market leader when it comes to achiev-
ing a balance of cost and fashion credibility.
Branch: 41-43 Nassau Street, Southside (677 4944).

O'Connor's

*23 Grafton Street, Southside (670 7606). All
cross-city buses.* **Open** 9.30am-6pm Mon-Wed, Fri,
Sat; 9.30am-8pm Thur. **Credit** AmEx, MC, V.
Map p313 H5.
O'Connor's is worth a visit if you're after clubwear
or denim, including gear by Red or Dead and Diesel.
Branches: ILAC Centre, Parnell Street, Northside
(872 9902); 148 Capel Street, Northside (873 3242).

Top Shop

*Jervis Centre, 125 Upper Abbey Street, Northside
(878 0477). All cross-city buses.* **Open** 9am-6pm
Mon-Wed, Fri; 9am-9pm Thur; 9am-6.30pm Sat;
noon-6pm Sun. **Credit** AmEx, MC, V. **Map** p313 G4.
Top Shop successfully nabs the best cutting-edge
trends from the catwalk and reproduces them at
very reasonable prices.
Branch: Liffey Valley Shopping Centre, Clondalkin,
Southern suburbs (623 4666); 1, Unit 22,
Blanchardstown Town Centre, Blanchardstown,
Northern suburbs (822 1874).

Urban Outfitters

*Cecilia House, Temple Bar, Southside (670 6202).
All cross-city buses.* **Open** 10am-7pm Mon-Wed, Sat;
10am-8pm Thur, Fri; noon-6pm Sun. **Credit** AmEx,
MC, V. **Map** p75.

Dedicated followers of fashion

Until recently, Dublin was a dreary
department store town. Brown Thomas,
Arnotts, Cleary's and Guiney's – in
descending order of chicness – were our only
fashion meccas, and the height of girl style
was a rugby shirt tucked into faded denims.

However, the Celtic boom brought with it an
enviable array of seriously stylish boutiques
selling a range of labels from high-end
international designers to local talent, in
spaces that are as well-designed as the
clothes they sell. The first wave of fashion
Glasnost – largely spearheaded by British
high-street chain stores – has been
supplemented by an indigenous scene that is
original, creative and diverse. And Dubliners'
style sense has benefited in consequence.
Looking good no longer means simply
blanket-buying the latest creations, but
instead a mix-and-match approach that
borrows from a diverse range of sources.

Beloved of Sharon Corr and Sinead
O'Connor, **Costume** on Castlemarket was
opened three years ago by Mrs Tucker and
sells a wonderfully diverse range of clothes
for grown-up fashionistas. Currently the only
outlet for London-based Irish designer Pauric
Sweeney's remarkable leather creations,
Costume is also the place for predominantly
European labels, like Parisienne Severine
Peraudin, pretty chiffons from Anna Sui and
wonderfully tailored suits by Mrs Tucker's
daughter, Leigh – definitely one of the
younger generation of designers to watch.

Around the corner on South William Street,
Platform Eile is an Aladdin's cave of avant-
garde fashion and to-die-for accessories.

A strong focus on the more established young
Irish designers, such as knitwear king Tim
Ryan, and cutting-edge European labels that
by-pass trends for enduring style, such as
Helena Christensen's favourites Munthe and
Simenson, make this relaxed boutique one
of the surest bets in town. Opened by Joan
Wood over ten years ago, is a fixture on
the Irish fashion scene, and somewhere you
can be sure of getting an absolutely honest
opinion on anything you try on.

For uncompromising urban cool, **Cuba** is
the place. Street-wear-gone-glamour is the
mantra and an impressive selection of cult
labels predominate. The only Irish outlet for
ultra-hip Spanish label Ropa Positiva, Cuba
stocks creations by Evisu, Boxfresh and Paul
Frank as well as home grown labels such as
Optix and David Poole.

If you're looking for something more
outrageous than practical, check out **Cuan
Hanley** in Temple Bar. Cuan's own range
of bespoke tailoring for men rubs shoulders
with a dynamic and eclectic mix of extremely
cutting-edge local talent – much of which is
directional rather than accessible – classic
items from John Rocha, casual wear from the
Coca Cola label and sexy, structured pieces
by local success story Antonia Campbell-
Hughes. The cool, minimal interior sets off
the unique selection of clothes to perfection.
Expect also Camper shoes, distinctive
accessories by Melissa Curry, a Dublin-based
designer currently the toast of Paris, and
charming head-pieces by Wendy Judge.

A stone's throw away, the latest addition
to Dublin's fashion renaissance is **Smock,**

A great one-stop shop. Funky, affordable clobber, cosmetics, gadgets and homewares under one roof. There's even a dance music section with club vinyl.

Children

Baby Bambino

41 Clarendon Street, Southside (671 1590). All cross-city buses. **Open** 10am-6pm Mon-Wed, Fri, Sat; 10am-7pm Thur. **Credit** AmEx, MC, V. **Map** p313 H5. A selection of funky clothes and accessories for young kids, plus more formal christening wear.

Freckles

1 Liffey Street Upper, Northside (873 1249). All cross-city buses. **Open** 9.30am-6pm Mon-Sat. **Credit** MC, V. **Map** p313 G4.

Freckles caters mainly for slightly older children, with a range of clothes for toddlers, schoolchildren and teenagers.

Gymboree

75 Grafton Street, Southside (670 3331/ www.gymboree.com). All cross-city buses. **Open** 10am-6pm Mon-Wed, Fri, Sat; 10am-8pm Thur. **Credit** AmEx, MC, V. **Map** p313 H5. Exclusive kids fashions.

Mothercare

St Stephen's Green Centre, Southside (478 0951/ www.mothercare.com). All cross-city buses. **Open** 9.30am-6pm Mon-Wed, Fri; 9.30am-8pm Thur; 9.30am-6.30pm Sat. **Credit** AmEx, MC, V. **Map** p313 H6. Kids' chain with practical accessories and clothes. **Branch**: Jervis Centre, Northside (878 1184).

a boutique that aims to replicate that cosy boudoir-like feeling of walking into a friend's bedroom and trying on clothes. It carries a simple, elegant mid-price range, with labels such as Jacob Tutu – created by owner Susan O'Connell, Justin Oh, Le Prairie de Paris and Dublin's golden boy, Ali Malek.

Vivien Walsh on Stephen's Street Lower is another fixture on the Dublin fashion scene. As well as gorgeous one-offs from exclusive designers such as L'essential, Sunjow Moon, Paul & Joe, plus shoes by Kte Keyte, the real treat here are the accessories, including tempting tiaras and costume jewellery designed by Vivien herself.

However, not all is roses in the world of Irish fashion. The recent, much-publicised departure of womenswear designer Marc O'Neill for London and the job of chief designer with Mulberry highlighted the concerns of the current generation of designers. With talent to burn and an enviable grasp of the mechanics of business, they are nonetheless finding it difficult to consolidate their success and to supply the quantities that would meet demand for their designs. O'Neill – whose departure was considered frankly overdue by a growing community of London-based Irish designers – wished to make a statement about the Irish government's unwillingness to support the struggles of the emerging Irish fashion scene. Those left behind are dismayed that this gesture wasn't treated more seriously. The difficulties faced, particularly on the level of production, mean that there is substantial scepticism as to whether the current fashion

explosion will go the distance, or give rise to yet another wave of talent haemorrhage from these shores.

Costume

10&11 Castlemarket, Southside (679 4188). All cross-city buses. **Open** 10am-6pm Mon-Wed, Fri, Sat; 10am-7pm Thur; 2-6pm Sun. **Credit** AmEx, MC, V. **Map** p313 G5.

Cuan Hanly

1 Pudding Row, Essex Street West, Temple Bar, Southside (671 1406). All cross-city buses. **Open** 10.30am-6pm Mon-Sat. **Credit** AmEx, DC, MC, V. **Map** p75.

Cuba

13 Trinity Street, Southside (672 7489). All cross-city buses. **Open** 9.30am-7pm Mon-Wed, Fri, Sat; 9.30am-8pm Thur; noon-6pm Sun. **Credit** AmEx, DC, MC, V. **Map** p313 H5.

Platform Eile

50 William Street South, Southside (677 7380). All cross-city buses. **Open** 10am-6pm Mon-Wed, Fri, Sat; 10am-8pm Thur. **Credit** AmEx, MC, V. **Map** p313 H5.

Smock

East Essex Street, Temple Bar, Southside (613 9000). All cross-city buses. **Open** 10.30am-6.30pm Mon-Fri; 10am-6pm Sat. **Credit** MC, V. **Map** p75.

Vivien Walsh

24 Stephen's Street Lower, Southside (475 5022). All cross-city buses. **Open** 10am-6pm Mon-Wed, Fri, Sat; 10am-7pm Thur. **Credit** MC, V. **Map** p313 G5.

Designer

None of the major design houses have yet set up their own stores in Dublin – undoubtedly by the time the fourth edition of the *Time Out Dublin Guide* is published, Versace, Calvin Klein et al will be scattered around the city (yeah, right). In the meantime, however, **Brown Thomas** (*see p144*) offers an unrivalled selection of clothes and accessories from top-flight designers, and you'll also find concessions in other department stores and shopping centres. For details of the best independent shops, with ranges by up-and-coming Irish designers as well as international names, *see p150* **Dedicated followers of fashion**.

Alias Tom

Duke House, Duke Street, Southside (671 5443). All cross-city buses. **Open** 9.30am-6pm Mon-Wed, Fri, Sat; 9.30am-8pm Thur. **Credit** AmEx, MC, V. **Map** p313 H5.
Dublin's most popular men's designer clothing store until BT2 (*see below*) opened. The emphasis is on European- rather than American-influenced designs, and the range is mouthwatering.

Boutique Homme

2 South Anne Street, Southside (671 5122). All cross-city buses. **Open** 9am-6pm Mon-Wed, Fri, Sat; 9am-7.30pm Thur; 1.30-5.30pm Sun. **Credit** AmEx, MC, V. **Map** p313 H5.
The place to go for exclusive men's clothing of the conservative, well-cut variety.

BT2

28-29 Grafton Street, Southside (605 6666). All cross-city buses. **Open** 9am-6pm Mon-Wed, Fri, Sat; 9am-8pm Thur. **Credit** AmEx, MC, V. **Map** p313 H5.
The offshoot of Brown Thomas (*see p144*), situated across the street, BT2 targets the younger, richer kids of the parents who shop at the above. It's the best shop in Dublin for all the latest top-flight labels. Bring your cheque book.

Design Centre

Powerscourt Townhouse Centre, 59 South William Street, Southside (679 5718). All cross-city buses. **Open** 9am-6pm Mon-Wed, Fri, Sat; 9am-7pm Thur. **Credit** AmEx, MC, V. **Map** p313 H5.
For the best of Irish design, climb the stairs in the Powerscourt and enter the Design Centre. This is by far the most popular of Dublin's designer fashion stores, where you'll find clothes by innumerable gifted designers of national and international renown in every fabric and style, and for every taste. Prices are high, though, so keep an eye out for sales.

Louis Copeland

39-41 Capel Street, Northside (872 1600). All cross-city buses. **Open** 9am-5.45pm Mon-Wed, Fri, Sat; 9am-8pm Thur. **Credit** AmEx, MC, V. **Map** p313 G4.
Men can match their latest shirt to a suit from Louis Copeland, one of Europe's most acclaimed tailors.

Pink

29 Dawson Street, Southside (670 3647). All cross-city buses. **Open** 9.30am-6pm Mon-Wed, Fri, Sat; 9.30am-7pm Thur. **Credit** AmEx, MC, V. **Map** p313 H5.
Situated at the southern end of Dawson Street, Pink offers some of the loveliest shirts for men and women in the city. They're popular with riskier and zestier young upstarts.

Platform

16 Creation Arcade, Lemon Street, Southside (677 7380). All cross-city buses. **Open** 9.30am-6pm Mon-Wed, Fri, Sat; 9.30am-8pm Thur. **Credit** MC, V. **Map** p313 H5.
A small but eclectic mix of designer brands, with a bias towards sensual fabrics and flowing lines.

Jewellery & accessories

Choose between traditional shops that specialise in beautifully cut diamonds and engagement rings, or the more contemporary arty stylings of the **Temple Bar** crowd. On **Anne Street South**, a selection of old-fashioned, friendly and open-minded stores stocks a broad range of new and antique jewellery, while **Johnson's Court**, at the side of Bewley's on Grafton Street, boasts every kind of jewellery store from **Appleby's** (*see below*) to the nameless shop at the end of the street that changes watch batteries more cheaply than anywhere else in town.

All the department stores have significant accessories sections, but there are also several well-stocked, reasonably priced accessory stalls on the ground floor of the **St Stephen's Green Centre** (*see p145*).

Appleby's

5-6 Johnson's Court, Southside (679 9572). All cross-city buses. **Open** 9am-5.30pm Mon-Wed, Fri, Sat; 9am-7pm Thur. **Credit** AmEx, MC, V. **Map** p313 H5.
The city's most exclusive jeweller.

Design Yard

12 East Essex Street, Temple Bar, Southside (677 8453). All cross-city buses. **Open** 10am-5.30pm Mon, Wed-Sat; 11am-5.30pm Tue. **Credit** AmEx, MC, V. **Map** p75.
For innovative jewellery, Temple Bar's Design Yard is the ultimate feast, with an extensive and fascinating range of beautiful contemporary Irish pieces. One thing is made clear, as much from the methods of display as from the prices: these items of jewellery are being sold as works of art, not trinkets.

Hat Shop

St Stephen's Green Centre, Southside (478 5185). All cross-city buses. **Open** 9am-6pm Mon-Wed, Fri, Sat; 9am-8pm Thur. **Credit** MC, V. **Map** p313 H6.
Formal and semi-formal wear, suitable if you're on for Ladies' Day at Leopardstown Races.

Hat Stand

*5 Temple Bar Square, Temple Bar, Southside
(671 0805). All cross-city buses.* **Open** 9am-7pm
Mon-Sat; 11am-6pm Sun. **Credit** MC, V. **Map** p75.
This hat shop stocks everything from traditional
to zany designs.

Weir's

*96 Grafton Street, Southside (677 9678). All cross-
city buses.* **Open** 9am-5.30pm Mon-Sat. **Credit**
AmEx, MC, V. **Map** p313 H5.
Weir's remains Dublin's best-known jewellers – and
often its most reliable, too. Products are of unim-
peachable quality, and there is a particularly strong
line in expensive wristwatches from
around the world. It also stocks quality silverware
and leather goods.

Laundry & dry-cleaning

Baggot Cleaners

*33 Baggot Street, Ballsbridge, Southern suburbs
(668 1286). Bus 10.* **Open** 7.45am-6.30pm Mon-
Wed; 7.45am-7pm Thur, Fri; 9am-6pm Sat.
Credit MC, V.
Specialists in leather, suede and sheepskin, with a
reliable same-day service. Collection and delivery
facilities are available.

Crown Dry Cleaners

*81 Camden Street Lower, Southside (475 3584).
All cross-city buses.* **Open** 8.30am-6pm Mon-Sat.
Map p313 G7.
Crown will dry-clean most garments.
Branches: throughout the city.

Rental

Black Tie

*Westmoreland Street, Southside (679 1444). All
cross-city buses.* **Open** 9am-6pm Mon-Sat; 2-6pm
Sun. **Credit** AmEx, DC, MC, V. **Map** p313 H4.
Men's suit and tuxedo hire
Branches: throughout the city.

Second-hand

Eager Beaver

*17 Crown Alley, Temple Bar, Southside (677 3342).
All cross-city buses.* **Open** 9.30am-5.30pm Mon-Wed;
9.30am-7pm Thur; 9.30am-6pm Fri, Sat. **Credit** MC,
V. **Map** p75.
A perennial favourite with students, the Eager
Beaver stocks an often bewildering array of second-
hand clothing. Cheap suits, jeans, retro skirts, and
all manner of accessories are packed into this
cramped store on two floors.

Flip

*4 Fownes Street, Temple Bar, Southside (671
4299). All cross-city buses.* **Open** 9.30am-6pm Mon-
Wed, Sat; 9.30am-7pm Thur, Fri; 1-6pm Sun.
Credit MC, V. **Map** p75.

Vintage chic at **Eager Beaver**.

One of the longest established shops in the Temple
Bar area, Flip is a particularly good place to find
second hand Levi's and other vintage Americana.
It's also a good source of leather and suede jackets.

Jenny Vander

*20 Market Arcade, South Great George's Street,
Southside (677 0406). All cross-city buses.* **Open**
10am-6pm Mon-Wed, Fri, Sat; 10am-7pm Thur.
Credit MC, V. **Map** p313 G5.
A firm favourite with those whose taste runs
towards the eclectic. Jenny Vander's delightful shop
specialises in highly distinctive retro dresses and
skirts, many of them dating from the 1950s. There's
a men's department upstairs, too, and the shop has
a good line in quirky accessories.

Wild Child

*61 South Great George's Street, Southside
(475 5099). All cross city buses.* **Open** 10am-6pm
Mon-Wed, Fri, Sat; 10am-7pm Thur. **Credit** MC, V.
Map p313 G5.
Vintage clothing for women, with a particularly
strong line in party wear.
Branch: 77 Aunger Street, Southside (475 7177).

Shoes

In addition to the shops listed below, don't
forget to check out the department stores,
particularly **Arnotts** (*see p143*) and **Brown
Thomas** (*see p144*).

Aspecto

*South Anne Street, Southside (671 9302). All cross-
city buses.* **Open** 8.45am-6pm Mon-Sat. **Credit** MC,
V. **Map** p313 H5.
Big stockists of Birkenstocks' many coloured shoes.

Market forces

As Molly Malone would probably testify, Dublin has a long history of lively street trading. The city's most famous street market, and one of its oldest, is to be found on **Moore Street** on the northside of the city. In recent years, the countless stalls of fruit, vegetables, portable radios and Christmas cards – in June – have been supplemented by African and Asian food stuffs and haircare products. You can listen for hours to the unconducted orchestra of street-traders. 'Mandarins, eight for feeftee!', or 'Sports socks, last pair, two pairs for a peeownd!'; or again, in the lower but more urgent voices of those selling contraband cigarettes, 'Jimmy! Pigs!'.

Across the river on **Meeting House Square** and **Cow's Lane**, every Saturday two food markets draw an altogether different crowd of people. These are D4s (called after Dublin's most desirable postcode) who mysteriously don't eat portable radios and give their favour instead to such staples as olives, organic bread and fresh south American enchiladas. The cries, too, are different: 'Tristan! Tea Rooms for an espresso?'.

Of course, there is an appealing middle ground in the world of Dublin markets. Being indoors is an immediate advantage for the **George's Street Arcade** (between South Great George's Street and Drury Street, also known as Market Arcade), undoubtedly Dublin's finest and most varied sheltered market. In addition to excellent vintage and used clothes shops, it also has some fine second-hand book and music stalls, a small print stand with a Republican leaning, a fortune-teller, a very good olive stand and some other foodie finds.

Food stalls line **Camden Street** further south, though the heavy traffic of recent years has affected it badly. Some of this traffic is no doubt crawling towards **Blackrock**, where every weekend an expansive and varied market – part indoors and part outdoors – opens to the public. The stalls vary with time, but on an average Sunday you can find crafts of all kinds and qualities, cushions, books, music, electrical goods, furniture, bean-bags, paintings and clothes. But no olives. Or dodgy ciggies.

Black Boot
28 Wicklow Street, Southside (679 5795). All cross-city buses. **Open** 9am-5.30pm Mon-Sat. **Credit** MC, V. **Map** p313 H5.
Dublin's best stockists of Doc Martens.

Carl Scarpa
25 Grafton Street, Southside (677 7846). All cross-city buses. **Open** 9.30am-6pm Mon-Wed, Fri, Sat; 9.30am-8pm Thur; 1.30-5.30pm Sun. **Credit** MC, V. **Map** p313 H5.
High-quality footwear at reasonable prices.

DV8
4 Crown Alley, Temple Bar, Southside (679 8472). All cross city buses. **Open** 10.30am-6pm Mon-Wed, Fri, Sat; 10.30am-8pm Thur. **Credit** MC, V. **Map** p75.
The most popular contemporary footwear designs are stocked here, plus Doc Martins in every colour, shape and flavour. Be prepared to ask where your foot goes in.

Korky's
47 Grafton Street, Southside (670 7943). All cross-city buses. **Open** 9am-5.30pm Mon-Sat. **Credit** AmEx, MC, V. **Map** p313 H5.
Mid-priced fashion footwear is Korky's forte.

Natural Shoe Store
25 Drury Street, Southside (671 4978). All cross city buses. **Open** 10.30am-5.30pm Mon-Sat. **Credit** MC, V. **Map** p313 G5.
As close as conservationists can get to going barefoot in the city.

Schuh
47-48 O'Connell Street, Northside (804 9420). All cross-city buses. **Open** 9.30am-6.30pm Mon-Wed, Fri, Sat; 9.30am-8pm Thur; noon-6pm Sun. **Credit** AmEx, MC, V. **Map** p313 H4.
Covetable shoes and trainers from Kickers, Red or Dead, Vans, Bronx and Airwalk are up for grabs in this well designed store.

Zerep
57 Grafton Street, Southside (677 8320). All cross-city buses. **Open** 9am-6pm Mon-Wed, Fri, Sat; 9.30am-8pm Thur; 1.30-5.30pm Sun. **Credit** AmEx, MC, V. **Map** p313 H5.
Mid-priced fashion footwear aimed at a young and reasonably funky crowd.

Flowers & plants

The easiest and quickest way to get some flowers is to buy them from one of the many street vendors scattered around the city. If you want something delivered, however, try the following florists.

The Egg Depot
34A Wexford Street, Southside (475 6506). All cross-city buses. **Open** 9am-6pm Mon-Sat. **Credit** MC, V. **Map** p313 G6.

This small and rather quirky store specialises in more unusual blooms, and has an unrivalled selection of rare and tropical flowers.

Justyne Flowers
Irish Life Mall, Talbot Street, Northside (872 8455). All cross-city buses. **Open** 8am-6pm Mon-Fri; 9am-6pm Sat. **Credit** AmEx, MC, V. **Map** p313 H3.
A pretty standard Interflora shop.
Branches: throughout the city.

Food & drink

Bakers & confectioners

Ann's Hot Breadshop
Mary Street, Northside (872 7759). All cross-city buses. **Open** 7.30am-6pm Mon-Wed, Fri, Sat; 7.30am-8pm Thur. **No credit cards. Map** p313 G4.
It's worth visiting this popular bakery first thing in the morning, when the smell of cooking and fresh bread entices you to sit down for a second breakfast. Tea, coffee and cakes are also served.
Branch: 26 North Earl Street, Northside (871 6796).

Kylemore
1 O'Connell Street, Northside (878 0494). All cross-city buses. **Open** 8.30am-5.30pm Mon-Sat. **Credit** MC, V. **Map** p313 313 H4.
Kylemore runs several cake shops around the city. It's almost as famous as Bewley's but not quite as appealing or atmospheric.
Branches: throughout the city.

Delicatessens

Don't miss **Caviston's** in Sandycove. *See p105.*

Big Cheese
St Andrew's Lane, Southside (671 1399). All cross-city buses. **Open** 10am-6pm Mon-Fri; 9.30am-6pm Sat. **Credit** MC, V. **Map** p313 H5.
BC stocks cheeses that have been sourced from around the world, plus bread, delicacies and a range of US imports. It's a very good shop, but beware the pungent smells.

Jones's Delicatessen
137 Baggot Street Lower, Southside (661 8137). All cross-city buses. **Open** 7am-7.30pm Mon-Sat. **Credit** MC, V. **Map** p313 J6.
A standard deli with branches around Dublin, selling bread, cheese, cold meats and the like.
Branches: throughout the city.

Sheridan's Cheesemongers
11 South Anne Street, Southside (679 3143). All cross-city buses. **Open** 9.30am-6pm Mon-Wed, Fri, Sat; 9.30am-7pm Thur. **Credit** MC, V. **Map** p313 H5.
Sheridan's sells lots of exotic cheeses, including some vegetarian and even vegan varieties. It also stocks a range of other food products, including honey, preserves and pasta.

Health food

You'll find spacious, well-laid-out branches of **Tony Quinn Health Stores** throughout the city, including one at Eccles Street on the northside (830 8588).

General Health Food Stores

93 Marlborough Street, Northside (874 3290). All cross-city buses. **Open** 9am-6pm Mon-Sat. **Credit** AmEx, MC, V. **Map** p313 H3.
This long-established organic shop offers a great range of health foods.
Branches: throughout the city.

Nature's Way

ILAC Centre, Parnell Street, Northside (872 8391). All cross-city buses. **Open** 9am-6pm Mon-Wed, Fri, Sat; 9am-8pm Sat. **Credit** MC, V. **Map** p313 G3.
Nature's Way specialises in health food, vitamins and skincare products, though the real treat is the informed staff, who are happy to advise on the right natural remedy for your complaint.
Branches: throughout the city.

Off-licences

There's a surprising lack of off-licences in Dublin city centre, so the food courts of the major department stores are often your best bet for off-the-shelf booze: try **Marks & Spencer** (*see p143*), **Roches Stores** (*see p144*), and **Tesco/Quinnsworth** in the Jervis Centre (*see p145*).

Quinn's

238 Harold's Cross Road, Southern suburbs (497 4239). Bus 65B. **Open** 10.30am-11.30pm Mon-Sat; 12.30-11pm Sun. **Credit** AmEx, MC, V.
With branches all over the city, Quinn's is rapidly turning into the place to buy all your party needs: beer, wine, spirits, videos, pizzas and snacks. For the terminally lazy, home delivery is also available.
Branches: throughout the city.

Furniture & homewares

Don't forget to check out the funky stuff at **Urban Outfitters** (*see p150*).

Foko

66-67 South Great George's Street, Southside (475 5344). All cross-city buses. **Open** 9am-6pm Mon-Wed, Fri, Sat; 9am-8pm Thur; 2-6pm Sun. **Credit** MC, V. **Map** p313 G3.
Foko is filled with quirky furniture for the ideal post-nuclear home plus ingenious and striking gimmicks for the gadget-lover.

Habitat

7 St Stephen's Green, Southside (677 1433). All cross-city buses. **Open** 9.30am-6pm Mon-Wed, Fri, Sat; 9.30am-8pm Thur; noon-6pm Sun. **Credit** AmEx, MC, V. **Map** p313 H6.

This long-established chainstore is renowned for its successful combination of functionality and award-winning designs. Prices are erratic, but, in the absence of its lower-priced Scandinavian arch-rival Ikea, Habitat continues to dominate in Dublin.

Health & beauty

Don't miss the beauty counters at **Brown Thomas** (*see p144*).

Bellaza Beauty Clinic

27 Ranelagh Road, Southern suburbs (496 3484). Bus 12, 44, 44B, 48, 61, 62. **Open** 9.30am-8pm Tue-Fri; 9.30am-5pm Sat. **Credit** MC, V. **Map** p309.
Aromatherapy and toning tables are available here, while turbo sunbeds offer the sort of realistic tan that doesn't come naturally in Dublin. Electrolysis and manicures form part of the service. Phone for details of treatments and rates.

Body Shop

82 Grafton Street, Southside (679 4569). All cross-city buses. **Open** 9am-6.30pm Mon-Wed, Fri, Sat; 9am-9pm Thur; 1.30-6pm Sun. **Credit** AmEx, MC, V. **Map** p313 H5.
This branch of the world-famous store sells all the usual eco-friendly unctions and creams.

Hair & Beauty Clinic

31-32 Mary Street, Northside (872 5544). Bus 24. **Open** 10am-6pm Mon-Wed; 9am-8pm Thur; 9am-7pm Fri; 9am-6pm Sat. **Credit** MC, V. **Map** p313 G4.
Aromatherapy, body wraps, Eurowave slimming, manicures and pedicures. Phone for details of treatments and rates.

Nue Blue Eriu

South William Street, Southside (672 5776). All cross-city buses. **Open** 10am-6pm Mon-Wed, Fri, Sat; 10am-8pm Thur. **Credit** MC, V. **Map** p313 H5.
This sleek, minimalist space, decorated with carefully placed flowers and fish tanks, is the yummiest cosmetics and beauty boutique in Dublin with goodies from Khiels, Dr Hauschka, Eve Lom, Nars, Prada skinwear and Phoebe Manners. There are treatments, too, including aromatherapy massage, Eve Lom facials and the blissful-sounding Field of Dreams. Expensive and exclusive, its bright blue carrier bags are a Dublin status symbol.

Hairdressers

Cowboys and Angels

4 South William Street, Southside (679 7654). All cross-city buses. **Open** 10am-6.30pm Mon, Tue, Fri; 10am-7.30pm Wed, Thur; 9.30am-5pm Sat. **Credit** MC, V. **Map** p313 H5.
Creative cutting and colouring. Phone for prices.

David Marshall Hair Studio

6 Dawson Street, Southside (677 0106). All cross-city buses. **Open** 9am-6pm Mon-Wed, Fri, Sat; 9am-8pm Thur. **Credit** AmEx, MC, V. **Map** p313 H5.

Book well in advance for David Marshall's Dawson Street salon, one of the most popular hairdresser's in the city. The other branch is a cheaper option where students from his school of hairdressing get the chance to screw up your hair. (Not really. They're actually pretty good.) Watch out for Mr Marshall's own lovely bouffant hair; a style recommendation if ever there was one. Phone for details and prices.
Branch: 27 South Great George's Street, Southside (677 7418).

Lunatic Fringe
69 Grafton Street, Southside (679 3766). All cross-city buses. **Open** 9.30am-5.30pm Mon-Wed; 9.30am-8pm Thur; 9.30am-6.30pm Fri; 9am-5pm Sat. **Credit** MC, V. **Map** p313 H5.
Creative colouring and some sharp cutting.

Peter Mark
Level 2, St Stephen's Green Centre, Southside (475 1126). All cross-city buses. **Open** 9am-6pm Mon-Wed, Fri; 9am-8pm Thur; 9.30am-6pm Sat. **Credit** AmEx, MC, V. **Map** p313 H6.
Peter Mark has branches almost everywhere. In addition to haircuts, extras include waxing, electrolysis, make-up tips and manicures. Phone for details and prices.
Branches: throughout the city.

Toni & Guy
27 South Anne Street, Southside (671 4401). All cross-city buses. **Open** 10am-6pm Mon, Tue; 10am-8pm Wed-Fri; 9.30am-5.30pm Sat. **Credit** AmEx, MC, V. **Map** p313 H5.
Toni & Guy may be more expensive than Peter Mark's, but it's also considerably more chic.

Opticians

For good quality budget eyewear and eye examinations, you'll find branches of **Specsavers** (www.specsavers.com) all over the city.

Optika
1 Royal Hibernian Way, Dawson Street, Southside (677 4705). All cross-city buses. **Open** 9.30am-6pm Mon-Wed, Fri, Sat; 9.30am-8pm Thur. **Credit** MC, V. **Map** p313 H6.
The list of designer frames stocked here is endless, and includes the likes of Dolce & Gabbana, Armani and Paul Smith. Frames start at around £100. Optika also sells an array of sunglasses from designers such as Kata and LA Eyeworks. Eye tests are also available.

Pharmacies

There are branches of **Boots** throughout the city. In addition to providing a pharmacy service, they stock everything from plasters to hair dyes and barley sugar to condoms. The branch in the Square in Tallaght (462 2155) stays open until 11pm daily.

Treat yourself at **Nue Blue Eriu**. *See p156.*

Donnybrook Pharmacy
8 The Mall, Donnybrook, Southern suburbs (269 5236). Bus 10, 46A. **Open** 8am-10pm Mon-Sat; 9am-10pm Sun. **Credit** AmEx, MC, V.
A late night pharmacy for all your pharmaceutical needs. It's closed only on Christmas Day, but reopens the next day for hangover cures.

O'Connells
21 Grafton Street, Southside (679 0467). All cross-city buses. **Open** 8.30am-8.30pm Mon-Sat; 11am-6pm Sun. **Credit** AmEx, MC, V. **Map** p313 H5.
A chain of pharmacies spread mostly around the city centre, selling the standard range of goods and offering prescription facilities.
Branches: throughout the city.

Music

CDs & vinyl

For dance music, check out the vinyl selection at **Urban Outfitters** (*see p150*).

Borderline
17 Temple Bar, Southside (679 9097). All cross-city buses. **Open** 10am-6pm Mon-Sat; 2-6pm Sun. **Credit** MC, V. **Map** p75.
A fine second-hand store, particularly good for bootlegs and other unofficial bits and bobs.

Celtic Note
12 Nassau Street, Southside (670 4157). All cross-city buses. **Open** 9.30am-5.30pm Mon-Sat; 11am-6pm Sun. **Credit** AmEx, DC, MC, V. **Map** p313 H5.
A dedicated Irish music store, offering everything from U2 and Joe Dolan to fiddly-diddly music of the *Riverdance* ilk. Recently noted for a massive Dido display in the window, bearing the legend 'Her grandmother was Irish'. Jack Charlton, where are you when we need you.

Claddagh Records
2 Cecilia Street, Temple Bar, Southside (677 0262). All cross-city buses. **Open** 10.30am-5.30pm Mon-Fri; noon-5.30pm Sat. **Credit** MC, V. **Map** p75.
Claddagh has an excellent collection of Irish music, plus a decent array of roots, country and folk titles.

Eat, Drink, Shop

Truly Optimistic

PHOTOGRAPHY JONATHON FOSTER WILLIAMS

Agent Provocateur

Freebird

1 Eden Quay, Northside (873 1250). All cross-city buses. **Open** 10.30am-6pm Mon-Wed, Sat; 10.30am-7pm Thur, Fri. **Credit** MC, V. **Map** p313 H4.
Probably the best place in the city for indie labels.

Golden Discs

8 North Earl Street, Northside (874 0417). All cross-city buses. **Open** 9.30am-6pm Mon-Wed, Fri; 9.30am-8pm Thur; 9am-6pm Sat. **Credit** AmEx, DC, MC, V. **Map** p313 H3.
The largest chain of music stores in Ireland, with 15 branches in Dublin. It tends to carry a reliable, mainstream stock, with an emphasis on the Irish music scene. The small size of the average GD outlet tends to cramp the range, but competitive prices and generous offers improve matters.
Branches: throughout the city.

HMV

65 Grafton Street, Southside (679 5334/ticketline 156 9569). All cross-city buses. **Open** 9am-7pm Mon-Wed, Fri, Sat; 9am-9pm Thur; 11am-7pm Sun. **Credit** AmEx, DC, MC, V. **Map** p313 H5.
The most reliably stocked of the megastores, with three large floors catering well for every genre of music and every format from vinyl to mini-discs. Though HMV usually has some breed of sale going at all times, some of the stock can be quite pricey. HMV is also the best place in Dublin to buy advance tickets for gigs in the city *(see p191)*.

Road Records

16B Fade Street, Southside (671 7340). All cross-city buses. **Open** 10am-6pm Mon-Wed, Sat; 10am-7pm Thur. **Credit** MC, V. **Map** p313 G5.
Stocks indie music, second-hand vinyl and a good selection of stuff by local Dublin bands.

Smile Records

59 South Great George's Street, Southside (478 2005). All cross-city buses. **Open** 10am-6pm Mon-Wed, Fri, Sat; 10am-8pm Thur; 2-6pm Sun. **Credit** MC, V. **Map** p313 G5.
A great range of second hand stuff at reasonable prices, with affable and knowledgeable service.

Spindizzy

Market Arcade, South Great George's Street, Southside (671 1711). All cross-city buses. **Open** 10.30am-6pm Mon-Wed, Sat; 10.30am-8pm Thur; 1-6pm Sun. **Credit** AmEx, MC, V. **Map** p313 G5.
Great name and some good second-hand stock, particularly reggae, jazz and indie.

Tower Records

16 Wicklow Street, Southside (671 3250). All cross-city buses. **Open** 9am-10pm Mon-Fri; 9am-11pm Sat; 11.30am-7.30pm Sun. **Credit** AmEx, DC, MC, V. **Map** p313 H5.
Tower has a terrific range of alternative and world music, as well as good jazz, traditional and country sections. The rear left of the ground floor houses an unequalled selection of music books, magazines and newspapers, including the best range of foreign papers in Dublin. Granted, they're often a couple of days behind their countries of origin, but at least they're there. Tower can also order any paper or magazine on request.
Branch: Eason's, O'Connell Street, Northside (873 3811).

Virgin Megastore

14 Aston Quay, Southside (677 7361). All cross-city buses. **Open** 9am-6pm Mon, Wed; 9.30am-6pm Tue; 9am-8pm Thur; 9am-7pm Fri, Sat; 1-5pm Sun. **Credit** AmEx, MC, V. **Map** p313 H4.
The grandest, friendliest and cheapest of the big music stores. There is a formidable classical room off the ground floor; upstairs are great ranges of videos and games.

Instruments & sheet music

Charles Byrne Musik Instrumente

21 Stephen Street Lower, Southside (478 1773). All cross-city buses. **Open** 9am-5.30pm Tue-Fri; 9am-5pm Sat. **Credit** AmEx, MC, V. **Map** p313 G5.
An atmospheric and charming instruments shop

McCullough Pigott's

25 Suffolk Street, Southside (677 3138). All cross-city buses. **Open** 9am-5.30pm Mon-Sat. **Credit** AmEx, MC, V. **Map** p313 H5.
Probably Dublin's most popular instrument and sheet music retailer, McCullough's is a fantastic place for a music lover to waste a couple of hours.

McNeill's

140 Capel Street, Northside (872 2159). All cross-city buses. **Open** 10am-6pm Mon-Sat. **Credit** MC, V. **Map** p313 G4.
A small and beautiful store, McNeill's has been in business for over 150 years, and its selection of and advice on traditional instruments is second to none.

Newsagents & stationers

For foreign newspapers, visit **Tower Records** *(see above)*. **Bus Stop**, with branches around the city including one in Grafton Street (671 4476/677 3661), stocks cards and 'Irish' gifts (leprechaun soft toys and their ilk) as well as newspapers and magazines. **News Express** (46 O'Connell Street Upper, Northside; 873 1028) and **Spar** are other popular newsagents; the Spar shop at 115 Grafton Street (670 4512) is open 24 hours daily.

Read's

Nassau Street, Southside (679 6011). Bus 10, 11, 13. All cross-city buses. **Open** 8.30am-6.30pm Mon-Fri; 9am-6.30pm Sat. **Credit** MC, V. **Map** p313 H5.
An excellent newsagent with one of the widest ranges in the city, Read's also has a basement floor stocked with every possible stationery item you could need, as well as a full photocopying service (including colour, pleasingly).

Rainbow Crafts: strictly retro.

Sports & outdoor equipment

Army Bargains

30 Little Mary Street, Northside (874 4600).
All cross-city buses. **Open** 8.30am-6pm Mon-Sat.
Credit MC, V. **Map** p312-3 F/G4.
Honest advice and tonnes of offers make Army
Bargains just too good to miss.

Beaten Track

16 Exchequer Street, Southside (671 2477). All
cross-city buses. **Open** 9am-5.30pm Mon-Wed, Fri,
Sat; 9am-7pm Thur. **Credit** MC, V. **Map** p313 G5.
Beaten Track promises to help adventurers 'face
the elements with confidence', though whether any
of the designer-labelled fleeces purveyed herein
ever actually make it beyond the landscaped
wildernesses of Killiney or Dublin 4 is a question
open for discussion.

Great Outdoors

Chatham Street, Southside (679 4293). All cross-city
buses. **Open** 9.30am-5.30pm Mon-Wed, Fri, Sat;
9.30am-8pm Thur. **Credit** AmEx, DC, MC, V.
Map p313 H5.
Quality mainstream sports goods, plus stuff for
scuba diving, canoeing and skiing.

Marathon

24 Henry Street, Northside (872 9808). All cross-city
buses. **Open** 9.30am-6pm Mon-Wed, Fri, Sat; 9.30am-
8pm Thur. **Credit** AmEx, MC, V. **Map** p313 G/H4.
This growing sports store stocks all the well-known
brands in clothes, shoes and accessories.
Branch: Marathon Junior 28 Henry Street,
Northside (872 1417).

Milletts

26 Little Mary Street, Northside (873 3571).
All cross-city buses. **Open** 9am-6pm Mon-Sat.
Credit MC, V. **Map** p312-3 F/G4.
Amazingly low prices on an extensive range of high-
quality tents and camping/survival equipment set
Milletts apart from the competition.

Stadium Sports

St Stephen's Green Centre, Southside (475 3525).
All cross-city buses. **Open** 9.30am-6.30pm Mon-Wed,
Sat; 9.30am-8.30pm Thur; 9.30am-7.30pm Fri; noon-
6pm Sun. **Credit** AmEx, MC, V. **Map** p313 H6.
A diverse range of sportswear is on offer here.

Toys

Baba Toymaster

48 Mary Street, Northside (872 7100). All cross-city
buses. **Open** 9am-6pm Mon-Sat. **Credit** MC, V.
Map p313 G4.
All the big names at keen prices, Baba's is nigh-on
essential at Christmas.

Early Learning Centre

3 Henry Street, Northside (873 1945/www.elc.co.uk).
All cross-city buses. **Open** 9am-5.30pm Mon-Wed,
Fri, Sat; 9am-8pm Thur. **Credit** MC, V.
Map p313 G/H4.
Primary-coloured educational and fun toys for
babies and younger children can be found at this
well-known chain.

The Model Shop

13 Capel Street, Northside (872 8134). All cross-city
buses. **Open** 9.30am-5.30pm Mon-Sat. **No credit**
cards. Map p313 G4.
Planes, trains and automobiles.

Rainbow Crafts

5 Westbury Hotel Mall, Grafton Street, Southside
(677 7632/www.teddybears-dolls.com). All cross-city
buses. **Open** 9am-6pm Mon-Wed, Fri, Sat; 9am-7pm
Thur. **Credit** AmEx, MC, V. **Map** p313 H5.
An old-fashioned shop, concentrating on all the old
faves: wooden toys, rocking horses, doll's houses,
traditional teddy bears and spinning tops. The
goods here are as popular with nostalgia-seeking
adults as they are with children.

Treasure Chest

Unit 23, Swan Centre, Rathmines, Southern suburbs
(496 4720). Bus 15, 15A. **Open** 9.30am-5pm Mon-
Sat. **Credit** AmEx, DC, MC, V.
Lots of toys of all sorts for all ages in a compact,
well-stocked shop.

Travel agents

For discounted fares and all-round good value,
try the two listed below.

Trailfinders

4-5 Dawson Street, Southside (677 7888/www.
trailfinders.ie). All cross-city buses. **Open** 9am-6pm
Mon-Wed, Fri, Sat; 9am-7pm Thur; 10am-6pm Sun.
Credit AmEx, DC, MC, V. **Map** p313 H5.

USIT Now

19-21 Aston Quay, Southside (679 8833). All cross-
city buses. **Open** 9.30am-6.30pm Mon-Wed, Fri;
9.30am-8pm Thur; 9.30am-5pm Sat. **Credit** AmEx,
DC, MC, V. **Map** p313 H4.

Arts &
Entertainment

Features

By Season

A diverse cultural calendar and plenty of excuses for a booze-up keep Dublin swinging all year long.

In keeping with Ireland's overwhelming urge to compete on the world stage, more and more of Dublin's festivals are developing an international flavour: the **French Film Festival** (*see p175*) draws nearly as much attention as the **Dublin Film Festival**; sporting events such as the **Six Nations** rugby tournament and the **Kerry Gold Horse Show** bring international competitors to the city, and visiting productions often threaten to outnumber home-grown drama at the **Dublin Theatre Festival**.

Yet despite the prestige of these events, **St Patrick's Day** remains by far the biggest event on the Dublin calendar – and the one that attracts the most international attention. This saint's day may now be celebrated with pints of Guinness all over the western world, but Dublin remains at the heart of global festivities. And as long as you can cope with the crowds and the queues, there's no better place to enjoy it.

Spring

For information on the Guinness-fuelled festivities of the **St Patrick's Day Festival**, *see p163* **Paddy's Day Ha Ha Ha**.

Six Nations Rugby

4 Lansdowne Road, Ballsbridge, Southern suburbs (information 668 4601/www.irfu.ie). Lansdowne Road DART. **Tickets** €18-€50. **Credit** AmEx, DC, MC, V. **Map** p314 M7. **Date** mid Feb-mid Mar.
This rugby competition between England, Ireland, Scotland, Wales, France and Italy is one of the biggest events in the Irish sporting calendar. Home games are played at Lansdowne Road, and the atmosphere of a big match affects the whole city. Even when Ireland are not playing at home, match days are so partytastic that fans have been known to travel to Dublin to watch the game in a Dub pub on a Dub screen. Accommodation is nigh-on impossible to find, so booking ahead is absolutely essential. Information is available from the Irish Rugby Football Union at the start of the season.

Celebrating an Irish win in the **Six Nations Rugby** tournament.

Paddy's Day Ha Ha Ha

On 17 March it seems, anyone who's even so much as inhaled the aroma of a pint of Guinness will resurrect an Irish granny from somewhere and claim allegiance to the green, white and orange. Ah yes, it's the world's best excuse for a drink: the feast day of a Welsh man who ran the snakes out of Ireland.

If you're born and bred Irish, it's a different story, of course. The memory of years of Patrick's Day celebrations come back to scare you like haunting nightmares. There was a time, before Dublin got all sophisticated and Eurocentric, when St Patrick's Day was celebrated by stapling a clump of mucky, wilting shamrock to your lapel and traipsing into the rain-sodden city centre to see rain-sodden American brass bands and homegrown majorette troupes shake their rain-sodden little pom-poms. And did we mention it always rained? Visitors thronged Dublin's streets to celebrate 'Irishness': cheering on marching bands from every corner of the US and waving little plastic flags with poles that gave you splinters. But the new millennium was fast approaching, the city was purring to the sound of its rapidly filling coffers and it

was only a matter of time before Dublin cashed in on the fact that for one day a year the whole world wants to be Irish.

Over the past four years, then, the St Patrick's Day festival has been comprehensively glammed up. The parade still forms the core of the celebrations and draws half a million people on to the streets, but now they are here to watch Europe's brightest street entertainers, Irish puppeteers and theatre groups, the world's best pyrotechnics and state of the art equipment. Surrounding the main event is a four-day festival of world-class entertainment, including the Guinness Fleadh (see p104), plus all manner of street performances, firework displays and general frivolity. Pubs and bars are packed to the rafters, the Guinness flows and it's a magical – if very crowded – experience just wandering the streets. Bizarrely, even the rain seems to stay away.

St Patrick's Day Parade & Festival
Information 676 3205/www.paddyfest.ie.
Dates 15-18 Mar.

Arts & Entertainment

In the swim

The Liffey may have been gentrified with bridges and boardwalks, it may have undergone refurbishments and facelifts, but it remains a pretty murky stretch of water, famed for its smell rather than its clarity. Yet every year for the last 80 years or so, normally sane people have voluntarily hurled themselves into the river's grimy depths in order to take part in the annual Liffey Swim. The bemused indifference of passers-by may make you doubt the popularity of this event, but some 250 men and about 120 women sign up for it every year. And with the spanking-new boardwalk now in place, spectators have a perfect viewing platform to witness the madness.

The idea for the swim came from a Dublin archivist and amateur swimmer named Fagin, who managed to gain the financial backing of the *Irish Times*. The first race was held in 1920 and attracted 50 (all-male) competitors. In the years that followed, the event became increasingly popular and drew vast crowds of spectators to the banks of the river. Jack Butler Yeats captured the excitement in his 1923 painting of the event, which hangs in the National Gallery.

Nowadays swimmers have to complete a number of qualifying events in order to participate in the big race – not least of which is being able to hold your breath in a sewer. Competitors assemble at Rory O'More Bridge near the Guinness brewery, dive in and make their way east, negotiating bridges, scaffolding, bemused swans as well as the odd barge, before emerging exhausted one-and-a-half miles downstream at the finishing line on Custom House Quay . Meanwhile, clowns, face painters, trumpeters and other entertainers keep the spectators amused on the sidelines.

If you're in town for the event, be sure to scream your encouragement from the quays: this is a race, after all, and the most unlucky losers can expect is a decontamination treatment from the fire brigade at the other end.

Liffey Swim
Rory O'More Bridge to Custom House Quay (information 833 2434). **Date** late Aug/ early Sept.

Guinness Fleadh
Various venues, Temple Bar, Southside (information 671 5717). All cross-city buses. **Admission** free. **Map** p75. **Date** 15-17 Mar.
For a feast of traditional Irish music in all styles and interpretations you don't get much better than the three-day Guinness Fleadh. Usually the single biggest musical event of the St Patrick's Day Festival, it consists of (mostly free) gigs and concerts held at over 20 venues in Temple Bar. Outdoor drinking is strictly banned, but the area is still packed to the gills with music fans and sightseers soaking up the atmosphere rather than the booze.

Dublin Film Festival
Information: Events Office, 1 Suffolk Street, Southside (679 2937/www.iol.ie/dff). **Tickets** phone for details. **Date** Mar-Apr.
The international reputation of the Film Festival has grown steadily since its launch in 1986. It celebrates the best of Irish and world cinema, with screenings across the city, plus lectures and debates that allow fans to meet successful Irish screenwriters, directors and actors. The festival has received a lot of criticism of late for poor organisation and programming, but it remains extremely popular, so book tickets well in advance. *See p175* **Festival fever: Film.**

Summer

The **Dublin International Organ & Choral Festival**, a triennial event, is next scheduled to be held in June 2002. For information, contact the festival organisers (677 3066 ext 416). Also of note is the **Beo Festival**, a trad-music event at the National Concert Hall in late August (*see p191*). Around the same time is the **Liffey Swim**, a chance to watch hundreds of (fool) hardy swimmers race down Dublin's river, *see p164* **In the swim.**

Diversions on the Square

Meeting House Square, Temple Bar, Southside (information 671 5717/www.esb.ie). All cross-city buses. **Admission** free. **Map** p75. **Date** June-Aug.
Throughout the summer, a wide variety of free open-air events take place in the heart of Temple Bar. There are lunchtime and evening concerts, innovative dance performances, plus a variety of family events every Sunday afternoon (*see p168*). Film buffs should look out for the IFC's Saturday night outdoor screenings of classic movies (*see p174*).

Music in the Park

Information 672 3388/www.dublincorp.ie. **Admission** free. **Date** June-Aug
The sun is shining, there's laid-back jazz in the background and all is right with the world. Dublin Corporation's programme of free open air concerts and recitals in the city's parks has been a huge success. Brass, reed and swing bands can be enjoyed on most afternoons at alternating venues, including the Civic Offices Park on Wood Quay, Merrion Square Park and St Stephen's Green.

Adidas/Evening Herald Women's Mini-Marathon

Information 670 9461/496 0861.
Date 2nd Sun in June.
The annual Women's Mini-Marathon is the largest event of its kind in the world, attracting upwards of 30,000 participants (and not all of them female, incidentally). It's a competition than an opportunity to raise money for charity, and the vast majority of competitors walk rather than run the 10km (six-mile) course. Each year, people comment on the electric atmosphere, though the sight of many suspiciously hairy-looking 'nuns' and 'schoolgirls' also raises a few eyebrows.

Bloomsday Festival

Information: James Joyce Centre, 35 North Great George's Street, Northside (878 8547/ www.joycecen.com). **Date** 16 June.
Held every year around the 16 June (the day on which *Ulysses* is set), and taking its name from the novel's central character, the Bloomsday Festival commemorates Bloom's famous 'walking out' with a week-long celebration of the writings of James Joyce. Readings, performances, excursions and meals help to re-create the atmosphere of Dublin,

circa 1904. Fans of James Joyce, and anyone with an historical or cultural interest in Edwardian Dublin will enjoy the events. Booking is strongly advised.

Anna Livia Opera Festival

Information 661 7544/www.operaannalivia.com. **Tickets** prices vary; phone for details. **Date** mid June.
Inaugurated in 2000, this festival stages full-scale opera productions in the Gaiety Theatre (*see p187*), alongside smaller-scale concerts in the National Concert Hall, and youth and educational events.

Pride

Information: Gay Community News, Unit 2, Scarlet Row, Temple Bar, Southside (www.gcn.ie). **Date** last Sat, Sun in June.
Highlights of this week-long gay festival include a gay céilidh (or a gaylidh), drag contests, various workshops, readings and theme nights all held in the city's gay and gay-friendly venues. The flamboyant centrepiece, however, is the Pride march itself, from the Garden of Remembrance at the top of O'Connell Street to the grass-covered amphitheatre beside the Civic Offices at Wood Quay.

Kerrygold Horse Show

Royal Dublin Society, Anglesea Road, Ballsbridge, Southern suburbs (668 0866/www.rds.ie). *Lansdowne Road DART/7, 8, 45 bus.* **Open** 9am-6.30pm Wed-Sun. **Admission** phone for details. **Credit** AmEx, MC, V. **Date** 1st wk in Aug.
Offering some of the richest prizes in the world, this five day long showjumping event attracts high-profile visitors and competitors. The famous Kerrygold Nations' Cup, where international teams compete for the prestigious Aga Khan Trophy, is traditionally held on the Friday; Thursday is Ladies' Day.

Autumn

For information on the **Dublin Jazz Festival**, *see p194* **Festival fever: Rock, pop & jazz.**

All-Ireland Hurling & Football Finals

Croke Park, Jones Road, Drumcondra, Northern suburbs (836 3222/www.gaa.ie). *Bus 3, 11, 11A, 16, 51A.* **Tickets** prices vary; phone for details. **No credit cards. Map** p309. **Date** *Hurling* 2nd Sun in Sept. *Gaelic football* 4th Sun in Sept.
The north side of the city traditionally grinds to halt on the second and fourth Sundays in September, as Gaelic football and hurling fans travel from all over the country to Croke Park for their respective finals (*see p220* **Going Gaelic**).

Dublin Theatre Festival

Information 677 8439/www.dublintheatrefestival. com. **Tickets** €15.25-€30. **Credit** MC, V.
Date early Oct.
The festival has been a showcase for the best of Irish and world theatre since its foundation in 1957. It not only provides a stage for emerging local talent, but also attracts productions of an international stature.

Come and out and celebrate at Dublin's **Pride** parade. *See p165.*

Most of the city's major theatrical venues host festival events and the programme is generally varied – though it sometimes follows a specific theme. Criticised in the past for being either too high- or low-brow, the festival always manages to provoke vigorous dramatic debate and has staged a few coups in its time. Almost as prominent as its older sister, the **Fringe Festival** provides a high-quality outlet for more alternative forms of theatre, while the **Children's Season** caters for the under-18 crowd. For further details of all these events, *see p206* **Festival fever: Theatre**. Advance bookings are recommended.

98FM Dublin City Marathon
Information 623 2250/623 2159/entry form hotline 626 3746/www.marathonadventures.com.
Date usually last Mon in Oct.
First run in 1980, the Dublin City Marathon is a hugely successful event, attracting several thousand runners each year. The 26-mile (42km) course starts and finishes at the top of O'Connell Street and traces a route through many of Dublin's historic streets and suburbs. You have to be an early bird to watch the start of the event at 8.30am, but you can cheer on the finishers a couple of hours later. Those hoping to compete should submit their entry form at least three weeks before the race.

Samhain Festival (Hallowe'en)
Information: Dublin Tourism, Suffolk Street, Southside (www.visitdublin.com).
Date around 31 Oct.
Hallowe'en in Dublin is based on the traditional pagan festival of Samhain ('sow in'), a celebration of the dead that signalled the end of the Celtic summer. The Samhain Festival in Dublin is one of Ireland's largest night-time events, attracting up to 20,000 people on to the city streets. The Hallowe'en Parade winds its way through the city from Parnell Square to Temple Bar and Wood Quay and is followed by a large-scale fireworks display.

Winter

The **Junior Dublin Film Festival** takes place in late November and early December. *See p175* **Festival fever: Film**.

Christmas Eve Vigil
St Mary's Pro-Cathedral, Marlborough Street, Northside (874 5441). Connolly Station DART.
Admission free. **Map** p313 H3. **Date** 24 Dec.
Despite the onslaught of consumerism, in Ireland the majority of Christmas events still centre on the religious festival itself. A Christmas vigil is held in St Mary's Pro-Cathedral every year by the Archbishop of Dublin, with the beautiful sounds of the Palestrina Choir flexing their vocal chords at 9.30pm. Stick around for the mass at 10pm, too.

Christmas Day & St Stephen's Day
Date 25, 26 Dec.
On Christmas Day the city goes to sleep, with shops, pubs, restaurants and the public transport system all closing down for the day. Limited public transport and most pubs reopen on St Stephen's Day (Boxing Day) leading to a big party night in the city. Expect to walk everywhere unless you've booked your transport far in advance. St Stephen's Day also sees the beginning of the historic Christmas Racing Festival at Leopardstown Racecourse (*see p218* **Horses for courses**).

Children

Big ideas for the smaller visitor.

More than just the bear necessities of life for the inhabitants of **Dublin Zoo**. *See p168*.

With its boozy reputation, Dublin might not leap to mind as the ideal city for a family holiday. Until recently, Dubliners themselves made do with the natural amenities of the city's parks and beaches, with a trip to the zoo or the Funderland funfair at Christmas thrown in for a special treat. However, Ireland's increasing prosperity has created a demand for more structured and ambitious amusements for children. This hasn't necessarily resulted in an upsurge in new venues specifically for kids, but it has meant that galleries and museums now have art clubs for children, and stately homes have home farms and adventure playgrounds – attractions developed with children in mind. In addition, some newer attractions have incorporated purpose-built areas to cater for the child's-eye view.

Of course, the beaches and the parks are still there, and there are always the Georgian squares, a terrific asset for the weary parent: College Park at Trinity, Merrion Square and St Stephen's Green all offer safe, traffic-free zones in the heart of town (and on the Green, there's the added bonus of ducks to feed).

However, there's still a long way to go to make Dublin a truly child-friendly environment. Dubliners like babies and children, but this doesn't always translate into the provision of nappy-changing facilities, child menus or in-store crèches.

TRANSPORT

Many family attractions are situated outside the city centre; if you're planning to use public transport, prepaid family tickets are available from **Dublin Bus** or from shops around the city. Family one-day rambler tickets offer unlimited bus travel for two adults and up to four children, while the family short hop ticket offers unlimited bus and suburban rail/DART travel for the day. For further details, *see chapter* **Getting Around**.

INFORMATION

For up-to-date information on activities for children, consult Saturday's *Irish Times* (or the Wednesday 'Ticket' section in the same newspaper), the *Event Guide* (distributed free in shops, pubs and venues around the city) or the children's pages of Aertel, the teletext service of RTÉ. Also, keep an eye out for special events: the five-day **St Patrick's Day Festival** has lots of activities for kids (*see p163* **Paddy's Day Ha Ha Ha**).

The **Dublin Tourism Centre** on Suffolk Street (www.visitdublin.ie) produces a handy booklet, 'Family Fun in Dublin', which details child-friendly sights and attractions in the area. It can also provide lists of family-friendly hotels and guesthouses.

Sightseeing

Children's tastes and interests are, of course, as eclectic as their parents', and there is plenty in Dublin to satisfy both. Numerous guided tours of the city are available, but the **Viking Splash Tour** (*see p60*) is particularly popular with children. At €12.60 for adults and €6.90 for kids (no family tickets available) it's not cheap, but the novelty factor and the chance to don a Viking helmet make it worth the money.

Southside

There's plenty of fun to be had strolling around the city centre. Aside from the shopping, **Grafton Street** is a great, if crowded, spot for a walk, where the kids can listen to the buskers (some of whom are kids themselves) or try to make the mime artists move. **Temple Bar** is fun, too, with pedestrian areas, market stalls and street performers adding to the relaxed atmosphere. On Sunday afternoons during the summer there's the added attraction of the free family events in **Meeting House Square**. Organised by Temple Bar Properties (677 2255; www.temple-bar.ie) in conjunction with the **Ark** (*see p171*), each week features dancers, musicians, puppeteers and circus performers from around the world. Performances are often interactive, with face painting, or an opportunity to try out some percussion instruments.

When it comes to more traditional sightseeing, both sites of the **National Museum** (*see p66* and *p93*) are great places to explore and offer activity sheets and carts containing crayons and paper to their younger visitors. The museum also runs a series of events and activities for children throughout the summer at each of its sites. These include talks, tours, art workshops and the opportunity to see ancient crafts such as silversmithing in progress. Events are free, cater for a variety of ages, and adults are welcome to accompany their offspring. Call ahead to reserve places. The **Natural History Museum** (*see p70*), with its stuffed animals, dinosaurs, and vaguely creepy air of pickled Victoriana, is a good bet for the inevitable rainy day, and the **Chester**

Beatty Library in Dublin Castle (*see p74*) has a regular programme of workshops where children can learn about various aspects of eastern cultures – from stories about figures in Islamic history to Japanese art forms like origami. Workshops are aimed at the seven to 11 age group and numbers are limited, so book in advance.

A couple of southside attractions offer an accessible introduction to the history of the city: **Dublinia** (*see p77*), in the Christchurch area, offers a multimedia look at the medieval city, while the **Dublin Viking Adventure** (*see p76*) goes even further back in time, with an interactive exhibition that re-creates the sights, sounds, even smells, of Dublin as it was 1,000 years ago, and a large collection of artefacts discovered during excavations at Wood Quay.

The **Irish Museum of Modern Art** (IMMA, *see p82*) makes a particular effort to make its exhibitions accessible to families. Twice-weekly guided tours are free and aimed at first-time visitors, and in the Process Room and the Response Room visitors of all ages can use the dry materials provided to write or draw their impressions of their visit and display them afterwards on the notice board.

Northside

Mini music fans will enjoy the **Hot Press Irish Music Hall of Fame** (*see p86*) where they can get up close and personal with their rock and pop idols. Also north of the Liffey, is the kitsch haven that is the **National Wax Museum** (*see p88*). It contains plenty of models recognisable to the under-50s, but bear in mind that this place is stuck strictly in the pre-interactive age, which might be a problem for those with short attention spans. Nearby, in the **Dublin Writers' Museum** (*see p88*), kids can find out about Ireland's favourite children's authors. If you fancy a breather, the **Garden of Remembrance**, just across the road, contains a poignant statue of Irish mythology's most famous offspring, the Children of Lir.

Young horror fans should venture along the quays to **St Michan's Church** (*see p90*) on Lower Church Street, where they can go down to the vaults to view some remarkably well-preserved bodies. Further along the river is the **National Museum** at Collins Barracks (*see p93*), followed by **Phoenix Park** (*see p93*), the largest park in Europe. It has acres of romping space, as well as a visitors' centre and the worthwhile **Dublin Zoo** (*see p94*). Recently enlarged with an acclaimed African Plains section, the zoo also runs a long-standing Meet the Keeper programme daily in summer

Arts & Entertainment

and at weekends in winter, where kids can help feed the animals. If the weather's good, bring a picnic and make a day of it. Alternatively, the **National Botanic Gardens** in Glasnevin (*see p97*) offer a civilised outdoor experience. The Gardens sometimes host children's events, including special activities for National Science Week in September.

Dublin Bay

The local coast is another great natural resource for children – **Howth, Malahide, Dún Laoghaire, Dalkey** and **Bray** are all on the DART line and make perfect day excursions. Most of the beaches around Dublin Bay have more pebbles than sand, but the small beach at **Sandycove** (*see p105*) is true to its name and perfect for toddlers. Take a boat trip from **Howth** to visit Ireland's Eye (*see p101*), or enjoy a bracing seaside walk along the coast road from the pretty town of Malahide to Portmarnock, but watch out for the strong undertow if you fancy a swim here. The **Fry Model Railway Museum** (*see p102*) in the grounds of Malahide Castle is great fun for budding trainspotters, while at **Newbridge House & Traditional Farm** (*see p103*), young visitors can learn about how rural life has been lived over the centuries, or play in the adventure playground.

Eating & drinking

You'll find no problem in assuaging children's appetite for junk food in Dublin, which has more than its fair share of fast-food outlets. Try **Supermacs** on O'Connell Street (872 1828), which offers pizzas, burgers, kebabs, chicken and ice-cream. American-themed diners are also plentiful. The **Bad Ass Café** (*see p110*) is a Temple Bar institution offering reliable pizzas, burgers, salads, and a kids' menu, while **Eddie Rocket's City Diner** (7 South Anne Street, Southside; 679 7340) offers a hint of tacky 1950s glamour with red leather seats and working jukeboxes in the booths. Its fries, which come with a variety of toppings, are a messy, tasty treat. **Captain America's Restaurant** (44 Grafton Street, Southside; 671 5266) is another stalwart that found its niche years ago with the burgers and noise brigade, or there's **Elephant & Castle** (*see p110*), which majors in burgers, chicken wings and omelettes, and has big wooden tables for that Walton's mealtime feel. (This is a good place to know about if you're out and about early, as it's open for breakfast and brunch.) **Thunder Road Café** (Fleet Street, Temple Bar, Southside; 679 4057) is a noisy variation on the diner theme, with huge video

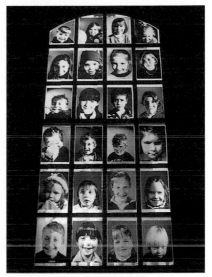

A child's-eye view at **Ark Children's Cultural Centre**. *See p171.*

screens and a Harley Davidson in the window, but it's rather overpriced and tends to get rowdy in the evenings. The New York-themed **Gotham Café** (*see p111*) can also get crowded, but it's a cut above the normal joint and serves excellent pizzas. If you're desperate, there's also **Planet Hollywood** (478 7827) and **TGI Friday's** (478 1233), both in the St Stephen's Green Centre at the bottom of Grafton Street. **Kitty's Kaboodle** (14 Merrion Row, Southside; 662 3350) close to the National Museum and Gallery may not have a kids' menu, but staff will happily serve smaller portions of its burgers, pasta dishes and salads, and the crayons on the table are there to be used: the walls are a gallery for diners who've eaten here before. If you're looking for something a little healthier, try the funky **Cornucopia Vegetarian Restaurant** (*see p120*) or **Chompy's Deli** (Powerscourt Townhouse Centre, William Street South, Southside; 679 4552), which offers sandwiches, bagels, pizzas and other hot meals. And you can people-watch from the balcony tables. For something completely different, slightly older children will enjoy Japanese noodle bar **Wagamama** (*see p117*).

When it comes to cafés, the **Bewley's** chain (*see p127*), though posher than it once was, can still be relied upon for sausage and chips and huge cream cakes. And, for afternoon tea with fabulous cakes, you can't do better than the **Queen of Tarts** (*see p128*).

Arts & Entertainment

Shops & services

For details of children's clothing outlets and toy shops, *see p152 and p160*.

Childminding

Most shopping and leisure centres have crèches that can look after your toddler for a while, but there are few officially sanctioned nannies in Dublin. **Childminders** (22 Kildare Street, Dublin 2; 678 9050) will look after kids at a cost of €55 (book in advance, two-day minimum), and some hotels offer babysitting services – as indicated in our **Accommodation** chapter.

Arts & entertainment

Activities & sports

Kart City (*see p221*) has indoor and outdoor circuits, and the **Irish National Sailing School** (*see p222*) runs courses during the school holidays for young sailing enthusiasts from eight to 17. The **Oldtown Riding Stables** (Wyestown, Oldtown, Co. Dublin; 835 4755) is a good choice for little riders, offering a flexible kids' club, which children can attend and pay for on a daily basis. For other riding stables and for swimming pools, *see p222*.

Fort Lucan

Off Strawberry Beds Road, Westmanstown, Lucan, Co Dublin (628 0166). Bus 25. **Open** *Mar-Easter* 1.30-6pm daily. *Easter-Sept* 10am-6pm daily. **Admission** €6.35 children; free under-2s, adults. **No credit cards**.

Fort Lucan, suitable for two- to 14-year-olds, features everything the adventure-hunter could wish for: assault course, high-tower walks, 40ft slides, trampolines, maze, suspension bridges, crazy golf, water slide, pendulum swing, two go-kart tracks and a tots' area. Opening hours depend on the weather.

Leisureplex

Old Bray Road, Stillorgan, Southern suburbs (288 1656). Bus 46A. **Open** 24hrs daily. **Credit** V.

Admission varies; phone for details. **Credit** V.

A noisy amusement centre: as well as the usual bowling, kids can play Quasar laser games, ramble around the adventure play area and scoff burgers at the café. In Stillorgan they can design and paint ceramics at Pompeii Paints, while Blanchardstown offers dodgems (adult and child cars available) for that old-fashioned fairground experience. All branches have bouncy castles, ball pools, slides and supervised play areas.

Branches: Blanchardstown Centre, Northern suburbs (822 3030); Malahide Road, Coolock, Northern suburbs (848 5722); Village Green Centre, Tallaght, Southern suburbs (459 9411).

Ramp'n'Rail Skatepark

96A Upper Drumcondra Road, Northern suburbs (837 7533). Bus 3, 11, 13, 33, 41. **Open** 11am-9pm Tue-Sun. **Admission** €7.60 per person per day. **Credit** AmEx, DC, MC, V.

If you're the kind of parent who lets your kids bring their skateboard on holiday, then this could be just what you're looking for. Purpose-built for boards but also suitable for rollerblades, it's colourful, well-designed and the kiddies' area keeps the little ones away from their more adventurous older siblings. Once you've signed in, your kids can skate for a day for a flat fee (they can even go off for lunch and

Get creative with ceramics at **Hey, Doodle, Doodle**. *See p171*.

come back at no extra charge). Helmets are compulsory and provided, but kids must bring their own board or rollerblades and protective pads.

Arts & crafts

Dublin's galleries offer a feast of child-centred activities and events. In addition to workshops and art lessons, the **National Gallery** (*see p70*) hosts free half-hour talks on Sundays that focus on a different painting each week, while the **Irish Museum of Modern Art** (*see p82*) operates the Explorer programme on Sunday afternoons from October to early December and from January to June, designed to help kids and parents get to grips with works on display; the programme is free and operates on a drop-in basis. The **Hugh Lane Gallery of Modern Art** (*see p87*) runs a Saturday morning Art Club for six- to 14-year-olds during the summer; places must be booked in advance.

Ark Children's Cultural Centre
11A Eustace Street, Temple Bar, Southside (670 7788). All cross-city buses. **Open** 9.30am-4pm Tue-Fri; 10am-4pm Sat. **Admission** free. **Map** p75.
A 1,500sq m (16,000sq ft) arts centre with a theatre, gallery and workshop, the Ark currently offers around ten programmes across the cultural spectrum. The emphasis is on art and culture by, for and about children aged four to 14. Specially commissioned plays for young people are also performed here.

Hey, Doodle, Doodle
14 Crown Alley, Temple Bar, Southside (672 7382). All cross-city buses. **Open** 11am-6pm Mon-Sat; 1-6pm Sun. **Rates** €8.99-€44 per piece of pottery; €6.35 studio fee. **Credit** AmEx, MC, V. **Map** p75.
Drop in, pick a piece of pottery, paint it and collect the completed masterpiece two to three days later (after firing and glazing).

Film

The **UCI** chain (*see p175*) offers the most child-friendly cinemas in Dublin, with a Kids' Club showing popular films every Saturday morning from 11am. The €2.50 charge covers the film plus popcorn and a soft drink and supervising adults get in free. Note that the UCI Coolock has a branch of Leisureplex beside it, so you could spend one whole entertainment-filled day in the area. For details of the **Dublin Junior Film Festival**, *see p175* **Festival fever: Film**.

Theatre

Much of the child-oriented theatre in the city is organised by travelling troupes that play primarily to schools. However, there are important exceptions. As well as the **Ark** (*see above*), there's the **Lambert Puppet Theatre**

& Museum (*see p209*), which has been telling stories to children for generations and continues to delight; it's open all year round. More recently, these old-timers have been joined by two new out-of-town venues that promise to cater for a younger audience. **Draíocht** (Blanchardstown Centre, Northern suburbs; 885 2622; *see p207*) has a programme for young people that includes storytelling sessions and performances by dance companies and the Dublin Youth Orchestra, while across the city in Dún Laoghaire, the **Pavilion Theatre** (Marine Road, Dún Laoghaire, Dublin Bay; 231 2929) offers summer workshops for kids in music, drama, storytelling, circus skills, dance, magic and more. These one-off sessions carry a small fee and cater for specific age groups, so call ahead for information.

For 20 years, the volunteer-led **Dublin Youth Theatre** (information 874 3687) has been performing specially commissioned pieces by established playwrights. Most productions are aimed at a teenage audience and take place in venues such as the Projects Arts Centre (*see p209*). Finally, the **Dublin Theatre Festival** runs a children's season in conjunction with the Ark, alongside the main festival in October (*see p206* **Festival fever: Theatre**).

Trips out of town

These two attractions are well worth a day trip. For other suggestions, *see chapter* **Leinster**.

Celbridge Abbey
Clane Road, Celbridge, Co Kildare (627 6608). Bus 67, 67A. **Open** 10am-6pm Mon-Sat; noon-6pm Sun. **Admission** €3.20 adults; €1.90 concessions; €7.60 family. **No credit cards.**
An outdoor centre owned by the St John of God religious order, with adventure playground, ecology trail, and a model railway, as well as a garden centre and some lovely walks and rare trees. The Abbey runs guided tours, and family-focused events are held throughout the year.

National Sea Life Centre
Strand Road, Bray, Co Wicklow (286 6939). Bray DART. **Open** *Summer* 10am-5pm daily. *Winter* varies; phone for details. **Admission** €7; €5 concessions; free under-4s; €25 family. **Credit** AmEx, DC, MC, V.
With the National Aquarium now defunct, the Sea Life Centre has become a slick commercial enterprise, though the emphasis remains focused, they tell us, on conservation. As well as the tanks displaying marine and freshwater creatures, the centre boasts 'touchpools', where children can reach out and stroke a crab or pick up a starfish, and Think Tank – a hi-tech interactive area. The centre also recently installed three new tanks to house its latest attraction, the Kingdom of the Seahorses.

Arts & Entertainment

Film

OK, so it's not exactly Hollywood, but the Irish film industry does have its moments of glory. Catch them all on Dublin's silver screens.

The Irish, undeniably, love to tell stories: whether they can afford to tell them on the big screen, though, is another matter entirely. The talent is certainly there, but the lack of an established cinematic culture dooms the handful of indigenous stories that are filmed to a rough ride at the box office. If film production in Britain is a small pool by comparison to LA, then film production in Ireland is a volatile jacuzzi, sometimes throwing out auteurs and actors into the big world beyond – the likes of Neil Jordan, Jim Sheridan, Liam Neeson and Colin Farrell – sometimes watching as they're dragged beneath the bubbles domestically.

Conversely, Dublin (and Ireland more generally) is a popular location for big-budget international productions. Wooed by tax incentives that considerably reduce the cost of most features, international filmmakers feel a pull to the city and its surrounds that goes far beyond aesthetic considerations.

The greatest beneficiary of the mini-boom has been the Ardmore studios in Bray, County Wicklow, where, among others, blockbuster *Reign Of Fire* and John Boorman's children's fantasy *Knight's Castle* were shot. In the city itself, Ewan McGregor could be seen giving his best James Joyce in *Nora*, with some exteriors filmed on North Great George's Street. Most commonly, though, Dublin pretends to be other cities, frequently Belfast, where the nationalistic subject matter of such films as *In The Name Of The Father*, *Nothing Personal* and *The Boxer* essentially guaranteed the non-cooperation of the Ulster security forces in film production. Dublin has acted the part of London (in *David Copperfield*), Liverpool (*Educating Rita*), and Limerick (*Angela's Ashes*). However, fear remains, in the local filmmaking community at least, that not enough indigenously developed films are being made in the city, or indeed the country as a whole.

Still, at least people keep trying: the fertile pen of playwright Conor McPherson has given us the delightful *I Went Down* and *Saltwater* (the latter of which he also directed), and for every international production such as *Michael Collins* there's a now low-budget, locally generated alternative like *About Adam* (written and directed by Gerard Stembridge) or *When Brendan Met Trudy* (written by Roddy Doyle,

directed by Kieron J Walsh). The film versions of the Barrytown Trilogy (*The Commitments*, *The Van* and *The Snapper*) demonstrated how a local script (Roddy Doyle), a local cast, British directors (Alan Parker, Stephen Frears) and international funding could be brought together to produce successful, popular cinema. More recently, the Irish Film Board and RTÉ collaborated with the UK's Channel 4 and Yellow Asylum Films on an ambitious project to produce film versions of Samuel Beckett's 19 plays, with directors including Neil Jordan, Antony Minghella, David Mamet and Conor McPherson – a commendable exercise that achieved critical acclaim if little popular appeal.

As for the cinemas themselves, central Dublin has a pretty sparse selection. The two that stand out are the **Irish Film Centre** (IFC) on Eustace Street and the **Screen** on d'Olier Street, the only spots in town where you're liable to catch anything other than standard Hollywood fare. The march of the multiplexes continues apace, their empty blandness now occupying a variety of out-of-town sites in addition to the **UGC** on Parnell Street. Spare a thought, too, for the **Savoy** on O'Connell Street, its 1970s setting is perfect for a trip down cinematic memory lane.

GENERAL INFORMATION

New films open on Fridays and movie listings appear daily in the *Irish Times* and the *Evening Herald*. The IFC also publishes its own guide, available from the tourist centres, city centre cafés and bars and the cinema itself. *The Dubliner* has reliable, intelligent reviews of current releases. Ticket prices vary very little, with afternoon shows around €3.80-€5 and evening shows €6.30-€7.60.

Cinemas

Classic

Harold's Cross Road, Southern suburbs (information 492 3324/bookings 492 3699). Bus 49, 49A. **Open** 3-9.30pm Mon-Thur; 3pm-12.30am Fri; 1-9.30pm Sat, Sun. **Tickets** €5.50; €4.50 matinées. **Credit** MC, V. A nondescript, slightly dingy two-screener, famed for the regular late Friday (11pm) showing of *The Rocky Horror Picture Show*, now in its 20th year, and featuring a dressed-up crowd with intimate knowledge of script and rituals.

Clockwise from above: **When Brendan Met Trudy** (2000), **Nora** (1999), **Michael Collins** (1996), **The Commitments** (1991).

Irish Film Centre

6 Eustace Street, Temple Bar, Southside (679 3477/www.fii.ie). All cross-city buses. **Open** 1.30-9.30pm daily. **Tickets** €6.50; €5.50 matinées. **Credit** MC, V. **Map** p75.

The IFC is a pleasing, well-converted 17th-century building with two screens, a café and the country's largest public film archive collection. Selection-wise, the IFC offers low-budget, foreign-language, indie, arthouse, specialist seasons, documentaries and the like – everything that you won't find anywhere else in the city. The bar serves excellent snacks and meals, and the whole place has a buzzing ambience. Membership is obligatory: the weekly membership is can cover up to three guests, while the annual version is also good for discounts at the small (but comprehensive) book and video shop. Open-air screenings in Meeting House Square are organised by the IFC during the summer (*see p165*).

Savoy

16-17 O'Connell Street Upper, Northside (information 874 8487/bookings 874 6000). All cross-city buses. **Open** 1.30-8pm daily. **Tickets** €5.50 before 6pm; €7.50 after 6pm; €4.50 concessions. **Credit** MC, V. **Map** p313 H3.

Dublin's most atmospheric cinema also contains the largest cinema screen in the city. It's old-fashioned and a bit tatty, and whether you think the '70s feel of the place is a good thing or not will depend how you like your cinemas. There's an almost small-town atmosphere about this very Irish picture palace that fits in well with the general decrepitude of O'Connell Street. Note that you may have trouble getting through on the phone, so drop into the box office in person to get tickets.

Screen

d'Olier Street, Southside (672 5500). All cross-city buses. **Open** 3-7.30pm daily. **Tickets** €7.50; €5 concessions; €5 matinées. **Credit** MC, V. **Map** p313 H4.

The Screen is nearly as old-fashioned and tatty as the Savoy, and shows an eclectic line-up somewhere between mainstream and arthouse. Two of the screens have seats for couples, so take someone you'd like to know better.

Stella

Rathmines Road, Southern suburbs (497 1281). Bus 14, 14A. **Open** 6.30-11pm Mon-Fri; 2-11pm Sat, Sun. **Tickets** €5; €4 matinées. **Credit** MC, V.

Small, not unpleasant cinema that could equally well be described as poky or quaintly cute.

UGC Cinemas

Parnell Centre, Parnell Street, Northside (information 872 8400/bookings 872 8444). All cross-city buses. **Open** 11.20am-9.30pm Mon-Thur, Sun; 11.20am-11.50pm Fri, Sat. **Tickets** €4 before noon; €5 before 6pm; €6.50 after 6pm; €4-€4.50 concessions. **Credit** AmEx, MC, V. **Map** p313 G3.

A multiplex with all the spick-and-spanness you'd expect from such a beast: rather soulless and over-priced, but at least it has a large number of screens on which to show the latest Hollywood production. Formerly a Virgin (but then weren't we all).

Out-of-town multiplexes

The following places have little to recommend them apart from big screens, reasonable sound and picture quality, easy parking and the fact

The **Irish Film Centre** is more than just a good place to catch a movie.

Festival fever Film

If you're in Dublin during the summer, don't miss the IFC's outdoor screenings in Meeting House Square (*pictured; see p174*).

Dublin Film Festival
Information: 1 Suffolk Street, Dublin 2 (679 2937/www.iol.ie/dff). **Date** Mar-Apr.
Unarguably the main cinematic event of the year in Dublin, with a good selection of old and new films, debuts, retrospectives and documentaries. *See also p162.*

Dublin French Film Festival
Information: Cultural Department, French Embassy in Ireland, 1 Kildare Street, Dublin 2 (676 2197). **Date** Nov.
An annual festival showing films and documentaries from France, Canada, Belgium, Vietnam, Algeria, Burkina Faso and anywhere else where French is spoken. The programme is published in mid-October and includes both premières and classics of French cinema. Information is available from the Festival office.

Junior Dublin Film Festival
Information: IFC, 6 Eustace Street, Dublin 2 (671 4095). **Date** Nov-Dec.
The Junior Festival shows new and classic films from around the world, targeting the nine to 18 age group. Well presented and unpatronising seminars, workshops and presentations on film-related skills and theory add to the festival's popularity.

Dark/Light Film Festival
68 Dame Street, Southside (670 9017/ www.darklight-filmfestival.com). **Date** May.
Four-day festival concentrating on the 'cutting edge of digital technology'. The emphasis is on screenings by up-and coming filmmakers, with a host of seminars, exhibitions and multimedia events.

that films usually run for longer here than at more central movie houses. They're generic multiplexes built in the last ten years, and as such are functional and almost entirely devoid of charm, although the **Ster Century** in Clondalkin does have the added attraction of the 'Big Fella' – currently Ireland's largest multiplex screen.

IMG Lower George's Street
Dún Laoghaire, Dublin Bay (280 7777/ www.filminfo.net). Bus 7, 7A, 45A, 46A, 46X, 59, 75, 111, 746. **Open** 1-8pm Mon-Fri; noon-8pm Sat, Sun. **Tickets** €7.50; €4.50-€6 concessions; €5 matinées. **Credit** MC, V.

Ormonde Stillorgan
Stillorgan Plaza, Kilmacud Road, Northern suburbs (278 0000/www.ormondecinemas.com). Bus 46, 46B, 63, 84, 84X, 86. **Open** 11.30am-7.30pm daily. **Tickets** €6.50; €3.50-€4.50 concessions; €3.50 matinées. **Credit** AmEx, MC, V.

Santry Omniplex
Old Airport Road, Santry, Northern suburbs (842 8844/www.filminfo.net). Bus 16, 16A, 33, 41, 41B. **Open** noon-8.30pm Mon-Fri; 11am-8.30pm Sat, Sun. **Tickets** €7; €4.50-€5 concessions; €5 matinées. **Credit** MC, V.

Ster Century
Liffey Valley Shopping Centre, Clondalkin, Southern suburbs (605 5700). Bus 78A, 210, 239. **Open** 11.30am-10.30pm Mon-Thur, Sun; 11.30am-midnight Fri, Sat. **Tickets** €7.50; €5 concessions; €5.50 matinées. **Credit** AmEx, MC, V.

UCI Cinemas
Malahide Road, Coolock, Northern suburbs (848 5122/www.uci-cinemas.ie). Bus 20B, 27, 42, 42B, 43, 103, 104, 127, 129. **Open** 12.30-8.30pm daily. **Tickets** €7.50; €4.50-€5 concessions; €5.50 matinées. **Credit** MC, V.
Branches: Blanchardstown Shopping Centre, Blanchardstown, Northern suburbs (1-850 525 354); The Square, Tallaght, Southern suburbs (459 8400).

Galleries

Dublin's contemporary art scene is growing in size and confidence. Go see.

Ireland may not have a celebrated visual arts tradition with a legacy of big-name superstars like some other European countries, but it does boast a remarkably long history of functional and devotional art stretching back to the prehistoric and early Christian periods. The decorated megalithic tombs at Newgrange (*see p233*), the Bronze Age jewellery on display in the National Museum (*see p66*) and the world-famous illuminated manuscripts in Trinity Old Library (*see p62*) are evidence of a long-standing artistic tradition that continues to this day. The National Gallery of Ireland (*see p70*) displays paintings from the early 18th century and a cast of supporting galleries show (and sell) the best locally produced art of the last three centuries.

In the 19th and early 20th centuries, Irish art was influenced by European stylistic developments: strains of Monet are apparent in the paintings of John Lavery and William Orpen, for example, while Evie Hone and Mainie Jellet studied with the Cubist Albert Gleizes. In the first decades of the 20th century,

the Celtic literary revival was mirrored by a similar development in the visual arts. The paintings of Jack B Yeats (brother of WB) and George Russell take their subjects from Celtic mythology and the ordinary life of the Irish.

In the last two decades, the Dublin art world has developed to such an extent that the city now has a thriving network of galleries. Publicly or part-funded galleries like the **RHA Gallagher Gallery**, the **Douglas Hyde Gallery** and the **Project Arts Centre** (*see p209*) coexist with a substantial number of independent commercial concerns, which are fairly evenly split between a commitment to fine art or landscapes, and modern work. Very contemporary work can also be seen annually (in early June) at the degree show of the **National College of Art & Design** (Thomas Street, Liberties, Southside; 671 1377). Founded in 1765, it's one of Ireland's most prestigious art schools and counts artists Jacki Irvine and Darragh Hogan, milliner Philip Treacy and designer Murray Scallon as alumni.

Admission to the following galleries is free.

The wide open spaces of the **RHA Gallagher Gallery**.

Exhibition spaces

Details of national galleries and major public
spaces are given in the Sightseeing chapters:
for the **Irish Museum of Modern Art**, *see
p82*; for the **Municipal Gallery of Modern
Art** (Hugh Lane Gallery), *see p87*; and for
the **National Gallery of Ireland**, *see p71*.

Douglas Hyde Gallery

*Arts Building (entrance Nassau Street gate), Trinity
College, Southside (608 1116). All cross-city buses.*
Open 11am-6pm Mon-Wed, Fri; 11am-7pm Thur;
11am-4.45pm Sat. **Map** p313 H5.
Created by a pairing of the ever-eager Arts Council
and Trinity College Dublin, the Douglas Hyde
Gallery has two levels, with the main exhibiting
space on the lower one. The gallery shows visiting
international artists or established Irish ones, with
a predominance of massive works that make the
most of the gallery's high ceilings. Exhibition-
related talks are held throughout the year (phone
for details), and all around is the lively atmosphere
of the Arts Building, which is stuffed full of
contemporary artwork.

Gallery of Photography

*Meeting House Square, Temple Bar, Southside (671
4654). All cross-city buses.* **Open** 11am-6pm Tue-Sat;
2-6pm Sun. **Map** p75.
Run in conjunction with the Arts Council and Dublin
Corporation, Dublin's premier photography gallery
hosts a permanent collection of 20th-century Irish
work as well as monthly exhibitions by contemporary
Irish and international photographers. The three-
level space is well-lit, purpose-built, and is the best
place in the city to browse for photography books
and arty postcards.

National Photographic Archive

*Temple Bar, Southside (671 0073). All cross-city
buses.* **Open** 11am-6pm Mon-Sat; 2-6pm Sun.
Map p75.
The National Photographic Archive has a wonderful collection of early Irish photographs from the
19th century and the beginning of the 20th century,
displayed alongside exhibits by contemporary photographers from all over the island.

RHA Gallagher Gallery

*15 Ely Place, Southside (661 2558). Pearse Street
DART/all cross-city buses.* **Open** 11am-5pm Tue,
Wed, Fri, Sat; 11am-8pm Thur; 2-5pm Sun.
Admission by donation; RHA Annual Exhibition
£2.50; £1 students. **Map** p313 J6.
A short stroll from the hustle and bustle of St
Stephen's Green, at the end of a quiet, classical
Georgian street is one of Dublin's finest exhibition
spaces. The RHA Gallagher Gallery was built to
replace the Royal Hibernian Academy of Art, care-
lessly destroyed during the 1916 Easter Rising, and
has become one of Ireland's main centres for modern
and contemporary art. The RHA has four galleries,
with extra space for an outdoor sculpture court: its
size means that many large-scale travelling exhibitions choose it for their stay in Dublin. The Ashford
gallery within the complex maintains a policy of supporting young artists; the gallery also hosts the RHA
Annual Exhibition every year in May.

Commercial galleries

Apollo Gallery

*51 Dawson Street, Southside (671 2609). All cross-
city buses.* **Open** 9.30am-6pm Mon-Wed, Fri, Sat;
9.30am-8pm Thur; 11am-6pm Sun. **Credit** MC, V.
Map p313 H5.
The Apollo Gallery, a brightly hued beacon on the
corner of Duke and Dawson Streets – unmissable
with frequently huge canvases in the window to
catch the eye – specialises in 19th-, 20th- and 21st-
century paintings, and is well worth a visit whether
you're a collector or merely a viewer. A plentiful collection includes work by Irish-born painter and
sculptor Graham Knuttel, whose large and colourful
works, featuring rather sinister-looking characters,
are in great demand among Hollywood celebrities.

Boulevard Gallery

*Merrion Square West, Southside. Pearse DART/
5, 7A, 8, 46, 62 bus.* **Open** May-Sept Sat, Sun.
Closed Oct-Apr. **No credit cards. Map** p313 J6.
The Boulevard Gallery is a grand name for the open-
air art perched on the fence surrounding Merrion
Square. It's reminiscent of Greenwich Village or
Montmartre (if slightly chillier), and the only
exhibitors are local artists selling their own work,
so it's a chance to meet the craftspeople instead
of just the salespeople. There are also occasional
exhibitions by newer artists.

Combridge Fine Arts

*17 South William Street, Southside (677 4652/
www.cfa.ie). Pearse DART/15A, 15B, 15C, 55,
83 bus.* **Open** 9.30am-5.30pm Mon-Sat. **Credit**
AmEx, MC, V. **Map** p313 H5.
On the go since the end of the 19th century, this
gallery features original contemporary Irish works
alongside good quality reproductions of the kind of
classic Irish art that (almost) no-one could afford to
buy in original form.

Davis Gallery

*11 Capel Street, Northside (872 6969/
www.liviaarts.com). Tara Street DART/all cross-city
buses.* **Open** 10am-5pm Mon-Sat. **Credit** MC, V.
Map p313 G4.
Situated one block north of the Liffey on the unattractive Capel Street, this bright and welcoming
space gives its surroundings a splash of colour with
a wide variety of exhibits and styles, mostly by the
gallery's own roster of artists, including its well-
known owner, Gerald Davis. A strong emphasis is
placed on Dublin scenes, wildlife and fauna, making
it a good place to choose a souvenir – if you have a
minimum of around £300 to spend.

The open-air art mart that forms the **Boulevard Gallery**. *See p177.*

Frederick Gallery
24 Frederick Street South, Southside (670 7055/ www. frederickgallery.net). **Open** 10am-5.30pm Mon-Fri. **No credit cards. Map** p313 H5.
The Frederick Gallery shows a mixture of traditional and contemporary Irish, alternating combined shows with solo efforts. Among the gallery's artists are Mark O'Neill, Phil Kelly and Peter Pearson.

Gorry Gallery
20 Molesworth Street, Southside (679 5319/www. gorrygallery.ie). All cross-city buses. **Open** 11am-6pm Mon-Fri. **No credit cards. Map** p313 H5.
The Gorry specialises in 18th-, 19th- and early 20th-century paintings and restoration work is also performed. It features the work of Paul Kelly, Gerald Brown and Noel Murphy.

Graphic Studio Gallery
Through the Arch, Cope Street, Temple Bar, Southside (679 8021/www.graphicstudiodublin.com). Tara Street DART/all cross-city buses. **Open** 10am-5.30pm Mon-Fri; 11am-5pm Sat. **Credit** AmEx, MC, V. **Map** p75.
The Graphic Studio Gallery deals solely in contemporary original prints by established and emerging Irish artists. A vast amount of work is on view over the two levels, including etchings, lithographs, monoprints, screen, relief and Carborundum prints. Works are available to buy, starting at £40.

Green Gallery
Top Floor, St Stephen's Green Centre, Southside (478 3122/www.sale-of-art.com). All cross-city buses. **Open** 8am-7pm Mon-Wed, Fri, Sat; 8am-9pm Thur; noon-6pm Sun. **Credit** AmEx, MC, V. **Map** p313 H6.

On the upper level of the usually packed shopping centre is this eclectic gallery with styles across the contemporary spectrum. A large list of featured artists include Ross Eccles, Brian Murtagh and the two generations of Knuttels, Jonathan and Peter.

Green on Red
26-28 Lombard Street East, Southside (671 3414). Pearse DART/all cross-city buses. **Open** 10am-6pm Mon-Fri; 11am-5pm Sat. **Credit** DC, MC, V. **Map** p313 J4/5.
A rather small, quiet gallery near-buried towards the back of Trinity college, this is nevertheless one of Dublin's best, with a new exhibition every month featuring the best of Ireland and Europe's up-and-comers. GoR specialises in contemporary art of an abstract, conceptual nature, covering various media, including video and photography.

Hallward Gallery
65 Merrion Square, Southside (662 1482/1483). Pearse DART/all cross-city buses. **Open** *Sept-June* 10.30am-5.30pm Mon-Fri; 11am-3pm Sat. *July, Aug* 10.30am-5.30pm Mon-Fri. **Credit** MC, V. **Map** p313 J6.
This basement gallery shows contemporary Irish art, with exhibitions lasting around three weeks. The gallery acts as agent for its artists, promoting their work both at home and abroad. Expect work from the likes of John Kelly, Sarah Walker and James Hanley.

Kerlin Gallery
Anne's Lane, South Anne Street, Southside (670 9093/ www.kerlin.ie). All cross-city buses. **Open** 10am-5.45pm Mon-Fri; 11am-4.30pm Sat. **No credit cards. Map** p313 H5.

Probably Dublin's most important commercial gallery, this large, well-lit space focuses on conceptual, minimalist and abstract work, and shows the country's most important contemporary artists including such figures as Sean Scully, Kathy Prendergast and Stephen McKenna. Established in 1988, the Kerlin moved to this John Pawson-designed minimalist space in the mid 1990s and has thrived ever since.

Kevin Kavanagh Gallery

66 Strand Street Great, Northside (874 0064/ www.kevinkavanaghgallery.ie). All cross city buses. **Open** 11am-5pm Mon-Sat. **No credit cards.** **Map** p313 G4.

This independent commercial concern run by the eponymous KK aims to provide a showcase for contemporary young Irish artists.

M Kennedy & Sons

12 Harcourt Street, Southside (475 1749/ www.kennedyarts.com). All cross-city buses. **Open** 9.30am-5.30pm Mon-Fri. **Credit** MC, V. **Map** p313 G7.

In addition to the excellent gallery upstairs, this super little shop has a great selection of books on Irish artists and works, as well as cards, postcards and art-bookmarks, making it a good choice for a classy souvenir reflecting the Irish art you'll have seen at the surrounding galleries.

Oisin Art Gallery

44 Westland Row, Southside (661 1315/ www.oisingallery.com). Pearse DART/all cross-city buses. **Open** 9am-5.30pm Mon-Fri; 10am-5.30pm Sat. **Credit** MC, V. **Map** p313 J5.

Virtually next door to Pearse Station, the Oisin Art Gallery was set up in 1990 and concentrates on contemporary Irish art, with the occasional retrospective thrown in, utilising its space well. Works by Marie Carroll, Markey, Eccles and Rabchinsky are available, though the Oisin also deals in limited-edition prints. In short, an excellent place to come art-hunting.

Original Print Gallery

4 Temple Bar, Southside (677 3657/www. originalprint.ie). Tara Street DART/all cross-city buses. **Open** 10.30am-5.30pm Tue-Fri; 11am-5pm Sat; 2-6pm Sun. **Credit** MC, V. **Map** p75.

Located in an identikit modern building next door to the Temple Bar Gallery & Studios, the OPG specialises in limited-edition prints including etchings, lithographs, woodcuts and silkscreens. Exhibits include works from a plethora of both well-known and emerging Irish and international print makers whose work covers every imaginable style. Also in the building, the Black Church Print Studio (677 3629) exhibits prints.

Rubicon Gallery

10 St Stephen's Green, Southside (670 8055). All cross-city buses. **Open** 11am-5.30pm Mon-Fri; 11am-4.30pm Sat. **Credit** MC, V. **Map** p313 H6.

Established in 1991, the Rubicon Gallery is a bright, well-lit gallery in a picturesque setting overlooking St Stephen's green. Holding a number of yearly exhibitions featuring work in all media from sculpture to photography, the gallery particularly supports young and emerging artists by means of an annual show.

Solomon Gallery

Powerscourt Townhouse Centre, South William Street, Southside (679 4237/www.solomongallery. com). All cross-city buses. **Open** 10am-5.30pm Mon-Sat. **Credit** MC, V. **Map** p313 H5.

One of Dublin's leading fine-art galleries, and a solid – if slightly conservative – influence on the local art scene, the Solomon Gallery, situated on the top floor of the Powerscourt Townhouse Centre, deals in contemporary Irish and international art. New exhibitions open every three to four weeks, and there are a large selection of gallery artists as well as early 20th-century paintings by artists such as Jack B Yeats (the poet's brother), Dan O'Neill, Sir William Orpen, Evie Hone, Sir John Lavery and Mainie Jellet. A strong selection of contemporary glass is also housed by the Solomon: featured works include those by Rowan Gillespie, Linda Brunker, Anna Duncan, Deborah Brown and US glass artist Dale Chihuly.

Taylor Galleries

16 Kildare Street, Southside (676 6055). Pearse DART/10, 11, 13 bus. **Open** 10am-5.30pm Mon-Fri; 11am-3pm Sat. **Credit** MC, V. **Map** p313 H6.

The successor to the Dawson Gallery, the Taylor is located in a fine Georgian building, with exhibitions held on three of the four floors. A permanent display of contemporary Irish art – which features painting, sculpture and graphics – includes artists such as (deep breath) Bourke, Brady, Brennan, Coen, Crozier, Delargy, Dennis, Doherty, Donnelly, Fallon, Farrell, Flanagan, Gale Harris, Harrison, Henderson, Hickey, Kiely, King, le Brocquy, Mulcahy, Scott, Shinnors, Souter, Tyrrell, Wynne-Jones and Yeats.

Temple Bar Gallery & Studios

5-9 Temple Bar, Southside (671 0073). Tara Street DART/all cross-city buses. **Open** 10am-6pm Mon-Wed, Fri, Sat; 10am-7pm Thur; 2-6pm Sun. **Map** p75.

Founded in 1983, the Temple Bar Gallery & Studios is one of the largest studio and gallery complexes in Europe, and holds more than 30 Irish artists at work on a variety of contemporary visual arts. This flagship of the Temple Bar propagates the next wave of Irish artists, offering exhibition space to artists with no link to commercial galleries, and its strong connections with many national and international organisations mean there's a rich diet of cutting-edge exhibitions. Although only the gallery section is open to the public it is possible, by prior arrangement, to view individual artists at work in their studios.

Arts & Entertainment

Gay & Lesbian

A few years down the line from legalisation, Dublin's gay and lesbian scene is offering more bang for its buck.

Dublin's legalised gay scene has been making up for lost time. As in Britain, lesbianism was never illegal in Ireland, but male homosexuality was only decriminalised in the Irish Republic in 1993 as part of the wave of liberalism that followed the election of Mary Robinson as President in 1990. Successive Irish governments had dragged their heels over this issue, arguing that because anti-gay laws were seldom enforced, there was no need to repeal them. Thankfully, this enlightened argument cut no ice with the European Commission and, faced with the threat of legal action in the European Court of Human Rights, the Irish government finally capitulated.

When legalisation came, it was with a whimper rather than a bang: gay rights, unlike the issues of divorce or abortion, appeared not to have the power to cause national turmoil. In a country already weary of political and financial scandals, and obsessed with polishing its image as a modern European state, gay rights seemed to fulfil both liberal and financial aspirations by harnessing the power of the pink punt. As a result, gay rights legislation passed through the Dáil with nary a word of complaint from the conservative elements in society.

Dublin, of course, had a fully functional scene before 1993, but decriminalisation brought about many changes. Most noticeably, the city witnessed a substantial increase in the number of gay and gay-friendly venues. Over the past five years, within the context of a burgeoning and upwardly mobile Dublin, the gay and lesbian community has become generally more confident, energetic and high profile: or, some might say, glossier and more self-satisfied. The developing gay and lesbian scene is entirely in keeping with the ostentatious prosperity of the Celtic Tiger generation and its hunting ground of coffeeshops and upmarket bars.

One consequence of this is that, in Dublin as elsewhere, the radical edge of the lesbian and gay community has been blunted. On the other hand, the scene in Dublin has developed a good reputation precisely because it is so accessible, attractive and manageable for visitors. While the scene remains comparatively small for a city of Dublin's size, it is growing steadily, it caters for most tastes and it still doesn't take itself too seriously. Visitors to Dublin may be struck

by the sense that the gay scene is integrated into the social life of the city to a much greater extent than is the case in many other places; the majority of venues are gay-friendly rather than exclusively gay although there are some notable exceptions. The city's lesbian scene is significantly smaller, but is also developing: check for new venues and events when you arrive. Unless otherwise stated, all the clubs, bars, cafés and restaurants listed below welcome both lesbians and gay men.

INFORMATION AND SPECIAL EVENTS

Media information on gay life in Dublin is easy to come by, with *Gay Community News*, Ireland's monthly gay and lesbian newspaper, available free in most of the establishments listed in this section, as well as in many bookshops. Aside from carrying information and reports about gay events and issues, *GCN* is also the place to look for details of bigger, annual events such as the **Alternative Miss Ireland** (St Patrick's weekend; *see p182* **Dublin's quare city**), **Pride** (late June; *see p165*) and the **Lesbian & Gay Film Festival** (held at the Irish Film Centre towards the end of July). The Gay & Lesbian pages of *In Dublin* contain regularly updated listings and features, and Irish glossies such as *GI* and *Scene In Ireland* are widely available, as are their British equivalents *Attitude*, *Diva* and the *Gay Times*. For further practical information and details of gay and lesbian support groups, *see chapter* **Resources A-Z: Gay & Lesbian**.

Accommodation

Frankie's Guest House

8 Camden Place, Southside (478 3087/www.
frankiesguesthouse.com). All cross-city buses. **Rates**
€34 single; €47 single with shower; €76 standard
double; €89 double en suite; €95 twin en suite.
Credit MC, V. **Map** p313 G7.
This comfortable hotel is a short walk from St Stephen's Green. All rooms include a TV and tea- or coffee-making facilities.

Inn on the Liffey

21 Ormond Quay Upper, Northside (677 0828). All
cross-city buses. **Rates** from €57 single, from €82.50
double, from €121 triple. **Credit** MC, V. **Map** p313 G4.

The George: the pulsing heart of Dublin's gay scene. *See p182.*

All 11 rooms at the Inn on the Liffey are en suite, and most have views overlooking the river. Rates include full breakfast and free admission to the Dock sauna *(see p184)*.

Cafés & restaurants

Of the numerous eateries reviewed in our **Restaurants & Cafés** chapter, the following are the most popular with gay customers

For breakfast or lunch go to **Café Irie** (11 Fownes Street, Temple Bar; 867 4381/ www.cafeirie.web.com), a small, relaxed and gay-friendly first-floor café, serving some of the best and most varied sandwiches and soups in Dublin. Off the George Street Arcade, you'll find **Simon's Place** *(see p128)*, which serves chunky sandwiches and scrumptious cinnamon buns in laid-back surroundings, while just around the corner, the **Stonewall Café** *(see p128)* is a great place for a lazy lunch and is very popular with the gay community.

In the evening the trendy set reserve a table at the **Mermaid Café** *(see p118)*. The café has a wonderful mirrored interior – perfect for checking your hair. Alternatively, stop in at **Juice** *(see p120)* on your way to or from the George *(see p182)* for excellent vegetarian food and a wide range of juices, exotic and freshly

squeezed. The service can be a little slow, but the food is usually worth the wait. For authentic Nepalese food, head for **Monty's of Kathmandu** *(see p115)* located opposite the Irish Film Centre.

Pubs & bars

The Bailey

2 Duke Street, Southside (670 4939). All cross-city buses. **Open** 11.30am-11.30pm Mon-Sat; 4-11.30pm Sun. **Credit** MC, V. **Map** p313 H5.

The Bailey is the latest reincarnation of an old Dublin pub, which has moved from the old-shabby-sofa look through the high-and-uncomfortable-bar-stools aesthetic to an elegant new streamlined model. Come here if you want to see, be seen, and experience the Bailey's gay-friendly buzz. The lunches are pricey but tasty, while the bar's location off Grafton Street makes it a good spot for a pint during the afternoon. *See also p131.*

The Front Lounge

33-34 Parliament Street, Temple Bar, Southside (670 4112). All cross city buses. **Open** noon-11.30pm Mon, Wed, Sun; noon-midnight Tue; noon-1.30am Thur, Fri; noon-12.30am Sat. **Credit** MC, V. **Map** p75.

The Front Lounge has bravely faced off tough competition from the plethora of glossy bars springing up on every street corner, and remains one of

Temple Bar's most attractive and airy hangouts. Sunday and Tuesday are perhaps the gayest evenings of all, but the ambience is decidedly relaxed all week long. On Tuesday, Miss Panti's Casting Couch (*see below* **Dublin's quare city**) packs wannabe Geris and Rickys on to the comfy sofas. Worth dropping in for a pose and a pint, and to eye the handsome clientele. *See also p133*.

The George

89 South Great George's Street, Southside (478 2983). All cross-city buses. **Open** 12.30-11.30pm Mon, Tue; 12.30pm-3am Wed-Sun. **Credit** AmEx, MC, V. **Map** p313 G5.

Continuing, despite all the competition, to draw the crowds, the George is the grand ol' dame of the Dublin scene, sporting gilt-framed portraits and garish scarlet wallpaper. It advertises itself as 'Dublin's best and soon to be Europe's No.1 gay venue', and while this might be overstating it slightly, the George remains one of Dublin's most popular gay bars: the gay bingo on Sunday nights has become a fixture on the circuit, and is something of a

GUBU: 'Do you come here often?'. *See p183.*

Dublin's quare city

Ireland has strong links with some of Britain's best-known drag acts: Danny La Rue was born Daniel Patrick Carroll in Cork; Lily Savage's alter(ed) ego, Paul O'Grady, comes from an Irish family; even ambiguous dresser Boy George (real name George O'Dowd), has strong Irish roots. It seems an abundance of Irish talent can be seen sashaying across British stages in eight-inch heels.

In contrast, the drag scene in Dublin hasn't had a very long life. Homosexuality wasn't decriminalised in Ireland until 1993 which meant the blonde wigs and full-length, sequinned gowns had to stay in the closet – at least, officially.

After decriminalisation, however, stages were erected in the city's small number of gay bars and the dragsters claimed the spotlight as their own. Among them was Kylie O'Reilly, a young pretender to the Aussie singer's crown, who regularly performed in the Parliament (now the **Turk's Head**; *see p139*). Also treading the boards at the time was the wonderfully named Mr Pussy. A friend to the famous, Mr Pussy was compère and bingo master at the sadly missed U2-owned restaurant Mr Pussy's Café De Luxe, just off Grafton Street. On a Saturday night, it was hard not to be impressed by the stars in the audience, with Naomi Campbell, Björk and members of Erasure counting themselves as regulars. Before calling bingo balls to the rich

and famous, Mr Pussy had worked her way around just about every working men's club and dance hall in the country. With a hardcore act aimed at a straight audience, Mr Pussy went on to became a regular on Irish telly, showcasing her Tina Turner routine.

After the café's demise, girls and boys who liked to be entertained by leggy men in dresses could be found at a very new type of club in Dublin. Through word of mouth (and the odd article in the Irish and British press), fetish club GAG became a sensation. The club introduced the naughty Miss Panti to the masses in a stage show that left little to the imagination. GAG led a short but successful life and was replaced by the mammoth production that was Powderbubble. Ireland had never seen anything like the decadent, screaming, glitter-filled club before; and must-visit. Space 'N Veda on Wednesdays and the Missing Link with the freakishly scary Miss Annie Balls on Thursdays are also not to be missed (*see below* **Dublin's quare city**). Adjoining the George upstairs is the Loft (*see p184*).

The Globe

11 South Great George's Street, Southside (671 1220). Bus 12, 16, 16A, 55. **Open** noon-11.30pm Mon-Thur, Sun; noon-midnight Fri, Sat. **Credit** MC, V. **Map** p313 G5.

This smart, fashionable bar, catering to a mixed gay/straight crowd, is pleasantly relaxed by day and thronged by night. The decent lunches include chunky sandwiches and tasty soups. Alternating art work gives you something to look at if the clientele aren't up to scratch. At night, it provides the bar for the club Ri Ra (*see p201*).

GUBU

7-8 Capel Street, Northside (874 0710). All cross-city buses. **Open** 5-11.30pm Mon-Wed; 5pm-12.30am Thur-Sat; 4-11.30pm Sun. **Credit** MC, V. **Map** p313 G4.

Relaunched as a gay bar in 2001, GUBU is giving the George (*see p182*) a run for its money. The decor immediately grabs the attention: subtle concrete angles, decent-sized tables and chairs, and Tardis-like toilets (making the most of a small space with mirrors). The clientele is well-dressed, young and funky. In case you're interested, the name refers to a phrase former prime minister Charlie Haughey used when he found out that a wanted murderer was staying at the home of the attorney general: Grotesque, Unbelievable, Bizarre, Unprecedented.

Hogan's

35 South Great George's Street, Southside (677 5904). All cross-city buses. **Open** 1-11.30pm Mon-Wed; 1pm-12.30am Thur; 1pm-2.30am Fri, Sat; 4-11pm Sun. **No credit cards**. **Map** p313 G5.

Hogan's is a popular, trendy bar with the added attraction of a downstairs club. Huge windows and subtle lighting make it the perfect place to pose. Hogan's caters to a similar, if younger, crowd as the Globe (*see above*), so come here with your straight friends. *See also p134.*

maybe never will again, but during its heyday, the people behind Powderbubble helped establish one of Dublin's most popular annual events, the **Alternative Miss Ireland**, a beauty contest for Ireland's transvestites held on St Patrick's Day weekend.

This pink pageant has become the breeding ground for the Dublin drag scene. Winners of the Alternative Miss Ireland crown inevitably end up on the city's drag circuit, often with their own show. Shirley Temple-Bar, a ribbon-twirling Irish girl with Olympic dreams, won the contest in 1997. Now Shirl power can be witnessed first hand at her **bingo night** on Sundays at the George (*see p182*).

Winner of the title in 1999 was Vada Bon Rev, a cross between *Absolutely Fabulous*'s Patsy Stone and Marilyn Manson. With a little help from Ireland's first drag king, Johnny

Silvino, Vada has successfully translated her distinct style into a Wednesday night show, **Space 'N Vada**, again at the George.

The undisputed queen of the drag scene, however, is Miss Panti. Although not a winner of the Alternative Miss Ireland, Miss Panti can claim a high-powered connection to the contest – she's the hostess. Miss Panti guides her glammed-up chicks through the highs and lows of drag life and still has time to host her own shows: the **Casting Couch** on a Tuesday at the Front Lounge (*see p181*) and the extremely popular **Gristle** every second Friday at POD (*see p184*). As for Annie Balls, she may never have won the Alternative Miss Ireland (she hasn't even bothered entering), but the black-clad, acid-tongued dominatrix is the star hostess of the **Missing Link** on Thursdays at the George.

Arts & Entertainment

Irish Film Centre

6 Eustace Street, Temple Bar, Southside (box office 677 3477/administration 679 5744). All cross-city buses. **Open** 10am-11pm Mon-Wed, Sun; 10am-2am Thur-Sat. **Credit** MC, V. **Map** p75.

Officially a 'cultural institute', but in reality many spaces under one glass roof: arthouse cinema (*see p174*), bookshop, bar and restaurant. The bar is attractive, popular with lesbians and gay men, and a pleasant place for a pint on a bright afternoon.

Out on the Liffey

27 Ormond Quay Upper, Northside (872 2480). All cross-city buses. **Open** 10.30am-11.30pm Mon, Tue, Sun; noon-12.30am Wed-Sat. **No credit cards.** **Map** p312/3 F/G4.

This pub on the north city quays has a low-key, quiet atmsophere that provides a relaxing antidote to Dublin's glammed-up gay scene. And though it's become a little rough around the edges of late, it's still popular and is usually fairly laid-back. Saturday nights are men only.

Club nights

Candy

Peg's, Earl of Kildare Hotel, Kildare Street, Southside (679 4388). All cross-city buses. **Open** 11pm-2.30am Tue, Thur, Sun. **Admission** €7.60. **No credit cards.** **Map** p313 H6.

The Sunday-night club at Peg's formerly known as Disko has transmogrified into a three-nighter called Candy. It caters for a heaving mass of predominantly young and predominantly male good time-getters, but if this sounds a little too hedonistic for you, then head upstairs and immerse yourself in the ambient vibes.

HAM (Homo Action Movies)/Gristle

POD, Harcourt Street, Southside (478 0225). All cross-city buses. **Open** 11pm-late Fri. **Admission** €7.60 members; €10.20 non-members. **Credit** MC, V. **Map** p313 G7.

The POD (it stands for Place of Dance; *see p199*) was once under-decorated and overrated. However, this illustrious venue has been refurbished, and Friday night's HAM now offers the well-oiled and well-muscled consumer the opportunity to rhythmically gyrate in a comfortable, sex-filled environment. The clientele is hunky and the door policy is totally queer. HAM's baby sister, Gristle, is held every second week at the club from 9 to 11pm. Hosted by Miss Panti (*see p182* **Dublin's quare city**) it's the place to watch Dublin's best dragsters lip-synching to anything from Britney to Placebo.

Hilton Edwards

Spy, Powerscourt Townhouse Centre, South William Street, Southside (677 0014). **Open** 10pm-3am Sun. **Admission** €7.60. **Credit** MC, V. **Map** p313 H5.

From the people behind HAM and Gristle, Hilton Edwards is an über-trendy paradise. The club is named after one half of Ireland's first famous

out couple, the other half being actor Michael MacLiammoir (*see p208*). Consisting of four main areas (the pink room, the black room, the lobby and 'dancefloor'), Spy (*see p201*) oozes class without the high admission price. The place noticeably fills up once the Bingo at the George is over (*see p182*) and the long queue for the bisexual toilets is annoying, but work it to your advantage and chat to that cutie in front.

Libida

Chief O'Neill's, Smithfield, Northside (817 3838/ www.chiefoneills.com). All cross-city buses. **Open** usually once a month, towards the end of the month. **Admission** free. **Credit** MC, V. **Map** p312 E4.

A great new club for women and their gay male chums: sexy, cruisy and full of cute chicks. The frequency of Libida varies from month to month, and seems to be held on something of an as-and-when basis. Your best bet is to check listings in *Gay Community News*, *In Dublin* or *GI*.

The Loft

The George, 89 South Great George's Street, Southside (478 2983). All cross-city buses. **Open** 12.30pm-3am Wed-Sun. **Admission** free before 10pm; €7.60 after 10pm. **No credit cards.** **Map** p313 G5.

The George (*see p182*) has spilled over into next door, providing much-needed additional space and a new dancefloor. The venue is open to all, but gay men tend to predominate.

SLAM

Switch, Eustace Street, Temple Bar, Southside (670 7655). All cross-city buses. **Open** 11pm-late Mon. **Admission** €6.35. **No credit cards.** **Map** p75.

Whoever said Monday nights were dead obviously hadn't been here. Slap, Lick And Munch or SLAM has recently launched itself onto the gay scene with two floors of funky to progressive house music to keep you dancing into Tuesday morning. The clientele is a mix of the young and the not-so-young.

Saunas

The Boilerhouse

12 Crane Lane, Temple Bar, Southside (677 3130). All cross-city buses. **Open** 1pm-5am Mon-Thur; entire weekend 1pm Fri-5am Mon. **Admission** €12.70. **Credit** AmEx, MC, V. **Map** p75.

This is the biggest sauna in Dublin, with a steam room, jacuzzi, café and solarium, and it's handily located slap-bang (as it were) in the city centre.

The Dock

21 Ormond Quay Upper, Northside (872 4172). All cross-city buses. **Open** 1pm-1.30am Mon, Tue; 1pm-3am Wed; 1pm-5am Thur; entire weekend 1pm Fri-5am Mon. **Admission** €8.90 before 7pm; €11.40 after 7pm. **Map** p312/3 F/G4.

Located at the Inn on the Liffey (*see p180*), the Dock is small, cosy and intimate, with non-stop opening hours at the weekend.

Music

Dublin's vibrant and varied music scene is sounding as good as ever. Tune in.

Classical & Opera

It has been suggested that the last great classical music performance in Dublin was the première of Handel's *Messiah* way back in 1742. An uncharitable assessment perhaps, but certainly indicative of the relatively low profile of classical music and opera in an otherwise vibrant musical city. There are no Irish composers of world renown and only a small handful of well-known classical performers – vocally, for example, Count John McCormack still reigns supreme nearly three-quarters of a century after his heyday. The city has no opera house, and although the occasional success of productions such as *Salome* and *La Traviata* at the **Gaiety** introduce some verve into the scene, there is a still a lot to be done before Dublin can hope to rival other European cities.

However, the situation is far from hopeless. There is decent classical music to be found in Dublin, even if it doesn't enjoy the high profile of other art forms. Much of the action takes place in the **National Concert Hall** (NCH), which is home to the **RTÉ Concert Orchestra** and the **National Symphony Orchestra.** Although the average age of the audience is nowhere near representative of the youthful demographic of the city, concerts here are usually well attended and of a reasonable standard. And, as the city becomes increasingly international in outlook, some fresher faces are beginning to make an appearance among the blue rinses. The economic boom has helped, too: more disposable income means that Dubliners are adopting a more adventurous outlook towards the arts.

One truly popular and populist classical music event is the free performance of Handel's *Messiah* every Easter in Fishamble Street. Other regular events include the annual **Anna Livia International Opera Festival,** the triennial **Dublin International Organ & Choral Festival** (for both, *see p163*) and the **RTÉ Proms** (208 3434), a feast of international music run by RTÉ each May. The Proms usually feature a selection of local orchestras leavened by one or two international names. Not much musical direction or thought goes into the whole affair, but it's an excuse for starved audiences to gorge themselves on international celebrity.

On a national scale, the gradual development of the classical music scene has been helped immeasurably by the continuing advancement of Limerick as a Centre of Excellence in Music, a title bestowed by the Arts Council of Ireland. As a result, the University of Limerick is now home to the **Irish Chamber Orchestra** (*see p186*), whose brief is to record, commission and perform pieces by Irish composers. The orchestra was also responsible for the founding of the **Killaloe Festival** (information 061 202620), an excellent chamber music festival that takes places in this tiny Limerick town in late July. What's more, there have been attempts by composers such as Michael U'Sulleabhain recently to develop indigenous classical music by cross-breeding it with traditional Irish music to create symphonic movements on such instruments as the Uillean pipes. Limerick is also home to **Lyric FM** (96-99FM), a national classical music radio station that has largely lived up to its optimistic remit. These dedicated institutions have greatly increased the significance of classical music, not only in Limerick but throughout Ireland.

Beyond the capital, musical entertainment is also provided by a number of prominent festivals. The **Kilkenny Arts Festival** (056 52176/www.kilkennyarts.ie) in mid-August has traditionally been the arts festival with the most consistent and highest-quality classical music content, and despite a drop in musical standards in the late 1990s, it remains worth a look. Opera buffs should head for the annual **Wexford Festival Opera** (053 22400/053 22144) in October, an exuberant event often showcasing rare or infrequently performed works, or the **Castleward Opera** (028 9066 1090) in June, where the idyllic setting at a National Trust property on the banks of Strangford Lough in Co Down usually compensates for any musical shortcomings. For chamber music, check out the **Killaloe Festival** (*see above*) and the **West Cork Chamber Music Festival** (027 61576/www.westcorkmusic.ie/festival.htm) in late June, an enterprising music festival, with a line-up of musicians who rehearse in Cork for a week prior to the event. Finally, the ecumenical **Two Cathedrals Festival**, held in Derry in October, offers a chance to hear the finest church and sacred music in lovely surroundings. Contact the Music Centre in Derry (028 7126 2312) for further information.

Chamber groups

Concorde Ensemble
Information 091 522 867.
The Concorde plays exclusively contemporary music, concentrating on works by Irish composers such as John Kinsella, Stephen Gardner and Deirdre Gribbin. Its free concerts at the Hugh Lane Gallery rank among Dublin's classical music highlights.

Irish Chamber Orchestra
Information 061 202 620.
Originally, the ICO was the hobby of a number of musicians from the RTÉ Concert Orchestra who wanted to play a little chamber music in their spare time. It's now a progressive outfit that often plays in Dublin despite having relocated to the University of Limerick.

Vanbrugh String Quartet
Information 208 3347.
Also run by RTÉ, the Vanbrugh combines faultless musicality with a progressive outlook and performs up to 100 concerts a year around the world. Based in Cork, the quartet is the force behind the West Cork Festival of Chamber Music, though the musicians are committed to the work of contemporary Irish composers and play regularly in Dublin.

Choirs

Coir Na nOg
Information 208 3347.
RTÉ's young people's choir has been a breeding ground for many of Ireland's current crop of singers. The concerts meander from baroque to pop.

Goethe Institute Choir
Information 661 1155.
A respectable choir made up of German-language students and other enthusiasts. The Goethe Institute Choir performs two to three concerts a year, covering the usual choral repertoire of masses and requiems as well as more offbeat works by contemporary Irish and German musos.

National Chamber Choir
Information 208 3347.
Ireland's only fully professional choir performs numerous concerts throughout the year, with a repertoire extending from Seiber and Thompson to Samuel Barber and even black church music.

RTÉ Philharmonic Choir
Information 208 3347.
Ireland's largest choir is made up of 120 part-time amateur singers. It has a standard choral repertoire, but has also been known to team up with the National Concert Orchestra on occasion for less frequently performed or contemporary works.

Robert Burt strikes a pose for **Opera Ireland.**

Opera companies

Opera Ireland
Information 453 5519.
Founded in 1941 and known until fairly recently as the Dublin Grand Opera Society, Opera Ireland is as close as Ireland gets to a national opera company. For years, the society served up concert-like performances of 19th-century Italian favourites, though strangely, the semi-professional chorus was joined during this 'golden' period by budding superstars including Placido Domingo, Jose Carreras and even the mighty Luciano Pavarotti, who made his international debut here in a 1963 Grand Opera Society production of *Rigoletto*. It was not until the mid '80s that the company began to transform itself into a professional outfit.

The major problem up until recently was a rabid conservatism on the part of both audiences and Opera Ireland personnel, which crippled the opera's

Arts & Entertainment

‹ ‹ ‹ ‹ can't get enough art? ‹ ‹ ‹ ‹ ‹ ‹ ‹ ‹ ‹ ‹ ‹ ‹ ‹ ‹ ‹ ‹

photo. yves klein, painting ceremony. shunk-kender

first-art.com

AFFORDABLE CONTEMPORARY ART

> > > drag your ass to www.first-art.com

repertoire for many years. While the need to sell tickets was understandable, Opera Ireland failed to challenge performers or the public. However, the recent move to mix Russian and German pieces in with the expected strains of Italian – for every *La Traviata* there's now a *Flying Dutchman* – not to mention the inclusion of the likes of Shostakovich (*Lady Macbeth Of Mtsensk*) and Mark-Anthony Turnage (*The Silver Tassie*), means that the company has, finally, to be applauded for its eclecticism. It plays two short seasons in autumn and spring, which are staged at the Gaiety (*see below*).

Opera Theatre Company
Information 679 4962.
Opera Theatre Company is the national touring company of Ireland. Based in Dublin, it has toured more than one hundred cities, towns and villages in Ireland and Northern Ireland since its first tour in 1986. OTC was founded to create high-quality opera productions on modest budgets that can be presented anywhere, filling a void in Ireland, a country with little or no operatic tradition. In addition to producing four new tours each year, the company has a lively education programme in schools, as well as the Opera Theatre Studio, a training facility for young singers. It has achieved national and international success with a number of baroque and early classical operas, as well as operas from the 20th century. In addition, the company has commissioned and performed nine new operas by Irish composers.

Rathmines & Rathgar Musical Society
Information 497 1577.
An almost legendary, enthusiastic amateur group that mounts Gilbert & Sullivan productions and popular musicals with a distinctive and endearingly unpolished approach. The R&R runs two seasons every year, one at the Gaiety Theatre, the other at the National Concert Hall.

Orchestras

National Symphony Orchestra of Ireland
Information 208 3347.
The National Symphony Orchestra was founded in 1926 to provide music for radio broadcasts, and is still run by the country's radio and TV station, Radio Telefís Éireann. Although the enormous contribution that RTÉ has made to Irish musical life has to be acknowledged, it is also true that the orchestra has suffered under the ad hoc care of an inflexible, bureaucratic organisation whose primary business is to produce TV and radio programmes .

The result has been an orchestra largely made up of world-class musicians but afflicted by erratic management. The repertoire of the NSOI consists of everything you would expect – Mozart, Strauss, Mendelssohn – plus more wilfully obscure pieces that often seem to have been included to prove a

point. That said, in the last few years the orchestra has seen a noticeable upswing in critical popularity. Following the departure of the poorly received Kaspar De Roo, the stewardship of the orchestra passed to Russian conductor Alexander Anissimov, whose services have been retained in an honorary capacity since the conclusion of his tenancy. The new man with the baton is Gerhard Markson, already wowing the locals with both his choice of repertoire and technique. The NSOI has the talent to break free from its traditional straightjacket, but it is possible that its environment is too restraining for much of an impact to be made.

RTÉ Concert Orchestra
Information 208 3347.
Though the Concert Orchestra suffers many of the problems of its big sister, the NSOI, the effects are cushioned by the less ambitious slant of its programming and by its defined role as a broadcasting outfit. It can at least lay claim to the largest audiences of any Irish classical music collective – thanks to Ireland's embarrassing winning streak in the Eurovision Song Contest in the '90s, when the orchestra was called upon to play to television audiences of 300 million. It can be heard on a more regular basis at the National Concert Hall playing anything from Brahms to Lloyd Webber.

Venues

Bank of Ireland Arts Centre
Foster Place, Southside (box office 671 1488/Mostly Modern 821 6620), All cross-city buses. **Open** *Box office* 11am-4pm Tue-Fri. **Credit** MC, V. **Map** p75.
A series of free lunchtime concerts are held here around twice a month for about half the year (usually November-April). There are also ticketed evening recitals throughout the year and the Mostly Modern series, which focuses on 20th-century works. The Arts Centre also hosts poetry readings (*see p35* **Word of mouth**) and art exhibitions.

Gaiety
South King Street, Southside (677 1717). All cross-city buses. **Open** *city buses.* 10am-7pm Mon-Sat. **Credit** (75¢ booking fee) MC, V. **Map** p313 H5.
Opera Ireland's regular venue is a 19th-century theatre. It has recently been revamped and spring-cleaned, but that doesn't alter the fact that it is highly unsuitable for the demands of a modern opera company. Apart from the slight seediness of the auditorium, the stigma attached to a venue that devotes the rest of the year to a mish-mash of club nights (*see p199*), musicals, pantomime and somewhat stuffy straight theatre (*see p208*) may prove instrumental in driving away younger audiences.

John Field Room
National Concert Hall, Earlsfort Terrace, Southside (475 1572). All cross-city buses. **Open** *Box office* 10am-7pm Mon-Sat. **Credit** AmEx, DC, MC, V. **Map** p313 H7.

Arts & Entertainment

National Concert Hall: bastion of the classical music scene.

The NCH annexe hosts performances of chamber, jazz, traditional and vocal music. Its versatility is marred only by its proximity to the main hall: concerts can't take place in both halls simultaneously.

Municipal Gallery of Modern Art (Hugh Lane Gallery)

Charlemont House, Parnell Square North, Northside (874 1903). All cross-city buses. **Open** 9.30am-6pm Tue-Thur; 9.30am-5pm Fri, Sat; 11am-5pm Sun. **Map** p313 G3.

This ample hall in the Hugh Lane Gallery hosts around 25 free concerts of contemporary music at noon on Sundays from September to June. For more on the gallery itself, *see p87.*

National Concert Hall

Earlsfort Terrace, Southside (475 1572/www.nch.ie). All cross-city buses. **Open** *Box office* 10am-7pm Mon-Sat. **Credit** AmEx, DC, MC, V. **Map** p313 H7.

Dublin's main venue for orchestral music was established in 1981, in the Great Hall of what was then University College Dublin. It still retains the bland flavour of a lecture hall, and reconversion has done little for the flat, leaden acoustics. A move north of the river has been touted several times recently.

RDS Concert Hall

Royal Dublin Society Showgrounds, Ballsbridge, Southern suburbs (information 668 0866/ tickets from TicketMaster). Buses 46, 57, 84. **Credit** *TicketMaster* AmEx, DC, MC, V.

An overlarge but fairly serviceable hall located in Ireland's main showjumping arena. In its favour, the venue is large enough to accommodate a modestly sized opera company without soaking up the more intimate sonorities of a chamber music quartet. The hall hosts around 20 concerts a year.

Occasional venues

The **Project Arts Centre** (671 2321; *see p209*) is better known as a dramatic venue, but it also sometimes hosts contemporary music concerts, events that should be able to take full advantage of the theatre's new acoustics. The **O'Reilly Hall** (706 1713) at University College Dublin is regularly used for concerts by all the RTÉ orchestras, and the **Irish Museum of Modern Art** in Kilmainham (612 9900; *see p82*) occasionally rents out an impressive annexe hall to independent ensembles.

St Stephen's Church, locally known as the 'Peppercanister' (288 0663; *see p72*), hosts a programme of orchestral and choral concerts. There are also beautifully sung daily services and choral concerts at both **St Patrick's Cathedral** (475 4817; *see p77*) and **Christchurch Cathedral** (677 8099; *see p76*). Finally, don't miss Latin mass at **St Mary's Pro-Cathedral** sung by the Palestrina Choir each Sunday at 11am (*see p86*).

Rock, Pop, Trad & Jazz

For proof of Dublin's international reputation as a city renowned for music, just make your way to Windmill Lane Studios in Dublin and read the wall outside, graffitied from end to end by crazed U2 fans. Despite persistent rumours that it will be painted over or demolished, the wall remains a mecca for music fans, with signatures from as far afield as Sydney, New York, Hong Kong and Prague.

Pop and rock music have been part of Dublin's cultural fabric since the formation of **The Dubliners** in the '60s – still revered as the original bad boys of Irish music. Since then, there has been a continual stream of bands with what has recently been labelled a 'Celtic perspective'. **Thin Lizzy**, along with less-celebrated acts such as the **Horslips**, acted as a bridge to electric music, with talented contemporaries from out of town such as Cork's **Rory Gallagher** also weighing in.

Following in the wake of these groups came the first wave of the articulate angry, led by the **Boomtown Rats** and, a couple of years later, **U2**. These Dublin groups had their Northern counterparts in **Stiff Little Fingers** and the magnificent **Undertones**, whose 'Teenage Kicks' can still lift the catatonic from a stupor.

U2 have since metamorphosed into the mammoth beast we know today. *The Joshua Tree*, effectively their breakout album, provided a highlight in an otherwise dreary decade, music-wise, in Ireland. During the 1980s, taste oscillated between **Daniel O'Donnell** and **The Four Of Us**, with not much else going on outside the traditional scene, where **Moving Hearts** and the still-around **Altan** made waves. The raw emotion of **Sinead O'Connor** struck a chord in the early 1990s, but during the rest of the decade, dance music became increasingly popular, and DJs came to dominate the bar and club scene. Even traditional music got in on the act, with **Afro-Celt Sound System** fusing Irish, African and electronic beats (topped off by the superb voice of Iarla O'Lionaird) and earning themselves a Grammy nomination in the process.

These days Dublin's most famous musical exports are aimed squarely at the teenybopper market. Manager extraordinaire Louis Walsh has followed the success of **Boyzone** with the equally huge **Westlife** and Dublin R&B diva **Samantha Mumba**. He's even aiming a shot at the Corrs' end of the market with new combo **Bellefire**. Those of us who thought this boy band lark couldn't last were proved both right and wrong: individual bands have a notoriously short shelf-life, but there's always a long queue of ravenously ambitious hopefuls waiting to take their place. **The Corrs** are, of course, another modern Irish success story, bringing a combination of saccharine pop and trad sounds to the masses.

But if Dublin is good at mass-producing bands for the corporate international market, its very credible local music scene also seems able to nurture and provide a showcase for less commercial musicians. In the city itself, you can hear a huge range of music on any given night, whether it's local pub rock, the a cappella world music of female vocal group **Yemanja**, or the dulcet tones of Athy man Jack L. The folk and trad scenes continue to thrive, with the ever-popular legend **Christy Moore** playing to a packed crowd at the Point in 1994, and 1970s stalwart **Paul Brady** selling out a whole month's residency at Vicar Street in 2001. Newer bands and singers are beginning to make their voices heard, too. While you're in town, listen out for gigs by the **Frames** (indie rock), **El Diablo** (alternative country), **Saville** (indie pop), **David Kitt** and **Gemma Hayes** (both folky pop).

Dublin diva? **Samantha Mumba**.

And of course, the daddies of them all, U2, continue to do their thing. In 2001, the band played to a record-breaking 160,000-strong crowd over two days at Slane Castle in Co. Meath. The concerts were a homecoming for the band in more ways than one; 20 years earlier almost to the day, they played the massive venue as support to Thin Lizzy.

TRADITIONAL AND FOLK
Dublin's reputation for traditional music doesn't quite rival the likes of Doolin in Clare or Gweedore in Donegal (which is where you'll hear Ireland's plaintive unaccompanied *sean*

nós singing), but there's more than enough going on in the city to occupy the folk fan. Whereas 'traditional' (or trad) means Irish traditional music, 'folk' can have several definitions: from acoustic covers bands to the best of the British or American folk scenes. Irish traditional music is played all over the city, generally for free and in far too many pubs to be listed here. The musicians are often in the background, and with such large numbers of them about, it's not always easy to predict quality. Keep an eye on local listings or even signs outside pubs for details of forthcoming gigs. The **National Concert Hall** (*see p188*)

Trad ain't bad

Trendy middle-class Dubliners tend to be condescending about traditional music. They term it 'diddly-aye', and dismiss it as the province of bearded rural types in dubious knitwear. Specifically, they associate it with the veneration of repressed and depressed bygone days – or alternatively, with a very twee theme-park 'Oirland'.

A particular bête noire of cosmopolitan urbanites is *sean-nós* singing. This is the unaccompanied vocal rendition of ancient Gaelic songs, and can sound like a grieving cow to the untutored ear. Still at least *sean-nós* is a recognised art form, and there can be no doubting its historical authenticity. Such excuses cannot be made for the maudlin mutation known as Country Irish – a mélange of trad and Country Western; prolonged exposure to this drivel could ruin your holiday. If you wish to avoid the worst trad, also beware the ersatz session where musicians with caged-hamster expressions churlishly rattle out the 'hits' ('Fields of Athenry', 'Danny Boy', and so on). One useful but not infallible rule of thumb is, if you see a keyboard player (and by God you will) you are very possibly in for dollop of aural marzipan.

Despite these cavils, there is more than a little of the baby and the bathwater about a wholesale rejection of Dublin's trad scene. And thankfully out-of-towners have helped local aficionados keep good music alive in the city. Indeed Irish life doesn't get much better than a 'mighty' session: creamy pints flow, and finger-flying, foot-tapping musicians lash out frenetic jigs, reels and hornpipes, occasionally counter-pointing this musical wildness with mournful laments of visceral beauty. Introduce your Dublin friends to such an evening and their cynicism tends to melt.

It is worth distinguishing between formal and informal sessions, although posters rarely do. The first are more performance-oriented and the best take place in venues such as the **Shelter** (*see p195*) and the **Harcourt** (*see p192*), where some of trad's finest exponents regularly perform. Although you may have to pay an entrance fee, such gigs are your best guarantee of quality music. Many other places offer regular, free formal sessions of varying quality. Some are excellent, while others aim to provide no more than background noise to the drinking.

Informal sessions are rarer, more organic affairs involving whichever musicians turn up on the night, resulting in sets that are unpredictable to say the least. The musicians tend to play for themselves as much as for the audience, but the adaptability required to take part usually ensures a high standard. The spirit engendered by quality players letting the music 'breathe', gradually complementing each other and then shifting gears as the session takes off, can be exhilarating.

A brief word on session etiquette. Pay-in gigs are for those who wish to appreciate the music and are not places to catch up with your mates. Audience chatter should be kept to a minimum, with total silence demanded during individual singing – talking over a *sean-nós* singer is ranked up there with flag-burning in some places. In some venues applause is welcome at the end of tunes, while in others, particularly informal sessions, it is unnecessary – take your lead from locals. Gaping at musicians will instantly identify you as a tourist. Finally, while it is possible to enjoy the music without alcohol, the fact that in Ireland the word 'session' is synonymous with the phrase 'piss-up' speaks for itself.

Arts & Entertainment

frequently features the bigger trad acts, and recently inaugurated the **Beo Festival** at which the best traditional Irish musicians take over the NCH for a week or so in August and September. For more information on the trad scene, see p190 **Trad ain't bad**.

JAZZ

Dublin's jazz scene has flourished in recent years. In the '60s, jazz clubs were a central part of musical life in the city and the popularity of the genre has now returned, with the likes of Louis Stewart performing regularly in town. The addition of the **Dublin Jazz Festival** to the city's events calendar has also raised the profile of the genre (see p194 **Festival fever: Rock, pop & jazz**). There are a small number of venues that specialise in jazz, but it also occasionally features at mainstream venues.

INFORMATION

To find out about the latest gigs, buy magazines In Dublin or Hot Press, or pick up The Event Guide, an excellent free listings guide that can be found in bars, clubs and record shops throughout the city. These publications also have ads for events at out-of-town venues such as Millstreet Arena in Co. Cork, Semple Stadium at Thurles in Co. Tipperary and Slane Castle in Co. Meath.

Rock and pop gigs start at about 8pm or 9pm, with the main act taking the stage between 9.30pm and 10pm. Schedules for trad sessions are more relaxed and so less predictable.

TICKETS

While the **Point**, the **Olympia** and SFX each have their own box offices, other major venues plus some of the smaller but established names like **Whelan's** and **Vicar Street** rely on agencies for ticketed concerts. You can get tickets at **Sound Cellar** (47 Nassau Street, Southside; 677 1940) and **HMV** (see p159), whose branch of **TicketMaster** deals with just about every big event (1-890 925 100/from outside Ireland 456 9569/www.ticketmaster.ie); call early as the lines tend to get jammed. There's also a ticket shop in the **Tourism Centre** on Suffolk Street that takes credit card bookings (605 7777).

Watch out for 'hidden' booking charges; recent court challenges to the way promoters advertise the price of concert tickets means that they're obliged to state where these will apply. This hasn't reduced the charges, though, so don't be surprised if you pay a per ticket charge for a credit card or Internet booking, or even a 'handling' charge if you pay by cash.

As for the smaller pub and club venues, admission to most gigs is by cash on the door on the night only.

Venues

Large-scale rock and pop concerts are occasionally held in outdoor sports arenas like Lansdowne Road (see p217) or Croke Park (see p216), but the majority of events take place in the venues listed below. As a visitor to the city, you're more likely to get into one of the smaller-to medium-sized gigs, which may not sell out as quickly as high-profile concerts, although the quality of music can vary hugely. A good night out can often be had via a tip-off from leaflets left in coffee shops and bars, but similarly, beware the flier that offers tourists the night of their lives for €2 before 11pm.

Apart from the big arenas, classifying venues in Dublin according to the type of music they offer is an almost impossible task. Most of the venues below, unless otherwise stated, feature an eclectic mix of artists and genres and are proud of the fact. Many also host club nights on certain days, or after the main gig has finished. Keep an eye on local listings for information on upcoming gigs, or phone the venues directly for details of what's on during your stay.

Ambassador Theatre

O'Connell Street, Northside (www.mcd.ie/ ambassador). All cross-city buses. **Credit** *TicketMaster AmEx, DC, MC, V.* **Map** p313 H3
At the time of going to press, the Ambassador Theatre had yet to acquire a permanent phone number, but early signs for this rejuvenated venue are good. The venue occupies what used to be the Ambassador Cinema – its conversion has been a relief to many Dubliners who hated seeing the beautiful old building lying idle. The new owners have kept many of the original features, including the balcony. With a 1,200 capacity, including the upstairs seating, the Ambassador is a much-needed larger venue for the northside of the city. A high-profile roster of gigs, including the likes of Mercury Rev, Zero 7 and the Afro Celt Sound System, mean that this place is bound to be worth a look.

Break for the Border

Grafton Plaza Hotel, Johnson Place, Southside (478 0300). All cross-city buses. **Open** noon-11.30pm Mon, Tue, Sun; noon-2.30am Wed-Sat. *Live music* midnight-2am Fri; 9-11pm, midnight-2am Sat. **Admission** free. **Credit** AmEx, DC, MC, V. **Map** p313 H5.
Cover bands of varying quality play late at night in this hotel chain venue in the heart of the southside city centre. See also p197.
Branch: Major Tom's, South King Street, Southside (478 3266).

Bruxelles

7-8 Harry Street, Southside (677 5362). All cross-city buses. **Open** 11am-1.30am Mon-Wed; 11am-2.30am Thur-Sat; 12.30pm-1.30am Sun. *Live music* from 9.30pm Mon, Tue; 6.30-9.30pm Sun. **Admission** free. **No credit cards**. **Map** p313 H5.

Arts & Entertainment

Cosy pub, friendly locals and great trad:
don't miss the **Cobblestone**.

Local rock and blues acts play upstairs early in the
week. Quality is variable, but it's a great pub, and
you'd do well to pop in for a drink anyway. There is
also some late-night music in addition to the standard band slots. *See also p132.*

Cobblestone

*77 North King Street, Smithfield, Northside (872
1799). All cross-city buses.* **Open** 4-11.30pm Mon-
Wed; 1pm-12.30am Thur-Sun. *Bar music* from 9pm
daily. *Upstairs venue* from 9pm Thur, Fri, Sat; phone
for details. **Admission** *Bar* free. *Upstairs venue*
varies; phone for details. **No credit cards.**
Map p312 E4.

Overlooking the vast square at Smithfield, the
Cobblestone is an old-fashioned, friendly boozer
that features traditional music every night in the
relaxed surroundings of the back bar. Upstairs is a
surprisingly comfortable and intimate venue that
specialises in more serious gigs by high-quality
traditional and roots groups, as well as the odd rock
act. Recommended. *See also p139.*

Eamonn Doran's

*3A Crown Alley, Temple Bar, Southside (679 9114).
All cross-city buses.* **Open** 11.30am-3am daily. *Live
music* phone for details. **Admission** usually €3.80
Mon-Fri; €6.35 Sat, Sun. **Credit** AmEx, DC, MC, V.
Map p75.

On the site formerly occupied by Dublin's Rock
Garden, Eamonn Doran's has made 3A Crown Alley
just a little bit more upmarket. There's trad Irish
music upstairs every night in summer and on
Sundays in winter, with rock acts, both Irish and
international, gigging downstairs most nights.

Eamonn Doran's is pretty big for a pub venue, and
there's music until 2am most nights if you fancy a
nightcap or nine. *See also p197.*

Foggy Dew

*1 Fownes Street Upper, Temple Bar, Southside (677
9328). All cross-city buses.* **Open** noon-11.30pm Mon-
Wed; noon-12.30pm Thur; noon-2am Fri, Sat; 1-11pm
Sun. *Live music* 6-8pm Sun. **Admission** free.
No credit cards. Map p75.

So-so rock, jazz and blues. *See also p133.*

Gaiety

*South King Street, Southside (677 1717). All cross-
city buses.* **Open** *Live music* 11.30pm-4am Fri, Sat.
Admission €10.20 Fri; €11.40 Sat. **Credit** MC, V.
Map p313 H5.

Strictly speaking, Friday and Saturday nights at the
central Gaiety Theatre are club nights, but head
down there on either evening and you're likely to see
some terrific live music. Salsa Palace on Fridays features Latin, salsa and world music, while Saturday
night resounds to the alternately groovy and slinky
Soul Clinic. *See also p199.*

Harcourt Hotel

*60-61 Harcourt Street, Southside (478 3677/1-850
664 455). Bus 15A, 15B, 15C, 20, 61, 62, 86.* **Open**
Live music 9.30-11.30pm daily. **Admission** varies.
Credit AmEx, DC, MC, V. **Map** p313 G7.

One of the premier trad venues in the city, the
Harcourt Hotel features high-quality, established
acts. Jazz and pop/rock groups also play regularly,
with Tomato, a late-opening nightclub, following
some gigs (*see p203*).

HQ

Hot Press Irish Music Hall of Fame, 57 Abbey Street Middle, Northside (878 3345/tickets from Ticket Master). All cross-city buses. **Open** *Live music* phone for details. **Tickets** varies. **Credit** *TicketMaster* AmEx, DC, MC, V. **Map** p313 H4.

Home of the Hot Press Music Hall of Fame (*see p86*), HQ preceded the new Ambassador Theatre in providing a quality venue north of the river. The intimate hall holds around 500, views of the stage are pretty much perfect no matter where you are, the roster of bands is varied, and sound and lighting systems are reputedly the best in town. Smokers beware though, puffing is only permitted in the smoking room behind the bar; it has a perfectly good view of the stage but it's not exactly friendly (although non-smokers will probably be relieved not to have to share the fug). HQ also hosts regular club nights (*see p199*).

International Bar

23 Wicklow Street, Southside (677 9250). All cross-city buses. **Open** 10.30am-11.30pm Mon-Wed, Sun; 10.30am-12.30am Thur-Sat. *Live music* from 9pm Tue-Sun. **Admission** €7.60. **No credit cards**. **Map** p313 H5.

There's music upstairs in this small but popular central venue. The menu is mainly blues and soul from bands with residencies, but Tuesday is jazz night and there are also regular performances by local singer-songwriters. *See also p134.*

Irish Film Centre Bar

6 Eustace Street, Temple Bar, Southside (679 8712). All cross-city buses. **Open** 11am-11.30pm Mon-Thur, Sun; 11am-2am Fri, Sat. *Live music* varies; phone for details. **Admission** varies. **Credit** MC, V. **Map** p75.

The Film Centre bar offers blues and some jazz in sophisticated surroundings. Not for jazz aficionados, maybe, but worth a listen, if you're catching a film here. *See p174.*

Olympia: late-night gigs and cover bands.

Isaac Butt

Opposite Busáras, Store Street, Northside (855 5021). All cross-city buses. **Open** 11am-1am Mon-Thur, Sun; 11am-3am Fri, Sat. *Live music* from 8.30pm daily. **Admission** varies. **Credit** MC, V. **Map** p313 J3.

Another relatively new northside venue, the Isaac Butt has a pleasant upstairs bar, while downstairs hosts up-and-coming local rock acts all week, with late club nights afterwards at the weekend. A good place to check out the next big thing in intimate surroundings. *See also p140.*

JJ Smyth's

12 Aungier Street, Southside (475 2565). Bus 12, 16, 16A, 55. **Open** *Live music* from 9pm daily. **Admission** €3.80-€6.35. **No credit cards**. **Map** p313 G6.

One of Dublin's longest-standing jazz and blues venues offers good-quality music seven nights a week. There's an acoustic open jam session on Mondays and blues on Tuesday, Wednesday and Saturday. On Thursday, Friday and Sunday jazz is the order of the night, with the Isotope and Pendulum clubs lining up some of the best acts in the business. A well-informed, friendly clientele make the atmosphere at Smyth's even better. Well worth a look. *See also p134.*

Mother Redcap's Tavern

40-48 Back Lane, Southside (453 8306). Bus 50, 78A. **Open** *Live music* from 9.30pm Mon, Tue, 10.30pm-12.30am Fri, Sat; 1.30-3.30pm Sun. **Admission** €3.80 Mon; free Tue-Sun. **No credit cards**. **Map** p312 F5.

This lively, modern pub in the Christchurch area has a busy live music schedule, kicking off on Mondays with a 16-piece big band. If that's not your thing, there's unplugged trad and folk gigs on Tuesday night and Sunday afternoon, and ballad sessions on Saturday. *See also p135.*

National Stadium

145 South Circular Road, Kilmainham, Southern suburbs (information 453 3371/tickets from TicketMaster). Bus 19, 22. **Open** *Office* 10am-5pm Mon-Fri. **Tickets** varies. **Credit** *TicketMaster* AmEx, DC, MC, V. **Map** p312.

The National Stadium isn't really a music venue at all: it's actually a boxing ring (*see p214*) that is occasionally leased to promoters. The venue is entirely seated, and for gigs, the ring is converted into the stage. Gigs are put on by anyone brave or foolhardy enough to believe that they can fill its 2,200 seats, and though the all-round view is good, the sound quality is often poor: the stadium, after all, was not designed with live music in mind.

Olympia

74 Dame Street, Southside (677 7124/tickets 1-890 925 130). All cross-city buses. **Open** *Box office* 10.30am-6.30pm daily. *Music* usually 8pm, midnight Tue-Sun; phone for details. **Tickets** varies. **Credit** AmEx, MC, V. **Map** p75.

Late-night gigs began at the Olympia in 1987, and since then everyone from the Orb to Hole has played here. It's also where you'll find dubious cover acts, from the Classic Beatles to the Australian Pink Floyd. There are early-evening gigs, too, generally for more established acts, but after midnight anything goes. It's a beautiful theatre in old-fashioned red velvet and brocade style; for some concerts, the seats downstairs are removed for dancing, which can be handy when '70s highlights such as Brutus Gold's Love Train or the Boogie Nights team steamroll into Dublin on a Saturday night. There are bars on all three floors, but these close as soon as the gig is over, when heavy-handed bouncers make sure you don't overstay your welcome.

O'Shea's Merchant

12 Bridge Street Lower, Southside (679 3797).
Bus 50, 78A. **Open** *10.30am-11.30pm Mon-Wed;*
10.30am-12.30am Thur-Sat; 12.30-11.30pm Sun.
Live music from 9.30pm daily. **Admission** *free.*
No credit cards. **Map** *p312 F5.*
This large pub and restaurant features live trad music and set-dancing every night. *See also p137.*

Pod/RedBox

Old Harcourt Street Station, Harcourt Street,
Southside (478 0225/www.pod.ie). **Open** *Live music*
phone for details. **Admission** varies. **Credit** AmEx,
DC, MC, V. **Map** *p313 G7.*

These two classy sister venues are known principally as big lights on the Dublin club scene, but in recent times both have begun to feature some high-quality live music too (Pod recently played host to Run DMC). *See also p199 and p201.*

The Point

East Link Bridge, North Wall Quay, Northside
(tickets 836 6777/group bookings 836 6790).
Tara Street or Connolly DART/rail. **Open** *Box*
office 10am-6pm Mon-Sat. **Tickets** varies.
Credit AmEx, DC, MC, V. **Map** p314 L4.
The Point used to be a train depot, a fact that's still apparent: the main downstairs area is barn-like, which affects the atmosphere and acoustics, with seating rearranged or removed for some shows. As well as hosting major pop and rock acts, it's also the main venue for musicals (*Riverdance* was staged here), but size restricts it from featuring anything too off-the-wall. Tickets are expensive, with bar prices to match. Bear in mind, too, that the Point is a 20-minute walk from the city centre, although buses are provided for some shows.

RDS Showgrounds

Ballsbridge, Southern suburbs (RDS 668 0866/
tickets from TicketMaster). Lansdowne Road
DART/5, 7, 7A, 8, 45 bus. **Open** *Office* 9am-5pm
Mon-Fri. **Tickets** varies. **Credit** *TicketMaster*
AmEx, DC, MC, V. **Map** p309.

Festival fever Rock, pop and jazz

For further details of all the following festivals, contact **Dublin Tourism Centre** on Suffolk Street (1-850 230 330).

Dublin Jazz Festival

Information 877 9001/www.esb.ie/jazz.
Date mid-late Sept.
A recent addition to the Dublin music scene – the inaugural event was in 1998 – the Electricity Supply Board-sponsored Dublin Jazz Festival offers a potentially excellent mix of international and local jazz and world music. Aside from the many gigs at venues across town, including Vicar Street (*see p195*) and the NCH (*see p188*), there's a nightly club, plus movies, workshops and exhibitions. The event is organised by the Improvised Music Company, which promotes a number of other events throughout the year.

Heineken Green Energy Festival

Information 284 1747/www.mcd.ie. **Date** late April-early May (May bank holiday weekend). Groups such as the Divine Comedy began their ascent to stardom at Green Energy, now Dublin's premier city-centre rock and

pop fest and the only time you get to bop on the hallowed cobblestones of Dublin Castle. In recent times, the likes of Beck have headlined to large crowds in a variety of venues ranging from the castle to the Olympia (*see p193*) and the Temple Bar Music Centre (*see p195*).

Witnness

Fairyhouse Racecourse, Co Meath
(284 1747/www.witnness.com). Special bus
service from O'Connell Street. **Tickets** check
website for details. **Credit** AmEx, DC, MC, V.
Date 1st Sat, Sun in Aug.
After years of wrangling over planning and venues, Witnness fills the gap left by the much missed Féile and provides Irish crowds with a good old-fashioned open-air festival. Over two days, the five stages host over 50 acts, from established stars like the Stereophonics and Fun Lovin' Criminals on the main stage to up-and-coming Irish and international acts on the Witnness Rising stage. Bring your own raincoat, buy an inflatable sofa, and take this opportunity to dance the weekend away.

Vicar Street: Dublin's essential gig venue.

The longest-standing open-air venue in Dublin is actually a showjumping arena and one-time football ground, with a capacity of 40,000. Seats in the stands provide a better view than if you sit or stand on the grass, but in the great tradition of the open-air gig, many people prefer to be in the thick of things. Video screens are occasionally used, but don't count on them. Irish weather being what it is, a raincoat is an essential accessory.

SFX City Theatre
23 Sherrard Street Upper, Northside (855 4090). Bus 3, 11, 13, 16, 40C. **Open** *Box office* 10am-6pm Mon-Fri. Tickets also available on performance nights. **Tickets** varies. **Credit** MC, V. **Map** p309.
Formerly the St Francis Xavier Hall (although always known as 'the SFX'), this venue has played a major part in Dublin's rock history. U2 shot part of the 'Pride' video here, and the venue has hosted gigs by all manner of domestic and foreign talent. Nowadays it functions principally as a theatre space, but still hosts the occasional moshfest. Despite rather basic facilities, the atmosphere at this 1,500-capacity space can be fantastic. Be careful walking to the venue: there are unpleasant areas nearby, and the nearest bus stops are on Dorset Street.

The Shelter at Vicar Street
99 Vicar Street, off Thomas Street, the Liberties, Southside (information 454 6656/tickets from TicketMaster). Bus 123. **Open** *Live music* from 8pm Mon-Thur; 7.30pm Fri, Sat. **Tickets** varies. **Credit** *TicketMaster* AmEx, DC, MC, V. **Map** p312 E5.
Next door to and under the same ownership as the Vicar Street complex, the newer Shelter is successfully managing to forge an identity in its own right. In intimate, modern surroundings you can see the cream of Irish trad musicians, as well as the best of local and international jazz, folk and whatever else you fancy. It would seem that the Shelter is on the way to becoming as indispensable to the Dublin gigging scene as its big sister.

Temple Bar Music Centre
Curved Street, Temple Bar, Southside (670 9202/ www.tbmc.ie). All cross-city buses. **Open** *Live music* 7.30pm, 11pm daily. **Admission** varies. **Credit** MC, V. **Map** p75.
The TBMC features a good mix of music, both local and international, from traditional Irish to dance and rock. There's a decent bar off the main auditorium that can double as your warm-up to a night in Temple Bar, and the easygoing door policy reflects the laid-back feel of the entire place. Sounds great in theory, but the acoustics at the Music Centre are terrible; some locals refer to it as the 'black hole'. *See also p202.*

Vicar Street
99 Vicar Street, off Thomas Street, the Liberties, Southside (information 454 6656/tickets from TicketMaster/www.vicarstreet.com). Bus 123. **Open** *Live music* from 7.30pm Mon-Sat. **Tickets** varies. **Credit** *TicketMaster* AmEx, DC, MC, V. **Map** p313 E6.
Situated in a historic part of Dublin, Vicar Street has firmly established itself as one of the premier venues in the city. The pub at the front is bright, airy and comfortable, and the hall itself holds around 500 seated (although seats and tables are removed from the floor for some gigs). It hosts a wide variety of high-quality local and international acts, while next door, sister venue the Shelter (*see above*), looks set to continue the trend.

Whelan's
25 Wexford Street, Southside (478 0766/tickets from TicketMaster). Bus 55, 61, 62, 83. **Open** *Live music* from 8.30pm Mon-Sat. **Tickets** €9.50-€19. **Credit** *TicketMaster* AmEx, DC, MC, V. **Map** p313 G6.
One of Dublin's essential venues, Whelan's is housed in a building that dates back to the 18th century. Though the venue at the back is a converted warehouse, it's designed to complement the pub, and with a balcony on the upper floor and murals from the Book of Kells on the walls downstairs, it's impossible not to be impressed. Music-wise, expect anything from Gypsy bands, English folk and Irish trad to international rock, jazz and blues in a venue that's small enough to be intimate but large enough to be comfortable. Recommended. *See also p139.*

Nightlife

Dublin lives up to its reputation as a party city – make the most of it.

The past few years have seen Dublin settle into its new-found role as one of Europe's premier party cities. Though the initial flood of visitors who came to see the 'new Prague' has subsided somewhat, on Friday nights, the city still fills up with those looking for long liquid weekends. It would seem that no matter how many new bars and clubs are built and regardless of how many square feet are added to the existing ones, everywhere is full to capacity by 8pm – or even earlier at the weekend. This disregard for the laws of physics means that clubbing in Dublin is strictly for those who like their dancefloors crowded and sweaty. That said, with a bit of care, you can avoid the generic tourist discos and discover some great clubbing venues.

If you are not familiar with Dublin, you will probably gravitate towards **Temple Bar**; its cobblestone streets and many restaurants, shops and bars have made it a tourist mecca by day, but by night it can be heaving and decidedly unpleasant, particularly at the weekend. Stag and hen parties may have been officially banned from the district, but the larger bars still attract hordes of rowdy revellers. However, there are some great places here, if you can pick your way through the crowds, and if you walk a short distance you'll find yourself in a whole different world. Day or night the stylish and the outlandish swagger and stagger between the bars on **South Great George's Street**, while one block over on **South William Street** is a new breed of spacious and stylish bars and clubs catering to those Dubliners who have the required cosmopolitan sense of cool. North of the river there's less choice, although on the right night, a number of places – both in the north city centre and further west along the quays – are worth seeking out.

Dublin is a small city: wander around for an hour or two before you decide where you are going to base yourself for the night, or sit at a bar and ask someone who looks like they should know, 'Where's good tonight?'. Most young Dubliners will pride themselves on pointing you in the right direction. For more formal information, consult *In Dublin*, *Hot Press* and the *Event Guide*, and keep an eye out for flyers promoting one-off club nights.

Good music and a fun-loving crowd are the essential mix at the **Voodoo Lounge**. *See p132.*

Arts & Entertainment

CLUB NIGHTS

All of the major city centre clubs run regular nights by promoters, featuring specific styles of music and DJs, which means that you could go to the same venue seven nights in a row and have a very different experience with a different crowd on each occasion. Alternatively, you can follow the hordes as they migrate from club to club in pursuit of one style of music.

It's also well worth checking out the many DJ bars, the best of which are reviewed here or in the **Pubs & Bars** chapter. Irish licensing laws mean that bars can stay open almost as late as nightclubs from Thursday through to Saturday, when you may well find yourself staggering home at 3am never having crossed the threshold of a club nor having paid a cover charge. Bars such as **Hogan's** (*see p134*), the **Modern Green Bar** (*see p135*), **No.4 Dame Lane** (*see p199*), **Spy** (*see p201*), the **Voodoo Lounge** (*see p141*) and **Viva** (*see p139*) all take on a decidedly clubby vibe as the evening progresses. These are great places to get an early start on the cocktails and warm up your dancing feet, but be warned: you may end up staying all night.

Clubs

The Ballroom

Fitzsimmon's Hotel, Temple Bar, Southside (677 9315). **Open** 11am-2.30am Mon-Thur, Sun; 10.30am-3am Fri, Sat. **Admission** €4-€5 Mon-Thur, Sun; €9-€10 Fri, Sat. **Credit** AmEx, MC, V. **Map** p75.
This large basement club in the centre of Temple Bar plays predictable chart hits. It gets incredibly crowded at the weekend with tourists who seem to have found themselves here by accident or because they aren't familiar enough with the city to have picked anywhere better. If you are drunk enough you might have a laugh.

Boomerang

Temple Bar Hotel, Fleet Street, Southside (670 8945). All cross-city buses. **Open** 11pm-2am Wed-Fri, Sun; 10.30pm-2am Sat. **Admission** €5 Wed; €6.50 Thur, Sun; €10 Fri; €13 Sat. **Credit** AmEx, MC, V.
Popular with large groups of loud weekend visitors, this spacious, run-of-the mill club offers shiny, poppy dance sounds to go with its shiny, poppy interior.

Break for the Border

Grafton Plaza Hotel, Johnson Place, Southside (478 0300). All cross-city buses. **Open** noon-11.30pm Mon, Tue, Sun; noon-2.30am Wed-Sat. **Admission** free Mon-Thur, Sun; €6.35-€8.90 after 9pm Fri; €6.35-€10.20 after 9pm Sat. **Credit** AmEx, MC, V. **Map** p313 H5.
After a few hours in here, you may well want to break for the border: this three-level pub/club hosts a full-on boozing and sharking crowd. On the other hand, the atmosphere is lively, mainstream chart

hits allow everyone to have a bop, and the fact that it is a bar that only later turns into a club means accessibility and a hassle-free schedule. It's popular with visitors wanting some lurid stories to tell on the journey home.

The Capitol Bar

12-14 Lower Stephen Street, Southside (475 7166). **Open** 10.30am-2.30am daily. **Admission** free. **Credit** AmEx, MC, V. **Map** p313 G5.
The Capitol Bar has leather seats, leather pants, leather hats and an endless supply of R&B. Dress skimpy, dress leather.

Club M

Blooms Hotel, Anglesea Street, Southside (671 5622). All cross-city buses. **Open** 11pm-2.30am daily. **Admission** €6.35 Mon-Thur, Sun; €12.70 Fri, Sat. **Credit** AmEx, DC, MC, V. **Map** p313 H4.
A long-standing club that aims for Ibiza glamour, but instead attracts lager-swilling groups who want to away to easy chart sounds. If you are prepared to stomach the effects of an undiluted oestrogen/testosterone cocktail, you'll enjoy yourself.

Club Mono

26 Wexford Street, Southside (475 8555/www.clubmono.com). Bus 16, 16A, 55. **Open** 4pm-2.30am Mon-Thur, Sun; 4pm-3am Fri, Sat. **Admission** €5-€6.35; €3.80 concessions Wed, Thur, Sun; €10.20-€12.70 Fri, Sat. **Credit** MC, V. **Map** p313 G6.
Formerly the home of the Mean Fiddler rock venue, Mono has successively transformed itself into a bar and club venue that's particularly popular with a youthful student contingent. The downstairs bar is spacious and dimly lit, with plenty of couches to lounge about on, while upstairs is the main club where resident DJs spin crowd-pleasing tunes from Wednesday to Sunday to a busy dancefloor. There are also frequent guest appearances by big-name DJs from the UK including Cream and Bugged Out.

Coyote Lounge

D'Olier Street, Southside (671 2089). All cross-city buses. **Open** 10pm-3am Wed, 9pm-3am Thur; 8pm-3am Fri, Sat; 9pm-late Sun. **Admission** free Wed, Thur, Sun; €6.35-€8.90 Fri; €8.90 Sat. **Credit** MC, V. **Map** p313 H4.
This bar/club is popular with the well-dressed officey crowd. It has loungey decor, a mixed music policy and a late licence all week, making it a good spot for a chilled-out late drink. There are some excellent mid-week club nights with free admission.

Eamonn Doran's

3A Crown Alley, Temple Bar, Southside (679 9114). All cross-city buses. **Open** 11am-3am Mon-Sat; noon-3am Sun. **Admission** €3.80-€7.60. **Credit** AmEx, MC, V. **Map** p75.
The original Eamonn Doran's is an Irish bar in Manhattan. This version, here in the heart of Temple Bar, is a popular live music venue (*see p192*) that also has some good club nights: Flava on Wednesdays blends '80s music and hip hop, while Monday's

Arts & Entertainment

pressing all the right buttons

After 21 years, i-D is still the world's most indispensable fashion magazine. Keep on smiling with us by picking up a copy on your travels... To find i-D visit any good newsagent. To find a subscription visit subscriptions@i-dmagazine.co.uk. To find the limited edition i-D badges visit merchandise@i-dmagazine.co.uk. To find the i-D website visit www.i-dmagazine.com

Melting Pot gives you everything from reggae to drum 'n' bass. ED's is rough and ready, and it's always full of serious drinkers, but it also boasts some of the best scratch DJs in town, and if you want to go nuts without anybody staring at you, then this is the place for you.

Gaiety

South King Street, Southside (679 5622). All cross-city buses. **Open** midnight-4am Fri, Sat. **Admission** €11.50, €10.50 concessions. **No credit cards.** **Map** p313 H6.

There are three main dance floors in the refurbished Gaiety, plus the theatre itself, where old movies and cartoons are shown, making it an ideal chill out space. Weekend events manage to combine a little bit of everything: live jazz, soul and salsa in the largest of the five bar areas, dance-orientated tracks played by the DJs upstairs, and retro '60s and '70s tunes in the basement. The crowd is as eclectic as the entertainment, so you can dress up or down as you please. Be warned, though: drinks are fairly expensive. *See also p192.*

HQ

57 Abbey Street Middle, Northside (878 3345). All cross-city buses. **Open** 11.30pm-2.30am Sat. **Admission** phone for details. **No credit cards.** **Map** p313 H4.

This very large live music venue runs club nights after 11.30pm. HQ is particularly good at the weekends, when the music is generally soul and disco orientated. As venues go, it's a little sterile, but on Saturdays the enthusiastic crowd at Neon more than make up for it. *See also p193.*

The Kitchen

The Clarence, Essex Street East, Temple Bar, Southside (677 6635/www.the-kitchen.com). All cross-city buses. **Admission** €6.35-€19 **Credit** AmEx, DC, MC, V. **Map** p75

When it opened seven years ago this U2-owned club was the most exclusive venue in town, but as Dublin moved upmarket, the Kitchen has become more relaxed and more fun: it's still a classy spot, but the door policy is less strict and the music has become more challenging – generally good quality techno and house, with some R&B and drum 'n' bass thrown in for good measure. The main bar area is rather small and can become uncomfortable when crowded due, in part, to its strange concrete Swiss cheese decor. However, the large VIP area only has the velvet rope across it if the band are entertaining their A-list guests. Tourists come here in the hope of catching a glimpse of Ireland's megastars and can be seen standing around wondering why the DJ won't play any U2 songs.

Lillie's Bordello

Adam Court, Grafton Street, Southside (679 9204). All cross-city buses. **Open** 11.30pm-late daily; phone for details. **Admission** €12.70 cover charge for non-members. **Credit** AmEx, MC, V. **Map** p313 H5.

If you want a stress-free night in Dublin, you should probably give Lillie's a wide berth. The door policy is quite strict, and once inside, there are several reserved areas to negotiate. In fact, the crowd seems to be mostly hairdressers who think they're VIPs, and if there are any celebs at all, they're safely tucked away in one of the suites being bored to death by Dublin's self-appointed elite. The staff are curiously precious, and though the music can be good, everyone seems far too worried about striking a pose to really let their hair down.

Lobo

Morrison Hotel, Ormond Quay, Northside (887 2400). All cross-city buses. **Open** 10pm 3am Fri, Sat. **Admission** free before 11pm Fri, Sat; €8.90 Fri; €12.70 Sat. **Credit** AmEx, MC, V. **Map** p313 G4.

The Morrison is possibly Dublin's most glamorous hotel and its nightclub, Lobo, is no slouch either, with its stunning John Rocha-designed decor, seriously scary cocktail prices and a door policy that's so strict that the club is often less than full – apparently there are just not enough beautiful people in this city. Having said that, the setting is superb, and the DJs play an eclectic range of top tunes. What a shame, then, that the dancefloor is not much bigger than an After Eight.

No.4 Dame Lane

Dame Lane, Southside (679 0291). All cross-city buses. **Open** 5pm-12.30am Mon, Tue; 5pm-2.00am Wed-Sun. **Admission** free. **Credit** MC, V. **Map** p313 G5.

It's rather tricky to find this bar-club, despite the fact that it's named after its address, but it's worth the effort. No.4's interior is minimalist and lofty with lots of exposed brickwork. It draws a fashionable twentysomething crowd who come for a pre-club drink but often end up staying for the night. The large upstairs has a small dancefloor area, the music policy is eclectic and No.4 manages to attract some of the best DJs in the city from Wednesday to Sunday night for one offs and residencies. Keep an eye out for any night promoted by Influx or Strictly Fish.

Peg's

47-49 Kildare Street, Southside (679 4388). All cross-city buses. **Open** 11pm-2.30am daily. **Admission** €9 Mon; €7.50 Tue-Sun. **No credit cards.** **Map** p313 J5.

Peg's is not the prettiest club in town, but great fun on the right night. A young crowd and regular drinks promotions make it a good place to go if you're on a budget. Until recently the sounds have been strictly chart and greatest hits but now some of the cooler DJs in town are using Peg's as a place to practise their sets; keep an eye out for flyers.

POD

Old Harcourt Street Station, Harcourt Street, Southside (478 0225/www.pod.ie). All cross-city buses. **Open** 11pm-3am Wed-Sun. **Admission** €6.50-€13; free-€6.50 concessions. **Credit** MC, V. **Map** p313 H7.

Arts & Entertainment

Bored of the black stuff?

Dublin without Guinness? It's like a dairy-free Paris, or Rome without pasta: unthinkable. But while you'll smell the hops and barley being magicked into a 'pint o' plain' at the Guinness Brewery, it is possible to get from one side of the city to the other without a drop of the black stuff ever passing your lips. Why you should want to do that is another matter, of course.

While the Guinness in this city is admittedly superlative, not everyone shares writer JP Donleavy's desire to 'decompose in a barrel of porter and have it served in all the pubs in Dublin'. And let's face it, Guinness is a heavy drink – not for nothing was a glass of stout traditionally given to nursing mothers and blood donors on doctors' orders. In the mid 1990s even the Guinness Brewery itself realised slimline Celtic kittens' tastes were changing and tried (unsuccessfully) to launch a white beer, Breo, to catch those once stout and loyal stout and ale drinkers.

Forget Breo and concentrate instead on the own-brand lagers and white beers from the city's microbreweries. At the **Porterhouse** (*see p138*) the beer is brewed on the premises and the process has become part of the decor. There are plenty of light beers to choose from, but there's also an oyster-flavoured stout for those who like eating and drinking their pints. The **Dublin Brewing Company** (*see p140*) produces four fresh, punchy beers, which you'll find on draught at bars in Smithfield, including the **Cobblestone** (*see p139*), the **Dice Bar** (*see p140*) and the **Voodoo Lounge** (*see p141*), or there's Wicked Apple cider, if you've had enough of hops. For global beers try Belgian restaurant **Belgo** (17-19 Sycamore Street, Temple Bar; 672 7555) or **Thomas Read** (*see p139*), both of which carry a world of choice – in fact, you could fairly circumnavigate the globe, with the proper branded glasses to match. Cool bars such as the **Bailey** (*pictured; see p131*), **Dakota** (*see p132*) and **No.4 Dame Lane** (*see p199*) also have a good international range

Spiritually speaking, Dublin has every home-produced whiskey and imported scotch a lush could wish for. The **Old Jameson Distillery** in Smithfield will offer you a free shot of the stuff at the end of its tour (*see p92*), but if you want to do it properly, the traditional pubs such as **McDaid's** (*see p135*) and the **Stag's Head** (*see p138*) do it best. Hunch

over a tumbler with two fingers of whiskey, and take just a tablespoon of water from the proffered jug – asking for ice in your whiskey is the one of the quickest ways to make a real barman weep. And if whiskey's not your poison, you can continue your alcoholic travels of the world at **Pravda** (*see p140*), a Russian-themed bar with a fairly hefty vodka list.

Perhaps because Dublin does the drink thing so well, the city has yet to get the cocktail concept quite right, and it's rather 'a little of what you fancy' when it comes to bar staffs' take on the traditional mixes. That said, places like the **Chocolate Bar**, **Velure** (for both, *see p132*) and **Spy** (*see p201*) have wicked ways with a cocktail shaker. You just might not end up with the drink you were expecting.

It's not all 40-proof imbibing in this city, though. The newly health- and fashion-conscious population has embraced all the latest drinking fads: smoothies for breakfast, juices with lunch and quality coffee for those on the go are the benefits of a much more cosmopolitan city. Anything and everything is available and it's all done terribly well, from the hazelnut syrup in your Columbian blend non-fat decaf latte to your mango and star anise smoothie. Dubliners have imported the juice bar concept and taken to it like carrots to a blender: a visit to **Nectar**, **Nude** and **Juice** (for all, *see p120*) will leave you feeling pious and pioneering and set you up nicely for the night of alcohol ahead.

Dublin's most established super-club is housed inside the old Harcourt Street station and has large dancefloors (5,000 sq ft) over several levels. POD and its sister venue Red Box (*see below*) consistently feature top DJs and live PAs, who play generally dance-friendly happy house to a fairly flashy crowd of party people. Friday night's gay club HAM (*see p184*) has a strictly no-straights door policy, but it's a great night out if you are gay or willing to fake it at the door and if you still have the strength, drag yourself along to Odyssey on Sunday for some of the best house music in town courtesy of DJ Bubbles. There's a strictly enforced dress code, so make an effort to smarten up, particularly at the weekend.

Red Box

Old Harcourt Street Station, Harcourt Street, Southside (478 0225/478 0166/www.pod.ie). All cross-city buses. **Open** from 10pm-3am most nights; phone or check website for details. **Admission** €6.50-€19. **Credit** MC, V. **Map** p313 H7.

Part of POD complex (*see above*), Red Box boasts the biggest dancefloor in the city centre, so you can freak out to your heart's content. The design means that an explosive atmosphere is guaranteed, especially on nights when big-name guests visit: keep an eye out for special events. Devotion on a Friday is a journey into tech-funk with the Red Box stage converted into a large chill-out area.

Renards

23-25 Frederick Street South, Southside (677 5876). All cross-city buses. **Open** 10.30am-3am Mon-Fri; 2pm-3am Sat; 6pm-1am Sun. **Admission** free. **Credit** AmEx, MC, V. **Map** p313 H5.

A good spot to mix a bit of glam with some happy house. Renard's door policy can be unnecessarily strict, so go in small-ish groups and dress up. There are three floors; two are for members only, but the main café-bar is open to members of the public, where there's a DJ playing popular tunes.

Ri Ra

Dame Court (off South Great George's Street), Southside (677 4835/677 4835). All cross-city buses. **Open** 11.30pm-2.30am daily. **Admission** €5-€9. **Credit** MC, V. **Map** p313 G5.

Adjoining the Globe (*see p134*), Ri Ra consistently produces quality nights, frequented by a trendy, enthusiastic crowd. The music policy is varied, ranging from reggae and '60s soul to trance and hip hop. It's always fun, always full and cool enough to attract a visit from David Bowie when he's in town. The relaxed door policy and spacey bar staff add to Ri Ra's charm, but get there early as it regularly fills to capacity. One of Dublin's longest running and best loved regular nights is Monday's Strictly Handbag. Resident DJ Dandelion plays '60s soul in the upstairs bar while the main dancefloor jumps to kitsch '80s and disco. On Sunday, DJs play energetic hip hop sets at Bass Monkey.

Spy/Wax

Powerscourt Townhouse Centre, South William Street, Southside (677 0014/677 0067/www. spydublin.com). All cross-city buses. **Open** 10pm-3am Tue-Sat; 10pm-3am Sun. **Admission** *Spy* free Tue-Thur; €10 non-members after 11.30pm Fri, Sat. *Wax* €5 Tue-Thur; €10 non-members after 11.30pm Fri, Sat. **Credit** MC, V. **Map** p313 H5.

Ri Ra: trance, hip hop, '80s disco, '60s soul – and baby football.

Arts & Entertainment

Endless weekend

Seven nights out in Dublin.

You can find packed dancefloors and busy bars in Dublin on every night of the week – to the extent that you could be forgiven for thinking no one has to get up for work. Most dedicated clubbers will go out mid-week rather than risk injuring the crowds of suburbanites and listening to the chart-oriented music that sets the tone in most clubs at the weekend.

Listed below are some of the best weekly club nights in the city: pick the evening's entertainment of your choice – or plan a seven-night club-athon.

MONDAY

If the weekend didn't kill you, or you just want more, Mondays are a popular night out for younger Dubliners.

Warm up at the **Modern Green Bar** (see p135) or with feel-good '80s tunes at the **Front Lounge** (see p133). Move on to the essential Strictly Handbag at **Ri Ra** (see p201).

TUESDAY

Tuesday is a big night out for students. This has both drawbacks – teenagers dribbling and vomiting on each other – and advantages – students love to dance and most of the clubs offer cheap drinks promotions.

Warm up with a Salsa Villa dance class at the **Temple Bar Music Centre** (see p202). Move on to Genius at the **Kitchen** (see p199) for some techno mayhem and €1.27 vodka shots or Damage at **Switch**, which lives up to its name in all the right ways (see p202).

WEDNESDAY

This is often a good night to see live music – and we don't mean two turntables and a microphone. Local performers, who draw huge crowds in the UK and the States, often play small intimate shows when they get home. Wednesday's post-gig partying possibilities are limited, but there are a couple of regular nights that draw a loyal crowd.

Warm up with a gig at **Whelan's** or **Vicar Street** (for both, see p195). Move on to Soul Riot at the **Temple Bar Music Centre** (see p202) or enjoy the excellent dub and reggae of Firehouse Skank at the **Parnell Mooney** (74 Parnell Street, Northside; 873 1544).

THURSDAY

Make the most of Dublin's late licensing laws, but bear in mind that Thursday is pay day for most of the city; finding a balance between a wild night out and a drunken riot can be difficult.

Spy screams understatement at the top of it's lungs: you probably wouldn't know it was there if it wasn't for the heavy-handed doormen. The interior is marble, light boxes and shag pile carpet, a perfect setting for Dublin's most stylish, who stand around pouting coquettishly. If you get bored of people-watching, go downstairs to **Wax** for a dance. Wax is more casual, with ultra-slick decor, clever tunes and show-off dancers. On Fridays and Saturdays Spy and Wax work as one venue, and if you get in before 11.30pm, you'll avoid the cover charge. Dress up, spend like you earn it, show off to house and R&B, and you'll have a ball. For the best full-on party on Sunday check out Hilton Edwards, the city's largest gay club night (see p184).

Switch

Eustace Street, Temple Bar, Southside (670 7655). All cross-city buses. **Open** 11pm-3am daily. **Admission** €6.50 Mon-Thur, Sun; €10-€11.50 Fri, Sat. **No credit cards. Map** p75.
Switch is small, dark and sweaty but still one of the best clubs in town for anyone who goes out to dance not to pose. Hardcore house and drum 'n' bass are

the specialities, and the crowd is usually young and enthusiastic. The club is about 70% dancefloor, but by about 2am it's more like 95%. Damage on Tuesday is one of the best techno nights in town, while Monday's SLAM is a big night for the city's gay clubbers (see p184). There's also a new break-beat night (Food) on Fridays. As for a dress code; let's just say no one has ever been turned away from Switch for wearing trainers.

Temple Bar Music Centre

Curved Street, Temple Bar, Southside (670 9202). All cross-city buses. **Open** 10.30pm-2.30am Tue-Sat. **Admission** €8 Tue; €6.50, €4 with flyer Wed; €6.50, €5 with flyer Thur; €10-€15 Fri, Sat. **Credit** AmEx, MC, V. **Map** p75.
This 1,000-capacity purpose-built venue hosts live gigs until 11.30pm (see p195) and club nights after that. It's generally worth paying to see the live show and then staying on for the club; you won't have to fork out the club cover charge and though the bar's not the most comfortable in town, the music is usually good enough to keep you on your feet. There's a Latin club night, Salsa Villa, on Tuesday, which

Warm up with young bohemians and hard-core clubbers at the **Globe** and **Hogan's** (for both, *see 134*), or join the R&B crew at **Viva** (*see p139*). Move on to the indie mess of Screamadelica in the **Temple Bar Music Centre** (*see p194*) or just spend the night looking cool at **No.4 Dame Lane** (*see p199*).

FRIDAY

Treat yourself to a bit of glam. Face the fact that everywhere will be jammed – but sometimes a snotty door policy can be your friend, as it keeps down the crowds. If you are looking for a less designer night out, then it's advisable to have at least three strong drinks before venturing into any of the more mainstream clubs.

Warm up with designer cocktails at **Lobo** (*see p199*) or **Spy** (*see p201*). Move on with the cool crowd to **Wax** (*see p201*), or get your fix of top-notch drum 'n' bass at the **Kitchen** or R&B at the **Temple Theatre** (*see p203*).

is preceded by a dance class (from 0.30pm), while on Wednesday is the high-quality Soul Riot, which features guest DJs playing funky soul sets . Those who feel the need of a deeper, darker experience can join the lank-haired ladies and spiky-haired boys who congregate to shuffle about to indie records at Screamadelica on Thursday.

Temple Theatre

St George's Church, Temple Street, Northside (874 5088). No bus. **Open** 9pm-3am Wed-Sat. **Admission** €13-€16; €9 concessions. **No credit cards. Map** p313 H2.

Despite its location away from the city centre, the Temple Theatre manages to attract large crowds by simply giving them what they want, including frequent visits from guest DJs. It's a large venue inside a converted church, and usually worth a visit for the house music energy of the main dance area and the smoochy ambience of the downstairs chambers. On Fridays, Temple Theatre hosts Rhythm Corporation, Dublin's largest and classiest R&B night, complete with podium dancers and extra-jiggy dancefloor antics.

SATURDAY

If you thought the bars and clubs got crowded on Fridays, Saturdays are enough to make a well-oiled sardine wince. However, there are some clubs that are worth the queue for the bar. Being the busiest night of the week, many of the larger clubs put on big-name DJs from the UK and the States; check local listings and keep an eye out for posters.

Warm up at the **Voodoo Lounge** (*see p141*). Move on to **POD** (*see p199*), **Red Box** (*see p201*), Soul Stage at the **Gaiety** or Neon at **HQ** (for both, *see p199*).

SUNDAY

There is no late licence on Sunday, but all the clubs are open for those determined not to get a fresh start on Monday morning. Most clubs take it easy on the ears, opting for smooth soul and nostalgic music policies to round off the week. Sunday is also gay night in Dublin, so if you're after a full-on party, the city's gay venues are your best bet.

Warm up with drag bingo at the **George** (*see p182*). Move on to hip hop-tastic Bass Monkey at **Ri Ra** (*see p201*), the glamorously gay disco Hilton Edwards at **Spy** (*see p184*) or groove to the house sounds of Odyssey at **POD** (*see p199*).

Tomato

Harcourt Hotel, 60 Harcourt Street, Southside (476 4900). Bus 15A, 15B, 15C, 20, 61, 62, 86. **Open** 10.30pm-3am Wed-Sun. **Admission** €7.50, €6.50 concessions Wed, Thur, Sun, €10, €7.50 concessions Fri, Sat. **Credit** MC, V. **Map** p313 H7.

Tomato is a loungey night spot that consists of several spacious rooms with plenty of comfortable alcoves. It has a mixed music policy and is rather more glamorous than the other clubs that line Harcourt Street. Tomato usually remains relatively quiet during the week, but watch out for large groups of post-work drinkers and sports fans who have a tendency to get sloppy.

Whelan's

25 Wexford Street, Southside (478 0766). Bus 55, 61, 62, 83. **Open** *Club nights* 11pm-2.30am Thur-Sat. **Admission** €6.50-€9; free before 10.30pm. **Credit** AmEx, MC, V. **Map** p313 G6.

This bar-style live music venue (*see p195*) hosts respectable post-gig indie discos most nights of the week, and admission is free to anyone who has attended the live show.

Arts & Entertainment

Performing Arts

As Irish playwrights, actors, dancers and comedians make their mark on the international scene, it would seem that in Dublin, all the world's a stage.

Theatre

Irishness has always been associated with an affinity for literature, and in particular a strong dramatic tradition. Until the 20th century however, literary or dramatic success was not measured here – in a city considered provincial even by those born locally – but across the water, where Irish playwrights such as Wilde, Sheridan and Shaw were the darlings of the London scene. This changed thanks to the vision of WB Yeats and Lady Gregory, who founded the Irish Dramatic Movement and established the Abbey Theatre in 1904 to cultivate a steady stream of indigenous plays that has not yet dried up. Dublin must have as many playwrights and wannabes as Hollywood has scriptwriters and starlets.

Dublin's affluence is just as apparent in its cultural life as it is in the city's bars and restaurants. There is new energy on the theatrical scene – new theatres inaugurated, old theatres revamped and money to explore the city's full creative potential. There are drama, dance and comedy performances almost everywhere you look, in venues that run the gamut from glamorous to grotty.

The state-funded centres suffer from an image problem – they are seen as hidebound and stuffy. However, these places do receive substantial subsidies and so – though they are hardly ground-breaking – their production values can be guaranteed. One rung down is the clutch of 'new establishment' centres, places that have achieved considerable success but which retain a slightly rakish air from their bohemian beginnings. The fringe is a further step down, with many occasional venues (usually pubs that double as stages).

Expensive productions of Irish theatrical milestones are regularly staged in one of the mainstream theatres, such as the Gate or the Abbey, particularly during the summer months. The plays that established the name of writers such as Synge, O'Casey, Behan, Friel and Beckett (with whom the Gate claims a special relationship) are still performed, sometimes with strict adherence to the original form, sometimes in modern, attention-grabbing interpretations. Such productions are a must: to see professional Irish actors performing the Irish classics is to witness a perfect marriage of form and content.

But these, although pleasant and a valuable nod to tradition, are not the most interesting work Dublin has to offer. Alongside this visible canon, there is also ambitious work produced by a handful of energetic young companies, and performed by fine local actors: Pauline Hutton is extremely capable and dedicated, so determined to get things right that she seldom disappoints; Peter MacDonald, who flits from stage to screen with ease, has a charismatic presence that ensures he is always watchable; while Olwen Fouere brings a brooding, almost menacing presence to her roles and is working hard to push the boundaries of conventional forms.

The number of new writers coming through is another indication of the rude health of Irish theatre, with Conor McPherson, Martin McDonagh, Mark O'Rowe and Marie Jones in particular carrying the torch into the next generation (*see p210* **Staging a coup**).

George Bernard Shaw. *See p32.*

Arts & Entertainment

Expect musicals, opera and popular Irish drama at the refurbished **Gaiety**. *See p208.*

TICKETS AND INFORMATION

The Event Guide, In Dublin and the *Irish Times* all contain listings and reviews; *The Dubliner* is more selective but carries intelligent reviews of the bigger productions. Most Dublin theatres and companies produce clear publicity leaflets, generally found in tourist centres, hotels, bars and cafés. In addition, the *Golden Pages* directory has a useful theatre information section, complete with diagrams of seating arrangements for the Gaiety, the Gate, Andrews Lane, the Tivoli, the Abbey, Peacock, Olympia and Civic theatres. Tickets for some theatres – including the Abbey – are available through **TicketMaster** at HMV on Grafton Street, though it does charge a booking fee (1-890 925 100/from outside Ireland 00353 1-456 9569/ www.ticketmaster.ie).

Theatres

The Abbey

26 Abbey Street Lower, Northside (box office 878 7222/TicketMaster 456 9569). All cross-city buses. **Open** *Box office 10.30am-7pm Mon-Sat.* **Tickets** €12.50-€23.50; €6.50 concessions Mon-Thur & Sat matinée; €10 previews. **Credit** MC, V. **Map** p313 H4.

When the Abbey finally relocates, as it is due to do soon, there will be mingled sighs of regret and relief. Established by WB Yeats in 1904, this was the vibrant centre of Irish drama for many years. Controversial productions established it as the talk

of the theatrical town. Most notable was JM Synge's *Playboy of the Western World*, which delivered a vision of Irish youth so unpalatable that the audience expressed its disgust by rioting. This was followed by O'Casey's *The Plough and the Stars*, which depicted Easter 1916 as the idiotic work of drunkards and bully-boys, set against the backdrop of an indifferent, callous, looting Irish public. The audience's reception of the play was so bad that Yeats was moved to berate the crowd from the stage: 'You have disgraced yourselves again,' he thundered (referring to the original *Playboy* riots).

A fire demolished the original building in 1951 and its replacement, on the same site, has never been loved. The exterior is remarkably undistinguished, while the auditorium, with too many pillars and weird pockets of muffled sound, is notoriously difficult (rows F-M, seats 8-15 provide the best view in the house). However, the Abbey is still a reliable source of Irish theatre – in 2001 it showcased the work of Tom Murphy, one of the country's most celebrated playwrights – though there's little cutting-edge drama to be found on the main Abbey stage: for that, you'll have to try the Peacock (*see below*). Production values are always high, the addition of a resident choreographer has done wonders for the visual quality of the plays, and the theatre both launches and plays host to the country's most famous actors. Recently, the theatre's protectionist attitude has also relaxed slightly to allow visiting directors a chance to show what they can do with the space. Katie Mitchell's *Iphigenia at Aulis* and Deborah Warner's *Medea* were both superb productions in recent times.

Arts & Entertainment

Festival fever Theatre

Dublin Theatre Festival

44 East Essex Street, Temple Bar, Southside
(677 8439/www.eircomtheatrefestival.com).
Tickets €10-€32; 20% reduction for
previews. **Credit** AmEx, DC, MC, V. **Date** Oct.
For two weeks every October, Dublin turns
into theatretown, as everyone tries to claim
some kind of involvement with Europe's
biggest theatre-dedicated showcase. Founded
more than 40 years ago in 1957, the festival
has plenty of glamour and kudos. Firmly
established on the international circuit, it
usually attracts a fair smattering of the
great and the good. Though it features a huge
number of talented foreign acts from as far
away as Moscow and Tokyo, the Irish content
is still undoubtedly the highlight. A couple
of productions are always snapped up by
international festival directors – who attend
expressly for this purpose – and the festival is
an excellent opportunity to see the cream of
the theatrical crop at its freshest. Increasingly
over the last few years, special events have
been scheduled around the festival, including
public interviews and post-show talks by the
more famous directors and actors involved.

A preliminary programme for the festival is
available around May each year, though the
full programme doesn't emerge until late
August. Booking begins three weeks before
the festival opens, by phone or in person.
Many shows still have tickets available only
a few days before the performance, though
it's advisable to book ahead if there's
anything you're particularly interested in.
The venues are all major Dublin theatres,
though occasionally special arrangements
will be made for particularly large shows or
those with unusual requirements.

Fringe Festival

5 Aston Quay, Temple Bar, Southside
(1-850 374 643/679 2320/fax 679 2790/
www.fringefest.com). **Tickets** free-€15;
€2.50 reduction for concessions. **Credit**
AmEx, DC, MC, V. **Date** Sept-Oct.
Now into its seventh year, the fringe is so
established it hardly deserves the term
'fringe' any more. One of the highlights of the
theatrical calendar, this is generally a mixed
bag with some genuinely dazzling moments.
Vibrant and sassy, with an increasing amount
of crossover with the more established Dublin
Theatre Festival, the Fringe is dedicated
to providing a focus for new companies,

although it frequently acts as a forum for well-
established companies wishing to try out new
material or change direction. The emphasis is
on the unusual, and performances are usually
innovative, avant garde and fun.

Shows are chosen on the basis of their
production and entertainment values, then
performed in a variety of offbeat venues:
galleries, cafés, pubs and clubs are all roped
in. The festival includes dance, comedy,
cabaret and music, but concentrates on
theatre: mainly Irish, though a few international
shows always find their way in. It runs for three
weeks, two of which coincide with the Dublin
Theatre Festival, and an information office is
open for its duration. The Fringe's programme
is published at the start of September: shows
usually run for one week and tickets (priced
pretty reasonably) are usually obtainable only
30 minutes before the show. Anyone wanting
more information – or even wishing to submit a
proposal or pitch an idea – should contact the
festival at the above address.

Children's Season

Information Ark Children's Cultural Centre,
11A Eustace Street, Temple Bar, Southside
(670 7788/box office 677 8439). All cross-
city buses. **Tickets** €5-€7.50. **Credit** AmEx,
DC, MC, V. **Date** Oct.
Running alongside the Dublin Theatre
Festival, the Children's Season provides
performances for children by international
and domestic companies. Mime, animation,
music and puppets make the festival
colourful and entertaining, so if you have to
go along with the kids, it won't be too much
of a hardship. The programme is issued in
September, with performances held during
schooltimes, and at evenings and weekends.

Festival Club

Information 677 8439. **Open** 11pm-2am
nightly during Dublin Theatre Festival.
Membership €25.50. **Credit** AmEx, DC, MC,
V. **Date** Oct.
Really just an excuse for a late-night drink,
the Festival Club runs – as its name suggests
– as a post-performance event during the
Dublin Theatre Festival. Venues are
announced soon after the festival publishes
its programme, and club membership is
available from the festival box office. How
better to relax after a performance than with
the cast and crew of the show you've just
seen? You never know who you might meet…

Arts & Entertainment

John Hurt in *Krapp's Last Tape* was a highlight of The **Gate**'s 2001 season. *See p208.*

Andrew's Lane Theatre

9-13 Andrew's Lane, off Exchequer Street, Southside (679 5720). All cross-city buses. **Open** *Box office* 10.30am-7pm Mon-Sat. **Tickets** €9-€19; €13.50 previews. **Credit** AmEx, MC, V. **Map** p313 G5.
One of only a few specifically commercial theatres in Dublin, Andrew's Lane hosts a variety of touring provincial companies and international acts offering both dramatic and musical works; the only criterion is that they are proven crowd pleasers. Shows are usually entertaining, although there can be an element of 'Oh no I didn't', 'Oh yes you did' mindlessness to them. The building is unattractive – rundown, featureless and cold in winter – but the atmosphere is easygoing and the crowd (mostly large groups and families on a night out) are clearly out to enjoy themselves.

Bewley's Café Theatre

Bewley's, Grafton Street, Southside (information 086 878 4001). All cross-city buses. **Open** *Shows* 1.10pm Mon-Sat. **Tickets** (at the door) €10 incl soup and sandwiches. **No credit cards. Map** p313 H5.
Dublin's only year-round venue for lunchtime drama, Bewley's Café Theatre re-opened in 1999 after major refurbishment. This elegant and intimate space has gained a reputation for showing innovative and exciting productions of established classics and new Irish writing.

Civic Theatre

Tallaght Town Centre, Tallaght, Southern suburbs (462 7477). Bus 49, 49A, 50, 54A, 56A, 65, 65B, 77, 77A. **Open** *Box office* 10am-6pm Mon-Sat. **Tickets** *Main auditorium* €12.50-€19; €10-€16.50 concessions. *Studio* €12.50; €10 concessions. **Credit** MC, V.

Tallaght may not be official theatreland, but this purpose-built 350-seater – a bright, lavish, state of-the art space that also includes a studio, restaurant, bar and first floor gallery showing work by new and established Irish artists – can be rewarding. Initially a receiving house for established provincial and international touring productions in theatre, dance and opera, the Civic has now branched out to become a producing house in its own right, staging new work by Irish writers and new translations of European plays. Children's entertainment is a regular feature on the Civic's calendar, with a lively selection of puppet shows and retellings of classic fairy tales.

Crypt Arts Centre

Dublin Castle, Dame Street, Southside (671 3387). All cross-city buses. **Open** *Box office* 10am-6pm Mon-Fri; 1-5pm Sat. **Tickets** €10; €7.50 concessions. **No credit cards. Map** p313 G5.
The Crypt is worth a visit for its location alone – in the old church crypt of Dublin Castle – and with all the atmosphere one would expect from such a venue. Often used by Dublin's younger companies, many of which perform material that is boisterously experimental, if occasionally too ambitious, it is well-liked for its intimate size and elegant appearance.

Draíocht

Blanchardstown Centre, Blanchardstown, Northern suburbs (885 2622/admin@draiocht.ie). Bus 38, 38A, 39, 39X, 236, 237, 239, 270. **Open** *Box office* 10am-6pm Mon-Sat. **Tickets** €10-€15. **Credit** AmEx, DC, MC, V.
This latest addition to the Dublin theatre scene, although far from the beaten track, has plenty to offer: two performance spaces – a main auditorium,

Project Arts Centre: the blue-eyed boy of the city's contemporary art scene. *See p209.*

seating 286, and smaller studio, which seats 100 – two gallery spaces, an artist's studio, rehearsal room and bar. The complex will host the gamut of performing and visual arts, both national and international, from stand-up comedy, dance and children's shows to music recitals and the more dynamic contemporary theatre productions. The opening line-up is sufficiently interesting to make this one to watch.

Focus

6 Pembroke Place, off Pembroke Street Upper, Southside (676 3071). All cross-city buses. **Open** *Box office* 11am-6pm Mon-Sat. **Tickets** €9-€11.50; €6.50 previews. **No credit cards. Map** p313 J7.
This small, high-minded theatre, an institution in Irish theatrical life for 30 years, is currently in limbo following the death of founder Deirdre O'Connell, who presided over the renowned actors' studio that turned out Gabriel Byrne, Jayne Snow and Tom Hickey. There is plenty of goodwill among those who have worked here, but the Focus was one woman's labour of love and it is doubtful whether anyone else has sufficient vision to maintain its high ideals. Despite a new production in late 2001, without Deirdre O'Connell at the helm, the Focus's future is unclear.

Gaiety

South King Street, Southside (677 1717). All cross-city buses. **Open** *Box office* 11am-7pm Mon-Sat. **Tickets** €16.50-€31 plays; €10.50-€65 opera. **Credit** AmEx, MC, V. **Map** p313 H6.
The Gaiety recently received a dramatic and much-needed facelift and the ornate foyer is now matched by the gleaming, restored façade. A new pedestri-

anised zone in front of the theatre adds an almost continental feel, but the auditorium itself is still pretty grotty. The Gaiety hosts all manner of entertainment, from the Spring Opera season, classic Irish plays and West End shows to concerts and variety acts. The unifying theme is populism, so don't expect anything too highbrow.

The Gate

1 Cavendish Row, Parnell Square, Southside (874 4045/874 6042). All cross-city buses. **Open** *Box office* 10am-7pm Mon-Sat. **Tickets** €19-€21.50; €15 previews. **Credit** AmEx, MC, V. **Map** p313 H3.
Dublin's most elegant theatre, the Gate Theatre is the legacy of Micheál MacLiammóir and Hilton Edwards, a flamboyant, talented homosexual couple whose blatant relationship openly mocked the homosexuality laws of the time (local wit christened them 'Sodom and Begorrah'). Housed in an opulent 18th-century building leased from the Rotunda Hospital, the Gate has an intimate stage and a democratic auditorium (no pillars, no balcony, no boxes) that is beloved of actors and audiences alike. It forged a reputation for daring productions early in its career – one of the first plays performed here was Oscar Wilde's *Salome*, banned in England at the time – and interval spats between critics and partisan fans provide plenty of off-stage entertainment.

Highly cosmopolitan since its foundation, the theatre has traditionally shown predominantly European and American dramas, and the Irish content is distinctly Anglo: Orson Welles and James Mason made their acting debuts here. A certain conservatism crept in in recent years but is being dissipated by an influx of works by new and established Irish playwrights. The Gate is synonymous with celebrities and regularly consolidates its evident box office success with Hollywood names such as Jason Patric and Frances McDormund, who have punters queuing for returns out into the street. A recent spat with the Arts Council over funding did the Gate no harm whatsoever, but may well have contributed to the demise of the Arts Council in its current form. Production values are solid, and the performances are generally reliable. Be sure to have a drink at the little bar; it's one of the most charming in the city.

Lambert Puppet Theatre
5 Clifton Lane, Monkstown, Dublin Bay (280 0974). Monkstown or Salthill DART/7, 7A, 8 bus. **Open** *Box office* 9.30am-5pm daily. *Shows* winter 3.30pm Sat; summer 3.30pm Sat, Sun. **Tickets** €7.50. **Credit** MC, V.
A year-round children's theatre that offers imaginative and enjoyable retellings of all the old fairy tales. *See also p171.*

Olympia
72 Dame Street, Southside (677 7744). All cross-city buses. **Open** *Box office* 10.30am-6.30pm Mon-Sat. **Tickets** €9.50-€32.50; 10% reduction for previews. **Credit** AmEx, MC, V. **Map** p75.
This old-style variety theatre, Dublin's first music hall, retains its physical characteristics (many of them authentically grimy) but has largely parted company with straight theatre. An occasional venue

Samuel Beckett. *See p33.*

for international stand-up comedy acts, its most reliable event is Midnight at the Olympia – late-night concerts that often feature big-name acts (*see p193*).

The Peacock
26 Abbey Street Lower, Northside (box office 878 7222). All cross-city buses. **Open** *Box office* 10.30am-7pm Mon-Sat. **Admission** €10-€15; €6.50 concessions Mon-Thur. **Credit** AmEx, MC, V. **Map** p313 H4.
The Peacock is the Abbey's contemporary, experimental second stage, and there is a great deal of kudos attached to having seen successful productions here before they hit the big-time. Set up to give new, young writers an opportunity to show their work, it is remarkably discerning and successful in its choice of performances. It is known for nurturing some of the city's best new talent (Frank McGuinness's *Observe the Sons of Ulster Marching Towards the Somme* started here in 1986).

Project Arts Centre
39 East Essex Street, Temple Bar, Southside (box office 1-850 260 027/administration 679 6622/ www.project.ie). All cross-city buses. **Open** *Box office* 10am-6pm Mon-Sat. **Tickets** €10-€19; phone for details of preview and concession prices. **Credit** MC, V. **Map** p75.
Though Project was established over 35 years ago – it began life as a visual arts project in the foyer of the Gate – the doors to the new building (built on the site of the old venue in East Essex Street, Temple Bar) opened in July 2000. Custom-designed by Shay Cleary Architects, the new building boasts three fully equipped, multi-functional performance and exhibition spaces. Home to theatre, dance, live art, video and film, contemporary and popular music, cultural debates and performance pieces, the Project is Dublin's premier venue for the new, the innovative, and the cutting edge. The main auditorium seats 180, the studio space 73. Both spaces are flexible, designed as modern, accommodating homes for all contemporary art forms.

Samuel Beckett Centre
Trinity College, Southside (608 2266). All cross-city buses. **Open** *Box office* 11am-6pm Mon-Fri. Week before a show starts 11am-6pm Mon-Fri; 10am-5pm Sat. **Tickets** €4-€19. **Credit** MC, V. **Map** p313 H5.
Located in the heart of Trinity College, the theatre at the Samuel Beckett Centre caters mainly for drama students, but also manages to attract many of the more interesting shows from outside the collegiate circuit, in both drama and dance.

Tivoli
135-138 Francis Street, Liberties, Southside (454 4472). Bus 50, 78A. **Open** *Box office* 10am-7pm Mon-Sat. **Tickets** €12.50-€19; 10% reductions for previews. **Credit** MC, V. **Map** p312 F5.
The gamut of live entertainment, from serious drama to musicals, is offered at this commercial theatre. Irish and international shows feature in equal measure but don't expect to see anything that is much of a gamble.

Arts & Entertainment

Theatre companies

For those interested in modern Irish theatre, locating a good production takes a degree of spade work. There isn't a consistent stream of new material being performed on Dublin's stages, since the younger, more innovative companies tend not to be attached to any particular venue and don't perform to regular schedules. However, most of the companies reviewed in this chapter make a great effort to keep themselves visible, and a regular flick through any listings magazine should unearth the necessary information. The theatres themselves will also be able to provide details of forthcoming productions.

Barabbas the Company

7 South Great George's Street, Dublin 2 (671 2013/ fax 670 4076/www.barabbas.ie).
Probably the most prolific and high-profile of the smaller companies – it participated in Ireland's Cultural and Events Programme for EXPO 2000 in Hanover – Barabbas is loved by both critics and children. The troupe began life as a simple clown act, though the company now undertakes bright, bubbly and colourful interpretations of new and adapted works, performed predominantly through physical theatre techniques. Most recently, in November 2001, Barabbas the Company hosted a mini-festival of its own work at the Project Arts Centre (*see p209*). Advance information on Barabbas's productions is available from its offices at the above address.

Staging a coup

Snapping at the heels of Beckett and Friel are a new breed of playwrights, whose plays are performed regularly at distinguished theatres at home and abroad. **Conor McPherson** (*This Lime Tree Bower, The Weir, Dublin Carol* and *The Port Authority*; *pictured*) and **Martin McDonagh** (*The Leenane Trilogy, The Lieutenant of Inishmore*) are the celebrities of this brat pack. Both are prodigious, possess a selection of coveted awards, and both have divided critical opinion.

The great McDonagh debate – as old as his career – shows no signs of fizzling out. By his own admission, McDonagh is intolerant of traditional theatrical forms, and consistently parodies established devices, conventions and conceits. His plots take traditional themes – land, loss and exile – and inject them with zany, surreal humour and brutal, anarchic violence. Detractors are irritated by his rebellious, knowing, post-modern style because it so clearly mocks the very genre it inhabits. Supporters, however, point out that the genre itself has become a cliché and therefore deserves to be satirised, and that the energy and humour McDonagh injects into a tired art form are well worth any loss of purity. Audiences sometimes miss the point of the debate entirely, simply finding the slapstick quality of his plays hilarious.

McPherson, though less controversial, also sparks off his share of antagonism. Again, purists quibble that his work isn't, strictly speaking, theatre. His most successful plays dispense with the conventional need for action on stage and take the form of the storyteller's monologue. His critics wonder snidely if he can actually work within the

traditional format of the play, and why he doesn't just write for the screen (he does that too. of course, rather successfully). The monologue form may not be physically theatrical, but it is very performable and has won McPherson enthusiastic support from audiences in Ireland and abroad.

Operating in the shadow of these two is **Mark O'Rowe**, whose award-winning play *Howie the Rookie* premiered at the Bush Theatre in London. It was here that McPherson's *This Lime Tree Bower* also found a home after being rejected by the Gate and the Abbey, an indication of the continued importance of the British theatre scene in nurturing Ireland's most talented. O'Rowe's most recent production, *Made in China*, confirmed him as a writer greatly interested in extremes of violence – indeed, his style is dubbed 'Tarantino-esque' with monotonous regularity. Like McDonagh and McPherson, O'Rowe rejects any attempt to force him into a theatrical tradition, insisting he is more influenced by cinema and just wants to write a good yarn. Other names to look out for include **Michael West**, who has garnered critical acclaim for his one-man play *Foley* about the Irish Protestant inheritance, and **Enda Walsh**, whose high-energy portrayal of Irish youth, *Disco Pigs*, was one of the most successful Irish plays of the 1990s.

Alongside this shooting gallery of tough guys, **Marina Carr** (*Bog of Cats*) appears as a throwback. She herself admits to being 'a generation behind everyone else', but insists this is deliberate. Family is central to her drama, which adheres to the traditional form, and the influence of JM Synge isn't

Bedrock

Halfpenny Court, 36-37 Ormond Quay Lower,
Dublin 1 (872 9300/fax 872 9478/bedrock@clubi.ie).
Bedrock performs raw, visceral interpretations of
modern British, European and American plays previously unseen in Ireland. It also works closely
with up-and-coming playwrights such as Alex
Johnson, Ken Harmon and Owen McCafferty, and
started the Fringe Theatre Festival (*see p206*
Festival fever) seven years ago.

Corn Exchange

43-44 Temple Bar, Dublin 2 (679 6444/
www.cornexchange.ie).
A talented, dedicated group whose performances are
mainly in a commedia dell'arte style. The company
was born in 1995 as part of the Fringe festival and
has appeared in every Fringe to date, although it
also tours nationally and internationally. The actors
perform a mixture of scripted work and pieces of
their own devising and work with guest directors,
although founder Annie Ryan takes a part in direct-
ing every production.

Fishamble Theatre Company

Shamrock Chambers, 1-2 Eustace Street, Temple
Bar, Dublin 2 (670 4018/fax 670 4019/
info@fishamble.com).
Fishamble has performed many times at the Dublin
Theatre Festival, as well as in Galway, Belfast,
London, Glasgow and Edinburgh. It produces sturdy
new plays by Irish writers with strong, contemporary
themes, which are buoyed up by enthusiastic acting,
lively direction and innovative design.

hard to spot. The work of the northern Irish
playwright **Marie Jones** is also less obviously
controversial, although its clever, high-quality
comedy overlays complex emotions. Her two-
man play *Stones in his Pockets,* a hilarious
but ultimately moving exploration of the effect
of a Hollywood film production on a small
rural community, has achieved international
popular success as well as critical acclaim.

It would seem, then, that new writing
remains the cornerstone of Irish theatre.
Despite increased experimentation from
Dublin companies like Barabbas (*see p210*)
and the Corn Exchange (*see above*), who
attempt to push back theatrical boundaries,
the reputation of Irish drama is more often
focused on the international (British and
American) success of Irish playwrights, with
local talent still crossing the water to make
its fortune on the London scene. There is
almost a sense of desperation noticeable in
the Irish media at the moment, as successful
new writers are hurriedly proclaimed as the
next big thing. Although Dublin's reputation
as a source and forum for theatrical talent
seems secure, it remains to be seen who
in the long run will take on the heavy mantle
of Beckett, Synge and Shaw.

Arts & Entertainment

Dance

One of the success stories of Celtic Tiger Dublin, dance is finally struggling out from under the shadow of theatre, long seen as the more credible art form. With no tradition of dance in this country (bar the hands-by-sides, heels-tapping variety), the passage from also-ran to player in the world of visual arts has been a difficult one. Increasingly, however, exciting works are being performed in mainstream venues such as the **Project Arts Centre** or the **Tivoli**, and international choreographers and performers are including Dublin on their tour maps. Highly conscious of the narrative tradition within Irish arts, local companies tend to incorporate poetry, drama, live music, literature, mythology and even sculpture into their performances, thereby attracting audiences who know little about contemporary dance, and increasing the entertainment value of shows.

And then, of course, there's *Riverdance* (www.riverdance.com), the unstoppable showbiz phenomenon that began life as a five-minute floorshow during the Eurovision Song Contest and went on to conquer the world. Along with its even more breathtakingly tacky relation *Lord of the Dance* (www.lordofthedance.com) *Riverdance* tours the globe almost constantly, and still regularly brings audiences to their feet in displays of spontaneous enthusiasm. If you actually want to see these sentimental corporate icons of Irish experience, check out their websites – fortunately you're far more likely to catch them in Japan and Germany than on any visit to Dublin.

Dance companies

It's also worth keeping an eye out for **Ballet Ireland**, **Rubato Ballet**, **CoisCéim Dance Theatre** and **Fabulous Beast Dance Theatre**. Although none have a venue of their own, they can be seen regularly at many of Dublin's theatres. For more information, contact the Association of Professional Dancers at the address below.

Dance Theatre of Ireland

Bloomfields Centre, Lower George's Street, Dún Laoghaire, Dublin Bay (280 3455/fax 280 3466/ info@dancetheatreireland.com).
Dance Theatre of Ireland, known for the arresting visual quality of its work, performs material devised by artistic directors Robert Connor and Loretta Yurick and international guest choreographers such as Janet Smith. Recently the dancers have added a multimedia dimension to their performances with interactive, digital technology and fantastic back-

drops. The company's state-of-the-art studio, Centre for Dance, opened in October 2000. It has sprung floors, disabled access, sky lighting and seating for up to 100, and offers classes to the public in contemporary, jazz, hip hop and salsa.

Irish Modern Dance Theatre

23 Upper Sherrard Street, Dublin 1 (874 9616/ fax 878 7784/www.irishmoderndancetheatre.com).
Irish Modern Dance Theatre, now in its tenth year, performs ambitious new work set to original music by young composers. Director John Scott collaborates frequently with other artists, including playwright Tom MacIntyre and photographer Chris Nash, and has established strong links with international dance companies, in order to break down the vacuum in which Irish dance has, until now, existed. The company tour nationally and internationally, and when in Dublin perform in a variety of venues, chosen according to the requirements of the particular show.

Traditional Irish dancing

Irish dancing is being gradually squeezed out of Dublin as traditional pubs give way to trendy cafés and bars and live music is replaced by DJs. However, you can still stumble across the odd impromptu session or one-off night, in fact even the regular nights seem largely improvised. For more information, contact the Tourist Board (602 4000) when you're in town. The two venues listed below are stalwarts of the genre.

Cultúrlann na hÉireann

32 Belgrave Square, Monkstown, Dublin Bay (280 0295). Bus 7, 8, 78. **Open** *Lessons* 8pm Fri. *Dancing* 9pm Fri. **Admission** €6.50. **No credit cards**.
The Cultúrlann na hÉireann hosts popular large ceilidhs or communal dances, just like in the good old dancehall days. They attract a mix of committed locals and curious tourists.

O'Shea's Merchant

12 Bridge Street Lower, Southside (679 3797). Bus 21, 21A. **Open** *Dancing* 9pm-12.30am daily. **Admission** free. **Map** p312 F5.
Trad music, songs and set-dancing seven nights a week at this nice pub (*see p194*).

Dance classes

The craze for line dancing that swept Dublin a few years ago has happily receded, to be replaced by an enthusiasm for salsa and belly dancing. The **Association of Professional Dancers** (Basement office, 1 Harrington Street, Dublin 8 (478 1130/fax 478 1137/info@prodance ireland.com) will provide details on request, but if you're in Dublin for an extended period, the following offer reliable classes.

Dance Theatre of Ireland

Bloomfields Centre, Lower George's Street,
Dún Laoghaire, Dublin Bay (280 3455/
info@dancetheatreireland.com). All cross-city buses.
Open 10am-6pm Mon-Fri. **Rates** €65 for 10 wks.
No credit cards.

Jackie Skelly's Studios

41-42 Clarendon Street, Southside (677 0040).
All cross-city buses. **Open** 6.30am-9.30pm Mon-Fri;
9am-6pm Sat; 10.30am-5pm Sun. **Rates** €43-€54.50
per month. **Credit** MC, V. **Map** p313 H5.

Comedy

Irish comedy springs from a tradition of storytelling, unlike British comedy, which derives
largely from the music hall tradition. It is
perhaps this difference that accounts for the
recent runaway success of Irish comics in the
UK. Tommy Tiernan, Dylan Moran, Ardal
O'Hanlon and Graham Norton are all household
names and faces, and now there is a new
generation set to make the breakthrough:
watch out for Jason Byrne, Dermot Carmody,
Kevin Gildea, Michael Mee, Des Bishop, David
O'Doherty and Tommy Nicholson.

The **Comedy Cellar**, upstairs at the
International Bar, was the cradle of Irish
comedy. Launched by three students, one of
whom was Ardal O'Hanlon, it is still running
and still holds a pivotal position on the scene.
Murphy's Laughter Lounge and the
Ha'penny Bridge Inn are also reliable in
terms of regularity and quality. In addition,
big-name comics can occasionally be found at
the **Olympia** (*see p209*) and **HQ**.

If you're inclined towards performing
yourself, try the Ha'penny Bridge Inn's
'Battle of the Axe' night; just don't expect
any favours from the crowd, who drink and
heckle in equal measure.

Venues

Ha'penny Bridge Inn

42 Wellington Quay, Temple Bar, Southside
(677 0616). All cross-city buses. **Open** *Comedy*
shows 9.30pm Tue, Thur. **Admission** €3-€4.50.
No credit cards. Map p75.

A small pub on the quays, the Ha'penny Bridge Inn
is now a pretty established venue on Dublin's comedy circuit. Tuesday nights offer Battle of the Axe,
a crazy, terrible, anything-goes talent night, featuring everything from stand-ups to musicians, spoken-
word rants and fire-eaters. The winner – chosen by
the audience – gets a plastic duck. Get there by
9.15pm if you want to take a spot. On Thursdays,
it's Ha'penny Laugh, basically a glorified amateur
night where the comics improvise on suggestions

from the audience. In addition to the improv, there's
one stand-up slot at Ha'penny Laugh. In addition, a
purely stand-up gig takes place once every three
months or so. The performers here are in good company: the likes of Jason Byrne and Perrier Award-
winner Tommy Tiernan have taken the stage here.

HQ

57 Middle Abbey Street, Northside (889 9499/
www.imhf.com/tickets also from TicketMaster).
Open *Box office* 10am-4pm Mon-Sat. **Tickets**
€11-€19. **Credit** *Ticketmaster* AmEx, DC, MC. V.
Map p313 II4.

As well as housing the Hot Press Hall of Fame (*see*
p87) and doubling as a club, this purpose-built performance space hosts regular comedy nights. These
usually take the form of an international headline
act supported by local talent. Seating, table service
and generally good views make up for the room's
distinct lack of character. *See also p193.*

International Bar

23 Wicklow Street, Southside (677 9250). All cross-
city buses. **Open** *Comedy shows* 9pm Mon, Wed,
Thur. **Admission** €3-€6.50. **No credit cards.**
Map p313 H5.

There are now three regular comedy nights a week
at this central bar. Monday nights' the Comedy
Improv, is where all visiting comics want to play.
It's basically a live-action version of TV's *Whose*
Line Is It Anyway?, with four or five local comics
taking suggestions from the audience for spoofs
and skits, While quality obviously depends on the
talent available on the night, more often than not
it's hilarious. Wednesday's Comedy Cellar is where
it all began. Known for good amateurs and pros
wanting to try out new material and stay in shape
by exposing themselves to a tough crowd, it also
attracts plenty of unexpected guests, lured by the
charm of auld lang syne. Ardal O'Hanlon, Dylan
Moran, Ed Byrne and Ross Nobel have all turned
up here in recent times. Thursday's Murphy's
International Comedy Club offers a rather more
generic – but just as funny – selection of stand ups,
most of them Irish.

Murphy's Laughter Lounge

Eden Quay, Northside (1 800 266 339). All cross-city
buses. **Open** *Box office* 10am-6pm Mon-Wed; 12.30-
9.30pm Thur-Sat. *Shows* 9.30pm Thur-Sat.
Admission €12.50; €6.50 concessions Thur.
Credit MC, V. **Map** p313 H4.

Opened in December 1997, Murphy's Laughter
Lounge was the first circuit club in Dublin. The acts
are split 50-50 between homegrown talent and international guests, mainly from Britain, and sessions
usually feature at least one big name. The place is
more intimate than its capacity of 400 would indicate, and the atmosphere is usually jovial and
friendly. However, many performers complain that
the comedy is simply a background to a night of
heavy boozing and dub their slots 'survival gigs'.
Tickets are also available from TicketMaster and
the Dublin Tourism Centre on Suffolk Street.

Arts & Entertainment

Sport & Fitness

Dublin's sporting life.

Despite its boozy reputation, Dublin is a keen sporting city with some decent facilities. The most obvious manifestation of sporting enthusiasm is the number of soccer tops to be seen on the streets: Glasgow Celtic's green and white hoops are perhaps most prevalent, but English Premiership teams also figure prominently, particularly Manchester United, Liverpool and Arsenal. As the indigenous sports of Gaelic football and hurling become increasingly fashionable, so county tops are also starting to make an appearance: Dublin colours are sky blue and navy while others can be recognised by their Irish county names printed on the back.

The hunger for international sporting success ensures public acclaim for victorious heroes, but the reality of the country's sporting heritage means the Irish have also developed an almost fetishistic appreciation for gallant losers. Horse racing may be the sport in which the country has had the greatest impact on the world stage, but it is international rugby and soccer matches and GAA rivalries that bring colour and excitement to the streets. Boxing, golf and cycling also have substantial followings in the city, while greyhound racing has been upgraded from a shady nocturnal activity to a corporate and family favourite. This transformation of a day at the dogs into a credible popular pastime reflects continuing improvements in Dublin's sporting facilities as a whole. Whether you prefer the sedentary pleasures of being a spectator or a more active approach, you'll find something here to suit your tastes.

SPORT FOR THE DISABLED

Many venues listed below have facilities for people with disabilities, but it is always wise to call ahead to confirm a venue's suitability. Ireland will be hosting the **Special Olympics** in 2003. For details, phone 882 3972 or check the website (www.2003specialolympics.com).

Spectator sports

Athletics

Athletic events are usually held at the **National Athletics Stadium** (Morton Stadium, Santry) in the north of the city. For details contact **Bord Luthchleas na hEireann** (830 8925/www.athleticsireland.ie), the governing body for athletics in Ireland.

Basketball

The male and female basketball Super Leagues are relatively new, and in comparison to the American NBA they possess all the glamour of a pair of sweaty socks. Still it's early days and the game is catching on. Sponsorship since 2000 from the Electricity Supply Board has vitalised the national cup competition and the Irish team's first-time qualification for the 2001 European Championships can only further raise the game's profile. Important games are played at the **National Basketball Stadium** in Tallaght. Contact the **Irish Basketball Association** for details of local teams (459 0211/www.IBA.ie).

National Basketball Stadium

Tymon Park, Tallaght, Southern suburbs (459 0211). Bus 54A, 56A, 65, 77, 77A. **Open** 9am-5.30pm Mon-Sat; later during sporting events. **Tickets** €12.70-€25.40. **No credit cards**.

Boxing

Boxing is Ireland's most successful Olympic sport, although the country has had a shortage of credible professional contenders recently. The **National Stadium** has been staging fights for over 60 years and is the world's only purpose-built boxing stadium. If you fancy watching men legally beat the living daylights out of each other, then this is the place to go.

National Stadium

145 South Circular Road, Kilmainham, Southside (453 3371). Bus 9, 16, 19, 122. **Open** *Office* 10am-5pm Mon-Fri. *Boxing events* usually 8-10.30pm Fri. **Tickets** €12.70-€25.40. **No credit cards**.

Cricket

Cricket remains a minority sport in Ireland, although it is gradually shaking off its elitist colonial image. Visiting teams provide the annual highlights: there is still much talk about the national team's most famous victory against a touring West Indies side in 1969. The visitors made the most of the legendary Irish hospitality laid on by their shrewd hosts, but suffered for it on the cricket pitch the next day. According to the *Daily Telegraph*, the Irish side 'dismissed the visitors for 25 with the assistance of a wet wicket and an even wetter hospitality tent'.

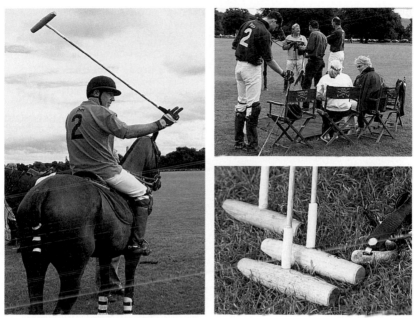

Chukkas away. The **All-Ireland Polo Club** gets into the swing of things in Phoenix Park.

There are international pitches in Clontarf, Rathmines and Malahide, but if you just want to watch an over or two on a summer afternoon, wander up to the south-east end of Phoenix Park (*see p93*) or hang out at the Pavilion Bar on Trinity College campus (*see p61*). For further information contact the **Irish Cricket Union** (www.cricketeurope.org/ireland)

Cycling

Cycling enjoyed a surge of popularity in the 1980s with the international successes of Sean Kelly and Stephen Roche, followed by the visit of the Tour De France in 1998. Interest has abated somewhat since, although crowds still turn out for the annual eight-day international **FDB Milk Race** in the last two weeks of May, which starts and finishes in Dublin. Contact the **Federation of Irish Cyclists** (855 1522/ www.icf.ie) for details. For more information on cycling in Dublin, *see chapter* **Getting Around**.

Equestrian

The premier event in the Irish showjumping calendar is the **Kerrygold Horse Show** (*see p165*). Held during August at the Royal Dublin Society (RDS) grounds in Ballsbridge, this event

is as much about high fashion as high fences. Horse-racing enthusiasts are well provided for too, with the famous **Leopardstown**, **Curragh** and **Punchestown** racecourses all within easy reach of the capital. *See p218* **Horses for courses**.

During the summer, spectators are welcome to attend **All-Ireland Polo Club** matches, which are held at weekends in Phoenix Park. It's a thoroughly pleasant way to spend a sunny afternoon.

All-Ireland Polo Club

near Aras an Uachtarain, Phoenix Park, Northside (677 6248/http://allirelandpoloclub.com). Bus 10, 25, 26, 51, 66, 67, 68, 69. **Matches** *May-Sept* 3pm Sat, Sun. **Admission** free.

Gaelic football & hurling

Run by the amateur **Gaelic Athletic Association**, Gaelic football and hurling are Ireland's national sports. Inter-county and major club matches are played at **Croke Park**, the home of the GAA. The All-Ireland hurling final takes place on the first Sunday in September, followed by the football final two weeks later. The Dublin side also plays at **Parnell Park** (Clantarkey Road, Donnycarney, Northern suburbs). *See p220* **Going Gaelic**.

Gaelic Athletic Association

Croke Park, Jones Road, Drumcondra, Northern suburbs (836 3222/www.gaa.ie). Bus 3, 11, 11A, 16, 51A. **Open** *office* 10am-5pm Mon-Fri. **Tickets** €3.80; €1.90-€2.50 concessions. **No credit cards.** **Map** p309.

Golf

The decision to award the 2006 Ryder Club to the exclusive **K Club** in Straffan, Co. Kildare (601 7300/www.kclub.ie) has provoked a flurry of excitement among the golfing community. The K Club also hosts the **Smurfit European Open** in July, which has added to Ireland's slightly inflated reputation as the 'golf mecca' of Europe. The other professional highlight in the Irish golfing calendar is the prestigious **Murphy's Irish Open** (662 2433), which takes place between the US Open and the British Open, at different courses around the country. It will take place in Cork in 2002.

Greyhound racing

Re-branded for the 21st century, greyhound racing promises a great night out that is cheaper and more accessible than horse racing. The two big tracks are at **Harold's Cross** and **Shelbourne Park**. Further information can be obtained from the **Bord na gCon** (Greyhound Board) at Shelbourne Park.

Bord na gCon

Shelbourne Park, Lotts Road, Ringsend, Southside (668 3502). Bus 3, 7, 7A, 8, 45, 84. **Open** *Racing* 7-10.30pm Wed, Thur, Sat. **Tickets** €6.40; €2.50 concessions. **No credit cards**. **Map** p314 M6.

Harold's Cross Racetrack

151 Harold's Cross Road, Harold's Cross, Southern suburbs (497 1081). Bus 16, 16A. **Open** *Racing* from 8pm Mon, Tue, Fri. **Tickets** €6.40; €2.50 concessions. **No credit cards**.

Rugby union

The restructuring of the professional game has meant the **All-Ireland Club League** is increasingly subservient to the demands of the provincial teams (Leinster, Ulster, Munster and Connaught). As well as competing against each other in the annual **Inter-Provincial Championship**, these four teams take part in the prestigious **European Shield** and the new **Celtic League** (against teams from Scotland and Wales). Local clubs complain that their players miss important matches on account of provincial commitments, and there are worries about the effect on the game at grassroots level. Nevertheless fans undoubtedly appreciate the international element of the big competitions. Lansdowne Road, where the national team plays, is the home of Irish rugby. Contact the **Irish Rugby Football Union** (668 4601/

Going to the dogs is no bad thing at **Shelbourne Park**.

Rugby fans at **Lansdowne Road Stadium**.

www.irfu.ie) for details of upcoming games. For details of the Six Nations tournament, *see p160*. The city's most successful clubs are clustered mainly in the affluent southern suburbs of the city. Division one sides include **Blackrock College RFC** (Stradbrook Road, Blackrock, Dublin Bay; 280 0151) and **Lansdowne RFC** (Lansdowne Road, Ballsbridge, Southern suburbs; 668 9300).

Lansdowne Road Stadium

4 Lansdowne Road, Ballsbridge, Southern suburbs (IRFU 668 4601). Lansdowne Road DART. **Open** 9am-5pm Mon-Fri. **Tickets** €3.80-€63.50. **Credit** AmEx, DC, MC, V. **Map** p311 M7.

Snooker

The top professional tournament is the annual **Irish Masters**, which recently moved to the Citywest Hotel in Tallaght. It was sponsored by a tobacco company until 2001, but owing to the Irish ban on tobacco sponsorship, the event is bizarrely now funded by the government's Office of Tobacco Control. Ken Doherty remains Ireland's top player. Contact the **Republic of Ireland Billiards & Snooker Association** (450 9850/www.oibsa.net) for more information.

Soccer

Ireland plays international home matches at **Lansdowne Road** (*see above*), and the national team has a huge following. When Ireland competes in the World Cup in Japan/Korea in 2002, expect the whole country temporarily to shut down as it focuses its attention and aspirations on the competition.

The **National League** (676 5120) is of a lower standard than elsewhere in Europe, but is a good way for visiting soccer addicts to get their fix. The top Dublin teams include **Shelbourne FC**, **Bohemians FC** (currently the only two professional teams in the league) and **Shamrock Rovers**. Local derbies between the northside Bohemians (known as the 'Gypsies') and the southside Rovers (known as the 'Hoops') are usually the most atmospheric and closely fought contests in town. The league traditionally runs from September to May, but there is much talk of changing to summer soccer in 2003. For further information contact the **Football Association of Ireland** (FAI; 676 6864/www.fai.ei).

Bohemians FC

Dalymount Park, Phibsborough, Northern suburbs (868 0923/www.bohemians.ie). Bus 10, 19, 19A, 124. **Tickets** €6.40-€12.70. **No credit cards.**

Shamrock Rovers

Information: 43 Parkway Business Centre, Ballymount, Dublin 24 (460 4105/www.shamrock rovers.ie). **Tickets** phone for details. **Credit** phone for details.
The Rovers are due to move into their new purpose-built stadium in Tallaght during 2002.

Shelbourne FC

Tolka Park, Richmond Road, Drumcondra, Northern suburbs (837 5536) Bus 3, 11, 11A, 13, 16, 16A, 41. **Tickets** €5.10-€13.60. **No credit cards.**

Active sports & fitness

Angling

There are ample opportunities for anglers who wish to get their tackle out around Dublin: inland there's the Grand Canal, the Royal Canal, the Dodder, the Liffey and Leixlip Reservoir, or try marine fishing in the Irish Sea. For information on permits and regulations contact the Central Fisheries Board on 837 9209 or try **Rory's Fishing Shop** (17A Temple Bar; 677 2351), which offers advice as well as equipment.

Athletics & jogging

Dublin's parks provide space for easygoing joggers and more serious athletes; some even have workout stations. For cross-country running, the beaches and coastal paths of Dublin Bay and the hill paths in the Wicklow Mountains offer picturesque routes. The **National Athletics Stadium** (*see p214*) has indoor facilities and an outdoor all-weather championship track, and is open to the public. For the **Dublin City Marathon** (*see p166*) and **Women's Mini-Marathon** (*see p165*).

Horses for courses

Horseracing has been a part of the Irish psyche since ancient times, when mythical heroes Fionn Mac Cumhaill and the Fianna are said to have raced each other on horseback over the Curragh, a swathe of fertile grassland in the heart of County Kildare. In 1673, Sir William Temple, writing to his Lord Lieutenant, remarked that 'horses in Ireland are a drug', and astutely identified the quality of the soil, the testing terrain and the luscious grass as factors in the country's particular suitability for breeding.

Boasting three famous racetracks and dozens of stud farms, County Kildare remains at the heart of Irish horse racing and breeding. The government-owned **Irish National Stud** in Tully is spread over 1,000 acres of prime Kildare countryside, and has been turning out top Irish stallions since 1900. Now open to visitors, the grounds include picturesque Japanese Gardens and the Irish Horse Museum, where the skeleton of all-conquering steeplechaser Arkle has pride of place. Male visitors to Tully seem particularly keen on purchasing T-shirts and sweatshirts with 'Irish National Stud' emblazoned across the front. Nearby is the **Curragh Racecourse**, the illustrious home of Irish flat-racing and host of five classic races during the season – the 1,000 Guineas, the 2,000 Guineas, the Oaks, the St Leger and the Irish Derby.

Flat-racing may attract the bigger prize money, but in Ireland, steeplechasing is considered the better sport and has produced some celebrated Irish-bred winners, including Prince Regent, Hattons Grace, Easter Hero, Cottage Rake, Dawn Run, Night Nurse, Red Rum and Arkle. The sport was invented in Cork in 1752 when two foxhunters – Mr Blake and Mr Callaghan – challenged each other to an open country race between Buttevant and Doneraile, with only the steeple of Doneraile church to guide them. The modern equivalent of Blake and Callaghan's seminal race, the **Irish Grand National**, has taken place annually at **Fairyhouse** in County Meath since 1870. Other important events on the steeplechasing calendar are the four-day **Irish National Hunt Festival** at **Punchestown Racecourse** in spring, and the hugely popular three-day **Leopardstown Festival** starting on 26 December at **Leopardstown Racecourse** in County Dublin (*pictured*).

A mammoth crowd turned up for the opening of Leopardstown in 1888: transport and other facilities were unable to cope, and the riot that almost ensued led one newspaper to write the course's epitaph. Fortunately reports of Leopardstown's demise proved premature: the course now stages flat- and hunt-racing throughout the year and attracts vast numbers of hopeful punters from the city.

The late Irish gambler Terry Rogers used to say that all men are equal over and under the turf. The democracy of Irish racing is one of its greatest assets and makes the racetrack a perfect place for people-watching. The champagne-swilling elite mingle with the Guinness-quaffing hordes in the bars, hardened gamblers rub shoulders with hopeful day-trippers in the betting rings, and legendary gambler owners like JP McManus and Barney Curley are seen as modern-day Robin Hoods by admiring punters. For a taste of Dublin society at play, a day at the races is hard to beat.

Bowling

Leisureplex

Malahide Road, Coolock, Northern suburbs (848 5722). Bus 42, 43. **Open** 24hrs daily. **Rates** €22.90-€33 per hour; €4-€4.80; €3.75-€4.80 concessions. **Credit** MC, V.
For those inevitable rainy days, the Leisureplex centres offer snooker, pool and video games in addition to 18-lane bowling arenas. The Tallaght and Coolock branches also have Quasar games and there are dodgems at Blanchardstown.
Branches: Blanchardstown Shopping Centre, Blanchardstown, Northern suburbs (822 3030); Village Green Centre, Tallaght, Southern suburbs (459 9411).

Diving

Great Outdoors Diving School

3 Clarendon Market, Southside (672 7160). All cross-city buses. **Open** 9.30am-5.30pm Mon-Wed, Fri, Sat; 9.30am-8pm Thur. **Rates** phone for details. **Credit** AmEx, DC, MC, V. **Map** p313 G5.
Based in a watersports shop, this outfit is PADI affiliated and offers beginners' and advanced courses and weekend excursions to the West Coast. In the summer there are also one-day dive trips for certificated divers, leaving from Dún Laoghaire harbour. Another branch of Great Outdoors on Chatham Street sells climbing gear, camping and skiing equipment (*see p160*).

The following racecourses are all easily accessible from Dublin city and have extensive facilities including restaurants, bars and children's play areas.

Bus Éireann (836 6111) and **Iarnród Éireann** (Irish Rail, 836 6222) both provide race-day transport to the Curragh, Fairyhouse and Punchestown.

Curragh Racecourse

Curragh, Co Kildare (045 441 205/ www.curragh.ie). **Open** *Race times usually 2.15pm or 2.30pm Sat, Sun; phone for details.* **Tickets** €13-€45. **Credit** AmEx, DC, MC, V.

Fairyhouse Racecourse

Ratoath, Co Meath (825 6167/www.fairy houseracecourse.ie). **Open** *Race days/times phone to check.* **Tickets** €10-€25.40; €1.30-€12.70 concessions. **No credit cards.**

Leopardstown Racecourse

Foxrock, Co Dublin (289 3607/www.leopards town.com). Bus 46A/Blackrock DART, then 114 bus. **Open** *Race days/times phone to check.* **Tickets** from €10; free under-14s. **Credit** AmEx, DC, MC, V.
For race-day transport to Leopardstown, contact **Dublin Bus** (872 0000).

National Stud

Tully, near Kildare, Co Kildare (045 521 617). **Open** *Feb-Nov 9.30am-6pm daily. Closed Dec, Jan.* **Admission** €7.60; €5.70 concessions. **Credit** MC, V

Punchestown Racecourse

Co Kildare (045 897 704/ www.punchestown.com). **Open** *Race days/times phone to check.* **Tickets** €10-€12.70; €5-€6.40 concessions. **Credit** AmEx, DC, MC, V.

Golf

There are over 60 courses in County Dublin, including some of the finest links in the world. Getting to play where and when you want, however, can sometimes be difficult, and it is advisable to always book your tee time well in advance. Most clubs accept visitors, but green fees vary greatly, from about €14 to €15 at the Dublin Corporation courses to €165 at the prestigious K Club.

Contact **Dublin Corporation** (862 0464/ www.dublincorp.ie) for details of its facilities and prices (including pitch-and-putt). A complete list of private courses can be obtained from the **Golfing Union of Ireland** (Glencar House, 81 Eglinton Road, Donnybrook, Dublin 4 (269 4111/www.gui.ie). The **Dublin Tourism Centre** on Suffolk Street (www.visitdublin.com) produces a leaflet, *Golfing Around Dublin*, with details of selected courses in the Dublin region.

Gyms & fitness centres

Many clubs are for members only and require a full year's membership, although some also offer health and fitness classes that are open to the public on a one-off basis. The more upmarket hotels may have their own gyms on site, or they may have arrangements with local

Going Gaelic

A mystery to the uninitiated, Gaelic football and hurling are Ireland's fast and furious national sports. Both are tough, skilful and have a huge national following. **Gaelic football** is perhaps best described as a cross between rugby and soccer, although its closest sporting relation is Australian Rules Football. (Notoriously physical compromise games between Ireland and Australia are played every two years.) **Hurling** resembles hockey or shinty and is one of the world's fastest field sports. The ball, known as the *slíothar*, is hit or carried along by the player's hurley stick; the clash of the ash and the aggressive momentum of the game make it incredibly exciting to watch.

In both disciplines 15 players a side play for 70 minutes on a pitch with rugby goalposts and soccer nets. Getting the football and *slíothar* over the crossbar gains a team one point, while a goal (getting the ball/*slíothar* in the net) is worth three points. A final score of 1-9 indicates that a team scored one goal and nine points (that is, a total of 12 points).

Fragments of the ancient Brehon Laws show that hurling was regulated in the country as early as the eighth century. It was proscribed by the English crown in the 12th century, but as is so often the case, the illicit game continued to thrive. It wasn't until 1884, however, that Michael Cusack and a group of fellow Irish nationalists formed the Gaelic Athletic Association.

Always intended to be more than just a sporting body, the GAA also supports activities that it regards as enriching Gaelic culture, including Irish language, music and dance. Resulting GAA policies have occasionally proved controversial, most notably the rule banning 'foreign sports', such as rugby and soccer, from being played in GAA grounds.

There are Gaelic football and hurling clubs in every town and village in Ireland, with the best club players selected for inter-county games. Each county competes in the league in winter and in Provincial Championships in summer; the latter are run on a knockout basis, although a rule introduced in 2000 allows losing teams a second chance to progress to the next round. Provincial champions and back-door qualifiers play for a place in the All-Ireland semi-finals.

The semi-finals and finals of the **Sam Maguire Cup** (football) and the **Liam McCarthy Cup** (hurling) are hugely colourful affairs played in Croke Park every September. While the games are strictly amateur, sponsorship from Guinness and the Bank of Ireland and some humorous advertising campaigns have improved the games' appeal considerably.

Unless you have roots in another county, supporting Dublin is a fast track to the natives' hearts. The true Dubs, sporting sky blue jerseys, with a dark blue collar and a

---

gyms or fitness centres in the city where guests can use the facilities. Otherwise your best chance of pumping some iron is to make use of the public facilities at one of the universities or at the new **Markievicz Leisure Centre** (*see p222*).

Crunch Fitness

UCD Campus, Belfield, Southern suburbs (260 3155). Bus 2, 3, 10, 11, 11B, 17, 39B, 46. **Open** 7am-10pm Mon-Fri; 10am-5.30pm Sat, Sun. **Rates** €12 per visit. **Credit** MC, V.
The UCD health centre, Crunch Fitness, has a fully equipped gym offering the usual range of cardiovascular machines and free weights. It also offers regular aerobics classes, and you don't have to be a member to make use of the facilities.

Sports Complex

Dublin City University, Ballymun Road, Glasnevin, Northern suburbs (700 5810). Bus 11, 13, 19, 103. **Open** 8am-10.30pm Mon-Fri; 9am-6pm Sat, Sun. **Rates** €3.20-€5 per visit. **No credit cards.**

As well as a full gym and fitness classes, the complex has squash, handball and racquetball courts, and a climbing wall. Membership also available.

Iveagh Fitness

Bride Road, Southside (454 6555). All cross-city buses. **Open** 6.30am-10pm Mon-Fri; 8am-9pm Sat, Sun. **Rates** €40.60-€53.30 per month. **Credit** MC, V. **Map** p312 F5.
Monthly membership allows unlimited access to a gym, swimming pool, fitness classes and a jacuzzi and steam room. No daily membership.

Luce Sports Centre

Trinity College, Southside (608 1812). All cross-city buses. **Open** *Summer* 8am-9pm Mon-Fri; 9am-2.30pm Sat. Closed winter. **Rates** €3.54 per visit. **Credit** AmEx, MC, V. **Map** p313 H5.
During the summer holidays the public can use the gym and weights room at Trinity College. There are also courts for badminton, squash, volleyball and five-a-side football. Monthly membership is available for long-term visitors.

managed by Kevin Heffernan, who fought legendary All-Ireland finals against Kerry. Dublin's Gaelic football fans have always viewed their team as invincible, and a reminder of the glory days will ensure you're welcomed into the fold.

Unfortunately results since 1980 have not been so spectacular, and Dublin usually struggles to beat Kildare and Meath (runners-up in 2001) to win the Leinster qualifying round. Overall, Kerry remains kingpin in football, although a host of Munster, Ulster and Connaught sides are also capable of winning the Sam Maguire Cup.

As for hurling, Dublin has never been as good as Cork, Tipperary (2001 champions) or Kilkenny, which may explain why many city dwellers dismiss the sport as 'sticktighting'. It may be the second fastest field sport in the world, but detractors regard it as a game for 'culchies' (country people). Certainly, it is the more rural counties that excel at hurling: great Munster teams like Cork, Waterford, Limerick and Clare are steeped in the game; supporters bring their own colours (blue and yellow for Tipperary, *pictured*) and loyalties to the big match at Croke Park in September.

three-castle crest will be found on Hill 16, their own famous terrace at Croke Park, now threatened to be turned into an all seater affair. If you find yourself among the local supporters, ask them about 'Heffo's Army', triumphant football teams of the 1970s,

Don't miss an opportunity to watch a Gaelic football or hurling match while you're in Ireland. You may not have a clue what's happening on the pitch, but the skill of the players and the sheer exuberance of the crowd will ensure a thrilling afternoon.

Horse riding

There are numerous riding schools situated in the Dublin suburbs or just outside the capital, and plenty of green spaces to enjoy on horseback. Kids may be particularly suited to the programme on offer at the **Oldtown Riding Stables** (*see p170*), but there are other options for riders of all abilities. Most schools offer a combination of lessons, trekking and cross-country rides. Hard hats and other equipment is usually provided.

Ashtown Riding Stables

Ashtown Navan Road, Ashtown, Northern suburbs (838 3807). Bus 37, 38, 38A, 39, 70. **Open** 9.30am-dusk daily. **Rates** €19; €15 concessions. **No credit cards.**
Readily accessible from the city centre, Ashtown Riding Stables offers hour-long rides through the attractive landscape of Phoenix Park, plus lessons and refresher courses for all abilities.

Brennanstown Riding School

Kilmacanogue, Holybrook, Bray, Co Wicklow (286 3778). Bray DART. **Open** Tue-Sat; times vary, phone for details. **Rates** €25.40 per hr. **No credit cards.**
Brennanstown offers trekking, hacking and cross-country rides in the lovely surroundings of teh Wicklow Hills. There are lessons for all abilities from absolute beginner to advanced.

Karting

Kart City

Old Airport Road, Cloghran, Northern suburbs (842 6322). Bus 33, 41, 41B, 41C, 230, 746. **Open** 11am-late daily. **Rates** *Adult track* €19 for 15min. *Junior track* €15.25 for 15min. **Credit** DC, MC, V.
Three tracks are available for four-wheel jeeps, kiddie karts, and adult kart and banger racing (supply your own banger, unfortunately). Feed your need for speed, and then celebrate on the winner's podium.

Arts & Entertainment

Snooker & pool

Snooker and pool are played throughout the city in a number of clubs, halls and leisure centres. Pubs with pool tables are increasingly hard to find as bar-owners cram in more and more drinkers. Many snooker clubs are for members only or frequently heavily booked, so always call ahead to check availability. Contact the **Republic of Ireland Billiards & Snooker Association** (450 9850/www.oibsa. net) for a full list of snooker and pool halls.

Jason's

56 Ranelagh Road, Ranelagh, Southern suburbs (497 5983). Bus 11, 11A. **Open** 24hrs daily. **Rates** £4.80 before 6pm; £6.40 after 6pm. **No credit cards.**
Jason's is the most famous snooker hall in Dublin, home-from-home since childhood to the 1997 world champion Ken Doherty.

Ned Kelly's

43 O'Connell Street, Northside (873 1016). All cross-city buses. **Open** 10am-10.30pm daily. **Rates** £5.50 per hr. **No credit cards. Map** p313 H4.
A handy snooker/pool hall close to the city centre, where it is nearly always possible to get a table.

Swimming

If your hotel doesn't have a swimming pool, then **Dublin Corporation** pools are often the best bet for public swimming. Most are fairly basic 25-metre, five-lane affairs, but the new **Markievicz Leisure Centre** is modern and well-equipped. Wearing a swimming hat is compulsory, but these are usually on sale at the ticket offices. Contact Dublin Corporation **Sports Section** (672 3362/www.dublincorp.ie) for information on your nearest pool. For details of seaside bathing spots, *see chapter* **Dublin Bay & the Coast**.

Markievicz Leisure Centre

Townsend Street, Southside (672 9121). Tara Street DART/all cross-city buses. **Open** 7am-10pm Mon-Fri; 9am-6pm Sat; 10am-4pm Sun. **Rates** *Swimming* €4.50-€5; €2.50 concessions; €7.60 family. *Gym* €5-€5.70. **No credit cards. Map** p313 J4.
Six-lane pool, plus a fully equipped gym and an aerobics studio.

Tennis & squash

Most tennis and squash clubs in Dublin are privately owned, and you need either to be a member or in the company of one to play. However, courts attached to hotels and less busy leisure centres are often open to the public. **Tennis Ireland** (668 1841/www.tennisireland. ie) and **Irish Squash** (450 1564) can provide information on where you might get a game.

Some Dublin parks also have public courts, which are generally open from 9.30am to 8pm (earlier in winter) and can be rented by the hour. These include **Albert College Park** (Glasnevin, Northern suburbs; 837 3891), **Bushy Park** (Rathdown Avenue, Terenure, Southern suburbs; 490 0320); **Eamonn Ceannt Park** (Crumlin, Southern suburbs; 454 0799); **Herbert Park** (Ballsbridge, Southern suburbs; 668 4364) and **St Anne's Park** (Raheny, Northern suburbs; 833 1859).

Watersports

Yacht and dinghy sailing are favourite pastimes along the Dublin coastline, and there are also opportunites for windsurfing, water-skiing and kayaking. Visitors with certification are welcome at many water-skiing clubs in Ireland, but sailing clubs tend to be strictly for members only. Contact the **Irish Sailing Association** (280 0239/www.sailing.ie) and **Irish Water Ski Federation** (285 5205) for further information. Sailing and windsurfing schools provide lessons throughout the summer. Lifejackets, wetsuits and other equipment can usually be hired on site.

Fingal Sailing School

Upper Strand Road, Malahide, Dublin Bay (845 1979). Malahide DART/rail/42 bus. **Open** *Apr-Oct* 9am-9pm daily. **Rates** *Dinghy/windsurf hire* €10.20-€25.40. *Lessons* €165 for 1wk. **Credit** MC, V.
Tuition is available in dinghy sailing, windsurfing, rowing, canoeing and power-boating. Boats and boards are also available for hire.

Irish National Sailing School

Marine Activity Centre, West Pier, Dún Laoghaire, Dublin Bay (284 4195/www.inss.ie). Dún Laoghaire DART/46A bus. **Open** *Mar-Nov* phone for details. **Rates** phone for details. **Credit** AmEx, DC, MC, V.
Weekend, daytime and evening sailing courses for all ages and abilities.

Surfdock

Grand Canal Dockyard, South Docks Road, Ringsend, Southside (668 3945). Grand Canal Dock DART/3 bus. **Open** *Summer* 10am-dusk daily. *Winter* 10am-dusk Sun. **Rates** phone for details. **Credit** MC, V. **Map** p314 M5.
Windsurfing, sea-kayaking and sailing lessons, plus equipment for hire for about €15 per hour.

Wind & Wave

16A The Crescent, Monkstown, Dublin Bay (284 4177/www.windandwave.ie). Salthill DART/7A, 45A, 46A, 59, 75 bus. **Open** *Windsurfing school* May-Sept 10am-6pm Mon-Sat. **Rates** €113 for 3 sessions. **Credit** AmEx, DC, MC, V.
This very well-stocked, popular watersports shop south of the city offers lessons for all abilities in windsurfing and canoeing.

Trips Out of Town

Getting Started

Done Dublin? There's plenty more to explore.

While there's much to see and do in Dublin, if you want a fully-rounded Irish experience, you'll have to travel beyond the city. Ireland is a small country, yet within its borders contains innumerable treasures: stunning scenery, beautiful beaches, prehistoric sites, grand houses and castles, lively towns and picturesque villages; what's more, the overall atmosphere, humour and pace of life can differ dramatically from county to county.

Whether you decide on a day-long sojourn in the Wicklow Mountains, a weekend in the medieval city of Kilkenny or a week driving around Kerry and West Cork, you'll find plenty to occupy yourself. And, wherever you choose to go, you'll find a warm welcome, hospitality to die for, and some unique landscapes. The Irish earned their reputations as hosts the hard way, and you can reap the benefits.

TRAVELLING AROUND

There are many ways to see Ireland, but if you intend to travel any distance from the urban centres, it's best to have your own transport. **Bus Éireann** and **Iarnród Éireann** (rail; for both, see p279) each have a relatively comprehensive network and provide a reliable, if often overcrowded service, but connections between rural stations are sometimes lacking. Coaches leave from the central bus station, **Busárus** on Store Street (see p279); south- and westbound trains leave from **Heuston Station** near Phoenix Park, while northbound trains depart from **Connolly Station** on Amiens Street. The important exception is the service to Rosslare in County Wexford (see p229), which also leaves from Connolly.

Bus Éireann and numerous independent operators such as **Gray Line Tours** (who have a desk in the Tourism Centre; 605 7705) offer guided excursions to destinations such as **Newgrange** (see p233), **Glendalough** (see p225) and the **Boyne Valley** (see p234). And, if you're short of time, **Dublin Airport** (see p279) has flights to Belfast, Galway, Kerry, Knock, Shannon, Derry, Cork and Waterford.

WALKING

Ireland has an extensive network of long-distance walking trails that provide access to some of the country's most impressive scenery. The trails are maintained by the **National Waymarked Ways Advisory**

Committee whose website (www.irishway markedways.ie) has further information about the routes we've highlighted in this guide.

INFORMATION

The **Irish Tourist Board** (Bord Fáilte; see p294) has local outposts in most major destinations; contact details are given in the following chapters. In the city, your first point of call should be the **Dublin Tourism Centre** (see p294), where you'll find reams of literature and plenty of helpful staff who'll assist you with accommodation, car hire, or just planning your itinerary. Those interested in Ireland's heritage are also advised to contact **Dúchas**, the Heritage Service of Ireland (see p58).

The best Trips

For a day's outing
Newgrange (see p233) and Glendalough (see p225) are fascinating destinations within easy reach of Dublin.

For a city break
Sample **Belfast**'s rejuvenated nightlife (see p271), the cultural attractions of **Galway City** (see p254), or the buzzing atmosphere of medieval **Kilkenny** (see p231).

For small town charm
Stuff your face in **Kinsale** (see p241), join the trad music fans in **Doolin** (see p253) and **Tubbercurry** (see p263), or go Yeats-mad in **Sligo** (see p263).

For gob-smacking scenery
Walk the **Wicklow Way** (see p225), explore the dramatic peninsulas of **West Cork** (see p242) and **Kerry** (see p246), marvel at the **Cliffs of Moher** (see p251) and trace the glorious **Antrim coast** (see p276).

For a touch of wilderness
Commune with the birds on the **Skellig Islands** (see p246), go walking in the **Connemara National Park** (see p257) and be inspired by the lonely landscapes of western **Mayo** (see p261) and **Donegal** (see p265).

Leinster

Before you head off to the west coast, make the most of the attractions closer to Dublin: mountains, beaches, gardens and unmissable ancient sites.

County Wicklow

Wicklow makes the Irish tourist board's job easy. Shingle-fringed beaches, rolling lowland meadows, immaculate gardens, heather-covered mountains and glistening lakes make it a perfect spot for cyclists and ramblers. Its proximity to Dublin is another major plus.

The Wicklow Mountains

The centre of the county is dominated by the granite **Wicklow Mountains**, with a series of deep glens and valleys on the eastern side. Experienced hillwalkers might consider walking the **Wicklow Way**, Ireland's first waymarked way (see p224), which starts in Marlay Park, Rathfarnham (see p96) and winds for a mountainous 120 kilometres (75 miles) to Clonegal in Co. Carlow. Allow eight days to walk the whole route, booking ahead at hostels and B&Bs. In 2001, **St Kevin's Way** one of the oldest pilgrimage routes in Ireland, incorporating 29 kilometres (18 miles) of breathtaking scenery from Holywood to Glendalough – was reopened and offers an attractive alternative.

If you are driving from the city your first stop might be **Glencullen** (still in Co. Dublin), home to Johnny Fox's Pub (see p141) and once a favourite haunt of the playwright John Millington Synge: 'Synge's Chair', a ridge separating the two glacial lakes, Lough Bray Upper and Lower, is named after him. Across the county border to the south-east is **Enniskerry**, a picturesque village that was built as an adjunct to the magnificent **Powerscourt Estate**, set at the foot of the Great Sugarloaf mountains. The house was designed by Richard Castle in 1743, and has been closed to the public since a serious fire in 1974. However, there is a new visitor centre on the estate, and more than enough to entertain you in the extensive formal gardens, laid out in the 18th and 19th centuries. Follow the signposts for a six-kilometre (four-mile) walk across the estate to the Powerscourt Waterfall, the highest in the British Isles. There are numerous bus tours to Powerscourt from Dublin; contact Dublin Tourism for details.

West of here at **Glencree**, join the Military Road, which cuts through the heart of some of Wicklow's finest scenery. The road was constructed in the early 19th century so that British forces would have access to rebel hideouts in the south of the county. A few kilometres south of Glencree is Sally Gap, one of the two main mountain passes in the area. From here you can turn on to the narrow R759 to **Lough Tay**, a dark lake at the bottom of a striking mountain chasm. It is overlooked by Luggala House, owned by a member of the Guinness family. South-east of Lough Tay is **Roundwood**, the highest village in Ireland and a good place to recover from strenuous walking in the hills.

Continuing on the Military Road south of Sally Gap will bring you through a desolate boggy landscape to the **Glenmacnass** waterfall, which crashes down from Mount Mullaghcleevaun to the west. Beyond here, the picturesque village of **Laragh** is the jumping-off point for the ancient monastic site of Glendalough.

Glendalough is a truly wooded glacial valley with two deep freshwater lakes. St Kevin came across the valley while seeking peace and solitude in the sixth century, and founded a monastic settlement here. During the Dark Ages Glendalough was one of the chief religious centres in Ireland, but it was repeatedly sacked by both the Vikings and the English in the following centuries. Today, a visitor centre provides information on the most important sites in the valley, including a round tower (fully restored in 1876), Celtic high crosses, beehive huts and the remains of a two-storey oratory that may date back to St Kevin's time. The mystical atmosphere of the valley can be severely diminished by crowds during the summer, so come early in the day and take time to enjoy the beautiful scenery around the Upper Lake. There are several walking trails in the area and the northern shore has remains of lead and zinc mines from the 19th century.

Glendalough is in the **Wicklow Mountains National Park**, which covers 200 square kilometres (77 square miles) of blanket bog and woodland, and shelters varied fauna and flora including rare orchids, deer, otters, badgers,

Magical **Glendalough**. *See p225.*

ravens and peregrine falcons. Phone 0404 45425 (summer) or 0404 45338 (winter) for more information about the park.

South-east of Glendalough, **Rathdrum** is the birthplace of one of Ireland's greatest leaders – Charles Stewart Parnell (*see p14*). **Avondale House**, set in a beautiful forest park, incorporates a museum to the man once known as the 'uncrowned King of Ireland'. Also in the vicinity is the **Greenan Farm**, where the farm animals, wild deer, farm museum and maze of Lawson Cyprus trees are fun for kids.

Further south, the Avonbeg and Avonmore rivers coincide to form the River Avoca at the **Meeting of the Waters**, a pretty spot that inspired Thomas Moore to write his celebrated poem. The village of **Avoca** was the location for the television series *Ballykissangel* and has become a tourist hotspot as a result. In 2001 the *Evening Herald* described the area as 'boring' and claimed that the villagers were out to 'fleece English visitors'. Although this judgement is more than a little harsh, there is certainly a strong element of paddywhackery about Avoca. The much-advertised **Avoca Handweaving Centre**, dating from 1723 and supposedly the longest-running business in Ireland, is blatantly aimed at tourists' wallets, but the stock is of high quality, and the café on site is extremely good.

The inland road south brings you to **Tinahely**, notable for its handsome Victorian courthouse that is now an arts centre. Down the road is **Shillelagh**, which gives its name to the knotted stick available from kitschy souvenir shops nationwide.

Avoca Handweaving Centre

Avoca (0402 35105). **Open** 9.30am-5.30pm daily. **Credit** AmEx, DC, MC, V.

Avondale House

Rathdrum (0404 46111). **Open** *mid Mar-Oct* 11am-5pm daily. Closed Nov-Feb. **Admission** €4.20; €3.80 concessions; €11 family. **Credit** MC, V.

Glendalough Visitors' Centre

Glendalough (0404 45325). **Open** *Summer* 9.30am-5.15pm daily. *Winter* 9.30am-4.15pm daily. **Admission** €2.50; €1.20-€1.90 concessions; €6 family. **No credit cards.**

Greenan Farm Museums & Maze

Ballinanty, Rathdrum (0404 46000/www. greenanmaze.com). **Open** *May, June* 10am-6pm Tue-Sun. *July, Aug* 10am-6pm daily. *Sept, Oct* 10am-6pm Sun. Closed Nov-Apr. **Admission** phone for details. **Credit** phone for details.

Powerscourt Estate Gardens & Waterfall

Powerscourt Estate, Enniskerry (01 204 6000). **Open** *House & gardens* Mar-Oct 9.30am-5.30pm daily; Nov-Feb 9.30am-4.30pm daily. *Waterfall* Apr-Sept 9am-7pm daily; Oct-Mar 10.30am-4.30pm daily. **Admission** €8 ; €4-€6.50 concessions; free under-5s. **Credit** AmEx, MC, V.

West Wicklow

In the north-west of the county are the **Blessington Lakes** (actually a reservoir) and **Russborough House & Gardens**. The house was built for the brewing magnate Joseph Leeson in the mid 18th century by Richard Castle and is one of the finest examples of Palladian architecture anywhere in the country. Sir Alfred Beit bought Russborough House in 1952 as a home for his magnificent painting collection, which includes Dutch, Flemish and Spanish masterpieces. In 1986 Dublin criminal Martin Cahill (aka the General) made off with a haul of these paintings, including a priceless Vermeer; the robbery is a key element in John Boorman's film *The General*. In the wake of the robbery some of the most valuable paintings were donated to the National Gallery in Dublin but there's still plenty to admire. However, in 2001 someone repeated Cahill's heist, so expect security at Russborough to be tight.

Further south, on the edge of the lovely Glen of Imaal, is a traditional whitewashed thatched **cottage**, which was the home of Michael Dwyer, a local rebel leader who disappeared in 1799. A statue to his lieutenant, Sam McAllister, who lost his life protecting Dwyer, adorns the neighbouring town of **Baltinglass**, which also boasts a ruined abbey from the 12th century. Above the town is a Bronze Age hill fort from which there are far-reaching views.

Dwyer McAllister Cottage

Derrynamuck (0404 45325). **Open** *Mid Mar-mid Oct* 9.30am-6pm daily. *Mid Oct-mid Mar* 9.30am-5pm daily. **Admission** €2.50; €1.20-€1.90 concessions; €6.30 family. **No credit cards.**

Russborough House & Gardens

Blessington (045 865239). **Open** (by guided tour only) *June-Aug* 10.30am-5.30pm daily. *Apr, May, Sept, Oct* 10.30am-2.30pm Sun. Closed Nov-Mar. **Admission** *Main rooms* €3.80. *Bedrooms* €1.90; 65¢ concessions. **No credit cards.**

The coast

The Christmas dinner scene from Joyce's *A Portrait of the Artist As A Young Man* takes place in No.1 Martello Terrace in **Bray**. The town, at the southern terminus of the DART line, used to be a fashionable seaside resort but is now rather run-down and seedy. However, children will enjoy the **Seaworld** centre (*see p171*) and there are fantastic views of the bay and the Sugar Loaf mountains from Bray Head. Near Bray, on the road to Greystones, is **Kilruddery House**, which has a lovely garden in the French classical style and the only sylvan theatre in Ireland (open in summer). Further down the coast is **Greystones**, a pretty fishing village that is now being swallowed up by encroaching housing developments, and the beautifully informal **Mount Usher Gardens** in Ashford.

The port town of **Wicklow** hosts the Round Ireland Yacht Race and has a popular summer regatta. There's not much to see here but the pubs are often good for Irish music sessions. Wicklow's restored **Historic Gaol** has exhibits relating to the 1798 rebellion, the famine, transportation and prison life in the 18th and 19th centuries. Along the coast on either side of town are miles of sandy beaches: Silver Strand and the small resort of Brittas Bay are particularly noteworthy.

Kilruddery House & Gardens

Between Bray & Greystones (286 2777). **Open** *House* May, June, Sept 1-5pm daily; closed Oct-Apr, July, Aug. *Gardens* Apr-Sept 1-5pm daily. **Admission** *House & gardens* €6.50; €2.50-€4.50 concessions. *Gardens only* €4.50; €1.50-€3.50 concessions. **No credit cards.**

Mount Usher Gardens

Ashford (0404 40205/http://homepage.tinet.ie/~gardens). **Open** *Mar-Oct* 10.30am-6pm daily. Closed Nov-Feb. **Admission** €5; €3.80 concessions. **No credit cards.**

Wicklow's Historic Gaol

Kilmantin Hill, Wicklow (0404 61599). **Open** 10am-6pm daily. **Admission** €5.70; €3.50-€4.40 concessions; €16 family. **Credit** MC, V.

Resources

Where to eat

The **Brook Lodge Inn** (Macreddin Village, 0402 36444, brooklodge@macreddin.ie, set menu €48) is the outstanding address in the county, with the Strawberry Tree restaurant dedicating itself to exciting cooking using wild and organic ingredients. For another culinary treat, try lunch outside on the terrace at the **Powerscourt Terrace Café** (Powerscourt House, Enniskerry, 204 6070, lunch only, main courses €6-€12), where the Avoca café team serve up beautiful cooking in a magnificent location. There's also a branch at the Avoca Handweaving Centre and at Kilmacanogue, on the N11 south of Bray.

The **Roundwood Inn** on Main Street in Roundwood (281 8107, main courses €12) is an award winning pub and restaurant serving rustic German-style food - get a good tramp in the Wicklow hills under your belt before you eat here. Also in Roundwood, the **Coachhouse** (Main Street, 281 8157, main courses €7-€12) offers good food, accommodation, web access and a beer garden.

In Wicklow town, the best choice is the **Bakery Restaurant** (Church Street, 0404 66770, closed dinner Sun, main courses €10-€12), housed in a pretty upstairs room and serving confident, feminine food. There's also an array of standard Irish-Italian dishes on offer at **Restaurant Del Forno** (The Mall Centre on Main Street, 0404 67075, closed Dec-Feb, €7-€10) and a decent, if unimaginative, selection of veggie food at the **Wicklow Arms** (Delgany, 287 4611, €7-€12).

Where to stay

Wicklow can easily be explored on day trips from Dublin. However, if you want to spend more time here, you should book your accommodation well in advance.

In Enniskerry try **Enniscree Lodge Hotel** (Cloon, 286 3542, rates €102-€115) or the **Summerhill House Hotel** (286 7928, rates €115). Both also serve good food, although the Enniscree Lodge restaurant is rather pricey. **The Heathers** (Poulaphouca, Ballymore-Eustace, 045 864554, rates €58) is a good choice in Blessington and there are a variety of accommodation at Glendalough. Try **Glendale** (0404 45410, rates €26 per person) or the **Glendalough International Youth Hostel** (Glendalough, 0404 45342, glendaloughyh@ireland.com, rates €19-€23 per person, €16 concessions), an excellent budget choice with Internet access.

Getting there

By car

Take the N11 Dublin–Wexford road and follow signs to Enniskerry. From Enniskerry, travel to Glencree and south towards Sally Gap. Turn right at Sally Gap to reach Blessington or continue south to Laragh for the turning to Glendalough. For an alternative route back to Dublin, continue west from Glendalough as far as Holywood where the road meets the N81. Turn right to head back to the city.

By bus

Dublin Bus 44 (€1.65 single) takes 1hr to travel to Enniskerry from Hawkins Street in Dublin. Bus 65 from Connolly Station runs to Blessington (€3 return). There are also **Bus Éireann** (836 6111) express buses to Wicklow town (from Store Street, 1hr 30min, €8.90 return) and Wexford. The privately run **St Kevin's Bus Service** (281 8119) has a twice-daily service to Glendalough via Roundwood from outside the College of Surgeons (St Stephen's Green) at 11.30am and 6pm.

By train

The DART terminates at Bray (€4.20 return), from where you can catch bus 85 to Enniskerry.

Tourist information

Tourist Office

Rialto House, Fitzwilliam Square, Wicklow (0404 69117). **Open** *Oct-May* 9.30am-1pm, 2-5pm Mon-Fri. *June-Sept* 9.30am-1pm, 2-6pm Mon-Fri; 9.30am-1pm Sun.
From early June to late August, tourist offices are also open in Blessington (Main Street, 045 865850) and Bray (286 6796).

County Wexford

The complex interconnectedness of Irish and British history has its roots in the Norman invasion of Wexford in 1169 (*see p7*). The Normans' legacy of castles, cathedrals and abbeys is everywhere in this county. Wexford was also at the epicentre of the 1798 rebellion against the British, with the roots of the uprising to be found in the local farmers' resentment at tithes exacted by the Church of Ireland. The United Irishmen rebels won a famous victory at Oulart Hill, but were finally routed at New Ross and made a desperate last stand on Vinegar Hill.

Today of course this whole area is relatively peaceful. The granite foothills in the north contrast nicely with the flat southern lowlands, and there are over 200 kilometres (124 miles) of coastline with several attractive beaches. Birdwatching, angling and walking are popular activities, and like neighbouring Kilkenny,

Wexford is a craft centre of some renown. There is also a range of cultural attractions on offer, most notably perhaps the **Wexford Opera Festival** in October (*see p185*).

Around Wexford Town

If you fancy a scenic walk, the **Wexford Coastal Path** covers the eastern and southern coastlines of the county from Kilmicheal Point (on the Wicklow border) down to Ballyhack, near Co. Waterford.

Travelling south by car on the N11, stop at **Enniscorthy** to visit the impressive **National 1798 Visitor Centre**, the best place in the country to understand the international context of the 1798 rebellion. Look out, too, for the **Wexford County Museum** on Castle Hill. It covers military, maritime, agricultural and ecclesiastical history and is housed in a 13th-century Norman castle. Walking tours of Enniscorthy start from the **Castle Hill Crafts Shop** (054 36800) on Castle Hill. They last roughly an hour and take place throughout the year on request (€5; €3 concessions).

About eight kilometres (five miles) north of Wexford Town at Ferrycarrig is the **Irish National Heritage Park**, a pseudo-historical theme park whose 90-minute tours will take you through the entire history of the country from Neolithic to Norman times and beyond – there's even a replica Viking longboat at anchor on the River Slaney just outside. On the coast east of Ferrycarrig is an area of low-lying land reclaimed from the sea. The public has access to hides and a visitor centre run by the **Wexford Wildfowl Reserve**, which protects the dozens of species of sea- and wading birds that breed and feed here. **Curracloe Beach**, to the north, is a long expanse of sand backed by dunes.

The Vikings arrived at the mouth of the River Slaney in about 850 and gave the area its name: 'Waesfjord', meaning 'estuary of the mud flats'. Apart from Waterford, **Wexford Town** is the principal town in the south-east and retains a maritime atmosphere, although silting has closed the harbour to larger vessels. On the waterfront at the Crescent is the tourist office and a statue of John Barry, who emigrated from Wexford to become a leading figure in the American navy and fired the last shot in the American War of Independence. Inland and running parallel to the waterfront, North and South Main Streets form the backbone of the town; **St Iberius Church** on North Main Street is an interesting example of Venetian Gothic architecture. Jane Francesca Elgee (aka 'Speranza', nationalist poet and mother of Oscar Wilde) was born near here at the corner of Common Quay and North Main Street.

A beacon at **Hook Head** has been guiding ships since the fifth century. See p230.

Only parts of the medieval town walls remain intact, but you can still visit the **Westgate**, one of six original tollhouses (contact Wexford Corporation for details; 053 42611), and the ruins of **Selskar Abbey** nearby. Henry II is reputed to have spent Lent 1172 at the Abbey doing penance for the murder of Thomas à Becket; it was destroyed by Cromwell in 1649. Free guided walks of the town, organised by the Wexford Historical Society, leave from outside the Talbot Hotel, Trinity Street and White's Hotel on George Street; contact the tourist office for details.

On the road to Rosslare, the 19th-century **Johnstown Castle** is now under state ownership and combines a research centre, the Irish Agricultural Museum, and beautiful Italianate gardens. Deep in the woods is a ruined medieval tower house. **Rosslare Harbour** is most notable for its ferry port with services to Wales and France, although there's also a popular sandy beach at **Rosslare Strand**. South of Rosslare Harbour, **Our Lady's Island** is a Catholic pilgrimage destination on account of its early Augustinian priory and also attracts a variety of birdlife to its saltwater lake.

Kilmore Quay on the south coast is the chief fishing port in the area, from where you can catch a boat to the **Saltee Islands**. These islands are home to a raucous collection of nesting sea birds, as well as a grey seal colony. Enquire at the tourist office in Wexford about booking a boat trip to the islands.

Irish National Heritage Park
Ferrycarrig (053 20733). **Open** *Apr-Sept* 9.30am-6.30pm daily. *Oct-Mar* times vary; phone for details. **Admission** €6.50 €5 concessions. **Credit** AmEx, MC, V.

Johnstown Castle & Gardens
south of Wexford Town (053 42888). **Open** *Garden* 9am-5pm daily. *Museum* Apr-Oct 9am-12.30pm, 1.30-5pm Mon-Fri; 2-5pm Sat, Sun; Nov-Mar 9am-12.30pm, 1.30-5pm Mon-Fri. **Admission** €4, €2.50 concessions; €13 family. **No credit cards.**

National 1798 Visitor Centre
Mill Park Road, Enniscorthy (054 37596/ www.1798centre com). **Open** 9.30am-5.30pm Mon-Sat. **Admission** €5; €3 concessions. **Credit** MC, V.

Wexford County Museum
Castle Hill, Enniscorthy (054 35926). **Open** *Mar-Sept* 10am-6pm daily. Closed Oct-Apr. **Admission** €3.80; €0.64-€2.50 concessions. **No credit cards.**

Wexford Wildfowl Reserve
North Slob, Wexford (053 231129). **Open** *Mid Apr-Sept* 9am-6pm daily. *Oct-mid Apr* 10am-5pm daily. **Admission** free.

Further west

Right on the Waterford border, New Ross on the River Barrow is not a particularly attractive place but does harbour the **Dunbrody Famine Ship**, a full-scale replica of a 19th-century 'coffin ship' that acts as a tribute to famine emigrants. Just south of New Ross, Dunganstown is the birthplace of Patrick Kennedy, grandfather of JFK. The **Kennedy Homestead** in the village has displays on the Kennedy dynasty and is developing a database of emigrants to the USA. Nearby is the 2.5-square-kilometre (one-square-mile) **John F Kennedy Park & Arboretum**, which opened in 1968 as a permanent memorial to the late president.

Heading south, towards the Hook peninsula, the next points of interest are the ruins of **Dunbrody Abbey**, a 12th-century Cistercian monastery, and **Dunbrody Castle**, which has one of the only full-size hedge mazes in the country. It's also worth stopping at 15th-century **Ballyhack Castle** and the star-shaped **Duncannon Fort** dating from 1586, which both overlook Waterford Harbour. (Ferry services to Passage East in County Waterford leave from Ballyhack; *see p237*.) Just to the east is the 12th-century **Tintern Abbey**.

South of here is the tapering finger of the Hook peninsula where you'll find the seaside village of **Slade**, overlooked by a ruined castle, and the **Hook Head Lighthouse**. There has been a beacon on this headland since the fifth century and its southerly position offers splendid views out to sea.

Ballyhack Castle

Ballyhack (051 389468). **Open** *June-Sept* 9.30am-6.30pm daily. Closed Oct-May. **Admission** €1.25; 50¢-€1 concessions. **No credit cards**.

Dunbrody Abbey, Castle & Visitors' Centre

Dunbrody Park, Arthurstown (051 388603). **Open** *Apr-June, Sept* 10am-6pm daily. *July, Aug* 10am-7pm daily. Closed Oct-Mar. **Admission** €1.90; €1.25 concessions; €3.80 family.

Dunbrody Famine Ship

JF Kennedy Trust, New Ross (051 425239/ www.dunbrody.com). **Open** *Apr-Sept* 9am-6pm daily. *Oct-Mar* 10am-5pm daily. **Admission** €5.70; €3.20 concessions; €12.70 family. **Credit** AmEx, MC, V.

Duncannon Fort

near Ballyhack, Co. Wexford. (051 389454/ www.thehook-wexford.com). **Open** 10am-5.30pm daily. **Admission** €4; €2 concessions; €10 family. **No credit cards**.

John F Kennedy Park & Arboretum

New Ross (051 388171). **Open** *Oct-Mar* 10am-5pm daily. *May-Aug* 10am-8pm daily. *Apr, Sept* 10am-6.30pm. **Admission** €2.50; €1.20-€1.90 concessions; €6.30 family. **No credit cards**.

Kennedy Homestead

Dunganstown, New Ross (051 388 264/ www.kennedyhomestead.com). **Open** *June-Aug* 10am-5.30pm daily. *May,* 11.30am-4.30pm daily. Closed Oct-May. **Admission** €4; €3.50 concessions; €10 family. **Credit** AmEx, MC, V.

Where to stay & eat

In Wexford Town choose between **St George Guesthouse** (George Street, 053 43474/ stgeorge@eircom.ie, closed Dec-Feb, rates €35 per person) or the 200-year-old surroundings of **Westgate House** (Westgate, 053 22167, rates €32 per person), where you can sleep in a four-poster bed. **White's Hotel** on George Street (053 22311/www.whiteshotel. iol.ie, rates €100) is the social centrepiece of the annual Wexford Opera Festival and gets very booked up. A good budget option is **Kirwan House Tourist Hostel** (3 Mary Street, 053 21208/www.hostels-ireland.com, closed Dec-Feb, rates per person €11.50 dorm, €15 double). Elsewhere, good B&Bs include **Arthur's Rest** in Arthurstown (051 389192, rates €63.50), and **Aisla Lodge** (053 33230, rates €52-€72) in Rosslare Harbour, for quick access to the ferries.

La Dolce Vita (Westgate, Wexford Town, 053 23935, main courses €10-€15) serves professionally executed Italianate cooking in a pleasant room. Local sea bass is a speciality. For about the same price you can try some of the finest food in the county at **La Marine Bistro** in Kelly's Resort Hotel in Rosslare (053 32114/www.kellys.ie, closed Dec-Feb), where Eugene Callaghan turns out some brilliant dishes at decent prices. The hotel is a four-star establishment in its own grounds with extensive leisure facilities (phone for rates).

Getting there

By bus

There are up to 11 **Bus Éireann** trips daily between Dublin and Wexford Town (€11.40 return, 3hrs), and 12 between Wexford and Rosslare Harbour (€4.45 return, 30min). **Ardcavan Coach** (053 22561) also runs a daily Dublin-Wexford Town service (€10.20 return, 2hrs 30min). Wexford bus station (053 22522) is next to the railway station.

By train

The Dublin-Rosslare Harbour service stops at Wexford Town's O'Hanrahan station (053 225220, €14.60 return, 3hrs). A local train service connects Rosslare Harbour and Wexford Town. Note that trains for Rosslare Harbour depart from Dublin's Connolly Station.

By boat

Irish Ferries (UK tel. 0870 517 1717) runs a ferry service from Pembroke in Wales to Rosslare; **Stena Sealink** (UK tel. 01233 647047) handles the Fishguard-Rosslare route. There are also ferries to Le Havre and Cherbourg in France; contact **Transport et Voyages** (042 669090).

Tourist information

Tourist Office
Crescent Quay, Wexford Town (053 23111). **Open**
Nov-Mar 9.30am-5.30pm Mon-Fri. *Apr-Oct* 9.30am-
5.30pm Mon-Sat. *July, Aug* 9.30am-5.30pm Mon-Sat;
11am-5pm Sun.
There are also offices in Rosslare (053 33232), New
Ross (051 421857) and Enniscorthy (054 34699).

County Kilkenny

Kilkenny town

Celts, Vikings, Normans and Anglo-Saxons have
all left their mark in Kilkenny. In the Middle
Ages, the city was the de facto capital of Ireland,
with its own Anglo-Norman parliament. The
Normans' assimilation of local culture gave rise
to the phrase 'Hibernicis ipsis hibernior' – 'more
Irish than the Irish themselves' – and resulted
in the infamous Statutes of Kilkenny in 1366,
which attempted to reverse this alarming
hibernicisation. The use of the Irish language
was forbidden and Normans were prevented
from marrying the native Irish. In the 16th and
17th centuries Kilkenny remained an important
political centre until it was ransacked by Oliver
Cromwell in 1650.

Today, Kilkenny's status – whether a city
or a town – is the subject of local heated debate,
but visitors might conclude that it offers the
best of both worlds. Compact and picturesque,
with cobbled streets and a singular medieval
atmosphere, the county town is nevertheless
lively, with numerous pubs and restaurants,
and an active cultural life. Kilkenny is also
a hurling mad county, a major craft centre,
and the locus for some of the country's best
festivals. On the May bank holiday is the
Kilkenny Country Roots festival, followed
by the **Cat Laughs** comedy extravaganza over
the June Bank holiday and the ten-day **Arts
Festival** in August, which incorporates film,
theatre, literary activity and music.

The main sightseeing attraction is the
imposing granite edifice of **Kilkenny Castle**,
overlooking the River Nore. Strongbow's son-
in-law built a timber or earth structure here
in the 12th century, and the site has been
repeatedly restored and renovated ever since.
The most recent work was completed in 2001
and has made the castle more impressive than
ever. The castle grounds form a well-manicured
public park and the **Castle Yard** is home to
the national Craft Council of Ireland (056
61804), with several artists', potters' and
jewellers' studios on site.

Kilkenny Castle.

Trips Out of Town

St Canice's Cathedral, the largest medieval cathedral outside Dublin, has also undergone many changes over the centuries, but the chancel, transept and the nave date from the 13th century. The tombs of long deceased local luminaries are contained inside and – for those who are fit enough to climb it – the adjoining tower offers a tremendous view of the surrounding countryside. Elsewhere, the Tholsel ('toll stall') on Main Street is an 18th-century council chamber that is still used as a corporation office. Further along on Parliament Street is the sturdy Elizabethan Rothe House, a beautiful merchant house (three houses to be precise) that has been tastefully restored. It is now home to a public museum and a library that can be visited by prior appointment. The tourist office building on Rose Inn Street is also of note, being one of the few remaining Tudor almshouses in Ireland.

Kilkenny Castle

The Parade, Kilkenny (056 21450). **Open** (by guided tour only) *Apr-May* 10.30am-5.30pm daily. *June-Sept* 10am-7pm daily. *Oct-Mar* 10.30am-5pm daily. Closed Nov-Feb. **Admission** €4; €1.90-€3.20 concessions; €10.20 family. **Credit** AmEx, MC, V.

Rothe House

Parliament Street, Kilkenny (056 22893). **Open** *Mar-Oct* 10.30am-5pm Mon-Sat; 3-5pm Sun. *Nov-Feb* 1-5pm Mon-Sat. **Admission** €3; €2 concessions. **Credit** MC, V.

St Canice's Cathedral

Irishtown, Kilkenny (056 64971). **Open** *Easter-Sept* 9am-1pm, 2-6pm Mon-Sat; 2-6pm Sun. *Oct-Easter* 10am-1pm, 2-4pm Mon-Sat; 2-4pm Sun. **Admission** €3. **No credit cards**.

Beyond Kilkenny town

The county is characterised by pretty villages and fertile countryside, meandering rivers and attractive stone buildings, with a number of key attractions. Kells (not to be confused with its more famous namesake in Co. Meath; *see p234*) is a delightful village on the River Nore with an old watermill and attractive stone bridge. Nearby are the ruins of Kells Priory, a remarkably complete monastic settlement dating from the 14th and 15th centuries. Not far away is Jerpoint Abbey in Thomastown, a Cistercian complex founded in 1160 and closed under Henry VIII. It may be in ruins, but the carvings on the cloisters and tombs are exquisite: look out for the bishops, dragons, long-faced, bearded saints and doe-eyed ladies. If you need refreshment in the area, Murphy's and Carrolls pubs in Thomastown are renowned as lively spots. There are further Cistercian settlements at Holy Cross Abbey

in Kilcooley, and Duiske Abbey at Graiguenamanagh – a delightful village near the Waterford border. Extensive restoration has spared Duiske the roofless indignity of Jerpoint, and it's now used as the parish church. Many medieval churches in Ireland feature *sheelagh-na-gigs* – carvings of splay-legged women aggressively displaying their genitalia; Duiske contains an interesting variant on this with a cross-legged knight who looks as if he's having difficulty finding a (medieval) bathroom.

Elsewhere in the county visit the exquisite village of Inistioge, with its ten-arch stone bridge spanning the River Nore, for a sense of rural Ireland at its most picturesque.

Jerpoint Abbey

Thomastown (056 24623). **Open** *Mar-May* 10am-5pm daily. *June-Sept* 9.30am-6.30pm daily. *Sept-Oct* 10am-5pm daily. *Nov* 10am-4.30pm daily. *Dec, Jan, Feb* by appointment only. **Admission** €2.50; €1.20-€1.90 concessions; €6.30 family. **No credit cards**.

Resources

Where to eat

Café Sol on William Street (Kilkenny, 056 64987) offers splendid lunches and beautiful afternoon teas in a delightfully feminine room. Pordylos is housed in a four-centuries-old building on narrow, medieval Butterslip Lane (off High Street, Kilkenny, 056 70660, main courses €14-€20). It's a pleasantly cosy restaurant, serving imaginative modern food. Lautrec's Bistro (9 St Kieran's Street, 056 62720, main courses €7-€19) offers a wide range of food incorporating French, Italian and Tex Mex, and there's decent Chinese on offer at Pearls (10 Irishtown, 056 23322, main courses around €13). For the hippest locale in the city, head for Zuni (26 Patrick Street, 056 23999/ www.zuni.ie). The bar is a cool place to hang out before enjoying some very slick cooking in the restaurant (main courses €13-€24). Everyone in the city and the county comes here, so book in advance.

Where to stay

During festivals it can be difficult to get accommodation in Kilkenny, so book well in advance. There are a lot of central B&Bs on Parliament Street, Patrick Street and the roads leading out of town. Alternatively consult Bedfinders on Rose Inn Street (056 70088). Again, Zuni (*see above*) has the most sought-after accommodation around, offering sleek modern rooms in soothing colours (€90-€150). If you can't get in there, try the Hibernian on Patrick Street, an upmarket guesthouse with a

good restaurant (056 71888/www.kilkenny
hibernianhotel.com, rates €95). A cheaper
option is the **Metropole Hotel** (High Street,
056 63778, rates €89), which offers B&B in
12 rooms, or the **Kilford Arms Hotel** (John
Street, 056 61018, rates €65-€102), which has
a decent restaurant and bar.

Getting there

By car

Take the N7 out of Dublin as far as Naas in County
Kildare; continue on the N9 through Carlow until
the junction at Paulstown. Here, take the N10 into
Kilkenny town.

By bus

Bus Éireann services (051 879 000) connect Dublin
with Kilkenny (2hrs, €10.20 return).

By train

Trains run daily from Dublin's Connolly Station to
Kilkenny (2hrs, €16 return).

Tourist information

Kilkenny Tourist Office

Rose Inn Street (056 51500).
Open *Nov-March* 9am-1pm, 2-5pm Mon-Sat.
Apr, Oct 9am-6pm Mon-Sat. *May, Sept* 9am-6pm
Mon-Sat; 11am-5pm Sun. *July-Aug* 9am-7pm Mon-
Sat; 11am-5pm Sun.

County Meath

Navan, the principle town in Meath, has the
distinction of having produced two winners of
the Perrier award for comedy at the Edinburgh
festival: Dylan Moran and Tommy Tiernan.
Tiernan's apocryphal tale about a local Navan
councillor asking why the town should need a
proposed new arts centre when it already had
a shopping centre, says much about the way the
town and county is viewed in the rest of Ireland.
A hilarious radio character called Navan Man
does little to improve the image of the town as
a provincial backwater.

However, the Meath countryside has a proud
history dating back to ancient times. Although
there are no urban centres of interest or any
stunning scenery, the prehistoric remains at
Newgrange and **Knowth** make Meath an
unmissable day trip destination from Dublin.

Situated on a low ridge eight kilometres (five
miles) east of Slane, **Newgrange** is the best-
preserved passage grave site in Europe. Built
between 3500 BC and 2700 BC – making it 500
years older than the Egyptian pyramids and
1,500 years older than Stonehenge – it was used
as a tomb where Stone Age peoples buried the
cremated remains of their dead. Newgrange is
an extraordinary feat of engineering that took
at least 40 years to build – the equivalent of the

New Agers' delight: celebrate the winter solstice at **Newgrange**.

Trips Out of Town

life's work of a whole generation. A huge stone cairn is surrounded by bulky monoliths, with a kerb of 97 more boulders forming a dry-stone wall around the base. The main entrance to the burial chamber is marked by the threshold stone, which admits you to the 'roof box' through which the sun's rays penetrate at daybreak on the winter solstice, 21 December, to spectacular effect. You won't get into Newgrange for the solstice, due to a massive waiting list, but you can visit on other days, albeit by guided tour only.

The tour leaves from the recently established **Bru na Boinne** visitor centre, located two miles off the Slane–Drogheda road. The visitor centre offers a seven-minute introductory audio-visual presentation, a walk-through replica of Newgrange that includes a simulation of the winter solstice, and a thorough explanation of why Newgrange is Ireland's best-known prehistoric monument. A minibus takes visitors to the tomb itself; expect delays in summer, and try to arrive as early as possible.

The visitor centre tour also covers nearby **Knowth**, which, stone for stone, outdoes Newgrange in the sheer quantity of its megalithic art, and also dates back even further to the earliest neolithic times. The smaller **Dowth** tomb was overrun in the 19th century by a group of eccentrics known as the British Israelites who were convinced that the ark of the covenant was buried on the site; it has not been properly excavated since.

The nearest attraction to the passage graves is the **Boyne Valley**, where the Battle of the Boyne took place in 1690. In 1688, the Catholic King James II was deposed in favour of his Protestant daughter Mary and her husband William of Orange. James sought to regain his throne and fought William's army at Oldbridge but his troops were routed and he had to flee to France (*see also p11*). Close by is **Slane Castle**. The castle grounds were landscaped by Capability Brown, but most young Dubliners know Slane for the large-scale rock concerts that are held here from time to time, including gigs by U2 in the summer of 2001 (*see p190*). On the **Hill of Slane** outside the town, St Patrick lit an Easter bonfire in 433 as a challenge to the authority of the Kings of Tara. The subsequent spread of Christianity eroded the power of the pagan rulers, and a statue of Patrick marks the spot today.

Elsewhere in the county, visit the **Hill of Tara**, south of Navan, where the High Kings of Ireland had their private domain. This was the centre of political and religious power in pre-Christian Ireland. Access to the hill is free and there's a visitors' centre in the church at the top of the hill. Nearby, **Trim** has the largest Anglo-

Norman castle in Ireland. Hugh de Lacy began its construction in 1172 but the keep was not completed until the 1220s. This 20-sided tower is three storeys high and was protected by a ditch, a curtain wall and a moat.

In the north-west of the county on the N52 is the market town of **Kells**, which was established as a religious settlement in AD 550: the market Cross, the Round Tower and St Colmcille's Cross are evidence of the town's ecclesiastical past. Kells' two greatest treasures, the Crozier of Kells and the Book of Kells (*see p61*), are kept in the British Museum and Trinity College, Dublin respectively.

Bru na Boinne Visitor Centre
Donore (041 988 0300). **Open** *Nov-Feb* 9.30am-5pm daily. *Mar, Apr, Oct* 9.30am-5.30pm daily. *May, Sept* 9am-6.30pm. *June-mid Sept* 9am-7pm daily. **Admission** €5; €12.60 family. **Credit** MC, V.

Slane Castle
Slane (046 49336). **Open** *Apr-Sept* noon-5pm daily. **Admission** €6.35. **Credit** MC, V.

Trim Castle
Trim (046 37111). **Open** *May-Oct* 10am-6pm daily. *Nov-Feb* 10am-6pm Sat, Sun. **Admission** €3.10; €7.60 family. **No credit cards**.

Resources

Where to eat

The **Cellars Bistro** in the Boyne Valley Hotel (041 983 7737, main courses €10-€19) offers French and Irish cuisine, including fresh fish and steaks. The **Ground Floor Restaurant** (Bective Square, 046 49688, main courses €18-€24) is a decent licensed bistro in Kells.

Getting there

By car
To reach Bru na Boinne take the N2 out of Dublin to Slane. The N3 leads from Dublin to Navan.

By bus
There are buses to Navan and Slane several times a day from **Busárus** (€10.80 return; 45min). Tour buses run from Navan to Newgrange and Knowth. There are also coach tours from Dublin; contact the tourism centre on Suffolk Street for details.

Tourist information

Navan Tourist Office
21 Ludlow Street (046 215181/www.meathtourism.ie). **Open** *Mar-Dec* 9.30am-5pm Mon-Fri. Closed Jan, Feb. The Dublin Tourism Centre on Suffolk Street (*see p294*) can also provide comprehensive information on the county's attractions.

Munster

Go west for some of the Emerald Isle's most strikingly beautiful scenery.

County Waterford

Waterford town & around

Waterford was founded as 'Vadrefjord' by the equally unpronounceable Sigtryggr in the ninth century. In 1170 Robert de Clair, aka Strongbow, arrived to bloodily enforce the Norman conquest of Ireland, followed shortly afterwards by Henry II, who made Waterford second in importance only to Dublin.

The most distinctive symbol of Waterford's past is the chess-piece-like **Reginald's Tower**. Built by Reginald the Dane in 1003 and later occupied by Strongbow, it has been an arsenal, a mint, a prison and a museum. Behind the tower are part of the original city walls. The best place to absorb Waterford's long history is on a self-guided tour of the **Waterford Treasures Museum**, located in the converted Granary on Merchant Quay. The building has been completely updated to provide a modern setting for its collection of artefacts from the Viking and medieval periods. The Granary is also the site of the town's main tourist office (see p237). To the east of the museum is Meagher Quay, named after Thomas Francis Meagher, who took part in the abortive 1848 uprising. He was transported to a penal colony in Tasmania, but escaped to the USA, and later became a hero of the American Civil War. There's a pub named after him on O'Connell Street, where you can sample the local Moondharrig whiskey.

In the city centre, it's hard to walk very far without stumbling upon the work of 18th-century local architect John Roberts. Cathedral Square holds two strikingly contrasting examples of his work: the opulent and ornate **Cathedral of the Most Holy Trinity** (Catholic) and the elegant **Christchurch Cathedral** (Protestant), the only neo-classical Georgian cathedral in Ireland. In the 12th century, Strongbow married the Irish princess Aoife in the medieval cathedral on this site, a union that marked the beginning of English involvement in Ireland. Christchurch underwent major restoration work in 2001 and will be open for guided tours from May 2002.

Traditional west coast **fishing boats** come in handy for keeping the rain off.

Trips Out of Town

Roberts also built **City Hall** on the Mall, a street of fine 18th-century buildings. It houses the Municipal Collection of Art, with work by Jack Yeats and Louis le Brocquy, but access is only possible as part of one of the infrequent guided tours (051 873 510). Next door is **Waterford's Theatre Royal**, another Roberts creation, which hosts an **International Festival of Light Opera** every September (contact the tourist office for details).

After Cork, Waterford is the busiest port on the south coast, a fact that has been crucial to the development and trade of **Waterford Crystal**. The first glassmaking factory in the town was founded in 1783, but its modern incarnation dates from 1947. A guided tour explains all the stages of production.

Christchurch Cathedral
Cathedral Square (051 585 958/www.christchurch waterford.org). **Open** *Guided tours* May-Sept; phone for details. **Admission** €4 donation. **No credit cards.**

Reginald's Tower
Parade Quay, Waterford (051 304 220). **Open** 9.30am-5.30pm daily. €1.90; €0.70-€1.20 concessions; €5 family. **No credit cards.**

Waterford Crystal Visitor Centre
Waterford (051 332 500/373 311). **Open** *Showrooms* Nov-Feb 9am-5pm daily. Mar-Oct 8.30am-6pm daily. *Tours* Nov-Feb 9am-3.15pm Mon-Fri; by appointment Sat, Sun. Mar-Oct 8.30am-4pm daily. **Admission** €6; €3.50; free under-12s. **Credit** MC, V.

Waterford Treasures Museum
The Granary, Waterford (051 304 5000). **Open** (last entry 1hr before closing) *Apr, May, Sept* 9.30am-6pm daily. *June-Aug* 9.30am-9pm daily. *Oct-Apr* 10am-5pm daily. **Admission** €6; €3-€4.50 concessions; €12-19 family; free under-5s. **Credit** AmEx, MC, V.

West of Waterford

The coast of Waterford is characterised by sandy beaches and plenty of opportunities for coastal walks. At the mouth of the harbour is **Dunmore East**, a picturesque fishing and holiday village set among sandstone cliffs and small coves, with a good view of Hook Head lighthouse in County Wexford (*see p230*).

About 12 kilometres (seven miles) south-west of Waterford is **Tramore**, one of Ireland's most popular tourist resorts since the 18th century. It now suffers somewhat from the usual blight of amusement arcades and other seaside distractions, although the five-kilometre (three-mile) beach with its high sand dunes remains a delight. The mascot of the beach is the Metalman, a colourful figure perched on the

headland in Westown since 1824 as a warning to shipping. For the best views of the bay, take the eight-kilometre (five-mile) Doneraile Walk.

The next big town along the coast is **Dungarvan**, though Annestown, Bunmahon and Clonea all offer pleasant beaches along the way. Dungarvan has plenty of facilites for the visitor, including golf courses, coastal walks and fishing, and is also a convenient location from which to explore the scenic **Monavullagh** and **Comeragh Mountains** in the north of the county. Further west, at the foot of the Knockmealdown Mountains is the beautiful small town of **Lismore**. St Carthage founded a monastic university here in 636, which remained an important seat of learning until the 12th century. **Lismore Castle** was constructed in 1185 by Prince John, Lord of Ireland, and in the 16th century was presented to Sir Walter Raleigh. Although the building is now private property, the magnificent gardens landscaped in the 17th and 18th centuries, are open to the public. In town, the **Lismore Heritage Centre** offers a 30-minute audio-visual show on the historical and natural attractions of the area.

North-west of here, the road affords fine views of the Knockmealdown Mountains. The viewpoint at **Vee** features the cyclopean tomb of Samuel Grubb, who asked to be buried standing up so he could keep an eye on the landscape that he loved so much.

In the far south-west of Waterford is the seaside town of **Ardmore**, overlooked by the ruins of **St Declan's Church & Oratory**. The ruins are supposed to mark the site where St Declan set up his monastery as early as the fourth century and include a delicate round tower, a church, an eighth-century oratory and some Ogham stones. (These standing stones, engraved with early Irish script, can be found throughout Munster. Most date from the fourth to the seventh centuries and denote a burial site.) South of town is **St Declan's Well**, a fresh water spring where pilgrims en route from Ardmore to the Rock of Cashel in Tipperary would wash. The five-kilometre (three-mile) cliff walk from the well, with views over the beach, is recommended.

Lismore Castle Gardens
Lismore (058 54424/www.lismorecastle.com). **Open** *Apr-June, Sept* 1.45-4.45pm daily. *July, Aug* 11am-4.45pm daily. Closed Sept-Mar. **Admission** €4; €2 concessions. **No credit cards.**

Lismore Heritage Centre
Old Courthouse, Lismore (058 54975). **Open** *Nov-Feb* 9.30am-5.30pm Mon-Fri. *Mar-Oct* 9.30am-6pm Mon-Sat; noon-6pm Sun. **Admission** €3.30. **Credit** AmEx, DC, MC, V.

Where to eat & drink

The most happening eaterie in Waterford city is the **Wine Vault** on the High Street (051 853 444), which combines a wine shop (closed Sun) with a good-value restaurant (main courses €13.30-€19.95). For classical cuisine in elegant surroundings, try dinner (main courses €15.90-€22.20) at **Dwyer's** (8 Mary Street, 051 877 478, www.dwyersrestaurant.com, closed Sun). **Egan's** (36 Barronstrand Street, 051 875 619) is a lively pub with a lunchtime carvery (€7.50) and a dinner menu (main courses €10), while **T&H Doolan's** (George's Street, 051 841 504) serves bar snacks (€6.30-€8.80), a traditional seafood menu (main courses €12.60 €17.70) and chilled pints of plain to the accompaniment of traditional live music. **McAlpin's Suir Inn** in Cheekpoint (just outside the city, 051 382220, closed Sun, also closed Mon & Tue in winter, main courses €12.10-€18.40) is a 16th-century riverside hostelry that is much loved by locals for its speedy service and tasty cooking.

Wherever you stay in the county, don't miss the cutting-edge cuisine on offer at The Tannery (Quay Street, Dungarvan, 058 45420, closed late Jan-early Feb, closed lunch Sat & dinner Sun). This is one of Ireland's most exciting culinary adventures (main courses €18.50-€23.50). In Lismore, the eaterie of choice is the uniquely characterful **Buggy's Glencairn Inn** (058 56232, closed Mon-Wed, Sun in winter, main courses €17.72-€22.25); it's also a very pleasant place to stay.

Where to stay

The most luxurious choice is **Waterford Castle Hotel** (Ballinakill, 051 878 203/fax 051 879 316/www.waterfordcastle.com, closed Christmas & Jan, rates €180-€310) located on a private island three kilometres (two miles) from the city. Facilities include a tennis court and an 18-hole golf course. In town, try the **Granville Hotel** on Meagher Quay (051 305 555, fax 051 305 566, www.granville-hotel.ie). This 18th-century merchant's house was the former home of Thomas Meagher (rates €140-€200). On the edge of Waterford in the grounds of the ruined Butlerstown Castle is the **Coach House** (Butlerstown, Cork Road, 051 384 656/fax 051 384 751/www.iol.ie/~coachhse), a beautifully restored 19th-century stone building offering cosy, rustic and excellent value accommodation (closed late Dec-late Jan, rates €71-€89).

For a proper seaside holiday, stay at the **Grand Hotel** in Tramore, (051 381 414/ www.grand-hotel.ie, rates €89-€114), which is five minutes' walk from the beach. A good budget option is the **Dungarvan Holiday**

Hostel (Rice's Street, Dungarvan (058 44340/ www.dungarvanhostel.com, rates €12- €15 per person), while the **Cliff House Hotel** in Ardmore (024 94106/www.cliffhotelardmore. com, closed Jan, Feb & Mon-Fri during Nov, Dec) has 20 rooms, all en suite, with spectacular sea views (rates €76.20-€107). **Buggy's Glencairn Inn** (see above) is the top choice in Lismore, but if you're here for the fishing try the lovely **Ballyrafter House** (058 54002/ www.waterfordhotel.com, closed Nov-Feb, rates €120), an 18th-century Georgian building, which organises salmon fishing trips from February to September (book well in advance).

Getting there

By car
The quickest routes to Waterford are via the N9 from Kilkenny and Dublin or the N25 from Wexford. However, more enjoyable is the route from Wexford to Ballyhack on the eastern side of Waterford Harbour, followed by the ferry to Passage East, a small harbour surrounded by thatched cottages. From here it is 11km (7 miles) into Waterford centre. The N25 links Waterford and Cork, though the coastal R675 from Tramore to Dungarvan is more interesting. To reach Lismore take the N72 north-west from Dungarvan.

By bus
In Waterford city, bus services operate out of Plunkett station on the north side of the river: there are regular services from Dublin (2hrs 45min) by **Bus Éireann** (051 879 000, €10.80-€11.40 return) and **Rapid Express Club Travel** (679 1549/051 872 149, €11.40 return). Over a dozen Bus Éireann buses run daily between Waterford and Tramore. Further services connect Dungarvan with Dublin, Killarney and Cork, while Ardmore has services to Dungarvan, Waterford and Dublin.

By train
Waterford train station (051 873 401) is next to the bus station, with daily trains to and from Heuston station in Dublin (2hrs 40min, €17-€21.60 return).

By air
You can fly to Waterford directly from the UK with **Euroceltic Airways** (051 875 020), which has a daily service from London Luton. Waterford airport is about 10km (6 miles) out of the city centre; a taxi should cost about €13.

Tourist information

Waterford Tourist Office in the Granary Building on Merchant's Quay (051 875 788/ 051 875 823/fax 051 877 388/www.southeast tourism.ie) is the main point of contact for the whole of the south-east. It is open all year round. For specific information about the city, also consult the Waterford website (www.waterfordtourism.org). Outside the city, there's a tourist office in the Courthouse in **Dungarven** (058 41741/www.amireland.com/ dungarvan, closed Sun) and a summer office in **Ardmore** (024 94444).

County Cork

Cork is Ireland's largest county, extending from the south-east to west coasts, with a whole host of attractions for the visitor. Historic links with Spain and France have encouraged Cork to identify more with continental Europe than neighbouring Britain, and its southerly latitude means it may surprise you with some positively balmy summer weather; palm trees and bamboo grow here in abundance. Highlights of this varied county include **Cork** city, the gourmet mecca of **Kinsale**, the sophistication of **Clonakilty** and **Bantry** and the untouched natural beauty of the **Beara Peninsula, Clear Island** and **Mizen Head**. You'll eat and drink handsomely in Cork, and the traditional music ensures that even on the rainiest nights you're unlikely to be without entertainment.

The harbour at **Cobh**. *See p239.*

Cork city & around

Cork is a compact city at the head of the largest harbour in Ireland. Its roots go back to St Finbarr, who chose a marshy area around the present-day cathedral for a monastery in the seventh century. The settlement was later destroyed by the Vikings and rebuilt on an island in the middle of the River Lee where it developed into a thriving locus for trade. Its fortified walls saved it from destruction by Cromwell in the mid 17th century, although it fell to William of Orange in 1690.

Modern Cork dates from the heyday of the 1800s, when it was a successful trade centre with an important butter market. However, its proximity to Cobh (*see p239*) also made Cork one of the principal plugholes through which the emigrant Irish population trickled away in the 19th and 20th centuries. During the early 20th century, Cork was strongly Republican and played an active role in the War of Independence. The mayor Thomas MacCurtain was killed by the Black and Tans in 1920, who also burned down much of the town, and Michael Collins was shot just west of the city during the Civil War (*see p17*).

Apart from Jack Lynch's years as Taoiseach, Cork suffered in the second half of the 20th century from the indifference of successive Dublin administrations. One benefit of this, however, was that its historic buildings tended

to escape the 'pull-em-down' approach that blighted Dublin. Cork is now a thriving city, with an appealing combination of flourishing commerce and lively arts, ironic self-deprecation and good, clean craic.

With a population less than a fifth of Dublin's, Cork has an intimate feel and can be easily traversed on foot. **Patrick Street** on the south side of the River Lee is the city's main thoroughfare, its curved lines marking what was once a waterway. It boasts all the usual British and Irish chain stores, though more distinctive shops, restaurants and pubs are tucked away on alluring sidestreets and alleys. Head north to reach Emmet Place, the location of the **Opera House** and the **Crawford Municipal Art Gallery**, a distinctive red-brick building topped by an octagonal turret. The gallery houses the most important Irish collection of 19th- and 20th-century art outside Dublin, including sculpture by Seamus Murphy and paintings by Harry Clarke and Jack Yeats (*pictured p240*). It's a delightful gallery with a pleasant café and shop.

Cross the river at St Patrick's Bridge or Opera House Bridge to reach Camden Quay on the north side, with its 18th-century Georgian houses. West of here is the **Shandon** area of Cork where people from all over the South-west would gather to sell butter at the Butter Exchange. It now houses a craft centre and the **Institute for Choreography & Dance** *(see p240)*. Shandon is dominated by the unusual limestone and sandstone steeple of **St Ann's Church**, from which there is a great view of the entire city. The steeple is topped by a seven-metre (11-foot) weathervane in the form of a salmon and is nicknamed the 'four-faced liar' after its clocks, which showed different times until the mechanisms were harmonised in 1986. As well as climbing the steeple, visitors are allowed to ring the bells; sheet music is provided if you fancy a turn.

South of the city centre, **St Finbarr's Cathedral** on Bishop Street marks the site of the original settlement. The current ornate cathedral was built by William Burgess in the 19th century to replace a structure destroyed in the Siege of Cork in 1690. Further west on College Road is **University College Cork** (Western Road; 021 490 3000/www.ucc.ie), founded in 1845. It has a fine quadrangle with a collection of Ogham stones, behind which is the 19th-century **Honan Chapel**, with beautiful Harry Clarke windows. Cross the river from the campus to reach Fitzgerald Park and the **Cork Public Museum**, which has interesting displays on the city's eventful political history, plus some less inspiring archaeological exhibits. Further north again is **Cork City Gaol**. The excellent audio tour of this 19th-century prison shows the cells with models of former inmates having a miserable time, and is accompanied by recordings of shuffling feet and clinking chains.

Cork City Gaol
Sunday's Well Road (021 430 5022). **Open** *Mar-Oct* 9.30am-5pm daily. *Nov-Feb* 10am-4pm daily. **Admission** €6; €3-€4 concessions; €14 family. **No credit cards.**

Cork Public Museum
Fitzgerald Park, Mardyke Road (021 427 0679), **Open** *June-Aug* 11am-1pm, 2.15pm-6pm Mon-Fri; 3pm-5pm Sun. *Sept-May* 11am-1pm, 2.15pm-5pm Mon-Fri; 3pm-5pm Sun. **Admission** free Mon-Sat; €1.25, €2.50 family Sun. **No credit cards.**

Crawford Municipal Art Gallery
Emmet Place (021 427 3377/www.synergy.ie/ crawford). **Open** 10am-5pm Mon-Sat. **Admission** free. **No credit cards.**

St Ann's Church
Church Street, Shandon (021 450 5906/ www.shandonsteeple.com). **Open** *Apr-Sept* 9.30am-5pm Mon-Sat. *Oct-Mar* 10am-4pm Mon-Sat. **Admission** €4.45; €3.80. **Credit** MC, V.

St Finbarr's Cathedral
Bishop Street (021 496 3387). **Open** *Apr-Sept* 10.30am-5.30pm Mon-Sat. *Oct-Mar* 10am-12.45pm, 2-5pm Mon-Sat. **Admission** free; €2.50 donation appreciated. **Credit** MC, V.

Around Cork city

About eight kilometres (five miles) west of Cork is **Blarney Castle**, a 550-year-old tower house set in beautiful grounds. A spiral staircase at the top of the castle will lead you to the quintessentially tacky Irish tourist ritual to beat all quintessentially tacky Irish tourist rituals. Apparently, being held round the waist by a local and lowered over a grating to kiss a none-too-clean looking slab of rock will imbue you with everlasting eloquence. If your money doesn't fall out in the process, you may want to spend some of it in **Blarney Woollen Mills**, a hit with the coach tours. Otherwise head to the **Ballincollig Gunpowder Mills** on the Killarney road, an 18th-century mill complex, which once produced as many as 16,000 barrels of gunpowder a year.

Cork harbour is dominated by Great Island, which is joined to the mainland by a causeway. The pretty small town of **Cobh** (pronounced 'Cove') on the island was traditionally the main port for Cork city and the point of exodus for two-and-a-half million Irish emigrants between 1848 and 1950. The 'Queenstown Story' at the **Cobh Heritage Centre** covers the 'coffin ships' of the Famine years, convict transportations to Australia, the growth of the liner business, the *Titanic's* visit in 1912 and the sinking of the *Lusitania* off the Cork coast in 1915. Under British rule, Cobh was known as Queenstown because Queen Victoria landed here on her first visit to Ireland in 1849. The town is overlooked by the 19th-century French Gothic **St Colman's Cathedral**, noted for its elaborate bell-ringing displays.

East of Cork is the conservation-conscious 16-hectare (40-acre) **Fota Wildlife Park** – one of the world's leading centres for cheetah breeding – and the small town of Midleton. Visitors to the **Old Jameson Distillery** here can see the world's largest pot still (holding 31,468 gallons – a good evening's worth), discover the use of such arcane implements as the bung flogger, the croove and the chiv, and test their palates with a blind tasting of Irish whiskey brands.

Further east still, **Youghal** ('Yawl') is a pleasant seaside town at the mouth of the River Blackwater. It makes a good stop en route between Waterford and Cork and was used as the location of the 1954 film *Moby Dick* with Gregory Peck. An 18th-century clocktower straddles the main street, though the town walls and the **Church of St Mary's** both date from the 13th century. Sir Walter Raleigh was mayor of Youghal for a time in the 16th century and is said to have planted the first potatoes in Ireland in the town in 1588.

The Small Ring by JB Yeats.

Ballincollig Gunpowder Mills Heritage Centre

Ballincollig, 12km west of Cork (021 487 4430).
Open *Easter-Sept* 10am-6pm daily. Closed Oct-Mar.
Admission €3.20. **No credit cards**.

Blarney Castle

Blarney (021 438 5252/www.blarneycastle.com).
Open *May* 9am-6.30pm Mon-Sat. *June-Aug* 9am-7pm
daily. *Sept* 9am-6.30pm daily. *Oct-Apr* 9am-dusk
Mon-Sat; 9.30am-5.30pm Sun. **Admission** €5.50;
€2-€4 concessions; €11.50 family.
No credit cards.

Blarney Woollen Mills

Blarney (021 438 5280/www.blarney.ie).
Open 9.30am-5.30pm Mon-Fri. **Admission** free.
Credit AmEx, DC, MC, V.

Cobh Heritage Centre

*Cobh Railway Station, Cobh (021 481 3591/
www.cobhheritage.com).* **Open** *Apr-Nov* 10am-5pm
daily. *Dec-Mar* 10am-4pm daily. **Admission** €5.
Credit MC, V.

Fota Wildlife Park

Carrigtwohill, Fota Island (021 481 2678). **Open**
Mar-Oct 10am-6pm Mon-Sat; 11am-6pm Sun. *Nov-
Mar* 10am-3pm Sat; 11am-3pm Sun. **Admission** €7;
€4.20 concessions; €27.90 family. **Credit** MC, V.

Old Jameson Distillery

*Midleton (021 461 3594/www.whiskeytours.ie/
www.jameson.ie).* **Open** *Nov-Feb* (by guided tour
only) 11.30am, 2.30pm, 4pm daily. *Mar-Oct* 10am-
6pm daily. **Admission** €5.75; €2.50-€5.10; €15
family. **Credit** AmEx, DC, MC, V.

Where to eat & drink

Café Gusto (3 Washington Street, 021 425
4446/www.cafegusto.com, closed Sun am) is
a good place for a snack lunch and serves the
best espressos in town. In the evening, don't
miss the haute vegetarian cuisine on offer in
the relaxed surroundings of **Café Paradiso**

(Lancaster Quay, Western Road, 021 427 7939,
main courses €11-€17.80). Another stand-out
spot is **Jacob's Mall** (South Mall, 021 425
1530, closed Sun, main courses €14.60-€21),
housed in a former Turkish baths. It's the best
place to eat in the city thanks to Mercy Fenton's
brilliant cooking.

Cork brews two excellent stouts, Murphy's
and Beamish, both noticeably sweeter than
Guinness. Other local brews can be tried at the
Franciscan Well Brew Pub (North Mall,
021 439 3434/www.franciscanwell brewery.ie),
which produces four own-brand beers. Another
good place for booze is the **Hi-B** (Oliver
Plunkett Street, 021 427 2758) an old-school,
upstairs bar with red leather couches, classical
music, erudite chat and creamy pints. Finally,
the **Long Valley** (Winthrop Street, 021 427
2144) is a splendidly eccentric boozer where
food is served all day. Be sure to indulge in a
doorstep sandwich.

Outside the city, there are two places in
Midleton deserving of your attention. At the
top end, **Ballymaloe House** (Shanagarry,
Midleton, 021 465 2531) is at the vanguard of
Irish country house cuisine, offering quality
ingredients, classically cooked (main courses
€24.70-€21.75, five-course dinner €55), while
the **Farm Gate** (Cool Bawn, Midleton, 021
463 2771, closed Sun & dinner Mon-Wed)
combines a shop with a restaurant that offers
particularly good lunches (main courses
€6.35-€8.90 lunch, €19 dinner).

Arts & entertainment

There is a lively entertainment scene in Cork
highlighted by the high-profile **Cork Jazz
Festival** in October (021 637 5219/www.cork
jazzfestival. com). Also at this time is the long-
running **International Film Festival** (021
427 1711/www.corkfilmfest.org), a prestigious
international showcase, specialising in short
films and new Irish cinema. Bear in mind
that hotels get booked up weeks in advance
for these events.

At other times of year you can expect
mainstream theatre at the **Cork Opera House**
(021 427 0022), and dance performances at the
Institute for Choreography & Dance in
Shandon (021 450 7487). The **Triskel Arts
Centre** (Tobin Street, 021 427 2022) is arguably
the most important of the city's cultural venues,
with a cinema, theatre, concert arena and art
gallery. For live music try one of the three
pubs on Union Quay – the **Donkey's Ears**,
the **Lobby** or the **Phoenix** – or the **Savoy
Theatre** (108 St Patrick's Street, 021 425 3000/
www.savoytheatre.ie), Cork's newest and best
gig venue and nightclub.

Where to stay

The **Imperial Hotel** (South Mall, 021 427 4040/ fax 021 427 5375/www.flynnhotels.com, rates €120) is a decent central option, or there's the **Victoria Inn** on Patrick Street/Cook Street (021 427 8788/fax 021 427 8790/www.thevictoriahotel. com, rates €76.20), where James Joyce once stayed. On the river, **Seven North Mall** (North Mall, 021 439 7191/fax 021 430 0811) is an attractive townhouse with pleasantly furnished rooms (rates €90-€120) and brill breakfasts.

If you don't want to stay in Cork City, try the **Blarney Castle Hotel** (021 438 5116/fax 021 438 5542/www.blarney-castle-hotel.com, rates €88), a small, family-run place, within kissing distance of its namesake. Elsewhere, the **Barnabrow Country House** in Cloyne, near Midleton (021 465 2534, fax 021 652 534, www.barnabrow house.com, closed Mon-Wed in winter, rates €114-€165) is good for a classic country house experience. All food is organic, including veggies from the hotel garden, and leisure facilites include a tennis court and donkey rides for children.

In Youghal, try **Aherne's** (163 North Main Street, 024 92424/fax 024 93633/www. ahernes.com), an upmarket choice with king-sized beds (rates €140-€260 suite) and a decent restaurant (main courses €11.40-€17.70).

Getting there

By car

Take the N11 out of Dublin, picking up the N25 at Wexford for a coastal route to Cork. If you're heading to West Cork use the Jack Lynch Tunnel to bypass the city centre.

By bus

Bus Eireann services connect Cork with Dublin (4hrs 30min, €26 return) and other major towns in Ireland. The bus station (021 450 8188) is at the junction of Parnell Place and Merchant's Quay.

By train

Train services from Dublin's Heuston station take 3hrs and cost €44.45-€53.35 return. Cork station (021 450 67665) is on Lower Glanmire Road.

By air

Aer Lingus (021 427 4331) connects Cork with Dublin and London Heathrow. The airport (021 431 3131) is 8km (5 miles) south of the city and there's a connecting bus service with departures every 30min (tickets €4.60 return). There's also a taxi rank outside the main terminal; the journey to the centre should cost about €10-€11.50.

By boat

There are daily ferry services Mar-Nov between Cork and Swansea in the UK with **Swansea Cork Ferries** (in Ireland 021 427 1166/in the UK 01792 456116/www.swansea-cork.ie) There are also weekly ferry connections to Roscoff in France with **Brittany Ferries** (021 427 7801/www.brittanyferries.com).

Tourist information

Cork & Kerry Tourism

Grand Parade (021 425 5100/www.corkkerry.ie). Open June, Sept 9am-6pm Mon-Sat. July, Aug 9am-7pm Mon-Sat; 10am-5pm Sun. Oct-May 9.15am-5.30pm Mon-Fri; 9.30am-4.30pm Sat.

Kinsale & around

Kinsale is the gateway to West Cork and one of Ireland's favourite tourist destinations. The prettiness of the town belies its tumultuous history: in 1601, Catholics from Ulster led by the Earl of Tyrone and Spanish troops fought alongside one another against the English in the infamous Battle of Kinsale. The Battle was a disaster for the Spanish and Irish, most of whom were bloodily slaughtered, and the event became a decisive moment in the English subjugation of Ireland. A pub on Pearse Street, the **1601**, commemorates the event.

Nowadays, Kinsale is better and rightly known as Ireland's gourmet capital – there's an annual festival to prove it – with seafood particularly prominent. The **Kinsale Gourmet Festival** (www.kinsale.ie/gfest.htm) is held for four days in October, with information and tickets available from the Kinsale Good Food Circle (*see p242*).

Desmond Castle on Cook Street is a 16th-century tower house that was occupied by the Spanish in 1601. It now houses a small wine museum. Other historic sites include the medieval **St Multose Church** and the **courthouse** on Market Square where the enquiry into the sinking of the *Lusitania* was held. **Charles Fort** at Summercove, to the south-east of town, is a substantial military structure dating from the 1670s. It was severely damaged during fighting in the 1922-3 Civil War but there are fine views of the harbour and the coast. For more stunning coastal scenery, make for the **Old Head of Kinsale**, a rocky headland that juts into the sea between Kinsale and Ballinspittle.

The coastline west of Kinsale is a pleasant muddle of villages and coves. **Ballinspittle** became briefly famous in the 1980s when locals claimed a statue of the Virgin Mary had begun to move. It still attracts pilgrims, but hasn't budged from its plinth lately. Next along the coast is **Timoleague**, where there are the ruins of a 13th-century Franciscan friary that was badly damaged by the British in 1642. It's also worth visiting **Timoleague Castle Gardens**,

Trips Out of Town

where Mediterranean plants thrive in sheltered conditions. The ruins of the 1920s castle can still be seen among the foliage.

Desmond Castle & International Museum of Wine
Cook Street, Kinsale (021 477 4855). **Open** (last entry 45min before closing) *Apr-June* 10am-6pm Tue-Sun. *June-Oct* 10-6pm daily. **Admission** €2.50; €1.20-€1.90 concessions; €6.30 family. **No credit cards**.

Timoleague Castle Gardens
N71, 11km south of Bandon (023 46116). **Open** *June-Aug* 11am-5.30pm Mon-Sat; 2-5.30pm Sun. **Admission** €3.80. **No credit cards**.

Where to eat

Some of the best restaurants in Kinsale club together to form the self-selected and self-promoting Good Food Circle (021 477 4026/www.kinsale.ie/kinsgour.htm). A complete list is given on the website, but we particularly like **Man Friday** (Scilly, Kinsale, 021 477 2260, closed Sun, main courses €17.50-€25) just outside town; a noisy, casual, fun setting for Philip Horgan's relaxed, full-flavoured food, and **Max's Wine Bar** (Main Street, 021 477 2443, closed Nov-Feb, main courses €15-€25) renowned for its outstanding menu and wine list. Another stand-out spot is the **Gourmet Store & Fishy Fishy Café** (Guardwell, 021 477 4453, closed Sun in winter, main courses €12), which offers some of the finest fish cooking you can find in Ireland, and plenty of seafood in the shop, too. The only problem is trying to get a table.

Where to stay

The **Blue Haven Hotel** (3-4 Pearse Street, 021 477 2209/fax 021 477 4268/www.bluehaven kinsale.com) is located in the centre of town and has 17 luxury en suite rooms (rates €140-€216). There's also a wine bar and a good nautically themed restaurant. Also in the centre is the well-equipped **Tierney's Guesthouse** (70 Main Street, 021 477 2205/fax 021 477 4363, rates €66). A top-quality bed and breakfast choice, with a superlative breakfast menu, is **Old Presbytery** (Cork Street, 021 477 2027/www.oldpres.com, rates €90-€115).

Getting there

By car
Kinsale is just south of Cork city on the N27.

By bus
Buses depart regularly from Cork three or four times a day. There are also two buses Monday to Friday from Cork to Timoleague.

West Cork

From Clonakilty to Mizen Head

Clonakilty is a pretty, bustling tourist town, with good nightlife and traditional music throughout the year, though its ultra-narrow main street makes the traffic troublesome. Michael Collins was born at Woodfield, west of Clonakilty. The family home was burned down by the Black and Tans, but it is still possible to visit the remains, which are marked as the **Michael Collins Memorial Centre**. For more on the struggle for independence in this part of Ireland, it's worth checking out the **West Cork Regional Museum** on Main Street, opposite the large gothic revival Catholic Church. East of town is the **Lisnagun Ring Fort**, a reconstructed tenth-century fortified settlement with a wattle and daub farmhouse and a souterrain (underground chamber), while to the south is huge, sandy **Inchydoney beach**.

The coast road from Clonakilty to Skibbereen snakes through a succession of villages and coves that are among the most charming in Cork. Stop off at **Castle Freke**, an 18th-century mansion in a romantically precarious state of decay and at **Drombeg Stone Circle**, a particularly well-preserved pre-Christian site thought to be aligned with the midwinter sunset. Near the small cathedral town of **Rosscarbery** is **Castle Salem**, an extraordinary edifice which combines a 17th-century farmhouse built onto the side of a 15th-century castle.

Skibbereen was founded in 1631 when the people of nearby Baltimore fled inland from Algerian raiders (strange but true). Its thriving atmosphere today belies the awful suffering and poverty with which it became synonymous during the Famine years. **Lough Hyne** (or 'Ine'), near Skibbereen, is a unique ecological halfway house, fed by the sea at high tide and by a freshwater stream at low tide. Its warm brackish water allows species from more southerly climes to thrive here. There are some lovely walks to be enjoyed in Knockomagh Woods beside the lake.

South-west along the coast is **Baltimore**, a pleasant fishing town that is overrun with deck-shoed yachties during the summer. From May to September it is possible to catch a ferry (028 39153/www.westcorkcoastalcruise.com, €13 return) from here to **Cape Clear Island**, a *gaeltacht* (Irish-speaking area; *see p257* **Gael talk**) with glorious scenic walks and vast numbers of migratory birds. There are also seven boats daily from Baltimore to **Sherkin Island** (028 20125), which has beautiful silver sandy beaches and lively pubs. The last boats return to the mainland quite early, and as pub opening hours on both islands are notoriously generous, it makes sense to stay overnight if you want to make the most of them.

Back on the mainland, the road winds through ridiculously pretty **Ballydehob**, where you can turn off the N71 for the Mizen Peninsula. **Schull** (pronounced 'skull') is overlooked by the towering peak of Mount Gabriel, topped by strange looking aircraft-tracking devices. There are boat services from here to Cape Clear Island, Sherkin Island and the **Fastnet Rock** (summer only). Beyond Schull the landscape becomes more barren, although the rock formations and steep cliffs along the coast are stunning.

At the end of the peninsula is an excellent but rarely crowded surfing beach at **Barleycove** and the atmospheric remains of a 13th-century castle at **Three Castles Head**. Ireland's southernmost tip is marked by **Mizen Head** lighthouse. The visitor centre houses an exhibition on the men who worked the lights before automation, but the views are far more attention-grabbing.

Mizen Head Visitor Centre

Mizen Head (028 35115/www.mizenvision.com). **Open** *Mid Mar-May, Oct* 10.30am-5pm daily. *June-Sept* 10am-6pm daily. *Nov-mid Mar* 11am-4pm Sat, Sun. **Admission** €4.50, €2.50-€3.50 concessions; free under-5s; €14 family. **Credit** *Gift shop only* AmEx, DC, MC, V.

West Cork Regional Museum

Western Road, Clonakilty (023 33104). **Open** *May-Nov* 10.30am-5pm Mon-Sat; 2pm-6pm Sun. **Admission** €2.50; €1.25 concessions; free children. **No credit cards.**

Bantry & the Beara Peninsula

Beyond Durrus is the **Sheep's Head Peninsula**, a beautifully green tract of land that forms the south-eastern shore of Bantry Bay. The lack of major sites or sandy beaches on the peninsula mean Sheep's Head is often missed by tourists, and villages such as Gearhies and Kilcrohane look as though the adjective 'sleepy' could have been invented just for them. Its spectacular scenery is best enjoyed by walking part of the 88-kilometre (55-mile) **Sheep's Head Way** – contact the tourist office in Bantry for details.

In 1796, a French armada left Brest for **Bantry** under the command of Dublin revolutionary Wolfe Tone (*see also p11*). Stormy conditions made landing impossible, but the aborted rebellion is still commemorated at the **French Armada Exhibition** at Bantry

House during the summer. The exhibition has some artefacts from the wreck of *La Surveillante* and a lifesize model of Wolfe Tone sitting in his cabin cursing the weather. It is ironic that the exhibition should be located in the grounds of **Bantry House**, the historic seat of the White family, since it was by notifying the English military in Cork about the impending invasion that Lord White gained his peerage. The house enjoys a magnificent position overlooking the bay and is well worth exploring, with Aubusson tapestries designed for Marie Antoinette and portraits of royalty in the Blue Dining Room. The beautiful gardens are also open to the public. Bantry House is the setting for the **West Cork Chamber Music Festival** in June (*see p185*).

Inland from Bantry is **Gougane Barra Forest Park**, which has a number of well-marked walks and is the most picturesque part of inland Cork. St Finbarr, the founder of Cork, once lived in an island hermitage here. To the west of Bantry are Glengariff and the Beara Peninsula.

Glengariff was a favourite tourist destination in the 19th century and remains popular with walkers. It's also a jumping off point for **Garinish Island**, which has an Italianate garden created by Harold Peto, who slipped over everything down to the soil. Boats leave every 20 minutes daily during the summer (027 63040, tickets €6.35-€7.60). Just outside the village is Cromwell's Bridge, allegedly built at an hour's notice, and the gentle peaks of Cobduff and Sugarloaf.

The **Beara Peninsula**, which Cork shares with Kerry, is one of the bleakest landscapes in Ireland, but also one of the most unspoilt and inspiring. It can be explored on the long-distance (197-kilometre/122-mile) Beara Way, which starts and finishes in Glengariff – contact the tourist office for details. Beyond Glengariff is **Castletownbere**, from where you can catch boats out to Bere Island. Just west of the town are the twin ruins of **Dunboy Castle** and **Puxley Mansion**. The first of these was the home of the O'Sullivan clan and was razed by the English in 1602, while the latter was built by the copper-mining Puxley family and burned down by the IRA during the Irish War of Independence. Daphne du Maurier's novel *Hungry Hill* is based on the Puxley family and named after the highest point on the peninsula (686 metres/over 2,000 feet). North of Castletownbere, the small village of Eyeries contains the largest Ogham stones in the country. At the end of the peninsula is **Allihies**, a pretty village with a single sandy beach. From here you can take a rickety cable car ride out to **Dursey Island**.

Bantry House & French Armada Exhibition

Bantry (027 50047). **Open** *Mar-Oct* 9am-6pm daily. **Admission** *House* €5; free under-16s. *Gardens & Armada exhibition* €4; free under-14s. **Credit** MC, V.

Where to eat

Fionnuala's in Clonakilty (Ashe Street, 023 34355, closed Mon, Tue from Sept to Easter) offers an Irish spin on Italian food in a great, humdinging room (main courses €8.90-€16.50). Further west, try the **Custom House** in Baltimore (028 20200, closed Oct-Mar, menus €23 or €33), which serves up well-crafted, free-spirited fish dishes at reasonable prices. For an unforgettable experience, though, catch the single boat at 7.55pm from Cunnamore (near Skibbereen) to **Island Cottage** on tiny Heir Island (028 38102, closed Mon, Tue & Oct-Apr) for a stunning set menu of five courses (€27), with highlights such as Cape Clear turbot. Don't miss the perennially popular and newly energised cooking at **O'Connor's Seafood Restaurant** in Bantry (The Square, 027 50221, main courses €15-€23) or the funky and good value modern lunches (main courses €6-€7) at **The Pantry** on New Street (027 52181, closed Sun). For simple pub food plus the odd eclectic delicacy, try **The Snug** (The Quay, Bantry, 027 50057, main courses €7, dinner €8.25-€17). Beyond Bantry, **Larchwood House**

Restaurant (Pearson's Bridge, Ballylickey, 027 66181, closed Mon-Wed in winter) serves hip cooking – lettuce and rhubarb soup for starters, for example, – in domestic, unhip surroundings (dinner €35.50).

Where to stay

The Lodge & Spa at Inchydoney Island, Clonakilty (023 33143/fax 023 35229/www.inchydoneyisland.com, rates €235) is the place for an utter treat, with extensive spa facilities, including a heated seawater pool, seaweed wraps, massages and beauty treatments. The newly refurbished **West Cork Hotel** (Glen Street, 028 21277/fax 028 22333/www.westcorkhotel.com) is a good choice in Skibbereen (rates €89-€130) with a terrific restaurant (lunch €15.90, dinner €21-€30). In Bantry, **Vickery's Inn Guest House** (New Street, tel/fax 027 50006/www.westcork.com/vickerys-inn, rates €70) has been a family-owned guesthouse since 1850 and has a fully licensed restaurant. More upmarket is **Ballylicky Manor House** (Ballylicky, 027 50071/www.ballylickey manorhouse.com, closed Nov-Feb, rates €178-€304), which has an outdoor heated swimming pool, a large garden and access to golfing, fishing and sailing nearby. In Glengarriff, try **Eccles Hotel** (027 63003/fax 027 63319/www.eccles hotel.com, rates €80-€120), which has a good seafood restaurant.

Rush hour on the lake in **Killarney National Park**. *See p245.*

Getting there

By car

The N71 runs from Cork city to Clonakilty, and on through Rosscarbery to Skibbereen, Ballydehob and eventually Bantry.

By bus

There are three buses daily from Cork to Clonakilty, with connections to Skibbereen, Ballydehob and Schull. Skibbereen is also served by buses from Cork and Killarney. Three buses a day run between Cork and Bantry, with summer buses to Killarney via Clonakilty, Skibbereen, Bantry and Glengarriff.

Tourist information

The Cork city tourist office can provide information for the whole county, but there are also offices in **Clonakilty** (Ashe Street, 023 33226), **Skibbereen** (Town Hall, North Street, 028 21766), **Bantry** (027 50229) and **Glengarriff** (027 70054), although opening hours may be slightly erratic out of season.

County Kerry

Kerry is a county of contrasts: staggering natural beauty and leaping leprechaun T-shirt shops, fine traditional music and tourist extravaganzas, outstanding gourmet restaurants and greasy chippers. Don't be put off, though. It takes little effort to peel back the plastic façade and dip into a treasure trove of panoramic scenery, historical sites, and cultural experiences that are hard to surpass.

Killarney & around

Many west coast towns have met economic decline by repackaging themselves as tourist attractions. Killarney is the exception: a tourist trap is all it's ever been, custom-built by Lord Kenmare in the peerless setting of its lakes and jagged mountains. Sir Walter Scott, Thackeray, Maria Edgeworth and Tennyson all passed through, but the apogee of Killarney's pastoral theming was reached when Queen Victoria took tea in a small cottage built specially for the few minutes she spent there.

August Pugin's St **Mary's Cathedral** on Cathedral Place is among his best work, but three other churches are also worth a visit. The Anglican **St Mary's Church** on Main Street is a neo-Gothic wonder, the diminutive **Methodist Church** on Countess Road has an unusual Lutyens-like interior, and the **Franciscan Friary** on Fair Hill has a spectacular Belgian-style altar containing

the skull of a 17th-century friar. The **National Museum of Irish Transport** in Scott's Gardens has a fine collection of antique bikes, carriages and cars, including a 1910 Wolsley driven by Ireland's first woman MP, Constance Markievicz, with WB Yeats in the passenger seat. While you're in town, take time to enjoy some good shops selling local woollen products, pottery and linens.

Immediately south-west of town (with pedestrian access from Cathedral Place) is **Killarney National Park**, which offers beautiful lake and mountain scenery that's perfect for walking and cycling, plus a number of historic sights. The park is studded with glacial lakes, the biggest of which is **Lough Leane** or 'the lake of learning'. The lake is dotted with over 30 small islands including **Innishfallen**, quarantine-cum-sanctuary for the seventh-century St Finan the Leper. The *Annals of Innishfallen*, now held in the Bodleian Library in Oxford, were written here in the 13th century. On the island are the ruins of a 12th-century oratory, while on the shores of the lake is the 15th-century **Ross Castle**. This was one of the last local fortresses to hold out against Cromwell before finally succumbing in 1652. There are excellent guided tours of the castle, and rowing boats (€3.20 per person per hour) or motorboats (€5) to Innishfallen can be hired from outside from April to October (064 34351).

On the eastern edge of the park, a few kilometres south of Killarney, you'll find **Muckross House**, a wonderfully restored estate house, with extensive gardens full of unusual flora and fauna. Also on the estate is the **Kerry Country Life Experience**, which offers glimpses into the past through recreated working farms and craft shops. From the house, a number of peaceful lanes and paths lead into the heart of the National Park. The remains of the 15th century Muckross Abbey, with its stunning cloisters, are a short cycle ride away. A little beyond Muckross is **Torc Waterfall**, where you can join the **Kerry Way** walking trail. This 214-kilometre (133-mile) route passes through the Macgillycuddy's Reeks – which include Carrauntoohill, the highest mountain in Ireland at 1,040 metres (3,411 feet) – and right around the Iveagh Peninsula, starting and finishing in Killarney. For further information, contact the Killarney Tourist Office.

Continuing further south on the Kenmare Road, **Ladies View**, overlooking the Long Range, offers a celebrated and stunning view that was much admired by Queen Victoria's ladies-in-waiting in 1861. At the very western edge of the park is the **Gap of Dunloe**, a dramatic mountain pass leading to the isolated Black Valley. The Gap is a very popular tourist

Trips Out of Town

outing from Killarney and often clogged with ponies and 'jaunting cars', but if you time your visit carefully, it is still possible to escape the hordes and make your way through the pass on foot. The rather silly jaunting cars (glorified horse-drawn carriages) wait for customers near Kenmare Place and Muckross House and have been transporting visitors around the area for over a century.

Muckross House & Kerry Country Life Experience

Kenmare Road, Killarney (064 31440). Open 9am-6pm daily. Admission €5-€6.35; €3.80 concessions. No credit cards.

National Museum of Irish Transport

Scott's Garden, East Avenue, Killarney (064 346 77). Open Apr-Oct 10am-6pm daily. Closed Nov-Mar. Admission €3.80; €2.55 concessions. No credit cards.

Ross Castle

Ross Road (064 35851). Open Apr-Oct 9am-6.30pm daily. Admission €3.80. No credit cards.

Where to eat & drink

Restaurants in Killarney are a mixed bag varying from low-grade fast-food joints to sleek, contemporary eateries. **Gaby's** (27 High Street, 064 32519, closed Sun & Feb-early Mar) offers casual dining with a range of mostly seafood and some meat dishes (main courses €21.60-€44), while **The Cooperage** (Old Market Lane, 064 37716) attracts fashionable, well-heeled locals with its innovative, modern menu (main courses €11.40-€21.50). Pub life in Killarney can be a bit frustrating, consisting of formulaic tourist sing-a-long sessions or bars full of singles seeking companionship.

Where to stay

At the top end, try the newly refurbished **Great Southern Hotel** in Killarney (East Avenue, 064 31262/fax 064 31642/www.greatsouthern hotels.com) for Georgian elegance and a hushed atmosphere, or the perfect period decor of **Muckross Park Hotel** in the heart of the National Park (064 31938/fax 064 31965/ www.muckrosspark.com, closed late Nov-mid Feb, rates €124-€178). Options close to the centre include **Orchard House** (Fleming's Lane, 064 31879, rates €25.40 per person) and **Ross Hotel** (Kenmare Place, 064 31855/fax 064 36399, closed Dec-Feb, rates €100-€130) where you'll find friendly staff and generally older guests. Most backpackers flock to the extraordinarily popular **Sugar Kitchen Hostel** (Lewis Road, 064 33104, rates €11.40 per person), although the quarters are cramped.

Getting there

By car

From Dublin, take the N7 to Limerick, the N21 to Castleisland, the N23 to Farranfore, then the N22 into Killarney. The journey takes about 5hrs. Cork to Killarney is a scenic drive of about 2hrs on the N22.

By bus

There are daily **Bus Eireann** services between Dublin and Killarney, although the journey takes a painfully slow 7hrs (€28.60 return). Services also run between Killarney and most major towns, including Cork, Limerick, Galway, Waterford and Rosslare.

By train

Trains to Killarney depart daily from Cork and Dublin via Mallow and Limerick (064 31067). The journey from Heuston station takes 4hrs and fares are about €45.

By air

Kerry County Airport (066 976 4644) is approximately 19km (12 miles) from Killarney and has daily services from Dublin (Aer Arran) and London Stanstead (Ryan Air). A taxi to the town centre costs about €19.

Tourist information

Killarney Tourist Office

Beech Road (064 31633/fax 064 64506/www. ireland.travel.ie). Open May-Sept 9am-6pm daily. Sept-Apr 9.15am-1pm, 2.15pm 5.30pm Mon-Sat. Also contact Cork & Kerry Tourism (see p241).

The Ring of Kerry & the Skellig Islands

Circuiting the Macgillycuddy Reeks mountain range and the Iveragh peninsula, the **Ring of Kerry** is the scenic drive to end all scenic drives. However, its beauty means it is also unbelievably popular; so popular in fact that it should be avoided altogether in high season, when geriatric tour buses trawl bumper to bumper along the roads. At other times of year, though, put some distance between yourself and the coaches and take in some of the finest countryside Ireland has to offer.

Kenmare at the southern head of the peninsula is home to the first suspension bridge of its kind in Ireland. Lace-making is associated with the town's Poor Clare nuns: examples can be seen in the local history exhibition at the **Kenmare Heritage Centre** in the Courthouse. Heading west, the countryside gets barer and more windswept as you approach **Sneem** ('knot' in Irish). For salmon and brown trout fishing, try nearby **Lough Fadda**, but for good sandy beaches, keep going for Westcove and Castlecove near **Caherdaniel**. Some 4,000 years ago, this small village exported copper ore to Spain for smelting, but its principal attraction today is **Derrynane House**, one time residence of Daniel O'Connell. The house is full of artefacts from the life of the 'Great Liberator', and is right next to an excellent beach. Chief among other attractions in the area is **Staigue Fort**, near Castlecove. This well-preserved Irish stone fort is 2,000 years old, with circular dry stone walls that are five and-a-half metres (18 feet) high and nearly four metres (13 feet) thick.

After **Waterville**, a left turn takes you on a scenic detour along the coast to Portmagee for access to the celebrated **Skellig Islands**. The furthest west of the Skelligs, **Skellig Michael**, harboured a religious community from the seventh to the 13th centuries in a cluster of tiny beehive huts. You can reach it by boat from Ballinskelligs, Portmagee and Valentia during the summer (weather permitting) for about €25. Expert local guides will help you explore the island, with its monastic buildings and rare birds. Like the other two islands, **Little Skellig** and **Puffin Island**, it's home to large colonies of puffins, gannets, guillemots and razorbills.

For more information on the Skelligs, visit the **Skellig Experience** on **Valentia**, a far larger island located just off the mainland coast to the north. The centre provides an insight into the life of the monks of Skellig Michael, a history of the Skellig lighthouses, and a look at the amazing wildlife on the islands today. In its Victorian boom years, Valentia's quarry produced slate for some of the finest building in the British Isles, including the Houses of Parliament, but it was closed down in 1884 and is now a rather eerie place. Valentia's other claim to fame is as the site of the first transatlantic telegraph cables in the mid-19th century. For several weeks it was possible to telegraph New York from here, but not Dublin. The eclectic and excellent **Valentia Heritage Museum**, on the road to the quarry, has an intact schoolroom and information on the local linen-making and dyeing crafts, plus lively displays on local history.

Back on the Ring of Kerry, the next town is **Caherciveen**, where the chief attraction is **Leacanabuaile Fort**, a round stone fort containing three beehive huts. Towering over Caherciveen is **Seefin**, seat of the legendary giant Fin. As you leave town, the ruins of Daniel O'Connell's birthplace, **Carhan House**, are on the right. The road becomes more mountainous en route to the old-fashioned seaside resort of **Glenbeigh**. The expansive beach has plenty of sand space, and adjacent

hill trails provide breathtaking views. **Killorglin** is the final stop on the Ring. Each August the town hosts the **Puck Fair**, the oldest festival in Europe, based on an ancient fertility rite. A wild mountain goat is crowned king for three days and keeps a watchful eye over non-stop merrymaking in the Town Square.

Derrynane National Historic House & Park

near Caherdaniel (066 947 5113). **Open** *Nov-Mar* 1-5pm Sat, Sun. *Apr, Oct* 1-5pm Tue-Sun. *May-Sept* 9am-6pm Mon-Sat; 11am-7pm Sun. **Admission** €2.50; €1.25-€1.90 concessions. **No credit cards.**

Kenmare Heritage Centre

Town Square, Kenmare (064 41233). **Open** *May-Oct* 9am-6pm Mon-Sat; 10am-5pm Sun. Closed Nov-Apr. **Admission** free.

Skellig Experience

Valentia Island (066 947 6306). **Open** *Apr-June* 9.30am-7pm daily. *July-Sept* 10am-7pm daily. *Oct-mid Nov* 10am-5.30pm Mon-Thur, Sun. Closed mid Nov-Mar. **Admission** €4.50; €2.25-€3.80 concessions. **Credit** MC, V.

Valentia Heritage Centre

Old School Road, near Knightstown, Valentia Island (066 947 6411). **Open** *Easter-Sept* 10am-5pm daily. **Admission** €1.50. **No credit cards.**

Where to eat

In Kenmare, try **An Leath Phingin** (35 Main Street, 064 41559, closed Wed), which offers refined, Italianate cooking (main courses €11.40-€17.80). In Killorglin, **Nick's Restaurant** (Bridge Street Lower, 066 976 1219, closed Nov) offers fresh seafood (main courses €15.25-€22.90) and a raucous atmosphere, while the **Bianconi** (Annadale Road, 066 976 1146) serves reliable pub food (main courses €7.60) and restaurant fare (€14-€21.60). It also has rooms (rates €82-€95). For a real treat, though, make your way to **Brennan's Restaurant** in Caherciveen (12 Main Street, 066 947 2021, closed Mon & Sun in winter). It's one of the best-kept secrets on the Ring of Kerry with incredible seafood (main courses €13-€22).

Where to stay

The **Sive Hostel** (15 East End Street, Caherciveen, 066 947 2717, rates per person €10.80 dormitory, €12.70-€15.90 room) is comfortable and welcoming, with pretty views, while **Sleepers Nest** in Glenbeigh (066 976 9666/fax 066 976 9667/www.glenbeigh.net, closed Oct-Mar, rates €78) is a popular summer

Trips Out of Town

spot with well-informed staff. In the centre of Killorglin you'll find **Bianconi** (*see above*), while on the outskirts of the village is the **Laune Valley Farm Hostel** (066 976 1488, launehostel@ireland.com, rates €10 per person dorm, €28). For travellers with money to burn, the only place to stay is **Sheen Falls Lodge** (Kenmare, 064 41600/fax 064 41386/ www.sheenfalls lodge.ie, rates €240-€485 double; €413-€585 suite). Regarded as one of the best hotels in the world, it offers guests unadulterated luxury.

Getting there & around

If you don't have your own transport, **buses** leave Killarney twice daily, stopping at Caherciveen, Waterville, Caherdaniel and Sneem. Contact the tourist office in Killarney (*see p246*) for details.

Tourist information

Kenmare Tourist Office

Kenmare Heritage Centre, Town Square, Kenmare (064 41233/www.kenmare.com). **Open** *June-Aug* 9am-6pm Mon-Sat; 10am-5pm Sun. *May, June, Sept, Oct* 9.15am-1pm, 2.15pm- 5.30pm daily. Closed Nov-May.

Dingle Peninsula & around

Jutting out far into the Atlantic, the Dingle Peninsula is the wildest and most Gaelic part of Kerry. It combines the stunning Conor Pass, the poignancy of the depopulated Blasket Islands and the majesty of Mount Brandon.

The best place to start is **Tralee**, which hosts the **Rose of Tralee Festival** in August, Ireland's softly-softly answer to Miss World. Otherwise, the main attractions are the **Kerry County Museum** and the **Siamsa Tíre** National Folk Theatre, whose new arts centre on the Town Park (066 712 3055/ www.siamsa tire.com) looks like a drive-through Newgrange. You can also visit **Kerry the Kingdom**, which combines a good museum with a silly ride around imaginary 15th-century Tralee. Sewer smells are piped in for authenticity. Outside the town is **Blennerville windmill** (built in 1800 and now restored to full working order).

The next town west, **Castlegregory**, is on a spit of land between Tralee and Brandon bays and has a fine sandy surf beach. Further west towers **Mount Brandon**, sacred to St Brendan and affording spectacular views of the bay. The narrow **Conor Pass** winds through a glacial valley, amid sheer cliffs and boulder-strewn wilderness, bringing you eventually to Dingle.

Fungi does his stuff.

Dingle was an important port in medieval times, but now depends chiefly on tourism. An Atlantic bottlenosed dolphin called Fungi arrived in the bay in 1984 and has been there ever since, inspiring a thriving line in T-shirts, mugs and keyrings. If the water isn't too cold, get in and introduce yourself: he's fond of human swimming partners, particularly women and children. Back on dry land, **Dingle Oceanworld** has a sea tank teeming with local sea life, plus a display of St Brendan's journey across the Atlantic. At night Dingle throbs with excellent traditional music: to sample some of the best try either **An Droichead Beg** or **O'Flaherty's** on any night of the week.

Beyond Dingle, make your way along the coast road to the **Celtic & Prehistoric Museum** in the tiny village of Ventry. It's one of the best small museums in Ireland, with an astounding collection of fossils, the head of a woolly mammoth, plus jewellery and tools from the Iron Age onwards.

On the tip of the peninsula, **Dunquin** is the jumping off point for the **Blasket Islands**. The islands are now uninhabited on a full-time basis, although one is the holiday home of former Taoiseach Charles Haughey. Boats leave Dunquin harbour daily for **Great Blasket** (the main island) from May to September (weather permitting). There's not much in the way of facilities once you get there, but it's pleasingly isolated and good for walking. An **Interpretive Centre** at Dunquin offers plenty of information on the communities that used to live on the islands.

From Dunquin, continue to **Ballyferriter** and follow the road signs for the **Gallarus Oratory**, the best-preserved early Christian church in Ireland. Perhaps best described as a minimalist chapel, the dry-stone building is 12 centuries old, and stands in near-perfect condition, every slate intact. There are a number of these religious structures – known

as 'beehive huts' – on the peninsula: the earliest
had a round shape, but the Gallarus Oratory
is boat-shaped. Nearby is **Kilmalkedar**, a
12th-century Romanesque church and part of
a complex of buildings thought to have once
housed a sophisticated religious community.
Also close to Ballyferriter is **Reasc**, an entire
monastic settlement that was excavated in
the 1980s. Among the remains are several
decorative pillar stones featuring early
Christian artwork. For a site with more recent
historical flavour, visit the **Dun An Oir
Promontory Fort** just north of Ballyferriter.
In 1580 it was held by an invading force of
Spanish and Italian mercenaries, who joined
with Irish rebels ready to take on the English.
English troops, led by Lord Grey, and including
Walter Raleigh and Edmund Spenser laid
seige to the fort for three days until the rebels
surrendered. Six hundred people were executed.

Heading back to Dingle, follow the south
coast of the peninsula to **Lough Annascaul** –
good for fishing and hikes – and **Inch**, which
has one of the best beaches in the whole county.

Blennerville Windmill

Blennerville, Tralee (066 712 1064). **Open** *Apr-Oct*
9.30am-6pm daily. Closed Nov-Mar. **Admission**
€3.80; €1.90-€3.20 concessions; €9.50 family.
No credit cards

Celtic & Prehistoric Museum

*Kilvicadownic, Ventry, Dingle (066 915 9941/
www.dinglewest.com)* **Open** *Mar-Oct* 9.30am-5.30pm
daily. **Admission** €3.80; €3.20 concessions; €12.70
family. **No credit cards**.

Dingle Oceanworld

*near Dingle Harbour, The Wood, Dingle (066 915
2111/www.dingle-oceanworld.ie)*. **Open** 10am-5pm
daily. **Admission** €7; €4.20-€6 concessions; €19
family. **Credit** AmEx, DC, MC, V.

Dunquin Interpretative Centre

*The Great Blasket Centre, Dunquin, Tralee (066 915
6444/6371/www.heritageireland.ie)*. **Open** *Easter-
July, Sept-Oct* 10am-6pm daily. *Aug* 10am-7pm daily.
Closed Nov-Mar. **Admission** €3.10; €1.20-€2.20
concessions; €7.60 family. **No credit cards**.

Kerry County Museum

*Ashe Memorial Hall, Denny Street, Tralee (066 712
7777/www.kerrymuseum.com)*. **Open** *Mar-Oct*
9.30am-5.30pm daily. *Nov, Dec* 11.30am-4.30pm
daily. Closed Jan, Feb. **Admission** €7; €3.80
concessions. **Credit** V.

Where to eat

In Dingle, the **Beginish Restaurant** on Green
Street (066 915 1321, closed Mon) serves smart
and delicious cooking (main courses €17-€27)
in a wonderful atmosphere. Another option is

the **Chart House Restaurant** (066 915
2255, closed Tue & Jan, Feb), which offers
contemporary cuisine with innovative
combinations (main courses €14.91-€22.79).
In Tralee you can dine in the former kitchen
and wine cellar of the ruling Denny family's
Georgian house: **Finnegan's Cellar
Restaurant** (17 Denny Street, 066 718 1400)
offers an exciting modern menu and superb
value (main courses €11.75-€21.50). If you're
heading towards Limerick, stop in at **Allo's
Bar & Bistro** at 41 Church Street, Listowel
(068 22880, closed Mon) for creative cooking
(main courses €7.55-€23.50) and a splendid bar.

Where to stay

There's farmhouse accommodation and
organic, vegetarian food on offer just south
of the peninsula at **Phoenix Farmhouse**
(Shanahill East, Castlemaine, 066 976 6284,
closed Nov-Mar, rates €42). In Dingle, try
Alpine House (Mail Road, Dingle, 066 915
1250/fax 066 915 1966, rates €52-€80), which
has a central location and good facilities or the
Dingle Skellig Hotel (066 915 1144/fax 066
915 1501/www.dingleskellig.com, closed Mon
& Sun Nov-Feb, rates €130). To the west is the
Smerwick Harbour Hotel (Gallarus Cross,
Ballyferriter, 066 915 6470/fax 066 915 6473/
www.smerwickhotel.com, closed mid Nov-Jan,
rates €76-€128), where a high standard of
accommodation is complemented by welcoming
staff. On the north coast, make for the **Conor
Pass Hostel** (Stradbally, near Castlegregory,
066 713 9179/fax 066 713 9533, closed Nov-Mar,
rates €11), where you'll enjoy a spectacular
location and comfortable beds.

Getting there & around

Buses travel from Tralee and Killarney daily
to Dingle. A further bus runs from Dingle
to Dunquin, passing the villages in between;
the earliest connects with the **ferries** leaving
Dunquin for the Blasket Islands. Another ferry
travels between Valentia Island and
Caherciveen twice daily.

Tourist information

Tralee Tourist Office

*Ashe Memorial Hall, Tralee (066 712 1288/
fax 066 712 1700/www.shannon-dev.ie/tourism)*.
Open *Mar-July* 9am-6pm Mon-Sat. *July, Aug* 9am-
7pm daily. *Sept-Nov* 9am-6pm Mon-Sat. *Nov-Feb*
9am-5pm Mon-Fri.
There is also a seasonal tourist office on the Quay
in Dingle (066 915 1188), which is open from March
to August only.

County Clare

First settled by the mysterious Fir Bolg, according to the *Old Irish Book of Invasions*, Clare is as rich in landscape and history as anywhere in the West of Ireland. The Anglo-Norman conquest only reached the area when Thomas de Clare (from Gloucester) built Bunratty Castle in 1277. The de Clares were expelled in 1318, and did not re-establish control over the area until the 16th century. The county was reduced to ruins by Cromwell's troops, but its Irish nobility still harboured hopes of restoring their rule. A number of Clare families fought on the losing side at the Battle of the Boyne, before going into exile on the continent. Thereafter Clare settled down to a century and a half of Protestant ascendancy, broken only by the emergence of Kerry-born Daniel O'Connell, who was elected member of parliament for Clare in 1828. Clare was also Eamon De Valera's constituency in a by-election of 1917. De Valera remained TD (Dáil deputy) for Clare until 1959, when he became President of Ireland.

Ennis & around

The cathedral town of **Ennis** is the largest town in Clare, and has a medieval flavour with narrow, one-way streets and shopfronts noted for their colour and style. Traditional arts are highly prized and cultivated here, and the town hosts the annual **Fleadh Nua** festival each May (065 684 2988/www.fleadhnua.com) featuring traditional music, song, dance and story telling. The town's focal point is the Daniel O'Connell **monument**. From here, it's only a short walk to the **Clare County Museum**, located in a restored convent, with a display devoted to De Valera, and **Ennis Friary**, a striking building dating from 1242, which boasts lancet windows and the impressive alabaster carved tomb of the MacMahon family.

Nine kilometres (six miles) north of Ennis is the early Christian site of **Dyseart O'Dea**. Remains include a church, round tower and the White Cross, featuring carvings depicting Daniel in the lion's den. There is a small museum on the site. To the south-east of Ennis meanwhile, is **Quin Abbey**, a well-preserved Franciscan friary with an attractive cloister and tower, and **Knappogue Castle**, which was spared destruction by Cromwell. It's worth a look for its skillfully restored interior with superb decorations, and there are medieval banquets to boot (phone for details).

Just off the Knappogue–Sixmilebridge road is **Craggaunowen**, a heritage site with reconstructed ancient dwellings, displays of craftwork and exhibits. The replica *currach* (leather-hulled boat) is much like the one purportedly used by St Brendan to sail to America. It was built by Tim Severin, who successfully crossed the Atlantic in it in 1976.

Compared to windswept Blarney Castle, **Bunratty Castle**, just outside Limerick City, is luxury itself, and hosts nightly banquets in the former great hall of the earls of Thomond. This tourist extravaganza should not detract from the value of visiting this 15th-century castle, though, which has an impressive range of original furniture and fittings. In the grounds, a folk park contains a reconstruction of an entire Tudor village, including a pub whose period decor looks unwittingly modern. During the summer, authentically dressed traditional craft workers demonstrate weaving and butter churning to rapt audiences.

Bunratty Castle & Folk Park

Bunratty, N18 (061 360 788/061 361 511/ www.shannonheritage.com). **Open** *Castle* June-Sept 9am-4.15pm daily; Oct-May 9.30am-5.30pm daily. *Park* June-Sept 9am-6.30pm daily; Oct-May 9.30am-5.30pm daily. **Admission** €7.35-€9.50; €4.20-€5.30 concessions. **Credit** AmEx, DC, MC. V.

Clare County Museum

Arthur's Row, Ennis (065 682 3382/ www.clarelibrary.ie). **Open** *Mar, May, Oct-Dec* 9.30am-5.30pm Mon-Sat. *June-Sept* 9.30am-5.30pm daily. *Jan, Feb* 9.30am-5.30pm Mon-Fri. **Admission** €3.50; €1.50-€2.50 concessions; €10 family; free under-5s. **No credit cards**.

Craggaunowen Project

Kilmurray, Sixmile Bridge, near Ennis (061 36778). **Open** *Apr-Sept* 10am-5.45pm daily. Closed Nov-Mar. **Admission** €6.35; €2.70-€3.80 concessions. **Credit** MC, V.

Ennis Friary

Town Centre, Abbey Street, Ennis (065 682 9100) **Open** *May-Oct* 10am-6pm daily. Closed Nov-Apr. **Admission** €1.25; 50¢-88¢ concessions; €3.80 family. **No credit cards**.

Knappogue Castle

near Ennis (061 368 103). **Open** *Easter-Oct* 9.30am-4.30pm daily. Closed Nov-Mar. **Admission** €3.80; €2.50 concessions; €9.50 family. **No credit cards**.

The Burren & around

Covering a total area of some 300 square kilometres (116 square miles), the karstic limestone plain of the Burren is one of the most unusual natural features of the Irish landscape. The limestone was formed a hundred million years ago into an alternating mosaic of slabs

Rock steady: **Poulnabrone Dolmen** on the Burren.

and crevices known as 'clints' and 'grykes', which have remained largely unaltered since the Ice Age and gave the area its name – in Irish, *An Bhoireann* means 'the rocky place'. There are relics of human habitation believed to date back to 4000 BC, including 60 wedge tombs. The most famous of these tombs is the **Poulnabrone Dolmen**, located between Ballyvaughan and Corofin, though tourists have been known to mistake it on brochures for a folksy Irish bus shelter.

Tim Robinson's map, which lists all the monuments, fairy forts and other curiosities of the area, is something of a must-purchase for Burren field trips of any length. You might also want to take part in an excellent guided walk led by **Burren Hill Walks** (065 707 7168).

One of Cromwell's commanders, Edmund Ludlow, said the Burren lacked 'water enough to drown a man, nor a tree to hang him, nor soil enough to bury him', but it would be wrong to assume the Burren is devoid of wildlife. While you're here, you might spot such rarities as the pearl-bordered fritillary butterfly, the bloody cranesbill, mountain avens, hoary rock rose and many kinds of orchids.

Over the millenia, rainwater has carved out underground rivers and caverns in the remarkable geology of County Clare, making the Burren hugely popular with pot-holing enthusiasts. Only **Ailwee Cave** is open to

the public, but it makes an good introduction to the underside of the county. The network of caves was once a hibernation site for bears. Don't panic, the last ones cleared out several thousand years ago.

If the Burren feels too lonely, **Lisdoonvarna** will provide the perfect antidote. This Victorian spa town hosts an annual matchmaking festival in September and October. Another attraction of sorts is the **Bath House**, where you can take a smelly, but supposedly recuperative, dip in the sulphurous water. Nearby the small cathedral town of **Kilfenora** boasts none other than the Pope himself as its bishop, though he hasn't been seen in the area any time recently. The impressive mini-cathedral has an 800-year-old Doorty High Cross, with a superbly rendered Celtic pattern. There's also a **Burren Display Center** here – a good spot for maps, literature and displays about the region. About two miles east of Kilfenora is **Leamaneh Castle**, which combines a 15th-century tower with a mid 17th-century house built by Connor O'Brien, who later died fighting Cromwell. Nearby, on the R476 north from Corofin, the ruined church in **Killanboy** is worth visiting for its *sheelagh-na-gig* (*see p232*), located over the doorway.

The road north from **Lahinch** leads to the spectacular **Cliffs of Moher**, rising majestically from the swirling sea to a height

On the edge: the mighty **Cliffs of Moher**.
See p251.

of 203 metres (656 feet). The vistas are consistently impressive and the sounds of the ocean beating against the cliffs below make for an exhilarating experience. The best panoramic views can be had from **O'Brien's Tower**, built as a lookout in the 19th century. North of here is the village of **Doolin**, a perfect base from which to explore this whole area. Doolin contains perhaps the greatest concentration of traditional musicians anywhere in the country, with most of them congregating in **McGann's** and **Gus O'Connor's** pubs. There are also some decent restaurants and accommodation options though they can get very booked up in high season. Ferry and flight services operate from Doolin to the Aran Islands in County Galway (*see p258*).

Ailwee Cave

South of Ballyvaughan, off N67 (065 707 7036/ www.ailweecave.ie). **Open** 10am-5pm daily. **Admission** €7.50; €4.50 concessions. **No credit cards.**

Burren Display Centre

Kilfenora (065 708 8030). **Open** *Mar-May, Oct* 10am-5pm daily. *June-Sept* 9.30am-6pm daily. Closed Nov-Apr. **Admission** €6; €5 concessions. **Credit** MC, V.

Resources

Where to eat

As an alternative to pub fare in Ennis try **Numero Uno** (3 Barrack Street, 065 684 1740, closed Mon) for fabulous pizzas (€6-€9.15). The **Sherwood Inn** (065 682 0255, closed Sun) also serves generous portions at budget prices (main courses €5-€8). Enjoy a traditional Irish tea at the **An Fear Gorta Tearooms**, Pier Road in Ballyvaughan (065 707 7077/ 707 7157, closed Oct-May, tea €5.70-€8.25) or, for something more innovative, try the interesting menu at **Doolin Café** (Upper Village, Doolin, 065 707 4795, closed Jan, Feb and Mon-Fri in Dec, main courses €12.70-€19).

Where to stay

Ennis has a variety of accommodation for most budgets. At the lower end, try the cheerful rooms and lively bar at the **Auburn Lodge Hotel** (Galway Road, 065 682 1247/fax 065 682 1232, rates €57 per person), or the **Queens Hotel** (Abbey Street, 065 682 8963/fax 065 682 8628, rates €57 per person), which enjoys a central location near the sights.

In Ballyvaughan you can live the luxurious life at **Gregans Castle Hotel** (065 707 7005/ fax 065 707 7111/www.gregans.ie, closed Mon-

Wed in winter, rates €196-€270 double, €350-€400 suite) or enjoy the friendly and comfortable **Gentian Villa** (Main Road, 065 707 7042, closed Nov-Mar, rates from €40). In Doolin, the **Ballinalacken Castle Country House** (Coast Road, 065 707 4025/ www.ballinalackencastle.com, closed Oct-Apr, rates €101-€150) is a charming 1840 estate house with spectacular views, while the **Aille River Hostel** (065 707 4260, closed Jan, rates €11 dorm; €23-€25 double) is relaxed, friendly and good value. Inland, **Kincora Hotel** in Lisdoonvarna (065 707 4300/fax 065 7074490/ www.kincora-hotel.com, closed Nov-Mar, rates €64-€124) is an elegant, welcoming choice.

Getting there

By car

Take the N7 from Dublin to Limerick, then on to the N18 to Ennis. The journey takes a little under 4hrs. The R476 runs north from Ennis to Corofin. At Leamaneh Castle, take the R400 north to Ballyvaughan, then east to the Burren.

By bus

Bus Eireann services link Ennis with Dublin (4hrs 30min; €20.30), Cork (3hrs; €21) and Galway (1hr 20min; €14.60). The bus station (065 682 4177) is a 10min walk from the centre of Ennis. There is also a direct service between Doolin and Dublin and, during the summer, between Ballyvaughan, Lisdoonvarna, Doolin and Galway. A local service runs between Ennis, Ennistymon, Lisdoonvarna and Doolin.

By train

There is a daily train service between Ennis and Dublin (3hrs, €31.75 return). The train station (065 684 0444) is next to Ennis bus station.

By air

There are flights to Shannon Airport in County Limerick from London Heathrow (Aer Lingus), London Stansted (Ryan Air) and from Manchester (British Airways Express). Aer Lingus connects Shannon with Dublin. A bus from Shannon airport to Limerick city takes 45min, and it's another hour from Limerick city to Ennis.

Tourist information

Ennis Tourist Office

Arthur's Row, off O'Connell Street, Ennis (065 682 8366/www.shannon-dev.ie). **Open** *Jan, Feb* 9.30am-5.30pm Mon-Fri. *Mar-June, Oct-Dec* 9.30am-5.30pm Mon-Sat. *Mid June-Oct* 9.30am-5.30pm daily.

For the Burren, the nearest tourist information office is at the Cliffs of Moher visitors' centre (065 708 1171/www.shannon-dev.ie). Local information is also available at the Burren Display Centre (*see above*) and at the Ennis tourist office. All these places sell Tim Robinson's exemplary map.

Connaught

Wet and wild Connaught remains enticingly remote. Enjoy the scenery and try not to worry about the weather.

County Galway

Visitors to County Galway have three major areas of interest to choose from: **Galway City**, the wild landscape of **Connemara** to the west, and the three **Aran Islands** off the coast. This is West of Ireland heartland and, despite many years of bungalow blitz, it remains one of the most elementally beautiful and unspoilt corners of the country.

Towards Galway City

If you're travelling up the coast from County Clare, there are a few sights worth stopping for on your way to Galway City.

The road along Galway Bay will bring you first to the fishing village of **Kinvara**, where traditional sailing boats known as Galway hookers are celebrated at the **Blessing of the Boats** festival each August. Further up the coast is 16th-century **Dunguaire Castle**, which was once owned by the surgeon and wit Oliver St John Gogarty. Different floors have

been restored to represent different historical periods and pseudo-medieval banquets are held here in summer.

Alternatively, the inland N18 provides access to the remains of the **Kilmacduagh** monastic settlement dating from the 11th to the 14th centuries. The home of Lady Gregory is a short drive away at **Coole Park**. Nothing remains of the house, which was often visited by WB Yeats, but the surrounding grounds are lovely and contain a tree, autographed with the initials of Yeats, Synge and Shaw. Nearby is **Thoor Ballylee**, a 16th-century tower that was used by Yeats as a summerhouse in the 1920s. Further north, the N18 passes through **Kilcolgan** and **Clarinbridge**, the focus for festivities during the county's **Oyster Festival** in September.

For much of the 20th century, **Galway City** was an easygoing west coast alternative to Dublin, a small, often picturesque city with plenty of elbow room. More recently though (as it never stops reminding itself) Galway has been one of the fastest developing cities in Europe, and has enjoyed industrial success powered by a combination of EU grant aid and

There's time and space for reflection in **Connemara National Park**. *See p257*.

international investment. As well as a thriving economy, Galway is the cultural capital of the west coast. The city is known for the quality of its local theatre and traditional music; pub sessions often feature *sean nós* singing (*see p190* **Trad ain't bad**). More accessible perhaps is the music on offer at the **Galway Arts Festival** (091 566 577/www.galway artsfestival.com), which attracts culture vultures from far and wide to the city each July. The 2002 event will mark the Festival's 25th anniversary; check the website, or contact the tourist office for up-to-date information.

In the heart of the town is **Eyre Square**, dominated on the south side by the limestone mass of the Great Southern Hotel. Sights in the square include the Browne doorway (all that remains of a 17th-century merchant mansion), two cannons from the Crimean War, an emblematic statue of Galway author Padraic O Conaire (1883-1928), and the John F Kennedy memorial, which resembles a rusting collection of scrap iron. Galway's lively nightlife has turned Eyre Square into a less than friendly place at night; in 1999 some drunken revellers decided to lop off Padraic O Conaire's head, though it was later recovered.

Galwegian Justice Lynch Fitzstephens would have been in no doubt about how to deal with such inexcusable rowdyism. the **Lynch memorial** on Market Street marks the spot where he hanged his own son for murder in 1493. Associated with the same prominent Galway family is **Lynch Castle** on Shop Street, now a bank. It is a splendid example of medieval town architecture (parts of the building date from the 14th century) and is covered in gargoyles, decorative stonework and coats of arms. More gargoyles can be found on the exterior of the **Collegiate Church of St Nicholas** on Market Street, where Columbus is reputed to have said a prayer on his way through the city. Its tombs contain fine examples of medieval stone carving. Across the road from the church on Bowling Green is **Nora Barnacle's House**, a small terraced dwelling that attracts committed Joyce fans, although the author only visited the cottage twice.

Galway's present prosperity and continental atmosphere is a resurgence of the spirit that characterised its past. In the middle ages, Galway developed into a major port on the Atlantic seaboard, establishing lucrative links with Portugal and Spain, although it declined after being besieged by Cromwell in 1651. A faint reminder of the era when Spanish was spoken on the quayside is provided by the **Spanish Arch** on the Old Quays. The 16th-century arch is thought to have been an extension of the city walls

through which trading ships would unload their cargo. Next door is the unspectacular **Galway City Museum** – worth considering on a wet afternoon. The maze of streets and alleys between Eyre Square and the Corrib River comprise the food and entertainment heart of the city, while the nearby docks are now the prime site for the process of urban redevelopment that has been so central to Galway's modernisation.

West of the centre on Nun's Island is the delicately named but rather grotesque-looking **Cathedral of Our Lady Assumed into Heaven**, dedicated in 1965 and commonly known as St Nicholas's Cathedral. The enclosed quadrangle of **University College Galway** across the road provides a refreshing contrast to the Cathedral's architectural excesses, and is a pleasant place to sit on the odd sunny day.

The west bank of the Corrib is known as the **Claddagh**, from the Irish word for shore. This primarily residential area used to house local fishermen and their families, and gives its name to the Claddagh ring, which depicts two hands encircling a crowned heart. If the ring is worn with the heart pointing in towards the hand, the wearer is romantically attached; worn the other way, the wearer is available. Beyond Claddagh lies **Salthill**, a coveted address on the coast. Salthill's seaside promenade is good for a bracing walk, though notoriously casual sewage arrangements make this part of Galway Bay less than ideal for a swim. The **Galway Irish Crystal Heritage Centre** can be found on the other side of the city near the suburbs of Merlin Park. Tours begin in the beautiful mansion and finish in the factory itself.

Coole Park

Coole, Gort (091 631 804). **Open** *Apr, May* 10am-5pm Tue-Sun. *June-Aug* 10am-6pm daily. *Sept* 10am-5pm daily. Closed Oct-Mar. **Admission** €2.50; €1.20-€1.90 concessions. **No credit cards**.

Dunguaire Castle

Kinvara (091 637 108/www.shannonheritage.com). **Open** *Castle* Apr-Sept 9.30am-5.30pm daily. *Medieval banquets* (book in advance) May-Sept 5.30pm, 8.45pm daily. Closed Oct-Mar. **Admission** €4 castle; €42 banquet. **Credit** AmEx, DC, MC, V.

Galway City Museum

Spanish Arch, Galway (091 567 641). **Open** *May-Sept* 10am-1pm, 2-5pm daily. *Oct-Apr* 10am-1pm, 2-5pm Wed-Sun. **Admission** €1.30; 60¢ concessions. **No credit cards**.

Galway Irish Crystal Heritage Centre

Merlin Park, Dublin Road, Galway (091 757 311/ www.galwaycrystal.ie). **Open** 9am-5.30pm Mon-Sat; 11am-5.30pm Sun. **Admission** free; €2.50 tour. **Credit** AmEx, DC, MC, V.

Trips Out of Town

Nora Barnacle's House

8 Bowling Green, Galway (091 564 743). **Open** 10am-1pm, 2.15-5pm Mon-Sat. **Admission** €3; €2 concessions. **No credit cards.**

Thoor Ballylee

Gort (091 631 436). **Open** *Easter-June* 10am-6pm daily. *July-Sept* 10am-6pm Mon-Sat. Closed Oct-Mar. **Admission** €5; €1 concessions. **Credit** MC, V.

Where to eat

In Galway city try the ever-popular **Le Doghouse Nite Café**, located above the Bunch of Grapes (2 High Street, Galway, 091 565 811, main courses €7.55-€10.80) with a good view of the streetlife below. Another top spot is **Nimmo's**, housed in an old stone building on the Long Walk (Spanish Arch, 091 562 353, closed Mon, Sun). It's a restaurant and a wine bar that serves some of the best seafood in Galway. **Kirwan's Lane Creative Cuisine** (Kirwan's Lane, 091 568 266, closed Sun, closed lunch Sept-May, main courses €19-€23.50) is not really creative, but serves very nice food nonetheless. For something different, there's **Da Tang** (2 Middle Street, 091 561443, closed lunch Sun, main courses €8.20-€10.20 lunch, €10.20-€18 dinner). This was Ireland's first Chinese noodle house and has an Asian deli next door.

Between Galway and Clare, stop in at the **Merrimann Inn** (Main Street, Kinvara, 091 638 222, main courses €9.50-€15.20 bar, €16.45-€22.20 restaurant). It boasts the largest thatched roof in Ireland, and the food's pretty special, too.

Where to stay

Ashford Manor at 7 College Road, Galway (tel/fax 091 563 941, rates from €30 per person including breakfast) is one of a series of B&Bs along College Road, within walking distance of the city. If you want to be slap bang in the centre, however, the **Imperial Hotel** is a comfortable choice right on Eyre Square (091 563 033, rates €108).

Those on a budget might like to try the dormitory at the **Corrib Villa Hostel** (4 Waterside, 091 562892, rates €12.70 per person) which enjoys access to the lovely river walkway. However, the best option is probably the centrally located **Jury's Galway** (Quay Street, 091 566444/fax 091 568 415/www.jurys doyle.com, rates €64-€94 room only). Rooms sleep up to three adults and four children. Finally, at the top end, is the spanking new **Radisson Hotel** (Lough Atalia Road, 091 538300/fax 091 538 380/www.radissonsas.com, rates from €102 or €122 including breakfast).

Getting there

By car

Take the N4 out of Dublin, and turn on to the N6 at Kinnegad, which heads directly to Galway city. The journey takes about 3hrs 30min, although there's often a bottleneck around Kinnegad.

By bus

Bus Éireann (01 836 6111) connects Galway city with Dublin (13 buses daily, 3hrs 40min, €15.23 return), Doolin, Limerick and Cork. Two private bus companies also offer a daily service between Dublin Airport and Galway: **City Link Buses** (091 564163, 9 buses daily, 4hrs, €25 return) and **Nestor's** (091 797144, 5 buses daily, 3hrs 30 mins, €19 return).

By train

There are several Dublin–Galway trains daily (01 805 4222). The journey from Heuston station takes about 3hrs and a return ticket costs €29.21-€34.29.

By air

Aer Arann (091 755569) run 5 flights daily during the week and 3 daily at weekends between Dublin and Galway airport, located east of the city. Flight time is 45min and tickets cost about €111 return.

Tourist information

Galway Tourist Office

Foster Street, Galway (091 537 700/fax 091 537 733/info@irelandwest.ie). **Open** *July, Aug* 9am-7.45pm daily. *May, June, Sept* 9am-5.45pm daily. *Oct-Apr* 9am-5.45pm Mon-Fri; 9am-12.45pm Sat.

Connemara

Divided from the rest of the county by Lough Corrib, Connemara is a land of dramatic coastlines, brooding mountains, sleepy pubs and wet afternoons. It's a remote place with clannish locals, and is also a *gaeltacht* (Irish-speaking area; *see p257* **Gael talk**): many road signs in the area are in Irish only.

You could do worse than head straight to **Oughterard**, a popular angling town at the base of Lough Corrib. Boats can be hired here to tour the lake (famed for its stock of salmon and trout) and to visit the uninhabited island of **Inchagoill**, where the ecclesiastical ruins feature ancient Latin inscriptions. Cinéastes can take a ferry right across the lake to **Cong** in County Mayo, where Maureen O'Hara and John Wayne starred in the blarney-esque 1956 film *The Quiet Man*. Two miles south of town is 16th-century **Aughnanure Castle**, an impressive tower house that was once home to the bellicose O'Flaherty clan.

From Oughterard, drive west on the N59 and then north on the R336 between the stunning Maamturk and Partry mountains to reach another film location. The 1989 film, *The Field,* was shot in **Leenane**, a small village on the edge of Killary Harbour, Ireland's only fjord. The **Leenane Cultural Centre** is dedicated to the history of spinning and weaving. At the tip of the Salrock peninsula is the **Killary Youth Hostel**, built around a cottage where Wittgenstein stayed in 1948. He wrote part of the *Philosophical Investigations* during his stay here and called Connemara 'one of the last pools of darkness in Europe'.

Alternatively, stay on the main N59 west as far as **Recess**, where you can turn north on the R344 through the ravishingly beautiful **Lough Inagh** valley, with the Twelve Bens mountain range looming down on the western side. The road rejoins the N59 to the north, leading east to Leenane, or west to Letterfrack and Clifden.

On the Clifden road stop off at **Kylemore Abbey** set on the shores of Kylemore Lough. South-west of here stretches the **Connemara National Park**, which includes part of the Twelve Bens and is the location of a 4,000-year-old megalithic tomb. The **visitor centre** in Letterfrack provides details of the park's wildlife, information on hikes and offers guided walks in July and August.

Further west, ferries (095 44642/095 44750) travel between **Cleggan** pier and **Inishbofin** (the Island of the White Cow). The island can't match the Aran Islands for tourist numbers, which makes it an extremely enticing place. Among its attractions are traces of a seventh-century monastery founded by St Colman, but most people come merely to enjoy its tranquility and some lovely sheltered beaches.

Gael talk

Although Ireland is officially a bilingual country, only a vanishingly small percentage of people remain who still speak Irish as their first language. Regions where Irish is predominantly spoken are known as *gaeltachts* ('Irish-speaking areas'). These are increasingly few and far between, and most of their inhabitants also speak English. The best known are in Donegal and Waterford, and in south Connemara in Galway, although the language has also recently undergone a resurgence in Dublin's troubled Ballymun estate. Irish comes from the same linguistic family as Scots Gaelic and is often called 'Gaelic' by tourists. Within Ireland, though, it is usually known as Irish.

Despite its decreasing usefulness in daily life, Irish is kept on life-support through a variety of cultural and financial incentives. The most obvious of these are road signs, which list destinations in both English and Irish. In addition, all Irish children learn Irish in school from the tender age of four and may study it for up to 13 years. It is perhaps strange, then, that most people under the age of 30 claim to have no working knowledge of Irish at all, despite being fluent enough when pressed. This mental block is often said to derive from a single teaching text called *Peig*, which describes the tragic life and times of Kerrywoman Peig Sayers. Although it is an intriguing cultural document in its own right, many students turn from the language in despair after finishing it.

Another cultural initiative has been somewhat more successful. Six years ago TnaG (Teilefís na Gaeltaoht), the nation's first exclusively Irish language television station, was launched. Now called TG4 (*see p289*), its headquarters remain located in the depths of the Connemara *gaeltacht*, where it continues to produce some of the country's freshest programmes, although it now also broadcasts several English-language programmes in the evening as a concession to audience ratings. While these attempts to revive the language are admirable, the majority of Irish people remain far more comfortable speaking English. Irish is a quirky, musical language with an intriguing history, but it hasn't really succeeded in shaking off its parochial image; the term *gaelgoir* (Irish-speaker) is even considered a term of abuse in some circles. Galway's literary, academic and broadcasting *gaelgoirs* sometimes converse in Irish when they meet on the city's cobbled streets, but this is an (occasionally pretentious) phenonemon peculiar to the west of the country. There remains a snobbery about Irish dialects among the *gaelgoir* intelligentsia, with TG4 initially preferring its presenters to use a Connemara dialect rather a Donegal one. In fact, many of the people who express most interest in the language these days are not even Irish. The old cliché about foreigners being more Irish than the Irish certainly applies in this context, and if a revival really takes off it seems likely that it will be spearheaded by outsiders.

It was in a bog near **Clifden** that Alcock and Brown touched down after their pioneering transatlantic flight of 1919. Had they seen the tourist trap that Clifden has since become, they might have been tempted to turn around and fly straight back again. Still, some decent restaurants and manifold opportunities for walking, pony-trekking and dinghy sailing all add to the town's appeal. Favourite local walks from Clifden include the coast road past Leo's Hostel or the beautiful Sky Road, which loops around the peninsula to the west and then north to the tiny village of **Claddaghaduff**, where there are some fine beaches.

Further round the coast, near Ballyconneely, magnificent white sand beaches, including Gurteen Bay and Trá Mhóir, make tempting detours en route to the village of **Roundstone**. The village is notable for its lobster fishing and for the local manufacture of traditional musical instruments such as the *bodhrán* (a drum, but also the Irish word for 'moron'). While you're in the area, don't miss the two-hour walk from Roundstone to the top of **Mount Errisbeg**, from where you will be rewarded with one of the best views in the county.

The scenic coast road back to Galway city will take you past **Pearse's Cottage** near Screeb, where the rebel leader Patrick Pearse (1879-1916; *see p14*) lived and wrote some of his short stories and plays. It's also worth detouring to the beaches and low-lying islands at **Carraroe**. Note that nearby **Rossaveel** is one of the main departure points for the Aran Islands (*see p260*).

Aughnanure Castle

N59, 2 miles south of Oughterard (091 552 214). **Open** *May-mid June, Oct* 9.30am-6pm Sat, Sun. *Mid June-Sept* 9.30am-6pm daily. Closed Oct-Apr. **Admission** €2.50; €1.20 concessions; €6.30 family. **No credit cards.**

Connemara National Park Visitor Centre

Letterfrack (095 41054/095 41006). **Open** *Apr, May, Sept* 10am-5.30pm daily. *June* 10am-6.30pm daily. *July, Aug* 9.30am-6.30pm daily. Closed Oct-Mar. **Admission** €2.50; €1.20 concessions; €6.30 family. **No credit cards.**

Kylemore Abbey

N59, 2 miles east of Letterfrack (095 41146/ www.kylemoreabbey.com). **Open** 9am-5.30pm daily. **Admission** *Abbey* €5; €3.50 concessions; €11 family. *Garden* €6.50; €4 concessions. **Credit** AmEx, DC, MC, V.

Leenane Cultural Centre

N59, Leenane, between Clifden & Westport (095 42233/42231). **Open** *Mar-Oct* 10am-7pm daily. Closed Nov-Feb. **Admission** €2.55; €1.30 concessions. **No credit cards.**

Pearse's Cottage

Rosmuc, off R340, west of Screeb (091 574292). **Open** *June-Sept* 10am-6pm daily. Closed Oct-May. **Admission** (incl guided tour) €1.20; €0.50 concessions; €3.80 family. **No credit cards.**

Where to eat & stay

West of Killary Harbour, **Renvyle House Hotel** (Renvyle, Connemara, 095 43511/fax 095 43515/www.renvyle.com, closed Jan-mid Feb, rates €70-€140 per person) enjoys a lovely setting with coastal views and has a fine restaurant (set dinner €38). There's more good food to tuck in to at the **Rosleague Manor House Hotel** in Letterfrack (095 41101, closed Nov-Mar, rates €70-€101), an elegant Georgian hotel overlooking Ballinakill Bay. Also in Letterfrack is the **Old Monastery** (095 41132, rates €12 dormitory, €32 double), a picturesque budget choice. In Clifden you'll find **Kingstown House** (Bridge Street, Clifden, 095 21470), which remains open throughout the year (rates €23-€27 per person). Summer visitors to the south coast will find the **Heatherglen House** in Roundstone (095 35837, closed Oct-Apr, rates from €20 per person) a convenient choice, with stunning views of the bay. Eat at **O'Dowd's** in Roundstone (095 35809, restaurant closed Mon-Thur in winter, main courses €7 bar, €12.70-€16.50 restaurant), where the fine pub food includes shark and chips. Further east is the elegant and comfortable **Zetland Country House Hotel** (Cashel Bay, Connemara, 095 31111, closed mid Nov-Mar, rates €85-€110 per person), surrounded by a dramatic landscape of lakes, mountains and white sand beaches.

Tourist information

Clifden Tourist Office

Market Street, Clifden (095 21163). **Open** *Apr-Sept* 9am-5.45pm Mon-Fri; 10am-6pm Sat, Sun. Closed Oct-Mar.

This is the main tourist office for the region. There's also a small tourist office in Oughterard (091 552 808), open weekdays in summer.

The Aran Islands

Seamus Heaney described the Aran Islands – Inis Mór, Inis Meáin and Inis Orr – as 'stepping stones out of Europe'. The three bean-shaped rocks, 48 kilometres (30 miles) off the Galway coast have been eroded to sheer cliff faces on their western coasts by the constant buffeting of the Atlantic. As untouched, non-English-speaking pockets of Gaelic culture, the Aran Islands became immensely symbolic during the Irish cultural and nationalist renaissance of the 19th century. Irish remains the main language on the islands.

The largest of the islands, **Inishmore** (Inis Mór), slopes upwards from the relative shelter of the inhabited northern shore to the sheer cliffs that mark its dramatic southern edge. The island is criss-crossed by a network of dry stone walls, some of which date back to pre-Christian times. In peak season, Inis Mór is an over-touristed, noisy, frenetic place, especially around the main town of **Kilronan**, but its jaw-dropping scenery and some astonishing archaeological sites justify its popularity. Hire a bicycle from the massed ranks in Kilronan and set off down a narrow boreen on the six-and-a-half-kilometre (four-mile) ride to **Dun Aengus** (Dún Aonghusa), a spectacular semicircular Iron Age fort on a cliff edge 91 metres (300 feet) above the Atlantic. The fort is ringed by perimeter ramparts and a menacing 'chevaux de frise' a barricade of viciously sharp rocks sticking out of the ground. Other prehistoric sites nearby include **Dún Dúchathair** and **Dún Eoghanachta**.

The two smaller islands miss most of the daytrippers, attracting a more moneyed class of visitor instead. **Inishmaan** (Inis Meáin) has successfully marketed its distinctive knitwear for international fashion consumption and many women on the island still wear traditional red flannel skirts. There are also two prehistoric forts here, **Dún Choncobhir** and **Dún**

Ferbhaigh. A short hop across Foul Sound takes you to the smallest of the islands, **Inisheer** (Inis Orr). There's not much to do here, which is what makes it so charming.

Where to eat & stay

On Inishmore most eateries are to be found in and around Kilronan. **Joe Watty's Pub** (Kilronan, 099 61155) serves excellent soups and pasta dishes (main courses €6-€13) in high season. Further west, the **Ard Éinne Guesthouse** (099 61126, closed Nov-Mar, rates €58) has a fabulous view across to the mainland. **Kilmurvey House** (099 61218, closed Oct-Mar, rates €35 per person) is an attractive old manor house on the path to Dún Aengus, or there's **Cregmount House** (Creig-An-Cheirin, 099 61139, rates €35 per person) at the north-western end of the island with panoramic views of Galway Bay.

Pick of the few options on Inishmaan is probably **Creig Mór**, a B&B (099 73012, closed Dec-Mar, rates €25 per person). On Inisheer try the friendly **Fisherman's Cottage** (099 75073, closed Oct-Apr, main courses up to €13 lunch, up to €25 dinner), which serves great seafood.

Getting there

There are many options to consider when travelling to the islands: intra-island tickets, fly/ferry combos and various package deals.

Cliffhanger: **Dun Aengus** on Inishmore.

Visit the Galway City tourist office (*see p256*) for all the information. Most boats depart from Rossaveel, west of Galway City; note that car parking charges are steep.

By boat
Island Ferries (4 Forster Street, Eyre Square, Galway, 091 561767/091 568903/www.aranisland ferries.com) services all three islands (35min, €19 return). Boats depart from Rossaveel, with a bus connection from Galway city. **Doolin Ferries/ O'Brien Shipping** (091 567283/www.doolinferries. com), based in the Galway tourist office, runs a service directly from the city (95min, €19 return). It also runs a summer service to the islands from Doolin in Clare (065 7074455; *see p253*).

By air
Aer Arann (091 593034) flies from Inverin near Rossaveel to all three islands (€44.45 return). The bus connection to Galway airport takes longer than the flight, which is under 10min.

Tourist information

Tourist Office
Kilronan, Inishmore (099 61263). **Open** *Oct-May* 10am-5pm daily. *June-Sept* 10am-7pm daily. There's no tourist office on Inishmaan, but Inisheer has a tourist information point at the harbour where maps of the island are available. Note that there are no cash machines on any of the islands; a travelling bank stops at Inishmore on Wednesdays only.

Counties Mayo, Sligo & Leitrim

Mayo

Mayo has a striking coastline and a wild interior that remains isolated and underpopulated, but is punctuated with an abundance of relics evoking the Gaelic past. It must also be one of the most popular fishing destinations in Europe. The **River Moy**, flowing from the Ox Mountains to the Atlantic at Killala Bay, provides superb trout and salmon fishing, while the great inland lakes of **Mask**, **Conn** and **Cullen** offer some of the best game fishing in the country. Sea-anglers will remember the exhilarating experience of beachcasting on Mayo's coasts or deep-sea angling around the off-shore islands.

Westport & around

If you're driving north into Mayo from County Galway, take the R335 via Delphi, which passes through the awesome scenery of the **Doolough Valley**, flanked by the Mweelera Mountains to

the west and the Sheefry Hills to the east. During the Great Famine starving tenants set out from Louisburgh to beg food and assistance from Lord Sligo at Delphi Lodge. They were turned away empty-handed and 400 perished in the Doolough Valley on the journey home.

Louisburgh itself is a delightfully laidback place with a **visitors' centre** dedicated to the pirate queen Grace O'Malley (Granuaile; 1530-1603). She was the fiercely independent daughter of a Connaught chief who established her own fleet, fighting off both rival chiefs and the English for control of the coast here. The landscape is distinguished by some marvellous beaches and ocean views at Louisburgh and **Killadoon**, and there are ferry services to the beautiful and unspoilt islands of **Clare** and **Inishturk** from Roonagh Quay (098 28288/098 25045). Clare has the ruins of a 15th century abbey, possibly the final resting place of Grace O'Malley, as well as her castle. Both islands offer peace, seclusion and breathtaking scenery, and are perfect for day trips from the mainland.

Just south of Westport is the mountain of **Croagh Patrick** (known as the 'Reek'). In 441, St Patrick is supposed to have spent 40 days on the top of it in order to perform his vanishing snakes trick. It is now a popular pilgrimage site with thousands making their way to the chapel at the summit on the last Sunday of July. Start the ascent of the Reek from the village of Murrisk.

Westport was laid out in 1780 by the architect James Wyatt and is a graceful example of early Georgian town planning that now attracts hordes of visitors in the summer. At the centre of town is the tree-lined Mall with the River Carrowbeg running down the middle, but the chief attraction is **Westport House**, a splendid Georgian mansion set in beautiful grounds overlooking the Atlantic just outside town. The house was built in 1730 by Richard Castle and is still the family home of Lord Sligo, but the addition of numerous 'attractions', including a zoo and a tourist train, have somewhat diminished its aesthetic appeal. Westport Quay to the west of town was the birthplace of 1916 rebel leader John McBride, husband of Maud Gonne (*see p16* **First ladies of Ireland**). The **Clew Bay Heritage Centre** here is stuffed with historical documents and artefacts relating to the nationalist struggles, as well as information on Granuaile and the O'Malley clan.

Clew Bay Heritage Centre
The Quay, Westport (098 26852/www.museums ofmayo.com). **Open** *Apr, May, Oct* 10am-2pm Mon-Fri. *June, Sept* 10am-5pm Mon-Fri. *July, Aug* 10am-5pm Mon-Fri; 3-5pm Sun. **Admission** €2.50; €1.25 concessions; free children. **No credit cards.**

Surfing IRE

Compared to their warm-water cousins, UK surfers have it tough: campsites crowded with grommets, lineups like Piccadilly Circus at rush hour, stinkeyes from the locals. Sound familiar? Well, before you dust off your board bag and hop on the next plane to California, consider some of the surf options on the Emerald Isle.

Ireland's coastline gets hammered by some of the north Atlantic's toughest swells, generating every kind of wave, from muscular beachbreaks to bone-crunching points and reefbreaks. OK, so the weather can be unpredictable and the water's not exactly bath temperature (you'll be needing your winter steamer), but when it's really going off, these green-fringed headlands and flat rock reefs might just serve you up the best rides of your life. And here's the best part: you won't have to share them with hordes of other riders, just a handful of some of the world's friendliest surfers.

For tips on where to catch the best Irish waves, contact the helpful **Irish Surfing Association** (096 494 280). Good spots around the country include: **Barleycove** (*see p243*) in Cork; **Castlegregory** (*see p248*) in Kerry; the beaches around **Lahinch** (*see p251*) in Clare; **Easky** (*see p263*) and the beaches around Sligo Bay in Sligo; **Rossnowlagh** (*see p265*) in Donegal, and **Portrush** (*see p276*) on the Antrim coast.

Granuaile Visitors' Centre

Louisburgh (098 66134). **Open** *June-Sept* 10am-6pm daily. Closed Oct-May. **Admission** €2.50; €1.50-€2 concessions. **No credit cards.**

Westport House

Westport (098 25141/www.westporthouse.ie). **Open** *May-Sept* 1-5.30pm daily. Closed Oct-Apr. **Admission** phone for details. **Credit** MC, V.

Achill Island

Up the coast beyond **Newport**, the road swings around the base of the extensive Nephin Beg range to the **Curraun Peninsula** and Achill Island, passing a turning to **Carrigahowley Castle**. This 15th-century stronghold is where Grace O'Malley lived at the end of her life after dissolving her marriage to Richard Burke by locking the castle against him. It's also worth stopping at the large and beautiful beach at **Mulrany** on the isthmus between Clew Bay and Bellacagher Bay.

Achill is the largest of Ireland's offshore islands, and is rich in archaeological remains, with some charming villages and a clutch of magnificent beaches. It is reached by a landbridge at Achill Sound. The longest beach on the island extends for four kilometres (two and a half miles) beside the village of **Keel**, which is Achill's main residential and commercial centre. There are other excellent beaches at Dooega, Doogort and Keem.

Just north of Keel is the deserted village of **Slievemore**, where the abandoned homesteads are a powerful symbol of the dereliction that affected rural Ireland in the 19th century. Mount Slievemore, behind the village, is the highest point on the island. It's a fairly easy hike to the summit for fab views of Blacksod Bay. To the west is Mount Croaghaun, whose north-west face has been eroded away by the Atlantic to create some of the highest sea cliffs in Europe around Achill Head.

Northern & central Mayo

The **Mullet Peninsula** in the far north-west of the county is one of the least populated areas of Europe and almost completely ignored by most visitors. The low-lying, wild and boggy peninsula forms part of the Mayo *gaeltacht* (*see p257*) and is home to large colonies of storm petrels, red-necked phalarope and barnacle geese. Boat trips are available to several islands off the west coast: one of which, **Inishglora**, is the setting for the legend of the Children of Lir, who were transformed into swans and cursed to wander the country for 900 years.

Between the Mullet peninsula and the Moy estuary is the North Mayo sculpture trail, featuring work by Irish and international artists. The major attraction on the north coast, however, is **Céide Fields**, an archaeological site dating from 3000 BC, located west of Ballycastle. This 1,500-hectare (600-acre) landscape of walled fields and dwellings was covered and preserved by a blanket bog, and provides one of the best insights into prehistoric farming methods. The audio-visual

Trips Out of Town

WB Yeats by Rowan Gillespie. *See p263.*

centre, housed in a striking pyramid, has regular exhibitions and there are also daily guided tours. If 5,000-year-old field systems leave you cold, take time to enjoy the view across to the dramatic sea stacks at **Downpatrick Head**. Further round the coast is the angling centre of **Killala**, most notable as the point where French forces first landed in Ireland in 1798 to join with Irish rebels in their fight against the British. Head south of here to reach the market town of **Ballina**, a focal point for fishing in the county.

Having fought off competition from various statue shrines that supposedly 'twitched' in the 1980s, **Knock** in the east of the county is the unchallenged Las Vegas of Irish spirituality. In 1879, so the story goes, the Virgin Mary appeared to two local women by the Church of St John the Baptist. Those with a weakness for religious kitsch will find an endless supply of knick-knacks, holy water dispensers and plaster saints here. Others may be more interested to know that Knock Airport has flights to Dublin, London and Manchester.

Céide Fields
Ballycastle (096 43325/www.heritageireland.ie).
Open *Mid Mar-May, Oct* 10am-5pm daily.
June-Sept 9.30am-6.30pm daily. *Nov* 10am-4.30pm daily. *Dec-mid Mar* group tours only, book in advance. **Admission** €3; €1.50-€2.50; €7.50 family. **No credit cards**.

Where to eat

The **Golden Acres** pub in Killala (096 32183) has lots of memorabilia from the filming of an RTÉ series about the French landing, and serves excellent food (main courses €6.35-€15.50 bar, €12.70-€23 restaurant). From Killala it's worth making the bleak drive to reach **Doonfeeny House**, one of the finest restaurants in the county, overlooking Ballycastle Bay (096 43092, closed Sun in winter, main courses €15.20-€20.25). The stand-out spot on the Mullet Peninsula is **Lavelle's Erris Bar & Restaurant** (Main Street, Belmullet, 097 82222), a triple award-winner that represents all that's best in the traditional Irish pub, with an excellent seafood restaurant (main courses €6.30-€19.70).

Where to stay

You can stay on the campsite at **Westport House** (*see p260*) from May to September – the website has details of rates – but for a bit more comfort, try the **Pontoon Bridge Hotel** (Pontoon, Foxford, 094 56120/fax 094 56688/ www.pontoonbridge.com), a superb family-run hotel overlooking Loughs Conn and Cullen and offering fishing and craft holidays (rates €60-€85 per person). To the north, in the centre of Ballina, **Hogan's Hotel** (Station Road, 096 21350/fax 096 71882, rates €20-€60 per person) is a handsomely restored provincial hotel, while on the north-west coast is the beautifully situated **Kilcommon Lodge Holiday Hostel** in the village of Pollatomish (097 84621/fax 097 84621/www.kilcommon lodge.net, rates per person €9.50 dorm, €10.80 room).

Getting there

By car
To reach Mayo from Dublin, turn off the N4 at Longford onto the N60 to Castlebar.

By bus
Bus Éireann (01 836 6111) services link Ballina, Westport and Castlebar with Dublin, Galway and Sligo. Dublin to Ballina takes 3hrs 45min and costs €18.41 return.

By train
There are daily trains from Dublin's **Heuston Station** to Westport (3hrs 55min) with a stop at Castlebar (3hrs 30 min); fares are €29.20-€34.28 return. The Dublin–Foxford–Ballina service costs the same but involves changing at Manulla junction.

By air
Knock International Airport serves flights from Dublin (Aer Arann, 1-890 462 726), London Stansted (Ryanair, 01 677 4422) and Manchester (01 609 7800).

Tourist information

Tourist Office

*James Street, Westport (098 25711/ireland@
irelandwest.ie).* **Open** *Sept-Feb* 9am-6pm Mon-Fri;
10am-1pm Sat. *Mar-June* 9am 6pm Mon-Sat. *July,
Aug* 9am-7pm Mon-Sat; 9am-6pm Sun.

Sligo & Leitrim

Sligo crams a rich history and a varied landscape
into a relatively small area. It is, of course, most
famous for its links to WB Yeats, who spent
much of his childhood here. The heart of Yeats
country – 'the waters and the wild' – is the
triangle of land just beyond Sligo town, between
Lough Gill, Rosses Point and **Benbulben**, a
mystical flat-topped mountain that dominates
the landscape, and exerts a brooding presence
over Yeats's poetry. The three great inlets of
Sligo Bay create a varied coastline with some
wonderful Blue Flag beaches that are good for
surfing. Whether or not you're a Yeats fan, the
lakes, mountains and coastline that inspired
his poetry are reason enough to visit.

South-west Sligo

Heading towards Sligo town on the N59 or
the N17 from the Mayo border, you have the
opportunity for a wonderful scenic tour of the
Ox Mountains and the expansive scenery
around **Lough Easky**. The area is a rich blend
of bogland, hills, lakes and open fields. Good
detours include **Tubbercurry** in the south
of the county, a great little market town with
a strong tradition of Irish music and some
excellent pubs, and the popular seaside village
of **Enniscrone**, which boasts a championship
golf course, a Blue Flag beach and a distinctive
Edwardian bathhouse, offering hot seawater
baths and cold seawater showers pumped
straight from the Atlantic, 50 yards away.
North of here is the village of **Easky**, famous
for sea trout and salmon fishing and the centre
for surfing in the county.

Kilkullen's Seaweed Bath

*Enniscrone (096 36238/fax 096 36895/
www.enniscrone.ie).* **Open** *May-Nov* 10am-10pm
daily. **Rates** €12.70 per session. **Credit** MC, V.

Sligo town

Sligo town, gateway to the north-west, is a
convenient base for exploring Sligo, Donegal,
Mayo and Leitrim. It's a thriving and rapidly
growing place, where the relaxed, small-town
atmosphere is imbued with an increasing sense
of expectancy and self-confidence.

The inevitable statue of Yeats, by Rowan
Gillespie, is on Stephen Street, cloaked in
engraved lines of verse. Also here is the
Sligo County Museum, a 19th-century
chapel building with a room chock-full of
Yeats manuscripts, letters, photographs and
other memorabilia, including his Nobel prize.
The Yeats Memorial Building on Hyde Bridge
also houses a **WB Yeats Exhibition**, as well
as the tourist information centre and the **Sligo
Art Gallery**, which hosts touring exhibitions.
On the Mall, in a rather sombre 19th-century
stone building, is the recently refurbished
Model Arts Centre, which has been
transformed into a focal point for arts in the
region. As well as hosting touring exhibitions,
it houses the **Niland Gallery**, one of the finest
art collections in the country. Paintings by Jack
B Yeats form the core of the collection, but are
supplemented by varied works by other Irish
artists. Other points of interest in the town
include the ruins of **Sligo Abbey** (071 46406),
with its unique medieval altar and beautiful
15th-century lancet windows.

Model Arts Centre & Niland Gallery

The Mall, Sligo town (071 41405). **Open** 10am-
5.30pm Tue-Sat. **Admission** free.

Sligo Art Gallery

*Yeats Memorial Building, Hyde Bridge, Sligo town
(071 45847/www.sligoartgallery.com).* **Open** 10am-
5.30pm Mon-Sat. **Admission** free.

Sligo County Museum

Steven Street, Sligo town (071 47190). **Open**
June-Sept 10am-noon, 2-4.50pm Tue-Sat. *Oct-May*
2-4.50pm Tue-Sat. **Admission** free.

WB Yeats Exhibition

*Yeats Memorial Building, Yeats Society, Hyde
Bridge, Sligo town (071 42693/www.yeats-sligo.com).*
Open 10am-4.30pm Mon-Fri. **Admission** €2.50;
€1.25 concessions. **No credit cards.**

North of Sligo town

The young Yeats spent much of his time at
Lissadell House, a Greek revival mansion
north-west of Sligo town. The house is the
ancestral home of the Gore-Booth family and
contains portraits, photographs and artefacts
relating to the family's history. (Constance
Gore-Booth became Countess Markievicz,
the first female MP; *see p16* **First ladies
of Ireland**.) Although he died in France,
Yeats is buried nearby in **Drumcliffe Church**.
Drumcliffe was also the site of a fifth-century
monastic settlement; the remains of the round
tower and a carved 11th-century high cross
can still be seen, and there's an excellent multimedia visitors' centre, where you can delve into

Trips Out of Town

the history of the area. Drumcliffe is less than five kilometres (three miles) from **Glencar Lough**, which straddles the border with Co. Leitrim. Walk to the impossibly picturesque waterfall, or explore the surrounding steep hillsides and fertile valleys.

Drumcliffe Visitors' Centre

Drumcliffe (071 44956/www.drumcliffe.ie). **Open** *Mid Feb-Apr, Sept-Dec* 9am-5pm Mon-Fri; 10am-5pm Sat. *May-Sept* 8.30am-6pm Mon-Fri; 10am-6pm Sat; 1-6pm Sun. Closed Jan-mid Feb. **Admission** *Audiovisual tour* €3.80; €2.50 concessions; €7 family. **Credit** AmEx, MC, V.

Lissadel House

Drumcliffe (071 63150/071 63150). **Open** *June-mid Sept* 10.30am-12.30pm, 2-4.15pm Mon-Sat. **Admission** €4; €2 concessions. **No credit cards.**

Lough Gill & around

South of Sligo town is **Carrowmore**, one of Europe's most significant megalithic burial sites, with over 60 stone circles and numerous dolmens and passage graves. Just to the east is **Lough Gill**. From Sligo town take the R286 along the north of the lake to reach the **Deer Park Court Cairn** dating from 3000 BC located up on a wooded hillside. Continue to **Parke's Castle** in Co. Leitrim, a restored 17th-century castle, which was constructed during the Plantation and is now a Dúchas site. South of here are the ruins of **Creevylea Abbey**, the last friary to be built in Ireland in 1508. The abbey was destroyed three times during the 16th and 17th centuries but retains some fine carvings. Nearby, a small island in the south-east corner of the lough was immortalised by Yeats in his poem 'The Lake Isle of Innisfree' and now attracts dozens of visitors, despite the fact that it's little more than a few tufts of grass just offshore.

Carrowmore Megalithic Cemetery

5km south of Sligo town (096 61534). **Open** *May-Sept* 9.30am-6.30pm daily. **Admission** €1.90; €0.75 concessions. **No credit cards.**

Parke's Castle

Fivemilebourne, Manorhamilton, Co Leitrim (071 64149/www.heritageireland.ie). **Open** *mid Mar-Oct* 10am-6pm daily. Closed Nov-Feb. **Admission** €2.50; €1.20-€1.90 concessions; €6.30 family. **No credit cards.**

Where to eat

En route to Sligo from Dublin, turn off the N4 for lunch at the **Leitrim Inn** (Leitrim Village, Co. Leitrim, 020460), a charming village pub, with excellent bar food (main courses €8.80-€18.40). In Sligo town itself, the popular

Garavogue Bar & Restaurant (15-16 Rear Stephen's Street, Sligo town, 071 40100/071 40104, main courses €3.20-€9.50) is a modern restaurant overlooking the river. To the south, **The Thatch** (Dublin Road, Ballysadare, 071 67288) is a fine pub with low beamed ceilings and plenty of nooks and crannies. There's good pub grub for under €3 and traditional music sessions, too. If you're driving around Lough Gill, stop off at the charming **Stanford Village Inn** (Main Street, Dromahair, Co. Leitrim, 071 64140), which offers excellent bar food (main courses €6-€13) and a restaurant menu (€25). In the north of the county, an Italian-influenced menu (main courses €16.50-€20.30) and wonderful views are the main attractions at **La Vecchia Posta** (Cliffoney, 071 76777/071 76788, closed mid Jan-mid Mar).

Where to stay

Sligo Park Hotel (Pearse Road, 071 60291/ fax 071 69556/www.leehotels.ie, rates €55-€160) is a decent three-star hotel in Sligo town with a swimming pool and leisure facilities, set in attractive landscaped gardens. Backpackers will be glad to find the **Harbour International Tourist Hostel** (Finisklin Road, Sligo town, 071 71547, 071 69256), a wonderful old house that offers comfortable accommodation in dorms (€14) and twin rooms (€33). The **Tower Hotel** close to the City Hall in Sligo town (Quay Street, 071 44000/fax 071 46888/www.tower hotelgroup.ie, rates €135) is an impressive and elegant hotel with a comprehensive range of facilities and a reputable restaurant.

Getting there

By car

The N4 from Dublin will take you all the way into Sligo town via Carrick-on-Shannon (the county town of Leitrim) in around 3hrs 30min.

By bus

The daily **Bus Éireann** service between Dublin and Sligo takes 4hrs and costs €14.50 return.

By train

Trains run from Dublin's Connolly Station to Sligo town daily (3hrs 20min, €25.40 return).

Tourist information

North-west Tourism

Temple Street, Sligo town, Co Sligo (071 61201/ irelandnorthwest@eircom.net). **Open** *Oct-Mar* 9am-5pm Mon-Fri; 10am-5pm Sat. *Apr-Sept* 9am-8pm Mon-Fri; 10am-8pm Sat.
This is the tourist headquarters for the whole of the north-west of Ireland.

Ulster

Leave your prejudices behind to explore the varied countryside, cities and scenery of Ireland's northern counties.

The **Giant's Causeway**. *See p276*.

County Donegal

Connected to the Republic of Ireland by only a thin strip of land on the coast, County Donegal has been somewhat marginalised by historical events. The fact that it is no longer served by rail adds to the county's isolation. Visitors can take advantage of this remoteness, however, to enjoy an unspoilt landscape, away from the tourist masses.

West Donegal

Bypass crowded Bundoran over the border from County Leitrim and drive straight on to **Ballyshannon**, birthplace of Victorian poet William Allingham and host to the annual **Ballyshannon Folk Festival** in early August (072 51453). Further north towards Donegal town is **Rossnowlagh**, a seaside village with a fantastic, never-crowded surfing beach. Donegal's large Protestant minority come to Rossnowlagh in summer for the Republic's only 12 July parade (celebrating the

Battle of the Boyne). The jovial atmosphere at this event couldn't be further removed from the tense confrontations at Drumcree and Belfast.

On the banks of the Eske, the town of **Donegal** is a pleasant base from which to explore the county. Its name (which means Fort of the Foreigners) refers to the Vikings who settled here in the 9th century. **Donegal Castle** was built in the 15th century by the ruling O'Donnell family, but was substantially rebuilt in the Jacobean style in the 17th century. In the centre of town is the Diamond (the word for town square in the north), with a monument commemorating four Franciscan friars who wrote *The Annals of the Four Masters* in the 1630s, one of the first histories of Ireland (now held in the National Library; *see p66*). Elsewhere, **Donegal Craft Village** offers a chance to meet craftspeople in their workshops, while railway enthusiasts will enjoy the restored steam engines and carriages at the **Donegal Railway Heritage Centre**.

Along the coast west of Donegal, take the picturesque detour to **St John's Point** at Dunkineely before continuing to **Killybegs**,

Ireland's premier fishing port – a fact that is immediately obvious from the smell. Beyond the town, the scenic coastal route leads to Kilcar, Carrick and Glencolumbcille and the heartland of south-western Donegal. The area's strong links with Scotland through migrant labour give Donegal's traditional music a hard-edged quality that sets it apart from that of Kerry, Clare and Sligo. Many bars and cultural centres present music sessions that are well worth catching.

From Carrick, signposts to Bunglas will lead you to the stunning **Slieve League** sea cliffs, which plunge 601 metres (1,972 feet) into the Atlantic, making them the highest in Europe. Intrepid (and experienced) walkers may want to venture beyond the cliffs to the Giant's Chair and One Man's Pass – a precipitous path with drops on both sides. Proceed with extreme caution and a vigilant eye on the weather.

The village of **Glencolumbcille**, overlooked by distinctive Glen Head, owes its survival in large part to James McDyer, a local priest who provided work for impoverished locals in the 1950s by introducing collective farming and opening canning and tweed factories. He also set up the **Folk Village**, which has dwellings from the 18th and 19th centuries. There are excellent beaches in the area, although you should beware of strong currents.

If the weather turns cold, as it frequently does in Donegal, you won't go short of a hand-knitted sweater if you head inland from Killibegs to **Ardara**, via the lonely but beautiful Glengesh Pass. Wool and tweed are big business in Donegal, and Ardara is a centre for the industry. On the way, turn off towards the coast to reach the spectacular **Assaranca Falls** and the **Maghera Caves**.

North of here, beyond the popular beach resorts at Dawros Head, is the Donegal *gaeltacht* (Irish-speaking area; *see p257* **Gael talk**) known as the **Rosses**. Not only is Irish widely spoken here, but English names are often painted over on the road signs. Such is the richness of Donegal Irish that Flann O'Brien boasted that some of its speakers 'know so many million words that it is a matter of pride with them never to use the same word twice in a lifetime'. The small town of **Gweedore** is the focal point of the region.

Towns in this part of Donegal are not so much urban centres as clusters of pubs and shops, surrounded by an endless succession of white bungalows. The scenery, meanwhile, epitomises the wild, dramatic landscapes for which the county is known. In addition to the rocky wilderness of the Rosses, there's a fantastic rugged coastal stretch between **Bunbeg** and **Dunfanaghy**.

To the west of Burtonport is the island of **Arranmore**, which combines startling cliffs on its northern and western coasts, with some lovely sandy beaches. Further north, off the coast of the **Bloody Foreland** (so-called for the redness of its rocks rather than anything more sinister) is **Tory Island**, the remotest of Ireland's offshore outposts. Tory is an exposed and isolated spot, but nevertheless boasts a school of Primitive artists and even a monarch. Locals have a strongly developed sense of their separate identity, and will often describe a trip to Bunbeg as 'going over to Ireland'.

Back on the mainland, stop off at the **Dunfanaghy Workhouse**, which now houses a small local history museum, including an exhibition on the Great Famine, before making your way to sandy Tramore Beach on **Horn Head**. It's not just one of the best beaches in the area but is also likely to be completely deserted out of season. Walk north from the beach to Pollaguill Bay for a view of the **Marble Arch**, a dramatic natural rock arch carved out by the waves, and take time to explore the stunning landscape of Horn Head by bicycle or on foot. South of the peninsula on the N56 to Letterkenny is **Doe Castle**, the remains of a fortress that passed into the hands of the MacSweeny clan before succumbing to English firepower in 1650.

Donegal Castle
Donegal Town (073 22405). **Open** *Mar-Oct* 10am-6pm daily; phone for details at other times. **Admission** €3.80; €1.50-€2.50 concessions; €9.50 family. **No credit cards**.

Donegal Craft Village
Ballyshannon Road, Donegal Town (073 22225). **Open** 10am-5.30pm Mon-Sat. **Credit** AmEx, MC, V.

Donegal Railway Heritage Centre
Old Station House, Donegal Town (073 22655). **Open** *June-Sept* 9am-5pm daily. **Admission** €2.50; €1.25 concessions. **No credit cards**.

Dunfanaghy Workhouse
Dunfanaghy (074 36540). **Open** *Mar-Sept* 9am-6pm daily. **Admission** *Famine exhibition* €4; €2 concessions. *Art gallery* free. **No credit cards**.

Glencolumbcille Folk Village
Glencolumbcille (073 30017). **Open** *Apr-Sept* 10am-6pm Mon-Sat; 1-6pm Sun. **Admission** €2.50. **No credit cards**.

Where to stay

In Donegal Town, the **Abbey Hotel** (073 21014, rates €114) in the main square, is an old-style establishment with loads of charm. The **Atlantic Guesthouse** (Main Street, 073 21187, rates €44) has the advantage of being close to the town's best bars and restaurants, while the **Independent Hostel Doonan** (073 22805, rates dorm bed €10, room €12) is a compact, friendly hostel located in picturesque surroundings.

On the coast, the **Bay View Hotel** (Main Street, Killybegs, 073 31950, rates €108-€152) is a luxury hotel on the harbour, with leisure facilities, or there's the **Lake House Hotel** in Portnoo near Dawros Head (075 45123, closed Oct-Mar, rates €38-€45 per person), which is set in private grounds two miles from a good beach. Inland, the **Green Gate** at Ardvally, near Ardara (075 41546, rates €60) has an flamboyant French owner, stupendous views and 15 types of home-made jam and marmalade to try at breakfast.

On the north coast, **Carrig-Rua Hotel** in Dunfanaghy (074 36133, rates €45-€60 per person) boasts a lovely, picturesque setting overlooking the bay and a good restaurant. Otherwise, those on a budget could try the **Corcreggan Mill Hostel** (Dunfanaghy, 074 36409, rates €8-€12 dorm, €10-€14 room), where guests have the chance to sleep in a renovated railway carriage.

Where to eat

The **Smugglers Creek** in Rossnowlagh (072 52366, main courses €10-€26) is a restored pub beside the beach with good bar food. In Donegal Town, **McGroarty's Pub** (the Diamond, 073 21049, main courses €3-€11) serves simple, tasty food, but for something a bit more upmarket head along the coast to **Castlemurray House** in Bruckless (073 37022, closed Nov-Mar, main courses €30-€42), which offers good modern French-Irish food, extraordinary views out across the bay and a number of inexpensive rooms.

Getting there

By car

From Dublin, take the N3 through Navan, Cavan and Enniskillen and on to Ballyshannon and then Donegal Town. From the Diamond in Donegal Town take the N56 road across the bridge to reach Killybegs. From here you can turn north to Ardara or stay on the coastal road to Glencolumbcille.

By bus

Bus Éireann services link Dublin with Donegal Town. Private bus companies include **Feda O'Donnell** (075 48114), which operates between Galway City and Donegal Town, and **McGeehan's** (075 46150), whose service runs from Dublin to Glencolumbcille. There are daily buses between Donegal and Glencolumbcille (1hr 30min, €11.43 return), stopping at Killybegs and Carrick.

By air

The 50min flight between Dublin and Donegal is operated by **Aer Arann** (in Dublin 814 1058) to Carrickfinn Airport on the upper west coast.

Tourist information

Tourist Office

Ballyshannon Road, Donegal Town (073 21148). **Open** *June-Aug* 9am-6pm Mon-Sat; 9am-5pm Sun. *Sept-May* 9am-5pm Mon-Fri.
The Lace House Centre in Glencolumbcille (073 30116, open May-Oct) is also a good source of information.

Central & eastern Donegal

Diagonally north-east of Donegal Town is **Letterkenny**, the largest population centre in the county and the ideal base from which to explore East Donegal. Despite its small size, Letterkenny has almost displaced Galway as the capital of cool in the west. In the summer, foreign visitors, English-language students and Irish tourists mix in the town's bars and restaurants, creating a cosmopolitan vibe. The Gothic cathedral of **St Eunan's** looks down imposingly from Sentry Hill, and the **Donegal County Museum** on the High Street is open year round with displays of local history. South of Letterkenny is the **Beltany Stone Circle** near Raphoe, whose 60 standing stones were once the focus of pagan spring festivities.

Head north-west from Letterkenny to reach one of Donegal's chief attractions, **Glenveagh National Park**. Some 16 square kilometres (six square miles) of forest and parkland extend from Dunlewy (at the foot of Mount Errigal) to Lough Gartan in the south-east, with Lough Veagh at their heart. There are nature trails throughout the National Park, which is also home to the largest herd of wild red deer in the country. The visitors' centre at the northern end of the Lough can provide information on the park's other wildlife. From the visitors' centre a free shuttle bus runs to **Glenveagh Castle**, which was donated to the state in 1983, while just outside the park, overlooking Lough Gartan, is **Glebe House & Gallery**, a former rectory restored by painter Derek Hill. The 40-minute tour of the house shows the wide range of artistic influences that inspired its decoration. Within walking distance of Glebe House, on the shores of Lough Gartan, is the **Colmcille Heritage Centre**, with displays devoted to the life and work of St Colmcille (Columba).

North of Letterkenny is the small and scenic **Rosguill Peninsula**, which has some lovely beaches, and **Fanad Head Peninsula**, which forms the western shore of Lough Swilly.

Trips Out of Town

Rathmullan on the edge of the Lough was the spot from where the last of the Ulster chieftains fled the country in 1607 in the Flight of the Earls, leaving the province defenceless against the Plantation that followed.

More isolated than either Rosguill or Fanad Head is **Inishowen Peninsula** further east. Extending as far as Ireland's northernmost point at **Malin Head**, it is a desolate and rugged part of the country with several ancient sites, plentiful birdlife and some secluded beaches. Moville, Carndonagh and Buncrana are the principal towns of this sparsely populated area.

At the base of the peninsula is the **Grianán of Ailigh**, a circular pagan temple dating from the fifth century, which was used as a fort in later centuries. From here, drive up the western side of the peninsula through the **Gap of Mamore** for spectacular views west across Lough Swilly to the Fanad Head Peninsula. When you reach Malin Head look out to sea to Inishtrahull – a remote rocky outcrop that is technically part of Greenland.

Colmcille Heritage Centre
Churchill, Letterkenny (074 37306). **Open** *June-Aug* 10.30am-6.30pm Mon-Sat; 1-6.30pm Sun. *Easter-May, Sept* phone to check. Closed Oct-Easter. **Admission** €2; €1 concessions. **No credit cards.**

Donegal County Museum
High Road, Letterkenny (074 24613). **Open** 10am-12.30pm, 1-4.30pm Mon-Fri; 1-4.30pm Sat. **Admission** free.

Glebe House & Gallery
Churchill, Letterkenny (074 37071). **Open** *Easter, mid May-Sept* 11am-6.30pm Mon-Thur; 11am-6.30pm Sat, Sun. **Admission** €2.50; €1.20-€1.90 concessions; €6.30 family.

Glenveagh Castle & National Park
Glenveagh (074 37088). **Open** *Park* free access. *Visitor centre* Mar-Nov 10am-5pm daily. Closed Dec-Feb. **Admission** *Visitor centre* €2.50; €1.25 concessions; €6.30 family. **No credit cards**.

Where to eat

The **Yellow Pepper** (36 Lower Main Street, Letterkenny, 074 24133, main courses €8-€20) has an amiable atmosphere and familiar food. On the Inishowen Peninsula, the **Corncrake** (Millbrea, Carndonagh, 077 74534, closed Mon-Fri from Oct to May, main courses €15-€32) is one of Donegal's outstanding restaurants. Don't miss the pannacotta or the rhubarb ice-cream. Further east, on Lough Foyle, **Kealy's Seafood Bar** (Greencastle, 077 81010, main courses €9-€12) serves fantastic fish feasts in a harbour location, while **Finnegans** in Muff, near the border with Derry (Main Street, 077 84455, main courses €16.50-€1.50) is snug and restful.

Where to stay

In Letterkenny, the **Ballyraine Guest House** (Ramelton Road, 074 24460, rates €28-€35.50) is five minutes' walk from the town centre. **Gallaghers Hotel** (100 Main Street, 074 22066, rates €31) is a great place to meet the locals, and the bar serves superb Guinness. The aptly named **Town View** (Leck Road, 074 21570, rates €25.50 per person) has a panoramic vista over the town; it has also won awards for its fantastic breakfasts.

Getting there

By car
To reach Letterkenny from Dublin, take the N2 heading north to Monaghan, then the A5 to Omagh and Strabane, then the N14 on to Letterkenny (journey time 4hrs). Letterkenny is north-east of Donegal town via the N15 and N13.

By bus
Bus Éireann (074 21309) run buses between Dublin and Letterkenny (4hrs; €19 return), and the useful Cork–Derry service connects Letterkenny with Galway (4hrs 40min; €23 return). Private bus companies provide the best local services: call **Lough Swilly** (074 22400) and **McGeehan** (075 46150) for details.

Tourist information

North West Tourism Authority
Derry Road, Letterkenny (074 21160). **Open** *Sept-May* 9am-5pm Mon-Fri. *June* 9am-6pm Mon-Sat. *July, Aug* 9am-8pm Mon-Sat; 10am-2pm Sun.

Dialling Northern Ireland

The UK area code for Northern Ireland is 028; to call Northern Ireland from the mainland dial 028 followed by the local code. If you're calling Northern Ireland from anywhere outside the UK and Ireland, dial the international access code, followed by the UK code (44) and drop the '0' from the Northern Ireland area code.

Confusingly, Northern Ireland has a different area code if you're calling from anywhere in the Republic of Ireland: dial 048, followed by the local code. The local code for Belfast is 90 and must be dialled within the city as well as from outside; the code for Derry is 71.

Northern Ireland

The Ulster Plantation began in 1604, when the province was presented by King James I to Sir Arthur Chichester. Over the next century, approximately 200,000 English and lowland Scottish farmers poured into the province of Ulster, appropriating land from its displaced Catholic population and transforming the religious and political make-up of Ireland irrevocably. Differences between Ulster and the other three Irish provinces intensified in the late 17th century when an influx of French Huguenots increased Ulster's importance as a trading centre. The Huguenots chose **Belfast** – improbable as this may sound – as a refuge from religious persecution. They brought linen manufacture with them, which rapidly became the major cottage industry of the 18th century, and by the 19th century, Belfast – the only Irish city touched by the industrial revolution – had been transformed into the linen workshop of the world as well as an international centre for ship building.

The link between Protestantism and Unionism in Northern Ireland has not always been as automatic as it may seem today. The Northern leaders of the 1798 rebellion (*see p11*) were idealistic middle-class Protestants, whose United Irishmen attempted to co-ordinate an alliance between Catholics and Presbyterians against the injustices of the ruling Anglicans. After the failure of the rebellion, Presbyterian and Catholic politics retreated behind sectarian barricades, where they have stayed with few interruptions ever since.

The present-day map of Northern Ireland dates from the Anglo-Irish Treaty of 1921 (*see p16*). The British Government insisted that the six counties in which Ulster Protestants formed a majority should stay part of the UK. Despite objections from nationalists throughout Ireland, Northern Ireland soon settled down to the 'golden age' of Unionist supremacism and simmering Nationalist resentment.

From 1922 to 1968 the province was ruled by the Unionist-dominated Stormont Assembly in Belfast and the rights of the Nationalist minority were consistently neglected. The Catholic civil rights movement in 1968 soon degenerated into widespread civil and political unrest that polarised the two communities, fuelled paramilitary armament and eventually resulted in the suspension of the Assembly and the imposition of direct rule from Westminster.

Since the Good Friday Agreement of 1998, Northern Ireland has sporadically enjoyed the benefits of devolution. However the thorny

West Belfast. *See p273.*

issue of IRA decommissioning, unwillingness to implement the Patton Report on policing, and systematic violations of the ceasefire by certain paramilitary groups on either side continue to undermine the chances of achieving a workable devolved government here. Initial optimism among the general population has certainly faded since the early days of the 1997 ceasefire announcement, though a full-scale return to what was Europe's longest running civil conflict remains unlikely.

Derry

The walled city of Londonderry – known to almost all as **Derry**, and called that hereafter in this guide (its full name is cracklingly politicised in Ireland) – is perched on a hill above the River Foyle. The streets climb up from the river, often so steeply that their footpaths have steps, and the city skyline is punctuated with the spires of **St Columb's Cathedral** (the first post-Reformation cathedral in Ireland) and the top of the ornate **Guildhall**, with the hills of Donegal forming an impressive backdrop. Northern Ireland's second city has a distinct, almost hybrid, ethos all its own. A border city in essence, Derry

Trips Out of Town

looks for its identity as much to neighbouring Donegal as to the rest of the North. Like Belfast, it has frequently been in the news for all the wrong reasons. The walled city was ravaged by bombs in the 1970s, but the city has been largely quiet since the mid 1980s, and has undergone considerable regeneration over the last 20 years. Visitors today will notice the sensitively restored terraces of townhouses and shops, and the substantial redevelopment of the walled city, which is now largely complete.

The date of the foundation of the city is traditionally set at 546, when St Columba set up a monastery on an island in the Foyle. The settlement flourished as a centre of learning before diminishing in size and influence in the middle ages. The western section of the Foyle gradually dried up and became a marsh (the Bogside), and the island of Derry became a site of considerable strategic importance.

In 1613, English and Scottish settlers, with financial assistance from the Guilds of London, established the new walled city of Derry (hence the prefix 'London'). Derry remains only walled city in the country and the one-mile circuit of the well-preserved **city walls** is an interesting walk. Enter at Magazine Gate and walk anti-clockwise for the best views. Contact the Visitor and Convention Bureau (71 267 284) or City Tours (71 271 996) for more details.

In the 19th century, Derry was one of Ireland's principal emigration ports, and in the 20th century it was crucial to the Allied Forces in World War II. The city's maritime history, including its role in the war, is traced at the **Harbour Museum**. If you want to learn more about Derry's history, try the **Fifth Province**, a rather over-the-top visitors' attraction that explores the city's Celtic past, or the **Tower Museum**, which has superb interpretative displays that tell the story of the city from prehistoric times to the present day. The building connects with the Craft Village, a self-contained complex of craft and gift shops.

Today, Derry proclaims its distinctiveness in mainly non-historical ways: the city is noted for its excellence in choral music, marked by the **Two Cathedrals Festival** in October (see p185), and, after years of decline, the city's pubs and clubs are now among the best in Ireland. A number of gallery and theatre spaces have been established in recent years, most notably the **Millennium Forum** (3 New Market Street; 71 264 455/71 264 426). This large performance auditorium, augmented by an outdoors entertainment space, should become the epicentre of the area's cultural resurgence. Other touches, such as the new river walk along the quay, have created an aura of revival in the city.

Fifth Province
Calgach Centre, Butcher Street (71 373 177). **Open** 10am-4.30pm Mon-Fri. **Admission** £3; £1 concessions. **No credit cards**.

Guildhall
Guildhall Square (71 377 335). **Open** 9am-5pm Mon-Fri. **Admission** free.

Harbour Museum
Guildhall Street, Derry (71 377 331). **Open** 10am-1pm, 2-4.30pm daily. **Admission** free.

St Columb's Cathedral & Chapter House Museum
London Street (71 267 313). **Open** *Nov-Easter* 9am-5pm Mon-Sat. *Easter-Oct* 9am-4pm Mon-Sat. **Admission** free.

Tower Museum
Union Hall Place (71 372 411). **Open** *Sept-June* 10am-5pm Tue-Sat. *July, Aug* 10am-5pm Mon-Sat. **Admission** £4.20; £1.60 concessions; £8.50 family. **No credit cards**.

Where to eat

An Bácús (The Bakehouse) at 37 Great James Street (71 264 678) is the only Irish-speaking café in the area. For views over the city, **Austin's Rooftop Restaurant** (2 The Diamond, 71 261 817, main courses £3.50-£5), on the top floor of Austin's department store, is a good choice. **Bean-there.com** (20 The Diamond, 71 281 303) is the city's only Internet café, and serves great coffee and snacks. And for excellent modern food in a serene setting, try **Brown's Restaurant** (1-2 Bonds Hill, 71 345 180, main courses £8.50-£14.95).

Where to stay

Aberfoyle (33 Aberfoyle Terrace, Strand Road, 71 283 333, rates £36) is a period townhouse, conveniently placed for the city's best bars. The Spirit Bar, which often has jazz evenings, is one of the main draws at the **Quality Hotel at Da Vinci's** (15 Culmore Road, 71 279 111, rates £59). For B&B accommodation, **Saddler's House** (36 Great James Street, 71 269 691, rates £45) is probably the city's most central option, with books and a television in every room. **Derry City Youth Hostel** (4-6 Magazine Street, 71 284 100) has ensuite rooms (rates £15 per person) as well as dorm beds (rates £8-£10).

Getting there

By car
Take the N2 north from Dublin via Monaghan, which turns into the A5 to Derry (journey time 3hrs 30min).

By bus

Ulsterbus (Foyle Street, 71 262 261) runs regular services from Belfast (40min; £8 return), Dublin (4hrs; £15 return), and other locations. **Lough Swilly Bus Company** (71 262 017) operates services from destinations throughout Donegal, and **Airporter** (71 269 996) operates an excellent shuttle service from the two Belfast airports.

By train

Northern Ireland Railways (Duke Street, 71 342 228) provides regular train services from Belfast, with connections to Dublin.

By air

City of Derry Airport, seven miles (11km) north-east of Derry (71 810 784), offers scheduled services from Glasgow and Manchester. **Ryanair** has low-cost flights from London Stansted, and **Loganair** operates a daily service between Derry and Dublin.

Tourist information

Tourist Information Centre

44 Foyle Street (71 267 284). **Open** *Mar-June, Oct* 9am-5pm Mon-Fri; 10am-5pm Sat. *July-Sept* 9am-5pm Mon-Fri; 10am-6pm Sat; 10am-5pm Sun.

Belfast

Belfast: a place like anywhere else in the world and like nowhere else in the world. The ceasefires and peace accords of the late 1990s have unleashed a wave of unparalleled prosperity, employment and multinational investment. But while new hotels, office blocks, call centres, restaurants and concert halls mushroom across the city centre and waterfront areas, tribal hatred fed by centuries of conflict continues to erupt spasmodically, threatening Belfast's most recent face-lift with the dogged energies of its turbulent past. Schizophrenic remains the best adjective to describe Belfast – split, as ever, between two antagonistic communities; between British and Irish cultural influences; and split, most visibly perhaps, between a brighter future and a nightmarish past. A 'peace-line' still slices through Belfast's suburbs, yet ten minutes away in the city centre, you'll find some of the best museums, art venues, restaurants and shops on the whole island of Ireland.

Belfast has also produced more than its fair share of writers and painters, composers and playwrights, and is the birthplace of popular heroes George Best and Van Morrison. Even at the height of the Troubles large areas of the city were not only untouched by the various terror campaigns, but almost devoid of petty crime. The newly self-confident city is now putting in a serious bid to become Europe's Cultural Capital in 2008.

Central Belfast

Donegall Square is the symbolic heart of the city and the site of the impressive and austere **City Hall**, a monument to the city's neo-classical respectability. Guarded on the outside by Queen Victoria, its main entrance incorporates a memorial chapel to Frederick Chichester, Earl of Belfast. A free guided tour will take you round the entrance hall, dome, robing room and the council chamber. Founded in 1788, the **Linen Hall Library** at 17 Donegall Square is a physical representation of the Enlightenment values of the United Irishmen, and houses an unrivalled collection of local publications and political literature; non-members are welcome to browse.

North of the City Hall on Rosemary Street is the location of the city's gracefully spartan **First Presbyterian Church**, built by Roger Mulholland in 1783, and with the original box pews still in place. Around the corner on Royal Avenue is the **Castlecourt Shopping Centre**, a bomber's paradise as a soft commercial target when it opened ('Buy now while shops last', as 1970s graffiti used to say). The shopping centre is now one of the city's greatest retail successes.

The waterfront where Belfast began as a permanent settlement is now an area glittering with post-ceasefire investment. **Lagan Weir** has been redeveloped to create an attractive pedestrian environment, and the **Lagan Lookout** affords a good vantage point for the shipyards of East Belfast. It was in these docklands that the *Titanic* was built in 1912; a commemorative plaque to the ill-fated liner can be found on the side of City Hall. Along the river is **Waterfront Hall**, a prime symbol of peacetime civic optimism that contains a bar, restaurants and a large performance space. Also here is the **Odyssey Arena** restaurant, entertainment and shopping complex, and **W5**, Ireland's only purpose-built interactive science and technology museum.

Away from the river, make your way to the rapidly developing area of the city known as the **Cathedral Quarter**, where 17th-century cobbled streets converge on **St Anne's Cathedral** (on the corner of Donegall Street and Talbot Street). Another church of interest is the **Sinclair Seamen's Church** on Corporation Square. Designed by the prolific Charles Lanyon (designer of Queen's University and many of the city's other landmark buildings), the church has a pulpit made from the prow of a ship and an amazing collection of maritime material.

The alleys around Cornmarket and Ann Street are also worth exploring, especially the area off High Street known as the **Entries**, which boasts some excellent bars, including the **Morning Star** (17 Pottinger's Entry, 90 323 976) and **White's Tavern** – the oldest pub in the city, established in 1630 (2-4 Wine Cellar Entry, 90 236 232). Neither of these establishments approaches the fame of the **Crown Liquor Saloon**, however (*see p74*), a legendary imbibing venue opposite the **Europa Hotel**, whose ornate interior comes courtesy of the Italian craftsmen who worked at the Harland & Wolff shipyard. Adjoining the Europa Hotel, the **Grand Opera House** is a gaudily eclectic piece of Victorian art nouveau.

Passing the **Ormeau Baths Gallery** – the most significant space for modern art in the city – and continuing along the Dublin Road brings you into the university district. The redbrick façade of **Queen's University** dates from 1849 and leads to a pleasant colonnaded quadrangle. The library here is named after Queen's Nobel Prize-winning graduate Seamus Heaney, one of a starry generation of Northern Irish poets that includes the likes of Michael Longley, Derek Mahon, Paul Muldoon and Ciaran Carson. The college is also the venue for the annual **Belfast Festival** (90 665 577),

which takes place annually over three weeks in November. Near the university are the **Botanic Gardens**, where people have been enjoying an oasis of peace in the metropolis since 1827. The highlight of the gardens is the white-painted, iron-and-glass Palm House by Richard Turner, who also designed the glasshouses in the National Botanic Gardens in Dublin (*see p97*).

On the edge of the gardens is the **Ulster Museum**, which houses a vast collection of history, ecology, art and technology exhibits, including work by the Dublin-born artist Francis Bacon. The so-called **Golden Mile** around the university is home to many of the city's best pubs, clubs and restaurants, as well as offering label-lovers specialist shopping just minutes away on Lisburn Road.

Botanic Gardens

next to Queen's University (90 324 902). **Open** *Gardens* 8.30am-6.30pm daily. *Palm House* Apr-Sept 10am-5pm Mon-Fri; 2-5pm Sat, Sun; Oct-Mar 10am-4pm Mon-Fri; 2-4pm Sat, Sun. **Admission** free.

City Hall

Donegall Square (90 270 456). **Open** *Tours* June-Sept 10.30am, 11.30am, 2.30pm Mon-Sat; 2.30pm Sun; Oct-May 2.30pm Mon-Sat. **Admission** free.

Out on the town

Belfast's traditional entertainment district stretches from Queen's University in the south to the city centre along the 'Golden Mile'. Post-ceasefire investment, however, has spawned two entirely new party districts that are well worth exploring on a night out: the waterfront redevelopment and its bohemian neighbour, the Cathedral Quarter. All the venues mentioned here are within easy walking distance of each other.

Start your night at the superbly-designed **Waterfront Hall** (*see p271*), which is always dazzling at night. Stop off for a quick drink in the high, glass-fronted bar, or take a walk along the sculpture-studded path to the floodlit lagoon of the **Lagan Weir**. Move on to an excellent pint of Guinness in **McHugh's** (29 Queen's Square; 028 9050 9990), a popular modern bar and restaurant housed in the oldest building in Belfast. Feeling peckish? Take a stroll through Hill Street, one of the oldest Entries in the city, towards **Ba Soba** (*see p274*) for excellent Far Eastern food in a buzzy communal setting. Now it's time for another drink and some live music. Make your way through cobbled side streets to the **John Hewitt** (*see p275*). Comfortable,

welcoming and stylish, without being glitzy, this new bar is renowned for its excellent live sessions of both Irish trad and jazz. If you're thirsting for a cocktail and some turntable rhythms, head to the **Northern Whig** (*see p274*) at the end of the street. Negotiate your way past three towering Soviet statues (shipped here from the Prague Communist Party headquarters) and you'll discover an enormous bar and restaurant, throbbing with city beats and young professionals. The fun here lasts till one o'clock, but if you don't feel like going home, head for **Milk** (*see p275*), Belfast's newest and coolest club, which will definitely keep you dancing till dawn. Belfast's oldest gay bar and club, the **Parliament**, (*see p275*) also runs into the morning and is just around the corner. All welcome.

Breakfast is served from 7am in the ultra-stylish **McCausland Hotel** (*see p275*), just a few minutes' walk away, but you'll need to book ahead. Alternatively, an hour later, head for **Bewley's Oriental Café & Bar** (Donegall Arcade; 90 234 955) for a cheaper version of the (in)famous Ulster Fry. Open fires in winter and excellent city views are on offer here from 8am.

Snuggle up with a glass or two in the beautifully ornate **Crown Liquor Saloon**. *See p272.*

Ormeau Baths Gallery
18 Ormeau Avenue (90 321 402). **Open** 10am-6pm Tue-Sat. **Admission** free.

Ulster Museum
Stranmillis Road (90 383 000). **Open** 10am-5pm Mon-Fri; 1-5pm Sat; 2-5pm Sun. **Admission** free.

W5
Odyssey Arena (90 467 700). **Open** 10am-6pm Mon-Fri; noon-6pm Sat, Sun. **Admission** £5; £3 concessions; £14 family. **Credit** AmEx, MC, V.

North Belfast

North Belfast is dominated by **Cave Hill**, a mountain resembling a giant on his back, where the United Irishmen swore their allegiance to the rebellion in 1795. The ancient seat of the Chichester Family, **Belfast Castle**, can be spotted nestling among the forested slopes of the hill. Cave Hill is also the location of **Belfast Zoo**, a pioneer in ethical zookeeping which gives all of its animals plenty of room to roam. Catch bus nos.45 to 51 to reach Cave Hill from the city centre.

Belfast Castle
Antrim Road (90 776 925). **Open** 9am-9pm Mon-Sat; 9am-5.30pm Sun. **Admission** free.

Belfast Zoo
Antrim Road (90 776 277). **Open** 10am-3.30pm daily. **Admission** £4.80; £2.40 concessions; free disabled, OAPs, under-4s. **No credit cards.**

West Belfast

Outside the Balkans, there aren't many places in Europe as tribally ghettoised as West Belfast. This area was the cauldron from which the Troubles spilled over in 1968, when mobs of rioting Protestants burnt Catholic families out of their homes. Protests at the inadequacy of the IRA response ('IRA, I Ran Away', one bit of graffiti used to read) provoked the movement into extremism, leading to the emergence of the Provisionals. At the height of the Troubles the IRA and Loyalist paramilitaries policed their areas with ruthless control; the lines of demarcation are still clearly drawn, with none clearer than the central 'peace line' that snakes between the Protestant residents of the Shankill Road and the Catholics of the Springfield Road and the . Despite the current ceasefire, sectarian harassment and firebomb attacks on home-owners in west and north Belfast continue at a shocking level, but this is a resilient and proud area that deserves to be seen. One of the highlights of the Belfast calendar is the **West Belfast Festival** held every August (90 242 028). If you're in town, this is the best time to explore everything the area has to offer.

The famous gable-end murals on the **Falls Road** cover an impressive range of subjects, from dead patriots to Che Guevara. At the end of the Falls, **Milltown Cemetery** (90 613 972) is worth a visit for its Republican plot, where the roll-call of patriots goes all the way back to 1798, and includes Bobby Sands and the other republican hunger strikers of 1981.

The murals on the **Shankill Road** tend to be more bellicose than on the Falls, featuring hooded men brandishing rifles and blood-curdling Old Testament quotations. There is a fervent evangelical scene in Protestant Belfast, best witnessed at one of 'Big Ian's' fire and brimstone Sunday services. As if you needed telling, people take their politics seriously here, so keep that Bobby Sands T-shirt covered up when you drop in for a pint on the Shankill and avoid striking up 'The Sash My Father Wore' in Andersonstown. Take Seamus Heaney's advice: 'whatever you say, say nothing'.

East Belfast

The predominantly Protestant area of East Belfast, over the river Lagan, has traditionally functioned as Belfast's industrial heartland, home to the **Harland & Wolff** shipyards and the aircraft manufacturing complex of Short's. Harland & Wolff's enormous cranes, Samson and Goliath, dominate the industrial landscape here. This area is also the birthplace of pop god Van Morrison and flautist James Galway.

The former home of the Northern Ireland government and current site of the Northern Ireland Assembly and Executive at **Stormont** is to be found at the top of Newtownards Road, four miles (six-and-a-half kilometres) from the city centre. It's an impressive structure, set in its own extensive grounds, which may be freely visited. Enquire at the tourist office or call Stormont about possible tours of the building's interior (90 520 600/90 520 700).

Where to eat & drink

Café society and cutting-edge cuisine have finally arrived in Belfast. Chinese restaurants also abound, and you'll find lots of **Clements** coffeehouses scattered throughout the centre; they're a pleasant choice for a quick snack.

Alden's

229 Upper Newtownards Road (90 650 079). **Open** 6-10.30pm Mon-Thur; 10am-2.30pm, 6-11pm Fri; 6-11pm Sat. **Main courses** £6.50-£15.95. **Credit** AmEx, DC, MC, V.
Cathy Gradwell's cooking is the epitome of contemporary Irish cuisine, and the room is fantastic, too.

Ba Soba

38 Hill Street (90 586 868). **Open** 11am-3pm Mon; noon-11pm Tue-Sat. **Main courses** £6-£9.50. **Credit** MC, V.
Belfast's only Japanese-style noodle bar serves an eclectic menu drawn from all over South-east Asia.

Cayenne

Shaftesbury Square (90 331 532). **Open** noon-2.15pm, 6-11pm Mon-Fri; 6-11pm Sat. **Main courses** from £9. **Credit** AmEx, DC, MC, V.
The Rankins' gorgeous room is splendidly hip, and the fab modern food lives up to its surroundings.

Crown Liquor Saloon

46 Great Victoria Street (90 279 901). **Open** 11.30am-midnight Mon-Sat; 12.30-10pm Sun. **Main courses** £3.75-£6. **Credit** AmEx, DC, MC, V.
A Belfast institution dishing up decent pub food. Get your Irish stew and oysters here.

Deane's

34-40 Howard Street (90 560 000). **Open** *Brasserie* noon-2.30pm, 5.30-10.30pm Mon-Sat. *Restaurant* 7-9.30pm Wed, Thur, Sat; noon-2pm, 7-9.30pm Fri. **Main courses** £9-£16 brasserie; £31-£55 set menus. **Credit** AmEx, MC, V.
There's informal cooking in the brasserie and much more complicated cuisine in the upstairs restaurant. Deane's is the only Belfast restaurant with a Michelin star; prices reflect this.

Ginger

217 Ormeau Road (90 493 143). **Open** 5-9.30pm Tue-Fri; noon-3pm, 5-9.30pm Sat. **Main courses** £10-£14. **Credit** MC, V.
This BYO restaurant has the most coveted tables in town: ace cooking, ace sounds and fantastic value are the winning combination here.

Nick's Warehouse

35-39 Hill Street (90 439 690). **Open** noon-3pm Mon-Fri; 6-9.30pm Tue-Sun. **Main courses** £6.50-£7.50 wine bar; £10.95-£13.95 restaurant. **Credit** AmEx, DC, MC, V.
Everything here is just right, from the ambience to the cooking. The atmosphere, especially downstairs in the wine bar, is thunderous.

Northern Whig

2 Bridge Street (90 509 888). **Open** 10am-1am Mon-Sat; 1pm-midnight Sun. **Main courses** £5.95-£11.95. **Credit** MC, V.
Welcome to Belfast's Socialist Realist experience at this recently opened café and bar. Statues of Soviet heroes dominate the enormous interior; good food and cocktails are served all day.

Sun Kee

38 Donegall Pass (90 312 016). **Open** 5-11pm daily. **Main courses** £6-£12. **No credit cards**.
Ignore the utilitarian decor; Sun Kee offers the best Chinese cooking in the whole of Ireland, served at scarily cheap prices.

Ta Tu Bar & Grill

701 Lisburn Road (90 380 818). **Open** noon-9.30pm Mon-Sat; noon-8pm Sun. **Main courses** £5.95-£11.95. **Credit** MC, V.
One of the most beautifully designed bars in Belfast has a spacious interior with exposed industrial piping. It also serves decent fusion food.

Arts & entertainment

Check *That's Entertainment*, available from the tourist office and some hotel lobbies, for the latest information. Popular music pubs include the **Eglantine Inn** (32-40 Malone Road, 90 381 994) and the **Botanic Inn** (23-27 Malone Road, 90 660 460), commonly known as the 'Egg and Bot'. For trad head to the **John Hewitt** (51 Donegall Street, 90 233 768), the **Duke of York** (4-11 Commercial Court, 90 241 062) and **Maddens** (74 Barry Street, 90 244 114). Good nightclubs include the **Limelight** (17 Ormeau Avenue, 90 325 968), the **Manhattan** (Bradbury Place, 90 233 131) and **Milk** (10-14 Tomb Street, 90 278 876). **Parliament** (2-6 Dunbar Street, 90 234 520) and the **Kremlin** (96 Donegall Street, 90 809 700) are the epicentre of the city's gay nightlife. *See also p272* **Out on the town.**

The **Grand Opera House** (2-4 Great Victoria Street, 90 241 919) has a busy programme all year. Classical and rock concerts are also staged at the **Ulster Hall** (Bedford Street, 90 323 900), the **Waterfront Hall** (2 Lanyon Place, 90 334 400) and the **Odyssey Arena** (2 Queens Quay; 90 451 055). The most significant Belfast theatres are the **Lyric** (Ridgeway Street, 90 381 081), which specialises in quality productions by Irish playwrights, and the **Old Museum Arts Centre** (7 College Square North, 90 235 053), which offers slightly more experimental material. The **Queen's Film Theatre** (Univerity Square Mews, 90 244 837) is the city's only arthouse cinema.

Where to stay

Credit card bookings can be made through the **Belfast Welcome Centre** (*see p276*).

Botanic Lodge Guesthouse
87 Botanic Avenue (90 327 682). **Rates** £25 single; £40-£45 double. **Credit** MC, V.
One of the most popular guesthouses in the city, this large premises is in the heart of the University and nightlife district.

Europa Hotel
Great Victoria Street (90 327 000/www.hastins hotels.com). **Rates** £70-£105 single; £100-£150 double. **Credit** AmEx, DC, MC, V.
Famed as the most bombed building in Europe until the Bosnian war, the Europa Hotel has since moved on to bigger and brighter things, such as providing former US President Bill Clinton with a bed for the night on his visit to Belfast.

Hilton Hotel
4 Lanyon Place (90 277 000). **Rates** £96-£110 single/double. **Credit** AmEx, DC, MC, V.

Set beside the Waterfront Hall, the Belfast Hilton was the first multi-national to brave Belfast after the ceasefire. It's also the only five-star hotel in the city.

Linen House Hostel
18-20 Kent Street (90 586 400/www.belfasthostel. com). **Rates** £6.50-£8.50 dormitory; £24 double. **Credit** MC, V.
An excellent, friendly city centre hostel, just minutes from the Belfast Welcome Centre, offering dorms and private rooms.

McCausland Hotel
34-38 Victoria Street (tel/fax 90 220 200). **Rates** from £110 single; £150 double; £190 suite. **Credit** AmEx, DC, MC, V.
Housed in two beautifully restored 19th-century warehouses, this boutique hotel is one of the most attractive places to stay in the city.

Tara Lodge
36 Cromwell Road (90 590 900). **Rates** £43-£60 single; £60-£68 double. **Credit** AmEx, DC, MC, V.
You'll pay slightly more for your bed and breakfast here, but it's worth it. The Tara is intimate and comfortable, with an excellent in-house restaurant.

Getting there

By car
From Dublin, take the N1, which eventually becomes the A1, north to Belfast.

By bus
Daily **Ulsterbus** (90 333 000) services connect Dublin with Belfast (3hrs; £12-£15 return). The main station in Belfast is on Glengall Street, beside the Europa Hotel.

By train
There are regular services (90 333 000) from Dublin to Belfast Central Station on East Bridge Street on board the excellent **Enterprise** service (2hrs, £30 return). Trains to and from all other destinations leave from Great Victoria Street station.

By air
There are two airports: the recently redeveloped **Belfast City Airport** (90 939 093), just 10min from the city centre, and **Belfast International Airport** (94 422 888), which is 32km (20 miles) outside the city in Co Antrim. BCA is used for flights from small British airports; BIA by most international airlines. There are a regular bus services from both airports to the city centre.

By ferry
The **Stena Line** catamaran from Belfast to Stranraer in Scotland docks at Belfast Harbour on Donegall Quay (087 057 0707). The **Seacat** (087 0552 3523) goes to Troon in Scotland and also to Heysham in England May-Sept. **P&O** services (087 0242 4777) from Scotland use Larne, 32km (20 miles) north of Belfast; there are also connections to Liverpool with **Norse Irish Ferries** (90 779 090).

Trips Out of Town

The glittering **Waterfront Hall** lights up Belfast. *See p271.*

Getting around

Buses depart from Donegall Square, with
timetables and route maps available from the
kiosks on the west side. **Taxis** are easily picked
up at the main rank on Donegall Square East, or
from: Fon-a-Cab (90 233 333); Jet Taxis (90 323
278) and Able Taxis (90 241 999).

Tourist information

Belfast Welcome Centre
47 Donegall Place (90 246 609). **Open** 9am-5.30pm
Mon-Sat.
The brand new centre offers an accommodation
service, bureau de change, shop, Internet café, plus
information on events, sights and attractions
throughout Northern Ireland.

Bord Fáilte
53 Castle Street (90 327 888). **Open** *Oct-May* 9am-
5pm Mon-Fri. *June-Sept* 9am-5pm Mon-Fri; 9am-
12.30pm Sat.

Northern Irish Tourist Board
*Postal address: St Anne's Court, 59 North Street,
Belfast BT1 1NB (90 231 221/fax 90 240 960/
www.ni-tourism.com).*

Other Ulster highlights

From either Belfast or Derry it is possible to
explore the other attractions of Northern
Ireland. In the far south of County Down, the
impressive **Mourne Mountains** do indeed
'sweep down to the sea' as Percy French
promises, and tempt serious hikers with
difficult but rewarding craggy terrain, while
in County Tyrone, the more gentle peaty
landscape of the **Sperrin Mountains** shelters
plentiful wildlife and dozens of prehistoric
relics. Also in Tyrone, close to the town of
Omagh, are the **Ulster History Park** and the
Ulster-American Folk Park, two of the
most impressive heritage sites in the country.
Further south, ancient relics, particularly Celtic
and early Christian remains, can be found
around the shores of **Lough Erne** in
Fermanagh, which also offers abundant fishing
opportunities and lovely lakeland scenery.

Perhaps most enticing of all is the stretch of
spectacular **coastline** between Portstewart in
Derry and Ballycastle in Antrim, and on south
to Cushenden. In addition to several good
beaches (those at Portstewart and Portrush are
favoured by surfers) and myriad wonderful
views, this coast is the location of the justly
famous **Giant's Causeway**, a cluster of basalt
rocks formed by a lava eruption 60 million
years ago. According to legend the causeway
was built by the giant Fionn McCumhaill who
was in love with a female giant on the Scottish
island of Staffa.

Contact the Northern Irish Tourist Board
and Bord Fáilte in Belfast (for both, *see above*)
for further information about these and other
attractions in the province.

Ulster-American Folk Park
2 Mellon Road, Castletown, Omagh (8224 3292).
Open *Oct-Mar* 10.30am-3.30pm Mon-Fri. *Apr-Sept*
10.30am-4.30pm Mon-Sat; 11am-5pm Sun.
Admission £4; £2.50 concessions; £10 family.
Credit MC, V.

Ulster History Park
Cullion Lislap, Omagh (8164 8188). **Open** *Apr-June,
Sept* 10am-5.30pm daily. *July, Aug* 10am-6.30pm
daily. *Oct-Mar* 10am-5pm Mon-Fri. **Admission**
£3.75; £2.20 concessions; £12 family. **Credit** MC, V.

Directory

Directory

Getting Around

Arriving & leaving

By air

Dublin Airport is located about 13 kilometres (eight miles) north of the city and is managed by **Aer Rianta** (814 1111). Flight information is also available on Teletext (**Aertel** pages 570-575). For details of duty and tax free shopping at the airport, call freephone 1 800 747 747; there's a great range, but the mark-up on food products is high, so buy your cheeses, whiskey marmalade and soda bread in advance in Dublin itself. For left luggage and lost property facilities at the airport, see p287.

The following airlines have regular services to Dublin:

Major airlines

Aer Lingus *886 8888/www. aerlingus.ie.* **Open** 8.30am-8pm Mon-Fri; 8.30am-6pm Sat; 10am-6pm Sun. **Credit** AmEx, DC, MC, V.
Alitalia *4-5 Dawson Street, Southside (677 5171/www.alitalia.it).* **Open** *Flights to Rome* 9am-5.30pm Mon, Thur, Sat. *Flights to Milan* 9am-5.30pm Wed, Sat, Sun. **Credit** AmEx, DC, MC, V.
bmi British Midland *407 3036/www.flybmi.com.* **Open** 8am-8pm Mon-Fri; 8am-6pm Sat; 9am-6pm Sun. **Credit** AmEx, DC, MC, V.
British Airways *reservations/ enquiries 1-800 626747/www. britishairways.com.* **Open** 24hrs daily. **Credit** AmEx, DC, MC, V.
City Jet *information/reservations 844 5566/www.cityjet.com.* **Open** 8am-7.30pm Mon-Fri; 8am-5.30pm Sat. **Credit** AmEx, DC, MC, V.
Ryanair *reservations 609 7800/www.ryanair.com.* **Open** 8am-9pm Mon-Fri; 9am-6pm Sat; 10am-6pm Sun. **Credit** AmEx, MC, V.
Virgin Atlantic *information/ reservations 500 5500/www. virginatlantic.com.* **Open** 9.30am-5.30pm Mon-Fri; 10am-1pm Sat. **Credit** AmEx, DC, MC, V.

To & from the airport

Dublin Airport is not served by rail, and taxis are notoriously expensive (€12.70-€19 into town), so the easiest way to get into the city centre is by bus. Dublin Bus's **Airlink** coach service (844 4265) has two routes: the **747** (5.45am-11.30pm Mon to Sat and 7.15am-11.30pm Sun) stops at the central bus station (Busárus) on Store Street (*see below*); the **748** (6.50am-9.30pm Mon to Sat; 7am-10.05pm Sun) stops at Heuston Station (*see below*). Both journeys take around 25 minutes and tickets, which can be bought from the driver, are €4.57 (€2.54 concessions). Three other non-express buses (41, 41B and 41C) also serve the airport (€1.46 single), with timetables displayed at the bus stops outside the airport's Arrivals terminal. The private **Aircoach** service (844 7118) runs from the terminal to Ballsbridge via O'Connell Street. It's more expensive (€5), but prompt and reliable.

Whether you're driving, taking a taxi or using one of the bus services, note that until the end of 2003 engineering works on the new Dublin Port Tunnel are likely to cause considerable delays on the main N1 airport road; always be sure to leave extra time for your journey.

By coach

Travelling by coach in Ireland is cheaper than travelling by rail, though the Irish road network is still not as good as it might be. The largest nationwide coach service is **Bus Éireann** (836 6111/ www.buseireann.ie), which operates out of Busárus, Dublin's central bus station. Other private companies, such as **Airbus** (671 5333), **Nestor Coaches Express Travel** (832 0094) and **Rapid Express** (679 1549) all offer similar services to Bus Éireann but their coverage is nowhere near as comprehensive.

Busárus

Store Street, Northside (information 703 2436). **Open** *Information desk* 9.30am-6pm daily. **Map** p313 J3/4. The Busárus information desk can provide details of local and national bus and coach services and tours, including services to Northern Ireland. For left luggage facilities and lost property, *see p287.*

By train

The national mainline railway network is run by **Iarnród Éireann** (836 6222/www. irishrail.ie). Trains to and from Dublin use either **Connolly Station** on the northside (*see p280*) or **Heuston Station**, near Phoenix Park (map p311 C4). As a quick guide, Connolly serves Belfast, Rosslare and Sligo; Heuston serves Galway, Westport, Tralee, Kildare, Cork, Ennis and Waterford. The Enterprise service to Belfast (*see p275*) is a pleasure (clean, fast and comfortable) but other InterCity services can be pretty grotty, slow and decidedly uncomfortable.

Bikes can be carried on most mainline routes: ask where to store them as regulations vary with the type of train. Rates for transporting bikes range from about €2.50 single or €5 return for journeys of up to 56

Directory

kilometres (35 miles) to €7.60 single/€15.25 return for trips over 138 kilometres (86 miles).

For details of left luggage and lost property at Connolly and Heuston Stations, *see p287*.

By ferry

The three main companies serving Dublin are **Irish Ferries** (Dublin–Holyhead), **P&O Irish Sea** (Dublin– Mostyn) and **Stena Line** (Dublin– Holyhead and Dún Laoghaire–Holyhead). Dublin Port is closer to town but Dún Laoghaire boasts a brand-new terminal and Stena's fast SeaCat service.

Irish Ferries

2-4 Merrion Row, Southside (reservations & enquiries 1-890 313 131/638 3333/recorded information 661 0715/www. irishferries.ie). **Credit** AmEx, DC, MC, V. **Map** p313 J6.
Irish Ferries also runs services from Rosslare to Pembroke, Roscoff and Cherbourg (*see p230*).

P&O Irish Sea

From the UK 0870 24 24 777/ from Rep. of Ireland 1-800 409 049/ www.poirishsea.com). **Open** 7.30am-10.30pm Mon-Fri; 7.30am-8.30pm Sat, Sun. **Credit** AmEx, MC, V.

Stena Line

Ferry Terminal, Dún Laoghaire Harbour, Dublin Bay (reservations & enquiries 204 7777/www.stena line.com). **Credit** AmEx, DC, MC, V. Stena Line also runs from Rosslare to Fishguard (*see p230*) and from Belfast to Stranraer (*see p275*).

Getting around

Dublin's city centre is remarkably compact. The main markers are **O'Connell Street** on the northside and **Trinity College** and **St Stephen's Green** on the southside. Even if you're told that some place is 'right on the other side of town', it will never be more than a 25-minute stroll away, but if your hotel isn't within walking distance of the city centre, you'll need to use public transport to get into town.

Public transport

Information

There are two types of public transport in Dublin: rail and bus. **Iarnród Éireann** runs the DART (electric rail) and suburban rail services, while **Bus Atha Cliath** (Dublin Bus) is responsible for the city buses. Several combined bus and rail tickets are available (*see below* **Pre-paid tickets**), so figure out where and how much you want to travel and see which type suits best. The offices listed below can sell tickets and give out maps and information.

Dublin Bus

Head Office, 59 Upper O'Connell Street, Northside (872 0000/ information & customer services 873 4222). **Open** 9am-5.30pm Mon-Fri; 9am-2pm Sat. **Map** p313 H3.

Iarnród Éireann (DART)

Head Office, Connolly Station, Northside (Iarnod Éireann 836 3333/ passenger information 836 6222). **Open** 8.30-6pm Mon-Fri; 9am-6pm Sat; 10am-6pm Sun. **Map** p313 J3.

Fares & tickets

Note that at the time of going to press, fares for 2002 had not been confirmed, although the Irish Government has said that the converted prices will be rounded down not up. **The Euro prices given here are conversions of the 2001 fares and are subject to change.**

Fares for both bus and rail travel are calculated on a 'stage' basis and range from 76¢ for up to three stages to €1.46 for long distances. Rail tickets are available from all DART/Suburban Rail stations and from the **Rail Travel Centre** (35 Lower Abbey Street, Northside; 836 6222). When purchasing a single or return rail ticket, specify the final destination, so that the ticket can be validated for a connecting bus service if

necessary. Tickets for both bus and rail travel can also be bought directly from the bus driver. However, be prepared for the **Autofare** system, which is now a feature of nearly all bus routes. Though it speeds up the process, you'll need the exact change in order to purchase a ticket. If you need to buy a ticket on the bus, get on through the left-hand side of the front entrance; the right-hand side is reserved for passengers who have **pre-paid tickets**, which are easier, quicker and cheaper. In addition to those listed below, weekly and monthly tickets are available. For these you will need a photo ID card (€2.54), from Dublin Bus Head Office. Combined pre-paid tickets can be purchased from the offices of Dublin Bus and DART, USIT (*see p293*), main newsagents and the Dublin Tourism Centre (*see p294*).

Pre-paid tickets

● **One-day Short Hop:** unlimited bus, suburban rail and DART travel – €7.24; €10.80 family.
● **One-Day Rambler:** unlimited bus travel – €4.45; €6.96 family.
● **Four Day Explorer:** 4 days unlimited off-peak bus, suburban rail & DART travel – €13.33.
● **Weekly rail pass:** €18.40; €13.97 concessions.
● **Weekly Short Hop:** unlimited bus, suburban rail and DART travel – €24.13.
● **Weekly Rambler:** unlimited bus travel for one week – €15.85; €5 children.
● **Child's ten-journey rail ticket:** €4.95-€11.43.

Buses

Bus stops look like tall green or blue lollipops. They usually (though not always) have a timetable attached but seldom feature a bus shelter. 'Set down only' means that the bus only lets passengers off there, so don't hang around waiting. Note that the middle doors of buses seldom open: get on at the front and off at the back.

There are about 900 buses on the road, serving well over

100 different routes, so you will usually find a bus stop close by. The frequency of buses, however, varies enormously: at best, buses may be anything from ten to 20 minutes apart, but on less-popular routes you could be waiting for over an hour. Timetables at bus stops are often defaced, so your best bet is to get up-to-date versions from Dublin Bus's head office (*see p280*). Buses only keep loosely to their schedules: sometimes they leave early or don't show up at all, so always allow plenty of extra time for your journey, especially in rush hour and during the whole of Friday afternoon.

Nitelink

General bus services end at around 11.30pm, but Nitelink buses run every night except Sunday from the city centre to the suburbs along 22 different routes. Services leave from d'Olier Street, Westmoreland Street and College Street (all on the southside), at 12.30am, 1.30am, 2.30am and 3.30am. The fare is set at €4, apart from route P to Maynooth, which costs €6. For further information, contact Dublin Bus.

Rail services

The **DART** (Dublin Area Rapid Transit) and **Suburban Rail** lines provide a cleaner and faster alternative to buses for journeys beyond the city centre, but they should be avoided during rush hour, when the carriages are usually overcrowded. Several DART stations offer connecting bus services, including one running between **Connolly Station** and **Heuston Station**, which means that even if the nearest station is further than walking distance from your destination, it may still be the best option. Apart from Connolly, the other city centre DART stations are **Tara Street**, **Pearse** and **Grand Canal Dock**.

The DART serves the north and south suburbs around Dublin Bay from Bray in the south to Howth and Malahide in the north. Note that it is sometimes necessary to change at Howth Junction to reach your desired destination north of the city. The DART is supplemented by Suburban Rail routes that range as far as Dundalk in Co. Louth, Arklow in Co. Wicklow, Mullingar in West Meath and Kildare in Co. Kildare. Consult the map on page 310 for details of intervening stations.

Taxis

There is a multitude of taxi companies in Dublin, but taxis are neither cheap nor (despite the industry's recent deregulation) particularly easy to get hold of. If you're getting a taxi at night, remember that most clubs finish at the same time (from around 2am), so it's worth leaving early to avoid the queues. Over Christmas, taxis are nearly impossible to come by, and an hour's wait is common. Even under normal circumstances, queues for taxi ranks can be very long. There are 24-hour taxi ranks at Abbey Street and Upper O'Connell Street on the northside, and at Aston Quay, College Green and St Stephen's Green (east and north) on the southside. In the southern suburbs try Lansdowne Road in Ballsbridge and Upper Rathmines Road. If you have any complaints or queries about the taxi service, contact the **Irish Taxi Drivers' Federation** (836 4166).

Fares

Some private companies offer fixed rates for certain journeys, and don't charge a pick-up fee, but licensed cabs all run on a meter. From 1 January 2002 the minimum charge was €2.75, for the first half-mile or four minutes. Each additional ninth of a mile or 30 seconds is charged at 15¢ (8am-10pm) or 20¢ (10pm-8am). There's an additional charge

of 20¢ on Sundays and public holidays. Extra charges of 50¢ are levied for additional passengers (excluding infants), animals (other than guide dogs) and each piece of luggage that has to stowed in the boot of the cab. You will be charged an additional €1.50 if you hire a taxi by phone or radio pick-up, or if you pick up a cab from the airport rank.

Phone cabs

Access & Metro Cabs 668 3333.
City & Eurocabs 872 2222/872 7272/844 5844
Co-Op Taxis 676 6666.
Pony Cabs 661 2233.

Chauffeur services

Execkars 830 5148.
The Limousine Company 872 3003.
Metro Limousine & Saloon Hire 667 0955.

Driving

EU and international driving licences are valid for driving in Ireland. In fact, as long as you're 17 or over and hold a provisional licence, you don't actually need to pass your test to drive unaccompanied in Ireland. Unsurprisingly, there are a shocking number of road deaths each year as a result – more than twice the toll in the UK. Speed limits are 48 kilometres per hour (30mph) in urban areas; 64 kilometres per hour (40mph) in suburban areas; 96kph (60mph) on primary roads (excluding urban areas and motorways); and 112 kilometres per hour (70mph) on dual carriageways and motorways. Written road signs are always bilingual. Seat belts must be worn by drivers and front seat passengers of cars and light vans; where rear seat belts are fitted these must also be worn. The alcohol limit, as in the UK and the majority of US states, is 80 milligrammes per 100 millilitres of blood. Drive on the left.

The traffic situation in Dublin is simply hellish. Tailbacks from 7am in the morning, and again in the evening, make the daily

Directory

commute a grind for most Dubliners. The situation is not helped by the fact that investment in public transport remains woefully low and parking fines are minuscule compared to the majority of other major European cities. However, the powers that be are finally getting their act together. Dublin now boasts the most sophisticated traffic monitoring system in the world – apparently – and the flashing lights of the clampers' tow truck have become a common sight on the streets of the city. There are also express bus services using dedicated bus lanes (Quality Bus Corridors) along certain major routes. Note that in the city centre, construction of the new LUAS (light rail system) is expected to cause considerable delays throughout 2002 and 2003.

If you are determined to join the motoring hordes, check out **Travel FM** (106.8FM), which broadcasts up-to-the-minute traffic information.

Outside the city, you'll find that the driving conditions are much more pleasant. Country roads may not always be of the highest standard, but they are rarely choked with traffic, and in recent years, their quality has greatly improved, thanks to European investment. Getting from A to B is not as vexing a procedure as it once was.

Breakdown services

The following places all offer 24-hour support.
Automobile Association *23 Suffolk Street, Southside (677 9481).*
Glenalbyn Motors *460 4050.*
RAC *freephone 1-800 535 005.*
Tom Kane Motors *833 8143/ after 6pm 831 5983.*

Filling stations

Maxol on Mespil Road in Ballsbridge (667 0450) is open 24 hours daily.

Parking

Parking in the city isn't outrageously expensive, at about €1.50 per hour with a flat rate in the evenings. You'll find computerised billboards dotted throughout the city detailing availability in the major car parks. All on-street parking within the city centre is now ticketed: there should be at least one of the necessary machines on each street.

Vehicle hire

Unless you're a committed (and patient) car driver there's no point hiring a car for your stay in Dublin. However, if you plan to tour the rest of the country, a vehicle becomes essential, since public transport is far less frequent – not to say sporadic – outside the city. You must have a valid driving licence and a credit card in order to hire a car. All the car hire companies listed here also have outlets at Dublin Airport. All advise that you pre-book your vehicle, giving at least 24 hours' notice, during the summer months.

Access
Unit 2B, Airport Business Park, Cloghran, Northern suburbs (844 4848). **Open** *Office 9am-5pm daily. Breakdown service 24hrs daily.* **Credit** DC, MC, V.

Avis
1 Hanover Street East, Southside (605 7555). **Open** 6am-11.30pm Mon-Fri, Sun; 6am-11pm Sat. **Credit** AmEx, DC, MC, V.

Budget
151 Drumcondra Road Lower, Northern suburbs (837 9611/837 9802/airport 844 5150/844 5919). **Open** 9am-5pm Mon-Sat; 10am-1pm Sun (summer only). **Credit** AmEx, DC, MC, V.
The airport branch is open 6am-midnight daily.

Hertz
149 Leeson Street Upper, Ballsbridge, Southern suburbs (660 2255/airport 844 5466).

Open 9am-5.30pm Mon-Sat; 9am-noon Sun (summer only). **Credit** AmEx, DC, MC, V.
The airport branch is open 6am-midnight daily.

National Car Rental
Cranford Centre, Stillorgan, Southern suburbs (260 3771/ airport 844 4162). **Open** 9am-5pm Mon-Sat; 9am-noon Sun. **Credit** AmEx, DC, MC, V.
The airport branch is open 6am-midnight daily.

Cycling

The biggest problem with cycling in Dublin is not the air pollution, nor avoiding the mad drivers, but rather finding a safe place to keep your bike: Dublin railings are filled with single wheels dangling from locks. If you have to park outdoors, try to use two locks – a strong one for the frame and back wheel and another for the front wheel – and take your lights, saddle and any other detachables with you.

Bicycle hire

Expect to pay around €12-€15 per day for bike hire, though weekly rates and group discounts will reduce the price.

MacDonalds Bike Rental
38-39 Wexford Street, Southside (475 2586). All cross-city buses. **Open** 9am-6pm Mon-Fri; 9am-5.30pm Sat. **Credit** MC, V. **Map** p313 G6.

Walking

Everybody walks everywhere in Dublin: the main shopping areas (Grafton Street, Henry Street and Temple Bar) are pedestrianised, and the city is ideal for meandering. You'll find a reliable series of street maps at the back of this guide, starting on page 311; otherwise try the very comprehensive Ordnance Survey maps of Dublin (available in any bookshop) or the array of pocket guides on sale at Dublin Tourism Centre (*see p294*).

Resources A-Z

Addresses

There is no system of postal or zip codes in the Republic of Ireland (Northern Ireland, of course, is covered by the UK postal code system) and addresses can often appear disconcertingly vague as a result. This is especially the case in rural areas, where an address can consist simply of the 'townland' and nearest town or village. This lack of precision notwithstanding, the Irish postal service is fairly quick and reliable (see p291).

Dublin is slightly different from the rest of the country in that it has a system of postal districts, numbered from 1 to 24, covering each area of the city. The system is simple: even numbers cover the area south of the river Liffey; odd numbers north of the river. As a quick guide, locations in the city centre will either have a Dublin 1 (northside) or a Dublin 2 (southside) post code. The area immediately west of Christchurch is Dublin 8; Ballsbridge, Ringsend and Donnybrook, just south-east of the centre, are Dublin 4, and the area around the Four Courts and Smithfield is Dublin 7.

For details of how addresses and area names are used in this guide, see p3.

Age restrictions

● Admission to pubs: officially 18, although children are tolerated before 5pm
● Admission to clubs: usually 18, although some may have an over-21 or over-23 policy
● Buying alcohol: 18
● Buying and consuming cigarettes: 16
● Driving: 17
● Marriage: 18 (or 17 with a Court Exemption)
● Sex (hetero- and homosexual): 17

Attitude & etiquette

Although, some people might argue otherwise, there are few, if any, national differences in behaviour between the Irish and the British. The Irish have traditionally prided themselves on a friendly and open attitude to life and their fellow human beings, but in some quarters, and especially in Dublin, this geniality is gradually and inevitably losing ground. In general, though, attitudes are still a little more relaxed here than in the UK.

Although recent political and financial scandals have given a public airing to the unorthodoxy of some Irish business practices (see p22), officially business etiquette is on par with that of other Western nations. You may well, however, notice more conviviality and less formality than in some other countries.

Business

Conventions & conferences

Incentive Conference Ireland

2 Pembroke Place, Ballsbridge, Southern suburbs (667 1711). The first point of contact if you are planning a conference in Dublin or elsewhere in Ireland.

Conference venues

The following venues have excellent conference facilities, suitable for varying sizes of group and budget.
Berkeley Court Hotel *Lansdowne Road, Ballsbridge, Southern suburbs (660 1711).*
Burlington Hotel *Leeson Street Upper, Ballsbridge, Southern suburbs (660 5222).* Map p309.
Dublin Castle Conference Centre *Dublin Castle, Southside (679 3713).* Map p313 G5.
Westbury Hotel *Grafton Street, Southside (679 1122; see p42).*

Couriers & shippers

Call freephone **DHL Worldwide Express** (1-800 725 725) or **Federal Express** (1-800 535 800).

Office hire & business centres

The following firms offer full office facilities, including ISDN, company voicemail and secretarial services.
Abbey House Serviced Offices *15-17 Abbey Street Upper, Northside (872 4911).* Map p313 G4.
Merrion Business Centre *20 Merrion Street Upper, Southside (676 1044).* Map p313 J6.

Secretarial services

The following offer the usual services: transcription, scanning and photocopying, proofing, Internet facilities and telephone answering.
ALISEC Secretarial Services *41 Lower Baggot Street, Southside (661 3824)* Map p313 J6.
Firstaff Personnel Consultants *85 Grafton Street, Southside (679 7766).* Map p313 H5.

Useful organisations

Business Information Centre

Ilac Centre, Henry Street, Northside (873 3996). **Open** 10am-8pm Mon-Thur; 10am-5pm Fri, Sat. Map p313 G/H4.
A reference service/library dealing with company and market information.

CFI Online

22 Northumberland Road, Ballsbridge, Southern suburbs (664 1111). **Open** 9am-5.30pm Mon-Fri. Map p314 L7.
Information on Irish companies and trade names.

Chamber of Commerce

22 Merrion Square, Southside (661 2888/www.chambersireland.ie). **Open** 9am-5.30pm Mon-Fri. Map p313 J6.

Directory

Ireland's national chamber of commerce. Visit the website for more information.

Dublin Chamber of Commerce

7 Clare Street, Southside (613 0800/661 4111). **Open** 8am-5.30pm Mon-Fri. *Documentation* 9.30am-12.30pm, 2.30-4.30pm Mon-Fri. **Map** p313 J5.

European Commission

18 Dawson Street, Southside (662 5113). **Open** 9am-5pm Mon-Fri;. *Library* (by appointment only) 11am-1pm, 2-4.30pm Mon-Fri. **Map** p313 H5.

Irish Stock Exchange

28 Anglesea Street, Southside (677 8808). **Open** 9am-5.30pm Mon-Fri. Not open to the public.

Consumer

If you have a consumer complaint contact the **Office of the Director of Consumer Affairs** (4-5 Harcourt Road, Dublin 2; 402 5500), which has the power to prosecute erring traders, with any resulting damages usually awarded to the complainant. Alternatively, you could contact the **European Consumer Centre** (13A Upper O'Connell Street, Dublin 1; 809 0600) for free legal advice. The Oasis website, **www.oasis.gov.ie**, has good information on consumer and citizens' rights.

Customs

Those visitors travelling to and from countries within the EU are no longer entitled to duty free. However, if you're entering Ireland from outside the EU, you are entitled to the following duty free allowances:

● 200 cigarettes or 100 cigarillos or 50 cigars or 250g tobacco

● 2 litres port, sherries or fortified wines or 1 litre spirits or strong liqueurs (over 22% alcohol)

● 2 litres of table wine

● 60 millilitres perfume

● 250 millilitres toilet water

● €184 worth of goods, including gifts and souvenirs.

There are restrictions in place on importing meat or meat products; the import and export of currency is unrestricted.

EU citizens of 18 years and over are not required to make a customs declaration, as long as they do not bring tax-free goods into the country; non-EU citizens aged 16 or over may bring in goods (for non-commercial use) on which tax has been paid, up to the value of €175. Those aged 15 have an allowance of €90.

Customs & Excise

Main office *Ship Street Gate, Dublin Castle, Southside (679 2777). All cross-city buses.* **Open** 9am-5pm Mon-Fri. **Map** p313 G5.
Also at *Second floor, Irish Life Centre, Abbey Street Lower, Northside (878 8811/fax 878 0836). All cross-city buses.* **Open** *Office* 9am-4pm Mon-Fri. *Telephone enquiries* 9am-12.45pm, 2-4pm Mon-Fri. **Map** p313 H4.

Disabled travellers

The Irish service industry is slowly coming around to the idea that potential customers are made up of all types of people. More and more places are now providing facilities for the disabled, so the easiest way to keep up to date is to call ahead and see if a venue can cater for your needs.

Some buses remain out of the question for disabled travellers, but Dublin Bus now has a growing number of wheelchair-accessible buses and more are being added all the time. Contact Dublin Bus for the latest details (*see p280*). Few railway or DART stations were designed with wheelchairs in mind, either, however, Iarnród Éireann (*see p280*) makes an effort to accommodate those disabled travellers who contact them in advance: staff will meet you at the station, accompany you to the train, arrange a car parking space and set up portable ramps. If you intend to remain

in your wheelchair for the journey, the train seat can be removed for you. The dining cars of all InterCity trains now have areas specifically designed for easy disabled access. For details of access to stations nationwide, call in to any DART station or train station and ask for the 'InterCity Guide for Mobility Impaired Passengers'. For further information, get in touch with the **Department of Transport** (44 Kildare Street, Southside; 670 7444).

Useful organisations

Catholic Institute for the Deaf 830 0522.
Enable (Cerebral Palsy) Ireland 269 5355.
Cystic Fibrosis Association of Ireland 496 2433.
Irish Deaf Society 860 1878/ 872 5748.
Irish Wheelchair Association 833 5366.

Drugs

The official Government and judicial attitude to drug abuse remains pretty draconian in Ireland. Although police attitudes on the ground are frequently quite relaxed, there are certainly no signs that soft drugs are about to be decriminalised in the Republic despite the change in attitude in the UK; and the drug problems in some of the city sink estates remain appalling.

It is easy enough to get hold of drugs in the city centre, although if you get caught in possession of illegal substances the result can be anything from an official caution to a night in a cell or worse, depending on the attitude of the police officer you encounter and the amount of drugs in your possession. However, there is no system of on-the-spot fines.

Drug Treatment Centre

30-31 Pearse Street, Southside (677 1122). **Open** 9am-4.30pm Mon-Fri; 10am-noon Sat, Sun. **Map** p313 J4/5.

Electricity

Like the rest of Europe, Ireland uses a 220-240V, 50-cycle AC voltage, with three-pin electrical plugs (as in the UK). Adaptors are widely available at airport shops. Note, too, that Irish and UK VCRs and TVs use a different frequency from those from the USA.

Embassies & consulates

It's advisable to telephone embassies to double-check opening hours, particularly regarding visa enquiries. For embassies and consulates not listed below, consult the Golden Pages (see *p294*). Note that many countries (such as New Zealand) do not maintain a full embassy in Dublin. In this case the embassy or high commission in London, UK, usually acts as the country's chief representative.

Australian Embassy *Fitzwilton House, Wilton Terrace, Dublin 2 (676 1517/www.australian embassy.ie).* **Open** 8.30am-12.30pm, 1.30-4.30pm Mon-Fri. *Visa enquiries* 11am-noon Mon-Fri.

British Embassy *29 Merrion Road, Ballsbridge, Dublin 4 (205 3775).* **Open** 9am-5pm Mon-Fri. *Visa enquiries* 10am-noon, 2-4pm Mon-Fri.

Canadian Embassy *65 St Stephen's Green, Dublin 2 (478 1988).* **Open** 8.30am-1pm, 2-5pm Mon-Fri. **Map** p313 H6.

New Zealand Consulate General *46 Upper Mount Street, Dublin 2 (660 4233).* **Open** 10am-12.30pm Mon-Fri. **Map** p314 K6. Contact the embassy in London outside office hours (020 7930 8422).

South African Embassy *Alexander House, Earlsfort Centre, Earlsfort Terrace, Dublin 2 (661 5553).* **Open** 8.30am-noon Mon-Fri. **Map** p313 H7.

United States Embassy *42 Elgin Road, Ballsbridge, Dublin 4 (668 8777).* **Open** 8am-5pm Mon-Fri.

Emergencies

In an emergency, telephone 999 or 112 and ask for the emergency service you require:

Fire, Garda (police), Ambulance, Irish Marine Emergency Service or Mountain & Cave Rescue.

Gay & lesbian

Help & information

The following are a good first point of call:

Gay Switchboard Dublin *872 1055.* **Open** 8-10pm Mon-Fri, Sun; 3.30-6pm Sat. Help and information for the gay community in Dublin.

Lesbian Line *872 9911.* **Open** 7-9pm Thur. Advice and information.

Other groups & organisations

Gay Men's Health Project

19 Haddingdon Road, Ballsbridge, Southern suburbs (660 2189/ 668 1577 ext 4221). Bus 45. **Open** 6.30-8pm Tue; 6-8pm Wed. **Map** p314 L6/7. Free and confidential drop-in health clinic for gay and bisexual men.

Outhouse

105 Capel Street, Northside (873 4932). All cross-city buses. **Open** 10am-6pm Mon-Fri. **Map** p313 G4 An accessible meeting place for the lesbian and gay community.

Health

If you need an ambulance, telephone 999 or 112. The national health service in Ireland is rightly maligned; although state investment has risen, this follows years of cutbacks. In Dublin, a number of city centre hospitals have moved to the suburbs, just as the population in the centre has begun to rise again. For details of health insurance and reciprocal agreements, see *p286*.

Accident & emergency

In the event of a medical emergency, call an ambulance (999/112). The following hospitals offer 24-hour Accident and Emergency

departments. Note that by law, all casualty patients must pay a flat fee of about €32 in order to be treated.

Beaumont Hospital *Beaumont Road, Northern suburbs (809 2714). Bus 27B, 51A.*

St James's Hospital *James Street, Kilmainham (416 2774). Bus 78A, 78D.* **Map** p311 C5/6

Complementary medicine

These centres offer a full range of treatments, including massage, acupuncture, reiki and reflexology.

Holistic Healing Centre *38 Dame Street, Southside (671 0813). All cross-city buses.* 9am-7.30pm Mon-Thur; 9am-6pm Fri; 10am-6pm Sat. **Map** p75.

Holistic Sourcing Centre *67 Camden Street Lower, Southside (478 5022). All cross-city buses.* **Open** *Office* 10am-8pm Mon-Fri. **Map** p313 G7.

Nelson's Homeopathic Pharmacy *15 Duke Street, Southside (679 0451). All cross-city buses.* **Open** 9.30am-5.45pm Mon-Fri; 9.30am-5.30pm Sat. **Map** p313 H5. Treatments and supplies.

Contraception & abortion

Condoms are available in pharmacies, newsagents, in vending machines in some pubs and from **Condom Power** (57 Dame Street, Southside; 677 8963).

Abortion is still illegal in Ireland, and a highly inflammatory subject. Its prohibition became part of Ireland's constitution in 1983, but debate raged once more in 1992 with the infamous 'X case' (see *p19*). Needless to say, Ireland is not exactly the ideal country in which to have an unwanted pregnancy; and with yet another referendum due in the spring of 2002, the subject is far from closed.

Directory

For anything relating to contraception or women's health, go to a **Well Woman Centre**. These offer services including breast exams, pregnancy counselling, smear tests, contraceptive advice and the morning-after pill. You don't need an appointment, and staff are friendly.

Well Woman Centres

35 Liffey Street Lower, Northside (872 8051). **Open** 9.30am-1pm, 5-7.30pm Mon, Thur, Fri; 8am-1pm, 5-7.30pm Tue, Wed; 10-3.30pm Sat. **Map** p313 G4.
Branches: 67 Pembroke Road, Ballsbridge, Southern suburbs (660 9860); Northside Shopping Centre, Coolock, Northern suburbs (848 4511).

Dentists

Unless you are an Irish citizen and hold a Medical Card, you must pay for all visits to a dentist. Charges start at €38 per visit, but can vary greatly from practice to practice. The expense means that lots of people go to Northern Ireland for dental treatment. Note that dental emergencies are not covered by European reciprocal health agreements.

Grafton Street Dentists

Grafton Street, Southside (670 3725). All cross-city buses. **Open** 9am-5pm Mon-Fri; 10am-noon Sat. **Map** p313 G5.

Molesworth Clinic

2 Molesworth Place, Southside (661 5544). All cross-city buses. **Open** 8.30am-5.30pm Mon-Fri. **Map** p313 G5.

Doctors

Unless you are an Irish citizen and hold a Medical Card, you must pay for all visits to a doctor. Doctors' charges range from €23 to €38.

Grafton Medical Practice

Grafton Street, Southside (671 2122). All cross-city buses. **Open** 9am-6pm Mon-Fri. **Map** p313 G5.

Mercer's Medical Centre

Stephen Street Lower, Southside (402 2300). All cross-city buses. **Open** 9am-6pm Mon-Thur; 9am-5pm Fri. **Map** p313 G5.

Hospitals

For hospitals with accident and emergency departments, *see p285*.

Children's hospitals

Children's Hospital *Temple Street, Northside (874 8763).* Bus 3, 11, 11A.
Our Lady's Hospital for Sick Children *Crumlin, Southern suburbs (455 8111).* Bus 50, 56A, 77, 77A, 150.

Maternity

The Coombe Women's Hospital *Dolphin's Barn Street, Southern suburbs (453 7561).* Bus 50, 56A, 77, 77A, 150. **Map** p309.
Rotunda Hospital *Parnell Square, Northside (873 0700). All cross-city buses.* **Map** p313 G3.

Pharmacies

Pharmacies are usually open from approximately 8.30am to 7pm Monday to Saturday. **O'Connell's Late Night Pharmacies** can be found throughout the city; *see p157*. For homeopathic remedies, try **Nelson's** (*see p285*).

Prescriptions

Unless you are an Irish citizen and hold a Medical Card, you will be required to pay for prescriptions. Charges vary but start at around €25; to avoid unnecessary expense, bring regular prescription medicines with you.

STDs, HIV & AIDS

AIDS Helpline *freephone 1-800 459 459.* **Open** 10am-5pm daily. Advice and counselling on HIV- and AIDS-related issues.
Dublin AIDS Alliance *873 3799.* **Open** 10am-5pm Mon; noon-5pm Fri. A care and education service for drug users and people affected by HIV and AIDS. The Dublin AIDS Alliance also runs community support services.

For women's support and services, *see p295*; for gay and lesbian helplines, *see p285*; for AIDS and HIV helplines, *see above*.

Alcoholics Anonymous *453 8998 in office hours/679 5967 at other times.* **Open** 9.30am-5pm Mon-Fri.
Asthma Line *freephone 1-850 445 464.* **Open** 24hrs daily.
Childline *freephone 1-800 666 666.* **Open** 24hrs daily.
Electricity Supply Board *(ESB) 676 5831.* **Open** 8.30am-5.30pm Mon-Fri.
Focus Ireland *freephone 1-800 724 724.* **Open** 24hrs daily. Emergency accommodation.
Gamblers Anonymous *872 1133.* **Open** 10.30am-12.30pm Mon, Wed, Fri; 24hr answerphone.
Gas emergency *freephone 1-850 205 050.*
Missing Persons Helpline *freephone 1-800 616617.* **Open** 9.30am-5pm Mon-Fri.
Narcotics Anonymous *830 0944/086 8629 308.* **Open** 24hrs daily.
National Poisons Information Centre *837 9964/873 9966.* **Open** 24hrs daily.
Parentline *873 3500.* **Open** 10am-9.30pm Mon-Fri.
Samaritans *freephone 1-850 609 090.* **Open** 24hrs daily.
Victim Support *freephone 1-800 661 771.* **Open** 24hrs daily.

There is no national ID system in the Republic of Ireland and you are not required to carry any form of identification once you are in the country. However, you will need ID to obtain certain transport passes, and it is usually a good idea to have a form of ID handy for cashing travellers' cheques and for other transactions.

If you're an EU citizen, an E111 form will cover you for most medical (though note not dental) emergencies. In the UK, get an application form from the post office. However, it is always advisable to take out medical insurance, too: it'll save you the effort of trying to wade through the red tape of EU health agreements and ensures more comprehensive coverage. It's also advisable to take out comprehensive travel insurance to cover your luggage and travel plans.

Always read the small print before agreeing to an insurance contract. There's usually an excess, and an upper claim limit may be imposed, too. If you're carrying anything of value, make sure that it is adequately covered. Organise your travel insurance before you leave your country of origin; it's impossible to sort out once you get to Ireland.

Internet

More and more hotels and hostels now offer some kind of Internet access; luxury hotels should have ISDN/Internet connection points in each room and hostels tend to have a clutch of terminals. If you want to set up an Internet account for your stay, good local ISPs include Eircom (701 0022/ www.eircom.ie) and Esat (freephone 1 800 924 924/www.esat.net).

Internet access

If you can't get online in your hotel, you can guarantee that Internet access won't be far away; Dublin is positively crawling with cybercafés, most offering a decent number of terminals and other services such as printing, faxing and photocopying.

Internet Exchange
Fownes Street, Temple Bar, Southside (635 1680). **Open** 8am-10pm Mon-Fri; noon-10pm Sat, Sun. **Rates** €2.50 per hr. **No credit cards**. **Map** p75.

Planet
13 St Andrew's Street, Southside (670 5183). All cross-city buses. **Open** 10am-10pm Mon-Thur, Sun; 10am-11pm Fri, Sat. **Rates** €1.90 for 15min; €6.35 per hr; 20% discount with student card. **No credit cards**. **Map** p313 H5.

Language

In the rush towards cultural homogenisation, much has been lost – but the English language as spoken in Dublin is still a breed apart. The real Dublin accent is rapid and clipped – note the dropped 't' – and can be heard to best advantage at the markets on Moore Street and Henry Street (*see p154* **Market forces**). Entirely different is the 'posh' southside 'DART' accent – so called because most exponents live near the coastal DART railway line. This accent is nasal and rather uptight; most real Dubs don't consider it part of the local vernacular at all.

For an ever-growing collection of words and phrases peculiar to Dublin, consult the Dublin Dictionary section of the **Blue Pages** website (www.bluepages.ie).

Left luggage

Busáras
Bus Éireann 703 2434. **Open** 8am-7.45pm Mon-Sat; 10am-5pm Sun. *Lockers* 7am-10.30pm daily. **Rates** €3.20 per item for 24hrs; €3.80 €8.90 locker. **No credit cards**. **Map** p313 J3/4.

Connolly Station
Platform 2 (Iarnod Éireann 836 6222/703 2363). **Open** 7.40am-9.30pm Mon-Sat; 9.10am-9.45pm Sun. **Rates** €2.50 for 24hrs. **No credit cards**. **Map** p313 J3.

Dublin Airport
Greencaps Left Luggage & Porterage 814 4633. **Open** 6am-11pm daily. **Rates** €2.50-€4.45 per item for 24hrs. **Credit** MC, V.

Heuston Station
next to the ticket office (Iarnod Éireann 836 6222). **Rates** *Lockers only* €3.20 small; €5 large. **No credit cards**. **Map** p311 C4.

Legal help

AIM Family Services
6 D'Olier Street, Southside (670 8363). All cross-city buses. **Open** 10am-1pm Mon-Fri. **Map** p313 H4. Provides legal information, counselling and mediation.

The Equality Authority
2 Clonmell Street, Southside (417 3336). All cross-city buses. **Open** 9.15am-5.30pm Mon-Thur; 9.15am-5.15pm Fri.

Legal Aid Board Centres
Head Office, St Stephen's Green House, Southside (661 5811). All cross-city buses. **Open** 9.30am-5.30pm Mon-Thur; 9.30am-5.15pm Fri. **Map** p313 H6. **Branches:** Law Centre, 45 Gardiner Street Lower, Northside (874 5440); Law Centre, 9 Ormond Quay Lower, Northside (872 4133).

Libraries

Colleges often allow foreign students a temporary reader's pass for library facilities. You'll need student ID, and, in some cases, a letter of introduction from your college. Non-students can use Dublin Corporation libraries, listed below. There is also a library at 138 Pearse Street, which is due to reopen in 2002.

Central Library *Ilac Centre, Henry Street, Northside (873 4333).* **Map** p313 G/H4. **Community & Youth Information Centre** *Sackville House, Sackville Place, Northside (878 6844).* **Map** p313 H4.

Lost property

Make sure you always notify the police if you lose anything of value, as you'll need a reference number from them to validate any subsequent insurance claims. To track down your lost property, call the following numbers:
Bus Éireann 703 2489.
Connolly Station 703 2363.
Dublin Airport 814 4480.
Dublin Bus 703 3055.
Heuston Station 703 2102.
Taxis Carriage Office Lower Yard, Dublin Castle (666 9854).

Media

Newspapers

Dublin is the centre of Ireland's publishing world and all but one of the Republic's newspapers are based here.

Directory

National broadsheets

The Irish Times acts as Ireland's serious intellectual broadsheet. Offering objective and insightful reporting of city, national and international affairs, it has transformed itself over its long life from an organ of the Anglo-Irish ruling class into the main voice of a relatively liberal and progressive Ireland – although it's now facing something of a financial crisis.

The *Times'* main rival, the *Irish Independent*, is tabloid in spirit, though it masquerades as a broadsheet. It's a more actively national paper, is more approachable than the *Times* and features less of that paper's metropolitan bias. This said, however, it is often sensationalist and sometimes lacking in objectivity. The third national broadsheet, the Cork-based *Irish Examiner*, provides decent reading.

National tabloids

The *Evening Herald*, peddled on the streets and newsstands from lunchtime on, is a tabloid, but is a little loftier in tone than some of the morning rags. In some circles, it's required reading: if you need a flat to rent, then look no further. *The Star* is Ireland's very popular response to Britain's *The Sun*, though with a little more conscience and a lot less cleavage. *The Irish Sun*, meanwhile, is the British *Sun* with a few pages of Irish news cunningly inserted to keep the locals happy. When the mother paper has one of its frequent fits of Irish-bashing, its Dublin equivalent quietly pulls the relevant pages.

Sunday papers

Of the many papers you will find lined up in a Dublin newsagent on Sunday morning, few will be Irish. The British press has saturated the Irish market in recent years, offering cheaper cover prices and more pages as a means of boosting circulation figures at home. Most of the papers follow the practice of *The Sun* (*see above*) modifying their editorial stance, where appropriate, for the Irish market: the *Sunday Times* is a particularly brazen offender. Of the indigenous newspapers, the *Sunday Tribune* and the *Sunday Business Post* both offer good news coverage, comment and columnists. The *Post*, like the *Financial Times*, is good for more than just money talk, and is, at times, the most outspoken of all the papers. The *Sunday Independent* is much like its daily stablemate. Sunday tabloids include the popular *Sunday World*.

Magazines

Listings magazines

The glossy *In Dublin* is the city's main entertainment listings magazine. Published every other Thursday, it offers comprehensive listings for all types of entertainment and a useful guide to what's on. This said, however, its features aren't great and its pages of sex ads at the back don't do much for its image. In 2000, it impressed the nation by being the first magazine in many years to be banned under Ireland's censorship laws: the sex ads went too far and the guardians of public morality reacted swiftly.

Hot Press, which also appears fortnightly, offers a slightly more intellectual take on things. After 20 years with more or less the same hard core of writers, however, it's starting to look tired and takes itself way too seriously. However, it's still the best guide to the Dublin music scene, with comprehensive listings and reviews, and its debate pages are pretty lively. Alternatives include *D-Side*, a lifestyle magazine in a similar vein to *Hot Press* but produced by a younger (although not necessarily more talented) team and the amiable and very comprehensive *Event Guide*, a freesheet available in most city-centre cafés and bars.

Other magazines

Dublin's shelves are as packed with glossy mags as any city's. All the international mainstays are there, some in special Irish editions, though titles unique to the Irish market include *U*, *Irish Tatler*, *Social & Personal* and *Image*. *Himself*, Ireland's first men's magazine was launched in 2000, but quietly folded after a few scornfully received issues. Good for a horrified laugh is *VIP*, which is modelled on *Hello!* and shares that publication's high-minded ideals, offering a fascinating insight into the exciting lives of Ireland's D-list.

For in-depth politics and current affairs, try the very excellent *Magill*; for buying and selling stuff, check out *Buy and Sell*. The *RTÉ Guide* offers the usual celebrity gossip plus full TV and radio listings; while the *Phoenix* offering a reasonable line in satire. For comprehensive, in-depth coverage of what's current in Irish literature and cinema, grab *Books Ireland* or *Film Ireland*.

Finally, three new entries in 2001: the *Dublin Review*, a literature and arts quarterly; the monthly *Dubliner*, a well-written and self-consciously upmarket glossy carrying intelligent reviews; and the equally glossy *GI*, which aims to cash in monthly on the spending power of Ireland's gay and lesbian community.

Television

Dublin is one of Europe's more heavily cabled cities and the full range of UK channels should be available wherever you stay. The national station,

RTÉ (Radio Telefis Éireann) runs three national channels: RTÉ1, Network 2 and TG4. The station is usually hard up for money, and recently it has been embroiled in a bitter row with the Government over whether its licence fee should be increased. Compared to many national stations, RTÉ offers fairly solid, reliable broadcasting; however, its perceived lack of adventurous programming and unflattering comparisons with the BBC make it a prime target for public criticism. Often this RTÉ-bashing is unwarranted: the station has a generally excellent current affairs output, creative children's programming and highly regarded sports reporting. Otherwise the schedule is made up of American sitcoms, gameshows, dramas bought in from the BBC and three-year-old blockbuster films.

RTÉ1

RTÉ1 seldom offers anything challenging or controversial. The daytime diet in Ireland largely consists of soap operas, undemanding chat shows and DIY programmes. Prime-time programming is slightly better. The most significant programme on Irish TV remains Friday night's *Late Late Show*, formerly hosted by national institution Gay Byrne and now in the hands of oily Pat Kenny. The *Late Late Show* is the longest-running chat show in the world and countless important events and interviews have taken place on the programme over the years. Today, however, it is a tired shadow of itself, and pressure is building on RTÉ to put it and its unctuous host out of their misery.

RTÉ's alternative prize programme is the Irish version of *Who Wants to be a Millionaire?*, hosted (innovatively) by Gay Byrne. Alarmingly for RTÉ, the

station has recently lost the rights to show *Coronation Street* (for decades the ratings-topper) to new upstart channel TV3 (*see below*), blasting great holes in the station's tried and tested schedule.

Although the excellent *Cursai Ealaine* arts series was foolishly axed in 2000, it was replaced by *The View*, a well put together arts show. The station also produces some fine one-off documentariess and excellent (subtitled) Irish-language shows. Look out, in particular, for the *Leargas* documentary series.

Network 2

RTÉ's second channel reinvented itself a few years ago, with largely successful results. Network 2 is now a smoother and more stylish operation than its sister channel. At night, music and chat shows aimed at a young, hip audience come to the fore, and the channel has also commissioned several new programmes, such as the well-received comedy drama *Bachelors Walk* (set in Dublin). You'll also notice that the most popular American imports, such as *Ally McBeal* and *Friends*, appear on RTÉ screens well before they show up on the United Kingdom's public channels.

Telefis na Gaeilge (TG4)

A predominantly Irish-language station, TG4 offers some imaginative home-grown drama and pretty good documentaries, punctuated by smartly selected arthouse movies dubbed for those who haven't mastered the native tongue. It's stylish and slick and well worth a look.

TV3

Ireland's newest (and first independent) station was born in 1998, and has used populist scheduling to carve a successful niche out for itself.

No nonsense about public service broadcasting here – its schedule is filled with low-budget American TV movies, excitable news broadcasts and low-budget sitcoms. It has also poached many of RTÉ's sporting contracts, however, and a link with Granada has meant that *Coronation Street* and a raft of other popular British shows have moved over to this channel.

Radio

RTÉ

RTÉ operates four national stations: **RTÉ Radio 1** (88.2-95.2 FM; 567, 729 AM) offers a fairly safe mix of news, sports programming and phone-in talk shows during the day, and an excellent range of interesting music slots and off-beat documentaries at night. **RTÉ 2FM** (90.4-97 FM, 612, 1278 AM) is aimed more at the kids, with pop and rock shows during the day and the ever-reliable *Hotline* request show at 7pm daily. **RTÉ Lyric FM** (96-99 FM), which is based in Limerick, offers a mix of arts programming and various kinds of music (*see p185*). **RTÉ Raidio Na Gaeltachta** (92.6-94.4 FM) is the national Irish-language station.

Other stations

A number of new licensed stations have challenged the hegemony of RTÉ in the last ten years. After a rocky start, **Today FM** (100-102 FM) has now successfully established itself, thanks mainly to Eamon Dunphy's high-profile *Last Word* (5-7pm Mon-Fri) talk show; Sunday morning's intelligent *Sunday Supplement* discussion slot is also well worth a listen. **Anna Livia FM** (103.2 FM) is Dublin's community station, putting out a good selection of programmes made by people who love radio; while chart enthusiasts will prefer the same-old, same-old diet of **98FM** (er, 98 FM), **FM104** (ah, find it yourself) and **Lite FM** (95.8 FM).

Pirate radio

The diet of blandness offered by the mainstream music stations, however, has meant that the city's handful of pirate stations have come to fulfil certain music needs in the city. Among the best are **Power FM** (97.2 FM) – a lot of techno and other dance music; **Phantom FM** (91.6 FM) – generally indie rock; **Jazz FM** (89.8 FM) – hip hop and jazz; and **XFM** (107.9 FM) – more indie rock. If you want originality, you're most likely to find it here.

Multimedia

Generally speaking, Ireland has spent the last decade enthusiastically embracing new technology, nowhere more so than in the capital. The country's economic boom was largely fuelled by the growth in information and media technology jobs and companies such as **Iona** (begun as a student initiative in Trinity College) continue to perform impressively on the world stage. However, Ireland has not been immune to the cold wind blowing through the virtual world. High-profile consultancy firm **Nua** went spectacularly bust in 2001, dragging its tourism and genealogy offshoot 'Local Ireland' with it. More successful is **Ireland.com** (www.ireland. com), which is linked to the *Irish Times*; and **iVenus.com** (www.iVenus. com), the 'website for women' that is now linked with *Irish Tatler*. Both of these are well worth a look and emphasise the importance of powerfully branding a product in order to stay afloat in tempestuous times. For other recommended websites, *see p297*.

Money

In February 2002, the euro became Ireland's sole currency. Ireland was one of the first countries to sign up to the single European currency, along with Austria, Belgium, Germany, Finland, France, Italy, Luxembourg, the Netherlands, Portugal and Spain. Greece joined later, taking the number of participating countries to 12.

The currency was officially launched on 1 January 1999 and cash in the form of euros (€) and cents (¢) came into circulation on 1 January 2002. The conversion rate was 1.26974 Irish pounds to the euro (0.787564 euros to the Irish pound). The Irish pound was withdrawn on 9 February, 2002, with the euro becoming the sole legal tender. The other euro countries phased out their local currencies at around the same time. Note that the United Kingdom did not join the euro and retains the pound as its sole currency.

The new currency features seven notes – €5 (grey), €10 (red), €20 (blue), €50 (orange), €100 (green), €200 (yellow) and €500 (purple) – and eight coins. One face of each coin features a communal map and flag illustration and the other a country-specific design (note: all can be used in any participating state).

Euro travellers' cheques are also available.

ATMs

Automatic cash machines can be found outside most banks and some building societies. Most are linked up to international networks (such as Cirrus), so you shouldn't have any problem withdrawing money directly from your account with your standard cash card, although you should expect a nominal charge for each transaction.

Banks

In general, banking hours in Dublin are 10am to 4pm Monday to Wednesday and Friday, and 10am to 5pm on Thursday (closed on Saturday and Sunday). The main Dublin branches of the major Irish banks are listed below.

AIB (Allied Irish Bank) *AIB Bank Centre, Ballsbridge, Southern suburbs (660 0311). All cross-city buses.* **Open** 10am-4pm Mon-Wed, Fri; 10am-5pm Thur.

Bank of Ireland *Baggot Street Lower, Southside (604 3000). All cross-city buses.* **Open** 10am-4pm Mon-Wed, Fri; 10am-5pm Thur. **Map** p313 J6.

Ulster Bank *33 College Green, Southside (702 8600). All cross-city buses.* **Open** 10am-4pm Mon-Wed, Fri; 10am-5pm Thur. **Map** p313 H5.

Bureaux de change

Nearly all banks, building societies and post offices have foreign exchange facilities, so you shouldn't have any trouble getting cash. There are desks at the airport and at the main bus station, **Busárus** (*see p279*; 878 7970), so you can stock up with euros as soon as you arrive. Another option is the bureau de change inside Clery's department store (*see p144*). Other useful addresses are:

American Express Travel Service

41 Nassau Street, Southside (679 9000). All cross-city buses. **Open** 9am-5pm Mon-Fri. **Map** p313 H5.

First Rate Bureau de Change

1 Westmoreland Street, Southside (671 3233). **Open** 9am-6pm Mon-Fri; 9am-8pm Sat, Sun. **Map** p313 H4.

Foreign Exchange Company of Ireland

12 Ely Place, Southside (661 1800). All cross-city buses. **Open** 9am-5.30pm Mon-Fri. **Map** p313 J6.

Joe Walsh Tours (JWT)

69 O'Connell Street Upper, Northside (872 5536). All cross-city buses. **Open** 8am-8pm Mon-Sat; 10am-6pm Sun. **Map** p313 H3.

Directory

Thomas Cook

*118 Grafton Street, Southside
(677 1307/1721).* **Open** 9am-5.30pm
Mon, Tue, Thur-Sat; 10am-5.30pm
Wed. **Map** p313 H5.

Credit cards

Ireland is still a cash culture,
but most places will accept
MasterCard and Visa, and
some also take American
Express and Diners' Club
cards. Although the Irish
debit card Laser is widely
used, debit cards from other
countries are not accepted.

Lost or stolen credit cards

Inform the police and the 24-
hour numbers listed below.
**American Express Customer
Services** *1-800 282 728.*
**American Express Travellers'
Cheques** *1-800 626 000.*
Diners' Club *1 800 409 204/
authorisation service 1 800
709 944).*
MasterCard *1-800 557378.*
Visa *1-800 558-002.*

Tax

Sales tax (VAT) in the Republic
is set at 20 per cent. Visitors
from outside the EU can get a
refund by filling in a tax-free
shopping cheque (available
from participating stores) and
handing it in to the Refund
Desk at Dublin Airport.

Natural hazards

None. Ireland doesn't even
have any snakes since St
Patrick drove them out.

Opening hours

General business hours
are 9am to 5.30pm Monday to
Friday. **Banks** are open 10am
to 4pm Monday to Wednesday
and Friday, and from 10am to
5pm on Thursday. City centre
shops generally open between
9.30am and 6pm on Monday,
Tuesday, Wednesday, Friday
and Saturday, and from 2pm
to 6pm on Sunday, with late-

night opening until 8pm on
Thursday. **Licensing hours**
were relaxed in 2000, meaning
that pubs are now usually
open from 11.30am to 11.30pm
on Monday and Tuesday;
11.30am to 12.30am from
Wednesday to Saturday and
from 4pm to 11pm on Sunday.
Many city centre bars now
have later opening hours at
weekends; *see chapters* **Pubs
& Bars** and **Nightlife** for
further details.

Police stations

The emergency telephone
number for police (called
Garda), fire and ambulance is
999 or 112. City-centre Garda
stations are located at the
following addresses; all are
open 24 hours daily. Non-
emergency confidential calls
to the Garda can also be made
on 1-800 666 111.

Garda stations

*Fitzgibbon Street, Northside (836
3113); Metropolitan HQ, Harcourt
Square, Southside (475 5555);
Pearse Street, Southside (677 8141);
Store Street, Northside (666 8000).*

Post

Post boxes are green and many
have two slots: one for Dublin
Only and one for All Other
Places. It costs 38¢ to post a
letter, postcard or unsealed
card (weighing up to 20g) to
the UK, 40¢ to anywhere in
the EU and 57¢ to elsewhere in
Europe and other international
destinations. All airmail letters
– including those to the UK –
should have a priority airmail
(Aerphost) label affixed: these
are free at all post offices.

Post offices

Post Offices are generally
open from 9am to 5.30pm
Monday to Friday and from
9am to 1pm on Saturday. Note,
however, that many smaller
post offices still close for lunch
from 12.45pm to 2pm.

General Post Office

*O'Connell Street, Northside (705
7000). All cross-city buses.* **Open**
8am-8pm Mon-Fri; 8am-1pm Sat.
Map p313 H4.

Poste restante

If you would like to have mail
retained in a post office for
collection, ask the sender to
address the envelope clearly
with your name and send it to
Post Restante, General Post
Office, O'Connell Street, Dublin
1 (*see above*). Take photo ID
with you when go to collect it.

Religion

Church of Ireland

Christchurch Cathedral

*Christchurch Place, Southside
(677 8099). Bus 50, 78A.* **Services**
Eucharist 12.45pm Mon-Fri (Lady
Chapel). *Choral evensong* 6pm Wed,
Thur; 5pm Sat (except July, Aug);
3.30pm Sun, *Sung Eucharist &
sermon* 11am Sun. **Map** p312 F5.

St Patrick's Cathedral

*Patrick's Close, Southside
(475 4817). Bus 50, 54A, 56A.*
Services *Eucharist* 11.05am Mon,
Tue; 8.30am 11.05am Wed; 11.05
Thur-Sat; 8.30am Sun. *Choral matins*
9.40am Mon-Fri (school term only);
11.15am Sun. *Choral evensong*
5.35pm Mon-Fri; 3.15pm Sun.
Map p312 F6.

Roman Catholic

Church of St Francis Xavier

*Gardiner Street, Northside (836
3411). All cross-city buses.* **Services**
Mass 7am, 8.30am, 10am, 11am, 1pm,
7.30pm Mon-Sat; 7am, 8.30am, 10am,
11am, noon, 7.30pm (Gospel Mass)
Sun. **Map** p313 H/J3.

St Mary's Pro-Cathedral

*Cathedral Street, Northside (874
5441). All cross-city buses.* **Services**
Mass 8.30am, 10am, 11am, 12.45pm,
5.45pm Mon-Sat; 10am, 11am,
12.30pm, 6pm Sun. **Map** p313 H3.

St Ann's Church

*Dawson Street, Southside (288
0663). All cross-city buses.* **Services**
Eucharist 11am Mon-Fri; 8am,
10.45am, 6.30pm Sun. *Evensong*
6.30pm Sun. **Map** p313 H5.

Other Christian

Abbey Presbyterian Church
Parnell Square, Northside (837 8600). All cross-city buses. **Services** 11am Sun. **Map** p313 G/H3.

Grace Baptist Church
28A Pearse Street, Southside (677 3170). All cross-city buses. **Services** 10am Sun. **Map** p313 J5.

Methodist church
Howth Road, Sutton, Dublin Bay (832 3143). Sutton DART. **Services** 10am Sun.

Islam

Islamic Centre Dublin
163 South Circular Road, Southside (453 3242). Bus 19. **Services** 5 prayers daily, plus Friday prayers.

Judaism

Dublin Jewish Progressive Congregation
7 Leicester Avenue, Rathgar, Southern suburbs (490 7605/298 7424). Bus 15A, 15B, 15C. **Services** phone for details.

Safety & security

Levels of street crime in Dublin have risen dramatically in the last decade. Pickpockets and bag-snatchers have always been fairly prevalent in the city, but in recent years some assailants have taken to using syringes as weapons. They have even been known to operate on city buses, walking the victim off at needle-point to get to a cash machine.

The majority of safety hints amount to little more than common sense. If you're worried about travelling on buses, then sit downstairs in sight of the driver. When wandering around town, avoid wearing ostentatious jewellery that says 'Rob me' and strap your bag across your chest with the opening facing towards your body. When withdrawing money from cash machines, don't stand around counting your money; put it away quickly, and, if there's a machine inside the bank, use that instead. Never leave your wallet in your back pocket. In bars, don't leave your wallet on a table, and keep your bag with you at all times.

Most of all, safety is about being aware and looking confident. This is especially important at night: if you're on your own, stay in well-lit, populated areas and try to avoid consulting a huge map every couple of streets. Arrange to meet people inside a pub or restaurant rather then waiting outside on your own.

Smoking

Attitudes to smoking are still fairly relaxed in Ireland. Most restaurants have no-smoking sections, but pubs remain definitely smoking zones. All shops are officially smoke-free, and so are all buses, though you shouldn't be too surprised if you see folk lighting up anyway. The DART too is smoke-free, but Intercity trains (except the Enterprise service service to Belfast) usually have one or two smoking carriages.

Students

Considering the sheer number of language schools, business colleges and universities in Dublin, it's not surprising that the city's student population is considerable. It's also diverse: over summer, thousands of people come to Dublin to study English, and for the rest of the year colleges are filled with academic students from Ireland and abroad. Citizens of roughly 60 countries (including all EU-member states) do not require visas to study here. However, the law requires long-term visitors to register with the **Immigration Department** at the Garda National Immigration Bureau, Harcourt Square, Southside (475 5555). For further information consult the website (www.iolgov.ie/iveagh) or contact the Irish Department of Foreign Affairs, Visa Section, Hainault House, 69–71 St Stephen's Green, Southside (408 2374).

Rents in Dublin have risen sharply in the last decade: expect to pay upwards of €80 a week for a reasonable place. The renting business gets cut-throat from September, when all the students returning to Dublin sort out lodgings, so summer is the best time to look for bargains.

The *Evening Herald* is probably the best paper to check for ads, though you might get lucky at USIT (*see p293*). You could also go through your college's accommodation service if it has one, or a letting agency. It may require a fee, but it can save a great deal of legwork.

Language schools

French
Alliance Française *1 Kildare Street, Southside (676 1732). All cross-city buses.* **Map** p313 H6.

German
Goethe-Institut *62 Fitzwilliam Square, Southside (661 8506). All cross-city buses.* **Map** p313 J7.

Irish
Gael-linn *35 Dame Street, Southside (676 7283). All cross-city buses.* **Map** p313 G5.

Spanish
Instituto Cervantes
58 Northumberland Road, Ballsbridge, Southern suburbs (668 2024). Lansdowne Road DART.

Universities & colleges

The three biggest colleges are as follows:

Dublin City University
Glasnevin, Northern suburbs (student services 700 5165/accommodation office 700 5646/5344).

Trinity College Dublin

College Green, Southside (students' union 677 6545/accommodation office 608 1177). **Map** p313 H5.

University College Dublin

Belfield, Southern suburbs (269 3244).

Other schools & colleges

American College Dublin

2 Merrion Square, Southside (676 8939). All cross-city buses. **Map** p313 J5/6.

Dublin Business School

Aungier Street, Southside (475 1024). Bus 10, 16A, 19, 19A, 83. **Map** p313 G6.

Dublin Institute of Technology

Cathal Brugha Street, Northside (402 3000/www.dit.ie). **Map** p313 H7.
There are six DITs, offering a wide range of courses, including architecture, music, engineering and tourism.

Griffith College Dublin

South Circular Road, Southside (454 5640). **Map** p309.

Useful organisations

International Student Travel

5 Merrion Row, Southside (676 4386). All cross-city buses. **Open** 9.30am-5.30pm Mon-Fri. **Map** p313 J6.

Union of Students in Ireland Travel (USIT)

19-21 Aston Quay, Southside (602 1600). All cross-city buses. **Open** 9.30am-6pm Mon-Wed, Fri; 9.30am-8pm Thur; 9.30am-5pm Sat. **Map** p313 H4.
USIT handles all student travel arrangements, so wherever you're going, it can tell you the cheapest way to get there. It's also very much a meeting of the ways: its noticeboards are filled with details of flatshares, language tuition, jobs and cheap flights. You'll probably have plenty of time to browse through the small ads while you're waiting to be served: you should allow for at least 30 minutes' queuing.

To avail yourself of student travel discounts in Ireland, you need to have a USIT International Student Card with a 'travel save' stamp. Bring student ID with you to USIT.

Telephones

Dialling & codes

The dialling code for Dublin is 01, though you don't need to use the prefix within the Dublin region itself. Local phone numbers in Dublin all consist of seven digits, though elsewhere in Ireland they may be shorter or longer. Phone numbers with the prefix 1-800 and 1-850 are free.

All Dublin numbers listed in this book have been listed without the city code of 01. To dial these numbers within Dublin, use the numbers as they appear in the listings. If you are dialling from outside Dublin but within Ireland, add 01 to the front of the numbers listed. If you are dialling from outside Ireland, you need to dial the international dialling code + 353, then the Dublin city code 1 (omitting the initial 0), then the number as it appears in the guide.

To make an international call from Ireland, dial 00, then the appropriate international code for the country you're calling (*see below*), then the number itself, omitting the first 0 from the area code where appropriate.

- Australia: 00 61
- United Kingdom: 00 44
- USA: 00 1
- South Africa: 0027
- New Zealand: 00 64
- Canada: 00 1

For information on calling Northern Ireland from the Republic and abroad, *see p268* **Dialling Northern Ireland**.

Making a call

If you have access to a private phone, the charges will be much lower than from your hotel or your mobile: a three-minute local call will cost around 15¢ during the day, and the same amount of money will net you 15 minutes' chat during off-peak hours.

Reduced rates are available 6pm to 8am Monday to Friday, and all day Saturday, Sunday and Bank Holidays. If you need to make international calls, try and wait until these off-peak hours, as it is considerably cheaper.

If you can't use a private phone, the next easiest way to make long-distance calls is to buy a phone card, available from most newsagents and post offices, to use in public phones, the majority of which take cards, not cash. They'll be especially useful outside Dublin, where payphones of all kinds are scarce.

If you intend to use your hotel phone, check rates in advance. It is unlikely that there will be any off-peak reductions.

Public phones

Cash- and card-operated public phones are found across the city. Local telephone calls from a public phone generally cost 40¢ for around three minutes during the day.

Operator services

Call 10 for operator services for Ireland and the UK, and 114 for international assistance. Reverse-charge ('collect') calls are also available but will cost about 77¢ extra.

For directory enquiries, dial 11811 for Ireland and Northern Ireland and 11818 for international numbers including UK numbers.

UK visitors planning their trip should note that when calling directory enquiries from the UK, Irish numbers are now listed under the usual directory enquiries number, 192, not under international directory enquiries.

Directory

Telephone directories

The Golden Pages is Dublin's equivalent of the Yellow Pages and fulfils the same function. The 'Independent Directory', distributed annually, is a smaller version, with the added bonus of fairly good restaurant listings.

Mobile phones

There are three networks in Ireland: **Eircell**, which is owned by Vodafone; **Esat**, which is owned by BT; and the latest arrival, **Meteor**. Each network has about 98% coverage across Ireland. Tariffs are expensive in comparison with the rest of Europe. Ireland's network uses the 900 and 1800 GSM bands. A UK handset will therefore work in Ireland if you have a roaming agreement with your service provider. Holders of US phones (usually 1900 GSM) should contact their provider to check compatibility.

If you need to buy a new handset or want to sign up to an Irish mobile phone network, contact one of the following:
Carphone Warehouse *30 Grafton Street, Southside (670 5265). All cross-city buses.* **Map** *p313 G5*
Let's Talk Phones *55 Grafton Street, Southside (679 9938). All cross-city buses.* **Map** *p313 G5.*

Telegrams

Or telemessages, as they are now called, are provided by Eircom – call 196. Messages can also be sent from post offices. A 12-word telemessage to the UK costs about €3.

Ireland is in the same time zone as Britain, and so runs according to Greenwich Mean Time. In spring, on a Saturday towards the end of March, the clocks go forward one hour for Summer Time, and return to normal towards the end of

October – on the same dates as the UK. For the 24-hour speaking clock, telephone 1191.

Tipping

You should tip between 12 and 15 per cent in restaurants. However, if a service charge is included on your bill, ask staff if they actually receive it: you can refuse to pay it if they don't. Always pay the tip in cash, too, to ensure your waiter or waitress receives it. It's generally accepted that hairdressers cent, as do taxi drivers for longer journeys. The posher bars and stores now have attendants in their loos: don't feel you have to tip them unless you want to.

Toilets

Clean and safe public toilets are thin on the ground in central Dublin; you should particularly avoid using the ones on O'Connell Street, which are often haunted by drug dealers. It's perfectly acceptable to use the toilets in bars and shopping centres. The toilets at Bewley's on Grafton Street (*see p127*) and in the Jervis Centre on Henry Street (*see p145*) are clean and pleasant.

Tourist information

Dublin Tourism Centre
St Andrew's Church, Suffolk Street, Southside (605 7700/www.visit dublin.com). All cross-city buses. **Open** *Sept-June* 9am-5.30pm Mon-Sat. *July, Aug* 8.30am-7pm Mon-Sat; 10am-3pm Sun. **Map** *p313 H5.* Located in a renovated church, the Dublin Tourism Centre is a drop-in centre offering numerous services, including a bureau de change, a car rental agency, a café, and a shop. Staff can book tickets for tours and travel excursions, and there's also a ticket reservations desk for concerts, theatre performances and other special events. Accommodation can also be booked through the Tourism Centre, though there is a booking fee for each reservation. To make a booking before you arrive, call ResIreland on 1-800 668 668 (within Ireland); 00800 6686 6866 from the

UK and the rest of Europe; or 00 353 669 792082 from all other countries.

Irish Tourist Board
Information 1-850 230330 from within Ireland/0800 039 7000 from UK & EU/00 353 669 792083 from other countries/ www.ireland.travel.ie. Visitors from the UK can also contact the Irish Tourist Board in London on 020 7518 0800.

Other Tourism Centres
Baggot Street Bridge. All cross-city buses. **Open** 9.30am-noon, 12.30-5pm Mon-Fri. **Map** *p314 K7. Dublin Airport. Bus 747, 748.* **Open** 8am-10pm daily. *Dún Laoghaire Ferry Terminal, Dublin Bay. Dún Laoghaire DART.* **Open** 10am-6pm Mon-Sat. *The Square, Tallaght, Southern suburbs. Bus 49, 49A, 50, 56A.* **Open** 9.30am-noon, 12.30-5pm Mon-Sat. *14 Upper O'Connell Street, Northside.* **Open** 9am-5pm Mon-Sat. **Map** *p313 H3.*

Visas & immigration

As with any trip, you should confirm visa requirements well before you plan to travel, either at the Irish embassy in your country or on www.irlgov.ie/ iveagh/services/visas/.

Citizens of the USA, New Zealand, Australia, South Africa and Canada do not need visas to enter Ireland and may stay for a maximum of three months. British citizens and members of all EU states have unlimited residency and employment rights in Ireland.

If you require a visa, applications should be made to the Irish embassy or consulate in your country well in advance of your trip. If there is no Irish representative in your country, apply directly to the Foreign Affairs Department in Dublin.

Consular Section, Department of Foreign Affairs
72-76 St Stephen's Green, Southside (478 0822/fax 668 6518). All cross-city buses. **Open** *Office* 9.30am-noon Mon-Fri. *Phone enquiries* 2.30-4pm Mon-Fri. **Map** *p313 H6.*

Average temperatures

Month	Maximum	Minimum
January	8°C/46°F	1°C/34°F
February	8°C/46°F	2°C/35°F
March	10°C/51°F	3°C/37°F
April	13°C/55°F	4°C/39°F
May	15°C/60°F	6°C/43°F
June	18°C/65°F	9°C/48°F
July	20°C/68°F	11°C/52°F
August	19°C/67°F	11°C/52°F
September	17°C/63°F	9°C/48°F
October	14°C/57°F	6°C/43°F
November	10°C/51°F	4°C/39°F
December	8°C/46°F	3°C/37°F

Public holidays

The following public (bank) holidays are celebrated annually in Ireland:
1 January New Year's Day
17 March St Patrick's Day
Good Friday
Easter Monday
First Mondays in May, June and August
The **Monday** closest to **Hallowe'en** (31 October)
25 December
Christmas Day
26 December
St Stephen's Day
29 December

Embassies of Ireland abroad

Australia
20 Arkana Street, Yarralumla, Canberra, ACT 2600 (06 273 3022/3201).

Canada
Suite 1105, 130 Albert Street, Ottawa, Ontario K1P 5G4 (613 233 6281).

New Zealand
Consular affairs are handled by the Embassy in Canberra (*see above*)

South Africa
First Floor, Sothern Life Plaza, 1059 Schoemann Street, Arcadia 0083, Pretoria; postal address: PO Box 4174, Pretoria 0001 (012 342 5062).

United Kingdom
17 Grosvenor Place, London SW1X 7HR (020 7235 2171).

United States
2234 Massachusetts Avenue NW, Washington DC 20008-2849 (202 462 3939).

Weights & measures

The Republic of Ireland is now (almost) fully metric, although imperial measurements are readily used and understood – most importantly, pints are still pints at the bar.

When to go

The high tourist season covers July and August; this is when most festivals and events take place across the country. Accommodation is at its most expensive during this time, special offers are few and far between and Dublin and other popular districts are at their most crowded. Prices are lower and the weather is generally better in May, June and September, so these months might be the best time to visit.

In winter, prices are lowest of all, but the weather is more likely to be wet (though it is seldom very cold). Note that over the St Patrick's weekend (17 March; *see p163*), Dublin is usually thronged, so do book well in advance if you're planning to visit at this time.

Climate

The Irish weather is notoriously unpredictable. There's little point in trying to summarise seasonal trends: just make sure that whatever time of year you visit, you pack a warm sweater and a raincoat because otherwise sod's law will dictate that you should have. For an up-to-date weather forecast for Dublin, telephone 1-550 123 854 (calls cost about 75¢ per minute).

Women

Although Ireland has made tremendous economic progress, changes in the fundamentally patriarchal social structure have been much more gradual, and women's issues remain, on the whole, neglected. The number of women in Irish politics is gradually increasing, no doubt thanks to Mary Robinson's groundbreaking presidency, and there has been a huge increase in awareness of women's rights over the last decade, but the legal system is slow to change, and public funding for women's aid is scarce. Though divorce is now legal, the predicted collapse of the marriage institution has not so far come to pass.

The organisations listed below offer support and/or information to women in need.

Albany Women's Clinic
Clifton Court, Fitzwilliam Street Lower, Southside (661 2222). **Map** p313 J6.

Rape Crisis Centre
70 Leeson Street Lower, Southside (661 4911). **Open** *Telephone lines* 24hrs daily. **Map** p313 H7.

Women's Aid
1-800 341 900. **Open** 24hrs daily. Advice and support.

Women's Refuge & Helpline
496 1002. **Open** 24hrs daily.

Directory

Further Reference

Books

Drama & poetry

Samuel Beckett *Waiting for Godot* Two blokes hang around for a couple of hours.

Brendan Behan *The Quare Fellow* A shocking drama from the notorious Dublin drinker.

Eavan Boland *In a Time of Violence* Collected poems.

Seamus Heaney *Opened Ground: Poems 1966-1996* The Nobel Laureate at his most powerful.

Patrick Kavanagh *The Great Hunger* The Famine as metaphor.

Frank McGuinness *Observe the Sons of Ulster Marching Towards the Somme* Award-winning play by a Dublin-based writer.

Sean O'Casey *Collected Plays* Politics and morality in 1920s Ireland, including *The Plough & the Stars*.

George Bernard Shaw *Selected Plays* 'My Fair Lady' wasn't really his fault. Honest.

JM Synge *The Playboy of the Western World* Championed by Yeats, loathed by 1920s Ireland.

Oscar Wilde *Plays, Prose, Writings and Poems* In which the 19th century's finest wit declares his genius.

WB Yeats *Collected Poems* The finest works of the mighty William Butler.

Fiction

John Banville *Ghosts* A haunting narrative with Beckett-like overtones.

John Banville *The Book of Evidence* A fine, introspective murder story.

Samuel Beckett *Murphy* A darkly humourous Irish portrayal of London life.

Samuel Beckett *Molloy/ Malone Dies/The Unnamable* Compelling – and compellingly odd – fiction.

Brendan Behan *Borstal Boy* An autobiographical novel of a Dublin childhood.

Maeve Binchy *Dublin 4* Decadence among the city's southside sophisticates.

Dermot Bolger (et al) *Finbar's Hotel* Bolger, Doyle and others collaborate to create a multi-layered image of a complex city.

Dermot Bolger *The Journey Home* A hard-hitting account of life lived on the edge.

Elizabeth Bowen *The Last September* Quintessential Anglo-Irish 'big house' novel.

Emma Donoghue *Stir-fry* A wry lesbian love story, and a fine debut.

JP Donleavy *The Ginger Man* The high japes of a drunken Trinity student; banned by the Catholic Church.

Roddy Doyle *The Commitments* The book's way better than the film.

Roddy Doyle *Paddy Clarke Ha Ha Ha* A Booker-winning tale of suburban adolescence.

Roddy Doyle *A Star Called Henry* First part of Doyle's ambitious historical trilogy.

Anne Enright *A Portable Virgin* Sympathetic, unusual stories about Dublin life.

Jeffrey Gantz (trans) *Early Irish Myths and Sagas* Don't myth this one.

Henry Glassie (ed) *Penguin Book of Irish Folktales* Fairies, leprechauns and big potatoes.

Seamus Heaney *Sweeney Astray/Buile Suibhne* The crazy King Sweeney updated.

Jennifer Johnston *How Many Miles to Babylon?* Protestant gentry and Catholic peasant bond.

James Joyce *A Portrait of the Artist as a Young Man* Cuts through superstition like a knife.

James Joyce *Dubliners* Compelling short stories from the master at work.

James Joyce *Finnegans Wake* This novel defines the phrase 'unreadable genius'.

James Joyce *Ulysses* Arguably, the most important 24 hours in literary history.

Pat McCabe *The Butcher Boy* A hilariously grotesque tale of an Irish childhood.

Colum McCann *This Side of Brightness* Intriguing tale of New York's tunnel people and the ties that bind them to Ireland.

Edna O'Brien *The Country Girls* Bawdy girlish fun that roused clerical ire.

Flann O'Brien *At-Swim-Two-Birds* A breathtakingly funny novel about a struggling student writer.

Flann O'Brien *The Poor Mouth* A satire on traditional Gaelic prose.

Joseph O'Connor *Cowboys & Indians* Emigration in modern Ireland.

Liam O'Flaherty *The Informer* Tense social comment from a civil war veteran.

Jamie O'Neill *At Swim Two Boys* A homosexual Bildungsroman set against the backdrop of the Easter Rising.

Bram Stoker *Dracula* The original horror novel. Garlic at the ready...

Jonathan Swift *Gulliver's Travels* The political satire to beat all political satire.

Colm Tóibín *The Heather Blazing* An elderly city judge is forced to confront history.

William Trevor *The Ballroom of Romance* Short stories by the Northern Irish master, set in rural Ireland.

Non-fiction

John Ardagh *Ireland and the Irish* An acute look at present-day Ireland.

Douglas Bennett *Encyclopaedia of Dublin* Packed with vital information on the city.

RF Foster *Paddy and Mr Punch* A media-savvy study of modern 'Irishness'.

FS Lyons *Ireland Since the Famine* A definitive text.

Frank MacDonald *The Construction of Dublin* Exploration of the city's architectural development during its Celtic Tiger days.

Robert Kee *The Green Flag* A chunky nationalist history.

Robert Kee *The Laurel and the Ivy* Parnell, Gladstone and the history of Home Rule.

Máire & Conor Cruise O'Brien *A Concise History of Ireland* A thorough overview.

Jacqueline O'Brien & Desmond Guinness *Dublin – A Grand Tour* A useful guide to the Irish capital.

Nuala O'Faolain *Are You Somebody?* Dublin memories from a respected columnist.

Seán O'Faolain *The Great O'Neill* Queen Elizabeth I, Hugh O'Neill and the battle of Kinsale.

Paul Williams *Gangland, The General* Two fine dissections of Dublin's organised crime.

Cecil Woodham-Smith *The Great Hunger* The definitive study of the 19th-century Famine.

Film

About Adam (dir Gerard Stembridge, 2000) A smart, funny drama with Celtic Tiger Dublin as its backdrop.

The Butcher Boy (dir Neil Jordan, 1998) Surreal but engaging adaptation of Pat McCabe's novel.

The Commitments (dir Alan Parker, 1991) Perky screen version of Roddy Doyle's novel.

The Dead (John Huston, 1987) Huston's final film is an atmospheric recreation of Joyce's short story.

The General (dir John Boorman, 1998) Gritty urban drama about Dublin's most notorious gangster.

I Went Down (dir Paddy Breathnach, 1997) Hilarious road movie scripted by playwright Conor McPherson.

Michael Collins (dir Neil Jordan, 1996) A fine bio-pic of the 'Big Fella' using lots of Dublin locations.

My Left Foot (dir Jim Sheridan, 1989) Engaging, occasionally sentimental, bio-pic about disabled Dublin writer Christy Brown.

When Brendan Met Trudy (dir Kieron J Walsh, 2000) Comic love story by Roddy Doyle about a mild mannered Dublin school teacher and his girlfriend, who's a thief.

Music

The Blades *The Last Man in Europe* (1984) Recently re-released, an angry response to the dark days of the 1980s.

The Dubliners *Original Dubliners* (1993) Collection of the band's first four successful albums: *Seven Drunken Nights*; *Seven Deadly Sins*; *More of the Hard Stuff* and *Whiskey on a Sunday*.

Jubilee Allstars (2000) *Lights of the City*. Dublin rock 'n' roll with a social conscience.

Luke Kelly *The Collection* (1994) Essential compilation by the much-missed former Dubliners balladeer.

Sinead O'Connor *I Do Not Want What I Have Not Got* (1990) Heartfelt musings by the outspoken Dublin vocalist-turned-priest.

Christy Moore *Live at the Point* (1994) The folk singer

at his best, in front of a massive (and rapturous) Dublin audience.

The Stars of Heaven (1984) *Speak Slowly* Country-tinged, vastly underrated songs by one of Dublin's finest '80s bands.

U2 *The Joshua Tree* (1987). Local heroes come of age and end up in the desert.

U2 *All That You Can't Leave Behind* (2000). The rock stars return to their roots.

Websites

www.bluepages.com Unofficial information about the city, including a dictionary of Dub lingo.

www.dublinbus.ie The official city bus website has a useful bus route search facility.

www.ireland.com Online version of the *Irish Times*, with supplemental features and an extensive section devoted to the capital.

www.cluas.com Excellent independent Irish music site.

www.dublinevents.com Online entertainment listings for the city.

www.eventguide.ie Dublin's best fortnightly guide.

www.evilgerald.com Satirical Irish 'zine in the style of 'The Onion' website.

www.fii.ie Official web home of the Irish Film Institute.

www.ireland.travel.ie The Irish tourist board.

www.local.ie If it's in Ireland, you'll probably find it on this website.

ww.rte.ie Online information from Ireland's much-maligned national broadcaster.

www.temple-bar.ie Guide to Dublin's 'cultural quarter'.

www.visitdublin.com Strangely unhelpful and badly designed site from the folks at Dublin Tourism.

www.wow.ie What's on Where. Comprehensive guide to events around Ireland.

Directory

Index

Advertisers' Index

Please refer to the relevant pages for
addresses and telephone numbers.

Place of interest and/or entertainment . . . . . .
Railway station . . . .
Hotel . . . .
Park . . . .
Hospital . . . .
Neighbourhood . . . . RANELAGH
Pedestrian street . . . .

Maps

Ireland

NORTHERN
IRELAND

Giant's
Causeway   Rathlin Is.

Dunfanaghy   Coleraine
                                                          ANTRIM
Aran Is.   Glenveagh   Londonderry
                National Park
              Letterkenny   Londonderry   Larne
              DONEGAL   LONDONDERRY   Ballymena
Glencolumbcille   Belfast
                    Donegal   Internt
        Killybegs   Omagh   Lough   BELFAST   Donaghadee
Donegal   Ballyshannon   Neagh
Bay   L. Lough   Harbour
                    Erne   Armagh Portadown Airport
        N15   LEITRIM   Enniskillen   ARMAGH
              Sligo   FERMANAGH   N2 Monaghan   DOWN
          Ballina   U. Lough   MONAGHAN   Newry
      Lough Conn   SLIGO   Erne   Dundalk
Achill Is.   MAYO   Lough   Dundalk
              Castlebar   Allen   Cavan   LOUTH   Bay
Clare Is. Clew   Knock   Carrick-on-   Drogheda
        Bay   Knock   Shannon   CAVAN
      Westport   ROSCOMMON   Kells   MEATH
                          Longford   (Ceanannas Mor)
C O N N A U G H T   Roscommon   LONGFORD   See p307
Clifden   N17   Lough Ree   Mullingar   N4   Dublin
    Connemara   Tuam   Athlone   WESTMEATH   DUBLIN
Oughterard   Lough Corrib   Ballinasloe   Dún Laoghaire
  GALWAY   L E I N S T E R   N7   Bray
    Galway   Galway   N6   OFFALY   Tullamore   KILDARE
Aran   I R E L A N D   Kildare   Wicklow
Islands   Doolin   The   Birr   Mtns
    Cliffs of   Burren   Port Laoise   Wicklow
    Moher   CLARE   N18   Roscrea   Athy   WICKLOW
      Ennis   Lough   LAOIS   Carlow   Arklow
          Shannon Derg   N7 Thurles   N8   CARLOW   N11
      Limerick   Kilkenny
              N24   TIPPERARY   KILKENNY
        LIMERICK   Tipperary   WEXFORD
    KERRY   N20   Wexford
      Tralee   Mallow   Rosslare
Great   Dingle Killorglin   Kerry County   M U N S T E R   IRISH
Blasket   SEA
Is.   Dingle Bay   Killarney   Waterford
Valentia   Lough   CORK   Dungarvan   WATERFORD
Is.   Cahirciveen Leane   N25 Waterford
    Sneem   Kenmare   Macroom   Cork   Youghal
        Glengarriff   N22 Cork
Dursey Is. Bear Is. Bantry   Kinsale
    Bantry Bay   Clonakilty   ST GEORGE'S CHANNEL
          Skibbereen
    Clear Is.

0   50   100 km
0   60 miles

© Copyright Time Out Group 2002

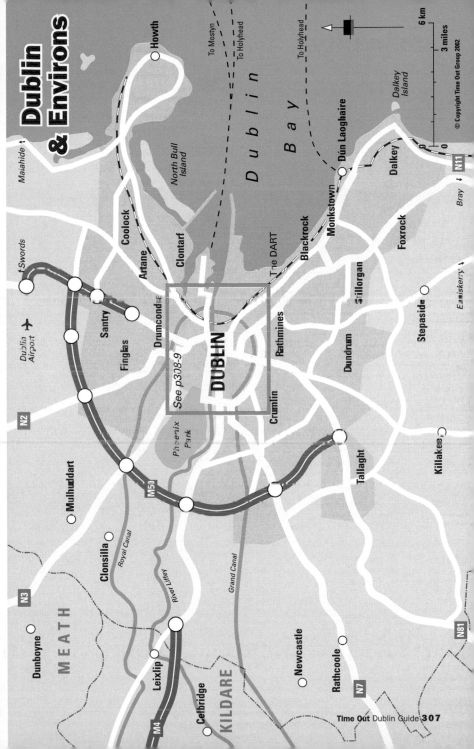

To Mostyn
To Holyhead
To Holyhead

6 km

3 miles

© Copyright Time Out Group 2002

Howth

North Bull Island

Dublin Bay

Dalkey Island

Dún Laoghaire

Dalkey

Bray ↓

N11

Malahide ↑

Coolock

Artane

Clontarf

The DART

Blackrock

Monkstown

Foxrock

↑ Swords

Santry

Drumcondra

Rathmines

Stillorgan

Stepaside

Dublin Airport ✈

Finglas

DUBLIN

See p308-9

Dundrum

Enniskerry ↑

N2

Phoenix Park

Crumlin

Tallaght

Killakee

Mulhuddart

M50

Clonsilla

Royal Canal

River Liffey

Grand Canal

N3

MEATH

Dunboyne

Newcastle

Rathcoole

KILDARE

Leixlip

Celbridge

N7

N81

M4

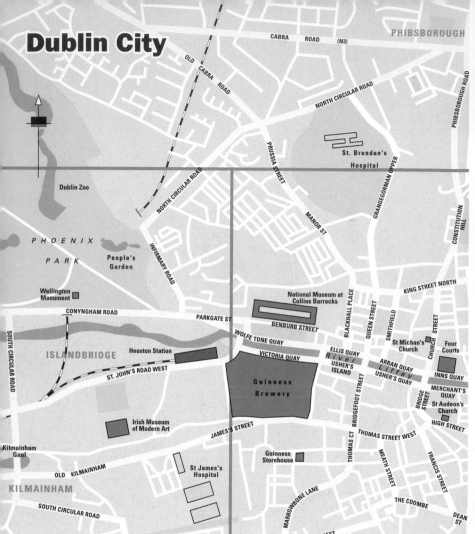

Dublin City

PHIBSBOROUGH

CABRA ROAD (N3)

OLD CABRA ROAD

NORTH CIRCULAR ROAD

PHIBSBOROUGH ROAD

PRUSSIA STREET

St. Brendan's Hospital

GRANGEGORMAN UPPER

CONSTITUTION HILL

Dublin Zoo

NORTH CIRCULAR ROAD

MANOR ST

INFIRMARY ROAD

P H O E N I X   P A R K

People's Garden

KING STREET NORTH

Wellington Monument

CONYNGHAM ROAD

PARKGATE ST

National Museum at Collins Barracks

BLACKHALL PLACE

QUEEN STREET

SMITHFIELD

CHURCH STREET

Four Courts

SOUTH CIRCULAR ROAD

ISLANDBRIDGE

Heuston Station

BENBURB STREET

WOLFE TONE QUAY

St Michan's Church

ST. JOHN'S ROAD WEST

VICTORIA QUAY

ELLIS QUAY

USHER'S ISLAND

River Liffey

ARRAN QUAY

USHER'S QUAY

INNS QUAY

MERCHANT'S QUAY

BRIDGE STREET

St Audeon's Church

HIGH STREET

Guinness Brewery

Irish Museum of Modern Art

JAMES'S STREET

THOMAS ST

BRIDGEFOOT STREET

THOMAS STREET WEST

Kilmainham Gaol

St James's Hospital

Guinness Storehouse

MEATH STREET

FRANCIS STREET

OLD KILMAINHAM

KILMAINHAM

SOUTH CIRCULAR ROAD

MARROWBONE LANE

THE COOMBE

DEAN ST

DAVITT RD

CORK STREET

CLANBRASSIL ST LOWER

See p311   See p312

DOLPHIN ROAD

DOLPHIN'S BARN

DOLPHIN'S BARN

SOUTH CIRCULAR ROAD

CLANBRASSIL ST UPPER

Brickfields Park

CRUMLIN ROAD

PARNELL ROAD

Grand Canal

GROVE ROAD

HAROLD'S CROSS

HAROLD'S CROSS RD

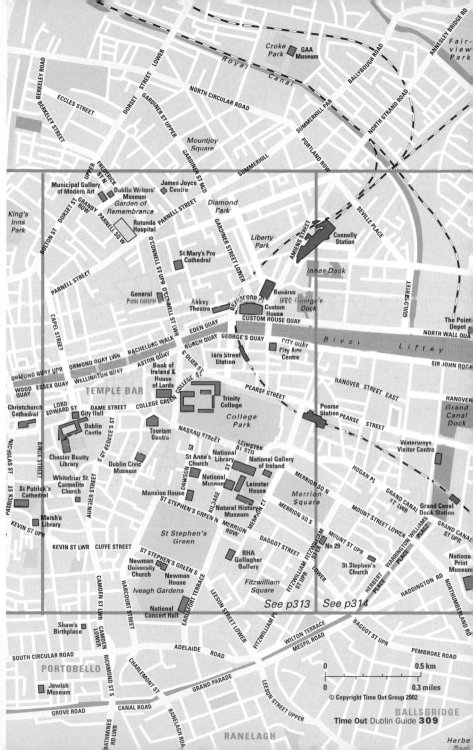

Croke
Park

GAA
Museum

Royal Canal

Fair-
view
Park

ANNESLEY BRIDGE RD

BALLYBOUGH ROAD

NORTH CIRCULAR ROAD

SUMMERHILL PAR

NORTH STRAND ROAD

BERKELEY ROAD

ECCLES STREET

BERKELEY STREET

DORSET STREET LOWER

GARDINER ST UPPER

Mountjoy
Square

PORTLAND ROW

SUMMERHILL

UPPER FREDERICK ST N

Municipal Gallery
of Modern Art

DORSET ST GRANBY
ROW

Dublin Writers'
Museum
Garden of
Remembrance

PARNELL SQ W

James Joyce
Centre

GARDINER ST MID

Diamond
Park

SEVILLE PLACE

King's
Inns
Park

Rotunda
Hospital

PARNELL STREET

GARDINER STREET LOWER

Liberty
Park

AMIENS STREET

Connolly
Station

BOLTON ST

PARNELL STREET

St Mary's Pro
Cathedral

O'CONNELL ST UPR

O'CONNELL ST LWR

Inner Dock

GUILD STREET

CAPEL STREET

General
Post Office

Abbey
Theatre

BERESFORD PL

Custom
House

Busárus

IFC
Custom
House Quay

George's
Dock

The Point
Depot

NORTH WALL QUA

ORMOND QUAY LWR

BACHELORS WALK

EDEN QUAY

CUSTOM HOUSE QUAY

River

Liffey

WOOD
QUAY

ORMOND QUAY UPR

ESSEX QUAY

WELLINGTON QUAY

ASTON QUAY

BURGH QUAY

GEORGE'S QUAY

CITY QUAY

SIR JOHN ROG

Christchurch
Cathedral

TEMPLE BAR

COLLIER ST

Bank of
Ireland &
House of
Lords

Iara Street
Station

City Arts
Centre

HANOVER STREET EAST

HANOVER

NICHOLAS ST

LORD
EDWARD ST

DAME STREET

ST GEORGE'S ST

City Hall

Dublin
Castle

COLLEGE GREEN

COLLEGE ST

Trinity
College

PEARSE STREET

Pearse
Station

PEARSE STREET

Grand
Canal
Dock

BRIDE STREET

Chester Beatty
Library

Dublin Civic
Museum

Tourism
Centre

NASSAU STREET

College
Park

Waterways
Visitor Centre

ST PATRICK'S
Cathedral

Whitefriar St.
Carmelite
Church

AUNGIER ST

St Anne's
Church

DAWSON ST

National
Library

LEINSTER ST S

KILDARE ST

National Gallery
of Ireland

HOGAN PL

Marsh's
Library

Mansion House

National
Museum

Leinster
House

MERRION SQ N

Grand Canal
Dock Station

KEVIN ST UPR

ST STEPHEN'S GREEN N

MERRION
ROW

Natural History
Museum

MERRION SQ S

Merrion
Square

MOUNT STREET LOWER

GRAND CANAL ST LWR

WILLIAM'S PLACE

GRAND CANAL ST UPR

KEVIN ST LWR

CUFFE STREET

St Stephen's
Green

BAGGOT STREET

FITZWILLIAM ST LWR

MOUNT ST UPR

No 29

St Stephen's
Church

WARRINGTON PLACE

HERBERT PLACE

National
Print
Museum

NORTHUMBERLAND RD

CAMDEN ST LWR

ST STEPHEN'S GREEN S

Newman
University
Church

Newman
House

Iveagh Gardens

RHA
Gallagher
Gallery

LEESON STREET LOWER

Fitzwilliam
Square

FITZWILLIAM PL

FITZWILLIAM ST UPR

HADDINGTON RD

HARCOURT STREET

EARLSFORT TERRACE

National
Concert Hall

See p313

See p314

Shaw's
Birthplace

CAMDEN ST LWR

ADELAIDE ROAD

WILTON TERRACE

MESPIL ROAD

BAGGOT ST UPR

PEMBROKE ROAD

SOUTH CIRCULAR ROAD

RICHMOND ST S

PORTOBELLO

Jewish
Museum

CHARLEMONT ST

GRAND PARADE

LEESON STREET UPPER

0   0.5 km

0   0.3 miles

© Copyright Time Out Group 2002

GROVE ROAD

CANAL ROAD

MATHMINES RD LWR

RANELAGH RD

RANELAGH

BALLSBRIDGE

Herbe

DART & Suburban Rail

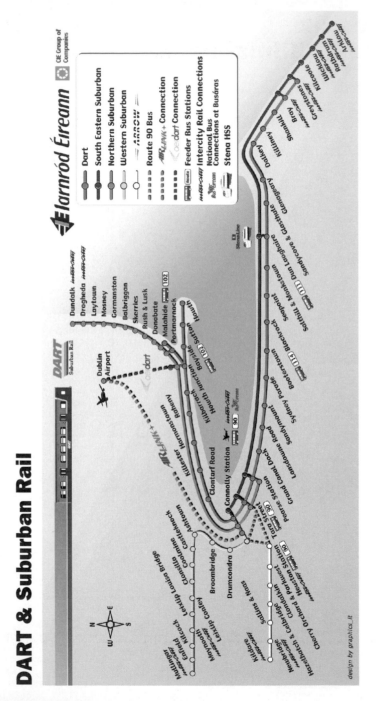

design by graphics_it

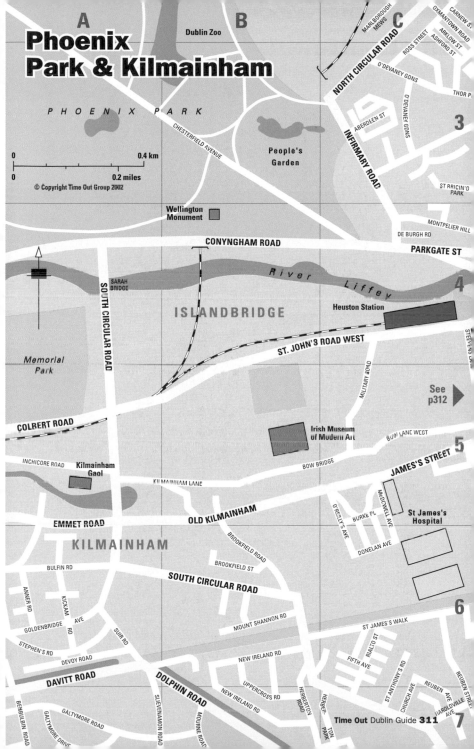

Phoenix
Park & Kilmainham

A   **B**   **C**

Dublin Zoo

MARLBOROUGH MEWS

CARNEW S.
OXMANTOWN ROAD
ROSS STREET
ARLOW ST
ASHFORD ST

NORTH CIRCULAR ROAD

O'DEVANEY GDNS

THOR P.

P H O E N I X   P A R K

CHESTERFIELD AVENUE

People's
Garden

ABERDEEN ST

O'DEVANEY GDNS

INFIRMARY ROAD

3

ST RRICIN'O
PARK

0   0.4 km

0   0.2 miles
© Copyright Time Out Group 2002

Wellington
Monument

MONTPELIER HILL
DE BURGH RD

CONYNGHAM ROAD

PARKGATE ST

River   Liffey

4

SARAH
BRIDGE

SOUTH CIRCULAR ROAD

Heuston Station

ISLANDBRIDGE

ST. JOHN'S ROAD WEST

STEE EAS LAN

Memorial
Park

MILITARY ROAD

See
p312

COLBERT ROAD

BOW LANE WEST

5

INCHICORE ROAD

Kilmainham
Gaol

Irish Museum
of Modern Art

BOW BRIDGE

JAMES'S STREET

KILMAINHAM LANE

EMMET ROAD

OLD KILMAINHAM

O'REILLY'S AVE

McDOWELL AVE

BURKE PL

St James's
Hospital

KILMAINHAM

BROOKFIELD ROAD

DONELAN AVE

BULFIN RD

BROOKFIELD ST

SOUTH CIRCULAR ROAD

ANNER RD

KICKAM

AVE

GOLDENBRIDGE

RD

SUIR RD

MOUNT SHANNON RD

ST JAMES'S WALK

RIALTO ST

6

STEPHEN'S RD

DEVOY ROAD

NEW IRELAND RD

FIFTH AVE

ST ANTHONY'S RD

CHURCH AVE

REUBEN AVE

REUBEN STREET

DAVITT ROAD

DOLPHIN ROAD

UPPERCROSS RD

NEW IRELAND RD

HERBERTON
ROAD

HERBER-

TON
PARK

HAROLDVILLE AVE

BENBULBIN ROAD

GALTYMORE ROAD

GALTYMORE DRIVE

SLIEVENAMON ROAD

MOURNE ROAD

Time Out Dublin Guide **311**

7

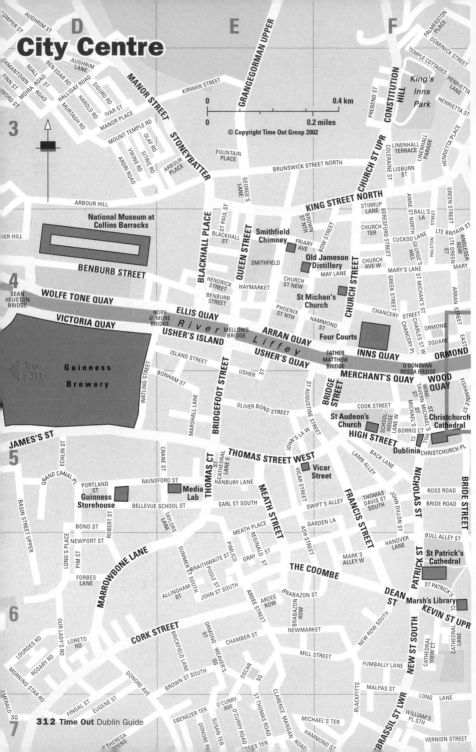

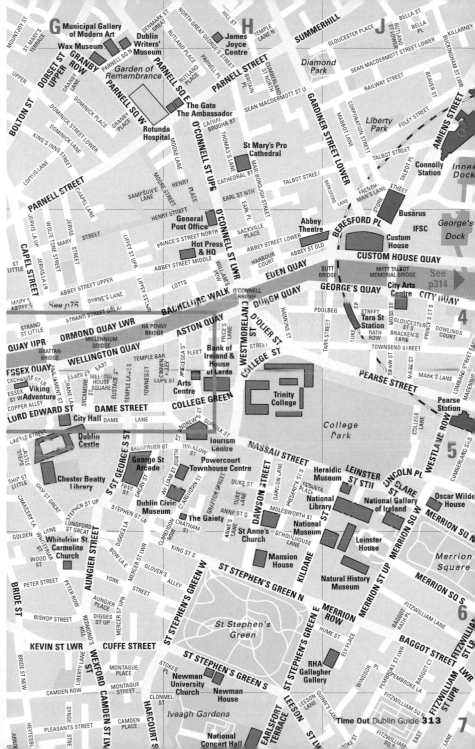

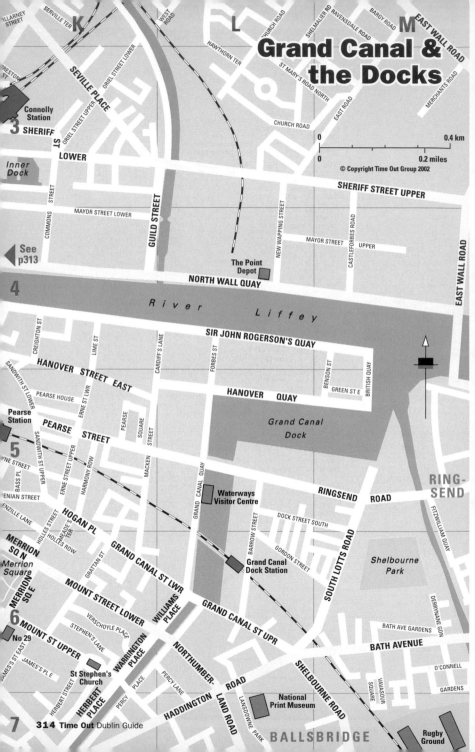

Grand Canal & the Docks

K L M

EAST WALL ROAD

ILLARNEY STREET

SERVILLE TER

WEST ROAD

CHURCH ROAD

HAWTHORN TER

SHELMALIER RD

RAVENSDALE ROAD

BARGY ROAD

MERCHANTS ROAD

SEVILLE PLACE

ORIEL STREET LOWER

ORIEL STREET UPPER

ST MARY'S ROAD NORTH

EAST ROAD

PRESTON ST

3

Connolly
Station

SHERIFF

CHURCH ROAD

0   0.4 km

0   0.2 miles

© Copyright Time Out Group 2002

*Inner
Dock*

LOWER

ST

STREET

COMMONS

MAYOR STREET LOWER

SHERIFF STREET UPPER

NEW WAPPING STREET

MAYOR STREET   UPPER

CASTLEFORBES ROAD

EAST WALL ROAD

◀ **See
p313**

GUILD STREET

The Point
Depot

NORTH WALL QUAY

4

River   Liffey

CREIGHTON ST

LIME ST

CARDIFF'S LANE

FORBES ST

SIR JOHN ROGERSON'S QUAY

BENSON ST

GREEN ST E

BRITISH QUAY

HANOVER   STREET   EAST

SANDWITH ST LOWER

PEARSE HOUSE

ERNE ST LWR

HANOVER   QUAY

**Pearse
Station**

PEARSE   STREET

SANDWITH ST UPPER

ERNE STREET UPPER

PEARSE

SQUARE

STREET

HARMONY ROW

MACKEN   STREET

*Grand Canal
Dock*

**RING-
SEND**

NE STREET

BASS PL

ENIAN STREET

ENZILLE LANE

HOGAN PL

HOLLES STREET

MEADE'S

TER

HOLLES ROW

GRAND CANAL QUAY

Waterways
Visitor Centre

RINGSEND   ROAD

FITZWILLIAM QUAY

**RING-
SEND**

**MERRION
SQ N**

*Merrion
Square*

GRAND CANAL ST LWR

GRATTAN ST

BARROW STREET

DOCK STREET SOUTH

GORDON STREET

SOUTH LOTTS ROAD

*Shelbourne
Park*

DERRYNANE GDN

Grand Canal
Dock Station

**MERRION
SQ E**

MOUNT STREET LOWER

GRAND CANAL ST UPR

6

MOUNT ST UPPER

VERSCHOYLE PLACE

STEPHEN'S LANE

WILLIAMS
PLACE

NORTHUMBER-

BATH AVENUE

BATH AVE GARDENS

O'CONNELL

GARDENS

No 29

JAMES'S ST EAST

JAMES'S PL E

St Stephen's
Church

HERBERT STREET

WARRINGTON
PLACE

PERCY   PLACE

PERCY LANE

LAND ROAD

SHELBOURNE ROAD

VAVASOUR
SQUARE

**HERBERT
PLACE**

PERCY

HADDINGTON   ROAD

LANSDOWNE PARK

National
Print Museum

*Rugby
Ground*

7

BALLSBRIDGE

Street Index

James's Place East –
   p314 K6
James's St East – p314 K6
James's Street – p311 C5
James's Street – p312 D5
Jervis Lane Lwr – p313 G4
Jervis Lane Upr – p313 G4
Jervis Street – p313 G3/4
John Dillon Street – p312 F5
John Street South – p312 E6
John's Lane West – p312 E5
Kevin Street Lwr – p313 G6
Kevin Street Upr – p312 F6
Kickam Road – p311 A6
Kildare Street – p313 H6, J5
Killarney Street – p313-4 J/K2
Kilmainham Lane – p311 A/B5
King Street North – p312 F3
King Street South – p313 H6
King's Inns Street – p313 G3
Kirwan Street – p312 E3
Lad Lane – p313 J7
Lamb Alley – p312 F5
Lansdowne Park – p314 L7
Leeson Lane – p313 H7
Leeson Street Lwr – p313 H7
Leinster Street South –
   p313 J5
Liberty Lane – p313 G6
Liffey Street Lwr – p313 G4
Liffey Street Upr – p313 G4
Lime Street – p314 K4
Lincoln Place – p313 J5
Linenhall Parade – p312 F3
Linenhall Terrace – p312 F3
Lisburn Street – p312 F3
Little Britain Street – p312 F4
Little Green Street – p312 F4
Loftus Lane – p313 G3
Lombard Street East –
   p313 J4/5
Long Lane – p312 F7
Longford Street Great –
   p313 G5/6
Long's Place – p312 D5/6
Lord Edward Street – p313 G5
Loreto Road – p312 D6
Lotts – p313 H4
Lourdes Road – p312 D6
Luke Street – p313 J4
Mabbot Lane – p313 J3
Macken Street – p314 K5
Magennis Place – p313 J4/5
Malpas Street – p312 F6
Manor Place – p312 D3
Manor Street – p312 D3, E3
Mark Street – p313 J4/5
Mark's Alley West – p312 F6
Mark's Lane – p313 J5
Marlborough Mews – p311 C2
Marlborough Street –
   p313 H3/4
Marrowbone Lane – p312 D6
Marshall Lane – p312 E5
Mary Street – p313
Mary Street Little – p312 F4
Mary Street Little – p313 G4
Mary's Lane – p312 F4 F4
Mary's Abbey's – p313 G4
Matt Talbot Memorial Bridge –
   p313 J4
May Lane – p312 F4
Mayor Street Lwr – p314 K3/4
Mayor Street Upr – p314 L/M4
Mcdowell Ave – p311 C5/6
Meade's Terrace – p314 K5/6
Meath Place – p312 E5
Meath Street – p312 E5/6
Meeting House Square –
   p313 G5
Mellows Bridge – p312 E4
Mercer Street Lwr – p313 G6
Mercer Street Upr – p313 G6
Merchant's Quay – p312 F5
Merchants Road – p314 M3
Merrion Row – p313 J6
Merrion Sq East – p314 K6

Merrion Sq North – p313 J5/6
Merrion Sq North – p314 K6
Merrion Sq South – p313 J6
Merrion Sq West – p313 J5/6
Merrion Street Upr – p313 J6
Michael's Terrace –
   p312 E7, F7
Military Road – p311 C4/5
Mill Street – p312 E6, F6
Millennium Bridge – p313 G4
Moira Road – p312 D3
Molesworth Street – p313 H5
Montague Place – p313 G6
Montague Street – p313 G6
Montpelier Hill – p311 C4
Montpelier Hill – p312 D4
Moore Lane – p313 H3
Moore Street – p313 G3, H3
Morning Star Road –
   p312 D6/7
Moss Street – p313 J4
Mount Shannon Road –
   p311 B6
Mount Street Lwr – p314 K6
Mount Street Upr – p314 K6
Mount Temple Road – p312 D3
Mountjoy Street – p313 G2
Mourne Road – p311 B7
Murtagh Road – p312 D3
Nassau Street – p313 H5
New Ireland Road – p311 B6/7
New Row South – p312 F6
New Street South – p312 F6
New Wapping Street –
   p314 L3/4
Newmarket – p312 E6, F6
Newport Street – p312 D6
Niall Street – p312 D3
Nicholas Street – p312 F5
North Circular Road –
   p311 C2/3
North Great George's Street –
   p313 H2/3
North Wall Quay –
   p314 K4, L4, M4
Northumberland Road –
   p314 L6/7
O'Connell Bridge – p313 H4
O'Connell Street Lwr –
   p313 H3/4
O'Connell Street Upr –
   p313 H3
O'Curry Ave – p312 E7
O'Curry Road – p312 E7
O'Donovan Rossa Bridge –
   p312 F4
O'Connell Gardens – p314 M6
O'Devaney Gardens – p311 C3
Olaf Road – p312 D3
Old Kilmainham – p311 B5
Oliver Bond Street – p312 E5
O'Reilly's Ave – p311 C5/6
Oriel Street Lwr – p314 K3
Oriel Street Upr – p314 K3
Ormond Quay Lwr – p313 G4
Ormond Quay Upr – p312 F4
Ormond Quay Upr – p313 G4
Ormond Square – p312 F4
Ormond Street – p312 E6
Oscar Square – p312 E6
Our Lady's Road – p312 D6
Oxmantown Road – p311 C2/3
Oxmantown Road – p312 D3
Palmerston Place – p312 F2
Parkgate Street – p311 C4
Parliament Street – p313 G5
Parnell Place – p313 H3
Parnell Square – p313 G/H3
Parnell Street – p313 G3, H3
Patrick Street – p312 F6
Pearse House – p314 K5
Pearse Square – p314 K5
Pearse Street – p313 J4/5
Pearse Street – p314 K5
Pembroke Lane – p313 J6
Pembroke Street Lwr –
   p313 J6/7

Pembroke Street Upr –
   p313 J7
Percy Lane – p314 L6
Percy Place – p314 K6/7, L6
Peter Row – p313 G6
Peter Street – p313 G6
Phoenix Street North – p312 E4
Pim Street – p312 D5/6
Pimlico – p312 E5/6
Pleasants Street – p313 G7
Poolbeg Street – p313 H4, J4
Poole Street – p312 E6
Portland Street – p312 D5
Prebend Street – p312 F3
Preston Street – p314 K3
Price's Lane – p313 H4
Prince's Street North –
   p313 H4
Prince's Street South –
   p313 J4
Queen Street – p312 E4
Quinn's Lane – p313 J7
Railway Street – p313 J3
Rainsford Street – p312 D5, E5
Rath Row – p313 J4
Ravensdale Road – p314 M2
Redmond's Hill – p313 G6
Reginald Street – p312 E6
Reuben Ave – p311 C6/7
Reuben Street – p311 C6/7
Rialto Street – p311 C6
Ringsend Road – p314 L5, M5
Robert Street – p312 D5/6
Rory O' More Bridge – p312 E4
Rosary Road – p312 D6
Ross Road – p312 F5
Ross Street – p311 C2/3
Rutland Place – p313 H2/3
Rutland Street Lwr – p313 J2
Rutledges Terrace – p312 F7
Sackville Place – p313 H4
St Andrew's Street – p313 H5
St Anthony's Road –
   p311 C6/7
St Augustine Street –
   p312 E/F5
St Bricin's Park – p311 C3
St Cathedral Lane East –
   p312 E5
St James's Walk – p311 C6
St John's Road West –
   p311 B4/5, C4
St Mary's Road North –
   p314 L2/3
St Mary's Terrace – p313 G2
St Michael's Close – p312 F5
St Michael's Hill – p312 F5
St Michan's Street – p312 F4
St Patrick's Close – p312 F6
St Paul Street – p312 E3/4
St Stephen's Green – p313 H6
St Theresa Gardens – p312 D7
St Thomas Road – p312 E6/7
Sampson's Lane – p313 G3
Sandwith Street Lwr –
   p314 K4/5
Sandwith Street Upr – p314 K5
Schoolhouse Lane – p313 H6
Schoolhouse Lane West –
   p312 F5
Sean Heuston Bridge –
   p312 D4
Sean Macdermott Street Lwr –
   p313 J2/3
Sean Macdermott Street Upr –
   p313 H3
Serville Terrace – p314 K2
Setanta Place – p313 H5, J5
Seville Place – p314 K2/3
Shaw Street – p313 J4/5
Shelbourne Road –
   p314 L6, M6/7
Shelmalier Road – p314 L/M2
Sheriff Street Lwr – p314 K3
Sheriff Street Upr – p314 L/M3
Ship Street Great – p313 G5
Ship Street Little – p313 G5

Sigurd Road – p312 D3
Sir John Rogerson's Quay –
   p314 K-M4
Sitric Road – p312 D/E3
Slievenamon Road –
   p311 A6/7
Smithfield – p312 E4
South Circular Road –
   p311 A4-6, B6
South Great George's Street –
   p313 G5
South Lotts Road – p314 M5/6
Steevens Lane – p311 C4/5
Stephen Street Lwr – p313 G5
Stephen Street Upr – p313 G5
Stephen's Lane – p314 K6
Stephen's Road – p311 A6
Stirrup Lane – p312 F3
Stokes Place – p313 H6
Stoneybatter – p312 E3
Store Street – p313 J3
Strand Street Great – p313 G4
Strand Street Little – p313 G4
Suffolk Street – p313 H5
Suir Road – p311 A6
Summer Street South –
   p312 E6
Summerhill – p313 H/J2
Susan Terrace – p312 E7
Swift's Alley – p312 E/F5
Sword Street – p312 D3
Sycamore Street – p313 G5
Synge Street – p313 G7
Talbot Place – p313 J3
Talbot Street – p313 H/J3
Tara Street – p313 J4
Taylors Lane – p312 E5
Temple Bar – p313 G/H4
Temple Cottages – p312 F3
Temple Lane North – p313 J2
Temple Lane South –
   p313 G4/5
The Coombe – p312 E6, F6
Thomas Court – p312 E5
Thomas Davis Street South –
   p312 F5
Thomas Street West –
   p312 E/F5
Thomas's Lane – p313 H3
Thor Place – p311 C3
Townsend Street – p313 J4
**Uppercross Road –
   p311 B6/7**
Usher Street – p312 E4/5
Usher's Island – p312 E4
Usher's Quay – p312 E4
**Vavasour Square –
   p314 M6/7**
Vernion Street – p312 F7
Verschoyle Place – p314 K6
Vicar Street – p312 E5
Victoria Quay – p312 D4
Viking Road – p312 D3
Warrington Place – p314 K6
Watling Street – p312 D4/5
Weaver's Square – p312 E6
Wellington Quay – p313 G4
West Road – p314 L2
Westland Row – p313 J5
Westmoreland Street –
   p313 H4
Wexford Street – p313 G6
Whitefriar Street – p313 G6
Wicklow Street – p313 H5
William Street South –
   p313 G/H5
William's Place South –
   p312 F7
William's Row – p313 H4
Williams Place – p314 L6
Windsor Place – p313 J6
Winetavern Street – p312 F5
Wolfe Tone Quay – p312 D4
Wolfe Tone Street – p313 G4
Wood Quay – p312 F5
Wood Street – p313 G6
York Street – p313 G6